The International Theological Library·

PLANNED AND FOR MANY YEARS EDITED BY

The Rev. Professor CHARLES A. BRIGGS, D.D., D.Litt.

AND

The Rev. Principal STEWART D. F. SALMOND, D.D.

THE THEOLOGY OF THE OLD TESTAMENT.

By A. B. DAVIDSON, D.D., LL.D., Litt.D.

International Theological Library

THE THEOLOGY

OF THE

OLD TESTAMENT

BY

A. B. DAVIDSON, D.D., LL.D., Litt.D.

LATE PROFESSOR OF HEBREW AND OLD TESTAMENT EXEGESIS
NEW COLLEGE, EDINBURGH

EDITED FROM THE AUTHOR'S MANUSCRIPTS

BY

Principal S. D. F. SALMOND, D.D.

EDINBURGH

T. & T. CLARK, 38 GEORGE STREET

PRINTED IN ENGLAND BY
LEWIS REPRINTS LTD.
TONBRIDGE
FOR
T. & T. CLARK LTD., EDINBURGH

0   567   27206   0

FIRST PRINTED .   .   .   1904
LATEST IMPRESSION .   .   .   1976

PREFACE.

THE master hand, it will easily be seen, has not put this work in order for the press. The subject was long in Professor Davidson's mind. He gave it a large place in his College Lectures. He was constantly engaged in writing upon it and in recasting what he had written, modifying his statements and revising his conclusions. He prepared a large mass of matter, but he did not survive to throw it finally into shape for publication.

It has been a difficult and anxious task to deal for the best with the abundant material. Dr. Davidson's manuscripts bear on every page impressive evidence of the immense pains he took with things, and the lofty standard he set before him in all his professional duty. Much of the matter came to me in a variety of editions,—four, five, or six in not a few cases,—the long results of unceasing study and searching probation of opinion. It has been far from easy to decide between one form and another, all being left undated, and to bring the different parts into proper relation.

I have not thought it right to take liberties with my departed friend's work. I have given it substantially as he left it, adding only an occasional note where that seemed specially appropriate or needful. Nor have I judged it within my province to depart from his ways in the use of Scripture or in anything else. When expounding any

Biblical truth he was in the habit of making copious quotations from the sacred text, referring to the same passages again and again as they offered themselves in different aspects and connexions. He did this, too, with much freedom, using sometimes the Authorised Version and sometimes the Revised, furnishing sometimes a translation of his own, and sometimes giving the sense rather than the terms. His methods in such things are followed as they are found in his manuscripts.

Had Dr. Davidson been spared to complete his work and carry it through the press, it would have been different, no doubt, in some respects from what it is. It would have been thrown into the best literary form. Its statements at some points would have been more condensed. It would have had less of that element of iteration of which he made such effective use in his class-room. But even without the last touches of the skilled hand, it will be seen to be a distinct and weighty contribution to a great subject. Fine thinking, penetrating exegesis, spiritual vision, a rare insight into the nature and operation of Revelation, make the book one which the student of Old Testament Scripture will greatly value.

One thing that gave Dr. Davidson much concern was the question of the plan on which a work of this kind should be constructed. His object was to bring the history and the ideas into living relation, to trace the progress of Old Testament faith from stage to stage, and to exhibit the course along which it advanced from its beginnings to the comparative fulness which it obtained at the end of the prophetic period. But he never carried out the scheme. He had an increasing distrust of ambitious attempts to fix the date of every separate piece of the Hebrew literature, and link the ideas in their several measures of immaturity and maturity with the writings as thus arranged. He

became more and more convinced that there was no solid
basis for such confident chronological dispositions of the
writings and juxtapositions of the beliefs. In his judgment the only result of endeavours of this kind was to give
an entirely fictitious view of the ideas, in their relative
degrees of definiteness, the times at which they emerged or
came to certainty, and the causes that worked to their
origin and development. The most that we had scientific
warrant to do, in view of the materials available for the
purpose, was, in his opinion, to take the history in large
tracts and the literature in a few broad divisions, and study
the beliefs and the deliverances in connexion with these.

My work is at an end. During its course the mist
has been often in my eyes. The sense of loss has been
revived. A voice has spoken to me out of the past. A
face that was darkened has seemed to be turned upon me
again with its old light. I have felt how long art is and
how short is life.

S. D. F. SALMOND.

ABERDEEN, *April* 2, 1904.

CONTENTS.

—◆—

I. THE SCIENCE OF OLD TESTAMENT THEOLOGY.

II. THE DOCTRINE OF GOD.

III. THE DOCTRINE OF GOD—THE DIVINE NATURE.

IV. THE DOCTRINE OF GOD—THE SPIRIT.

V. THE DOCTRINE OF GOD—THE DIVINE ATTRIBUTES.

VI. THE DOCTRINE OF MAN.

VII. THE DOCTRINE OF MAN—SIN.

VIII. THE DOCTRINE OF REDEMPTION.

IX. DOCTRINE OF REDEMPTION—SUPRAHUMAN GOOD AND EVIL.

X. DOCTRINE OF REDEMPTION—PRIESTHOOD AND ATONEMENT.

XI. THE DOCTRINE OF THE LAST THINGS—THE MESSIANIC IDEA.

XII. DOCTRINE OF THE LAST THINGS—IMMORTALITY.

THE THEOLOGY

OF THE

OLD TESTAMENT

and in its principal turning-points during the ages preceding. This at once suggests to us, therefore, when we consider that God's operation extended over this long period, and yet that it took end at last in the coming of His Son, that two characteristics belong to it. It is historical, and it is progressive; it covers a long period, and it advances from less to more, and finally culminates. And the Bible keeps pace, so to speak, with this operation, reflects it, and gives us the knowledge of it in this form.

In its fullest sense the kingdom of God was only introduced in the Coming of the Son of God into the world; and in this sense all that went before might seem only capable of being regarded as preparation for this kingdom, or at most shadows of it. And this is the view which has often been taken of what is called the Old Testament dispensation, namely, that it is a designed shadow or adumbration of the new. But this is not the view which it takes of itself; the consciousness of Israel as reflected in the minds of its prophets and highest men was that it was the kingdom of God already. The apparent discrepancy disappears on a little consideration of what the kingdom of God is. It is the fellowship of men with God and with one another in love. In a perfect sense this could not be till the Coming of the Son in whom this fellowship is fully realised. And in a sense all that went before was preparation for the kingdom rather than the kingdom itself. But how was the perfect kingdom prepared for? Not by mere predictions of it and references to it as a thing to come, nor by setting up a thing which was a shadow of it; but by setting itself up in as perfect a form as was possible to begin with, awakening within men both a sense of dissatisfaction with its imperfections then, and lofty ideals of what its true condition would be, and thus kindling in them an enthusiasm which made them not only long for the perfect kingdom, but struggle for its attainment. For as the kingdom of God in its perfect form does not lie in mere knowledge, but rather in the life which the knowledge awakens, so it could not be prepared for by the mere knowledge that it was approaching, nor even by the knowledge outwardly communicated of what it was. It could be prepared for only by bringing in, and that in ever fuller tides, the life of which it consists. That life no doubt depended on the knowledge of what the kingdom truly was; but this knowledge could be learned by men only by living within the kingdom itself.

Thus the perfect kingdom was gradually prepared for by setting up such a kingdom in an imperfect state and under temporary forms, and by administering it in such a way as progressively to suggest to men's minds the true ideal of the kingdom, and communicate to them in broader streams the true life in such a kingdom. And each step of this communication was a more perfect bringing in of the kingdom itself, an advance towards its perfect form. Thus a life and a thought were awakened within this kingdom of God set up in Israel, which grew and expanded till they finally burst and threw off from them the imperfect outward form of the kingdom in which they were enclosed. Now the Old Testament Scriptures exhibit to us the growth of this life and this thought. We can observe the stream of life and ideas flowing from the Exodus at least, or even from a source higher up, ever broadening as it proceeds, and finally pouring itself into the sea of life and thought in the New Testament age. We can fathom this stream here and there along its course, mark the velocity and breadth of its current, observe the changing colour of its waters as it pursues its way through region after region of the people's history, and perceive what subsidiary streams poured their contents into it and helped to swell it. To do this and present the results to ourselves is to be Old Testament theologians.

What we shall have to look for is a point of view; and that point of view will be this, that in the Old Testament we have presented to us an actual historical religious life,—men filled with the profoundest thoughts of God, and living to God a most close personal life, and, having such thoughts of God and such experiences of life to Him, importunate in their desires and attempts to awaken in those around them the same thoughts and the same life. This is the strange scene, full of the intensest reality, which the Old Testament exhibits to us,—a scene continued down through a long historical period, changing in some ways, but always presenting the same main feature —namely, that of a body of profoundly religious men speaking the truth to their countrymen, and seeking to turn them to God. Thus we do not go to the Old Testament with any general conception that it is the word of God spoken to us. We do not go to it with this conception, but we rise from it with this conception. This is the thing which will be made plain to us,—the personal religion of all the writers of Scripture, their life to God and with God. This becomes plainer the lower down we come,—in the Psalter, for example, and in such books as Job. In the period after the Exile we shall find problems raised by the conditions of life,—problems touching God's rule of the world, His relation to Israel, the people who knew Him, and were the representatives of His cause in the world ; problems, too, of His relations to the godly in an ungodly generation. To the intellect these questions might be insoluble. But we shall see something that enabled men to live without a solution. This was their religion, their conscious fellowship with God. We shall find that more and more religious certainty was based on this consciousness. It was the only thing the pious mind possessed, but it was at last always found enough. "Nevertheless," said the Psalmist, tried by misfortune and intellectually paralysed before the riddles of providence,—"nevertheless, I am continually with thee" (Ps. lxxiii. 23). The consciousness of God becomes the other side of self-consciousness, and this in- ward assurance will be seen to be strong enough to face all the difficulties raised by what is external.

2. Studies preliminary to Old Testament Theology.

This conception of what Old Testament Theology is at once suggests that certain studies must precede it. If it be the presentation to ourselves of the gradual advance of the kingdom of God as exhibited to us in the successive books of Scripture, it is necessary that we should see how these books follow one another, and know the age to which they belong, and of which they reflect the life and the thought. Criticism or Introduction must precede any attempt at a scientific Old Testament Theology. And this fact is what legitimates Criticism and gives it a place as a handmaid to Theology. As a mere literary science whose object was to settle the ages of the various literary components of the Bible, and describe their characteristics, and indicate their connections with the history of the People of Israel regarded as any other ancient people, Criticism would have no proper place among our theological disciplines. But when it is not pursued simply for its own sake, so to speak, but is used as an instrument for disposing the books of the Old Testament in their proper place so that we may correctly perceive how ideas arose and followed one another in Old Testament times, and may observe how history reacted upon the thought and life of the people, then Criticism has a very important place to fill.

Obviously, too, Old Testament Theology must be preceded by scientific exegesis of the literature in its length and breadth. We cannot create a trustworthy theology of the Old Testament by merely picking out a text here and there in an Old Testament book. We must know the whole scope of the book. Individual passages always derive their meaning from the context. Torn from their surroundings their mere language might suggest to us much more or sometimes perhaps much less than they really mean. Such passages have usually some bearing on the circumstances of the author's time. This bearing often greatly modifies their meaning, and it is seldom that we can really discover the true sense of any single passage in a book unless we have made a study of the whole book and learned to estimate the author's general modes of thinking, the broad drift of his ideas, and discovered to what matters in the history of his people and what

condition of their minds it is that he is directing his whole
work.   Such studies of whole books are useful and almost
necessary preliminaries to Old Testament Theology.   Such
studies, exhibiting what the Germans call the *Lehrbegriff*,
the general drift of the teaching of a book, have not been
uncommon in connection with the New Testament.   They
have been less attended to with regard to the Old
Testament.

3. *Definitions and Characteristics of Old Testament Theology.*

Old Testament Theology has been defined to be the
historical and genetic presentation of the religion of the
Old Testament; or as others express it, it is that branch
of theological science which has for its function to present
the religion of Revelation in the ages of its progressive
movement.   These definitions do not differ from the one
already suggested, namely, that it is the presentation of
the great operation of God in bringing in the kingdom of
God, so far as that operation was carried on in the Old
Testament period.   The one definition speaks of the
religion of the Old Testament, and the other of God's
operation in bringing in His kingdom.   But these two
things are in the main the same.   The kingdom of God
is within us.   To bring in the kingdom was to awaken a
certain religious life in His people, and to project great
thoughts and hopes before their minds.   This life and
these thoughts are reflected to us in the Old Testament
Scriptures.   These various definitions all imply the same
distinct characteristics.

They all imply, *e.g.*, that Old Testament Theology is a
historical science.   It is historical in the same sense as that
in which the Old Testament is historical, *i.e.* in the sense that
its parts follow one another down through a long period of
time.   We can readily perceive reasons sufficient to explain
the gradual and historical inbringing of the kingdom of God.
For instance, one of the first necessities to one who will
take his place in the kingdom of God is that God should

be known to him, at least on the moral side of His being. But God could not make His moral nature known by mere statements concerning Himself delivered at once. His power He could reveal in one terrible act, but the principles lying behind His power, and governing the exercise of it,—His justice, His goodness, His grace, in a word His moral nature,—could not be shown except by a prolonged exhibition of Himself in relation to the life of men. When we look at the Divine names we observe that the attribute which the Shemitic mind earliest laid hold of was the Divine power. The Shemitic people were slower to learn His other attributes, especially to learn the constancy and unchangeableness of these attributes, in other words, to rise to the conception of God as a transcendent moral Person. They could be taught this only by observing how God acted in their history with a terrible consistency, punishing evil with an inflexible uniformity, and making righteousness on their part the condition of His being their God and protecting them. When we read the Prophets we perceive that they considered that this was the chief lesson which the people's history was fitted to teach them. In opposition to their superficial hopes, founded on Jehovah's being their national God, and their expectation that they could at any time secure His favour by making their burnt sacrifices fatter and more abundant, these prophets insist upon the ethical uniformity of the Divine Mind, which cannot be bribed by gifts, but demands rectitude : " I hate, I despise your feasts . . . let judgment roll down as waters, and righteousness as a mighty stream " (Amos v. 21–24, R.V.). This lesson in regard to the nature of God is the chief lesson which the prophets draw from the history of the people. But one can conceive many other uses served by the long preliminary history of Israel. Its many vicissitudes threw individuals into very various circumstances, often trying, sometimes joyous, and thus we have those beautiful pictures of the life of the individual with God which are contained in the Book of Psalms, almost the most precious heritage which the Church has derived from Israel, and to which there is almost nothing similar in the New Testament period.

These definitions also all imply that the presentation of the Old Testament religion in Old Testament Theology is *genetic*. This means not only that Old Testament Theology shows us the religion of the Old Testament *in genesi*, that is, in the condition of actually arising or originating, but that its progress was, so to speak, organic. It grew, and that not by mere accretion or the external addition of truth to truth. The succeeding truth rose out of the former truth. This was due to the fact that the kingdom of God was planted into the life of a people, and thus its progress was inseparably connected with the progress and destiny of the nation of Israel. We cannot get a religious progress without a religious subject in whose mind we observe the progress. Now, the religious subject in the Old Testament was the people of Israel—and the progress can be studied in the mind of this subject as influenced by its history. Revelation of truth was not, so to speak, communicated from without; but the organs of revelation rose within the people in the persons of its highest representatives, men in whom its life beat fullest and its aspirations were most perfectly embodied. Thus the truths concerning the kingdom of God which they were enabled, stage after stage, to reach, had a connection with one another parallel to the connection between the stages of the life of the people. The truths regarding the kingdom of God appearing in the Old Testament are all given in terms, so to speak, of the history, institutions, and life of the people of Israel. It is customary to regard the institutions of Israel, its offices and ordinances, as all prearranged parallels to the things of the Christian Church, shadows and adumbrations or types, as they are called, of the realities of the New Testament kingdom. Now, of course, it must be maintained that the perfect form of the kingdom of God, the form which it was to have in the New Testament, was contemplated from the beginning. There was a determinism impressed on the Old Testament kingdom toward its perfect form; it was a growth, an organism of which we see the complete stature only in the New Testament kingdom. But we must not regard those institutions in Israel as only having this use of foreshadowing the future. They were real institutions and offices there, and their reference to the future was probably, in many instances, not understood or even surmised. The way they bore reference to the future in the minds of the people was rather this. The highest thinkers among the people, such as the prophets, perceived the idea lying in the offices and institutions, and expressed their longing and certainty that the idea would be yet realised.

Thus it was, for instance, with the kingship. Its idea was a king of God's kingdom, a representative of God sitting on the throne in Jerusalem. Such an idea of the kingship led to the most brilliant idealising of the king and his office. Being king for God and in God's kingdom, he had attribute after attribute assigned to him, all reflections of the Divine attributes, till at length he was even styled the 'mighty God,' he in whom God Himself would be wholly present. And not only the kingship, but other offices and other characters appearing among the people were idealised; and as it by and by came to be felt that such ideals could not be realised in the present, the realisation of them was thrown into the future. One of the most remarkable of these ideals is the Suffering Servant of the Lord, which is rather a personification of the suffering people idealised. But, in general, everything significant in the people's history and life was, as it were, abstracted from its relations in the present; it was held up and magnified by a process of moral idealisation—and the realisation of it thrown into the future. Thus the people's minds were directed to the future, not, as is often thought, because they understood beforehand or ever were taught that their institutions were all predetermined shadows of a reality to come, but because they perceived that the ideals which their institutions suggested to them, and which their history and experience had called up before their mind, were ideals that could not be realised in the present, in the conditions of the people and the world that then existed, nor even under those institutions which had been the very means of suggesting the ideals to their minds.

But, again, these definitions all imply that Old Testament Theology is a *development*. It is not a thing complete, it is but the earlier part of Biblical Theology, and is completed in New Testament Theology. Still, Biblical Revelation being an organism, Old Testament Theology is not a torso. It is a growth which, though it has not attained perfection, has attained a certain proper development. All its parts are there, though none of it is yet in full stature. There is perhaps no truth in the New Testament which does not lie in germ in the Old; and conversely, there is perhaps no truth in the Old Testament, which has not been expanded and had new meaning put into it in the New. The Old Testament contains the same truths as the New Testament, but in a less developed form, and we must avoid two errors which are not uncommon. The one is the mistake of separating the Old Testament from the New in such a way as leaves us with no authoritative truth in the Old. The other is to confuse the New and the Old so that we shall find the Old equally advanced with the New. The difference between the New and the Old is not that the same truths are not found in both, but that in the one the truths are found in a less degree of development than in the other. The Old Testament is as good authority for a truth as the New; only we must not go beyond the degree which the truth has yet reached in the Old Testament.

This fact, however, that the progress of the kingdom was organic and at last culminated, suggests that the Old Testament should be read by us always in the light of the end, and that in framing an Old Testament Theology we should have the New Testament completion of it in our view. What we shall be engaged in is mainly discovering the thoughts and estimating the life of the Old Testament people in its various stages. But it is obvious that at no time was the consciousness of the Old Testament Church able to take in the whole meaning of the development in the midst of which it stood. It must be our first object to discover what views the prophets and other Old Testament writers had, to present them to ourselves, and to take care not to impose New Testament conceptions upon them. Still, it will be of interest to ourselves to compare the two together, and to see how far the Old Testament Church had been able to realise to itself the point towards which the development was moving; and, knowing this goal, we shall be in a better position to estimate the meaning of the Old Testament from the light in which it is thus set for us.

4. *The Relation of Old Testament Ideas to the Old Testament History.*

If the view which we have taken of our subject, then, is correct, it will appear that, though we speak of Old Testament *Theology*, all that we can attempt is to present the religion or religious ideas of the Old Testament. As held in the minds of the Hebrew people, and as exhibited in their Scriptures, these ideas form as yet no Theology. There is no system in them of any kind. They are all practical religious beliefs, and are considered of importance only as they influence conduct. We do not find a *theology* in the Old Testament; we find a *religion*—religious conceptions and religious hopes and aspirations. It is we ourselves that create the theology when we give to these religious ideas and convictions a systematic or orderly form. Hence our subject really is the History of the Religion of Israel as represented in the Old Testament. We have seen, too, that the presentation or exhibition of the religious ideas is to be historical. This is the systematic form under which the religious ideas are presented, and which the Old Testament itself supplies. The historical character of the Old Testament religion is one of its chief characteristics, that is, its continuance and growth during a long period of history. And, further, we have seen that the presentation is organic. This, indeed, is contained in the fact that it is historical. The history of any individual consciousness must be organic, whether the mind be that of a nation or that of a person. Our successive experiences and the phases of mind which we go through during a lifetime are not isolated occurrences. They rise each out of the other. They are connected with our external history ; many times they are due to it. But even our external history has a unity and an organic character in it. And this is no doubt truer of a nation, or at least its truth may be more distinctly perceived in national life. When, therefore, it is said that the Old Testament religion is to be presented organically, it is meant that each step of progress was intimately connected with the people's history—with their experiences. Revelations of this truth or that were not made sporadically, but were given in continuous connection with the national life and experience, and so the truths are interlinked with one another in the same way as the successive stages of evolution in the national history are.[1]

5. *Divisions of the Subject.*

Now, the question arises, What divisions of the subject shall we adopt ? If we employed the ordinary threefold division,—Theology, Anthropology, and Soteriology,—we

[1] "From an evolutionist point of view, men speak of the development of the religion of Israel. From a different point of view, the history of Israel's religion is called a progressive revelation. We must remember that a progressive revelation from the Divine side must exhibit itself among men as a persistent struggle to realise new truths. Every new thought of God is first understood in a soul which has been made receptive for it ; and, once grasped, it maintains itself in him who is illumined by it, as well as in those around him, only by conflict. This conflict appears to one man as a progressive development ; to another, who, by experience, has learned to know the gulf between God and the human heart as a terrible reality, it appears as a progressive revelation. But, however it be regarded, all are agreed that from the Tora and Nebîim [Law and Prophets] we can understand how the precious treasure of Israel's religion came more and more fully to light, and maintained itself ever more firmly " (Wildeboer, *Canon*, p. 162).

should have to take each of these subjects and trace it down, step by step, through the whole length of the nation's history, marking the points at which the current of thought on the subject received new additions or a new momentum. Perhaps, however, the easier way would be to divide the history into periods, to cut it into zones, as it were, and examine in each of these zones the whole religious thought of the people during the period, as it is reflected in the literature of that period. This method preserves better the historical character of the study, and this is the method usually adopted by writers on the subject of Old Testament Theology. In point of fact, the three-fold theological division — Theology, or doctrine of God; Anthropology, or doctrine of man; and Soteriology, or doctrine of salvation—is somewhat too abstract for a subject like ours. What we meet with in the Old Testament are two concrete subjects and their relation. The two are: Jehovah God of Israel, on the one hand, and Israel, the people of Jehovah, on the other; and the third point, which is given in the other two, is their relation to one another. And it is obvious that the dominating or creative factor in the relation is Jehovah. The Old Testament contains almost exclusively a *theology* (λόγος περὶ Θεοῦ) or doctrine of Jehovah the God of Israel. It is to be observed, too, that what we have to do with is not a doctrine of God, but a doctrine of *Jehovah, Israel's God.* We have reached now such a stage of thinking on the Divine that, while some may doubt whether there be a God at all, nobody supposes that there is more than one. But this point is just one that has to be inquired into regarding Jehovah—how far Israel's God was believed to be God alone. At all events, as I have said, He was the normative factor in the relation. He moulded the people, and the mould into which He cast them was that of His own nature. The conceptions of the people regarding Jehovah immediately reacted on the people and created corresponding conceptions regarding themselves. The people must be what their God, Jehovah, was.

Now, thoughts of Jehovah or revelations regarding

Him,—for the two things are the same, seeing that a revelation is no revelation until it takes the shape of human thought,—might run on two chief lines. One would be ethical or spiritual conceptions of Jehovah—conceptions which immediately reacted on the people and made them feel that the same ethical character was demanded from them, if they were to be His people. And a second would be thoughts of how Jehovah was to be served in acts of worship—in other words, thoughts regarding the sacred ritual. Now, these are the two lines on which most of the sacred writings of the people run. The first line of conceptions, the ethical or spiritual, whether in regard to the nature of Jehovah or the conduct of His people, was chiefly developed by the prophets. The line of ritual service naturally was developed mostly by the priests, or at least by men who were more practical than the prophets. But even the ritual legislation was influenced by the prophetic teaching—it was often an embodiment in a practical form of their ideas. This second line, then, is that of the legislation, for all the legislation relates to the worship or ritual service of Jehovah—at least in the main. These two streams of thought might be called objective, so far as the body of the people was concerned. For, though the prophetic thoughts were, of course, profoundly subjective to the prophets themselves, that is, rose up out of their own hearts with the greatest intensity and fire of conviction, yet the prophets were a small body compared with the whole mass; they were the organs of revelation to the general body. And in like manner the legislation, which was many times a mere practical embodiment of prophetic teaching, was formulated by small bodies of priests, and was imposed upon the mass by authority.

Besides these two objective streams there were two others, which might be called subjective. One of these was the expression of personal devotion, or the spiritual experience and exercise of the individual mind, such as we have in the Psalms. There is no reason at all to suppose that the bulk of the Psalms are the production of one individual

They are the expression of the devotion, and many times of the religious conflicts of the individual mind, throughout the whole of the people's history, particularly during its later stages. And, secondly, the other subjective stream of thought was that embodied in the Wisdom. This is the expression of the religious reflecting mind, as the other was of the devotional mind. The pious emotions responded to the prophetic truth, and to the demands of the law, in words that run through the whole scale of religious feeling. The reflecting mind delighted itself by observing how the great ethical truths of Jehovah's nature were everywhere verifying themselves in His providence in the world and in men's lives. Or it was startled at a later time, when even the godly lay under grievous calamities, to find that the prophetical teaching was contradicted by events of actual providence. This gave rise to doubts and questionings, by which men were sometimes almost driven to despair. This Wisdom we have in the Proverbs, many of the Psalms, Job, and Ecclesiastes; and, of course, to all these have to be added many expressions of religious faith and many examples of religious conduct in the historical writings.

Keeping, then, all these general lines of thought in view, which are in the main four,—prophecy, or religious politics; legislation, or the ritual of worship; devotion, and reflection,—we have the literary materials which we have to divide into periods, so as to exhibit the historical growth of the conceptions which the materials embody. Naturally, any division will to some extent break in upon things closely connected, because the growth of thought or the stream of history cannot be cut into sections. For it is a thing continuous and uninterrupted. But with this admission the following division marks the great points in the literary history of Israel.

6. *The great Historical Periods.*

(*a*) *A preliminary or introductory period terminating with the Exodus.*—The Old Testament religion hardly begins till the Exodus.   Therefore the religious subject in Old Testament times with whom Jehovah's covenant was made was the people Israel, not individual Israelites, and the people was the creation of the great act of redemption at the Exodus. This period, then, would be preliminary.   We have no literature *from* this period itself.   What we have is the *view* of this period taken in the ninth and eighth centuries.   This *view* contains many elements—particularly *two*, national traditions of early human history not peculiar to Israel, but shared in by most Shemitic nations; and, secondly, the penetration and modification of these traditions by the principles of the religion of Jehovah—*e.g.* in the narratives of the Creation, the Fall, the Flood, etc.   So the patriarchal period is the period of tradition, and of tradition possibly religiously coloured.   What is perhaps most important for us is this religious colouring, rather than the mere details of the history.

(*b*) *The period from the Exodus to written prophecy,* B.C. 800.—The beginning of written prophecy in the deliverances of Amos and his successors is a point of such importance that it is natural to make it an era.   Apart from the religious truths taught by the canonical prophets there is one thing which characterises them all from Amos downwards.   They have completely broken with the nation, whose condition they condemn and pronounce to be hopeless, and on the eve of destruction.   This destruction is inevitable, Jehovah their God being what He is.   No doubt earlier prophets express the same judgment, but less universally.   Even as early as Solomon, Ahijah of Shiloh predicted the downfall of his kingdom (1 Kings xi. 31–39). And Elijah's attitude was the same towards the kingdom of the north.   Perhaps during this period we can trace only two of the four great streams of thought with much certainty.

1. Of Prophecy, we have examples in Deborah, Samuel, Elijah, and Elisha.   Except the Song of Deborah, there is no literary prophecy.   Under prophecy, however, according to the Jewish modes of classification, fall historical writings, *e.g.* Judges, the Books of Samuel.

2. The other stream is that of Legislation. Here we can put with certainty the so-called Book of the Covenant, Ex. xx.–xxiii. It may be the case that more should be placed here; but this is disputed. It is probable, however, that there were both Psalms and Proverbs during this period—the latter certainly, as, *e.g.*, in the fable of Jotham. But it is difficult to identify those of this age As to this oldest legislation, however, all scholars are agreed, and with it goes, of course, a good deal of the history in Genesis, Exodus, Numbers, and Joshua. It is very probable that laws more strictly ritual than those in the code Ex. xx.–xxiii. existed. But it is not certain that they were yet reduced to writing, being merely traditional among the priests. If written, they were kept within the priestly circles.

(c) *From 800, written prophecy, to 586, the Exile of Judah.*—1. Prophecy. The stream of prophecy beginning with Amos gradually widens out to be a broad and imposing river. The great prophets whose names we know belong to this period—Amos, Hosea, Micah, Isaiah, and Jeremiah. Perhaps it would be safest to close the period with Jeremiah, who survived the Exile only a very short time, and to carry Ezekiel into the next period. He survived the Exile a number of years, and for other reasons he rather belongs to the post-Exile sphere.

2. In Legislation we have belonging to this period the Book of Deuteronomy. This may be said apart from any theory of its origin or even its date of composition. It ought to be placed in this period on other grounds. It was discovered in the Temple in the year 621. Made public in this year, it exercised immediately a powerful influence upon the worship, and also upon the general current of the people's thoughts. This period of its discovery was that when its teaching really became a factor in the public life and the religious conceptions of the nation. It became public law, and powerfully influenced both religious practice and religious literature from this date. It is also the general impression among writers on the Old Testament

2

that Deuteronomy follows the great prophets Amos, Hosea, and Isaiah, and reflects in its spirit their teaching. So far as its legislative contents apart from its spirit are concerned, they are an expansion of Ex. xx.–xxiii.

(*d*) *From the Exile,* 586, *to* 400, *the close of the prophetical Canon.*—This might be called the period of the Restoration and Reconstruction of the State. It deserves to be considered a distinct period, because undoubtedly new conceptions and a new way of reading the past history of the nation arose, and also a new ideal for the future. The prophet Ezekiel belongs to this period, at least as a powerful influence, though in point of fact he lived mainly during the preceding period.

It includes : 1. Prophecy—Ezekiel, II Isaiah, Zechariah, Haggai, Malachi.   2. Legislation—the Levitical legislation of Ezra and Nehemiah.   3. The Psalter.   4. The Wisdom.

(1) As to Prophecy. The second half of Isaiah is usually placed in this era. Its contents refer it to this period. If Isaiah was its author, he was enabled to project himself in spirit into the Exile, and see and estimate that period, with its personages and forces, precisely as if he had lived during it in the body.

(2) The Legislation of this period is the so-called priestly or Levitical legislation, contained now in Ex. xxv.–xl., Leviticus, and good part of Numbers. It is disputed, indeed, whether this legislation as a whole belongs to this period. And it may be allowed to be probable that there were written ritual laws as early as other laws. There were customary ritual actions—a ritual praxis, consuetudinary and practised—embracing the various kinds of sacrifice, though the numbers of victims, etc., might not be fixed. This ritual praxis gradually expanded, and became more splendid, more refined, more expressive in details of the underlying ideas. We see it in great grandeur in the time of Amos and Isaiah ; it was about complete in the time of Ezekiel. It is not at all probable that these ritual laws were for the first time written at this late period, but at this period they appear to have been

brought together and codified, and no doubt additions were made to them to give them theoretical completeness. They are probably the result of the ritual practice throughout the history as it was modified and improved. It appears to me that the Book of Ezekiel shows that before his day the ritual was almost the same as it became after the Restoration. But how far the ritual customs had been reduced to writing before this period is difficult to ascertain. Being largely for the guidance of the priests, they had less public importance.

Apart, however, from other considerations, there are, at any rate, these two reasons for placing the priestly legislation here—first, it was certainly not completed or codified in the form in which we have it till this period ; and, secondly, what is more important, it did not become an element in the national life till this era. Whether it existed before or not, it was not obeyed, the nation did not subject themselves to it. From the year 444, when Ezra and Nehemiah read the Law before the people, it is certain that this Levitical law, as a ritual, and the hierarchical system as a government, became the ritual and government of the community. The theocracy, which was, so to speak, ideal before (*i.e.* Jehovah was king), now became hierarchical : the theocracy was a government by priests ; the high priest was the head of the community.

(3) The Psalter. The Psalter must be placed here for various reasons. It was only now that the Psalms were collected together, and as a whole made the medium of the devotional service in the temple. Not before this time did the Psalter enter into the people's life as the expression of their devotions, and as a powerful influence upon their life. In estimating the progress of religious thought and devotional life, we must recognise the public acceptance of the Psalter as the expression of this thought and life to be one of the most important events with which we have to deal. Many of the Psalms, of course, may be ancient. It would be as untrue to say that the Psalmody of Israel took its rise with the Second Temple, as to say that the Thames rises

at London Bridge. But though the Thames rises higher up, it begins at London Bridge to bear on its bosom the commerce and the industrial life of the nations; and the Psalter, too, begins with the Second Temple to express the religious life, not of individuals, but of Israel. And the national use of the Psalter shows how completely all the conflicts which the prophets had to wage against idolatry and the like, had been fought out and the battle won. The providence of God had set its seal on the prophetic teaching, and it was accepted by the restored nation.

(4) The Wisdom. The Proverbial literature probably would fall largely into the preceding period. But some of the most splendid fruits of the reflective mind of Israel, such as the Book of Job, probably belong to this epoch. The Wisdom belongs to the literature of the individual's religious life; Prophecy and Legislation to the sphere of the national life. Consequently the Wisdom literature is mainly late.

(e) *From* 400 *to the Christian era.*—This embraces: 1. Prophecy—Daniel; 2. Wisdom—Ecclesiastes; 3. History—Chronicles. This is the period of the Law.

The division which we have followed gives five periods, a preliminary one, and four others—From Moses to prophecy, 800; from 800 to 586, the fall of Jerusalem; from 586 to 400; and from 400 to our era. But perhaps the whole period from the Exodus might be divided into three characteristic stages—1. Pre-prophetic period, down to 800; 2. Prophetic period, down to 586; and 3. Levitism, down to our era. Of course, these names are general. Prophetism is but the development of Mosaism on one side; but it is a distinct development and a literary development. Similarly, Levitism is a development of Mosaism on another side, but it is no doubt an expansion; and historically the Levitical system during this period actually made itself master of the people, and brought them into subjection to it, which historically had not been true at an earlier period.

The prophets, being statesmen in the kingdom of God, stand in closest relation to the history, and in their pages the significance of the various momenta and turning points in the national career can best be estimated. And it is their teaching that we should chiefly have before us. From 850 or 800 to 400 B.C. they are the main figures in the history of Israel; and unquestionably the prophetic literature is the most characteristic, and has most affinities with the New Testament. We are able to receive a better general idea of the religion of the Old Testament by studying the Prophets than by reading any other part of the Hebrew Scriptures. The literature of the period ending with 800 or 750 B.C. is scanty, being chiefly contained in the part of the Pentateuch called J, or the united elements JE. It is different with the prophetical period, 800–586, which is the most important for an Old Testament theologian, *i.e.* for one who wishes to understand the development of Revelation or the religion of Israel historically—in other words, to understand the faith and hopes of Israel as they existed actually in the minds of the prophets and the people. All the great religious conceptions of the Old Testament come to view in this period. An exception might be made in regard to the doctrine of immortality. But there are two doctrines of immortality in the Old Testament—that of the people, the kingdom of God; and that of the individual person. The former is fully developed in the prophetic age; that of the individual, perhaps not until the period of Judaism. For the prophetic teaching is, so to speak, national; it was only on the downfall of the State that the meaning and worth of the individual life began to be adequately felt, and consequently that the destinies of the individual began to be earnestly pursued and reflected upon. But very much of the Christian doctrine of immortality—*e.g.* the concomitants of it, the judgment; the result of it, eternal peace and fellowship with God, and the like—is taught in the Old Testament in connection with the eschatology of the kingdom or people of God.

But if the prophetic period be the most important period for the Old Testament theologian, the period of

Judaism, from the Restoration in 537 to our era, is of supreme importance for the Christian theologian or exegete. Because, although this period is not so rich in original productions, it is the period of reflection and generalisation on the prophetic teaching, and of appropriation and assimilation of it into the individual life. This process in great measure stripped off the nationalism from the prophetic truths, and brought them under individualism. But individualism is universalism. The individual is of no nation.

But this way of looking at the ancient literature generalised the contents. The circumstances in which a truth was uttered ceased to be of importance, while the person who uttered it or to whom it was uttered was equally unimportant. All those things ceased to have meaning. The things that had meaning—and had universal applicability — were the ethical and religious principles. These were the Word of God. So that in a sense it is true that the better historical Old Testament theologians we are, the worse fitted are we to comprehend the New Testament writers. It is admitted that the sense put by New Testament writers on much of the Old Testament which they quote is not the true historical sense, *i.e.* not the sense which the original writers, prophets, or wise men had in their mind. The sense which the New Testament writers express is the sense which arose during the period of Judaism—which experience and reflection and personal piety put upon the Old Testament. Hence is it that to the Christian theologian or exegete the period of Judaism is of the utmost importance.

7. *General Course and Drift of the History.*

The literature of Israel, then, being so closely connected with its history, it is of importance to understand the general course and drift of the latter. As in all ancient States, the religion was national. The religious unit or subject was not the individual in the State, but the ideal unity formed by the State as a whole. Now, this unity came into existence at the Exodus from Egypt. From that hour Israel was conscious of being a people, and Jehovah, who had delivered them, was their God alone: "I am Jehovah thy God, who brought thee out of the land of Egypt" (Ex. xx. 2 ; cf. Hos. xiii. 4). The sense of being a people, and the sense of being the people of Jehovah, if not identical feelings, reacted very powerfully on one another ; and hence the religious literature of the people reflects from age to age all the changing hues of its history. That history ran very much such a course as we should have expected.

(1) The migration of the ancestors of the people from the East, the descent into Egypt, the oppression and bondage there, and the delivery under Moses, are events testified to not only in the formal history of the Penta-teuch, but by frequent incidental allusions in other writing. These allusions express the fundamental historical feeling of the people, the very basis of their national and religious consciousness (Amos ii. 9 seq. ; Hos. xii. 13 ; Mic. vi. 4).

(2) Disintegration under the Judges. It was natural that the unity into which the tribes[1] had been welded at the Exodus by the necessity of facing a common danger, or sharing a common enterprise, should become relaxed when the danger was over and the enterprise had in great measure succeeded ; and, accordingly, after the settlement in Canaan, we find the unity in some degree disintegrated, and the various tribes fighting each for its own hand, and only entering into combinations when some danger more serious than usual threatened. Such is the history as reflected in the Book of Judges. No doubt a religious disintegration in some measure ran parallel to the political one. Even in this troubled period, however, although

---

[1] The tribes entered Canaan, or at least conquered a place in it, not in common, but independently, or in smaller combinations. There were two Canaanite belts—between Judah and the northern tribes, and between the northern tribes themselves, *i.e.* the plain of Jezreel.

practically the tribes are often seen acting independently, and settling with a strong hand their own local differences with the native population, the sense of the ideal unity of all the tribes as one 'Israel' inspired the higher minds in the nation, as, *e.g.*, the prophetess Deborah (Judg. v. 2, 3, 5, 7, 9, etc.); and the need of some single head, such as a king, to represent this unity is often felt and expressed by the people (Judg. viii. 22).

(3) The Monarchy. When a danger, so pressing that it threatened the national existence of Israel, arose in the Philistine [1] power, the need of a visible head to bind the tribes together, and animate them with a common impulse, and lead them against the common enemy, was universally recognised, and the people demanded that Samuel should give them a king to "go out before us and fight our battles" (1 Sam. viii. 20). The aged seer, though reluctant to see the ideal sovereignty of Jehovah, the feeling of which should have been enough to secure the national unity, brought down and materialised in the form of an earthly representative king, was sagacious and patriotic enough to perceive the necessities of the time, and to take them under his direction. And thus arose the Monarchy, a partial attempt in the same direction having already been made by Abimelech (Judg. ix.). The history of this period is recorded in the Books of Samuel.

This period is of extreme importance in the literary and religious history of Israel. Three powerful streams of influence take their rise in it, and run through the whole succeeding history, fertilising and enriching it. These were, first, the prophetic order; a class of men who probably

[1] The origin of the Philistines is yet far from certain. They came from Caphtor (Amos ix. 7 ; Deut. ii. 23 ; Jer. xlvii. 4, 5), supposed by some to be Cappadocia, by others to be Crete, or Cyprus, or the northern Egyptian Delta. They either were Semites, or they speedily adopted the language and religion of the country. Their chief god appears to be allied to the Aramaic Marnas and the Babylonian Dagan. The time of their settlement on the coast of Palestine must have been during the time Israel was in Egypt.

existed from the earliest times along with the Nazirites
(Amos ii. 11), but who acquired an influence in the State
at this period, first as counsellors and seers of the early
kings (Nathan, Gad, 2 Sam. xii. 1, xxiv. 11), and ultimately as an independent order who took the religious
destinies of the nation into their own hands, and in whose
writings, the Prophetical Scriptures, we have the fullest
exposition of that lofty spiritual religion in Israel to which
the New Testament directly attaches itself. Secondly, the
elevation of the Davidic dynasty to the throne. The
brilliant reign of David, whose arms extended the limits of
the Jewish State till for those days it might justly be
named an empire, became the ideal of after ages; and
when, amidst disaster and religious decline, men looked
back to it and transfigured it in the light of the religious
hopes which filled their minds, it became the type both of
a future king and a future universal kingdom of God that
would arise upon the earth in the latter days. These
special predictions of the perfection of the kingdom of the
Lord, named Messianic prophecies, all borrow their form and
colours from this powerful reign. And, thirdly, the choice
of Jerusalem as the centre both of the national and the
religious life of the people. The influence of the Temple of
Solomon, both in purifying and in elevating the ritual worship, as well as in leading ultimately to its concentration at
one shrine, cannot be overestimated. But the step taken by
David gave a colour to all succeeding literature. Patriotism and religion were once more wedded together. Jerusalem was not only the perfection of beauty, the joy of the
whole earth (Ps. xlviii. 2), it was also the 'hearth' of
Jehovah, who dwelt in Zion at Jerusalem (Isa. xxix. 1).
National sentiment mingled with religious emotion in one
powerful stream, and the union has given to the religious
poetry of Israel, which celebrates 'Zion,' or longs to revisit
it, or tells that its dust is dear, not only a religious value,
but a never-dying human pathos.

(4) Disruption of the Kingdom. There had existed
from of old a jealousy between the North and the South,

between the powerful tribe of Ephraim, which always aspired to the leadership of the tribes, and the great tribe of Judah. We see already in the Song of Deborah the smaller tribes clustering around Ephraim, and learn from the fact that Judah receives no mention that this great family had already begun to pursue its own course and go its own way. Naturally, therefore, when the unity of the tribes under the Monarchy was subjected to a great strain under Rehoboam, it broke asunder, and two kingdoms arose, existing side by side, sometimes hostile to one another, but in the main friendly.[1] Though either of the two kingdoms might prove itself sufficiently strong to hold in subjection the petty States of Edom and Moab, and even to maintain its own against the more powerful kingdom of Syria, when the time came that they were confronted with the imposing empires of Assyria and Babylon, they naturally lost their independence, first Israel at the hands of Assyria (721 B.C.), and then Judah at the hands of Babylon (586 B.C.), and became merged in these empires as provinces. The internal history of the two kingdoms is told in the Books of Kings; and the internal condition of the people, the relaxation of morals, the struggles of contending parties, and the cruel idolatries to which despair had recourse, are reflected in the pages of the prophets— in the writings of Amos and Hosea during the last years of Samaria; in Isaiah and Micah during the conflict of Judah with Assyria; and in Jeremiah during the death struggle of Judah with Babylon.

(5) The Exile and Restoration; Israel a religious community. As one colossal empire followed another and succeeded to the inheritance of its predecessor,—Babylon,

---

[1] Though the nation now formed two kingdoms, not always friendly, the conception of the higher unity of all parts of Israel still filled the religious minds of the country. Hosea, a prophet of the North, has the tenderest regard for Judah. Amos, a native of Judah, felt called to preach to Samaria. And all Isaiah's earlier prophecies have regard both to Judah and to Israel, which to his mind are one people of Jehovah; and he addresses his oracles to both the houses of Israel—Israel and Judah (viii. 14). Even Jeremiah and Ezekiel still continue to speak of one Israel—North and South.

Persia, Greece, and Rome,—the people of Israel, no longer independent, existed as a community governed internally in the main in accordance with its own conceptions, but forming externally part of the heathen empire for the time. Only after a successful revolt against the Græco-Syrian rule of the Seleucids did the people again attain to independence, and become ruled by native princes for about a century (167–63 B.C.). It then fell under the influence of Rome, which finally destroyed the city and temple, 70 A.D.

No internal history of the Babylonian Exile has been written; but the picture of the desolation of the land, the sad silence in the streets and gates of Jerusalem, which used to ring with the joy of the feasts, and the sense of abasement and contempt into which the people had fallen as a nation among the nations, together with the flickerings of a faith in the sure mercies of the Lord that refused to be quenched (Lam. iii. 22),—all this may be seen in the exquisite collection of elegies known as the Lamentations, written not many years after the fall of the city; while the delirium of hope raised somewhat later by the victories of Cyrus, and the approaching downfall of Babylon, and the brilliant religious anticipations of the destruction of idolatry and the conversion of the nations to the true religion of Jehovah through the ministration of Israel restored, "the servant of the Lord," fill the pages of the second half of Isaiah (chs. xl.–lxvi.).

The fortunes of the returning exiles are described in Ezra and Nehemiah, and their hopes and despondencies in the three prophets of the Return (Zechariah, Haggai, Malachi); while the aims and faith and hopes of the godly Israel during the Maccabean struggles are reflected in the Book of Daniel. Thus, amidst all the vicissitudes of its eventful history, the literary activity of Israel knew no intermission. The great literary period extends from 800 to 400 B.C.; but much of the finest historical writing is anterior to this period, while several important books, as Chronicles, Ecclesiastes, and Daniel, fall later.

8. *Literary and Historical Criticism in relation to Old Testament Theology.*

It is admitted that the *order* in which the Old Testament literature now exists is not the historical order, and that traditional ideas regarding its date and authorship require sifting. For example, it is acknowledged that the Pentateuch is not a homogeneous work, the composition of a single person at a very early date, but consists of a number of distinct writings, originating at different periods, all down the people's history, and brought together at various times, so that it gradually assumed its present shape not earlier than about 500 B.C.; and that there are elements in it later than this period. Similarly, in regard to the prophetical writings, though the dates of the main parts of the prophetical literature are less liable to discussion, still it is a fact that the prophets themselves were less careful to collect their own prophecies than one might have expected. Jeremiah, for example, dictated to Baruch an outline of his prophecies for the first time more than *twenty* years after he became a prophet. The prophecies, as we have them, are the work of collectors or editors, and they are often grouped together according to subjects, though the individual prophecies may be of very different dates, or even different ages; and, further, the collectors, occasionally at least, made insertions in order to make the prophecies applicable to the thought and religious needs of their own time. Edification, not strict literary exactness and discrimination of dates, was the object they pursued.

The newest criticism is partly *textual* criticism and partly *literary*. It moves mainly in three lines.

1. It is acknowledged that the early history of the world (Gen. x., xi.), and the patriarchal history, and even partly the history of the Exodus, were not written down till very long after the events happened which are recorded. It is traditional or legendary. The question arises, How

much real history is it possible to extract from this? The narrative has affinities with early Babylonian traditions, and it is largely coloured by the religious sentiments of the age when the traditions were written down. How far, *e.g.*, are the Patriarchs real persons, or ideal types of nationalities (Esau = Edom; Laban = Arameans, etc.), or how far are they ideal types of the true Israel or the true Israelite?

2. Textual criticism. To take one example. Besides the formally poetical books, Psalms, Job, and Proverbs, it is certain that much of the early prophecy is poetical. Now, in criticising and attempting to restore the text of a classical poet, the metre would be a powerful instrument for use in the hand of the critic. Any current text where the metre was defective, making the line too long or too short, would certainly be false. The line, if too long, must he restored by some omission; or, if too short, by some insertion or change of words. Must the same process be applied to Hebrew poetry? Many scholars reply that it must. Hence enormous changes are introduced—by Duhm, for example—into the early prophetic texts, and into such books as Job and the Psalms.

3. As to *literary* criticism, *two* principles are assumed as undeniable. (1) The language, like all languages, has a history. The vocabulary changes in process of time, and to some extent also the syntax. After Jeremiah the Aramaic language begins to influence the Hebrew, both in vocabulary and in style. (2) It is not only the language that has a history, but also the thought of the nation. New thoughts arise. Modes of contemplating things are seen in later ages which were unknown in earlier times; and, in particular, ideas which might be called eschatological hopes and outlooks into the future destiny of the nation and of the other nationalities of the world become very prevalent.

Now, these principles being admitted, and it being further admitted that the literature, as it stands, has been collected by scripturalists—I use that word rather than scribes—in a way not chronological, and without discrimination with regard to what is ancient and what is modern,—the newest criticism feels that it has the task before it of applying these principles,—particularly those relating to the progressive changes in the language and the progressive changes in the religious ideas, and by their application separating the elements out of which the present texts of the prophecies have been composed, and showing which is ancient and which is recent. Now, these processes are, in principle, quite legitimate. No other method is open. But, at the same time, a door is opened to subjective and individual judgment, and the operation is necessarily a precarious one. The literature is very limited. An idea that is found now only in a late writing might really belong to an earlier time, if we only had a more extensive literature covering that time. But the effect of the criticism referred to is to cut up the writings, particularly the prophecies, into a multitude of fragments, and to introduce the greatest uncertainty into the exegesis. I cannot help thinking that this kind of criticism has gone to extremes in recent times, and has had the effect of discrediting the criticism which is legitimate.

II. THE DOCTRINE OF GOD.

1. *General Character of the Old Testament Conception of God.*

On the subject of *God* the ideas of the ancient world are in many respects different from our own. And the ideas of the Old Testament have, in these points of difference, naturally greater affinity with those of the ancient world in general than with ours. One such point of difference is this, that it never occurred to any prophet or writer of the Old Testament to prove the existence of God. To do so might well have seemed an absurdity. For all

Old Testament prophets and writers move among ideas that presuppose God's existence. Prophecy itself is the direct product of His influence. The people of Israel in their character and relation are His creation. It is not according to the spirit of the ancient world in general either to deny the existence of God or to use arguments to prove it. The belief was one natural to the human mind and common to all men. Scripture does indeed speak of men who say in their heart there is no God, but these are the *fools*, that is, the practically ungodly; and their denial is not a theoretical or speculative one, but merely what may be held to be the expression of their manner of life. Even the phrase " there is no God " hardly means that God is not, but rather that He is not present, does not interfere in life; and counting on this absence of God from the affairs of the world, and consequently on impunity, men become corrupt and do abominable deeds (Ps. xiv.). And for their wickedness they shall be cast into hell, the region of separation from God, along with all the nations that forget God (Ps. ix. 17). Yet even this forgetfulness of God by the nations is regarded as something temporary. It is a forgetting only; it is no obliteration of the knowledge of God from the human mind. That is impossible, and these nations shall yet remember and turn unto the Lord. Scripture regards men as carrying with them, as part of their very thought, the conception of God.

This being the case, the Old Testament naturally has no occasion to speculate on how this knowledge that God *is* arises in the mind. Its position is far in front of this. It teaches how God who is, is known, and is known to be what He is. But it seems nowhere to contemplate men as ignorant of the existence of God, and therefore it nowhere depicts the rise or dawn of the idea of God's existence on men's minds.[1] In the historical period the

---

[1] The origin of the idea of God, the origin of religion, is a question of great interest. As the origin lies so far beyond the horizon of history, little but conjectures regarding it need be looked for. We perhaps perceive two stages, the one the full historical stage, such as it meets us in all the Old

idea of God's existence is one of the primary thoughts
of man. He comes possessed of this thought to face and
observe the world. His conception of God already possessed
explains the world to him; the world does not suggest to
him an idea hitherto strange, that of the existence of God.
And, of course, the bare idea of the existence of God is not
the primary thought which Scripture supposes all men to
possess. This abstract idea gathers body about it, namely,
a certain circle of ideas as to what God is.

And with these ideas the Hebrew took up his position
over against the world. To him God and the world were
always distinct. God was not involved in the processes
of nature. These processes were caused by God, but were
quite distinct from God.

The Hebrew thinker, however, came down from his
thought of God upon the world; he did not rise from the
world up to his thought of God. His primary thought of

Testament writings; the other, one lying behind this, some dim traces of
which we may perceive in practices occasionally appearing in Israel, or
referred to in the history of the Patriarchs (such as Jacob's anointing with
oil the stone which he called Beth-el, the place of God); and in some things
treated and announced as superstitions in the historical period, such as
seeking for the living unto the dead, necromancy, witchcraft, and the like
(Isa. viii. 19). It has been thought that several sources of the religious idea
might be discovered, as, *e.g.*, animism, reverence for deceased ancestors, or
for heroes of the tribe, etc. The forces of nature, and man's subjection to
them, suggested powers, or more particularly spirits, as they were unseen.
These were located in various natural objects. In stones—generally natural,
but afterwards artificial, places were prepared for the spirit. These artificial
stones were the Maççebas or pillars. They either became altars or were
placed beside altars. We find them standing beside the altars of Jehovah,
and denounced by the prophet Hosea. Other objects to which the spirit
attached itself were trees and fountains. Hence some explain the part
played by trees in the patriarchal history, as the oak of Mamre near Hebron,
and the place given to the well Beersheba, long a sanctuary, as Amos
shows (v. 7). The sacred tree was, no doubt, common in Canaan, and was a
seat of the god, and a place where oracles were given; hence the name the
Oak of the Soothsayers (Judg. ix. 37). A later substitute for this sacred
tree was the Ashera—or wooden stock. This was also always naturally
beside an altar. Possibly many practices observed in mourning, such as
cutting off the hair, may have reference to dedication of the hair as a sacrifice
to the dead. Setting food before the dead is forbidden in Deuteronomy
(xxvi. 14). These practices in historic times are all treated as heathen
superstitions in Israel, and forbidden.

God explained to him the world, both its existence and the course of events upon it; these did not suggest to him either the existence or the character of God, these being unknown to him. The thought of the Hebrew, and his contemplation of providence and life, were never of the nature of a search after God whom he did not know, but always of the nature of a recognition and observation of the operation of God whom he already knew. There seems no passage in the Old Testament which represents men as reaching the knowledge of the existence of God through nature or the events of providence, although there are some passages which imply that false ideas of what God is may be corrected by the observation of nature and life. When the singer in the xixth Psalm says that " the heavens declare the glory of God," all that he means is that the glory of God, who is, and is known, and is Creator, may be seen reflected on the heavens. But the Psalmist only recognised on the heavens what he already carried in his heart. When, however, in Isa. xl. 25, 26, Jehovah, asks " To whom then will ye liken Me ? . . . Lift up your eyes on high, and see who hath created these things, that bringeth out their host by number," it is implied that false views of what God is may be corrected, or at least that they may be brought home to men's consciousness. There is an approximation to the arguments of Natural Theology in some of these passages. And even more in a passage in one of the Psalms (xciv. 5–11), when, speaking probably of the excuses of the heathen rulers of Israel, the writer says : " They break in pieces Thy people, O Lord, and afflict Thine heritage. They slay the widow and the stranger, and murder the fatherless. And they say, The Lord doth not see, neither doth the God of Jacob observe. Consider, ye brutish among the people : and ye fools, when will ye be wise ? He that planted the ear, shall He not hear ? He that formed the eye, shall He not see ? He that instructeth the nations, shall not He correct ? *Even* He that teacheth men knowledge ? The Lord knoweth the thoughts of men."

The Old Testament as little thinks of arguing or proving that God may be known as it thinks of arguing that He exists. Its position here again is far in front of such an argument. How should men think of arguing that God could be known, when they were persuaded they knew Him, when they knew they were in fellowship with Him, when their consciousness and whole mind were filled and aglow with the thought of Him, and when through His Spirit He moved them and enlightened them, and guided their whole history? There is nothing strictly peculiar, however, here.

The peculiarity of the Old Testament conception rather comes out when the question is raised, *how* God is known. Here we touch a fundamental idea of the Old Testament— the idea of *Revelation*. If men know God, it is because He has made Himself known to them. This knowledge is due to what He does, not to what men themselves achieve. As God is the source of all life, and as the knowledge of Him is the highest life, this knowledge cannot be reached by any mere effort of man. If man has anything of God, he has received it from God, who communicates Himself in love and grace. The idea of man reaching to a knowledge or fellowship of God through his own efforts is wholly foreign to the Old Testament. God speaks, He appears; man listens and beholds. God brings Himself nigh to men; He enters into a covenant or personal relation with them; He lays commands on them. They receive Him when He approaches; they accept His will and obey His behests.[1] Moses and the prophets are nowhere represented as thoughtful minds reflecting on the Unseen, and forming conclusions regarding it, or ascending to elevated conceptions of Godhead. The Unseen manifests itself before them, and they know it.

Such a revelation of God is everywhere supposed in the Old Testament. God is not a God that hides Himself in the sense that He is self-engrossed or self-absorbed. His Spirit streams through the world, producing all life and

[1] Cf. Schultz, *Alttest. Theol.*, fünfte Aufl. pp. 397, **398**.

maintaining it, and begetting in men a fellowship with the life of God. His word goes forth to the world that it shall be, and shall be upholden, and to men that they may know Him and live in Him. He appears and manifests Himself to the patriarchs in angelic forms, to the prophets in the inspiration of their minds, in visions and dreams or spiritual intuitions, and to Moses speaking face to face. The form of His manifestation of Himself may change, but the reality of it remains the same. The conviction in the mind of the prophet that God revealed Himself and His word to him when the truth broke upon his mind, was not less vivid than that of the patriarch who was visited by angelic forms when sitting in the door of his tent. The prophet speaks the word of God, has his ear awakened by God, is the messenger and interpreter of God, as much as Moses who saw the God of Israel on the mount. And this is not because the prophet rose to the conception of God, or attained to know His will by reflection. It was because God called him and put His words in his mouth.

But, however much the Old Testament reposes on the ground that all knowledge of God comes from His revealing Himself, and that there is such a true and real revelation, it is far from implying that this revelation of God is a full display of Him as He really is. An exhaustive communication of God cannot be made, because the creature cannot take it in. Neither, perhaps, can God communicate Himself as He is. Hence Moses saw only a form, saw only His back parts. His face could not be beheld. Thus to the patriarchs He appeared in the human form. So in the tabernacle His presence was manifested in the smoke that hung over the Ark. So, too, in Eden He was known to be present in the cherubim, who were the divine chariot on which He rode. All these things signified His presence, while at the same time intimating that in Himself He could not be seen. Yet this may refer only to a bodily vision of Him. There is no trace of the idea in the Old Testament that God, as revealed to men, is not really God as He is in Himself.

There is no such idea as that His revelation of Himself is meant merely to be regulative of human life, while what He is in truth remains far away in a transcendental background, out of which it is impossible for it to advance, or unto which it is impossible for men to approach. The revelation God gives of Himself is a revelation of Himself as He is in truth. Yet it may be impossible to reveal Himself fully to men, and it is impossible for any form appreciable to the senses either to contain Him or do much more than indicate His presence. The Hebrew idea of God, however, is not physical; it nowhere speculates on His essence; its idea of Him is ethical.

This conception of revelation is just the characteristic conception of the Old Testament. It reposes on such ideas as that Jehovah is a living God, and that He rules by His activity all the life of men. And it reposes on the idea that the religious life of men is mainly their practical conduct. And revelation is His ruling practically the whole life of the people by making known His will. This must be done to individual persons, not to the whole people directly. Hence all revelation is oral, because it is continuous—the constant impression by Himself of the living God. Even the priests' decisions on questions of right between man and man—their *torah*—were oral, and always caused by occasions. Now, on man's side this revelation was an operation of Jehovah in the mind. Revelation was the arising in the mind of man of thoughts or impulses accompanied by the conviction that the thoughts and impulses were from God. In such thoughts the mind of man and God coalesced, and the man was conscious of meeting God.

2. *The Idea of the Divine Name.*

In so far as God reveals Himself He acquires a *name*. Men call that which they know by a name. God, in revealing Himself, proclaimed His own name—Jehovah, Jehovah merciful and gracious. Among the Hebrews the name was never a mere sign whereby one person could be distinguished from another. It always remained descriptive; it expressed the meaning of the person or thing designated. The name bore the same relation to the significance of the thing or person as a word does to a thought. It was always the expression of it. Hence when a person acquired a new significance, when he began to play a new rôle, or entered into new relations, or was in some sense a new man, he received a new name. Therefore Abram became Abraham; Jacob, Israel; Solomon, Jedidjah—'beloved of God' (2 Sam. xii. 25). So even to God men have a name. Thus He calls Moses and Cyrus by their name. That is, He conceives to Himself what their significance is, what meaning they have in His redemptive providence; and He recognises this, and enters into relations with them as men having this meaning. And the same is true of God's own names. Such a name expresses that which is known to men of the nature of God. When a new or higher side of the Being of God is revealed to men there arises a new name of God. Any name of God expresses some revelation of His Being or character. When the word *name* is used absolutely as God's name, it describes His nature as revealed, as finding outward expression. So when the Psalmist in Ps. viii. exclaims, " How excellent is Thy name in all the earth!" he means how glorious is God's revelation of Himself, or God as revealed on the earth,—that is, among the family of men, whom He has so dignified as to put them over the work of His hands, with all things under their feet. His grace to men is His name here, His revelation of Himself. So when Israel is warned to give heed to the Angel of the Lord that leads them, for His name is in him (Ex. xxiii. 21), the sense is that the significance of God is present there; what God is, His majesty and authority, is there embodied. So His name is holy and reverend; He, as being what He is known to be, is *reverendus.*

Occasionally, perhaps, as the name is properly a full description of the nature, the expression *name of God*

may refer rather to what God is in Himself than to that
which He has revealed Himself to be. But ordinarily,
at least, the latter idea is predominant; and even when
he swears by His name, or when, 'for His name's sake,'
He blots out transgression, or will not cast off Israel, the
idea is that on account of what He has given men to know
that He is, because He has manifested Himself to Israel,
and in relation with Israel to the world, therefore He will
not cast away Israel (Ezek. xxiii.–xxxviii.). This use of
'for His name's sake' is comparatively late — in Isaiah
only in the prose; in Second Isaiah, and often in Ezekiel,
and later Psalms. The ideas connected with this expression appear to be these: (1) In the mind of the writer
Jehovah is God alone. But (2) He is known to the world,
the nations of mankind, as Jehovah, God of Israel. All
the knowledge they have of Him is of Him as God of
Israel—who had led Israel out of bondage, and done great
things for them in the wilderness and in their history.
(3) Jehovah's purpose is to reveal Himself to all mankind.
This revelation has already begun in Israel and through
Israel. It is only as God of Israel that the nations know
Him—the one God. It is only, therefore, through Israel
that He can reveal Himself to them. The name, therefore,
for whose sake He is besought to save Israel, is the name
Jehovah, known to the nations, and revealed in His
redemption of Israel of old, and in Israel's history. Hence,
when He finally redeems Israel, His glory appears to all
flesh.

3. *Particular Names of God.*

Though the *Name* of God has this significance, it is
rather descriptions of Him as Jehovah merciful and gracious,
and such like, that carry with them this meaning and
express this insight into what He is, than what is known
as strictly the Divine names. Not much can be drawn
from these. They are chiefly two, *Elohim* and *Jehovah*;
the one a general name for God, that is, an appellative

expressing the conception *God*, and therefore having no special significance; the other Jehovah, the *personal* name of the God of Israel.

But these are not the only names. There is the term *El* (אֵל), which, like *Elohim*, expresses the general idea of God. There are also the terms *El-Shaddai*, *El-Elyon*, which are descriptive titles applied to God; and there is the singular *Eloach*. The names *El*, *Elohim*, *El-Shaddai*, and the term *Jehovah* itself, appear all to be prehistoric. The most widely distributed of all these names is *El*. It appears in Babylonian, Phœnician, Aramaic, Hebrew, and Arabic, especially South Arabic. It belongs, therefore, to the whole Shemitic world. Gesenius and many more have taken it to be a part of a verb אוּל = *to be strong*. But other explanations have been advanced. Nöldeke, *e.g.*, would connect it with the Arabic root *'ûl* = to be *in front*, whence *awwal = first*; according to which the idea would be that of *governor* or *leader*. Dillmann would refer it to a supposed root אלה, with the sense of *power* or *might*; while Lagarde would seek its explanation in a root supposed to be related to the preposition אֶל־, so that it would designate God as the *goal* to which man is drawn, or toward which he is to strive. This last explanation is entirely impossible. The idea of Deity implied in it is too abstract and metaphysical for the most ancient times. No satisfactory derivation has as yet been suggested.

Equally obscure is the name שַׁדַּי, which we translate *Almighty*. In poetry the word is used alone; in prose it is usually coupled with אֵל, = *God Almighty*. The derivation and meaning are uncertain. It is an archaic term. According to P, it was the name of God that was used by the patriarchs (Gen. xvii. 1 ; Ex. vi. 3). It marked in that case an advance upon *El* and *Elohim*. The tradition that it is an archaic name is supported by the Book of Job, where the patriarchal and pre-Mosaic speakers use it. It is also supported by such names among the people of the Exodus as Zurishaddai = 'Shaddai is my rock' (Num. i. 6). Some have suggested an Aramean root, שׁדא =

to pour out, and have taken the name to designate the *rain-* or *storm-god*. Others would derive it from שדד, giving it the sense of 'the destroyer,' or more particularly the *storm-god* or the *scorching sun-god*. But there is little probability in such derivations. The oldest Babylonian names for God are all equally unresolvable. The meaning of Ishtar or Astarte, Marduk (Merodach), and the like, cannot be ascertained. The Jewish scholars resolve שַׁדַּי into שׁ דַּי (אֲשֶׁר) = *he who is sufficient*; but whether self-sufficiency is meant, or sufficiency for others, is left uncertain. It is probable that the Sept. translators, or some of them, already knew this etymology, as they occasionally render the term by ἱκανός. Some Assyrian scholars would now refer it to the Assyrian *Shadu = mountain*, taking it to be a designation of God either as the 'Most High' or as 'the Mountain,' on the analogy of the Hebrew term for God, *the Rock*. The most that can be said of it is that *Shaddai* may be an epithet with the idea of *Almighty*, as *Elyon* is an epithet of *El* with the idea of 'Most High.' The phrase *El Shaddai* may be simply an intensification of *El* itself, and it is possible that this intensification might express the clarification of the idea of the Divine which took place in Abraham's mind at the time of his call. It may have been this idea that his faith took hold of, and which sustained him when committing himself to an unknown way—'God the Omnipotent'—able in all places to protect him.

As to the term *Eloach*, אֱלֹהַּ (Aram. *êlah*, Arab. *ilah*), it may be an augmentation of *El*, and express, as is commonly understood, the idea of *power, might*. But even this is uncertain. Some suppose it to be a literary formation taken from the plural *Elohim*. But the Aramaic and Arabic forms are against this; for these are similar singular forms, and there is no reason to suppose them to be late forms. The term *Eloach* occurs in poetry, and now and then in late prose.

The word *Elohim* is a plural, and probably a plural of that sort called the plural of *majesty* or *eminence*, more accurately the plural of *fulness* or *greatness*. It is common in the East to use the plural to express the idea of the singular in an intensified form. Thus the Egyptian *fellah* says not *rab* for *master*, but *arbāb*; so in Hebrew the name Baal = *Lord, owner, ruler*, is used in the plural though the sense be singular; cf. Isa. i. 3, "the ox knoweth his owner, and the ass his master's crib" (אֲבוּס בְּעָלָיו). The singular of Elohim means probably *strength, power*, or *might*, and the plural merely intensifies this idea — the might *par excellence*, or the plenitude of might, is God. The name is common to Israel with most of the Shemitic peoples. The plural form is unquestionably prehistoric, *i.e.* it was in use before Israel became a people. In use it is, though a plural, regularly construed with a singular verb or adjective, except that occasionally, in E, it has the plural verb and adjective.[1]

Some have regarded the plural form *Elohim* as a remnant of Polytheism. But to speak of 'the gods' is not natural in a primitive age, and this can scarcely be the origin of the plural. No doubt it is the case that the angels or superhuman beings are also called *Elohim*, just as they are called *Elim*; and there might lie in that the idea that the superhuman world, the ruler of man's destiny, was composed of a plurality of powers. This would not point to Polytheism, however, but rather to the earlier stage of religion called Animism or Spiritism, when men thought their lives and destiny were under

---

[1] The name אֵל is the oldest name for God; Babylonian *ilu*, where *u* is nominative case; Arabic, *'ilāh*; Aram. *'elāh*. Some think that אֱלֹהִים is plural of אֵל, through insertion of an *h*, as אָמָה, אֲמָהוֹת, *maids*. I have not seen any examples of this insertion except in feminine nouns, and the *h* in Arabic *ilah* seems to indicate that it is not peculiar to the plural. The Syriac *Shemohîn* is probably artificial, as *Shem* has the fem. pl. in Hebrew and Aramaic. The attempt to connect *El Elohim* with *elah, elon*, names of trees (Marti-Kayser), scarcely deserves notice. The general idea has been that אֵל is connected with אוּל = to be *strong*; if this were the case the vowel *e* would be long, but it does not seem to be. The suggestion that the plural was first used of the deities of some particular locality (W. R. Smith) has its difficulties, as usually each locality had only one deity. The idea that *Elohim* meant the *fulness of powers* contained in God (Dillmann), is too abstract.

the influence of a multitude of forces or powers, which, being unseen, were conceived of as spirits, inhabiting stones, trees, and waters, or the like. If this were the origin of the plural, it would point to a far back pre-historic time. It would express in a sense an advance upon Animism, inasmuch as the various spirits were no longer considered independent and multifarious, but were combined into a unity, and thought of as acting in concert. The next step to this would be the individualising of this unity, and the rise of Monotheism; or, at any rate, there would perhaps arise the idea that among these *Elohim* one was monarch and the rest subsidiary and his servants. This is not unlike the representation in many parts of the Old Testament, where Jehovah in heaven is surrounded by a court, a multitude of other beings who are His messengers. This idea is frequent in Scripture; but whether it arose in the manner just suggested may be doubtful.   If we compare the names employed by the Shemitic nations surrounding Israel, we discover that they all express very much the same idea, namely, that of *power* or *rule*. They express a high level of thought regarding God.   None of them is a name for the heavens, or any of the forces of nature in its more material aspect.   They are all abstractions going beyond phenomena; they express the idea of a Being who is over phenomena, who has a metaphysical existence.   They are altogether unlike such names as Ζεύς (*Dyaus*), the bright sky, or *Phœbus Apollo*, or *Lucina*.   Such names as *El*, *Elohim*, when we remember that the Shemite attributed all force or power to spirit, immediately lead to the conception of a spiritual being.

Such names as *El-Elyon*, *El-Shaddai*, do not of them-selves imply Monotheism, inasmuch as one God Most High, or Almighty, might exist though there were minor gods; yet when a people worshipped only one God, and conceived Him as Most High, or Almighty, the step was very short to Monotheism.

Again, such names as 'Eternal God,' 'Living God,' at once suggest spirituality; for to the Shemitic mind, at least to the Hebrews, life lay in the spirit—which they called the spirit of life. Without, therefore, committing ourselves to the opinion that the abstract conceptions of Monotheism or spirituality were in the mind of the worshippers in the patriarchal age, we can perceive that their conceptions of God at least did not differ greatly from those which we now have.

The stage of religion which these Divine names suggest was probably not the first stage of Shemitic religion, nor was it the last. It is always difficult to arrive at the first conceptions of God among any people. Possibly in the main they originate in impressions produced on man by the heavens in their various aspects. These aspects awaken feelings in man of a power above him, or it may be of many powers. This is probably the primary conception of God. This primary conception may be monotheistic, if the phenomena observed be considered due to some power above them,—and this is the stage to which the Shemitic names for God belong; or polytheistic, if the phenomena themselves be considered powers, or the manifestation of separate powers. But the Shemitic religions did not remain on this level. So far as we know them, they either advanced, like the religion of Israel, or declined. One can readily perceive how Polytheism would arise at a later stage by the mere fact of different names existing. It was forgotten or not observed that these names originally expressed very much the same idea, although one tribe used one name and another a different one. The names used by different tribes were naturally considered different gods. By length of time their worship had taken different forms of development among the different tribes; and this variety of cultus, coupled with the different name, suggested a different deity.

The most various and contradictory conclusions have been reached on the question, What was the primary form of the Shemitic religion? and on the question, What was it that suggested the conception of God which we observe existing? There is no doubt that among the Canaanites and Phœnicians, Baal was connected with the sun; the sun was Baal, or Baal resided in the sun. And attempts have been made to connect the God of Israel either with the Sun, the god of fire, or with Saturn. These attempts have little foundation, and cannot be said to have had much success. It is, no doubt, true that the God of Israel is often compared to a fire,—His feet touch the land, and it melts (Amos ix. 5). But that is in metaphor. Others, again, have pursued a different line. It is certain that some of the Shemitic tribes, such as the Arabs, worshipped stones; and it has been supposed that the primary religion of Israel was this stone-worship. Jacob set up a stone. Jehovah is often named 'Rock,' and even called the 'Stone of Israel.' Professor Dozy, of Leyden, thought that the passage in Isaiah, "Look unto the rock whence ye were hewn, and to the hole of the pit whence ye were digged " (li. 1),—the reference being to Abraham and Sarah,—showed that Abraham and Sarah were two stone deities of early Israel. Von Hartmann, again, took a different line, supposing that Abram means *High Father*, and Sarah *princess, queen* ; and that the two are still deities, names for the supreme god and his consort—the sun and moon. And Kuenen considered Saturn to have been the original object of Israel's worship, according to the passage in Amos: " Ye have borne . . . the star of your god." (v. 26). But Kuenen was probably mistaken in his opinion that the prophet describes the events in the wilderness in that passage.

These instances are sufficient to show the worth of attempts of this kind. There is absolutely no material, and the imagination has unlimited scope.

Our position must be this : We have no knowledge of the early Shemitic worship. How the ideas of God arose it is impossible to say ; their origin lies beyond the horizon of history. So far as Israel is concerned, the comparison of God to a rock, or a stone, or fire, or anything material, is now entirely figurative, and meant to express ethical properties.

The names I have referred to are scarcely elements of

revelation. They are names preceding revelation, at least to the family of Israel, which have been adopted by Scripture. Neither *Elohim* nor *El* is a revealed name. They are, however, names that truly express the attributes or being of God, and could be adopted by Scripture. It is possible, however, in view of what is said in Ex. vi. 2, that the name *Shaddai* may be an element of revelation. The statement given there as to God appearing to the fathers of the Hebrew race as *El-Shaddai*, is made by the writer who is usually known as the Elohist. There is every reason to regard the statement as historical. And if we look into the 1st chapter of the Book of Numbers, which refers to the time of the Exodus, we find certain names compounded with *Shaddai*. The author of the Book of Job also shares the idea of the Elohist, and puts *Shaddai* into the mouth of his patriarchal speakers.

4. *The Name Jehovah.*

Much has been written on the subject of the name *Jehovah*, but little light has been cast upon it. A few things may be mentioned in regard to it. (1) It seems a name peculiar to the people of Israel, to this branch of the Shemitic family. This is no more remarkable than that *Chemosh* should be peculiar to Ammon, another branch, or *Moloch* to Moab, still another. The word does appear in proper names of other tribes, but when used by them it seems borrowed. (2) From prehistoric times it is probable that God was worshipped by this family under this name, or at least that the name was known in Israel; the mother of Moses has a name compounded with it, and it is certain that the name became at the Exodus the name of God in covenant with Israel. But the fact that Moses could come before Israel with this name as known to Israel, implies that it was not new in his day. (3) The real derivation and meaning of the name are wholly unknown. Its true pronunciation has also been lost, from the rise of a superstition that

it was unlawful to pronounce it. This superstition probably is earlier than the Septuagint translation, which
renders it by κύριος, just as the Massoretes substitute
Adhonai for it. (4) In the Pentateuch the word is brought
into connection with the verb *to be*. This, however, is
not an account of the actual origin of the name, but only
a play at most referring to its significance, or perhaps
more probably connecting a significance with it. But the
significance thus connected with it is of extreme importance, because it expresses, if not the original meaning of
the name, which probably had been lost, the meaning
which it suggested to the mind of Israel during their
historic period.

And this, not its primary sense, is, of course, what
is important for us. As connected with the verb *to
be*, it is the third singular imperfect. When spoken by
Jehovah Himself this is the first person אֶהְיֶה, or in a
longer form, which merely makes more absolute the simple
form, אֶהְיֶה אֲשֶׁר אֶהְיֶה. The verb *to be* in Hebrew hardly
expresses the idea of absolute or self - existence; it
rather expresses what *is* or *will be* historically, and the
imperfect tense must mean not *I am*, but *I will be*.
In Ex. iii. 11–14 the revelation of the name יהוה is described—" And Moses said unto God, Who am I, that I
should go unto Pharaoh ? " And God said, " I will be
with thee, כִּי אֶהְיֶה עִמָּךְ " . . . And Moses said unto God,
Behold, when I come unto the children of Israel, and shall
say unto them, The God of your fathers hath sent me
unto you ; and they shall say unto me, What is His name ?
what shall I say unto them ? And God said unto Moses,
אֶהְיֶה אֲשֶׁר אֶהְיֶה : and he said, " Thus shalt thou say unto the
children of Israel, *Ehyeh* hath sent me unto you." That
is, God when speaking of Himself is אֶהְיֶה, and when spoken
of is יהוה. In the time of Hosea the etymological signification of Jehovah was still present to men's minds. Hence
He says : " I will not be to you, לֹא אֶהְיֶה לָכֶם " (chap. i. 9):—
" ye are not My people, and I am not, אֶהְיֶה, to you."

It seems certain that in Isa. xl. seq. the name Jehovah

is not used as having any special significance etymologically, but is the name for God absolutely. Ere these chapters were written the idea of God had passed through various stages. The unity of God had become a formal conception. It had been discussed, and the opposite idea of there being more Gods had been set against it. 'Jehovah' in the prophet's mouth expresses the idea of the one true God. And is not יהוה (simply) in this prophet (Isa. xl. seq.) = to יְהוָה צְבָאוֹת or הָאֵל הַקָּדֹשׁ, קְדֹשׁ יִשְׂרָאֵל in the earlier prophets? It is not an ontological name, but a redemptive one. It does not describe God on the side of His nature, but on that of His saving operations, His living activity among His people, and His influence upon them. Yet it is probable that it is a description of Jehovah in Himself, and not merely as He will manifest Himself to Israel. "I will be that I will be," expresses the sameness of Jehovah, His constancy — His being ever like Himself. It does not express what other attributes He had,—these were largely suggested by the fact of His being God; it rather expresses what all His attributes make Him, —the same yesterday and to-day and for ever, the true in covenant relation, the unchanging; hence it is said, "I am Jehovah, I change not" (Mal. iii. 6).

The pronunciation *Jehovah* has no pretence to be right. It was not introduced into currency till the time of the Reformation, about 1520.[1] It is a mongrel word, which has arisen from uniting the vowels of one word with the consonants of another—the vowels of the word אֲדֹנָי with the consonants of this sacred name. This name began, for whatever reasons, early to fall into disuse. Already it is avoided in some of the latest books of the Old Testament, as Ecclesiastes. In the second Book of the

---

[1] When *vowel* signs were invented and written in MSS. (600–900 A.D.) the practice, when one word was substituted for another in reading, was to attach the vowels of the word to be substituted to the consonants of the original word. Thus the vowels of *'ădōnāy* were attached to the consonants *yhvh*. In 1518 A.D., Petrus Galatinus, confessor of Leo X., proposed to read the vowels and consonants as one word, and thus arose *Yěhōvāh*—Jehovah— *y* requiring to be spelled with *ĕ* instead of *ă*.

Psalms it is little used, and it is evident that here in many cases it has been removed from places where it stood, and the name Elohim substituted in its room (compare Ps. xiv. with Ps. liii.). It is probable, as we have said, that a superstitious dread was the cause of the disuse. We found in Amos the sentiment that the name of Jehovah must not be mentioned, lest He should be provoked to inflict new calamities. In Lev. xxiv. 11 we read that the son of an Israelitish woman whose father was an Egyptian *blasphemed the name,* וַיִּקֹּב הַשֵּׁם, as we translate it. But in ver. 16 the Septuagint already translates it as if = *he named the name* (ὀνομάζων τὸ ὄνομα); and the exegesis of the Jewish commentators on the passage is—" he who names the name יהוה shall be killed." This superstitious reverence of later Judaism appears in many ways; for example, in the Targums instead of " the Lord said," it is always " the word of the Lord said." Gradually the name became altogether avoided, and the word Adhonai, *Lord,* substituted in its place. According to the tradition, the pronunciation of the name lingered for a time on the priests' lips, in sacred places and things, after it was banished from the mouths of common men; and it is said to have been still uttered in the first times of the Second Temple in the sanctuary at the pronunciation of the blessing, and by the high priest on the Day of Atonement. But from the time of the death of Simon the Just, that is, from the first half of the third century B.C., it was exchanged here also for Adhonai, as had long been the practice outside the Temple. The Jews maintain that the knowledge of the true pronunciation has been quite lost since the destruction of the temple. As the name Adhonai was substituted for it by the Jewish readers, this passed into the Septuagint as κύριος, and into modern versions as LORD. It is not quite certain what induced the Jews to substitute the word *Lord* for this name; but it is almost certain that no inference can be drawn from this substitution with regard to the meaning of the word *Jehovah.* The name ultimately became = the true God, God absolutely,

as even in Isa. xl. ff. Hence *Lord* was a good substitute
for it. Various reasons conspire together in favour of the
pronunciation now current יַהְוֶה, *Ya'wé* (variously spelled
Jahvé, Jahveh, Yahve, Yahveh, Yahweh, etc.) First, the
name became early contracted. The common contraction
יְהוּ at the end of names points to יַהְוּ (as שִׁחוּ = שָׁחוּ), which
is the ordinary form of contraction such words undergo.
Again, the ancient transcription into Greek is either *iaβé*
or *iaώ*, which express respectively the long or the contracted form. Theodoret transliterates the pronunciation
of the Samaritans (who continued to speak the word) *iaβé*;
and similar transliterations are given by other writers,
e.g. Clement of Alexandria. The traditional etymology
points in the same direction.[1] According to this derivation the word is third singular imperfect of the verb הוה
in its archaic form—the old imperfect of which would be
spelled יַהְוֶה equally in Kal and Hiphil. We may assume
that this is the true pronunciation of the word.

As to its origin and meaning, it may be assumed on
various grounds that the name, although it somehow
received new currency and significance in connection with
Israel from Moses, is far older than his time. One ground
is the form of the word. It seems to be an archaic form
in which *v* fills the place of the more modern *y*. But
certainly in Moses' time the change into *y* in the verb היה
had already long taken place. In the cognate languages
the *v* remains, and the name must belong to a time when
Hebrew had not dissociated itself so far from its sister
tongues as it had done by the time when Israel had become a nation. The second ground is the general repre-

[1] Various etymologies have been suggested. Some have referred the name
to the Arab *havah, to breathe* or *blow*, Yahveh being the god who is heard in
the storm, whose breath is the wind, and the thunder his voice. Others
think of *havah* in the sense of *to fall*, causative *to fell*, and take Yahveh to
be he who *falls* (the meteorite or Baitylion), or he who *fells*, *i.e.* prostrates
with his thunderbolt,—again the Storm-god. Others, again, refer the word
to *havah* (archaic form of *hayah*)=*to be*, in the causative=*to make to be*;
thus Yahveh would be he who brings into existence, either nature or events
—the Creator or the providential Ruler. These and other conjectures
however, have little value.

sentation of the history, according to which the name is ancient. Not only is Jahweh the same God as the fathers worshipped, for He says to Moses, "I am Jahweh" —and again, "I am the God of thy fathers"; but the history declares expressly of the time of Enos, "then began men to call on the name of Jahweh" (Gen. iv. 26); and the writers of the history put the name into the mouths of the forefathers of Israel. Added to this is the fact that the name appears already in a contracted form יָהּ in the Song at the Red Sea, which implies some considerable term of existence; and that it enters into composition in the name *J*ochebed, the mother of Moses. No doubt these inferences as to the antiquity of the name may seem difficult to reconcile with that other statement made in Exodus, that the name was not known to the patriarchs: " I appeared unto the fathers as El Shaddai, but by My name Jahweh was I not known to them." But this can hardly mean that the name was unknown, but only that its real significance had never yet been experienced by them, and that now God would manifest Himself fully in the character expressed by this name, which from henceforth became His name as God of Israel.

Some scholars have endeavoured to make it probable that the name was learned by Moses from the Midianite or Kenite tribes, into a priestly family of which he had married. They argue that the name was used by these tribes for the god whom they worshipped, and whose seat they supposed to be on one of the high mountains in the desert, where they roamed and pastured their flocks. It was when Moses had led the flocks of his father-in-law to the back of Horeb that Jahweh appeared to him in a burning bush. It was to the same locality that Moses led the people to worship this God, and to receive from Him His law. It is not at all certain where Sinai or Horeb lay; the traditional modern site is not beyond question. In the ancient hymn, the Blessing of Moses, in Deut. xxxiii., it is said: " Jehovah came from Sinai, and rose from Seir unto them; He shined forth from Mount Paran."

Seir is Edom, and Mount Paran is very considerably north of the present Sinai. The same representation occurs in the very ancient Song of Deborah: " Jahweh, when Thou wentest forth out of Seir, when Thou marchedst out of the field of Edom . . . the mountains flowed down at the presence of Jahweh, even yon Sinai at the presence of Jahweh, the God of Israel" (Judg. v. 4, 5). And there are other similar passages. The question of the situation of Sinai, however, is of little consequence. More interesting is the question whether Sinai was thought to be the local seat of Jehovah, and whether He and His name were known to the tribe to which Moses was related by marriage. Elijah, the great upholder of Jehovah's sole worship in Israel, fled from Jezebel, and went to the mount of God. But the prophet, who said : " If Jehovah be God, follow Him ; but if Baal, then follow him " (1 Kings xviii. 21), would scarcely fancy that Jehovah had any particular seat. His seeking the mount of God is sufficiently explained by the historical manifestation at the giving of the Law. Might we suppose that the fact that Moses led the people to Sinai was sufficiently explained by Jehovah's manifestation to himself in the bush ? Or is it not possible that at that time Jehovah was thought to have a connection specially with this region. If He had, then it would be natural that the tribes about the mountain worshipped Him. When the people sought leave of Pharaoh to go and sacrifice to their God, Moses said : " The God of the Hebrews hath met with us ; let us go, we pray thee, three days' journey into the wilderness, and sacrifice to Jehovah our God, lest He fall upon us with pestilence " (Ex. v. 3). This might seem to imply that Jehovah was specially to be found in the wilderness. As the Israelites sojourned in the south of Palestine, on the borders of the desert, before going down to Egypt, and as their abode when in Egypt was in the east of the country bordering still on the desert, it might be that some of the tribes were allied with them in religion. It is, of course, known that the Kenites attached themselves to Israel; and in Judg. iv. 11 the Kenites appear identified with the Midianites, the relatives of Moses; for it is said: "Now Heber the Kenite had severed himself from the Kenites, even from the children of Hobab, the father-in-law of Moses, and had pitched his tent near by Kadesh." Hebrew tradition, however, nowhere shows any trace of the idea that Jehovah was worshipped by any tribe except Israel itself. When Hobab came to visit Moses and the camp of Israel, and Moses narrated to him the wonders done by Jehovah in Egypt, and His redemption of Israel, he exclaimed: "Now know I that Jehovah is greater than all gods" (Ex. xviii. 11). In the description, too, of the manifestation of Jehovah on Mount Sinai at the giving of the Law, it is said that He had *come down* upon the mountain; a method of speaking which does not imply that He had His permanent seat there.[1]

[1] It is held by some that the word *Jahweh*, or a similar term, occurs in Assyrian. Hommel claims to have found a Divine name *I*, *Ai*, or *Ya*, in Western Shemitic, the original, he thinks, of which the Hebrew יהוה was a later expansion. The Rev. G. Margoliouth regards the Babylonian IA, EA, HEA, and the Hebrew *Yah* as forming an equation (*Contemporary Review*, Oct. 1898). President Warren, of Boston, takes substantially the same view, only refusing to identify, as Mr. Margoliouth does, the Babylonian EA with *Sin*, the Moon-god. He looks upon the shorter form JH, *Yah*, as the West Shemitic form of the East Shemitic EA, or Proto-Shemitic EA, and applies this account of *Jah*, *Jahweh*, to the explanation of the call of Moses (the serpent being Ea's familiar symbol), the changing of water into blood, the unlevitical libation of water to Jehovah mentioned in 1 Sam. vii. 6, the signs asked by Gideon (Judg. vi. 36–40), the healing of the waters of Marah, the production of water from the smitten rock, etc. (*Methodist Review*, January 1902; also a paper by Dr. Hans Spoer in the *American Journal of Semitic Languages and Literatures*, xviii. 1). Carrying out to its utmost length the disposition, represented by Winckler, Radau, and others, to regard Israel as dependent for most things on Babylonian civilisation and religion, Professor Friedrich Delitzsch now claims that even the idea of God is Babylonian, and revives the theory that *El* originally expressed the conception of *goal*. He thinks that this 'goal' was held to be *one*, and asserts that he finds even the Divine name *Yahweh*, and the phrase "Yahweh is God," in early Babylonian texts (see his *Babel und Bibel*). He reads the words in question as *Ia-ah-ve-ilu*, *Ia-hu-um-ilu*, and takes the rendering to be "Jahweh is God." But the translations are of the most doubtful kind. See Gunkel's *Israel und Babylonien*, Köberle's *Babylonische Cultur und biblische Religion*, König's *Bibel und Babel*, Kittel's *Der Babel-Bibel-Streit und die Offen-*

In an interesting essay on the name, Baudissin proves, I think, conclusively these two points: first, that the many forms and examples of the name to be found in Greek, on amulets and in other inscriptions, are all derivable from the word as pronounced Yahweh, *i.e.* as used among the Jewish people; and second, that there is no trace of the term as a name for God among other Shemitic speaking nations.[1] It is often found used by such nations, but always seems derived from Israel. This would seem to imply that the name is a peculiar heritage of Israel; though this would not in any way interfere with the antiquity of the name, nor with its derivation from a root common to all the Shemitic languages. The word *amlak* used for God in Ethiopic is peculiar to this division of the Shemitic races; but it may probably be very ancient, and is certainly formed from a root common to them all. But since the name is peculiar to Israel, we are thrown entirely upon what information we can glean from statements made in the Old Testament regarding its meaning, and upon our own conjectures from the sense of the root and the form of the word.

As to the fact that the Old Testament connects the name with the verb היה *to be*, it is extremely difficult to say in such cases of apparent etymologising whether there be a real derivation or only a reference by way of play to a root of similar sound. Thus Eve called her son קַיִן, for she said, "I have gotten (קָנִיתִי) a man from the Lord" (Gen. iv. 1). The word קיץ has a similar sound, but probably a different sense from קנה. The daughter of Pharaoh called the child whom she rescued Moshe— "because I have drawn him out of the water, מָשִׁיתִי " (Ex. ii. 10); but the name Moses is probably purely Egyptian, and the reference to the Hebrew verb a mere play. The same may certainly be the case with the word

barungsfrage, Leimdorfer's *Der Jhwh-Fund von Babel in der Bibel*, etc. etc. On the *Tetragrammaton*, see Driver in *Studia Biblica*, 1885 ; T. Tyler in the *Jewish Quarterly Review*, July 1901, etc.—ED.

[1] See his *Studien zur Semitischen Religionsgeschichte.*—ED.

Jahweh; its connection with the verb היה in its ordinary sense may be merely a play. Still, even if this were so, we have in this play, if not certainty as to the origin of the name, an indication of what it meant. At the time when this etymology arose and was current, the meaning of the name Jahweh to Israel could be expressed by the imperfect of the verb היה, *to be*—the modern אהיה, or at least the fuller formula א אֲשֶׁר 'א was felt to give the signification of the ancient Jahweh. We cannot be certain, of course, when the passage in Exodus was written. But even if in its written form it is the product of a much later age, it most probably expresses an old historical tradition. Much of the Pentateuch may be in its present form of comparatively late date, and not unnaturally a writer living in a late age may mix up some of his own conceptions with those of a former time, and colour his delineations of the past with ideas that belong to his own time. But wholesale fabrications of a past history from the point of view of a more modern age are very improbable. And this improbability is indefinitely heightened in the domain of ancient Shemitic literature.

To Moses the name Jahweh, which he elevated into such prominence, must have had a meaning of its own, and he is just as likely to have connected that ancient name with the verb היה as the prophet Hosea, who certainly does so. It is to be noticed that the Old Testament connects the name with the verb היה in its modern sense. The imperfect Qal of the verb היה, as used in the times of Moses and Hosea, expresses the meaning of Jahweh. It is certainly possible that the ancient name Jahweh is derived from this verb in its more ancient and primary sense. This sense is probably *to fall*; and some, as we have said, have supposed the name יהוה to be a Hiphil from this, and to mean the *feller*, the *prostrator*—a name which would be allied to אֱלֹהִים and שַׁדַּי (if the last were derived from שדד, which is not likely); just as others have supposed it to be a Hiphil, in the sense of to *cause to be*, and meaning the *Creator*. But such inquiries lie without the Old Testament horizon. To the Israelites of history the covenant name Jahweh has a meaning which may be expressed by the first singular imperfect Qal of היה, *to be.* Now, *two* things must be premised about this verb. *First,* the imperfect of such a stative verb as היה must be taken in the sense of a *future.* I do not think there is in the Hebrew Bible a case of the imperfect of this verb having the sense of the English *present.* This is expressed by the perfect. The word means *to fall, fall out, become* ; hence its perfect is equivalent to *to be.* The imperfect must be rendered, *I will be.* Second, היה does not mean to *be essentially,* but to *be phenomenally* ; it is not εἶναι, but γίνεσθαι. It cannot be used ordinarily to express 'being' in the sense of existence. Now these two facts regarding היה exclude a large number of conjectures as to the meaning of Jahweh. In the first place, the translation *I am* is doubly false: the tense is wrong, being present; and the idea is wrong, because *am* is used in the sense of essential existence. All those interpretations which proceed upon the supposition that the word is a name of God as the self-existent, the absolute, of which the Septuagint's ὁ ὤν is the most conspicuous illustration, must be set aside. Apart from the fact that such abstract conceptions are quite out of keeping with the simplicity and concreteness of Oriental thought, especially in the most early times, the nature of the verb and the tense peremptorily forbid them.

Second, the translation *I will be,* or *I will be what I will be,* while right as to tense, must be guarded also against having a metaphysical sense imported into the words *will be.* Some have supposed that the expression denoted the *eternity* of God, or the *self - consistence* of God, or His absolute *freedom* and His *inviolability* from all sides of the creature universe; but these constructions also put a sense upon היה which it cannot bear. The expression *I will be* is a historical formula; it refers, not to what God will be in Himself; it is no predication regarding His nature, but one regarding what He will approve Himself to others, regarding what He will show Himself to be to those in covenant with Him. The name is not a name like Elohim, which expresses God on the side of His being, as essential, manifold power; it is a word that expresses rather relation—Elohim in relation to Israel is Jahweh. In this respect the word has almost the same signification as the term קָדוֹשׁ *holy*; the "יֹשׁ 'ק and Jahweh are one. It is in this sense that Hosea says to Israel: לֹא א' לָכֶם *I will not be to you*; but I " will save them by the Lord their God" (בַּיהוָה)—*i.e.* as Jahweh their God (i. 7, 9).

In Exodus the formula appears in two shapes—the simple אהיה, *I will be*, and the larger 'א אֲשֶׁר א', *I will be that I will be*. But it is evident that the lesser formula is a full expression of the name—" say unto the children of Israel that 'א hath sent me unto you." The name is, *I will be*. Thus it is equivalent almost to ὁ ἐρχόμενος—he who is to come; it premises God, a God known; it promises His fuller manifestation, His ever closer nearness, His clearer revelation of His glory. And the burden of all the Old Testament prophets is: The Lord shall come:—" Say unto the cities of Judah, Behold your God! Behold, the Lord God will come with strong hand;" " the glory of the Lord shall be revealed, and all flesh shall see it together" (Isa. xl. 9, 5). *I will be*, or, *I will be it*; but what He will be has to be filled up by a consciousness of God already existing, and always receiving from every new manifestation of Him new contents. But it is clear that if אהיה be really the name, then the second part of the longer formula 'א אֲשֶׁר, *what I will be*, is unimportant, and cannot sustain the emphasis of the proposition. It can do nothing more than give body to the first *I will be*. It may mean *I will be, I who will be*. Or if it mean " I will be what I will be," it resembles the expression in Ex. xxxiii. 9, " I will have mercy on whom I will have mercy," the meaning of which would appear better if it were read, " On whom I will have mercy, I will have mercy"; I will have mercy fully, absolutely. The idea of selection scarcely lies in the formula; it is rather the strong emphatic affirmation, *I will have mercy.*

It may occur to one that such a sense of Jahweh can hardly be its primary one. But we must recall results already reached, *e.g.* that the name is purely Israelitish; that Israel had a name for God in general, namely, Elohim, common to it and the other Shemitic peoples; and that what it now needed was not a new name for God in His nature or being, but a name expressive of His new relation to itself. Israel did not need to be instructed that there was a God, or that He was all-powerful. It needed to know that He had entered into positive covenant relations with itself; that He was present always in Israel; that the whole wealth of His being—of what He was, He had promised to reveal, and to give to His chosen people. Elohim says to Israel אהיה לכם; and in this relation He is יהוה. He *who will be* is already known; what He will be is not expressed; it is a great inexpressible silence—contents immeasurable, blessing unspeakable—in a word, אלהים.

It is certainly possible that another construction may be put upon the words, which, though somewhat different, leaves the truth expressed very much the same. *I will be* may express something like uniformity in God, the constant sameness of God in His relation to Israel. This gives a sense not unlike the translation *I am*, namely, that of the unchanging nature of God. But in the one case, in the translation *I am*, the reference is more to God's essential being, in the other more to His unvarying relation to Israel. This latter is far more likely, in view of the ancient manner of speaking, especially among Eastern nations, and it is far more pertinent in the circumstances. The words express not that Israel had God among them, one who was unchangeable, self-existent in His nature, but rather what kind of God they had—one constant, faithful, ever the same, in whom they could trust, to whom they could flee, who was their dwelling-place in all generations. And hence a prophet says, "I am Jehovah; I change not" (Mal. iii. 6). At all events this is to be held fast, that the name expresses not God's essential nature, but His relation to Israel as the God of the covenant.

But speculations on the meaning of this name are less fruitful than observation of what Scripture says in regard to Him. It is from this we can gather the ideas entertained by the people.

5. *Jehovah the God of Israel.*

A question of great interest now arises, What is involved in saying that Jehovah was the *God of Israel* ? How much meaning in relation, say, to the general idea of the absolute unity of God, or to Monotheism, may we suppose to lie in the phrase ?

We have said that Jahweh and Elohim are not names parallel ; Jahweh is Elohim in relation to Israel, Jahweh is Elohim saying אהיה. And Elohim saying אהיה is Elohim of Israel. But thus Jahweh became the name of the Elohim of Israel—or rather of Elohim in Israel. This is certainly the way of thinking among the great prophets of the eighth and ninth centuries before Christ. Jahweh is not to them a God among other gods, neither is Jahweh God simply. He is God in Israel—God saying *I will be*, God in the act of unveiling His face more and more, in the act of communicating the riches of Himself more and more, in the act of pouring out all His contents into the life of Israel; or God as the constant One, the same yesterday, to-day, and for ever.

It is not easy to state with certainty what is included in the expression "Jahweh, God of Israel," and excluded by it. In order to estimate it fairly, we have to take into account not merely the form of expression, but the facts of history bearing on its meaning, and the conduct of those who professed this belief. But in taking into account history, a multitude of considerations have to be attended to. Israel was a numerous people; its past history had made it not a homogeneous, but a composite nation. Narratives, the veracity of which we have no reason to doubt, represent the people in the wilderness as a mixed multitude. Egyptian elements no doubt entered to some extent into the nation. Then it must have gathered foreign though kindred elements from the Shemitic tribes whom it encountered in the wilderness. The Kenites, who play an important part in Israel's history, attached themselves to it there. Moreover, it is plain that Israel on entering Canaan neither put to the sword nor dispossessed in any great measure the native races, but merely subjected them to tribute, and ultimately absorbed them into itself. It is evident that into the Israelitish nation which history deals with, elements of the most diverse kinds entered, and that classes existed differing very widely from one another in culture and morals. When it is asked, therefore, what is meant by saying " Jahweh was God of Israel," the answer may be that it meant very different things among different classes. And history may bring too often to light this unfortunate divergence. But manifestly we ought to ask, What did it mean in the minds of those who were the religious leaders of the people, such as Moses, and Samuel, and David, and the like ?

Now it is plain, first of all, that it meant that Israel was to worship no other God. The first commandment is, " I am Jahweh ; thou shalt have no other gods in My presence." Israel's worship was confined to one God— to God under one name, Jahweh. Not only the first commandment, but every element in the constitution bore this meaning. The expression and idea of a covenant had this in view—it made the people Jahweh's. And so was it with all the separate provisions of the covenant. The Sabbath, which was but an intensification of the idea that Israel's whole life was dedicated ; the offering of the first-born, which meant the nation in its strength (implying all its increase); the first-fruits of the harvest, and much else, particularly the appearing of all the males before Jahweh three times a year,—all these things were but expressions of the fundamental idea that Israel was Jahweh's—His סְגֻלָּה or peculiar possession, His alone.

But it becomes a question, Did this particularism amount to Monotheism ? Was Jahweh, whom alone Israel worshipped, God alone ? Such a question can be answered only by an induction of the attributes of Jahweh and of the facts of history. And this is not easy to make. On the one hand, it is known that each separate people of antiquity had its national god, and that one god worshipped did not necessarily imply one god believed in. The separate peoples, while each worshipping its own god, did not deny the existence of the gods of their neighbours. And in all likelihood among Israel very many stood on no higher platform than this — Jahweh was God of Israel; but Chemosh was god of Ammon. It is scarcely possible to explain Israel's history and the persistent falls into idolatry of a large part of the nation, unless we start with some such supposition as this—that to a great number in the nation Jahweh was merely the national God. If any higher idea was laid before them, they had not been able with any depth or endurance to take it in. But the question is, Was it laid before them by Moses and the founders of the Theocracy ? The first commandment contents itself with prohibiting Israel from serving a plurality of gods; it does not in words rise to the affirmation of Monotheism. But in like manner the seventh prohibits merely Israel from committing adultery, and the sixth from murder; they contain no hint that these injunctions have a universal bearing, and are fundamental laws of human well-being. The laws are all cast into the form of particular prohibitions. But who can doubt that the comprehensive mind which ministered to Israel those profound abstractions concerning purity and regard for life and truth and respect for property, perceived that they expressed the fundamental principles of human society ? And is it supposable that with such insight into morality he stood on so low a platform in religion as to rise no higher than national particularism ?

Of course, we must take such evidence as we have, and must not judge antiquity and the East by our modern ideas in the West. A Shemitic mind would rise to the idea of *unity* probably very gradually, and through attaching attributes to his national god which excluded all rivals. If we look down the Decalogue a little further, we come in the fourth commandment to a remarkable statement regarding Jahweh :—" In six days *Jahweh made the heavens and the earth.*" Jahweh, God of Israel, is Creator of the universe. He who wrote this sentence was certainly a virtual monotheist. Perhaps the thought did not rise in his mind as it does in ours, that the existence of such a Being excluded all other beings who might be called Elohim. But one with such a practical faith stood to Jahweh much as believers in the unity of God stand to Him now. And it cannot be doubted that all the leading minds in Israel, and many of the people, had from the beginning reached this high platform.

Perhaps we may observe even in the patriarchal age a tendency in an upward direction and an advance upon the stage indicated by the names which were common to Israel and the kindred races at the beginning. While the family of Abraham maintained the common name *Elohim* for God, as expressing the general idea, and *El*, used also as a personal name, we notice what might be called a potentiation of the latter name, a tendency to unite it with epithets which both elevate the conception expressed by it, and distinguish the Being whom the patriarchs called *El* from others who might be so named. Such names are, *El Elyon*, " God most High " ; *El Hai*, " the living God " ; *El Shaddai*, " God Almighty," or " God of overpowering might." Even in such names as *Adon, Baal, El*, there is already a step made towards Monotheism, the Being named *God* has been abstracted from nature. He is no more the mere phenomenon, nor even the power in the phenomenon. He is the power above the phenomenon. And the *particularism*, as it is called, of the Shemitic peoples, or their *monolatry*, which is so peculiar to them as distinguished from the Western nations, that is, the fact that they had each a national or tribal god, whom they worshipped alone

as their god, without, it may be, calling in question the
existence of other tribal gods whom their neighbours
worshipped, or inquiring whether other gods than their
own existed or not,—this peculiarity, if it cannot be called
Monotheism, forms at last a high vantage ground from
which a march towards Monotheism may commence. And
it is probable that we see in the patriarchal names just
referred to, particularly in *El Shaddai*, the advance in the
family of Abraham towards both the unity and the spirituality of God. He who called God *El Shaddai*, and
worshipped Him as the 'Almighty,' might not have the
abstract or general conception in his mind that He was
the only powerful Being existing. But, at least to him
He was the supreme power in heaven and in earth, and He
had given him His fellowship, and was condescending to
guide his life. And when one named the Being whom he
served the *eternal God*, or the *living God*, though he might
not have present before his mind the general conception of
what we call the *spirituality* of God, yet practically the
effect must have been much the same. For He who existed
from eternity and had life in Himself could not be part
of that material world everywhere subject to change, nor
could He exist in flesh which decayed.

The manner of thinking among these ancient saints of
God was very different from ours. We are the heirs of
all the ages. There lie behind us centuries of speculation
regarding God; and we have reached an abstract and
general conception of God to which, if there be any actual
God, He must correspond. But these men were pursuing
the opposite course. They started from the assurance of
the existence of a Being whom they named God, whom
they considered a person in close relation with their life;
and their general thoughts of Him were few, and only rose
to their mind gradually, one after another, as their life and
history suggested them. And the history of the people of
God enables us to observe how these great thoughts of
what God was rose like stars, one in succession to another,
upon their horizon; thoughts which we, who have inherited

the mental riches of these great men, now are able to unite together into one great constellation and call it *God*.

The religion of Israel was practical, not speculative; and while a practical Monotheism prevailed, and gave rise to all that profound religious life which we see in such men as Moses and Samuel and David and the prophets, it perhaps needed that internal conflict which arose through the slowness of the popular mind, and the degradation of the popular morals arising from absorbing the native Canaanite, to bring into speculative clearness the doctrines of Monotheism and Spirituality. The whole history of Israel is filled with this internal conflict between the strict worshippers of Jahweh and those who showed a leaning to other gods. And while all the leading minds held, and when they were writers expressed, conceptions of Jahweh which to our minds would have excluded the existence of all else named God, it is not perhaps till the age of Jeremiah that the speculative truth is clearly announced that there is no God but Jahweh. I exclude from consideration here the Book of Deuteronomy, the age of which is contested.

In estimating evidence on this question, however, we must always take the state of thought in those ages into account, and the condition of religion among the neighbouring peoples. Much is said in Scripture which reflects not the point of view of Israel, but that of the heathen peoples about, and the facts of religious practice in the world at the time. For example, in the hymn sung at the Red Sea it is said: "Who is like unto Thee, O Jahweh, among the gods? who is like Thee, glorious in holiness, fearful in praises, doing wonders?" (Ex. xv. 11). There it is certainly said, as elsewhere, of Israel's God, that He is incomparable. But it seems admitted that though supreme, He is just one God among others. Yet this last inference might be very mistaken. The language reposes upon the fact that the heathen nations had gods whom they worshipped, and is based merely upon the general religious conditions of the time. In a late Psalm (Ps. xcvii.),

certainly written after the expression of a theoretical
Monotheism by such prophets as Jeremiah and the Second
Isaiah, we read : " Great is Jahweh ;—He is to be feared
above all gods." And had we no more we might suppose
the author to admit the existence of other objects of
worship along with Jahweh, although he might put them on
a meaner level. But he immediately adds : " For all the
gods of the nations are vanities,"—אֱלִילִים, non-existences ;
" but Jahweh made the heavens." And David, who was
certainly a monotheist, uses similar phraseology when he
identifies being banished from the land of Israel with
serving other gods (1 Sam. xxvi. 19). Such language
arises from the religious conditions of the age, and we
cannot draw any conclusions from it as to the actual
views of the persons in Israel using it. We ourselves
still speak of the gods of the heathen, and our classical
education makes us many times refer to them as actual
entities. But this arises from identifying ourselves in
thought with the ancients ; we do not, when the matter
is seriously before our minds, give any weight to the
language we ourselves employ. A great deal too much
weight has been attached by writers like Kuenen and
others, whose object is to demonstrate a progressive advance from a mere national particularism to a true
Monotheism, to such expressions as those which we have
been considering. Such formulas may mean much or
little, according to the position of the persons in whose
mouths they occur ; and certainly much more discrimination
needs to be practised in estimating their value than is done
by Kuenen.

This class of writers admit that from the age of
Jeremiah a theoretical Monotheism prevailed in Israel.
And this may be held as conceded on all hands. Two
questions, however, arise in regard to this theoretical Monotheism. *First*, was it a view held by the older prophets,
by the prophets from the beginning, or may we observe
the rise of the view among the prophets whose writings we
possess ? And *second*, suppose we find that it was virtually

the view of the prophets from the beginning, though they may not have occasion to express the view in a very general way, being only interested on insisting on a practical Monotheism in Israel, was it the view current in Israel from the foundation of the commonwealth, *i.e.* from the Exodus?

In the age of Jeremiah such things are said of the heathen gods as leave us in no doubt that the prophets had reached the idea of a theoretical Monotheism; for, *e.g.*, these gods are named 'nothing,' מְאַיִן, Isa. xli. 24; 'chaos,' תֹּהוּ, Isa. xli. 29; 'falsehood,' שֶׁקֶר, Jer. x. 14; 'vanity,' שָׁוְא, Jer. xviii. 15; 'wind' or 'vapour,' הֶבֶל, Jer. ii. 5; 'nonentities,' אֱלִילִים, Ezek. xxx. 13; 'no gods,' לֹא אֵל, Jer. ii. 11, abomination,' תּוֹעֵבָה, Jer. xvi. 18; 'to be loathed,' שִׁקּוּץ, Jer. iv. 1; 'shame,' בֹּשֶׁת, Jer. iii. 24.

But long before Jeremiah, terms of a similar kind are employed. In Hos. xiii. 4 we read: "Thou knowest no God but Me; there is no saviour beside Me." And again he says of the idols, "They are no god," לֹא אֵל (viii. 6); and he even calls them לֹא absolutely or אֵל, *i.e. not*. Jehovah is the universal Governor. He brought the Syrians from Kir as well as Israel from Egypt (Amos ix. 7). In Mic. iv. 13 He is called "the Lord of the whole earth." In Amos His rule and judgment apply to all nations, whom He chastises for their infringements of the common laws of humanity. In Isaiah Jehovah moves on a swift cloud and flies to Egypt, and all the idols of Egypt are moved at His presence; and speedily Egypt shall be part of His Kingdom, and Israel shall be a third with Egypt and with Assyria, even a blessing in the midst of the earth, whom the Lord of hosts shall bless, saying: "Blessed be Egypt My people, and Assyria the work of My hands, and Israel Mine inheritance" (xix. 25). The only difference between the earlier and the later in regard to this subject seems to be that while the same doctrine of the unity of God is professed and taught by all, in the earlier prophets it is presupposed and expressed more in concrete form; while in the later, on account of conflicts that had

5

arisen within the nation, and from the political relations into which the people had entered with idolatrous nations abroad, the subject had become more one of abstract thought, and the prophets had occasion to formulate the faith of the nation more sharply in opposition to tendencies of thought that came in upon Israel from without, and currents originated by these tendencies from within.

But even during all the prophetic period, no less after than before Jeremiah, that mode of speaking still prevailed which referred to the idols of the nations as having a real existence and as being real gods. This way of speaking was one natural to the ancient world. It less readily occurred to an ancient thinker, who observed nations around him devoutly attached to their gods, to imagine that these had no existence, or to present to his own mind the idea that such deities were mere impersonations of the religious notions of the human mind. But when the prophets have the question before their own mind they are at one in denying any reality to the gods of the nations—there is one God, Jehovah, God of Israel. We observe, indeed, the same twofold method of speaking in the New Testament. At one time St. Paul says: "An idol is nothing in the world" (1 Cor. viii. 4), and hence meat sacrificed to idols is neither better nor worse than other meat, if a man have understanding and faith to perceive that this is the case. But as this is not the case with all men, the idol becomes to the apostle that which those who believed in it held it to be, something that had a real existence; "But I say, the things which the Gentiles sacrifice, they sacrifice to devils, and not to God: and I would not that ye should have fellowship with devils. . . . Ye cannot be partakers of the Lord's table, and of the table of devils" (1 Cor. x. 20, 21).

What is said of the prophets before Jeremiah is true of the writers who preceded these prophets. They profess not only faith in Jehovah as alone God of Israel, but faith in Him as the only God. Thus in the xviiith Psalm, the undoubted composition of David, we find it said: "Who is

God save Jehovah? and who is a rock save our God?"
(ver. 31). Cf. also Ps. vii. 8 and Ex. xix. 5. In the
former passage, part of an ancient Psalm, Jehovah judges
the nations; in the latter—a passage belonging to the
oldest literature—Jehovah has all the earth as His own.

God in giving His revelation to Israel was, first of all,
intent that this people should worship Him alone, that
they should be practically monotheists. It was religion
that was first necessary, a practical faith, in order to a
pure life. Hence expression of the doctrines of this faith
in a theoretical form was little attended to. With the
practice, the life, there gradually rose to the surface of the
mind the theoretical form of the truth. This explains the
form in which the commandments are given; how for
long the doctrines regarding God are expressed in the
practical concrete form; and how only late in the history
of Israel and as occasion occurred did these doctrines
acquire a theoretical expression. But the doctrines were
the same from the beginning.

6. *The historical occasion of the application of the Name Jehovah.*

If we could realise to ourselves the circumstances in
which the name *Jehovah* came into prominence in connection with Israel, it would undoubtedly help us. We have
two narratives of these circumstances, one in Ex. vi. and
another in Ex. iii. Modern scholars recognise different
writers in these two passages, and it is not quite easy to
reconcile the two statements made by them with one
another. The account in Ex. vi. is brief, that in Ex. iii.
circumstantial; and it is in the latter that we have what
appears to be an explanation of the name. The former (Ex.
vi. 2–4) is as follows: " And God 'א spake unto Moses, and
said unto him, I am *Jahweh*; and I appeared unto Abraham,
unto Isaac, and unto Jacob as El Shaddaἰ ('שׁ בְּאֵל), but (as
to) My name Jahweh I was not known to them " (or, " I did
not let Myself be known by them "). The writer who uses

these words is supposed to be the same who in Gen. i. says,
"In the beginning God created, בָּרָא אֱלֹהִים, the heavens and
the earth"; and who in Gen. xvii. 1 represents God in His
appearance to Abraham as saying, "I am *El Shaddai*";
and now he introduces God saying, "I am *Jahweh.*" In
other words, he is supposed to have a general view of the
progress of revelation and of the Divine names: first, in
the times before Abraham the name of God was Elohim,
or El; second, in the Patriarchal age it was El Shaddai,
from Abraham onwards; and in the Mosaic age and hence-
forward it was *Jahweh.* And in conformity with this view
it is supposed that the writer avoided the name *Jahweh*
in his historical sketch of ancient times, till he reached in
his narrative this revelation to Moses, when God called
Himself *Jahweh.*

If this be an accurate account of the facts, we may be
obliged to assume a certain difference of tradition, for in
other parts of Genesis the name *Jahweh* is assumed to exist
in pre-Mosaic times. Thus it is not only freely put into
the mouth of the Patriarchs, which might be due merely to
usage; but it is expressly said of men in the times of Enos,
the son of Seth: "Then began men to call upon the name
of *Jahweh*" (Gen. iv. 26). Looking at these facts, it is
certainly more probable that the author of Ex. vi. does not
mean to deny that the name *Jahweh* was older than Moses,
or unknown before his day. He denies rather that it had
Divine sanction before his day, and regards it as appropriated
by God now and authorised as part of His manifestation of
Himself,—as that which He revealed of Himself at this
new turning-point in the history of redemption. This is
probably the meaning, because the words are not "My name
Jahweh was not known to them" (נוֹדַע), but "*in* or, *as to*,
My name Jahweh, I was not known by them," or, "I did
not become known (נוֹדַעְתִּי) to them." This interpretation
admits the view, which is certainly likely, that the name
was old; it introduces no discrepancy into the various
narratives in Genesis; and it is in harmony with the other
passage in Exodus. On all hands it is admitted that in His

revelation to Moses, God appropriated the name *Jahweh* to Himself, and stamped it as the name expressive of His relation to Israel now about to be entered into and manifested in deeds of redemption, and in memory of these deeds to be henceforth His peculiar name as God in Israel.

It is in the other passage, however, Ex. iii., that more details are supplied, and where there is given what some have supposed to be an etymology of the name. There it is narrated how, as Moses kept the flocks of Jethro on Horeb, the angel of *Jahweh* appeared to him in a bush that burned, but did not consume. The angel of *Jahweh* here, according to the usage, is not any created angel; it is Jehovah Himself in manifestation, for He immediately says: "I am the God of Abraham." Moses turned aside to see the great sight, and the Lord addressed him from the bush, and said: "I am the God of thy father, the God of Abraham, the God of Isaac, and the God of Jacob." This is the first point, God who now appeared to him was the same God who had appeared to the fathers, and led them. The Being is the same, but as yet there is no reference to His peculiar name. But the cause of His manifestation of Himself now lies in His relation to the seed of Abraham, His friend: "I have seen the affliction of My people, . . . and am come down to deliver them out of the hand of the Egyptians"; in which great operation Moses must serve him: "Come now, therefore, and I will send thee unto Pharaoh." Moses shrank from the great task, and pleaded his unfitness: "Who am I, that I should go unto Pharaoh?" The reply of the Lord to him is significant, and the phraseology of it of great importance: "Surely I will be with thee" אֶהְיֶה עִמָּךְ—כִּי אֶהְיֶה, *I will be*. And in token of this great promise of His presence with him the Lord proposes to Moses a sign. Now, as I have said, it is of consequence to notice the phraseology used, אהיה, *I will be*, because it recurs immediately. Moses is still reluctant to undertake what seemed to him so hazardous an enterprise; he pictures to himself not only the dangers he might encounter from the Egyptians, but the incredulity with which he is likely to be met on the part of the Hebrews—"Behold, when I come unto the children of Israel, and shall say unto them, The God of your fathers hath sent me unto you; and they shall say unto me, What is his name? what shall I say unto them?" And God said unto him אֶהְיֶה אֲ אֶהְיֶה; "and he said thus shalt thou say unto the children of Israel, אֶהְיֶה hath sent me unto you." And God added finally: "Thus shalt thou say unto the children of Israel, *Jahweh*, the God of your fathers, the God of Abraham, the God of Isaac, and the God of Jacob, hath sent me unto you: this (*i.e. Jahweh*) is My name for ever, and this is My memorial unto all generations." Then follows an amplified form of the promise to deliver the people, and work great signs and wonders in Egypt, and do great judgments upon that people.

Now, here the name appears in three forms: אהיה א אהיה, the simple אהיה, and *Jahweh*. *Jahweh* is merely the third person, of which *Ehyeh* is the first; He who says *Ehyeh* when speaking of Himself is *Jahweh* when spoken about. But does it not seem manifest, as has already been indicated, that the name *Ehyeh* or *Ehyeh asher Ehyeh* cannot be translated differently from that former expression: "Certainly I will be with thee," אֶהְיֶה עִמָּךְ; that it is nothing else but that promise raised into a title, and that we must render *I will be*, and *I will be that I will be*, and, in the third person, *He will be?* It is evident that the whole meaning of the larger phrase, "I will be that I will be," אה' א אה', may be expressed by the shorter phrase *I will be* 'אה, or, in the third person, 'יה. The addition, "that which I will be," or as it might be rendered: "I who will be," only adds emphasis to the preceding *I will be*. The expression resembles the other declaration: "I will have mercy on whom I will have mercy," the meaning of which would be clearer if put in this order: "On whom I will have mercy I will have mercy." That is to say, when He has mercy, then, indeed, He has mercy; and so, "that which I will be, I will indeed be." But the point of the phrase lies in the circumstances of misery and bondage on the part of the people in which it was spoken, in the very vagueness of the promise of interference and presence, and in the continuousness of that presence which is suggested. The name is a circumference the contents of which cannot be expressed. He who relies on the same has the assurance of One, the God of his fathers, who will be with him. What He shall be to him when with him the memory of what He has been to those that have gone before him may suggest; or his own needs and circumstances in every stage and peril of his life will tell him. Or his conception of God as reposing on the past and on his own experience, and looking into the future, may project that before his mind.

The name Jehovah does not reveal a God who was not known. Jehovah is אל saying: "I will be"—I will approve Myself.

The name is not one expressing special attributes of Jehovah; it is rather a name expressive of that which all His attributes make Him—the same at all times, the true in covenant, His being ever like Himself, the unchanging.

The name supplies two things absolutely necessary in this age. (1) A personal name for God. Without this it may be said that the people could not have been educated into Monotheism. It brought strongly into relief His personality—His particular personality; and (2) a strong expression of His union with this people. The name did not express any attribute of God, or describe God as to His essence; but it described Him in this relation to Israel— "I will be with thee."

The same general principles apply to the discussion of another question, namely, the *spirituality* of Jahweh. There also the commandment merely prohibits the representation of Israel's God under any material form. It does not state directly that He has no such form. This could not have been expected from a practical religion, the object of which was to initiate men into the truth in practical life, that gradually they might ascend to its principles in speculation. Except the evidence of the second commandment, there is naturally not much to rely upon as evidence in favour of the spirituality of Jahweh. Some evidence of an indirect kind may be found in such statements as those in the fourth commandment. The Creator of heaven and earth can hardly be one capable of being presented under the *species* or תמונה of anything which He has created. But this, though an inference that *we* should make, may not have occurred to peoples whose mode of thought was less exact. More trustworthy evidence, though only of a confirmatory kind, may be found in the history of the Ark and the Tabernacle. It is certain that no form was permitted in the Tabernacle. Jahweh was worshipped as a formless being. The injunctions of the law were there carried out in practice. In Judah almost always, we might say, the worship of Jehovah without any image prevailed, and in Jerusalem this worship was never interrupted.

But we may readily conceive how a coarse-minded people had difficulty in accommodating themselves to this abstract religion. The idea under which they conceived God was the *powerful*; the symbol of might, strength, was the *ox*. Even in the prophets the mighty One of Israel, אַבִּיר, is called by the same name by which the ox is called. A sensuous race could ill be restrained from giving Jahweh a sensible form in order to realise Him to themselves. We know how early this occurred, and how even the weaker leaders of the people were drawn into the error. All down the history of the people this tendency manifested itself, and it is to be presumed that the private sanctuaries so common in the north, particularly in the time of the Judges, contained images of Jahweh in the form of an *ox*. This was the type of power. And the familiarity of the people with this form explains the readiness with which Jeroboam's religious innovations were accepted. But all this does not imply that the spirituality of Jahweh was not a doctrine of all the higher minds in the nation and of Mosaism itself. It merely implies that the crass imagination of the masses had not been penetrated

temporarily eclipsed; it is rather forgetfulness than final loss—they shall remember and turn unto the Lord.

It may seem hardly to be another thing, but rather something involved in the above, when we say that Scripture does not teach, but assumes, that God may be *known*. We do not mean *known to be*, but *known*, seeing that He is. Scripture does not teach that God may be known, but it teaches these things—in what ways He is known, and that He is known so far as He gives Himself to be known. But it always assumes as a thing undeniable that He may be known. The doctrine of Scripture on the *knowability* of God is much more extensive than its doctrine regarding His existence. Two things have to be considered here, namely, first, what Scripture teaches about the possibility of knowing God; and, second, what Scripture teaches about God thus known. In dealing with these questions it is not necessary to distinguish between what Scripture asserts and what it assumes, inasmuch as its assumptions may be considered its teaching even more than its direct affirmations. Now, regarding this doctrine of our knowledge of God, we find these four positions: (1) Scripture assumes that God may be and is known by men. (2) This knowledge of God on the part of men is man's fellowship with God. (3) The avenues through which this knowledge reaches man's soul, or the regions within which man moving meets and knows God, are many—such as nature, the spiritual life of the soul, the redemptive history, prophecy, miracle, and so on. And (4) Scripture denies that God can be known by man. Perhaps Scripture is even more particular than what is here laid down. It may also be thought to state what element or organ of man it is that knows God immediately—whether the soul or the spirit. But if it do, that question need not be raised by us here, because, by whatever organ or side of his nature man knows God, it is not accurate to say that it is that organ or side that knows. It is man that knows through or by that organ or side; and we are concerned meantime with the possibility and reality of man's knowing God, not with any question of what element of man it is by which he knows,—which is a question concerning anthropology.

Now, *first*, it is hardly needful to prove that Scripture teaches or assumes that God may be known—*i.e.* not that God may be known to be, but that God who is may be known; not that He may be known as being or to be what He is, but that being what He is He may be known. If I say I know the king, I do not mean I know that the king is, or I know what the king is; but that the king being, and being all that he is in office and person, I know him—I, a person, know him personally. To know in Scripture is to be acquainted with, to have familiarity and acquaintance with whoever is known. The Bible certainly recognises all these four degrees of knowledge: (*a*) to know that God is, (*b*) to know what God is; (*c*) to know that a certain Being, or a Being who manifests Himself in a certain way, is God, and (*d*) to know God, who so manifests Himself. Thus Scripture says: "He that cometh to God must believe that He is, and that He is a rewarder of them that diligently seek Him" (Heb. xi. 6), though I am not sure whether that text means to describe the attributes of a person who does come unto God, or the requisites of a person who shall come; whether it means to say: "He who cometh unto God shows himself, by coming, to be possessed of a belief in God's existence and in His moral government; or to say: "If any one will come to God, he must, in order to come, believe in God's existence and in His moral government." But, in any case, the distinction between the idea that God is and what God is, is clearly recognised.

As to what God is, — all that God is, — this is generally embraced in Scripture under the expression the '*name* of God.' That term embodies all His characteristics—is the summary of *what He is*. Hence it is said, "they that know Thy *name*—what Thou art—will put their trust in Thee" (Ps. ix. 10); and "the name of the Lord is a strong tower: the righteous runneth into it, and is safe" (Prov. xviii. 10). And nothing is more common in Scripture than the idea that certain acts, or words, or manifestations, show the Actor or Speaker to be God—" Be still, and know that I am God " (Ps. xlvi. 10); " Believe Me for the very works' sake " (John xiv. 11); " Unto thee it was showed, that thou mightest know that Jehovah is God. Out of heaven He made thee to hear His voice; and upon earth He showed thee His great fire " (Deut. iv. 35). And it is said that God's wonders in Egypt brought both the Israelites and the Egyptians to know that the worker of them was God:—Israel shall know—the Egyptians shall know that I am the Lord— the heathen shall know that I am the Lord. And that this Being, who is known by His works to be God, may Himself also be known, is manifest in every line of the Bible. Indeed, it is the object of the Bible to make Him known—the object of the Incarnation to declare Him— " that they might know Thee the only true God, and Jesus Christ, whom Thou hast sent " (John xvii. 3). And while Scripture shows how all along history God made Himself known to men, it predicts that the time is at hand when all shall know Him—" they shall all know Me, from the least of them unto the greatest of them " (Jer. xxxi. 34).

Further, as to the *second* thing the Scripture was said to teach regarding this knowledge, namely, that it was fellowship with God, it may perhaps be questioned if that statement be strictly accurate. At least, if it be not accurate to say that Scripture identifies knowledge of God with fellowship with Him, it considers the two inseparable, and so allied that the one may be put for the other. Christ Himself says : *to know Thee is eternal life* (John xvii. 3), and calls this knowledge and life the object of His mission. And His apostle calls the object of his mission *fellowship*—" that ye may have fellowship with us : and truly our fellowship is with the Father, and with His Son Jesus Christ " (1 John i. 3). But what I am concerned to say is that Scripture does not present God as an object of abstract contemplation, or anticipate His being made such. He is always a historical Being, with a history, with a particular sphere of manifestations in specific relations, and exhibiting a certain character in these relations. No doubt there is a background,—an *unseen*,—but that is rarely before the eye of the saint or prophet. Occasionally, however, it is, and when it is, he can only speak of it in negatives like ourselves. God in that case cannot be made the subject of positive speech or thought: "Canst thou by searching find out God?" (Job xi. 7). "Who hath measured the Spirit of Jehovah?" (Isa. xl. 13). Scripture does recognise this distinction, which the Germans have made so much of, between *immanent* and *economic*; that is, God as in Himself He is, and God as in revelation He has shown Himself to us. But while many theologians and philosophers, in maintaining that distinction, have asserted either that God immanent is different from God economic (a singular position to assume, seeing the term *economic* must embrace the whole circuit of our knowledge of God), or have contented themselves with the position that we are unable to say whether He be the same or different, Scripture never contemplates the idea that He is different. He is the same as we know Him to be; only He is all that we know Him to be, heightened so as to exceed our reach of thinking.

It is rare, however, that Scripture deserts the region of revelation, the very idea of which implies that God can be known; or the region of spiritual experience, which is but another name for fellowship. The occasions when it does desert this empirical realm are chiefly two: first, when showing the absurdity of idolatry it holds up the *Incomprehensible* before the idol-maker, and asks if his idol be a proper presentation of Him; and second, in cases of religious desertion, or other awful and unwonted experience in the soul, when the spirit moving amidst mysteries is brought often to question the truth of its ideas of God, and always to recognise that, whether true or not, they go but a little way to express Him;—"Verily,

Thou art a God that hidest Thyself, O God of Israel"
(Isa. xlv. 15). Thus, what Scripture means by knowledge
of God is an ethical relation to Him; and, on the other
side, when it says that God knows man, it means He has
sympathy and fellowship with him. All Israel's history
is filled with this reciprocal knowledge, rising up from
strength to strength, till One came who knew the Father,
and whom the Father knew in fulness:—"No man knoweth
the Son but the Father; neither knoweth any man the
Father save the Son, and he to whomsoever the Son will
reveal Him" (Matt. xi. 27).

Now, *thirdly*, as to the channels through which this
knowledge reaches man, or the regions moving in which
man knows or comes to the knowledge of God. Those
that Scripture recognises are very much what we insist
upon to this day, viz. *nature, history*, the human *soul*. But
I think Scripture does not make quite the same use of
these things as we do in our Natural Theology. For example, I doubt whether it regards these as primary sources
of our knowledge of the existence or of the character of God.
The position it assumes is not this: Contemplate nature
and you will learn from it, both that God is and what He
is; but rather this: You know that God is, and what He is;
and if you contemplate nature, you will see Him there—
the heavens declare the glory of God. This, at least, is
the position of the Old Testament revelation, though in the
New I am not sure but some further use is made of nature.
And, in any case, if God's character be manifest in nature,
then that memory of God and that knowledge of Him
which we have otherwise may be refreshed, and if needful
corrected by the contemplation of nature. I need not say
that Scripture neither contemplates any one destitute of
the knowledge of God, nor describes the process whereby
any one destitute of this knowledge comes to reach it. It
merely mentions certain regions in which, or media by
which, God is in fact and actually known; without assert-
ing that any of them occupies the first place, much less
the only place; without saying of any of them that it

is the medium through which we first know or begin to know God, or is the only medium through which God can be known.

Now in regard to *nature*, Scripture has been thought to teach or assume not only that God may be recognised in nature, but that He may be known from nature, *i.e.* not only that we may see God there whom we already know, but that we may discover God there though formerly unknown. The Old Testament, as it spoke chiefly to a people having a knowledge of God from revelation, insists mainly on recognising that God of revelation in nature ; but it also appeals to nature to correct the ideas of God given by revelation when the people had perverted them. It is merely exhibition of an already known God which we find (Ps. viii. and xix.); but it is a heightening of the conceptions already had of God when Isaiah points to the starry heavens, saying, " To whom then will ye liken Me, or shall I be equal ? saith the Holy One. Lift up your eyes on high, and behold ! Who hath created these things ? " (xl. 25). And in a remarkable passage in Ps. xciv. an inference is drawn from the nature of man to the nature of God who made him, and an argument somewhat similar to what we call our argument from design [1] is conducted. The writer in that Psalm denounces, first, the wickedness of certain men ; and, second, their foolishness in thinking that God cannot or does not see their wickedness :—" They say the Lord shall not see, neither shall the God of Jacob regard it. . . . Ye fools, when will ye be wise ? He that planted the ear, shall He not hear ? He that formed the eye, shall He not see ? " While, of course, it is always assumed that God created the capacities, it is argued that the existence of certain capacities in man implies their existence much

---

[1] What is called the ontological argument is probably not touched in Scripture. The cosmological may be supposed to be touched in Paul's statement, " In whom we live, and move, and have our being," although, as usual, the fact is assumed. It is not put so as to be proof. The physico-theological or teleological argument is often alluded to.

more in the Creator of man ; and the Apostle Paul conducts
a similar argument before the Athenians when, from the
fact that we are the offspring of God, he infers the absurdity
of representing God by images of gold or silver :—" Foras-
much, then, as we are the offspring of God, we ought not to
think that the Godhead is like unto gold or silver or stone,
graven by art and man's device" (Acts xvii. 29). All
these passages speak of discovering, or recognising, the
character of a Being supposed to be already known ; so
that while it is mainly recognition, it in no case goes
further than correction of false ideas of Him, or inference
as to His true character from His works.

There is one passage, however, which many have
thought to go further, and to teach that it may be discovered from nature *that* God is, as well as what He is—
the well-known passage in Rom. i. 19. Now that passage
certainly teaches or assumes that in nature certain things,
or so much, of God, may be or is known,—" that which
may be known of God (τὸ γνωστόν) is manifest in them,—
for God showed it unto them." Apart from revelation, so
much is known of God,—it is known in men's hearts,—for
God has made it known to them. And it is known thus :
the invisible things of God, the invisible attributes which
form His character, are seen from His works, νοούμενα
being = things perceived by the reason, even His power and
Godhead, θειότης. But it is doubtful if θειότης include
existence—it is all the attributes that make up Godhead.
It is questionable whether the passage contemplates proof
of the Being of God. The Scripture does not seem to
contemplate men without a knowledge of the existence
of God, or without certain ideas regarding His nature.
It does contemplate them as possessed of perverted ideas
regarding Him ; and it affirms, both in the Old Testament
and in the New, that so far right notions of God may be
derived from nature apart altogether from supernatural
revelation.

But Scripture regards *Revelation*, particularly as historical, as the main source of our knowledge of God, or the

main region wherein God is known. I have already quoted passages to this effect, and I need not repeat them. But there are two elements in the history of revelation which Scripture singles out as spheres wherein God is specially known—*miracle* and *prophecy*. The miracle is not only a proof that God is there; the complexion of the miracle is an exhibition of some aspect of the character of God. "According to Josh. iii. 10, it is shown by the wonderful subjugation of the Canaanites that Jehovah is the *living* God; according to Ex. vii. 5, the Egyptians shall know by the plagues He sends upon them that Jehovah is God; according to Deut. vi. 21, the miracles are meant to draw the eyes of all nations to Jehovah, just as in Ex. ix. 29 they are intended to produce the conviction that the earth is the Lord's" (Steudel, *Vorlesungen über die Theologie des AT.*, p. 170). And very frequently Scripture sets forth prophecy as a sphere in which God may be known. This mark of God's presence is very much insisted upon in the second half of Isaiah, and in chap. xli. it is coupled with the extraordinary, if not miraculous, history of Cyrus, as manifesting the activity of God—"Who raised up the righteous man from the East—gave the nations before him, and made him rule over kings? I the Lord, the first and with the last, I am He." And idols are challenged to demonstrate their Godhead by predicting some event near or distant :—"Let them show us what will happen—let them show the former things, or the things that are to come hereafter." Such is the tenor of the passage.

But now, *fourthly*, in opposition to all this, Scripture denies that God can be known. It moves here among natural contradictories or antinomies, which only need to be cited to be understood. Thus it says of the angels that they see God—"their angels do always behold the face of My Father who is in heaven" (Matt. xviii. 10). But of men in their present bodily life it says, "no man shall see God and live" (Ex. xxxiii. 20; cf. John i. 18, etc.); while again, on the other hand, David comforts himself with the hope that he shall see God: "As for me, I will behold Thy face in righteousness: I shall be satisfied, when I awake, with Thy likeness" (Ps. xvii. 15); and Jesus promises the same thing to those who are pure in heart (Matt. v. 8); and John says: "We shall be like Him; for we shall see Him as He is" (1 John iii. 2). Again, it is said (Ex. xxiv. 9, 10): "Then went up Moses and Aaron, Nadab and Abihu, and seventy of the elders of Israel: and they saw the God of Israel." There is the statement: "No man hath seen God at any time" (John i. 18); while again it is said: "In the year that king Uzziah died I saw the Lord seated on a throne, high and lifted up" (Isa. vi. 1). Paul speaks to the Athenians of feeling after God and finding Him, though He is not far from any one of us (Acts xvii. 27); while Job says: "Who can by searching find out God?" (xi. 7). Scripture speaks of possessing the Spirit of God in the soul, and then it says: "Who can measure the spirit of the Lord?" (Isa. xl. 13). These contradictories explain themselves. Scripture does not say in what sense God may be seen and may not be seen, how He may be known and may not be known. It assumes that men themselves understand this, and merely alludes to the two facts as things undoubted in men's thought and experience.

2. *The Essence and the Attributes of God.*

With respect to what Scripture teaches of this God who may and may not be known, two things are in view here—first, what may be known of the essence of God; and second, what may be known of His attributes, or of God Himself. As to the essence of God, Scripture teaches directly in the New Testament and assumes in the Old that God is *Spirit*. Christ says, "God is Spirit, and they that worship Him must worship Him in spirit and in truth" (John iv. 24). But the same truth is presupposed in the Old Testament in many ways; for example, in the prohibition to represent God by any material likeness; and

also, not obscurely in the history of man's creation, in which
God is said to have formed man's material part out of the
dust of the ground, but to have drawn his spiritual part out
of Himself; and again, perhaps in the name given to the
angels as spirits, *sons of God, i.e.* altogether in His likeness,
both as to essence and as to moral nature. Yet more
perspicuously the spirituality of God is seen to be an idea
underlying all Old Testament thought from a significant
passage in Isa. xxxi. 3 : "Now the Egyptians are men, and
not God; and their horses flesh, and not spirit." There
the parallelism shows that man is to God as flesh to spirit;
that as man is a corporeal being, so God is spiritual. It
has indeed been maintained that the Old Testament, or the
Israelites, at first at least contemplated God as possessed
of a corporeal form, and that gradually the conception of
Him clarified till He was recognised as formless spirit.
It is difficult to see how such a theory can be fairly
maintained in the face of the above passages. Some of
the early Fathers, such as Tertullian, fancied that God
possessed a form; yet they denied it to be material.

As to what is taught about this Being Himself, that
may be found in Scripture in various forms—chiefly two,
namely, statements or assumptions regarding God, and
names applied to God. It will be found, I think, that all
other designations of God, and all other assertions respect-
ing Him, and all other attributes assigned to Him, may be
embraced under one or other of the two names given to
God in the opening chapters of Genesis. What is taught
of God in these chapters is, *first*, that God is the absolute
Cause and the absolute Lord of all things—heavens and
earth; which terms embrace not only the upper and lower
matter, but the superior and inferior spirits. And, *second*,
that God is the absolute personality—over against finite
personalities, not absorbing personalities in Himself, nor by
His personality excluding personalities besides Himself.

This personality is self-conscious—it is not undetermined till it becomes what it is in the finite personality
but it is free before the finite comes into being, and

conscious of itself as over against the finite when it has
called the latter into existence. Before the existence of
the finite it deliberately purposes to make it :—" Let there
be light "; " let us make man "; " let him have dominion."
And when created, it conceives of itself in opposition to
the finite :—" Hast *thou* eaten of the tree of which *I*
commanded thee not to eat ?   *I* will put enmity between
thee and the woman."

This person is perfectly ethical, and is in an ethical
relation of undisturbed love-communion with the innocent
spiritual beings whom He has made.

To speak shortly, the truths contained in these names,
the *names* by which God is known in the account of
Creation, are these two—first, that God is the power to
whom the world belongs ; and, second, that He is at the
same time the Eternal, the Person who stands in a fellowship of love with the spiritual beings in the world.[1]   The
first truth is contained in the name *Elohim* and the cognate
names ; the second, in the name *Jehovah* and others allied
to it ; and all other assertions regarding God in Scripture
may be reduced to one or other of these two.   But of this
more hereafter.

There is no reason to deny that some elements of
truth, or many elements, may have been found in the
primeval Shemitic religion held by the ancestors of
Abraham, or by himself before his call—fragments of a
primitive knowledge of God more or less pure, generalisa-
tions more or less profound regarding God and morality,
hopes and aspirations more or less exalted, like those of
Job.   We cannot form a very complete idea of the condition.   But these stages in the development of the knowledge of God in Israel may be detected : *first*, the primeval
Shemitic religion, in which each family had its particular
god, whom it worshipped, if not in images, at least in connection with sensuous forms, as groves, trees, pillars.
Second, a very important development from this primitive
Shemitic religion which took place at a far back period

[1] See Hofmann, *Schriftbeweis*, p. 75 ff.

towards a high morality and faith in a spiritual omnipotent God. This development we know as the call of
Abraham and the foundation of the Patriarchal religion.
Third, even a higher development which took place at
the end of the Patriarchal time and the beginning of the
national life. This we know as the legislation of Moses,
in which the spirituality and unity of God are set forth
in the fundamental laws of the constitution. Jacob is
represented as having found God in a certain place, and
as rearing a pillar, on which he poured oil, as a visible
representation, if not of God, yet of the place of God.
The idea of God as One everywhere present seems far from
this. But all similitudes were forbidden by Moses. The
second and third of these stages are not to be regarded
as natural developments of the primary religion, for the
surrounding tribes did not share in the development, but
sank deeper into idolatries of the most degrading kind.
The Scriptures represent God as revealing Himself to
Abraham and Moses, and there seems no way of accounting for their knowledge except by considering this statement of Scripture to mean that God revealed Himself to
these men in another manner than to the Gentiles.

The distinctive title of God as known and worshipped
by the patriarchs—El Shaddai, God Almighty; El Elyon,
Most High God—shows that the omnipotence of God was
the attribute to which most prominence was given. This
was very natural, seeing that the primary idea of God in
the Shemitic mind was *power*. But if the idea of the unity
of God was not already in the worshipper's mind, these
names were very well fitted to suggest it. And in like
manner, if the first commandment of the Decalogue—
which beyond doubt is Mosaic—did not directly inculcate
the unity, it immediately suggested it—"thou shalt have
no other gods with Me."

Again, if the second commandment—"thou shalt not
make unto thee any תְּמוּנָה of anything in heaven above,
or in the earth beneath, to fall down to them and worship
them," did not directly inculcate the spirituality of God, it

immediately suggested it. And there can be no hesitation in saying that all the men of insight in Israel read these commandments as meaning that there was but one God, and that He was a spiritual being who could not be represented under any form.

But it is very evident that two lines were thus opened up, on which there might be divergence and conflict in Israel—the *unity* of God and the *spirituality* of God. The denial of the one, or the failure to recognise it, led to the introduction of other gods along with Jehovah, particularly of Baal; and the denial of the other led to the worship of Jehovah through sensuous forms, particularly the *calf*. This was made the distinctive form of the worship of the Northern Kingdom. This officially sanctioned mode of worshipping Jehovah must not be confounded with pure idolatry, such as the Baal worship. The one not unnaturally led to the other; but the prophets of Jehovah drew a clear distinction between the two, and, though they denounced the calf worship, they did not leave the kingdom, or hold that those who practised it cut themselves quite off from being the people of God. But with the Baal worship they would hold no terms. Against the prophets of Baal they waged a war of extermination. There is perhaps no more singular phenomenon in the history of Israel than the repeated outbreaks into idolatry. There was even the attempt, under the dynasty of Omri, to suppress the worship of Jehovah and extirpate His followers out of the country. These repeated falls into idol worship, exhibited throughout the whole history of Israel, especially in the Northern Kingdom, but even also in the Southern, and there in an aggravated form toward the close of the monarchy under Manasseh, require some explanation.

And, as might be expected, the explanation that many have given has been, that we have in the history of Israel as established in Canaan the spectacle of a people slowly emerging by natural means out of the darkness of idolatry into the clear light and freedom of a spiritual monotheism. The leaders of the people in this splendid march, in which Israel were the pioneers of mankind, were the prophets. There in Canaan, and in this people Israel, humanity achieved its most glorious triumph; it trod down under its feet those debasing embodiments of its own passions and vices called gods; and prostrated itself before that loftiest conception of one spiritual being, Lord of the universe, who is God. But the victory was not reached without many temporary defeats; and the progress of the conflict may be watched in that history which records the changes from Jehovah worship to idolatry, and from idolatry to Jehovah worship, till, finally, the refining process of the Exile purified the people's conceptions of God, so that idolatry utterly disappeared from among them.

Now these things are true in this representation, namely, that there was a conflict between the worship of Jehovah and idolatry; that the prophets were the leaders on the side of Jehovah; that the conflict lasted during the whole history of Israel; and that the victory was won only under the purifying sorrows of the Exile. This, too, is true, that in this splendid march Israel became the pioneer of humanity, or, as it may be put, humanity was in Israel making this triumphal march. For humanity is no doubt a unity, and no theory of revelation requires us to break up this unity or deny that what God was showing to one people and enabling it to perform, He was achieving once for all in the race. So far is this theory from being contrary to revelation, that it is itself part of revelation, which teaches that God founded His Church once for all in Abraham; that He took the Jewish people into His covenant of salvation, not for themselves merely, but for the salvation of the world. All this is certainly true, and there may even be more truth still in the representation. For unquestionably such a conflict could never have been fought unless there had been many born idolaters among the mass of the people, unless large masses of the general surface of the nation had been continuously sunk in idolatrous doctrines, and the light of the true faith in its purity had shone only on those elements that rose up high above the common level. The history throughout its whole length shows a polluted stream of idolatrous worship. They were idolatrous in Canaan ; even David's wife had teraphim ; they were idolatrous in the wilderness ; they were idolatrous in Egypt ; they had been idolatrous in Ur of the Chaldees. But this is what is false in the representation above given, that the struggle was carried on in the field of natural religion. What natural religion contributed was the idolatry. The worship of the spiritual God came from revelation.

The case can be accounted for best by supposing the Jehovah worship something impressed from without, and the mass of the people only imperfectly penetrated by it. The conflict itself came to a head in the kingdom of Israel, under the rule of the monarchs of the house of Omri. That vigorous ruler, more intent on strengthening his kingdom by alliances without than by purity of national faith at home, had entered into treaties with the kingdoms about, especially the Syrian, and married his son to Jezebel, a daughter of Ethbaal the king of Sidon. Ahab was not so much vicious as weak ; one who, like a wilful child when refused his wishes, fell sick, and would not eat. And thus he fell completely under the guidance of his self-willed and unscrupulous wife. At her instigation he introduced the worship of Baal. Baal worship became thus a State religion. For a time, probably, it subsisted peaceably side by side with the worship of Jehovah. But collisions naturally ensued between the partisans of the two, and the royal power seems to have been used to put down the worship of Jehovah. An order was issued for the murder of Jehovah's prophets, and the throwing down of His altars. This is nowhere expressly recorded. But Elijah, who alone of the Lord's prophets escaped, says : " The children of Israel have forsaken Thy covenant, and thrown down Thine altars, and slain Thy prophets with the sword ; and I, even I only, am left ; and they seek my life, to take it away " (1 Kings xix. 10). The history here is very defective.

but the representation of the prophet is corroborated by a statement given as made by Obadiah, who represents himself as hiding one hundred of Jehovah's prophets by fifty in caves.

The commanding genius of this era was Elijah. In the long period from the Judges to the times of Elijah and the downfall of the house of Omri, proceedings were going on of which no record has been preserved.

David was a fervent Jehovist. Solomon perhaps was not fervent in any direction. He can hardly have been a theoretical monotheist when he erected temples to the deities of his wives. Nor can Ahab, when he raised a house to the Sidonian Baal served by his wife. Still Ahab called all his sons by the name of Jehovah. There was evidently great want of clearness of thought in men's minds.

It is very useful for us if we can here and there find an epoch in the course of events signalising a new turn and a new victory in the higher conception of God. We have such an epoch in the reign of Ahab and the downfall of the house of Omri before Jehu.

What is included in the expression *Jehovah, God of Israel*, has been much disputed by modern writers, as we have said, and we have already remarked that we must take into account the existence of various elements in Israel since its settlement in Canaan. In Israel, as history deals with it, there were sections differing very widely from one another in culture and morals; and when it is asked what is meant by saying *Jehovah is God of Israel*, the answer may be that it meant different things among different classes, or to different minds. History or prophecy may bring to light this divergence. But it seems clear, as we have said, that the phrase meant at least that Israel was to worship no other God but Jehovah. Unquestionably the people entered upon national existence with the consciousness of having been delivered or redeemed from Egypt by Jehovah. He was not unknown to the people before this deliverance, but now

He had made them free, and created them a people. They owed their existence to Him, and He was their God. This was the positive fact; but no deductions are drawn from the fact in reference to other gods, nor are any general conceptions as to Godhead connected with it. Each separate people about Israel had its national god, and one god worshipped did not necessarily imply the belief in the existence of no other gods: "For all the nations walk every one in the name of his god," says the prophet Micah, "and we will walk in the name of the Lord our God for ever and ever" (iv. 5). The separate peoples, while worshipping each its own god, did not deny the existence of the gods of their neighbours—though they may have considered their own the most powerful. And it is probable, as we said, that many in Israel stood on no higher platform than this, that Jehovah was God of Israel, while Chemosh was god of Ammon. But it is certain, at least, that the national consciousness was at one with the prophets on this point, that Jehovah was God of Israel. This was a common faith, though it was, of course, a faith that might be held in very different senses, that is, with very different conceptions of the Being called Jehovah, as we perceive from the prophets Amos and Hosea. The first commandment might seem to leave the question whether there were gods besides Jehovah undecided, for it merely prohibits the worship of other gods in Israel.[1] By mention-

[1] The question is one of great interest, What deduction are we entitled to draw from the words, "Thou shalt have no other gods before Me"?

If we looked at the Commandments as simple objective revelation and as ordinances given to Moses, without, so to speak, any exercise of his own mind, then perhaps questions need not be raised about the enigmatical form, "Thou shalt have no other gods before Me." But if we suppose that the mind of Moses concurred in this revelation and was not inactive, but that the commands came through his mind, just as the revelation to Amos or any of the prophets was reached not without all that activity of mind which we cannot help perceiving, then the question, how the command took this shape, and what is implied in it, at once rises. The command is unique in antiquity. What induced Moses, the founder of the new religion, to give it this shape? It must have been his conception of what Jehovah was. It has been suggested that it arose from the idea that Jehovah was a 'jealous God.' But if Moses conceived Jehovah as a jealous God, which He is often named, this

ing other gods it might even appear to admit their existence, at least it might be thought not to rise to the affirmation of Monotheism. But in like manner, as we have already noticed, the seventh commandment prohibits merely Israel from committing adultery, and the sixth from doing murder; they contain no hint that these injunctions have any universal validity, and are fundamental laws of human wellbeing. A Shemitic mind, we repeat, would rise to general conceptions such as we cherish very slowly; and while practically Jehovah was the only God to the Hebrew, he might not have risen to the theoretical notion that He was God alone. But one with such a practical faith in Jehovah

conception only throws the difficulty a step further back. How did he conceive Him as jealous? Jealousy is the reaction of the consciousness of one's self—of being what he is, when this consciousness is hurt or touched. How did Moses fancy that the presence of other gods would wound Jehovah's consciousness of Himself? What conception had Moses of Jehovah's nature which would make him attribute jealousy to Him? The deities of the nations were not jealous. They were sometimes contemptuous, sharing the spirit of the nations themselves; but from all we observe they were perfectly tolerant of the existence of other deities beside them. With Jehovah it was otherwise. This intolerance of His requires some explanation, that is, some explanation of Moses' way of conceiving Him which made him impose upon the people such a law.

The explanation must lie in his conception of Jehovah's nature—His ethical nature. Certainly Moses regarded Jehovah as the God of righteousness. When he sat and judged the people, he did so in Jehovah's name— he only interpreted and expressed His mind. He was the guardian of right and moral order. Hence the curious phrase, that the people were to bring their causes before Elohim, when they came to the priests or judges for decisions. But mere ethical quality in Jehovah will not explain the exclusiveness, unless on the supposition that this differentiated Him from other gods, who were not ethical, or else that He was ethical in such degree that He was the one Being that men should worship. When the form of the other commandments is considered, the natural conclusion is that Moses was a monotheist, and not merely what is called a monolatrist. The peculiar thing about Israel is not that it had one God, but that it had an evil conscience when it served other gods. This is unique. The mere existence of a *law* will hardly account for this. No doubt the law had been reinforced by the history, by the redemption which their God had wrought for the people. At all events we must attribute to the Exodus the planting in the popular mind of the truth that Jehovah was God of Israel. So far as we see, Israel never had any native God but Jehovah. If it fell into the worship of the Baals as local deities, it found these. No proper name is compounded with such a name as Astarte.

stood to Him much as believers in the unity of God stand
to God now.   The religion of Israel was practical, not
speculative; and while a practical Monotheism prevailed, and
gave rise to all that profound religious life which we see
reflected in such men as Moses, and Samuel, and David,
and the prophets, it perhaps needed that internal conflict
which arose through the slowness of the popular mind,
and that outward collision with idolatrous nations which
occurred in the days of the great prophets from Isaiah
downwards, to bring into speculative or theoretical clearness
the doctrines of the oneness and the spirituality of God.
My impression is that this conflict, whether within the
State or with foreign nations without, did not suggest to
the prophets the doctrines of God which they express, but
only furnished the occasion which demanded the expression
of them.

Perhaps we lay too much stress upon the meaning
in religion of a mere theoretical Monotheism, i.e. upon this,
that the worshipper had in his mind the idea that the
Deity he stood before was God alone.   Probably even now
this feeling is little present to the mind of worshippers.   It
is what God is to the worshipper, and what are His attributes in Himself, that is important, not whether there be
other beings to be worshipped.   Of course, at other times
we have in our minds the fact that the Being we worship
is God alone; and this no doubt influences the mind when
it comes to the act of worship, though the idea be not present
in the act.   And perhaps this consideration may lead us to
judge more favourably of the worship even of heathen and
polytheistic nations.   As a rule, the individual worshipper
did not adore more gods than one.   He selected some one
of the deities worshipped in his country.   Practically this
god was the only one to him.   He gave this god his adora-
tion, and sought from him alone the help he needed.
Religiously, his mind towards this deity was just as if no
other deity existed.   Even when he admitted the existence
of other deities, they took, in regard to the deity he
worshipped, a lower place.   His god was the supreme god,

and the others were merely his agents, or, it might be, intercessors with him for the worshipper. Cyrus, when he conquered Babylon, restored to their ancient seats the gods which had been collected there by the previous king, and he begs that these minor gods would intercede with the supreme God Bel for him and his son Cambyses. Both in Egypt and in Babylon there is visible a tendency to elevate one deity into a supreme place,—not always the same deity by name,—and to concentrate on one all the attributes of all the others, so that the one embodies the exhaustive conception of Deity.

There are various classes of passages in which the gods of the nations are mentioned: one class consists of passages put into the mouth of persons whose history or conduct is being described by Old Testament writers. Thus in Judg. xi. 23, 24, Jephthah is represented as saying to the king of the Ammonites: "So now Jehovah the God of Israel hath dispossessed the Amorites from before His people Israel, and shouldest thou possess them? Wilt not thou possess that which Chemosh thy god giveth thee to possess?" Another class of passages consists of expressions used by Old Testament writers themselves in which the gods of the nations are referred to, and Jehovah is contrasted with them, or said to be superior to them, and the like. Now in estimating all these passages we must take the state of thought in those ages into account, and the condition of religion actually existing in the world at the time. Even the passage in Judges can hardly show that Jephthah conceded any existence to Chemosh. He could hardly speak otherwise than he did to one whose national god Chemosh was. Jeremiah himself, as we have seen, uses phraseology analogous: "Woe to thee, O Moab: the people of Chemosh perisheth" (xlviii. 46); and again: "Hath Israel no sons, hath he no heir? Why then doth Milcom inherit Gad, and his (i.e. Moloch's) people dwell in his cities?" (xlix. 1). Evidently such language means nothing in Jeremiah's mouth. It is argued, however, that though in the mouth of such men as Jeremiah such ex-

pressions have no meaning, reposing merely on the belief
and the condition of things in Moab itself, and on the
notorious fact that Chemosh was worshipped there, it may
have had meaning in the popular mind; and that, though
in later times such phraseology had merely become a
current mode of speech, with little significance, at the
time when it first arose it must have expressed the belief
in the existence of Chemosh.   It is no doubt difficult
to estimate the value of this kind of language.   But it
may be said, I think, that the use of it is far from con-
clusive as to the belief in the reality of the gods spoken
of.   Take a passage from the Chronicles, a very late book,
probably of the age of Alexander the Great, the end of the
fourth century before our era (2 Chr. xxviii. 23).   Speaking of Ahaz, the writer says that he sacrificed to the gods
of Damascus, who had smitten him, saying: " Because the
gods of the kings of Syria helped them, therefore will
I sacrifice to them, that they may help me."   But the
writer adds: " But they were the ruin of him and of all
Israel."

It is certain that at that time of day neither the
Chronicler nor any educated man in Israel ascribed reality
to any object called god except the God of Israel.   In
ancient times a stranger must attach himself to some tribe
or family in order to be protected.   But attachment to a
tribe or family meant partaking in its *sacra*—its religious
rites; for this was what constituted a tribe's distinction,
or that of a family.   Hence the stranger who went to
a foreign country must perforce take part in the religion
of the country and serve its gods.   A great deal has been
made of an expression used by David (1 Sam. xxvi. 19).
Appealing to Saul not to pursue him out of the country,
he says : " They have driven me out this day from abiding
in the inheritance of the Lord (*i.e.* the land of Israel),
saying, Go serve other gods."   According to these words,
abiding in a foreign land is equivalent to serving other
gods.   But, again, we are supplied with analogous phraseology in Jeremiah—the man who counselled the exiles in

Babylon to build houses and plant vineyards, to seek the peace of the city whither they had been carried captive, and to "*pray unto the Lord for it*, for in the peace thereof shall ye have peace" (xxix. 5). While men may pray unto the Lord in foreign lands, He threatens Israel: "Therefore will I cast you forth out of this land into the land that ye know not . . . and there shall ye serve other gods" (Jer. xvi. 13). And similarly in Deut. iv. 28: "The Lord shall scatter you among the nations . . . and there ye shall serve gods, the work of men's hands, wood and stone." The phraseology rests merely on the fact that in foreign lands other gods were worshipped; it contains no proof that these gods had any reality. At most it might be supposed to imply that Jehovah was God only of Israel, and could not be found in a foreign land. It is possible that the phrase might have had this meaning; but it had no such sense in Jeremiah's days, for he counsels the exiles to pray unto the Lord for the peace of the land of their exile.

It is admitted on all hands that from Jeremiah downwards there are abundant expressions of a theoretical Monotheism. The circumstances of the prophets from Isaiah onwards differed from those of the earlier prophets. The great prophets, such as Isaiah and Jeremiah, were confronted by the world powers, and the question of the relation of Jehovah to them was forced upon them. These powers were embodiments of idolatry, and they were the oppressors of Israel. The antithesis between their gods and the God of Israel pressed itself upon men; the relation of Jehovah to the world, and His relation to the idols, the gods of the world, could not be evaded. The prophets solved the question of the conquest of Israel by the world power, by the great conception that the world power was Jehovah's instrument to chastise His people—the Assyrian was the rod of His anger, Nebuchadnezzar was His servant. And this was already also a solution of the relation of the idols to Jehovah. It was not the idols, but Jehovah that gave Assyria and Babylon its victories. Much more, it was not the idols that had raised up Cyrus to destroy the idolatrous Babylon. And when these powers forgot that they were but instruments in the Lord's hand, they were acting as if the saw should magnify itself against him who *shook it*, or as if *the rod should say it was not wood* (Isa. x. 15). But even in this age the same way of speaking still prevailed,—of speaking of the gods of the nations as if they had reality; as St. Paul also speaks of idols at one time as 'nothing in the world,' and at another time as 'devils.'

Perhaps the citation of these passages may suggest that some caution is necessary in founding inferences upon expressions which at first sight might seem to imply belief in other gods besides Jehovah, on the part of those who used them.

3. *The Unity of God.*

The simplest notion of God among the Semitic peoples was, as we have said, the idea of *power, force.* If we consider ourselves at liberty to inquire how this idea was reached, we should presume that it was through the processes and phenomena of nature. The power that worked in Nature, that changed her face, that conducted the gigantic movements of the heavens above and the waters beneath, was God. There cannot be a doubt that among the peoples about Israel there appeared the tendency to confound Nature herself with God, to regard individual forces in Nature as gods. We do not find such a thing among the Jews, except occasionally and by imitation. But how shall we regard this tendency? As a degeneration of a Monotheism retained by Israel? Or as a Polytheism out of which Israel rose to Monotheism? Was the first step to regard the forces of nature as gods, and the next to abstract and unite the forces into one, and spiritualising this force name it God? Or was the tendency downward, to break up this grand simple power into a multitude of forces, and out of the one God to frame many gods? The question probably cannot be answered with certainty, either on Shemitic or on Indo-Germanic data. But in point of fact we find Israel agreeing with the related peoples in the Name it gave to God and the idea it had of Him, and occasionally falling into their way of idolatry, which identified some natural force with God, as the force resident in the sun, or the generative power of nature, etc.

If the idea of a Supreme Being was first impressed on men, or impressed anew after being lost, by the operations of some single great force in nature, they would be very apt to identify this force with the Being, or to regard the two as inseparable. Such an identification would operate in two ways on the conception of God. It might prevent the mind rising easily to the unity of God. And it might make it slow to reach the idea of the spirituality of God. This was but a single force, there were many; the Being who so showed His power might not be the only powerful being. And the Being who showed Himself through this material symbol might not readily be conceived abstractly and unclothed in the physical energy. Yet He might have to the worshipper a very distinct personality. A pantheistic conception of nature is quite foreign to the Shemitic mind. Hence even where we cannot be sure that the conception of God in any particular case implied His unity or spirituality, we may assume that His personality was always part of the conception. It is true that in Homer, while some of the gods are undoubtedly and always persons, others of them appear sometimes as forces or phenomena and sometimes as persons, such as Iris, Dream, etc., and sometimes even Apollo 'far darting,' as if the statue were partly formed out of the block, or the living bird half out of the shell. But among the Shemitic races this condition does not appear to present itself. God is always personal.

Now, if we suppose that the condition of the idea of God among the Shemitic peoples prior to the call of Abraham, or even after his call, was this, that He was a personal power, there are materials in it for that profound religious experience which we know to have been his. The power may easily rise to omnipotence; the personality may easily pass into spirituality, and the union of these two easily into unity. But we must not judge the ancients by ourselves. With this Personal Power, Lord of men, ruler of nature — without raising questions, as we should, whether He was Lord of all men or ruler of all nature—there might be a fellowship, and towards Him a reverence, and on Him a dependence, and in His intercourse a training and an elevation, that together made up the elements of a fresh and deep religious life. The personal bond to a governing personal power—or, as it was called, the *covenant*—was the essence of religious life. How God by His training of Abraham purified his faith and strengthened it, we see from the history.

It is probable that among the family out of which Abraham sprang there had come a great degeneration, or at least there prevailed a low condition of religion prior to his time. This is the universal supposition of the Scriptures. Joshua in his last speech exhorts the people thus: "Now therefore fear the Lord, and serve Him in sincerity and in truth: and put away the gods which your fathers served on the other side of the flood, and in Egypt; and serve ye the Lord" (Josh. xxiv. 14). And the same appears from the story of Jacob's flight from Padan-Aram, in which his wife Rachel is represented as stealing the gods of her father, and carrying them with her in her flight.

And thus it is certain that through God's revealing of Himself to Abraham a great purification and elevation took place in his conception of God. The fundamental thought of God did not alter, but it was more firmly grasped and sharply conceived, and probably carried to such a degree of clearness as to involve, if not the spirituality, at least the unity of God. That fundamental thought common to all the Shemitic peoples was, as we have seen, *power*, expressed in the words *El, Elohim*; but we are expressly informed that the prevailing conception of God in the Patriarchal age was that of *almightiness*:—" I appeared to your fathers as *El Shaddai—God Almighty*." This is a potentiation of the simple idea of *mighty*, which seems to carry with it the exclusion of other powers, and to lead directly to the conception of the *Unity of God*. We should probably be right in considering the Patriarchal idea of God as embracing these two ideas within it.

The plural form of the word *Elohim* might be supposed to have some bearing on the question of unity. And, indeed, by many it has been supposed to bear testimony to the plurality of gods originally worshipped among the Shemitic peoples; and by others, who seem to consider the name Elohim part of God's revelation of Himself, to the plurality of persons in the Godhead. The real force of the plural termination, as we have already said, is not easy, indeed, to discover. But a few facts may lead us near it. In Ethiopic the name of God is *Amlāk*, a plural form also of a root allied to *melek — a king*. All Shemitic languages use the plural as a means of heightening the idea of the singular; the precise kind of heightening has to be inferred from the word. Thus *water*—מַיִם—is plural, from the fluidity and multiplicity of its parts; the *heavens*—שָׁמַיִם—from their extension. Of a different kind is the plural of *adon—lord*, in Hebrew, which takes plural suffixes except in the first person singular. Of this kind, too, is the plural of *Baal*, even in the sense of *owner*, as when Isaiah uses the phrase אֲבֻם בְּעָלָיו (i. 3). Of the same kind also is the plural *teraphim, penates*, consisting of a simple *image*. And of this kind probably is the plural *Elohim*—a plural not numerical, but simply enhancive of the idea of *might*. Thus among the Israelites the *might* who was God was not an ordinary might, but one peculiar, lofty, unique. Though the word be plural, in the earliest written Hebrew its predicate is almost universally singular. Only when used of the gods of the nations is it construed with a plural verb; or, sometimes, when the reference is to the general idea of the Godhead. This use with a singular predicate or epithet seems to show that the plural form is not a reminiscence of a former Polytheism. The plural expressed a *plenitude of might.* And as there seems no trace of a Polytheism in the name, neither can it with any probability be supposed to express a plurality of persons in the Godhead. For it cannot be shown that the word is itself part of God's revelation; it is a word of natural growth adopted into revelation, like other words of the Hebrew language. And the usage in the words *baal, adon, rab,* and such like, similar to it in meaning, leads us to suppose that the plural is not numerical, as if *mights,* but merely intensifying the idea of might. Nor can it be shown to be probable that the doctrine of a plurality of persons should have been taught early in the history of revelation. What the proneness of mankind to idolatry rendered imperative above all and first of all, was strenuous teaching of the Divine Unity.[1]

4. *The Doctrine of the sole Godhead of Jehovah in later Prophecy.*

We have noticed certain forms of speech used with reference to Jehovah, the God of Israel, which seemed to suggest that, though God of Israel, and greater than all gods, He was not considered God alone. The phraseology in which other gods are spoken of may not be quite easy to estimate justly. But if writers on the religion of Israel are not unanimous on the question as to how such phraseology is to be interpreted in the earlier books of Scripture, they are entirely at one in the view that from Jeremiah downwards the prophets give undoubted and clear expression to a theoretical Monotheism. The circumstances of the prophets from Isaiah onwards

---

[1] It is probably a return to the literal sense of the word when the term *Elohim* is used of men or angels, or of what we call the supernatural : " I said, Ye are gods " (Ps. lxxxii. 6) ; "Thou hast made him a little lower than the Elohim " (Ps. viii. 5) ; " I saw Elohim coming up out of the earth," said by the witch of Endor of the ghost of Samuel (1 Sam. xxviii. 13).

differed from those of the earlier prophets. In the time of the earlier prophets, Israel came into connection with nothing but the petty States lying immediately around. These States were many, and their gods many. And over each of them Jehovah was the Saviour of Israel. In point of fact Amos, the oldest of the prophets, except in one obscure passage, makes not the faintest allusion to the gods of the nations; he represents Jehovah as ruling immediately over all the peoples neighbouring on Israel, and chastising them, not only for their offences against Israel, but for their cruelties to one another. Still this prophet's world was composed of a multitude of small peoples—the world did not yet form a unity in opposition to Israel. But when Israel was confronted by the great empires of Assyria and Babylon, empires which virtually embraced the world and presented it as a unity, then the question of the relation of Jehovah their God to this unity was forced upon them. These empires, too, were embodiments of idolatry; for, of course, as in all ancient States, the culture, and the law, and the social fabric of the empire reposed on the religion. And thus, when Israel was confronted with the world as a unity in these empires, Jehovah was felt to be confronted also with idolatry as a general faith and conception. And thus the prophets were led to form, or at all events to express, abstract and theoretical judgments regarding these matters.

Now the judgments which they do express regarding Jehovah and the idols are remarkable. So soon as Northern Israel came into collision with Assyria, it fell before the great Eastern empire; and in like manner Southern Israel, Judah, succumbed before Babylon. Now, if the prophets had learned their conceptions of Jehovah from history, the natural inference would have been that the gods of Assyria and Babylon were more powerful than Jehovah, the God of Israel. This was the inference of the foolish king Ahaz when defeated by the Syrians: " Because the gods of the kings of Syria help them, therefore

will I sacrifice to them, that they may help me " (2 Chron.
xxviii. 23). And this was the inference no doubt of
Manasseh also, and of many in Judah during its later
years, when the worship of the host of heaven and many
other idolatries were introduced from Assyria and Babylon.
Men worshipped the gods of their conquerors. But the
inference of the prophets was a wholly different one.
They solved the problem of Israel's humiliation by the
idolatrous nations on these two principles: first, these
nations were Jehovah's instruments—they were not more
powerful than the God of Israel, on the contrary, the
Assyrian was the rod in His hand to chastise His people,
and Nebuchadnezzar was His servant; and, secondly, it
was because Jehovah was holy and His people sinful that
He gave them up to the destroyer. The great events of
Israel's history did not suggest to the prophets their conceptions of Jehovah. On the contrary, their conceptions of
Jehovah already held, solved to them the enigma of the
events that happened. But no doubt these events also led
them to express their thoughts of Jehovah and the idols in
a more general and abstract—one might say almost—
dogmatic way.

Here an important place belongs to the Second Isaiah,
the finest, but also the most difficult, part of Old Testament
prophecy. Here the name of *Jehovah* has no *special* meaning; it is the highest name of God. Though the prophet
is a monotheist in the strictest sense, his Monotheism is no
mere dead article of belief or inoperative conviction. It
is the most living and powerful of truths that Jehovah,
God of Israel, is God alone. Being God alone, He must
make Himself known to be God alone: " My glory will I
not give to another, neither My praise to graven images "
(Isa. xlii. 8). In the words *Jehovah, God alone*, is heard
the death knell of all idolatry: " I have sworn by Myself
. . . that every knee shall bow " (Isa. xlv. 23). But on
another side the sole Godhead of Jehovah opens up wide
prospects of thought to the prophet. He who is God
alone is God over all—He is the God of the nations as

well as of Israel. And that which He is to Israel as God
of Israel, He must be to the nations also as their God.
His purposes, which are in the main purposes of grace,
must extend to the peoples also as well as to Israel. Yet
Jehovah is primarily God of Israel, and He remains so
always. His relation to the nations is manifested only
through Israel. Israel is His servant to make Him
known to the nations, to mediate His grace to all mankind.

The doctrine of Jehovah is stated in the broadest and
most developed manner in this section of prophecy. Still
this is done with such religious fervour, and in a way so
brilliant with all the hues of a poetical imagination, that
to state the several points in that doctrine in cold and
naked propositions of the mere intellect, seems to desecrate
them. We need only mention a few things, and refer to
one or two passages.

Jehovah, God of Israel, is God alone. This is frequently stated explicitly and in so many words; usually,
however, it is based on certain kinds of evidence, or it takes
the form of contrasting Jehovah with the idols. In chap.
xli. Jehovah challenges the idol worshipping nations to
meet Him before a tribunal, that a question whether He or
the idols be God may be decided: " Let the nations renew
their strength; let us come near together to judgment!"
Opening the plea on His own side, He asks them two
questions: " Who raised up Cyrus ? " and, " Who predicted it from of old ? " The idol gods of Babylon have
hardly brought Cyrus on the stage of history, who will
lead Bel and Nebo away captive (chap. xlvi.). And if
they are gods, let them show what will happen. Let
them point to former things, prophecies already uttered,
that they may be compared with events, and be seen to
be true predictions; or let them now in the present
declare things that are to come; yea, let them do good
or do evil, that they may be seen to have life in them.
They are silent, and judgment is passed on them that they
are of nothing and their work of nought (Isa. xli. 21).

In a word, Jehovah appeals to history and to prophecy in proof of His sole Godhead.

This appeal to prophecy fully justified Apologetics in making the same appeal, however arguments of another kind may be used now in addition to this order of evidence. And no doubt the argument from prophecy has considerably changed its form; it is now less an argument based on the literal fulfilment of predictions of contingent individual events. It has become more an argument from prophecy than one from prediction, an argument based on a broad, general movement of the religious mind taught of God in Israel,—a movement that revealed itself in religious presentiments, in aspirations of the pious heart, in momentary flights of faith too lofty to be sustained, in a certain groaning and travailing under the sense of inadequate life and a cry for fuller life, in a sense of imperfection that was often far from seeing clearly how it was to be satisfied, how the imperfection was to be removed. It is all these things and many more put together now that form the argument for prophecy; for with the widening of the conception of prophecy as not mere prediction, the argument from prophecy has widened in proportion.

And in this prophet the reference to prophecy is more for the purpose of showing that Jehovah is, unlike the idols, a living, intelligent Being, who is working a work the end of which He foresees and declares from the beginning. Being living and conscious, He has before Him the whole scope of His great operation; and He might carry it on, leaving men in darkness as to what it is. But from the nature of His operation men must be enabled to enter into it also with intelligence. Israel is His Servant in carrying it out, and it is Jehovah's relation to Israel that makes them prophesy. Men cannot live unless they have some knowledge of what the end of life shall be. They cannot strive unless a goal be set before them, nor run for the prize unless there be a mark. Prophecy was an absolute necessity in a redemptive history;

though, of course, it might be enough to give great general conceptions of the future, and less necessary to supply knowledge of contingent occurrences. This prophet evidently refers to special events in history, such as the destruction of the Babylonian empire. But what makes his general conception of interest is that he connects prophecy and history together as but the inner and outer sides of one thing. History is Jehovah in operation; prophecy is His mind, conscious of its purpose, breaking out in light around Him, and enabling men to see Him operating.

The prophet's references to prophecy in proof of Jehovah's sole Godhead are confined to chaps. xl.–xlviii. After these chapters this argument, being sufficiently well developed, is no more pursued. I need not do more than mention a few of the passages where the sole Godhead of Jehovah is explicitly stated: xliv. 6 ff.: "I am the first, and I am the last; and besides Me there is no God"; "Is there a God besides Me? yea, there is no rock; I know not any." Being God Himself, He thinks He would know the other gods; but He has no acquaintance with them. Similarly xlv. 6, 21, xlvi. 9; cf. also lxiv. 4. In xliii. 10 it is said: "Before Me there was no God formed, neither shall there be after Me . . . beside Me there is no saviour." Besides prediction and history, the Creation in its unity is proof of the sole Godhead of Him that formed it: "Thus saith the Lord that created the heavens: He is God" (xlv. 18).

Such passages as these indicate why it is that the prophet so much insists on the Godhead of Jehovah alone. It is no mere formal intellectual Monotheism that He preaches. To Him the knowledge of the true God is the source of all truth and all life to men, that alone which allows the nations of the earth to have any destiny before them. Having no true God in the midst of them, the nations have no goal before them, no elements of true progress; they are without the conditions of attaining the destiny set by God before men. Yet they are included in His purpose of grace, and they shall be brought into the stream of it by His servant Israel : " Behold my Servant, . . . he shall bring forth right to the nations. . . . He shall not faint . . . till he have set right in the earth, and the countries shall wait on his instruction " (xlii. 1). It is here that to the prophet lies the significance of the sole Godhead of Jehovah ; the knowledge of it is the condition of salvation for mankind. Hence Jehovah says : " Look unto Me, and be ye saved, all the ends of the earth : for I am God, and there is none else " (xlv. 22). This forty-fifth chapter is one of the most important in the prophecy in this point of view.

5. *The Personality and Spirituality of God.*

The question which naturally follows that of the *Unity* of God, is that of the *Personality* and *Spirituality* of God.

Unquestionably the most distinct and strongly marked conception in regard to God in the Old Testament is that of His personality. This appears on every page. A God identical with nature, or involved in nature, and only manifesting Himself through the blind forces of nature, nowhere appears in the Old Testament. He is always distinct from nature, and personal. In the first chapter of Genesis He stands over against nature, and perceives that it is *good*. He stands also over against man, and lays His commands upon him : " Of the tree of the knowledge of good and evil thou shalt not eat." He puts Himself as a moral person over against men as moral persons, and enters into covenant of moral conduct with them. Not only is He conscious of men, but He is conscious of Himself : " By Myself have I sworn " (Gen. xxii. 16 ; Isa. xlv. 23). He is not only conscious of Himself as existing, but of what character He Himself is. He resolves with Himself to make man, and to make him in His own image.

In Amos He swears not by Himself, but by His *holiness* (iv. 2). The idea of some modern writers, that the conception of God among the people of Israel was first that of some power external to themselves which they perceived in the world, a power making for a moral order or identical with it, and which they afterwards endowed with personality and named God, inverts the Old Testament representation, according to which the personality of God was the primary idea, and the secondary idea the moral character of this person; for this latter idea, no doubt, became clearer and more elevated. This representation of modern writers to which I have referred is not a historical account of the origin of the conception of God's personality among the people of Israel,—at all events in the historical period which the Old Testament embraces. It is rather a description of movements of thought in regard to God, peculiar to modern times, when men, having lost the idea of God's personality which once prevailed, are making a new effort to regain it.

From the first historical reference to God in Scripture the idea of His being a *person* is firmly reached, and little advance takes place along this line.

This is so much the case that, on the other hand, the question arises whether this very vividness with which the personality of God was realised in Israel did not infringe upon other conceptions necessary to a true idea of God, such as His transcendence and ubiquity and spirituality. Did not Israel so strongly conceive God as a person, that He became to them a mere magnified human person, subject to the limitations of personality among men, so that true attributes of Deity were obscured? Now, in going to the Old Testament and seeking to estimate its statements about God, we have to remember that it is not a piece of philosophical writing, that its statements about God are all given in the region of practical religious life, and that they are the expressions of this vivid religious life among a people strongly realistic and emotional. A theology of the schools, where the laws of exact thought prevail, was unknown in the Old Testament period.

We observe, indeed, the beginnings of such a theology in the Alexandrian translation of the Scriptures, and in the

Chaldee translation, and in Jewish writings of later times. These express themselves, in regard to God, in a form that seeks to be more severe and exact, using circumlocutions for the anthropomorphisms of the Old Testament,—a fact which indicates that these caused some offence to the minds of this age. Even in the so-called Priests' Code, while there are some anthropomorphisms, anthropopathisms are avoided. In the Old Testament generally, however, such anthropomorphisms are freely used, as we use them still, when not meaning to be scientific, and when expressing our religious life and feelings. It may be made a question, no doubt, whether, in the popular religion, among ourselves they may not be carried to excess, and whether the strong realising of the personality of God there may not obscure some other conceptions of God which also have their rights. This may well be. Still the use of anthropomorphisms is inevitable if men will think of God; and it has usually been argued that they are legitimate, seeing men were made in the image of God. We are in some measure at least entitled to throw back upon God the attributes of man when speaking of His action and thought.

Yet just as in the popular religion among ourselves—the true religion of men animated with a true religious life—it is possible that the powerful feeling of the personality of God may obscure some of God's essential attributes and lead to a narrow conception of Him, so it is quite possible that among the people of Israel the same narrowing effect may have arisen from the same cause. So far, however, as the Old Testament is concerned it cannot be said that its expressions go this length. When it speaks of the hand, arm, mouth, lips, eyes of God, of His speaking, writing, laughing, mocking, and the like; when, as in Second Isaiah, He makes bare His holy arm in the sight of all the nations (lii. 10); when in His eagerness to deliver the people He pants like a woman in travail (xlii. 14); when, as in the 2nd Psalm, He that sits in the heavens laughs; when He lifts up a signal to the nations (Isa. xlix. 22); when He is seen at the head of the Medians mustering His hosts,—all this is but vivid conception of His being, His intelligence, His apprehension, His activity, and His universal power over the movements of the nations which He directs. The human is transferred to His personality, as it could not but be; it is transferred graphically, as could not but happen when done by the vivacious, poetical, powerful phantasy of the people of Israel. But under all this what we observe is the vivid realisation of the true, free, intelligent, active personality of God. Such language only certifies to the warmth and intensity of the religious feeling of the writer.

Another class of passages may perhaps require more consideration: those in which manifestations of God are described which seem to imply that He was confined within the limitations of space, or that the human form really was proper to Him. He is said to have walked in the garden in the cool of the day; to have come down to see the tower which men did build; to have been one of three men that appeared to Abraham, and to have eaten that which was set before Him. Jacob thought Bethel a house, *i.e.* a place or abode of God; and in Israel His presence was inseparably connected with the Ark of the Covenant. Under all these things there lies at least not only a vivid conception of His personality, but a vivid conception of a profound and more strictly redemptive truth, namely, that He reveals Himself and enters into the closest friendship with men.[1] It may be the case that ideas of God's spirituality were less clear in the Patriarchal age, and that some of these narratives preserve this fact. It was but a short step from the Unity to the other essential element in the conception of God, His Spirituality. Yet this step has always been found very hard to take. The whole history of Israel shows how hard the struggle was in the popular mind between this idea and the sensuous conception of God.

[1] Of course, different minds may estimate these narratives differently. So far as we consider the experiences, say, of Jacob at Jabbok real, we may suppose that a spiritual impression always reflected itself in an accompanying extraordinary physical condition; just as among the early prophets the ecstasy was usual, while, although still occasional among the later prophets (Isa. vi. 8), it became rare.

And when the sense of God's spirituality was lost, there followed speedily the loss of the sense of His unity.

Throughout the whole Patriarchal time the prevailing sense of God was that of a lord, an owner, an almighty ruler whose commandments must be obeyed, who tells his servant to leave his country and he leaves it, who gives the barren children, who subdues kingdoms, and rebukes kings for his servant's sake. If Abraham had a clear thought of His spirituality, this clearness became obscured in the minds of his descendants. Even in Abraham's history God is attached to places. Jacob found Him at Bethel—and said, " Surely God is in this place—this is a house of God —a gate of heaven." And this patriarch reared his *stone*, which, if it did not represent God, was called by him Bethel, and conceived by him as something to which God would attach Himself. These localisations of God show an imperfect conception of His spirituality. Hence such high places were rigidly forbidden in the Mosaic constitution. And it is certain that even the conceptions of the Patriarchal time became greatly obscured among the people in Egypt. Idolatry was practised largely there. Ezekiel in several places chastises the people for their idolatrous practices in this land. " Then said I unto them, Cast away every man the abominations of his eyes, and defile not yourselves with the idols of Egypt " (xx. 7).

We may consider these two things ascertained from a study of the history of Moses. First, that he gave great prominence to the idea of the *spirituality* of God ; and, second, that he connected the idea of the spiritual God with the name Jehovah. The new elevation given by Moses to the idea of God cannot be regarded as anything but the result of a special revelation. God appeared to him. He did not reach a purer conception of God by study or thought. God showed Himself to him. But the conceptions of the Patriarchal time which were then loosely held, and which had been almost lost entirely in Egypt, were brought back by him in full luminousness, and laid as fundamental conceptions at the basis of his constitution. One might raise doubts, though hardly with good reason, as we have already seen, in regard to the first command, as to whether it in so many words prescribed the absolute unity of God, or only the relative unity of God to Israel: "I am Jahweh thy God, which have brought thee out of the land of Egypt . . . thou shalt have no other gods before Me." Israel shall have no God but Jahweh ; but whether there be other gods is not certainly declared ; and in a hymn contemporary with this law, the hymn after the passage of the Red Sea, we read: "Who is like unto Thee, Jahweh, among the gods ? " But there can be no doubt that the second commandment teaches the spirituality of God in the sharpest manner : "Thou shalt not make unto thee any graven image, or any likeness of any thing that is in heaven above, or that is in the earth beneath, or that is in the waters under the earth" (Ex. xx. 4) ; and in the repetition of the law in Deuteronomy : "Take ye therefore good heed unto yourselves ; for ye saw no manner of similitude on the day that the Lord spake unto you in Horeb . . . Lest ye corrupt yourselves and make you a graven image" (Deut. iv. 15, 16). And very singularly that very act which Jacob did is expressly prohibited in Lev. xxvi. 1—"neither shall ye set up any image of stone in your land." What is forbidden in the commandment is not worshipping other gods than Jahweh, but worshipping Jahweh under any similitude. That does not expressly declare that Jahweh has no similitude, but the inference is immediate.

Jehovah is represented as having a *dwelling-place* But He is no local God. That dwelling-place is usually conceived to be *heaven*. But though His abode is there, He visits the children of men, and appears wherever His people are. He appeared to the patriarchs often and in many places in Canaan. But though Canaan be the land of Jehovah, and His house, He is not confined to it. He says to Jacob : "Fear not to go down into Egypt ; for I will there make of thee a great nation : I will go down with thee into Egypt" (Gen. xlvi. 3, 4). To Moses in the wilderness He gave the promise: "Mine angel shall go before thee" (Ex. xxiii. 23); and Moses said: "If Thy presence go not with me, carry us not up hence" (Ex. xxxiii. 15). In one place He appeared to Joshua as the leader of the Lord's host; in another, to David.

So far as His dwelling among the people was concerned, He abode in the Ark. The Ark of the Covenant is not to be conceived as an idol, or as an image of God. No deity could be represented in the form of a small chest. But neither is it enough to say that the Ark was a symbol of Jehovah, whatever that might mean, or a symbol of His presence. It was more than that. Jehovah's presence was attached to it. It was in some sense His dwelling-place. But although it was so, and the people had thus an assurance that He was present among them there in some special sense, His presence was not confined to the Ark. He appeared in the form of the Angel of the Lord in many places; and when the Ark was captured by the Philistines, the priests offered sacrifices to Jehovah at Nob, and set the shewbread before Him as had been done in Shiloh. Everywhere in the old histories as well as in the prophetic writings, the supersensuous abode of Jehovah, and His condescension, nevertheless, and entrance into the life of men, were both well understood.

We cannot say that from the time of Israel's becoming a nation any belief in a local limitation of God can be traced. The sanctuaries scattered up and down the country were hardly places to which God was confined; they were rather places where, having manifested Himself, He was held to have authorised His worship. Such facts as that men, *e.g.* Gideon, Saul, etc., reared an altar anywhere, and that Absalom when an exile in Geshur outside of Palestine made a vow to Jehovah, show that they conceived of Jehovah as without local limitations. Finally, the multiplicity and variety of the combinations of the manifestation of God with nature show that the idea lying at the root of them was not that God was locally confined, but that He was present in all the phenomena of the world. This is the religious idea lying under such descriptions. The rest is but clothing thrown around this idea by the religious phantasy. And when, as in Ps. xxix., the thunderstorm is specially regarded as a theophany, this, of course, arose from the fact that majestic phenomena, like the thunderstorm and earthquake, brought more impressively before the mind the conception of the great Person who was the cause of the phenomenon, and who revealed Himself through it. But it does not need to be said again that the phenomenon did not suggest the idea of God, and cause the mind to rise to the idea of a person; the idea of a person was there already, and explained the phenomenon.[1]

We pass into another and somewhat higher region when we take into account another class of passages—those in which human emotions and modes of conduct are thrown back upon God. The first class of passages referred to mainly suggested the personality of God. The next class added the deep religious idea of His manifesting Himself to men. This new class brings in the idea of the moral in God's personality. Thus He repents that He made man, and also of the evil He intended to do; He is grieved; He is angry, jealous, gracious; He loves, hates, and much more; He breaks out into a passion of anger (Isa. liv. 7, 8), and again He feels as if His chastisements had been excessive (xl. 2). All the phenomena of the human soul of which as men we are conscious, and all the human conduct corre-

[1] Two beliefs characterise the Hebrew mind from the beginning; first, the strong belief in causation,—every change on the face of nature, or in the life of men or nations, must be due to a cause; and, secondly, that the only conceivable cause is a personal agent. The unseen power under all things, which threw up all changes upon the face of the world, which gave animation to the creature or withdrew it, which moved the generations of men upon the earth from the beginning (Isa. xli. 4), bringing Israel out of Egypt, the Philistines from Caphtor, and the Syrians from Kir (Amos ix. 7), was the living God. Some phenomena or events, such as the thunderstorm or the dividing of the sea, might be more striking instances of His operation than others. They were miracles, *i.e.* wonders, but they did not differ in kind from the ordinary phenomena of nature, from His making the sun to rise, and His sealing up the stars; His clothing the heavens with blackness, and making them bright with His breath. Everything is supernatural, *i.e.* direct Divine operation. There is no idea of Law to be broken.

sponding to these emotions, are thrown back upon God
It may be that here there is a certain imperfection,—that
when we conceive Him from another point of view we
must hold Him free of all passion, and not subject to such
changes as are implied in one emotion succeeding another.
This may be true; but it is equally true that this other
mode of conception, however much it may have its rights,
reduces God to a Being absolutely unmoral, and even impersonal, if it be carried to its fair issue. Scripture takes
the other line. Starting with the idea of personality, it
adds that of moral personality, and this can he expressed
in no other way than by attributing to God such emotions.
Scripture is conscious that this mode of conception may be
abused : " God is not a man, that He should lie; nor the
son of man, that He should repent" (Num. xxiii. 19)—
" I am Jehovah, I change not " (Mal. iii. 6).

But, again, what is to be observed is that it is the
general truth lying under all these expressions that really
makes up their meaning; that the real force of these
expressions does not lie in the *form* or in the detailed
variety of the emotions, but in the general conception
which they combine to suggest, namely, the moral Being
of God; that men are in relation with a Being between
whom and them there is a moral reciprocity,—a Being
to whom men's conduct and thought have a meaning, such
a meaning that they seem to reflect themselves upon His
nature, and determine it according to their quality. In
one sense such language used of God gives more a piece
of anthropology than of theology ; it testifies to the meaning
of human life, to its moral character, to the essential
distinction between one act of man and another. These
distinctions are so real and of such influence, that they
repeat themselves upon the nature of God. Man is not
related to an impassive nature force which his actions leave
unaffected. The moral voices of his conduct do not fall
on the dead walls of a prison in which he is immured.
They reverberate in heaven. But while the language
elevates the meaning of man's life and conduct, it also

states something about God. It describes Him as the sensitive moral Spirit in the universe,—sensitive because He is perfect moral personality, and His sensitiveness visible because He is the Being to whom all stand related. But we should be doing the same wrong to the writers of Scripture that we should do to ourselves or to another, if we charged them, when expressing the moral Being of God through such language, with infringing by it the passionless nature of God.

IV. THE DOCTRINE OF GOD—THE SPIRIT.

1. The Spirit of God.

It is under the aspect, then, of perfect ethical personality that the Old Testament conceives of God. It has little to say of His essence. He is a free, active, moral person. And to this attaches what the Old Testament says of the *Spirit of God*. The question whether the Old Testament teaches the *personality* of the Spirit of God is not one that should be raised apart from the other—What is its *conception* of the Spirit of God? We are very apt to raise these formal questions when we ought first at least to raise the material ones. The sphere of the Old Testament is the practical religious sphere, out of which it never wanders into the sphere of ontology. The whole question is the question of the relation of a living, active, moral, personal God to the world and men. It asks as little what the essence of God is as it asks what the essence of man is.

The question regarding the Old Testament idea of the Spirit of God presents itself in another way. As we have seen, there are uncertainties attaching to the terms *El, Elohim, Jehovah*, which prevent us from getting all that we might expect from these ancient designations of God. More instructive are the general statements which occur of what were the prevailing thoughts regarding God.

These statements bear that He was conceived to be the source of all things to Israel—of things spiritual specially, but also of other advantages; and that He ruled Israel. He was King in Jeshurun, and He was Judge. Men brought their causes to Elohim, as it was said; that is, they brought them to the priests, to whom through an oracle Jehovah gives a decision. A later writer sums up all when he says: "The Lord is our judge, the Lord is our lawgiver, the Lord is our king; He will save us" (Isa. xxxiii. 22). It becomes, then, an interesting question how Jehovah exercises His rule in Israel, and His guidance of it in all the spheres of its life.

There are two ways in which the Old Testament conceives this to be done. *First*, by external manifestation of Himself to men, and the giving of commands. This external manifestation of Himself is called the *Angel of the Lord* (מַלְאַךְ יְהוָה). This Angel is not a created angel—He is Jehovah Himself in the form of manifestation. Hence He is identical with Jehovah, although also in a certain sense different. We have such expressions as these: "The angel of God spake unto me (Jacob) . . . and said, I am the God of Bethel" (Gen. xxxi. 11, 12); "Behold, I send an Angel before thee . . . My name is in Him," *i.e.* My revelation of Myself is in Him" (Ex. xxiii. 20, 21). The "Angel of the Lord" redeemed Jacob, led Israel into Canaan, and directed Israel's armies in the conflict with Sisera. *Second*, by God's Spirit. As Jehovah's operations in ruling His people were chiefly through men, they are regarded as the operations of His Spirit. The "Spirit of Jehovah" is Jehovah Himself *within* men, as the "Angel of Jehovah" is Jehovah Himself *without* men. This Spirit raised up judges, *i.e.*, inspired men. He fell on Saul, and Saul was changed into another man. He raised up Nazarites and other special persons. In particular, He animated the prophets. The whole public life of Israel was thus inspired by Jehovah. Jehovah ruled, and He ruled through His Spirit.

Further, the idea of the Spirit of God, like other ideas

of God, is probably formed upon the idea of the spirit of man. The spirit of man is not something distinct from man, but *is* man. The thinking, willing life within man, manifesting itself in influences on what is without, is his spirit. So the fulness of life in God, active, effectual on that which is without, is His Spirit. The Spirit of God, however, may be spoken of as outside His being or as within it. It is His nature, not conceived, however, as *substance* or *cause*, but as moral, personal life. It may feel within Him, or be efficient without Him. It corresponds to the spirit of man. Hence it may be physically conceived just as man's is. As man's spirit manifests itself in his breath, so God's Spirit is the breath of His nostrils, His fire-breath. Hence it is represented as *poured out*, as *breathed*, as *coming from the four winds*, etc.

Now there are two questions which have to be put here. *First*, What is said of the Spirit of God in the Old Testament? and, *secondly*, What is that Spirit of God of which such things are said? On this second question it may not be possible to say very much. The answer to it is in the conclusion suggested by the answer to the other. The first question itself has two branches, namely, first, What is said of the Spirit of God in God, within God Himself? and secondly, What is said of the Spirit of God not in God Himself, but in connection with the world or human life?

2. *The Spirit of God within God Himself.*

As what is said of God is for the most part of necessity secondary, that is, a reflection upon His being and application to Him of what is said and thought in regard to men, it may be useful to look at the general idea connected with *spirit* in the Old Testament, and at what is said of the spirit of man in man. The passage in Isaiah (xxxi. 3) perhaps comes nearer expressing the idea of spirit in a general way than any other : " Now the Egyptians are men, and not God, and their horses flesh, and not spirit." The general scope of the passage is to show the impotence of the Egyptians: they

are men, and not God; their horses are flesh, and not spirit
Flesh is weak and liable to decay, it has no inherent
power in it; spirit is power, or has power. This seems
everywhere in the Old Testament the idea attached to
spirit. It is quite probable that the idea is not primary,
but derived. The physical meaning of spirit (רוּחַ) is *breath*.
Where breath is present there is life and power; where it
is absent there is only flesh and weakness and decay. And
thus the idea of life and power may have become connected
with רׄ from observation. But if we should suppose this to
be the case, the connection of the idea of life and power
with spirit is of such ancient date that it precedes that use
of language which we have in the Old Testament.

Now, in harmony with this general idea of *spirit* is all
that is said of the spirit of man in man in the Old Testament. The original meaning of spirit is breath. This was
the sign of life, or was the principle of life. But by a step
which all languages seem to have taken, this merely pheno-
menal life or visible sign or principle was, so to speak,
intensified into an immaterial element in man, the spirit
of man. Now, avoiding as far as possible anthropological
questions which do not concern us here, when the immaterial element in man is called *spirit* it is in the main
either when it is put in opposition to flesh, *or* when its
strength or weakness in respect of power and vitality is
spoken of. Hence we have such expressions as these:
" God of the spirits of all flesh " (Num. xvi. 22); " In whose
hand is the spirit of all flesh of man " (Job xii. 10); " The
spirit of Jacob their father revived " (Gen. xlv. 27); " To
revive the spirit of the humble " (Isa. lvii. 15); " My spirit
is quenched, my days are over, graves are mine " (Job
xvii. 1). So it is said that there was " no more spirit "
(1 Kings x. 5) in the Queen of Sheba when she observed
the wisdom of Solomon; *i.e.* she was overcome, and felt
weak. Hence, too, the spirit is " overwhelmed " and
" faileth " (Ps. cxliii.); " by sorrow of the heart the spirit
is broken " (Prov. xv. 13 ; " I will not, saith the Lord,
contend for ever, neither will I be always wroth; for

the spirit would fail before Me, and the breaths that I
have made" (Isa. lvii. 16).

The spirit, then, being that in which resides vitality,
power, energy in general, the usage became extended somewhat further. First, any predominating determination or
prevailing direction of the mind was called a *spirit* of such
and such a kind; what we call a mood or temper or frame
of a temporary kind. Thus Hosea speaks of "a spirit of
whoredoms" being in Israel (iv. 12); and Isaiah, of a
"spirit of deep sleep" being poured out on them (xxix. 10);
and of "a spirit of perverseness" being in the Egyptians
(xix. 14); and another prophet speaks of "a spirit of grace
and supplications" (Zech. xii. 10). So one is "*short* in
spirit," that is, impatient; *grieved* in spirit, *bitter* in spirit,
and the like.

This powerful determination of mind, however, might
be not of a temporary, but of a permanent kind. This is
also called *spirit*, and corresponds to *character* or disposition,
whether it be natural or ethical. Hence one is of a
haughty spirit, of a *humble* spirit, of a *steadfast* spirit; and
the Psalmist prays to be upheld with a *free* spirit (li. 12).
Thus the spirit in man expresses all the activities and
energies of life and mind: the strong current of emotion;
the prevailing determination of mind, whether temporary or
permanent, and whether natural or ethical.

And the usage is entirely the same in regard to the
Spirit of God in God. The term expresses the fulness
of vital power, and all the activities of vital energy,
whether, as we might say, emotional, or intellectual, or
moral,—whether temporary or permanent. In regard to
His emotional nature Micah asks: "Is the spirit of the
Lord short, impatient?" (ii. 7). Another prophet asks:
"Who directed the spirit of the Lord?" that is, His
intelligence, which presided over His power in giving
weight and measure to the infinite masses of the material
universe. "Who weighed the mountains in scales, and the
hills in a balance? Who directed the spirit (or mind) of
the Lord (when He did so), or being His counsellor taught

Him? Who . . . instructed Him in the path of judgment, and . . . showed to Him the way of understanding ? " (Isa. xl. 13, 14). One Psalmist (Ps. cxxxix.) expresses by the term Spirit His whole omniscient and omnipresent mind: "Whither from Thy spirit can I fly ?" And one of the Psalmists, by the same term, expresses His unchanging ethical disposition: "Thy spirit is good, lead me into the land of uprightness" (Ps. cxliii. 10). Thus the Old Testament language as to the Spirit of God in God Himself corresponds to its language in regard to the spirit of man in man.

3. *The Activities of the Spirit.*

The other branch of the general question was, What is said of the Spirit of God not in God, but in relation to the world and men? Now, as in the first half of the question it was of consequence to ascertain what general idea attached to *spirit*, so here it is of importance to remember the general ideas entertained of *God*. The conception of secondary causes is almost entirely absent from the Old Testament; what God does He does directly and immediately. And He is over all and in all. All phenomena are due to Him, all changes on the face of the material world, all movements in history, all vicissitudes in the life of men. The Old Testament doctrine of God is not more strongly monotheistic than it is theistic and not deistic. That universal power within all things which throws up all configurations on the face of the world, of history, and of man's life is *God*. When general language is used these phenomena are said to be due to God ; when more precise language is used they are said to be due to the Spirit of God. The Spirit of God *ab intra* is God exerting power, God efficient, that is, actually exerting efficiency in any sphere. And His efficiency pervades all spheres, the physical and moral alike.

Some instances may be given by way of illustration. First, in the cosmical sphere. The Spirit of God moved upon the face of the waters—the watery chaos (Gen. i. 2). This is a realistic image which expresses the idea that God's creative power was engaged in educing life and order out of the primal chaos. It is of some consequence to distinguish between this Spirit of God and the successive creative feats—"let there be light," etc. These latter express God's conscious will and determination. These are movements of the Spirit of God according to the passage in Isa. xl. 13, already referred to, *ab intra*. The pervading Spirit expresses God's efficient presence and operation *ab intra*, carrying out His voluntary determinations.

In Job (xxvi. 13) it is said that "by the Spirit of God the heavens are made bright,"—a bold, though not unnatural figure identifying the wind that carries off the clouds through God's efficiency with the Spirit of God. In like manner Isaiah (xl. 7) says "the grass withereth when the Spirit of the Lord breatheth or bloweth upon it," identifiying the hot withering wind of the desert with the Spirit of God; and Ezekiel (xxxvii. 9) uses the figure of breath or wind from the four quarters of the heaven for the vitalising Spirit of God, in animating the dead. This operation of the Spirit of God upon the material world, however, is rarely spoken of, and it appears to be but an extension of the idea which is referred to next.

Second, there is the Divine operation in the sphere of *life* or *vitality*. God in His power and efficiency, or the Spirit of God, is much dwelt on in the sphere of life, whether in giving vitality or in reinforcing it. In the Creation narrative it is said of man that he was formed "of the dust of the ground," and that man being thus formed, God breathed into his nostrils "the breath of life, and he became a living being" (Gen. ii. 7). This again appears to be exceedingly realistic imagery. Breath in man's nostrils is the sign of life; it may be said to be life in man. Hence also God has a breath of life in Him like man—as indeed the breath of His nostrils in anger is frequently spoken of. When this breath or spirit of life was breathed into man, man also lived. Obviously we must throw away the imagery and seek the idea—which is, that God is the source of life ; and in any particular case of producing life, it is God's Spirit that produces it. Man's life is the presence in man of God's Spirit. Hence Job says : " The spirit of God is in my nostrils " (xxvii. 3) ; and Elihu says, " The spirit of God made me, and the breath of the Almighty giveth me life " (xxxiii. 4). Hence as the source from whence life comes, this Spirit is called the Spirit of God ; but, as it is in man, it is also said to be *man's* spirit : " Thou hidest Thy face, they are troubled ; Thou takest away *their* spirit, they die, and return to their dust ; Thou sendest forth *Thy* spirit, they are created " (Ps. civ. 29, 30). And Elihu says in another passage : " If God should set His mind on Himself (*i.e.* cease to think of the creature) and withdraw His spirit, all flesh would perish " (Job xxxiv. 15).

Of course, we must beware of imagining that the Spirit of God is divided or divisible. The spirit of life in man is not a particle of God's Spirit enclosed in man, which, when released, returns to the great original source ; it is not a spark separated from the primary fire. And it is equally inept to ask where this spirit of life goes when withdrawn. It goes nowhere. As the ocean fills the caves on the shore, and again when it recedes leaves them empty, so the indivisible Spirit of God gives creatures life, and when withdrawn leaves them dead. Stripped of all these scarcely to be avoided figures, and of that tendency so ineradicable in the Eastern mind to turn general conceptions into *things*, all this seems to mean that vitality in all creatures is due to God, to God's operation. God is the source of life, and as God He is continually communicating His life. But God in operation or efficiency is the Spirit of God, and God's operation in giving the creature life is the entrance of His Spirit into the creature. His continuous efficiency in upholding life is the continuous presence of His Spirit ; His cessation to uphold life is the withdrawal of His Spirit.[1]

---

[1] The above exegesis of the passage in Gen. ii. may seem doubtful. There is room for dissent ; for the word רוּחַ means both the life-breath, mere vitality,

Third, there is also the Divine operation in a region perhaps somewhat higher, being one in human experience and history. This embraces those cases in which extraordinary feats of strength and daring are referred to the Spirit of God. Thus the Spirit of the Lord came upon Othniel, and he judged Israel and went out to war (Judg. iii. 10); upon Gideon, and he blew a trumpet, and Abiezer was gathered unto him (vi. 34); upon Jephthah, and he passed over Gilead against the children of Ammon (xi. 29); on Samson, and he rent the lion in pieces as one rends a kid (xiv. 6); on Saul, when the Ammonites besieged Jabesh-Gilead, and his anger was kindled exceedingly (1 Sam. ii. 6). Some of these cases may be referred to again. What struck the beholder in these cases was the presence of a power and efficiency superhuman. These heroes were acted upon, and showed a power not their own. The power of acting on them was God—the Spirit of God.

And perhaps to this division belongs the ascription of prophecy at first to the Spirit of God. The early prophets, as we see from what is related in connection with Saul, were the subjects of a lofty enthusiasm, which sometimes became an uncontrollable excitation or ecstasy. This visible external affection of the prophet was probably what attracted attention and was ascribed to the Spirit of God, *i.e.* the inspiration of which the excitation was the symptom was due to the Spirit of God. I do not allude here to any question whether or how God was present with these prophets. I merely say that it was probably the phenomenon of excitation which was observed, and which suggested

and the immaterial element in man. And it may seem that it was this latter that God breathed. I have never been able to see my way through these two uses of ר in the Old Testament. The point of union between them is, I think, here, that רוח is spoken of the immaterial part when special reference is made to vitality. I think when the phraseology I have referred to—that of the spirit being taken, was used the question was not pursued where it went. Later the question was asked, as in Ecclesiastes : "Who knows whether the spirit of man goeth up, and the spirit of beast goeth down ?" (iii. 21). On the exegesis adopted above the connection between the Spirit of God and life or vitality in the creature is evident.

to the observer the presence of God—the Spirit of God. It is probable that it was the external excitation and elevation of the prophet that was described as the effect of the Spirit of God, and not as yet anything ethical or spiritual in the contents of what the prophets uttered. We may infer this from the remarkable passage in 1 Sam. xviii. 10, where it is said that an "evil spirit of God fell upon Saul, and he prophesied in the midst of the house."

In later times, when prophecy threw off this excitation and became an ethical intercourse of the mind of man with God, a thing almost normal,—as in the case of Jeremiah, who repudiates all such things as prophetic dreams, and claims for the prophet simple entrance into the counsel of God,—the phraseology formed in earlier days still remained, but with another sense. The prophet is still called in Hosea the man 'of the Spirit'; and Micah says in significant language: "Truly I am full of power by the Spirit of the Lord . . . to declare to Jacob his transgressions, and to Israel his sin (iii. 8). The power which seemed formerly physical had now become moral.

Fourth, there is the same in the sphere of intellectual gifts. "There is a spirit in man," says Elihu, and "the breath of the Almighty giveth him understanding." Intellectual powers are regarded as the product of God's Spirit, *i.e.* of God. Artistic skill, as in the case of Bezaleel, is ascribed to the Spirit of the Lord.

Fifth, so, too, in the sphere particularly of moral life. All the religious emotions and vitality of man, the endowments which we call *spiritual*, are said to be due to the Spirit of God. Hence the Psalmist prays: "Take not Thy holy Spirit from me" (li. 11), which is almost equal to a prayer that his mind may not cease to be religious, to have thoughts of God, and aspirations towards God. Of course, connected with this, the Spirit of God is the source of all theocratic forces or capacities in the mind of man. Here God is personally most active; here He communicates Himself in most fulness. Hence the prophet is full of might by the Spirit of Jehovah to declare to Israel his sins (Mic. iii. 8). And the Messiah has poured out on him the Spirit of Jehovah, not only as a spirit of the fear of the Lord, but as a spirit of wisdom and government (Isa. xi. 2).

This is by far the largest of the various spheres. But it is familiar, and it is not necessary to enlarge upon it.

Now, perhaps this slight induction might justify the general remark that the Spirit of God is, so to speak, the constant accompaniment of God, the reflection of God. The Spirit of Jehovah is Jehovah Himself—the source of life of all kinds, of the quickening of the mind in thought, in morals, in religion, particularly the last. God is all, and all comes from Him. The ideas, God and Spirit of God, are parallel, and cover one another. This calling what is really God by the term the *Spirit of God*, is the strongest proof that the idea of the *spirituality* of God underlay the idea of *God* ; just as 'the spirit of man' indicated that in man spirit is the main element. Hence, whatever development we may trace in the Old Testament in the doctrine of God, there will be a corresponding development in that of the Spirit of God. The Spirit of God being God in operation, an advance on the conception of God, a tendency to give the thought of God a prevailing direction, as, *e.g.*, the ethical or redemptive, will be followed, or rather accompanied, by the same advance and tendency in regard to the Spirit of God.

And here perhaps a distinction should be alluded to which no doubt is connected with such a tendency—the distinction between the *Spirit of God* and the *Spirit of the Lord*, or *Jehovah*. The distinction has no bearing on general principles, inasmuch as Jehovah is God under a certain aspect. But the aspect is important. Jehovah is God as God of Israel, God as King of the redemptive kingdom of God in Israel. And the Spirit of the Lord is the Lord operating as redemptive God in Israel. This very idea in itself gave a particular direction to the thought of God, and therefore to that of the Spirit of God. The ethical and spiritual naturally came to the front. The

Spirit given to men such as Gideon, Jephthah, and others was this theocratic redemptive Spirit; it was Jehovah operating in men for redemptive purposes—saving and ruling His people. And the Spirit of prophecy became almost exclusively ethical. And, of course, the further down we come the more this conception of God, and consequently of the Spirit of God, became the prevailing one, until it became almost the exclusive one. The Spirit of God under the name of the 'Holy Spirit' occurs very rarely, only three times in the Old Testament, in Ps. li. and twice in Isa. lxiii. Both these compositions may be late. Judging from usage, *e.g.* holy hill, holy city, holy place, holy arm, etc., which mean hill of God, city of God, etc., the phrase 'Holy Spirit' probably at first merely meant Divine Spirit, Spirit of God, emphasising the fact that He was the Spirit *of God.* But, of course, as the ethical being of God more and more became pro-minent, the same advance in the ethical quality of the Spirit also took place, and the expression *Holy Spirit* was specially employed to express this idea.

The general conclusion which seems to follow from these things is: that the Spirit of God *ab intra* is God active, showing life and power, of the kinds similar to those exhibited by the spirit of man in man; that the Spirit of God *ab extra* is God in efficient operation, whether in the cosmos or as giving life, reinforcing life, exerting efficiency in any sphere,—according to the nature of the sphere, whether physical, intellectual, or spiritual; and that the tendency towards limiting the Spirit of God to the ethical and spiritual spheres is due to the tendency to regard God mainly on those sides of His being.

4. *What the Spirit is.*

But now, on the *second* question, What is the Spirit of God of which the above things are said? If the Spirit of God be God exercising power or efficiency, does He work it *per se* or *per alium*? Is the Spirit of God numerically another, distinct from God in the Old Testament? This question is exceedingly difficult to answer. Of course, the language used, whether of the Spirit of God *ab intra* or *ab extra*, might be used, and no doubt is used now, to express the conception of the Spirit as a distinct person. But it is doubtful if any Old Testament passage can be found which requires this sense; and it is doubtful if any passage of the Old Testament *has* this sense, if by the sense of the Old Testament we mean the sense intended by the writers of the Old Testament.

It should be said further, that the idea of the *personality* of the Spirit is not one that we should expect to be prominent in the Old Testament. For we have to start from the idea that the Spirit of the Lord *is* the Lord—not an influence from Him, but the Lord Himself. This is the first step to any just doctrine of the personality of the Spirit.

The Old Testament, however, seems to teach these things: (*a*) The Spirit of God is always something, as we say, supernatural, and it is always God. The Spirit of God is not an influence exerted by God at a point from which He is Himself distant. God is always present in the Spirit of God. The Spirit of God is God actually present and in operation. And this lays the foundation for the New Testament doctrine. (*b*) The Spirit of God is not a substance communicated to man. The Old Testament knows nothing of a spiritual substance. God is not anywhere called a Spirit in the Old Testament: He has a Spirit; but Spirit is not a substance. It is an energy. The various figures used of the communication of the Spirit, as to *fall on*, to *pass on*, to *rest on*, and the like, express either the supernaturalness of the gift, or its suddenness and power, or its abiding influence. One peculiar expression is used, the Spirit of God *clothed* him, implying the complete enveloping of all the human faculties in the Divine. This phrase is still used by the Mohammedans. When they whirl or jerk their heads back and forward till they fall down in a faint, then they are 'clothed.' **The** figure is quite intelligible. Job says: "I put on justice, and it clothed me" (xxix. 14)—he was himself hidden and lost behind justice. (c) And with this second point, that the Spirit of God is not a substance, is connected the other conclusion, that, as all the passages and examples show, the influence exerted on man in His communication is, as we say, dynamical. It does not give thoughts, e.g., but it invigorates and elevates the faculty of thought. It is not a material, but a formal gift, sending power into all the capacities of the mind, and thus it is in a sense re-creative.

There are, indeed, a very considerable number of passages in the Old Testament which might very well express the idea that the Spirit is a distinct *hypostasis* or person. We might refer specially to such passages as Hag. ii. 5 : "My Spirit is in the midst of you"; Zech. iv. 6 : "Not by might . . . but by My Spirit"; Isa. lxiii. 10 : They rebelled, and vexed His holy Spirit "; Isa. lxiii. 11 : Where is He who put His holy Spirit within it (Israel) ?," etc. But, on the other hand, it must be said that little can be made of most of those passages in which a distinction appears to be made between God and His Spirit. For men also distinguish between themselves and their spirit, and speak of their souls, their spirits, etc. This way of speaking, it must, however, be added, is much developed in the Old Testament, so that we may say the *beginnings* at least of the distinction between the Lord and His Spirit are to be seen. But, at the same time, it is doubtful whether there are any passages which *must* be so interpreted. That moral attributes, such as goodness and holiness, are ascribed to the Spirit, hardly goes any way to *prove* distinction. Of more force, perhaps, is such a passage as the one in Isa. lxiii. 10. But then another passage (Isa. liv. 6) speaks of a woman forsaken and grieved in spirit. Of some significance, however, is Isa. xlviii. 16 : "Jehovah hath sent me and His Spirit"—He and His Spirit have sent me, or perhaps, He hath sent me *with* His Spirit. The question here is whether the Spirit is *subject* or *object*. But even if the latter is the case, it may still be said that the Spirit becomes an agent parallel to man — whoever the speaker be, whether prophet or Servant.

There is one more point on which a word will suffice. We hear it said sometimes in regard to such passages as that in Gen. i. 26 : " Let us make man " ; or Isa. vi. 8 : " Who will go for us ? "—that there is there a vague or obscure intimation of the doctrine of the Trinity. Now this is unfortunate language. It is unhappily the case that there are many passages of the Old Testament which we must call *obscure* ; that is, we are unable to say whether this, or that, or some other thing be the meaning. But we never have any doubt that they have some one perfectly clear sense, if we had the means of reaching it. They are not vague in themselves. There is no vagueness or obscurity in either of the passages referred to. If God, who speaks in these passages, uses the word *us* of Himself, there is a perfectly clear statement to the effect that the Godhead is a plurality—whether that plurality be a duality, or a trinity, or some other number is spoken of. But so far the sense has no vagueness or obscurity. The point, however, is whether the Divine speaker uses the word *us* of Himself, *i.e.* of the Godhead alone, or whether He does not rather include others, *e.g.* His heavenly council along with Him. The opinion of most expositors is to the latter effect.

V. THE DOCTRINE OF GOD—THE DIVINE ATTRIBUTES.

1. *The Righteousness of God.*

The etymological meaning of the root צדק may not be now ascertainable. Like קדש, holy, the word, no doubt, once expressed a physical action ; but in usage it seems now to occur only in a moral sense, or when used of things in the sense of our word 'right.' It has been suggested that the Hebrew idea of 'right' was what was conformable to a standard; but there seems to be little in this. It was not conformity to a standard that made things right, but conformity to a right standard. The idea of a standard is secondary—the idea of right precedes it. A standard is only a concrete embodiment or expression of right in a particular sphere. An ephah is a standard in measurement, but only a right ephah. The prophet Micah speaks of the cursed scanty ephah, to measure according to which was not right (vi. 10).

All that it is of consequence to keep in mind is that long before we find judgments on conduct passed, the person or mind passing them had already the ideas of right and wrong, and the further ideas what things were right and what things were wrong in the particular spheres to which his judgment applied. And long before judgments are passed and predications of righteousness or unrighteousness made, whether in regard to God or to man, the persons making them were already so far morally educated. The question how persons found passing judgment became morally educated is not of much consequence, because it refers to something anterior to the point at which we must begin. The judgments which we find passed in regard to righteousness or unrighteousness are made from the *mind* of the person judging, and as a rule bear no reference to any source from which he may have learned to judge as he does.

That is 'righteous,' whether in God or in man, which is right in the circumstances, *i.e.*, judged by the person who pronounced the judgment to be right. Righteousness is one, whether in God or in man. It would be wrong in a human judge or ruler to condemn the righteous with the wicked, or destroy them indiscriminately; and Abraham asks in reference to such a thing: "Shall not the judge of all the earth do right?" (Gen. xviii. 25). Of course, there is great difference between God and man, seeing man's righteousness may largely consist in a right relation to God, while God may not be conditioned in this way.

But the fact that God is God does not withdraw Him and His actions from the sphere of moral judgment. Nothing would be right in God because He is God, which would not be right in Him were He man. Again, naturally this statement is general, and has to be limited in many ways. He is right, for instance, in demanding obedience from man, and man is right in obeying Him; still it is always understood in the particular instances that the act required and rendered is an act right in itself, though it may be that in details some actions might at an early time be considered right, or not wrong, which would not be considered right now. But while men may be found in plenty who are described as doing those things not now considered right, it may be doubtful if there are cases where they are commanded by God to do them.

It is sometimes argued that because God is sovereign He has a right to do with His creatures as He pleases, and He is right or righteous in so doing. The abstract question does not concern us here; I do not think it is touched upon in the Old Testament. The Old Testament certainly teaches that God does "according to His pleasure in the armies of heaven and among the inhabitants of the earth" (Dan. xi. 16); but I think it is always assumed that His pleasure is a benevolent and moral one, at least in the first instance, and that when it is otherwise this is due to the evil of men. The figure of the clay and the potter is frequently used. Now this figure means that it is God that does shape the history and destinies of mankind, particularly of His people; but it says nothing of the principles according to which He shapes them. In Isa. xlv. 9–12 the people of Israel are represented as criticising the methods of God's dealing with them, the instruments He is using for their deliverance. They disliked the idea that a heathen conqueror like Cyrus should be God's agent in giving them freedom, or they were incredulous as to the results. And God replies to them : "Woe to that which strives with Him who makes it! . . . Shall the clay say to the potter, What makest thou? or shall thy work say in regard to thee, He has no hands? . . . Thus saith Jehovah, the Holy One of Israel, Ask Me concerning My children, and commit to Me the work of My hands. I have made earth, and man upon it: My hands stretched out the heavens." What God claims here is not the right to do as He pleases; what He claims is superior power and understanding, and as having this He claims that He, the Creator of earth and man upon it, and of the host of heaven, may be trusted to deal with the people's destinies in wisdom and with success. It is the same idea as is expressed in another place: "Your ways are not My ways, nor My thoughts your thoughts. As the heavens are higher than the earth, so are My thoughts (or plans) higher than your thoughts" (Isa. lv. 8, 9).

The paragraph in Jer. xviii. about the potter supplies a further element. The prophet went down to the potter's house, and behold he wrought his work on the wheels. And when the vessel that he was making of the clay was marred in the hands of the potter, he made it again another vessel, as seemed good to the potter to make it. Then the word of the Lord came to the prophet: "Behold, as the clay in the potter's hand, so are ye in Mine hand, O house of Israel." The potter's design was to make a vessel, but the clay was marred in his hand. The cause, no doubt, lay in the clay; it was due to some flaw or intractability in it. It was not suitable for the potter's first intention, and he made of it that which could be made of it. This is the whole scope of the chapter. It is meant to show that God deals with men and nations on moral principles, one way or another, according to their character; that, if His first intention fails with them, He has recourse to another: "At what time I speak concerning a nation to build and to plant it, if it do evil in My sight, then I will repent of the good, wherewith I said I would benefit them." But the opposite is equally true: "At what time I speak concerning a nation, to pluck up, and to destroy it; if that nation turn from their evil, I will repent of the evil that I thought to do unto them." Jeremiah's figure teaches these two things:

first, that He can deal with nations as the potter deals with the clay; but, second, also the principles on which He deals with them.[1]

God is righteous when He does what is right in any particular case, or in any of the characters in which He acts as Judge, Ruler, God of His people. Righteousness is not an abstract thing; it is right conduct in particular relations. God is not very often said to be righteous in regard to His whole character, so to speak, though there are examples. The term is more often said of men. But a righteous man is one who has done or always does right actions. And God's righteousness is judged in the same way. Now it is evident what is right in a judge or ruler; it is to clear the innocent and condemn the guilty, to find out and give effect to the truth in any particular cause. It is particularly right in the judge or ruler to see that right be done to those who are weak or without human helpers, to stand by them and plead their cause, such as the widow or the orphan. Justice is to be done to all, and the judge is warned against favouring the poor unjustly because they are poor; but it is a sacred duty to see that right is done to those whose means of doing themselves justice are limited. Job claims this kind of righteousness for himself: "I was a father to the needy: and the cause of him that I knew not I searched out" (xxix. 16). And God is the father of the fatherless and the judge of the widow.

The function of the judge was wider than with us; he was both judge and advocate; not judging as judges do now, on evidence set before him by others, but discovering the evidence for himself. So the Messiah in His function as judge does not judge after the sight of His eyes, nor decide after the hearing of His ears, but judges the poor with righteousness—with an insight given to Him by the Spirit of God which fills Him (Isa. xi. 3). But the actions of God are judged in His various relations to men,

---

[1] On this see further in the author's *The Book of Ezekiel the Prophet* p. 36 (*Cambridge Bible for Schools and Colleges*).—ED.

just as the actions of a man would be judged. The dog-matic principle that men being sinners nothing is due to them, is not the foundation on which judgments in regard to God are based. No doubt this idea is often recognised, and in the earliest times : "I am unworthy of the least of all the mercies . . . which Thou hast showed unto Thy servant" (Gen. xxxii. 10). The principle of His grace is frequently emphasised. But in passing judgment on His actions in relation to men this principle lies further back, and His actual relations to men are made the basis of the judgment,—the fact that He is God of His people, father of His children, and the like.

And the principle of judgment applied is very much what would be applied to men. It is 'right,' for example, among men to forgive on confession of wrong, and God is righteous in forgiving the penitent: "Deliver me from bloodguiltiness, O God, Thou God of my salvation : and my tongue shall sing aloud of Thy righteousness" (Ps. li. 14). This language is also used in the New Testament: "If we confess our sins, He is faithful and righteous to forgive us our sins" (1 John i. 9); and again: "God is not unrighteous to forget your work, and the love which ye shewed toward His name" (Heb. vi. 10). There is therefore no antithesis between righteousness and grace. The exercise of grace, goodness, forgiveness may be called righteousness in God. Thus : "Answer me in Thy faithful-ness and in Thy righteousness, and enter not into judgment with Thy servant: for in Thy sight shall no man living be found righteous" (Ps. cxliii. 1). Here righteousness is opposed to entering into judgment, *i.e.* to the very thing which technically and dogmatically is called righteousness.

When the relations of God to His people Israel are considered, the question of His righteousness becomes more complicated. There are two or three points to be noticed. *First*, His relation to His people internally, when the other nations of the world are not considered. Here He acts as a righteous ruler. He punishes their sin. As Isaiah (xxviii. 17) expresses it, He "makes judgment (justice) the line and righteousness the plummet" with which He measures and estimates the people. His afflicting them may be only chastisement up to a certain point, but it may go further and become judgment, and all His judgments are done in righteousness. His being God of Israel does not invalidate the general principle of His righteous dealing with men. So far from invalidating it, it rather confirms it: "You only have I known of all the families of the earth, therefore will I visit your transgressions upon you" (Amos iii. 2). The relations of God and people are altogether moral. When, however, His chastisements produce repentance, He is again righteous in returning to His people and saving them. These two principles apply to the people as a whole; they apply also to the individuals of the people, as is seen in the case of David, when he greatly sinned and greatly repented of his sin. But, of course, the solidarity of the individuals and nation often involved those who were innocent in the national judgments, and this became the cause of extreme perplexity to the minds of many in later times.

Second, there is the case when the other nations are drawn into His operations with His people. So far from Israel being insured against the nations because it was in name His people, the nations are represented as being used as instruments in chastising the people. And these chastisements are an illustration of God's righteousness. "The Lord of hosts shall be exalted in judgment, and God the Holy One sanctified in righteousness" (Isa. v. 16); "For though thy people Israel be as the sands of the sea, only a remnant of them shall return: a consummation is determined, a stream flooded with righteousness" (x. 22). The moral character of the nations who are used to chastise Israel does not come into account. They are mere instruments in God's hand: "O Assyrian, the rod used by Mine anger" (x. 5). And when the purpose they served was effected they were flung aside; or when they overstepped their commission, and cherished purposes of conquest of their own, they fell themselves under God's anger, particularly when they dealt harshly with Israel, and oppressed where they were only used to chastise. So it is said to Babylon: "I was wroth with My people . . . and gave them into thine hand: thou didst show them no mercy; upon the aged hast thou very heavily laid thy yoke. Thou didst not lay such things to heart, neither didst consider the issue thereof" (Isa. xlvii. 6); and in Zech. God says: "I am very sore displeased with the nations that are at ease: for I was but a little displeased [with My people], and they helped forward the affliction" (i. 15).

In all the earlier prophets the calamities that befall Israel are illustrations of God's righteousness. They are all absorbed in the idea of Israel's sin, and the character of the heathen nations used to chastise the people little occupies their attention. No doubt they all, especially from Isaiah downwards, have an outlook; and the time of the nations will come, and Assyria shall be broken upon the mountains of Israel, when the Lord shall have performed His short work, *i.e.* His work of chastisement upon Jerusalem. But naturally when Israel had been long in exile the hardships they suffered at the hand of the nations were regarded as oppressive. They were so. As against the nations, Israel felt itself to be righteous: the nations were injurious and unjust. Jehovah's interposition therefore for His people was claimed as right: it was righteous. Hence in the second part of Isaiah, Israel complains that her God has forgotten her right: "Why sayest thou, O Jacob, and speakest, O Israel, My way (*i.e.* what I suffer) is hid from the Lord, and my right is disregarded by my God?" (Isa. xl. 27). And in another place, "They ask of Me judgments of righteousness" (lviii. 2); and again, "Therefore is judgment far from us, neither does righteousness accrue to us" (lix. 9), *i.e.* they do not enjoy God's interposition, which would be on His part righteousness. Hence, in general, God's interpositions to save His people are called His righteousness,—a way of speaking, however, which is very old, occurring in the Song of Deborah,—the righteous acts of His rule in Israel. The assumption underlying this usage is that the people as against the nations that oppressed them were in the right, and Jehovah's vindication of them was a righteous act.

But this leads on to what is perhaps the most interesting usage of the term *righteousness*, whether it be of God or man ; for God's righteousness and man's come into contact or run into one another. For Israel to claim God's interposition on their behalf because they were righteous, even as against the nations, might be thought to imply on their part a superficial conscience. Even if they were superior to the nations in morals, as no doubt they were, their sense of their own sin before God, it might be supposed, would restrain them from pleading their righteousness, which at the best was but comparative. But this was by no means their plea, as it is expressed in such a prophet as the Second Isaiah. In the last years of Judah and in the Exile Israel's religion had attained its maturity. Virtually no more growth can be observed in it. What we observe is not enlargement or addition in the religion, but its arrival at self-consciousness. From being before naïve, and instructive and unconscious in its utterances and life, it now attains to reflection on itself and the consciousness of its own meaning. The conflict of the nation with other nations, and their mixture among the peoples of the world, gave the people knowledge of the world religions, and compelled comparison with their own. And their own was true, the others false. They had in them the true knowledge of the true God. It is quite possible that this conviction was an ancient one ; indeed, it is certain that it was, if, at any rate, Isa. ii. belong to that prophet. Because there the nations are represented as all exhorting one another to go up to Jerusalem to the house of the God of Jacob, that He may teach them of His ways, and that they may walk in His paths. The author of this was already conscious that his religion was the true one, and that it would become universal.

But, in the age of the Exile and later, the conditions of the world and of the people caused this consciousness

to be much more widely spread and vivid. When, therefore, Israel pleads before God that it is in the right as
against the nations, the meaning is not that the people
are as persons or as a nation morally just or righteous.
The meaning is that their cause is right. In the conflict
of religions their cause is righteous. As a factor in the
world, in the destinies of mankind, they have the right
to which victory is due. The cause of Jehovah is contained within them. They possess the true knowledge
of the true God, and the revolutions of the nations, the
conflicts of opposing forces, going on then and at all times,
are but the great drama, the *dénouement* of which is the
victory of Jehovah's cause, which Israel has within it.
This is what is meant when Israel is called the Servant of
the Lord—His public servant on the stage of the world to
bring His purpose to fulfilment. The consciousness and
the faith of this Servant are expressed in the exquisite
passage, Isa. l. 4–9, where the Servant says: "The Lord
God hath given me the tongue of disciples, that I should
know how to uphold him that is weary. . . . The Lord
God opened mine ear, and I was not rebellious, neither
turned away backward. I gave my back to the smiters,
and my cheeks to them that plucked off the hair. . . .
For the Lord God helpeth me; therefore I have not been
confounded: therefore do I set my face like a flint, and I
know that I shall not be put to shame. He is near that
will justify me; who will contend with me? Behold, the
Lord God helpeth me; who is he that shall put me in
the wrong? Behold, they shall all wax old as a garment;
the moth shall consume them." This is the cause, the
cause as wide as the world; indeed, the world-cause, the
cause of Israel against the world—in truth, Jehovah's cause.
The Servant is conscious of its meaning, and his faith
assures him of victory—He is near that will justify me.
To give this cause victory is an act of God's righteousness.

" He is near," the Servant says, " who will justify me ";
that is, the justification is imminent, close at hand. To
justify is to show to be in the right. Now the idea

prevailing in those days was that the relation of God to a man or to a people was always reflected in the outward circumstances of the man or nation. Prosperity was the token of God's favour, and adversity of His displeasure. Hence Job, speaking of a man who had been sick unto death, but was restored, says: "He prayeth unto God and He is favourable unto him: so that he seeth His face with joy; and He restoreth unto man his righteousness" (xxxiii. 26), *i.e.* his restoration to health is a giving back to him his righteousness,—it is the token that he is now right before God. Similarly, when the great calamities of drought and locusts to which the people had been subjected are removed, and rain bringing fertility and plenty is again sent from heaven, it is said: "Be glad, ye children of Zion, and rejoice in the Lord your God: for He shall give you the former rain for righteousness" (Joel ii. 23)—לִצְדָקָה, *i.e.* in token of righteousness, right standing with God. In no other way could God's justification of the Servant be approved to the eyes of the nations or verified to the heart of the people except by the people's restoration to prosperity and felicity in their own land. Then Israel would be the righteous nation among the nations. Then would begin to operate all the redemptive forces within Israel, and to flow out among the peoples. Then she would be as the dew among the nations, not breaking the bruised reed nor quenching the glimmering light, till she brought forth right also to the nations— "Arise, shine; for thy light is come. . . . And the nations shall come to thy light, and kings to the brightness of thy shining" (Isa. lx. 1–3).

Hence in the Old Testament justification has always this outer side of prosperity and restoration, at least when spoken of the people. It does not consist in this, but this is an essential element in it; this is that which verifies it to the heart of the people. And this was usually the case also with the individual man. Even ordinarily the individual probably was slow to realise his sinfulness or God's displeasure except he fell into sickness or misfortune, and on the other hand he craved that God's favour should approve itself to him in his external life; when his circumstances reflected it, then his heart felt it. No doubt in some instances the individual saint rose to be at least for moments independent of all that was outward. His faith and right standing before God was a self-verifying thing, it reflected itself in his consciousness; and this evidence of his conscience might be so strong as to overbear any contrary evidence which men or adverse circumstances brought against him. So it is represented in Job, and so the surprising words of a psalmist overwhelmed with calamities: " Nevertheless I am continually with Thee " (Ps. lxxiii. 23).

There are two further points which may be briefly referred to in regard to the righteousness of God. The mere righteousness of God as an attribute of His nature does not require much investigation. It is to be understood. But His righteousness is said of His redemptive operations. It is a strange thing that from the fall of Jerusalem onwards Israel never attained again to a condition of prosperity. It was not only never again an independent people, but its condition was in general greatly depressed and miserable. No doubt for about a century it was ruled by the Maccabean princes, but the period was perhaps the most barren of any age of its history. Many scholars, indeed, have found Maccabean Psalms, but it must be acknowledged that there is little certainty here. At any rate, there is absolutely no evidence that the highest hopes of the people in regard to the incoming of the perfect kingdom of God among them were ever connected with any of the Maccabean princes. It was not when prosperous, but when under the deepest afflictions, that they reached the highest thoughts of God and themselves. Their long-continued calamities, the delay in the realising of their hopes concerning their redemption and God's coming in His kingdom, turned their thoughts back upon themselves to find the cause of such protracted disappointment. And all the deepest problems of religion rose before them—wrath and grace, sin and forgiveness, justification and righteousness. Israel, of course, never doubted that it had within it the truth of the true God, but the brilliant hopes which this consciousness created at the period of the return from exile became greatly dimmed and faded. Even to the great prophet of the Exile, in spite of his faith, the outlook seemed often very clouded. Between Israel, the ideal servant of the Lord with a mission to the world, and the Israel of reality the contrast was almost absolute—"Who is blind, but my servant ? or deaf, as my messenger whom I send ? " (Isa. xlii. 19). Israel was unrighteous. Its salvation could not come from itself, but from an interposition of God on its behalf. All the prophets of this age—Jeremiah, Ezekiel, and Second Isaiah—are at one in this. The first prophet asks in reference to his people, " Can the Ethiopian change his skin ? " (xiii. 23). Can they who are habituated to do evil do well ? And he can solve the problem only by the faith that Jehovah will yet write His law on the people's hearts. But it is only the Second Isaiah that calls this interposition of God, and His deliverance of His people, God's righteousness. In this use of it righteousness is frequently parallel to salvation : " I bring near My righteousness, and My salvation shall not tarry " (xlvi. 13). Only in the Lord, shall they say, is righteousness and strength : " In the Lord shall all the seed of Israel be justified, or be righteous, and shall glory" (xlv. 24, 25).

When this is called righteousness and also salvation, the two words are not quite equivalent. Salvation is rather the negative side—deliverance ; righteousness, the positive. And this includes, as was said before, the external felicity which is the guarantee to the nation's heart that it was justified or righteous. This is the outside of righteousness, indispensable, but only the outside. The inside is true righteousness of heart and life—" My people shall be all righteous " (lx. 21); " In righteousness shalt thou be established ; thy children shall be all taught of the Lord " (liv. 13); " He hath clothed me with the garments of salvation, He hath covered me with the robe of righteousness " (lxi. 10). This righteousness is thus sometimes called the people's and sometimes God's. It is the people's because they possess it, though it has been freely given to them. There is considerable approach to New Testament phraseology and thought here, though this righteousness of God which He bestows upon the people is not mere forensic justification. Besides the forgiveness of sin, it includes inward righteousness of heart, and the outward felicity which reflects God's favour, and is the seal of it to the people.

But why is this called *God's righteousness*? Scarcely merely because He gives it. Neither can this interposition and deliverance of Israel be called righteousness because it was right to interpose in behalf of Israel, the righteous nation. This cannot well be, *first*, inasmuch as Jehovah brings this righteousness of His to manifestation just because Israel is utterly unrighteous. In Isa. lix. 12 ff. the people confess this : " Our transgressions are multiplied before Thee, and our sins testify against us . . . in transgressing and denying the Lord, and turning away from following our God, speaking oppression and revolt, conceiving and uttering from the heart words of falsehood. Yea, truth is lacking ; he that departeth from evil maketh himself a prey." This is the condition of the people. And the Lord saw it, and it displeased Him that there was no judgment : " He saw that there was no man, and wondered that there was none to interpose : therefore His own arm brought salvation to Him ; and His righteousness, it upheld Him. He put on righteousness as a breastplate, and an helmet of salvation upon his head." . . . And, *secondly*, because this righteousness of His is given by Him not only to Israel but to the nations : " Attend, O My people, unto Me : for *torah*, teaching, shall go forth from Me, and I will make My judgment, *i.e.* justice or right judgment, to rest for a light of the peoples. My righteousness is near ; My salvation is gone forth, and Mine arms shall judge, *i.e.* justly rule, the nations ; the isles shall wait for Me, and on Mine arm shall they trust " (Isa. li. 4, 5).

These passages seem to give the key to this use of the word righteousness. It is not a Divine attribute. It is a Divine effect—it is something produced in the world by God, a condition of the world produced by God, a condition of righteousness, called His not only because He produces it, but also because when it is produced men and the world will be in attributes that which He is. This righteousness of God appears to the prophet to be something in itself, something independent and eternal: "Lift up your eyes to the heavens, and look upon the earth beneath: for the heavens shall vanish away like smoke, and the earth shall wax old like a garment: but My salvation shall be for ever, and My righteousness shall not be abolished" (Isa. li. 6).

To this prophet what characterised the world was unrighteousness, violence, bloodshed, devastating wars, cruel idolatries. This, in his view, was due to the false gods which they worshipped. Only knowledge of the true God would remedy it. For this was not the will of Him who in truth created the world: "Thus saith the Lord that created the heavens—He is God; who formed the earth and made it; He created it not to be a wilderness, He formed it to be inhabited" (Isa. xlv. 18). And in like manner the mission of the Servant of the Lord was to "bring forth judgment to the nations" (Isa. xlii. 1), *i.e.* not the true religion, but civil right, equity, humanity among the nations. This could only be, no doubt, by making them know the true God; but judgment was not this knowledge, but the secondary effect of it—it was righteousness as conduct and life. This is the thing called by the prophet *Jehovah's righteousness*; it is a condition of the earth, of mankind. It is Jehovah that brings it in; to bring it in is the goal of all His operations, and it is the final effect of them. It is not His own righteousness as an attribute; though, of course, it corresponds to His own being, for "the righteous Lord loveth righteousness" (Ps. xi. 7). Only by the knowledge of Him can it be attained. When attained it is salvation: "Look unto Me, and be saved, all the ends of the earth: for I am God, and there is none else

—a righteous God and a Saviour" (Isa. xli. 22). The antithesis which in dogmatics we are familiar with is a righteous or just God and *yet* a Saviour. The Old Testament puts it differently,—a righteous God, and *therefore* a Saviour. It is His own righteousness that causes Him to bring in righteousness. All His redemptive operations are performed in the sphere of this righteousness. Israel's first call: " I have called thee in righteousness " (Isa. xlii. 6); His raising up Cyrus: "I have raised him up in righteousness " (Isa. xlv. 13), and all His operations, have for their goal this condition of men and the world, and all are performed with a view to it. And when the great movement has reached its final goal, righteousness on earth is the issue: " Behold, I create new heavens, and a new earth wherein dwelleth righteousness " (Isa. lxv. 17).

2. *The Holiness of God.*

The " Holiness " of Jehovah is a very obscure subject, and the most diverse views regarding it have prevailed among Old Testament students. It is not possible to discuss these different views. I will rather set down first, in a few propositions, the results which comparison of the Old Testament passages seems to give; and then refer to these propositions briefly by way of illustration. The terminology is as follows:—

קָדַשׁ, to be holy; *Pi.*, *Hiph.* to sanctify, hallow, consecrate, dedicate; קָדוֹשׁ, holy, also as noun, ' Holy One ' (of Jehovah), 'saint' of men, or 'holy ones' of angels; קֹדֶשׁ, holy thing, holiness, thing hallowed, sanctuary, and frequently in combination, as 'holy hill,' hill of holiness, holy arm, people, cities, etc.; מִקְדָּשׁ, sanctuary, holy place. Now, with regard to this term, these things may be said—

(1) The word ' to be holy ' and the adjective ' holy ' had originally, like all such words, a physical sense, now completely lost, not only in Hebrew but in all the other Shemitic languages.

(2) Whatever this meaning was it became applied very

early to Jehovah in Hebrew, and to the gods in Shemitic heathenism. It is so much peculiar to the gods, *e.g.* in Phœnician, that the gods are spoken of as the 'holy gods'; the term *holy* being a mere *epitheton ornans*, having no force. The same phrase occurs also in the Book of Daniel.

(3) The word is applied, however, also to men and things, not as describing any quality in them, but to indicate their relation to deity. 'Holy' said of men and things originally means merely *belonging to deity*, sacred. It is probable that this use of the word, though naturally also very ancient, is secondary and applied. That this sense should be ancient as well as the other is natural; for wherever gods were believed in and worshipped there were persons and things employed in their worship, and dedicated to them, and therefore also 'holy.'

(4) In its original use the term 'holy,' when applied either to God or to men, does not express a moral quality. Of course, when applied to things it could not express a moral quality, though it might express a ceremonial quality; but in the oldest use of the word, even when applied to men, it expresses rather a *relation*, simply *belonging to Jehovah* or *the gods*; and when applied to Jehovah it rather expresses His transcendental attributes or that which we call Godhead, as opposed to the human.

(5) In use as applied to Jehovah it is a general term expressing Godhead. But, of course, 'Godhead' was never a mere abstract conception. Some attribute or characteristic was always in the person's view which betokened Godhead. Hence the term 'holy' is applied to Jehovah when manifesting any attributes which are the token of Godhead, or which men consider to be contained in Godhead; *e.g.* transcendent majesty, glory, greatness, power, righteousness, or in later prophets as Ezekiel 'sole-Godhead,' when Jehovah is spoken of. None of these attributes are synonyms of holiness strictly; they are rather elements in holiness. But Jehovah reveals Himself as 'holy' when He manifests any one of these attributes; and He is

'sanctified' among men when they attribute to Him any of these Divine qualities; just as, on the other hand, He is 'profaned' or desecrated when men fail to ascribe these attributes to Him, or act in forgetfulness of them. Thus 'holy' acquired contents, and one prophet puts in one kind of contents into it and another another. But it is important first to seize the general idea; the development of details which the idea may contain was, no doubt, a historical process.

(6) Similarly 'holy' in regard to men or things, originally expressing a relation merely, namely, the *belonging* to Jehovah, naturally became filled out with contents precisely parallel to the contents put into 'holy' when applied to Jehovah. Men who belonged to Jehovah must have the same character, so far as was possible to men, as Jehovah; the same ethical character, at least, and the same purity. Things that belonged to Him must have at least that purity which things are capable of having.

(7) In order to get a background for the idea of *holiness* and throw it into relief, the opposite ideas need to be looked at. These are חֹל, profane, and חִלֵּל, to profane, both also old words. 'Profane' is the opposite of 'holy' when applied to things; and to 'profane' is to desecrate, to take away, or at least detract from the 'holiness' which belongs to Jehovah, or anything that being His is holy, such as His sanctuary, His name, His Sabbath, His people, and His land. Of course, words like 'sanctify' and 'profane' always acquire in language an extended use, less exact than their primary use. Hence writers speak of sanctifying a fast or a war, *i.e.* a fast *to* Jehovah, and a war *for* Jehovah, in a somewhat general sense (Joel i. 14, ii. 15, iii. 9). The heathen 'profane' Jehovah's sanctuary when they enter it, and His land when they overrun it or take possession of it. Jehovah 'profanes' His people by casting them out of His land, and making them to appearance no more His; He 'profanes' or desecrates the prince of Tyre, a being who arrogated deity to himself, saying, "I am God, I dwell in the seat of God," when He cast him down out of his fancied

Divine seat, and gave him into the hands of Nebuchad-nezzar, the terrible one of the nations (Ezek. xxviii.).

(8) The consequences of these last propositions are easily seen. On the one hand, Jehovah's presence sanctifies, because it makes to be His all around it—primarily, the house in which He dwells, which becomes a 'sanctuary'; then in a wider circle Zion, which becomes His 'holy' hill, and Jerusalem the 'holy city'; and then in the widest circle the land of Israel, which is the holy land—and His people Israel, the holy people. On the other hand, an opposite effect may be produced by the presence of that which is opposed to Jehovah, sin and impurity. The sins of Israel in their worshipping other gods than Jehovah, and worshipping Jehovah in a false manner, 'profaned' the land, that it spued them out (Lev. xviii. 28). Much more did their sins, adhering to them, and their practices even in the Temple precincts, desecrate Jehovah's sanctuary, so that He could no more abide in it, but forsook it and gave it over to destruction; cf. Ezek. xxxvii. 28: "The heathen shall know that I the Lord do sanctify Israel, when My sanctuary shall be in the midst of them." Even Jehovah Himself may be profaned or desecrated, but particularly His holy name. Especially is it so when that reverend name 'Jehovah, the God of Israel,' is compromised in the eyes of the heathen through the calamities which befall Israel. Israel by their unfaithfulness compelled Jehovah to send severe judgments on them, and cast them out of their land. The heathen, observing this, concluded that Jehovah the God of Israel was a feeble Deity, unable to protect His people. They naturally were unable to rise to the idea that Jehovah's rule of His people might be a moral one,—they inferred at once His want of power, saying, "These are the people of Jehovah, and lo, they are gone forth out of His land." Thus Israel profaned Jehovah's holy name, caused it to be detracted from in the eyes of the nations.

(9) Finally, the development of the idea of holiness may be regarded as moving on two lines, the ethical, and the æsthetic or ceremonial. The word 'holy' while expressing

'Godhead' did not express this idea altogether abstractly, but always seized, on each occasion when used, upon some attribute, or connoted some attribute which betokened deity, such as majesty, or purity, or glory, and the like. In the older prophets and in the older literature outside the Law, these attributes are usually the ethical attributes; *e.g.* in Amos ii. 7 a man and his father go in to the same maid to "profane My holy name." This immorality on the part of those who were His people desecrated the name of their God; it brought the name of Him who is of purer eyes than to behold iniquity, down into the region of mere nature gods like Baal, who were served by a mere following of the unrestrained natural instincts and appetites of men. Similarly, Isaiah when he beholds Jehovah, whom the seraphim unceasingly praise as 'holy,' instinctively thinks of his own uncleanness. But he uses the word 'uncleanness' of his lips, as that through which the heart expresses itself, and in an ethical sense; and hence when the uncleanness showing itself in his lips is consumed by a Divine fire, it is said that his iniquity is removed and his sin is forgiven (vi. 5–7). So in chap. i. 16, 17 : "Wash you, make you clean; put away the evil of your doings from before Mine eyes; cease to do evil; learn to do well; seek justice, relieve the oppressed, judge the fatherless, plead the cause of the widow,"—where uncleanness is again exclusively *moral*.

This development on ethical lines can, no doubt, be traced through all the following literature. It is perhaps to be specially observed in the phrase 'holy Spirit.' Strangely this phrase, so common afterwards, occurs, as we have seen, only *three* times in the Old Testament, once in Ps. li., and twice in Isa. lxiii. (10, 11). Primarily, the phrase 'holy' merely emphasised the relation of the Spirit to Jehovah, just like 'His holy arm'—and meant very much 'His Divine Spirit'; but more lately it specially denoted the ethical side of Jehovah's being, or that which we now call His 'holiness.'

But alongside of this ethical development there ran

unquestionably a development on another line, which is to
be called æsthetic or ceremonial. There were taken up
under the idea of holy, or the reverse, a number of things
and actions which to us now have no moral significance,
but some of which have still æsthetic meaning, *i.e.* have a
reference to feeling, taste, and natural instinctive liking or
disliking. In this use 'holy' becomes nearly equivalent to
'clean,' and 'unholy' to 'unclean.' The words, however,
are by no means synonymous. The clean is not holy in
itself, although only that which is clean can be made holy.
But as the unclean cannot be made 'holy,' unclean comes
to be pretty nearly synonymous with unholy. This, however, is a very obscure region.

(10) There are two points which come in as appendix
to these preceding points: first, the meaning of the expression 'Holy One of Israel,' so often used by Isaiah;
and, secondly, the meaning of what is called the *jealousy*
(קִנְאָה) of Jehovah.

Now, in the phrase 'Holy One of Israel' the element
'of Israel' forms no part of the idea of 'holy.' The
phrase 'Holy One of Israel' is exactly equivalent in construction to the phrase 'God of Israel'; so in Isa. xxix. 23,
"Sanctify the Holy One of Jacob, and fear the God of
Israel." The phrase 'Holy One of Israel' means that He
who is *Kadosh* has revealed Himself in Israel—has become
the God of Israel. It is this strange twofold fact that to
Ezekiel gives the clue to human history. Jehovah is the
true and only God; but He is also God of Israel; and the
nations know Him only as God of Israel. Hence in revealing Himself to the nations He can only do so through
Israel; for the nations know Him only in that relation,
not in His absoluteness as the true and only God, which,
however, He is at the same time. For 'Holy One of
Israel' Ezekiel says 'Holy One *in* Israel' (xxxix. 7).
More rarely we have 'His Holy One' (Isa. x. 17), or 'my
Holy One'=my God (Hab. i. 12).

The 'jealousy,' קִנְאָה, lit. 'heat,' of Jehovah may be
any heightened emotion on His part, *e.g.* military ardour

(Isa. xlii. 13). But when used in the sense of jealousy
proper it is almost equivalent to injured self-consciousness;
it is the heightened emotion accompanying the sense of
having suffered injury either in Himself or in that which
belongs to Him, as His land, His people. Hence His
jealousy is chiefly awakened by the worship of other gods,
by want of reverence for His 'holy name,' *i.e.* His recognition as God alone, or by injury done to that which is His.

A few further notes may be added illustrative of the
various points referred to. First, as to the meaning of
the word 'holy' and its appropriation to designate deity,
or that which pertains to deity. The form קָדוֹשׁ is an
adjective or a participle of a neuter verb, just like גָּדוֹל, great;
רָחוֹב, broad; אָרֹךְ, long, and numberless others. Though no
more applied in a physical sense, it had originally, no
doubt, such a sense. Possibly its primitive meaning was
to be *separated*, or to be *elevated*, or to be *lofty*, or something of the kind.[1] Whatever exact idea it expressed, the
idea was one which could be held pre-eminently to characterise deity or the gods as distinguished from men. It
was so suitable for this that it was almost appropriated to
this use. It is certain that this was not a moral idea first,
but rather some physical one; at least we may say this is
probable, because the Phœnician gods are not moral beings,
and yet in Phœnician (Eshmunazar's inscription) the gods
are called the '*holy gods.*' The same expression is used several
times in Daniel, *e.g.* iv. 8, 9, "in whom is the spirit of the
holy gods"; so v. 11, and quite parallel to this v. 14, "the
spirit of the gods is in thee." Possibly the passage ii. 11
might interpret the term 'holy' — none other can show
it except the gods, whose dwelling is not with flesh. At
all events the word contained a meaning which was felt
appropriate to express the characteristic of the gods, or of
Jehovah as distingushed from men. The word in its use
bears a certain analogy to the ordinary word אֱלֹהִים for God.

---

[1] On this see more at length in the article on *Holiness* in Hastings' *Dict.
of the Bible*; also Baudissin's *Studien z. Sem. Religionsgeschichte*; Robertson
Smith's *Religion of the Semites*, pp. 91, 140 ff.—ED.

'The holy one,' הקדש, is God; a usage which went further. And the simple word קדש, without the article, was used like a proper name—"To whom then will ye liken me, saith Kadosh?" (Isa. xl. 25). And just as the plural Elohim is used, so the plural *Kedoshim* is used for God: "Surely I am more brutish than any man. . . . I have not learned wisdom, nor have I the knowledge of Kedoshim" (Prov. xxx. 2, 3; and perhaps so early as Hos. x. 12. And to this has to be added the fact that the angels are frequently called *Kedoshim*, just as they are named *Elohim*, or *Bene-Elohim*, sons, *i.e.* members, of the *Elohim*,—both epithets designating them as a class of beings in opposition to what man is.

'Holy,' therefore, was not primarily an epithet for 'god' or 'the gods'; it expressed the idea of god or the gods in itself. No other epithet given to Jehovah is ever used in the same way. For example, Jehovah is righteous; but 'the righteous one,' in the absolute or abstract sense, is a term never applied to Him—nor 'the gracious,' and the like. It seems clear, therefore, that *Kadosh* is not a word that expresses any attribute of deity, but deity itself; though it remains obscure what the primary idea of the word was which long before the period of literature made it fit in the estimation of the Shemitic people to be so used. The same obscurity hangs over the commonest of all words for God. But two things, I think, are clear: *first*, that it was a term describing the nature of Jehovah rather than His thoughts, what He was in His being or person. And, *second*, it was therefore a word that was mainly used in connection with worship. Jehovah's holiness was felt when men approached Him. When they were in His presence His being or nature, His personality, displayed itself; it showed sensibility to what came near it, or it reacted against what was incongruous, or disturbing to it. Hence, perhaps, there was originally a feeling that to approach Jehovah, or to touch that which was holy, was dangerous. So Isaiah exclaims, "I am undone; for mine eyes have seen the King" (vi. 5); and Uzzah, who put out his hand to touch the holy ark, was smitten with death. This may have been the older view. In the oldest view of all, the reaction of Jehovah may, so to speak, have been physical —the creature could not come into His presence; but in Isaiah's mind the reaction or influence of Jehovah's nature was of a moral kind. It is not quite certain whether in the Law it was thought that there was danger to the unclean person who approached Jehovah, or merely that such approach was intolerable to Jehovah.

Passing over some other points that do not need further illustration, it may be remarked that the probability is that the application of the term 'holy' to *things* is secondary. Things are called 'holy' as belonging to deity. It might be that the name holy was applied to things, just as it was applied to deity, to express something that characterised them. If 'holy' meant 'separated,' the things might be so called as separated and lying apart. But the term is never used in the general sense of separate or lying apart; it always signifies separated for deity, belonging to the sphere of deity. In Phœnician, just as in Hebrew, the Hiphil of the verb is used in the sense of to dedicate or consecrate to deity. All this being sufficiently plain, I may refer to the usage of the term 'holy' as applied on the one hand to things and men, and on the other hand again to God.

(*a*) With regard to things and men. Of course, 'holy' or 'holiness' said of things cannot denote a moral attribute. It can only express a relation; and the relation is, belonging to Jehovah, dedicated to Godhead. No thing is holy of itself or by nature; and not everything can be made holy; only some things are suitable. But suitability to be made holy and holiness are things quite distinct. For example, only the clean among beasts could be devoted to Jehovah, and a beast so devoted is holy; but all clean beasts were not so devoted. The ideas of 'holy' and 'clean' must not therefore be confused; cleanness is only a condition of holiness, not holiness itself. As the unclean was, however, incapable of being made holy, the case is somewhat different here, and the term *unclean* became, as we have said, almost synonymous with *unholy*, or all that was incompatible with and repugnant to the Holy One of Israel. According to the nomenclature in use, everything belonging to Jehovah, whether as His by nature or as dedicated to Him, is called *holy*. Thus writers speak of His holy arm, His holy Spirit, His holy word. In a wider way, the tabernacle, the place of His abode, was holy; Zion was the holy hill; Jerusalem, the holy city; Israel, His holy people; the cities of Palestine, His holy cities. All sacrifices and gifts to Him were holy things, the tithes, the first-fruits, the shewbread, the sacrifices, particularly the sin-offering and the trespass-offering.

In that which was holy there might be gradations; the outer part of the temple was holy, the inner most holy. All flesh-offerings were holy, but the sin-offering was most holy. The meaning does not seem to be this, that these things being dedicated to God, this fact raised in the mind a certain feeling of reverence or awe for them, and then this secondary quality in them of inspiring awe was called holiness. The word 'holy' describes the primary relation of *belonging to* Jehovah; and things were 'most holy' which belonged exclusively or in some special way to Him. The sin-offering, for example, was partaken of exclusively by the priests, His immediate servants. It was wholly given over to Jehovah; while the peace-offerings were in large part given back to the laity, to be used by the people in their sacrificial feasts. The idea of holiness appears in the terms in which those are described who are to be priests; as indeed it appears quite evidently in the passage where Israel is called an 'holy' nation (Ex. xix. 6), which is parallel on the one hand to a 'kingdom of priests,' and on the other to the word 'private possession,' סְגֻלָּה. Korah and his company objected to the exclusive priesthood of Aaron, saying, "Ye take too much upon you, seeing all the congregation are holy, every one of them, and Jehovah is among them"· His presence makes all alike holy, *i.e.* His. To which

Moses answered: " To-morrow will Jehovah show who are His, and who are holy " (Num. xvi. 5). Hence the priests are said to be holy unto Jehovah; His special possession.

The term ' holy ' applied to things, therefore, signifies that they are the possession of Jehovah. Naturally out of this idea others arose of an allied kind. That which is His, *e.g.*, is withdrawn from the region of common things. Thus in the legislation of Ezekiel, a part of the holy land, 25,000 cubits square, the portion of the priests, is called a holy thing, and distinguished from all around, which is חֹל, *profane*, or common—that which lies open, is accessible. Hence ' holy,' that which is peculiar to Jehovah and not common, is looked at as elevated above the ordinary. And, in like manner, belonging to Jehovah it is inviolable, and those who lay their hands upon it desecrate it, and Jehovah's jealousy reacts against them and destroys them. So it is said of Israel in her early time, in the beautiful passage Jer. ii. 2, 3 : " I remember of thee the kindness of thy youth . . . Israel was a holy thing of the Lord, and the first - fruits of His increase," *i.e.* His nearest property; all that devoured her incurred guilt.

In a similar way, when ' holy ' was said of men, the term gathered a certain amount of contents into it. Though expressing originally merely the idea of dedication to Jehovah, or possession by Him, all the conceptions of that which Jehovah was naturally flowed into the term, because men dedicated to Jehovah must be fit for such a consecration, and fitness implied that they must be like Jehovah Himself—partakers of the Divine nature. Hence Isaiah (iv. 3, 4) speaks of the holy seed being the stock of a new Israel of the future; and what ideas he expresses by ' holy seed ' appears from chap. iv. 3, in which he describes the regenerated nation of the time to come, in those last days when all nations shall pour in pilgrimage to the house of the God of Jacob: " And it shall come to pass, that he that is left in Zion, and he that remaineth in Jerusalem, shall be called holy, every one whose name is inscribed among the living in Jerusalem :

when Jehovah shall have washed away the filth of the
daughters of Zion, and shall cleanse away the bloodshed of
Jerusalem from the midst thereof."

(*b*) A few passages may be cited in illustration of the
application of the term 'holy' to Jehovah. *Holy* as
applied to Jehovah is an expression that in some way
describes Him as God, either generally, or on any particular
side of His nature the manifestation or thought of which
impresses men with the sense of His Godhead. Generally
the term describes Jehovah as God. For example, in one
place (Amos vi. 8), "Jehovah God hath sworn by Himself";
in another (Amos iv. 2), "Jehovah God hath sworn by His
holiness," the two phrases having virtually the same sense.
Again (Hos. xi. 9), "I am God, and not man, Kadosh in the
midst of thee," where Kadosh is equivalent to God and
opposed to man. So in Isa. vi. 3, the cry of the seraphim,
"Holy, holy, holy is Jehovah of hosts," the term 'holy'
expresses the same conception as *Adonāi*, the sovereign,
or *melek*, the king; it expresses the conception of Deity
in the highest sense. But usually more than the mere idea
of Godhead is carried in the term. That it also connotes
the attributes always associated with Godhead, appears even
in this passage, where the vision of Jehovah immediately
suggests to the prophet the uncleanness of his lips and
those of his people. Still it was not any particular side of
Jehovah's Godhead, or any one special attribute, that *Kadosh*
expressed; Jehovah was seen to be *Kadosh* when He manifested Himself on the side of any of those attributes which
constituted Godhead.

Thus there may be among the prophets considerable
difference in regard to the application of the term 'holy';
one prophet, such as Isaiah, may call Jehovah *Kadosh*,
when His moral attributes are manifested, as His righteousness; another, such as Ezekiel, may consider His
Godhead revealed more in the display of other attributes
which are not distinctively moral, such as His power.
In Isa. v. 16 we have this: "Jehovah of hosts shall
be exalted in judgment," and "God, the Holy One (*hak-*

kadosh), shall be sanctified in righteousness." The Niphal, rendered *to be sanctified*, means either to show one's self *Kadosh*, or to get recognition as *Kadosh*. Here then Jehovah shows Himself as *Kadosh*, or is recognised as *Kadosh* by a display of His righteous judgment upon the sinners of Israel. An exhibition of righteousness shows Him to be *Kadosh*. In other two passages of Isaiah Jehovah is ʻsanctifiedʼ — recognised or reverenced as *Kadosh*—by religious fear or awe: "Fear ye not that which this people fear, nor be in dread thereof. Jehovah of hosts, Him shall ye sanctify; and let Him be your fear, and let Him be your dread" (viii. 13); and, "They shall sanctify the *Kadosh* of Jacob, and shall stand in awe of the God of Israel" (xxix. 23). In Num. xx. 12 a remarkable instance of the general use of the term *sanctify* occurs. Jehovah says to Moses and Aaron: "Because ye believed not in Me to sanctify Me in the eyes of the children of Israel," *i.e.* because Moses apparently doubted the Divine power to bring water out of the rock. In Lev. x. 3, referring to the profane act of Nadab and Abihu, Jehovah says: "I will be sanctified (recognised and reverenced as *Kadosh*) in them that come nigh Me, and before all the people I will be glorified"; being ʻglorifiedʼ is not synonymous with being ʻsanctified,ʼ but it is a part of it. So Ezek. xxviii. 22: " I am against thee, O Zidon; and I will be glorified in the midst of thee: and they shall know that I am Jehovah (*i.e.* God alone), when I have executed judgments in the midst of her, and I shall be sanctified in her"; where to be ʻsanctifiedʼ or recognised as Kadosh is parallel to "they shall know that I am Jehovah,"—which in Ezekiel means the only true God, and all that He is.

Passages might be multiplied, especially from Ezekiel, but it is not necessary. The words *holy, sanctify*, and their opposites, *profane* and the like, are the terms usually employed. It is a remarkable thing that never in Ezekiel, any more than in the Levitical law, is the term ʻrighteousʼ applied to Jehovah. Men are *righteous*, but Jehovah is *Kadosh*. This is particularly remarkable when the usage of Jeremiah is observed. Except in chaps. l. and li., which are usually considered in their present form later than Jeremiah, that prophet does not use the word 'holy' in any of its forms in reference to Jehovah (except xxiii. 9, where he applies it to the *words* of Jehovah). There are two prophets contemporary with one another differing totally in their phraseology in regard to God—Jeremiah following the example of the earlier prophets, and avoiding the phraseology of the ritual law, Ezekiel following it. The fact shows that we must be very cautious in inferring from a writer's usage of language and from his conceptions the date at which he lived. Ezekiel knows and uses all the terminology of the ritual law; his contemporary Jeremiah avoids it as much as prophets two centuries before him, such as Amos or Isaiah. The peculiarity is due to personal idiosyncrasy and associations, and is not a criterion of date. And it is precarious, as a rule, to rely much on the argument from silence. The fact that Jeremiah has no interest in the ritual with its terminology, and ignores it, while the mind of his contemporary Ezekiel is full of it, leads us to ask whether there may not have been contemporary with the older prophets, Amos, Isaiah, etc., who ignore it, a body of persons like-minded with Ezekiel, godly men as well as he, who cherished the same class of thoughts—in a word, a priestly class among whom the term 'holy' was used where among another class 'righteous' was employed, among whom 'sin' and all evil were conceived of under the idea of *uncleanness* and *impurity* and such-like— men, I say, as godly, and pursuing ends as holy and as truly theocratic as the prophets, but dominated by a different class of conceptions and by different ideals.

To what shall we ascribe the domination of this class of ideas, and, particularly, how shall we account for the drawing of the æsthetic or ceremonial into the idea of holiness, and the strange conception—strange to us, at least —that certain creatures were obnoxious to the Deity, that certain acts perfectly innocent morally incapacitated a person for worshipping Him acceptably?

Now, this is a large question. But, in the first place, the place of æsthetic in religion is undoubtedly ancient. It pervades antiquity, and is seen very early in Israel. The priest who gave the holy bread to David and his followers insisted on knowing whether the young men were clean. Among all ancient peoples the sexual relations, the offices of nature, the giving birth to children, inferred uncleanness, and in Israel, at least, contact with death. There was something in all these things which to decency or refinement or taste was repulsive. Further, human feeling recoils in many instances from some of the lower creatures, such as the reptiles, and those designated in the wider sense vermin, such as the smaller quadrupeds. Men shrink from contact with all these creatures, and they have a feeling of defilement in regard to the actions just referred to. Undoubtedly this feeling, which men shared, was attributed by them also to God.

Again, this æsthetic or ceremonial side of holiness was greatly promoted by the other conception that Jehovah was located in a certain place—His Temple. This created the possibility and the danger that some of these things should be brought near Him, or that men being in that state which the above mentioned acts brought them into, should come into His presence. This æsthetic or ceremonial element in holiness was thus undoubtedly an ancient element, as ancient as the notion of the existence of a place where Jehovah abode. It was essentially connected with the idea of worship rendered to Jehovah in a place of His abode.

Once more, undoubtedly, this idea of Jehovah's being connected with a particular place was strengthened by the destruction of all the local shrines, and the confining of ritual to Jerusalem. There He was present in person. The destruction also of the local shrines destroyed all private sacrifice, and made ritual officially religious; and the idea pervaded the minds of men more and more of being a congregation, a body of worshippers, and the question was raised as to their condition and fitness to appear before the presence of Jehovah. By all these things probably the æsthetic or ceremonial was drawn more and more into the idea of holiness. The conception of ceremonial cleanness was old, as old as that of the existence of a place of worship; and the class of conceptions would be cherished among the priestly order, and developed by them; and as the idea of Israel's being a State was lost, and it appeared merely a worshipping community, the conceptions would gain greater ground. Thus probably the multiplication of ceremonies, defilements on the one hand and purifications on the other, may have gradually increased, until it reached the dimensions which it has attained in the ritual law.[1]

But one may perceive from all this that there was no distinction in the Law between moral and what we have been accustomed to call ceremonial. The idea of ceremonial, i.e. rites, such as washings, etc., which have no meaning in themselves, but are performed in order to express or suggest moral ideas, has strictly no existence in the Old Testament. The offences which we call ceremonial were not symbolical, they were real offences to Jehovah, against which His nature reacted; and the purifications from them were real purifications, and not merely symbolical. That is, what might be called æsthetic or physical unholiness was held offensive to the nature of God in the real sense, in a sense as real as moral offences were offensive to Him; and the purifications were true removals of these real causes of offence. This æsthetic or physical holiness is an ancient idea. But the prophets made little of it, insisting on moral holiness. On the other hand, the idea receives a great extension in the Law. And hence at the return from Captivity, when the people were no more a nation but a worshipping community, serving God who abode in a house in the midst of them, this idea of 'holiness' was the fundamental idea, both of God who was worshipped and of men who worshipped Him, and the con-

[1] Did not purifications take place before sacrifice, even at the high places? No doubt.

ception lies at the basis of the new constitution after the Restoration.

In this connection we may advert also to the point of view from which the *people* are regarded. In the extra-ritual books *atonement* is very much equivalent to forgiveness of sin,—after Jehovah's exhibition of His righteousness by the chastisements inflicted on the people who sin, and on their acknowledging their sin and repenting. The conception of God is that of a moral Mind who regards sin as morally wrong, deserving of punishment, and who as a moral Ruler inflicts punishment; though His long-suffering and mercy are ever ready to forgive.

The same conception of Jehovah appears in Isa. liii.; but there the chastisement of sin falls upon another than those whose sin is forgiven. He bears the chastisement of the sins of the people, and they are forgiven and restored. But though this be the case, God continues to be considered the author of salvation. This laying of the sins of the people upon another was His act: "It pleased the Lord to bruise Him," with the view that if He made an offering for sin, the work of the Lord should prosper by Him. This is the view in the Law and Ezekiel. It re-appears in the Epistle to the Hebrews. Perhaps this view of God and of atonement is that expressed in St. Paul's Epistles.

There is, however, another view of God in the Old Testament. He is not regarded so much in the character of a righteous ruler as in that of a sensitive being or nature which reacts against sin. Sin, however, is conceived as uncleanness. In this view Jehovah is called *holy*, and *atonement* is removal from men of all uncleanness disturbing to Jehovah's nature.

3. *The Natural Attributes.*

When the prophets speak of Jehovah as God alone they also state in many ways what His attributes are. Not that they ever speak of the attributes of Jehovah abstractly or as separated from Himself. They speak of a great, living person who shows all the attributes of moral Being. Jehovah, who is God alone, is a transcendent moral person. He is such a person as we are ourselves; His characteristics do not differ from ours, except that they exceed ours. To say that Jehovah is a transcendent moral person, is to express the whole doctrine of God; for that which is moral includes mercy and love and compassion and goodness, with all that these lead to, not less than rectitude and justice.

What needs to be said on this subject may be best said by looking specially at the representations given in Second Isaiah. In the first nine chapters of the prophecy, in which the prophet, in order to sustain the faith of Israel and the hope of deliverance, enlarges upon the antithesis between Jehovah and the idols, it is mainly what have been called the *natural* attributes of Jehovah that he dwells upon, such as His power, His foresight and omniscience, the unsearchableness of His understanding or mind, and the like. But in the succeeding chapters, where not the opposition between Jehovah and the idols and idol-worshipping nations is dwelt upon, but the relations of Jehovah to His people Israel, it is naturally chiefly the redemptive attributes of Jehovah that become prominent, His *love*, as in calling the people and redeeming them of old; His memories of Abraham His friend; His *compassion* when He beholds the miseries of the people, and remembers former times before they were cast off, as a wife of youth, who had been rejected, is remembered; or His *mercy* in restraining His anger in pity of their frailty: "He will not be always wroth; for the spirits would fail before Him, and the souls which He has made"; or the freedom of His *grace* in blotting out their sins for His name's sake: "I am He that blotteth out thy transgressions for Mine own sake, and I will not remember thy sins" (xliii. 25).

In these chapters, especially from the forty-ninth onwards, the prophet descends to a depth of feeling, in two

II

directions, to which no other prophet reaches—first, in his feeling of the love of Jehovah for His people. He becomes, as we might say, immersed in this love, placing himself in the very Divine mind itself, and expressing all its emotions, its tender memories of former union, its regrets over the too great severity of the chastisement to which the people had been subjected. She has "received of the Lord's hand double for all her sin" (xl. 2); "In an overflow of anger I hid My face from thee" (liv. 8). He tells of returning love, and the importunity with which it desires to retrieve the past: "Comfort ye, comfort ye My people: speak to the heart of Jerusalem" (xl. 1, 2); and makes the announcement of the unchangeableness of His love for the time to come: "This is the waters of Noah unto Me: as I have sworn that the waters of Noah shall no more overwhelm the earth, so have I sworn that I will no more be angry with thee" (liv. 9).

And in another direction the depth of the prophet's feeling is without parallel—his sense of the people's sin. It is no doubt the unexampled sufferings of the people, especially the godly among them, that mainly suggested to him the depth of their sin. It is usually held that it was the Law that gave Israel its deep sense of sin. The Law was, no doubt, fitted to suggest to men the exceeding breadth of God's commandments, and the inability of man to fulfil them, and thus to lead them to feel that they must cast themselves upon the grace of God. Yet, historically, it is probable that this educational influence of the Law began later than the prophetic age. At whatever time the Law, as we understand it, was actually given, it certainly did not draw the people's life as a whole under its control till after the restoration from the Exile. So that as a matter of history the sense of sin was impressed upon the people by their experiences. Their sufferings were Jehovah's chastisement of them, they were due to His anger. And they measured His anger by the terribleness of their calamities; and their sin they estimated according to the terribleness of His anger. It is in the sections where the sufferings of the Servant are touched upon that the prophet's sense of the people's sin most clearly appears.

But it is proper to refer to some of those attributes of Jehovah usually called *natural*. These may be dealt with very briefly. First, His *power*. In Isa. xl. the prophet, in order to comfort the people and assure them of Jehovah's ability to redeem them out of the hand of their enemies, presents before them His might as Creator—His immeasurable power. He measured in the hollow of His hand the oceans. The nations to Him are as a 'drop of a bucket,' and as 'the small dust upon the balance'—inappreciable. So great is He that to make a sacrifice to Him that would be appreciable 'Lebanon would not suffice' for the wood, nor all the beasts there for an offering. All nations are from His point of view nothing; in a word, His greatness is such that no comparison can be instituted between Him and aught else; He and the universe are incommensurable. As an instance of His power in nature good for all, the prophet points to the motions of the starry heavens: "Who created these, bringing out their host by number? He calls every one by name, for the greatness of His power not one faileth." He is the Lord of hosts, calling out His armies on their nightly parade, and not one fails to answer His call. This is physical power. But His mental power is equally immeasurable: "Who regulated or directed His mind in creating?" the prophet asks, "who was His counsellor?" The infinite masses of the universe are there by His wisdom in their just proportions: "He weighed the mountains in His scales." He is an everlasting God; the sources of His life and power well up eternally fresh; He fainteth not, neither is weary; there is no searching into His understanding.

And it is not only that He possesses this power; He may be observed continually wielding it in history. He sits upon the circle of the heavens overarching the earth, and the "inhabitants thereof are as grasshoppers"; and He "bringeth princes to nought," withering up, as the hot wind of the desert does the vegetation, the most powerful combinations of men in armies and in empires, and scattering them as dust abroad; dissolving kingdoms and States, and causing their elements to enter into new combinations (xl. 22). And not only in the past does He so act, but in the present He raises up Cyrus from the East, making him come upon rulers as upon mortar, and as the potter treadeth clay (xli. 25); subduing nations before Him, breaking in pieces the doors of brass, and cutting asunder the bars of iron (xlv. 1, 2). And this is no mere sporadic exhibition of power, no inbreak merely into history; for He dominates all history and the life of mankind upon the earth; He calleth the generations from the beginning, each to come upon the stage of life, and when its part is played to depart (xli. 4). His sovereignty over nature and men and the nations is absolute and universal, and He makes all serve His ends. Over nature His sovereignty is beautifully expressed in the passage where, making all things to help the restoration of His people, He says: "I will make all My mountains a way, and all My highways shall be paved" (xlix. 11); "I will say to the north, Give up; and to the south, Keep not back: bring My sons from far, and My daughters from the ends of the earth" (xliii. 6). His sovereignty over men, over His people, in like manner is expressed in the passage: "Woe to him that striveth with his Maker! Shall the clay say to him that fashioneth it, What makest thou? or thy work, He hath no hands?" (xlv. 9). And in chap. lv. 8: "My thoughts are not as your thoughts." And not only over men or His people, but over the nations: "I will give Egypt for thy ransom, Ethiopia and Sheba instead of thee" (xliii. 3).

But the further multiplication of passages is unnecessary. There are three names used by the prophet under which these various conceptions of Jehovah might all be summed up. These are: (a) *Kadosh*, קָדוֹשׁ, the 'Holy One,' as we might say, the *transcendent*. (b) צְבָאוֹת 'י, *Jehovah of Hosts*, the omnipotent. And (c) רִאשׁוֹן וְאַחֲרוֹן, *the first and the last*.

The expression 'Holy One of Israel' is common to these

chapters with the first part of Isaiah; in these chapters, however, the simple קָדוֹשׁ is used even without the article as a proper name: "To whom then will ye liken Me? saith *Kadosh*" (xl. 25). The word is derived from a root קַד meaning to *cut*, or *cut off*; hence the meaning of קָדוֹשׁ, as we have seen, is possibly *separate, removed*. As applied to Jehovah it comes nearest our term *transcendent*. It signifies Jehovah as removed from the sphere of the human or earthly. Naturally, though this removal might first of all apply, so to speak, to Jehovah in His physical nature, so far as usage goes, it is employed mainly of His moral nature.

But of the first of these three names enough has been said already. The second, the phrase 'Jehovah of hosts,' or 'Jehovah, God of hosts,' was probably first used in connection with the armies of Israel. But later, the hosts were understood of the stars; and the commanding of these, and causing them to perform their regular movements, was held the highest conceivable exercise of power. Hence 'Jehovah of hosts' is nearly our *Almighty* or omnipotent, as the Septuagint in some parts renders it παντοκράτωρ.

The third expression, 'the first and the last' (Isa. xliv. 6), is a surprising generalisation for a comparatively early time. It is not a mere statement that Jehovah was from the beginning and will be at the end. It is a name indicating His relation to history and the life of men. He initiates it, and He winds it up. And He is present in all its movements: "Since it was, there am I" (xlviii. 16). Even the last book of the New Testament has nothing loftier to say of Jehovah than that He is 'the first and the last': "I am the Alpha and the Omega, the first and the last, saith the Lord, the Almighty" (Rev. i. 8).

The prophet's doctrine of Jehovah on this side of His Being is very lofty and developed, more so than is seen in any other book except Job; and most writers are inclined to conclude from this highly advanced doctrine of God that the prophecies cannot be earlier than the time of the Exile. The unity of God and the universality of His power and rule are inferred from His being Creator: "Thus saith the Lord, who created the heavens, He is God" (xlv. 18). It is to be remarked, however, that the prophet's interests were never abstract or merely theoretical. All his exhibitions of the *unity* or *power* or *foresight* of Jehovah have a practical end in view, namely, to comfort the people of God amidst their afflictions, to sustain their faith and their hopes, and to awaken them to those efforts on their own part, that forsaking of their sin and their own thoughts, which are needful to secure their salvation. "Why, when I am come, is there no man? when I call, is there none that answereth? Is My arm shortened, that it cannot save? Behold, by My rebuke I dry up the sea, I cover the heavens with blackness" (l. 2). Thus all the teaching of the prophet regarding Jehovah and regarding the people is strictly religious. When he insists on the unity of Jehovah, it is not the unity as a mere abstract truth about God, but as the very basis and condition of salvation for Israel and all men. And the same is true in regard to all the attributes of Jehovah which he touches upon, and all the operations which he represents Him as performing. His whole interest is summed up in such words as these which the Lord speaks through him: "There is no God besides Me, no Saviour." To mention one or two particulars:

(1) Even creation is a moral work, or has a moral purpose. In it Jehovah contemplated the peace and well-being of men. "Thus saith the Lord who created the heavens; He is God, who formed the earth: He created it not a chaos, He formed it to be inhabited" (xlv. 18). The world is a moral constitution. The devastations introduced by wars, the miseries of men due to idolatry, with its pride and cruelty and inhumanity, are perversions of His primary conception in creation. This idea of the universality of Jehovah's sovereignty—which the prophet expresses so often by calling Him Creator—compels him to take into account not only Israel, but all mankind in his view. Jehovah, God alone, is God of all men. Hence He is the

Saviour not of Israel only, but of all men. Earlier prophets, such as Isaiah in his second chapter, in the prophecy of the 'mountain of the Lord,' to which all nations shall go up that Jehovah may teach them of His ways, and that they may walk in His paths, already teach that the Gentiles shall be partakers with Israel of the knowledge of the true God. But the present prophet has a much securer hold of the truth, or at least expresses it much more formally: "The Servant of the Lord shall bring forth right to the nations; they shall wait on his instruction" (xlii. 1–4); "He shall be the light of the Gentiles" (xlii. 9, xlix. 9); "The nations shall come to Israel's light, and kings to the brightness of her rising" (lx. 1); "Jehovah's arms shall rule the nations" (li. 5).

(2) As in creation Jehovah contemplated men's good and salvation, so all His operations, all the exhibitions of His power and foresight, have the same end in view. All His operations on nature, for instance, when He trans-figures it and makes the desert pools of water, are for the sake of His people: "The poor and needy are seeking water, and there is none, and their tongue faileth for thirst; I will open rivers on the bare heights, I will make the wilderness a pool of water" (xli. 17, 18); "Behold, I will do a new thing, I will give waters in the wilderness, and rivers in the desert, to give drink to My people, Mine elect" (xliii. 20). And that all things form a unity, and that it is in salvation that their unity and their good are realised, appears from the jubilations which the prophet puts into the mouth of universal creation, men and nature, when he refers to the salvation of God. Thus, when Jehovah announces that He will not give His glory to another, nor His praise to graven images, but that His Servant shall be the light of the Gentiles, the prophet makes all mankind break into song over the announcement: "Sing unto the Lord a new song, and His praise from the ends of the earth, ye that go down into the sea; the isles, and the inhabitants thereof. Let the wilderness and the cities thereof lift up their voice . . . let them shout from the

top of the mountains" (xlii. 10). And so all nature
is to burst into singing over the redemption of Israel,
because that is the first step towards the evangelising of
the world: "Sing, O ye heavens, for the Lord hath done
it; shout, ye lower parts of the earth . . . for the Lord
hath redeemed Jacob, and will glorify Himself in Israel"
(xliv. 23 ; cf. xlv. 8, xlix. 13).

(3) And it is not only Jehovah's operations on nature
which have salvation in view, but also all His operations
on the stage of history; such, for example, as His raising
up of Cyrus. This great act of providential history contemplates the widest scope. It has, no doubt, narrower
objects in view, but even these narrower purposes look
towards a universal one. Jehovah raises up Cyrus, first,
that Cyrus may know Him: "That thou mayest know that
I am the Lord"; secondly, that His servant Jacob may be
set free: "For My servant Jacob's sake, and Israel My
chosen, I have called thee by thy name"; but, thirdly,
these two are but steps in the direction of the universal
object in view: "That men may know from the rising of
the sun, and from its going down, that there is none besides
Me. I am the Lord, and there is none else" (xlv. 1–7)
And the same idea is expressed in the name 'First and
Last' given to Jehovah. He has a purpose from the
beginning, which He brings to completion; and this is none
other than that they may "look unto Him and be saved,
all the ends of the earth" (xlv. 22). And the same is the
meaning when it is said so often that Jehovah is performing some great act in 'righteousness,' as when He says of
Cyrus: "I have raised him up in righteousness" (xlv. 13).

(4) And corresponding to this exclusively religious conception of Jehovah, all whose attributes and operations are
conceived as working to one end, is the prophet's conception
of the people Israel. Though he still holds fast to the
idea of the people or nation, as all the prophets operate
with nations, the religious unit being to them the people,
not the individual;—though he still retains this conception,
his idea of Israel and its meaning is a purely religious one.

This he expresses by calling Israel the *Servant of the Lord*. All other conceptions of the people have been dropped, and its sole significance is as a religious unity, serving the Lord as His people, and in a public mission to the world on His behalf. Though Israel remains a people, the prophet's conception of it is that of a Church. And that which makes Israel the 'Servant of the Lord' is that He has put His word into its mouth; Israel is the prophet of the world. In earlier writings the antithesis was between the individual prophet and the people of Israel. The individual prophet was the servant of the Lord sent to the people of Israel. Now the antithesis is a wider one. The universalism of the prophet's conception of Jehovah compels him to formulate Jehovah's relations to all nations, and he expresses his conception of this by saying that *Israel* is the Servant of the Lord, His messenger and prophet to mankind. Israel is the Lord's Servant, because Israel is the word of the Lord incarnate; and the greatness of the scope which Jehovah had in view in putting His word into Israel's mouth is expressed in the words: "I have put My words in thy mouth, that I may plant the heavens and lay the foundations of the earth (*i.e.* the new heavens and the new earth), and say unto Zion, Thou art My people" (li. 16). The prophet's redemptive or religious conception of Israel exhausts Israel. This appears in the remarkable passage in chap. lxi., where Israel's relation to the nations in the new world is described: "Strangers shall stand and feed your flocks, and aliens shall be your plowmen and vine-dressers. But ye shall be named the priests of the Lord; men shall call you the ministers of our God" (lxi. 5).

4. *The Redemptive Attributes.*

These general remarks lead us to refer more particularly to those of Jehovah's attributes that are usually called *redemptive*. It is unnecessary to dwell on these: the mention of one or two things will suffice. There is one preliminary point, however, on which a remark may be made.

The prophet's statements are concrete and not general. He speaks of Jehovah as Redeemer mainly in relation to Israel. Israel was then His people, and no other was. His redemptive attributes therefore are manifested in His relation to Israel. To interpret the prophet rightly this must always be kept in mind. Yet now when the Church or people of God has a wider sense, and belongs to all mankind, we are, no doubt, entitled to apply to this universal Church that which this prophet says of Israel, the Church in his day. Though he regards Jehovah's purpose of salvation as universal, embracing the nations, he does not represent Jehovah as loving the nations, or choosing them, or redeeming them. The Lord does not use those terms regarding them which He uses regarding Israel. Jehovah has compassion on their miseries; He sees that the flame of life burns low in them, and His Servant in bringing forth right to them will deal gently with them, and quicken and heal their decaying strength: "The bruised reed He will not break, and the dimly burning flame He will not quench" (xlii. 3).

(a) First, then, Jehovah *loved* Israel. This is not a common expression; it occurs, however, several times, as in xliii. 4: "Since thou hast been precious in My sight . . . and I have loved thee." And Abraham is called the *friend* or *lover* of God (xli. 8). The word אהב is not much used by the prophets of Jehovah's mind towards His people. But there is another word, namely, חסד, which we render by 'loving-kindness.' This is oftener employed, as, *e.g.*, in the beautiful passage: "I will make mention of the loving-kindness of the Lord, and the great goodness which He bestowed on the house of Israel, according to His mercies and according to the multitude of His loving-kindnesses" (lxiii. 7). And this word really expresses the idea of *love*. Again: "In an overflow of wrath I hid My face from thee for a moment, but with everlasting love will I have mercy upon thee" (liv. 8). This love of Jehovah to Israel is entirely inexplicable. It was certainly not due to any loveliness on Israel's part, for Israel has been a "transgressor from the womb" (xlviii. 8), and her "first father sinned against the Lord" (xliii. 27). The prophet might seem to give an explanation when Jehovah addresses Israel as "the seed of Abraham my friend" (xli. 8). Israel is "beloved for the father's sake." But this only thrusts the difficulty a step back, for His love of Abraham himself cannot be explained: "Look unto Abraham your father . . . for when he was but one I called him, and blessed him, and made him many" (li. 2). Jehovah's love is free, and we cannot explain it. We can see, indeed, why He should love some one people, and enter into relations of redemption with them, and deposit His grace and truth among them ; but we cannot see why one and not another. It helps us, however, somewhat if we perceive that His choice of one was only temporary, and for the purpose of extending His grace unto all. And we are assured that His love is not arbitrary, nor a mere uncalculating passion ; but, seeing it is said that God is love, His love is the highest expression of His ethical being, the synthesis and focus of all His moral attributes.

(b) He *chose* or *elected* Israel. It is difficult to say whether this choice follows God's love, or is contemporaneous with it, or is but another way of expressing it. The *choice* or *election* of Israel is one of the most common thoughts of the prophet: "But thou, Israel, My servant, Jacob whom I have chosen" (xli. 8), and a multitude of other places. The familiarity of the idea to this prophet is remarkable when the other fact is taken into account that the idea finds expression in no ancient prophet. It occurs in a single passage of Jeremiah (xxxiii. 24), and also once in Ezekiel (xx. 5), and in some passages in Deuteronomy. Otherwise, it occurs only in late psalms, such as Ps. cv. and cvi. The reason why this prophet insists upon Israel's election so much is easily perceived. It is part of the 'comfort' which he is charged to address to the people. Israel seemed dissolving away under the wearing forces of the time. It was dispersed among all peoples, itself no more a people. In its despondency it could only complain: " Jehovah hath forsaken me, and the Lord hath forgotten me." To which Jehovah answers: " Can a woman forget her sucking child ? . . . I have graven thee upon the palms of My hands; I have chosen thee, and not cast thee off" (xlix. 15, 16).

(c) This choice realises itself in *calling*, or, as it is otherwise expressed, in *creation* or *redemption*. " I called thee from the ends of the earth,"—which probably refers to Egypt, as the prophet, in all probability, wrote in Babylon (xli. 8, 9). And to this same event, namely, the Exodus, the terms *create* and *redeem* usually refer. Jehovah is called the *Creator* of Israel, because He brought Israel into existence as a people of the Exodus; and for the same reason He is called the *Redeemer* of Israel. No doubt the term ' Redeemer ' is more general. It expresses a constant relation which Jehovah bears to His people—a relation illustrated in the Exodus, and to be again illustrated in the deliverance from Babylon: " Say ye, The Lord hath redeemed His servant Jacob " (xlviii. 20).

(d) A characteristic of this love of Jehovah to His people is its *unchangeableness*: " Can a woman forget . . the son of her womb ? Yea, they may forget, yet I will not forget thee " (xlix. 15); and many similar passages. The flow of this love may be interrupted for a small moment by an access of anger; yet it but returns again to its channel to run in an everlasting current: " For a small moment have I hid My face from thee; but with everlasting love will I have mercy upon thee " (liv. 8). Indeed, the interruption was but apparent. There was no real separation between the Lord and His people: " Where is your mother's bill of divorcement, with which I sent her away ? " (l. 1).

(e) There is another affection of Jehovah towards His people which is but a complexion or aspect of His love —His *compassion*. This is love modified by some other element, chiefly the wretchedness of those loved. Thus in the beautiful passage, " In all their affliction He was afflicted, and the angel of His presence saved them: in His love and in His pity He redeemed them; and He bare them, and carried them all the days of old" (lxiii. 9); and in the similar passage chap. xlvi. 3 : "Hearken unto me, O house of Jacob . . . which have been carried from the womb: and even to old age I am He; and even to hoar hairs will I carry you." And His anger is kindled against Babylon for its severe treatment of His people: "I was wroth with My people, and gave them into thine hand . . . thou didst show them no mercy; upon the aged hast thou very heavily laid thy yoke . . . therefore, these two things shall come upon thee in one day: the loss of children and widowhood" (xlvii. 6, 9). Most frequently the compassion of Jehovah arises when He chastises His people, or it awakens in His breast to arrest His chastening hand: "I will not be always wroth: for the spirits would fail before me, and the souls which I have made" (lvii. 16).

(f) There is one thing else to notice. That the salvation of Israel is of the *free grace* of God is consistently taught, *e.g.*, in the declaration, "Thou hast wearied Me with thy sins. I, even I, am He that blotteth out thy transgressions for Mine own sake; and I will not remember thy sins" (xliii. 24, 25); and in many other passages. In one passage, however, there is an idea introduced which deserves attention. It is there said, "For My name's sake do I defer Mine anger, and for My praise do I refrain from thee, that I cut thee not off: for how should My name be profaned? and My glory will I not give to another" (xlviii. 9, 11). Here the idea seems expressed that Jehovah's motive for saving Israel is lest His name should be profaned—that is, lest His power to save and His glory as God should be little esteemed, probably among the nations. This shade of idea seems to occur first in Ezekiel, in whom it is very common. There the motive of salvation is not found in the condition of those saved, nor in the love, or mercy, or goodness of God, but in the respect which He has to His own glory or name—as we might almost say, His reputation. Now, no doubt, God must be conceived as Himself the end of all His operations; as all things are by Him, so all things are unto Him. The idea, however, is one which

requires to be very carefully expressed. Otherwise we
may be in danger of introducing a certain egoism into our
conception of God which would be fatal to it. When
Moses asked to see Jehovah's *glory*, He replied that He
would "make all His *goodness* to pass before him"; and
He proclaimed His name, "The Lord merciful and gracious"
(Ex. xxxiv. 6). The glory of God is His goodness, and His
goodness is His blessedness. He is glorified, therefore, not
when His goodness is revealed to men, and they admire or
praise it; for that would still involve a certain egoism.
He is glorified when by revealing His goodness He attracts
men unto Himself, and His own goodness is reproduced in
them, and they are created anew in His image; for to be
this is blessedness.

Finally, when it is said that salvation is of God's free
grace, this does not exclude atonement for sin, such as that
rendered by the Servant of the Lord. For this comes in
as the instrument of God's grace: "It pleased the Lord to
bruise him; He put him to grief" (Isa. liii. 10).

These points are all mere commonplaces of Christian
doctrine. But it is of interest to see that they are here
already in the Old Testament—at all events six hundred
years before the Christian age. Christianity brought something absolutely new into the world, but much that it
embraces was already prepared for it.

When we consider the very lofty and highly-developed
doctrine of God found in this prophet, it is somewhat surprising to find him more addicted to the use of anthropomorphisms than any other prophet. This is, no doubt,
due to his highly imaginative mind, and the strength of
his religious fervour.

5. *God's Relations to Nature and to Men.*

Much more might be said in this connection of God's
relations to nature and to men. With respect to the
former, He is always represented as the Maker of all things,
heavens and earth, and all creatures; and on the highest

scale He commands nature, sending a flood upon the sinful world, opening the windows of heaven above, and breaking up the fountains of the great deep beneath; overthrowing the cities of the plain by a convulsion of nature; making the stars in their courses to fight against Sisera. All earthly forces are obedient to Him. He caused the east wind to blow and roll back the sea that His people might pass through; and at His word the sea returned and overwhelmed the Egyptians. The plagues were brought by Him on the land of Egypt and on the royal house. For the idolatry of Israel under Ahab and Jezebel, He scourged the land with drought three and a half years; and when Elijah prayed earnestly with his head between his knees, He gave rain. Perhaps the two greatest wonders of Deity to the ancient mind were that He set bounds to the sea and that He gave rain. So Jeremiah says: "Let us now fear the Lord our God, that giveth rain, both the former and the latter, in his season" (v. 24); and again: "Are there any among the vanities of the heathen that can cause rain? . . . Is it not Thou, O Lord God?" (xiv. 22). In punishment of Saul's attempt to exterminate the Gibeonites, in defiance of the solemn oath by which Israel, under Joshua, had bound itself to spare their lives (Josh. ix.), He sent a drought and a famine, which were only alleviated when expiation was made for the blood which Saul had shed. And to chastise the pride of David in numbering the people, He devastated the people with a pestilence (2 Sam. xxiv.). In all these cases His rule of nature, although absolute, appears to be for moral ends, as in the instances of the Flood and Sodom.

With respect to God's relation to men—nations and individuals—in the early period of the Old Testament history, Israel had not yet entered greatly into connection with the nations. The definite teaching of Scripture in regard to Jehovah's rule of the nations, therefore, first appears in the Prophets, when the great Assyrian and Babylonian empires came upon the scene of the world's history. But the conception of Jehovah's relation to the nations is the same in the early history as in the Prophets, although it is not so broadly expressed. He showed His power over Egypt when He brought Israel out with a high hand and an outstretched arm ; when He laid on Egypt the terrible stroke of the death of the firstborn, and over-whelmed its army in the sea. He declared war for ever against Amalek, and gave Israel the victory over that power. And that the victory was of Him, was shown by the symbol, that when the hands of Moses, uplifted in prayer, became relaxed and hung down, Amalek prevailed, and when they were held up Israel prevailed. The view is everywhere expressed that Israel's victories over the Canaanites were due to Jehovah.

There is a point of great interest here, however, in regard to the conception of the Lord in the early histories, namely, the representation of Jehovah as *predetermining* and *revealing* all these dispositions of His in regard to the nations long before they actually occurred. To Abraham and to his seed He promised by covenant the land of Canaan. The territories of Moab and Ammon He assigned to them ; and Israel's conflicts with Edom and victory over it were foreshadowed in the struggles of the two children, Jacob and Esau, before their birth. Now, most modern writers regard all this as just the actual situation which history brought about reflected back upon a much earlier time. Jacob and Esau were never children ; they are brothers, because kindred peoples. Their struggles before birth, and the prediction that the elder should serve the younger, reflect the history of David's time. Edom or Esau was the elder, because he found a settled abode earlier than Israel. Jacob robbed his brother of the birth-right—meaning, in other words, that Israel inherited the good land of Canaan, while Edom had his portion in the stony desert. And the promise to Abraham of the land of Canaan is a reflection of the actual possession of Canaan by Israel, Abraham being their greatest, and, above all, their spiritual, ancestor. How much truth there may be in these representations I do not stop here to discuss. There

may be some in regard to Jacob and Esau. This, however, is a question by itself. The point deserving of notice
is that in the age when these histories were written these
conceptions of Jehovah prevailed. He was a God who saw
the end from the beginning, who purposed and, though
He long delayed, eventually executed His purposes. In
Gen. xv. Jehovah is represented as making a covenant with
Abraham, promising that the land of Canaan should be his,
and that in him all the families of the earth should be
blessed. The two essential things in a covenant are, *first*,
the disposition or engagement on the part of God to do
some act of goodness or grace to men; and, *second*, His
making this purpose known to men. This revelation of
His purpose of goodness is necessary, because it can only be
carried out through the intelligent and spiritual co-operation of men. The covenants are *momenta* in the religious
history of man; and as this history is a redemptive history,
they are *momenta* in man's redemptive history. This being
so, they are more than successive steps in the revelation of
a purpose; they are *momenta* in the history of God's
redemptive indwelling among men, and His entrance into
their life. Now, undoubtedly, when the narrative in
Gen. xv. was written this idea was current in Israel of an
engagement on the part of Jehovah to give Canaan to
Israel as his abode, and to bless all nations through him.
Is it anything incredible that this should have been
revealed to Abraham ? Amos says: " Surely the Lord
God will do nothing, but He reveals His secret unto His
servants the prophets " (iii. 7). The characteristic of the
Israelitish mind was an outlook into the future. In
Isa. xli. prophecy, even prediction, is regarded as an
essential in redemptive history. Jehovah is ' the first and
the last.' He is conscious of His own purposes. But it is
His indwelling in Israel that causes Him to declare them.
Because they concern Israel, and because Israel, His
servant, must co-operate towards their fulfilment, they
must be made known to him. Was the case different with
Abraham ? If he was anything like that character which

these early histories describe him to have been, nothing would seem more natural than that he should be made to know what the goal was to be to which his history looked. One can scarcely explain how Israel came to direct its atttention to Canaan when it escaped from Egypt, unless it had some tradition of its destiny alive in it.

More interesting than Israel's views of the way in which Jehovah judged and ruled the nation, and approved Himself its God, whether in giving it victory over its enemies, or in visiting its sins upon it, are those indications that are given of how Jehovah's relations to *individuals* were thought of. The truth that God's covenant at Sinai was made with Israel as a people, and that the prophets deal mainly with the State and its destinies, rarely with individuals, and of these mainly with the ruling classes, obscures, for the time being, the question of Jehovah's relation to individual persons. Indeed, it has been asserted that down to the time of the prophet Amos, no individual mind in Israel was conscious of a personal relation to Jehovah. This is serious exaggeration. From the nature of the case less is said of such relations than we might wish. But enough is said to enable us to see that the thought of Jehovah entered into every circumstance of the people's life. That Jehovah is conscious of the meaning of the individual is sufficiently plain. He calls Moses by name, *i.e.* He conceives his meaning as a person and a servant. He chooses David, calling him from the sheep-cotes, and finds him a man after His own heart. He loves Solomon. It is, however, in certain relations of life that the feeling reveals itself how intimately Jehovah is connected with the life of men, and enters into it. Such relations are those, *e.g.*, of family life. It is when children are born into the world that the pious feelings of parents are most strongly evoked and expressed. So the names of most children are compounded of the Divine name. Thankfulness is expressed, and the child is accepted as a Divine gift, and is called, *e.g. Jonathan* = " Jehovah has given," etc. ; or some hope is expressed which God will grant; or some happy omen is seized indicative of God's purpose with regard to the child. The story of the naming of Jacob's children in Padan-Aram is full of indications how closely men and women felt Jehovah to be bound up with their history. And there is perhaps nothing more striking in Israel's history than this—that it is chiefly a history of great individuals—Abraham, Moses, Elijah, David, etc.

One other point, illustrating how Jehovah entered into the life of men, may be mentioned. That is, the making of contracts or covenants. Into these Jehovah is represented as entering as a third party—the Guardian of the contract. Men mutually swore by Him. Or they offered a sacrifice, of which part was given to Him, while the rest was eaten together by the contracting parties; and so all three were drawn into the bond, and bound by it. When Laban left his daughters to Jacob in Gilead, they made a covenant, raising a cairn in witness of it; and Laban on parting said : "The Lord watch between me and thee when we are absent from one another" (Gen. xxxi. 49). "God is witness betwixt me and thee." So Sarah, when enraged by Hagar, her maid, said to her husband : "The Lord judge between me and thee" (Gen. xvi. 5). The Lord everywhere upholds right. Sometimes it seems that the conception held of Jehovah was very severe, and sometimes His action seemed to show great jealousy of any familiarity with anything specially His or holy, as when He struck down Uzzah for putting his hand to the ark to uphold it when it tottered (2 Sam. vi. 6, 7), and slew seventy men of Bethshemesh for looking into the ark (1 Sam. vi. 19). Yet His pious servants show the profoundest humility before Jehovah and submission to His will. When Eli heard from Samuel that his house was doomed to forfeit the priesthood and perish, he said: "It is Jehovah, let Him do what seemeth good" (1 Sam. iii. 18). When David fled before Absalom, and was cursed by Shimei, whom his servants wished to be allowed to slay, he said : "Let him curse: for the Lord hath said unto him. Curse David"

(2 Sam. xvi. 10). And it is in these histories that the Lord proclaims His name : " The Lord God, merciful and gracious, forgiving iniquity and sin," pardoning the sin of David in the matter of Uriah (2 Sam. xii. 17), and graciously granting the prayer of the afflicted Hannah at Shiloh (1 Sam. i. 10, 17). My impression is that even in the most ancient passages of the Old Testament essentially the same thought of Jehovah is to be found as appears in the Prophets and the later literature.

The doctrine of Jehovah receives few developments during the course of the Old Testament period. It is stated more broadly in the later books, but in the oldest writings the germs of it are contained. Instead of quoting separate passages, it will be enough, in bringing this statement to an end, to refer to one passage which gives a very vivid picture of what may be called the consciousness of God in the mind of Old Testament saints. That is the cxxxixth Psalm. Here we see, *first*, how the Psalmist begins with the expression of God's general knowledge of man, even of his heart: " Thou hast searched me, and known me." The writer feels himself standing before One who *knows*. The knowledge and the whole relations expressed are properly ethical, but the ethical at times—so strong is the feeling of the presence of the Person who knows, and of His scrutiny pervading the whole nature—seems to pass into the physical, and the image of one substance or element surrounding and compressing another is used to body out the almost physical feeling of God's presence. But that this is only a powerful way of expressing the ethical, is seen from the concluding prayer: " Search me, . . . and lead me in the way everlasting."

Second, this one general feeling of being known is broken up into particulars : " Thou knowest my *sitting down* and my *rising up*, . . . Thou hast sifted my *going* and *lying down*." The outward is known, sifted, every mode in which existence expresses itself is seen through. But it is not so much the things themselves as that out of which they come : " Thou knowest my thought afar off," long ere it be formed ; ere the word be on my tongue, Thou knowest it all. This feeling of being known by One present is so strong that it expresses itself in the figure of physical pressure; this piercing eye, this seeing Person is so near that He thrusts Himself against the Psalmist—"Thou pressest me before and behind"; the faculties of his soul, not to speak of his body, have not room to play, to move, for this impinging element about them, bearing in upon them, and hampering them in their action. And this figure is varied by another, that of the grasp of a hand laid upon the man, by which he is carried about, and from beneath which he cannot move: "Such knowledge is too deep for me"; he is unable to grasp it.

Third, this surrounding, compressing element bears in upon him with such terrors and causes such awe, that the thought rises in his mind whether he might not flee from it. But that cannot be: "*Whither from* Thy spirit can I go? If I ascend into heaven, Thou art there: if I descend into Sheol, Thou art also there: if I take the wings of the morning, and dwell in the uttermost part of the earth, there will Thy hand hold me." The physical figure, by which the Divine omniscience was expressed, leads through the thought of the escape from it, if that were possible, to the expression of the Divine omnipresence. The two are hardly distinct things; He who knows, God as knowing, is an all-pervading presence. This surrounding element, how shall he escape it? this inbearing, oppressing spirit, that thrusts itself close unto him, how shall he elude it? "Whither from Thy spirit can I go?" In heaven, in hell, in east or west—though he should pass from the highest heaven to the deepest Sheol, or through space as swift as the light from east to west, the hand that lies on him will still lie—"Thy right hand holds me." Even in the darkness he is conscious of a face beholding him—to God the darkness is as light.

Fourth, the Psalmist adds words which seem partly meant to be an explanation of this knowledge of God—"for Thou hast possessed my reins," or "hast made my reins.'

If the former, as the *reins* denoted what we mean by the *conscience* or *consciousness*, the meaning is, that God had settled down in his consciousness. If this were the meaning, the figure would be deserted, and the literal meaning expressed. It is perhaps more likely that the meaning is, "Thou hast made my reins." This both explains God's knowledge, and deepens the expression of it. God knows him; for He was present at the beginning of his being, and foresaw and designed all that it should be—all his members before they were "written in His Book." God formed him, and prescribed and looked forward to all that he should be; His knowledge of him is not new. And to the mind of the Psalmist there is a certain awfulness in this thought: "Such thoughts are too heavy for me"; he is fascinated by this sense of God, and cannot dispel it from his mind. When he awakes in the morning, it still haunts him and fills his mind—"when I awake I am still with Thee"; still occupied with Thee. His consciousness of God has become the other half of his consciousness of himself.

Yet, that all this conception of God, however much expressed in physical figures, is mainly ethical, appears, as we have said, from the prayer with which the Psalmist concludes: "Search me, and know my heart: try me, and know my thoughts: and see if there be any wicked way in me, and lead me in the way everlasting." Though he fears the searching, yet he invites it. The Divine, although awful, yet attracts. He is fascinated by the Divine light, almost as the insect by the lamp; and he must move towards it, even though there be danger that it should consume him.

VI. THE DOCTRINE OF MAN.

1. *Human Nature and its Constitution.*

On the subject of Old Testament Anthropology the first question that presents itself is the question of human nature itself and its elements, as they are spoken of in Scripture. Much has been written on the subject of the Psychology of the Old Testament. Many systems of Biblical Psychology have been constructed, and the points signalised in which this Psychology differs from ordinary Psychology. Two points have generally been much insisted on. One is that the Bible teaches a trichotomy, or threefold division of human nature, *body, soul,* and *spirit*; and the other is that the *spirit* is the highest element in man, the element allied to God, the element endowed with the power of receiving God and Divine influences. It is not easy to bring into system or order the statements of Scripture regarding the nature of man, and its several elements or sides. But the following remarks may be made:

(1) What we may expect in the Old Testament is not scientific, but popular phraseology. Any such thing as a science of the mind, whether just or false, is not to be looked for among the people of Israel in Old Testament times. A Biblical Psychology of the same class as other psychologies of a philosophical or natural kind, but distinct and different from them, is not to be expected. It is the purpose of the Old Testament to impress practical religious truth on men's minds, and with this view it speaks their ordinary language, not the language of the schools, if, indeed, we could suppose such a language to have existed at the time.

(2) If the Old Testament speaks the popular language, its usage will reflect all the varieties of that language. We cannot expect a more constant use of terms in particular senses than actually prevailed among the people. If the popular language contained distinctions, these will appear in the Old Testament; and if words were used without discrimination and indifferently in the mouths of the people, this indiscriminate usage will appear in the Scriptures. It is not probable that in the Old Testament there is any advance over popular usage in the direction of a fixed or scientific phraseology.

(3) In this connection it is proper to refer to the New

Testament and its ideas. The New Testament phraseology is not purely Jewish, but has been influenced by Greek thought. And in the New Testament there may be observed an approach towards a more fixed or definite use of terms. But even in the New Testament there is no Biblical Psychology in a scientific sense. The New Testament Psychology is not meant to be a psychology of the mind as regards its substance or elements, or even its operations, except on a certain side of these operations. All that we have is an ethical and religious phraseology. The Psychology of the New Testament is part of its ethics, and cannot be pursued further back so as to be made strictly a *psychology* or physiology of the mind. It remains a description of the mind or its attitudes ethically and religiously. It might, no doubt, be legitimate and useful to inquire whether the New Testament phraseology, applied there exclusively in an ethical way, might not have partly arisen from previous speculations of a more purely psychological kind. It is not unlikely that such speculations in some degree influenced the language of the New Testament writers. But a distinction should be drawn between the New Testament usage, which is exclusively ethical, and previous usage of a more strictly philosophical kind which such inquiries might reveal. The latter should not be mixed up with what is called Biblical Psychology. And perhaps such a phrase should not be used at all; for it suggests the idea, for which there is no foundation, that the Scriptures contain a peculiar psychological nomenclature distinct from that of popular usage, which is not true in any sense, and that this nomenclature might be compared or contrasted with that of secular systems of philosophy of the mind, which is only true in this sense, that terms which in secular systems are used in a strictly psychological way, are in the Scriptures used ethically or religiously.

There are certain passages in the New Testament that might seem, and by many have been held, to establish a distinction between *soul* and *spirit* of a kind to be named substantial, and consequently to teach a trichotomy of human nature, a division into three distinct elements. In 1 Thess. v. 23 occur the words : " And the very God of peace sanctify you wholly : and may your spirit and soul and body be preserved entire, without blame, at the coming of our Lord Jesus Christ." The commentary of a writer, not undeserving of attention, on this passage is as follows : " The position of the epithet shows that the prayer is not . . . that the *whole*, spirit, soul, and body, the three associated together, may be preserved, but,—that each part may be preserved *in its completeness*. Not mere associated preservation, but preservation in an individually complete state, is the burden of the apostle's prayer. The prayer is, in fact, threefold : *first*, that they may be sanctified by God, the God of peace,—for sanctification is the condition of outward and inward peace,—wholly (ὁλοτελεῖς) in their collective powers and constituents ; *next*, that each constituent may be preserved to our Lord's coming ; and *lastly*, that each so preserved may be entire and complete in itself, not mutilated or disintegrated by sin ; that the body may retain its yet uneffaced image of God, and its unimpaired aptitude to be a living sacrifice to its Maker ; the appetitive soul, its purer hopes and nobler aspirations ; the spirit, its ever blessed associate, the holy and eternal Spirit of God." [1]

This New Testament passage certainly names three constituent elements of human nature, names them all co-ordinately, and speaks of each as needing sanctification, and as capable of preservation. And it might be plausibly argued that, as the three are specially named, there is as good reason for considering the *spirit* distinct from the *soul*, as there is for considering the *body* distinct from either. But this reasoning would be seen to go further than it ought ; for the distinction between *soul* and *spirit*, even admitting it, can hardly be one of essence. And on the other side it may not unfairly be represented that the apostle's language does not require, in order to justify it,

[1] Ellicott, *Destiny of the Creature*, p. 107.

a distinction of organs or substances, but may be accounted
for by a somewhat vivid conception of one substance in
different relations or under different aspects.   In ordinary
language we certainly speak of *soul* as well as of *spirit*; and
in his fervid desire for the complete and perfect sanctification of his disciples, the apostle accumulates these terms
together, so as to give an exhaustive expression to the
whole being and nature of man.

In Heb. iv. 12 there occurs a similar passage: " For
the word of God is quick, and powerful, and sharper than
any two-edged sword, piercing even to the dividing asunder
of soul and spirit, of both joints and marrow, and quick to
discern the thoughts and intents of the heart." The word
of God has four attributes assigned to it: it is *quick*, that
is, living, as we speak of the quick and the dead; it is
powerful, that is, active; it is *sharp*; and being so, it *pierces*
even to the dividing of soul and spirit. The word ' dividing ' means here the act of dividing rather than the place
of division. The meaning does not seem to be that the
word of God, like a two-edged sword, enters so deep as to
reach the place of division, the seam, or boundary line between soul and spirit, but that it goes so deep as to effect
a division of them. Some doubt may remain whether the
sharp word of God effects a division between the soul and
spirit, or a division within them—whether it separates
between the two, or cuts asunder each, as we might say
dissects both the soul and spirit.

In comparison with the question, indeed, whether the
soul and the spirit be distinct things, this other question is
of less consequence. The passage recognises two things, one
called *soul*, and another called *spirit*. Are these conceived
to be separated by something introduced between them,—an
operation delicate enough, but one which an instrument so
sharp as the word of God is qualified to accomplish ? Or
is it that each of them is divided and cut open into its own
elements ? Probably the view that the division is made
not between the soul *and* the spirit, but within each of
them, is the true one. If the other view were correct,

that according to which a division is effected by the word
of God between soul and spirit, a relation between soul
and spirit would be suggested which is injurious to the
latter, a sensuous sinking of the spirit into the soul, where
its higher energies become drowsy, and expire in the soft,
voluptuous lap of the lower psychical nature; and the
word of God comes to dissever and divorce this depressing
union, and elevate the spirit again to a position of freedom
and command.   This interpretation, however, is less probable.   The meaning is rather that the word of God is so
sharp that it pierces and dissects both the soul and spirit,
separates each into its parts, subtle though they be, analyses
and discerns their thoughts and intents.

But in any case the question forces itself upon us—
Are we here on the ground of literal speech or of
metaphor ?   A writer whose imaginative and rhetorical
manner endows the word of God with life and activity
may very readily conceive one thing in its various states
and connections as various things.   We need to remember
that the writers of Scripture were Oriental, or we shall
be in danger of taking figures of speech for statements of
doctrine.   Perhaps, too, the vivid grandeur of the conceptions of Scripture is not altogether due to their authors
being children of the East.   The time when these conceptions were formed was one of profound excitement.   Old
systems of thought and life were breaking up under the
fresh influence of Christian thought like an ice-bound
river, and the strong currents newly released were dashing
the fragments against one another.   A new moral world
had suddenly been created, more real, and to the earnest
imagination of the time almost more substantial, than
the world of matter.   It was not mere conceptions amidst
which men stood ; it was things, almost beings.

Even to a man of the character of St. Paul the words
sin, death, law, and the like represented personalities rather
than abstract ideas.   He wrestled with them, as they
wrestled with one another.   And it was not outside of him
alone, or for him, that the conflict was carried on, but

within him. He found himself divided. One less conscious than he was, that the influence which gave men
power to be at any time victorious over the evil within
them came from without, might have described his moral
sensations by saying that he felt himself sometimes on the
side of good and sometimes on the side of evil. But the
apostle was not sometimes one *kind* of man and sometimes
another; he was *two men*, or there were two men within
him. There was an *old* man and a *new* man, an *inner* man
and another. And where the fervour of the religious
imagination produced creations like these, it may easily be
conceived to have spoken of two aspects of the one thing,
the mind, as if they were two things. Elsewhere, both with
St. Paul and with the author of *Hebrews*, we find human
nature spoken of as consisting of two elements only. The
one speaks of " cleansing ourselves from all filthiness of the
flesh and *spirit*, perfecting holiness in the fear of God "
(2 Cor. vii. 1); and the other, of our drawing near unto
God, " having our *hearts* sprinkled from an evil conscience,
and our bodies washed with pure water " (x. 22). It is
most likely, therefore, that the trichotomy which appears
in some other passages is rhetorical, and not to be taken
literally.

2. *The terms 'Body' and 'Flesh.'*

If we return now to the Old Testament and inquire
how the three terms, *body, soul*, and *spirit*, are employed
there, the following may be taken as an outline of what
the usage is :

As to the *body*. The Hebrew word for 'body' is גְּוִיָּה,
which is sometimes used for the *living* body (Ezek. i. 11,
" bodies of the Cherubim "; Gen. xlvii. 18; Neh. ix. 37),
but usually for the *dead* body or carcase. This term hardly
corresponds to the Greek σῶμα. Properly speaking,
Hebrew has no term for 'body.' The Hebrew term
around which questions relating to the body must gather
is *flesh*, בָּשָׂר. Now, the only question really of interest in

regard to this term is the question whether in the Old Testament an ethical idea had already begun to attach to it? Such an ethical use of the word 'flesh,' σάρξ, is very characteristic of the New Testament, at least of the Pauline Epistles; and it is of interest to inquire whether it be found also in the Old Testament.

The word 'flesh' is found in the Old Testament used of the muscular part of the body in distinction from other parts, such as skin, bones, blood, and the like, especially such parts of animals slain for food or for sacrifice. Hence it is used for food along with bread (Ex. xvi. 3), or wine, —eating flesh and drinking wine (Isa. xxii. 13),—and forms the main element of the sacrifice. The fact that it is used for sacrifice, and offered to the Lord as His fire-food, shows that no uncleanness belongs to the flesh as such. The distinctness of clean and unclean among animals is not one due to the flesh, for they are all alike flesh. The flesh in itself has no impurity attaching to it; it is of no moral quality.

In living creatures the same distinctions are drawn between the flesh of the body and other parts of it—" this is bone of my bone, and flesh of my flesh." But the flesh being the most outstanding part of the living creature, covering the bones and containing the blood, it naturally came to be used, the part being taken for the whole, of the living creature in general. In this sense it represents the creature as an organised being, flexible, smooth, and possessing members. In Arabic the corresponding word is used of the surface of the body as smooth and fresh; and it is curious that in Hebrew *flesh* in this sense does not seem to be employed of animals covered with feathers or hair, and probably the soft, fresh muscle and the smooth surface of the animal body is the prominent notion. Hence a usage which is as far as possible from casting any aspersion of an ethical kind upon the flesh, in the prophet Ezekiel, who says: "A new heart will I give unto you . . . I will take away the stony heart out of your flesh, and I will give you an heart of flesh" (xxxvi. 26).

This usage forms the transition to a wider one, according to which sensuous creatures, particularly mankind, are called *all flesh*. This remarkable expression for mankind, or for sensuous creatures in general, is usually, however, employed in a way that may suggest its origin. It is generally, or at least very often, used when there is an antithesis of some kind suggested between mankind and God. And it is possible that this antithesis gave rise to this way of naming mankind. The suggestive passage Isa. xxxi. 3, " The Egyptians are men, and not God: and their horses are flesh, and not spirit," perhaps gives a key to the kind of idea underlying the usage. The idea must be carefully observed. The passage begins : " Woe to them that go down to Egypt for help; that stay (trust) on horses, and look not unto the Holy One of Israel." The question with the prophet is a question of help, or where real strength lies. Therefore when he says, " their horses are flesh, and not spirit," his point is not what the horses are composed of, but what they are able to accomplish.

When Jehovah is called *Spirit*, it is not a question of His essence, but of His power. And when men are spoken of as *all flesh*, the emphasis does not fall on that which they are made of, but it rather expresses a secondary idea, no doubt suggested by this, the idea of their weakness. Flesh as one sees it is perishable, and subject to decay ; when the spirit is withdrawn it turns into its dust. As thus feeble and subject to decay, in contrast with God who is eternal, mankind and all creatures are spoken of as *all flesh*. The primary sense may perhaps be seen in Deut. v. 26 : " For what is all flesh, that it might hear the voice of the living God speaking out of the midst of the fire, as we, and live ? " And, similarly, Isa. xl. 6, 7 : " All flesh is grass . . . the grass withereth . . . but the word of our God shall stand for ever." Naturally, supposing this to be the origin of the expression, it came also to be used when no such antithesis between mankind and God was designed to be expressed. The phrase might have arisen from the fact that the flesh or body of animated creatures is the prominent thing about them to the eye; but in any case the expression denotes usually the weakness and perishableness of those creatures called 'flesh.' Mankind is also called כל נפש; but this phrase denotes every individual of mankind, whereas *all flesh* is rather the whole race; the characteristic of which is that it is flesh, and therefore weak and perishable.

Now this leads to the last point, namely, whether the term 'flesh' is used in an ethical sense, to imply moral defect, or to be the source of moral weakness. The Hebrews are rather apt to confuse the physical and the moral. There was, of course, no tendency among them, as with us, to resolve the moral into the physical, and obliterate the moral idea altogether. The tendency was the contrary one, to give moral significance to the physical or material; to consider the physical but a form or expression of the moral. So specific forms of disease acquired a moral meaning, and were religious uncleannesses. To touch the dead created a religious disability. This arose from their mixing up the two spheres, and their thinking of them in connection with one another; or it led to it. And this being the case, it might be very natural for them to give to the physical weakness of mankind as 'flesh' a moral complexion. Whether they did so is difficult to decide. They often couple the two together—man's moral and his physical weakness. The Psalmist, in Ps. ciii., blesses God, who healeth all our diseases and forgiveth all our sins. Yet here the things, though combined, are still distinct. And so in another beautiful passage, Ps. lxxviii. 38, 39 : " But He, being full of compassion, forgave their iniquity . . . yea, many a time turned He His anger away. . . . For He remembered that they were but flesh; a wind that passeth away, and cometh not again." Here flesh and iniquity are by no means confounded; on the contrary, He forgave their iniquity because He remembered that they were flesh—that is, transitory beings, a wind that passeth away and cometh not again.

It is possible that in such passages, where sin and flesh

go together, the feeling appears that it is to be expected
that beings so weak physically should be weak morally, and
liable to sin.   This seems to be the view in Job xiv. 1–4:
" Man, born of woman, is of few days, and full of trouble.
He cometh forth as a flower, and withereth: he fleeth as a
shadow, and continueth not.   And dost thou open thine eyes
upon such an one, and bringest me into judgment with thee ?
O that a clean could be out of an unclean ! there is not
one."   Here the two things, physical frailness and moral
uncleanness, again go together; but they do not seem confused.   Neither are they confused in the words of Eliphaz,
chap. iv. 17–19: " Shall man be righteous with God ?
. . . Behold, He charges His angels with error; how much
more man, that dwelleth in houses of clay, which are
crushed before the moth."   And there is a similar passage
in chap. xv. 14.   In all such passages the universal sinfulness of mankind is strongly expressed, and his physical
weakness and liability to decay serve to strengthen the
impression or assurance of his moral frailty.   It is this
moral fallibility that is insisted on.   There is also reference
to his physical frailty and brief life; he is called *flesh*, and
said to dwell in houses of clay and the like.   It is considered natural that one physically so frail should also be
morally frail and sinful.   Physical frailty is pleaded as a
ground of compassion for moral frailty.   But the two do
not seem to be confounded; neither is it taught that the
cause of man's moral frailty is to be found in his physical
nature, or that the flesh is in itself sinful, or the seat
of sin.

3. *The term 'Spirit.'*

The words *spirit*, רוּחַ, and *soul*, נֶפֶשׁ, are often put in
antithesis to the *flesh*, and express the invisible element in
man's nature—the separation of which from the body is
death.   In the Old Testament the word רוּחַ, *spirit*, is the
more important term.   In the New Testament, *spirit*,
πνεῦμα, is little used of any natural element in man; it

chiefly refers to the Divine Spirit communicated to men in fellowship with Christ.

In the Old Testament the word רוּחַ is used of the *wind*; the characteristics of this are impalpableness and force; it is invisible, but a real energy.

Then the word is used of the *breath*. The breath is the sign of life in the living creature. When he no more breathes he is dead—his breath departs, and he falls into dust. Man is a being in whose nostrils is a ' breath '— the sign of the feeblest existence. When this breath is sent out in a violent way it implies passion; hence the word is used for *anger, fury*. So even God's breath is spoken of, and His wrath, which is seen in His nostrils like a fiery smoke.

Now, here we meet an extension of the use of the term *spirit*, common in all languages, the various steps of which need to be distinctly noticed, though it is difficult to keep them separate. There are three steps: (1) the רוּחַ is the breath—the sign of life; (2) it becomes not merely the sign of life, but, so to speak, the principle of vitality itself; and (3) this principle of vitality being considered the unseen spiritual element in man, it comes to mean man's spirit. Reference to certain passages may show this ascent of three steps.[1]

(1) All life, whether in man, or in the lower creatures, or in the world, is an effect of the רוּחַ, the Spirit of God. God's Spirit is merely God in His efficiency, especially as giving life. The Spirit of God is hardly considered another distinct from Him; it is God exercising power, communicating Himself, or operating. This power may be simply vital power, physical life; or it may be intellectual, moral, or religious life. These are all communicated by the Spirit or רוּחַ of God. This Spirit of God communicated to man gives him life. Now, though this רוּחַ or Spirit of God be properly no substance, but a mere power, it is very

---

[1] Compare what has been said above on the subject of "The Spirit of God." Some of the points developed in the following statements are referred to there.—ED.

hard, perhaps impossible, to avoid conceiving it in some substantial way, or to escape the use of language which seems to express this. But we must guard against being misled by such phraseology. In the beginning of Genesis (ii. 7) the creation of man is set forth graphically, and in a very realistic way: "The Lord God made man out of the dust of the ground, and breathed into his nostrils the breath of life; and he became a living creature—*nephesh.*"

The passage is of interest in various ways: *first*, it distinguishes between man and the lower creatures. The earth and waters at the command of God brought forth the other creatures, but man's formation was the workmanship of God's own hand. *Secondly*, man's body being formed, God breathed into his nostrils the breath of life. The source of life does not belong to the body, life is not a manifestation of organised matter. It is a product of God's Spirit. *Thirdly*, man thus became a living *nephesh*— the soul or *nephesh* lives. Now, here we are on the ground of a representation which is very realistically put. Into the still, lifeless, unbreathing form of man God breathed a breath, and straightway the lifeless form exhibited the symptoms of life—breath in the nostrils, and was a living creature. God's רוּחַ, which is the source of life, is here considered God's own breath; the passage of the spirit into man is represented as God's breathing it; and, that being in man, man lived. Now all that seems in question here is just the giving of vitality to man. There seems no allusion to man's immaterial being, to his spiritual element. It is a picture of his endowment with vitality. Vitality is communicated by God, and He is here pictorially represented as communicating it by breathing into man's nostrils that breath which is the sign of life. The anthropomorphism of the author is very strong. He represents God Himself as having a breath which is the sign or principle of life in Himself; and this He breathed into man, and it became the same in him.

Now, this vital spirit, coming from God, but now belonging to man, not, it is to be observed, considered as a spiritual substance in man, but simply as a vital principle or as vitality, is called in Scripture the "Spirit of God," because it is a power of God or a constant efficiency of His; and the "spirit of man," because belonging to man. Hence Job says: "The spirit (or breath) of God is in my nostrils" (xxvii. 3), parallel to the other clause: "My breath is yet whole in me." And Elihu says: "The spirit of God hath made me, and the breath of the Almighty hath given me life" (xxxiii. 4). And again, arguing that the creation and upholding of life in creatures demonstrates the unselfish benevolence of God, he says: "If God should set His mind upon Himself—make Himself the sole object of His consideration and regard, and withdraw unto Himself His spirit and His breath, all flesh should perish together, and return again into dust" (xxxiv. 14). Again, Ps. civ. 29: "Thou takest away their רוח, they die, and return to their dust. Thou sendest forth Thy רוח, and they are created." All these passages are realistic ways of describing life and death; the one is caused by an efflux of God's spirit, which is represented by or identified with the breath in the nostrils, the sign or the principle of life; and the other, death, is caused by God's taking away His spirit, the previous continual sending forth of which was the cause of life. One can readily perceive how two things are mixed up in these representations: *first*, the belief that all life is communicated by God's Spirit, or by God who acts and is everywhere present as spirit, and as such is the giver and upholder of vitality in all that has life; and, *secondly*, a tendency to represent this sensuously by dwelling upon the breath in man, the sign, and presumably the principle, of their life.

When the spirit is spoken of as being withdrawn by God and going forth from man, in other words, when, as we say, he *expires* and dies, there is no question raised as to *where* the spirit of life which he had goes to. The spirit of life is not a substance, it is the mere principle of vitality, as we say. The question did not occur, when the spirit of life was spoken of in this sense, where it was when it went

out or was withdrawn. It really had no existence as anything in itself. It is not considered as gathered into a world
of spirits. Neither does it seem regarded as a part of the
Divine Spirit, which is reabsorbed into the Spirit of God.
This conception would be nearer the truth. If one wished
a figure, he might imagine it thus : As the ocean runs up
upon the shore and fills every cave and hollow in the
rocks, and thus, though each of these cavities has its own
fulness, yet this fulness is not separated from the rest of
the ocean, but is only the universal ocean, communicating
itself ; so God's spirit of life becomes the spirit of life in
all flesh, yet His spirit is not divided. And just as when
the ocean retreats the caves and hollows are left empty
and dry, so when God withdraws His spirit of life the
living creatures fall into dust. A better illustration,
because a scriptural one, is given in Ezek. xxxvii., in the
vision of the dry bones : " As I prophesied, there was a
voice, and the bones came together, bone to his bone.
And I beheld, and, lo, there were sinews upon them, and
flesh came up, and skin covered them ; but there was no
breath in them. Then said He unto me, Prophesy, and
say unto the wind (רוח), Come from the four winds, O breath
(רוח), and breathe into these slain, that they may live. So
I prophesied, and the breath (רוח) came into them, and
they stood up upon their feet an exceeding great army. . . .
Behold, I will open your graves, O My people, and I will
put My רוח in you, and ye shall live, and I will place you
in your own land."

(2) All the preceding illustrations have been given on
the plane of mere life or vitality. But an advance is
made on this in a use of the word רוּחַ which is common to
all languages. The spirit means the intellectual or mental
element in man. It could not but occur to men that the
breath was not the life or living principle in man ; there
was something unseen which was the source or seat of
life and also of thought. Still it was probably the breath
that suggested this, or the same word would hardly have
been used for both. There are still some passages where

the distinction between the breath and the immaterial
principle or mind is scarcely maintained. Thus Elihu
says: "There is a spirit in man, and the breath of the
Almighty giveth them understanding" (xxxii. 8). And
while in earlier books the question is not raised as to what
becomes of the life-spirit in man when he dies, in later
books this spirit is spoken of more as if it had an independent
being of its own. That is, the immaterial element in man
is identified with the spirit of life or principle of vitality in
him : "Then shall the dust return to the earth as it was,
and the spirit shall return unto God who gave it" (Eccles.
xii. 7). And in another passage in the same book : "Who
knoweth the spirit of man, whether it goeth upwards, and
the spirit of the beast whether it goeth downward to the
earth ?" (iii. 21). In general, however, the difference
between 'spirit' as *vitality* and 'spirit' as *immaterial
element* in man is pretty well preserved, though an affinity
between the two usages must be acknowledged.

The term spirit (רוּחַ) is used for the mental element in
the nature of man, especially in *three* aspects: first, when
put in opposition to flesh; *secondly*, when considered as
drawing its origin from God, when He is thought of as its
source; and, *thirdly*, when the strength or weakness in
respect of vitality of man's immaterial nature is spoken of.
The first two are illustrated by such passages as these:
"God of the spirits of all flesh" (Num. xvi. 22, xxvii. 16);
"In whose hand is the soul of all that liveth, and the spirit
of all flesh of man" (Job xii. 10). Examples of the third
are numerous : "The spirit of Jacob their father revived"
(Gen. xlv. 27); "To revive the spirit of the humble" (Isa.
lvii. 15); "My days are over, my spirit is extinguished"
(Job xvii. 1); hence the spirit "is overwhelmed and
faileth" (Ps. cxliii. 4); "by sorrow of heart the spirit is
broken" (Prov. xv. 13); "the sacrifices of God are a
broken spirit" (Ps. li. 17); and this other passage, "For I
will not, saith the Lord, contend for ever, neither will I
be always wroth: for the spirit would fail before me, and
the breaths which I have made" (Isa. lvii. 16).

This connection of רוּחַ with the idea of *life*, and consequently of *strength, power*, is very remarkable, and needs further investigation.   It seems, however, to be the foundation for two very interesting extensions of the use of the term רוּחַ, to which some allusion may be made.

First, as vitality, power, energy resided in the spirit, the term רוּחַ came to be used of a predominating *state* or *direction* of the mind, that which when it is temporary we designate a mood or humour or frame or temper, and when natural or habitual, a disposition or character.   In the former sense Hosea speaks of "a spirit of whoredoms" being in Israel (iv. 12, v. 4), and Isaiah of "a spirit of deep sleep being poured out on them" (xxix. 10), *i.e.* of insensibility, and of "a spirit of perverseness" being in the Egyptians (xix. 14); and in the same sense, perhaps, another prophet speaks of "a spirit of grace and supplications" (Zech. xii. 10).   In the latter sense, that of a prevailing disposition or character, the Old Testament speaks of those who are "proud in spirit" (Eccles. vii. 8), "haughty in spirit" (Prov. xvi. 18), "hasty in spirit" (Eccles. vii. 9); and, on the other hand, of a "humble spirit" (Prov. xvi. 19), of a "patient spirit" (Eccles. vii. 8), a "faithful spirit," and the like (Prov. xi. 13).   The word נֶפֶשׁ or 'soul' could hardly have been used in any of these examples.

Secondly, it is this same conception of power or energy or fuller life which is expressed when it is said that the Spirit of God is *given* to men, or when He *comes upon* them and *moves* them.   It is said, for example, in reference to Samson, that the *Spirit of God began to move him* at times in the camp at Dan (Judg. xiii. 25); that the *Spirit of God came upon* him, and he rent the lion as he would a kid (xiv. 6)—the reference being to the great display of strength which he put forth.   Similarly, it is said of Caleb that the "Spirit of God came upon him, and he judged Israel, and went out to war" (iii. 10).   It is probable that the nomenclature regarding the *Spirit coming on* the prophets originated in this way.   All exhibitions of power or energy whether bodily or mental, are ascribed to the Spirit; and the excitation which characterised prophecy in its earlier stages was spoken of as the result of the Spirit——as Ezekiel still speaks of the "hand of the Lord" being on him (iii. 14, 22, viii. 1, etc.). As prophecy became more purely ethical, and threw off excitement of an external kind, the internal revelation and moral elevation continued to be ascribed to the Spirit. But this revelation is not usually considered to be mere thought communicated, but rather an elevation and greater power of mind, which may, as in Isa. xi. 2, ramify into many directions as wisdom, judicial discernment, counsel, executive, and fear of the Lord.

4. *The term 'Soul.'*

Less needs to be said in regard to the *soul* or נֶפֶשׁ. The *soul* as well as the spirit is used to designate the whole immaterial part of man—though with certain shades of difference in the conception. That the two are identical upon the whole appears from Job vii. 11 : "I will speak in the anguish of my נֶפֶשׁ; I will complain in the bitterness of my רוּחַ." Compare also iii. 20 · "Why giveth He life to the bitter of נֶפֶשׁ?" When God "breathed into man the breath of life," man became a "living נֶפֶשׁ." A creature that has life is נֶפֶשׁ, an individual, a creature, or person. Even a dead person is נֶפֶשׁ. Hence נֶפֶשׁ being the actual living creature that we see, with its many varieties, its form, its sensibilities, and the like, in a word, the living concrete individual, when the word was applied to the immaterial substratum of this life, the *soul*, the same concrete individual character, marked by sensibilities, desires, affections, still adhered to it. Therefore to the נֶפֶשׁ belongs the personality of the individual. The 'soul' longs, pants, desires, melteth for heaviness, fainteth for God's salvation, abhorreth dainty meat, loathes, is satisfied, is bound down, cleaveth to the dust, quiets itself like a weaned child. The same epithets might be used of the רוּחַ and of the נֶפֶשׁ; but they would scarcely have the same force. Applied to the רוּחַ they would describe the condition more objectively as a condition of mental power, *e.g.* a broken spirit; applied to the נֶפֶשׁ they would describe the condition more reflexively as one *felt* by the נֶפֶשׁ or individual.

Any distinction of a substantial or elemental kind between רוּחַ and נֶפֶשׁ is not to be understood. Neither is the רוּחַ higher than the נֶפֶשׁ, or more allied to God. But the idea of רוּחַ is *vitality, strength, power*, which is also the idea attached to the רוּחַ of God; and such influences coming from God are influences of the רוּחַ, and are רוּחַ in man, or a strengthening of רוּחַ in man, because רוּחַ is man's nature on the side of its vitality, power, prevailing force, and the like.

The נֶפֶשׁ is the bearer of the individual personality; but it is not modified רוּחַ, as if רוּחַ concretised were נֶפֶשׁ. There seems no such idea in the Old Testament.

As it *has* or *is* the personality, most importance attaches to the נֶפֶשׁ in questions of immortality: "Thou wilt not leave my נֶפֶשׁ to Sheol" (Ps. xvi. 10); "He hath brought up my נֶפֶשׁ from Sheol" (Ps. xxx. 3). But with this we shall have to deal later.

To put it more exactly, the case is this:

(1) All influences exerted by God upon man are influences of the Spirit of God. God exerting influence is the Spirit of God. The kind of influence which God exerts is dynamical; as we might say, it is a communication of life, or a potentiation of life; or of strength, power, in some region—particularly in the ethical and religious spheres.

(2) As God communicates power as רוּחַ, so the soul of man, in its nature as רוּחַ, receives the communication, *i.e.* it is affected with new power, energy, elevation; and as exhibiting power, energy, elevation, the soul of man is רוּחַ.

(3) This does not imply that the רוּחַ in man is different from the נֶפֶשׁ, much less that the רוּחַ is higher than the נֶפֶשׁ The רוּחַ is the נֶפֶשׁ as possessing or showing power, elevation, etc. For we have seen that when man's mind moved in any direction with a strong current, whether the

current was temporary or permanent, it was described as a רוּחַ of such and such a kind; being a mood or temper or mental tendency when temporary, and being a character or disposition when permanent.

(4) Neither, finally, is the נֶפֶשׁ the רוּחַ individualised, or the רוּחַ modified and made concrete in the individual. No doubt the individuality or personality is attributed to the נֶפֶשׁ; hence נֶפֶשׁ often means 'a person.' And also the רוּחַ is spoken of more abstractly. But the רוּחַ is not first general and impersonal, and then impersonated in the נֶפֶשׁ; rather the נֶפֶשׁ is spoken of as רוּחַ when exhibiting determination, indicating power, strength, and elevation; while as נֶפֶשׁ it is more simply the individual. Hence נֶפֶשׁ can be used even of a *dead* person. Hence, also, two concurrent ways of speaking of death: the רוּחַ *returns* to God who gave it (Eccles. xii. 7); or as in Job: "If God should gather to Himself His spirit and His breath, all flesh would perish together, and man turn into his dust" (xxxiv. 14). But, on the other hand, the נֶפֶשׁ *descends into Sheol.* If נֶפֶשׁ were רוּחַ individualised, it is evident that man would not possess a רוּחַ at all, only a נֶפֶשׁ. But the fact that his רוּחַ as well as his נֶפֶשׁ is spoken of, implies that רוּחַ and נֶפֶשׁ are the same things under different aspects. If man's נֶפֶשׁ were רוּחַ individualised, then the taking away the רוּחַ would really leave nothing at death; while, in fact, the נֶפֶשׁ is left, and *descends* into Sheol. In our modes of thought we operate with substances, but the Hebrew mind operates rather with abstract conceptions which it treats and speaks of as things.

Thus it is saying very little to say that the רוּחַ ' returns to God who gave it.' For that may mean nothing more than that the vitality which flowed from God is withdrawn by God, and the living person falls into weakness and death. It is altogether another thing when Psalmists go the length of saying that the נ׳ is *taken* by God, or that He *redeems* the נ׳ from Sheol. Because the נ׳ is the *person*, while the ר׳ was but some vital energy, the withdrawal of which by God was death.

The main points reached, therefore, are these:

(*a*) That the flesh is not a moral term,—the flesh is not regarded as the source of sin,—and is not a term for sinful nature.

(*b*) The spirit of man and the soul of man are not different things, but the same thing under different aspects. 'Spirit' connotes energy, power, especially vital power; and man's inner nature in such aspects, as exhibiting power, energy, life of whatever kind, is spoken of as *spirit*. The same way of speaking prevails in regard to the Spirit of God. The Spirit of God is God operating powerfully, imparting life, communicating influence. Hence such influences of God when communicated to man affect the spirit of man, *i.e.* man's inner nature, in those aspects in which it is thought of as spirit.

(*c*) The soul, on the other hand, is the seat of the sensibilities. The idea of 'spirit' is more that of something objective and impersonal; that of 'soul' suggests what is reflexive and individual.

(*d*) Upon the whole, taking into account both what is stated in the beginning of Genesis and what appears elsewhere, the impression left on us is that Scripture adds nothing on this subject of Biblical Psychology to what is taught us by common sense. Besides the general doctrine that human nature is the work of God's hand, it gives special prominence to the fundamental dualism of man's nature. He is a compound of matter and spirit. The term 'matter' does not indeed occur in Scripture, but the particular matter of which man's body is composed is named *dust*. And man's spirit is drawn from a quite different quarter. Spirit or mind is so far from being the result of material organisation, that the organisation is represented as existing without spirit. And equally independent of the spirit is the material organisation in its origin. However popular the representation may be considered to be, and however much we may be inclined to regard the account written, so to speak, *post-eventum*, a description of man's creation conceived from the point of view of what man appears in life and in death, it is impossible to

eliminate from the account the belief in the dualism of
human nature and the essential independence of matter
and spirit, the two elements of his nature.

(e) There is nothing very difficult in the phraseology
employed in the Old Testament for the parts of human
nature. The material part, spoken of in itself, is עָפָר, *dust*
from the ground; the spiritual part, spoken of by itself, is
נְשָׁמָה or רוּחַ, *breath* or *spirit*. When united to the spirit,
dust becomes *flesh*, בָּשָׂר, which may be defined *living*, or
ensouled matter; and spirit when united to the dust, now
flesh, becomes *soul*, נֶפֶשׁ, which may be called *incarnate
spirit*. There is no more ground for Delitzsch's opinion
that soul is a *tertium quid*, a substance distinct from spirit,
although of the same essence,[1] than there is for an opinion
that בָּשָׂר is something different from עָפָר, *dust*. The *body*
is hardly spoken of in the Old Testament, but the idea of
the body is *organised* flesh—flesh under a special *form*.
Hence the form being inalienable, the body will rise from
the dead: flesh and blood shall not inherit the kingdom of
God, but the body shall.

VII. THE DOCTRINE OF MAN—SIN.

1. *Sin—its Nature and Extent.*

In all the prophets the conception or doctrine of God,
of Jehovah the God of Israel, is the primary subject, while
the idea of *sin* is secondary, and the obverse, so to speak,
of the other idea. In Amos, whose conception of Jehovah
is that of a supreme righteous ruler of the world and
men, the idea of sin is generally *unrighteousness, injustice.*
In Hosea, whose idea of God is that He is unchanging
love, sin is the alienation of the heart of the community
from Him; while in Isaiah, who conceives Jehovah as
the sovereign Lord, the transcendent Holy One of Israel
the sin of man is *pride* and *insensibility* to the majesty

[1] See his *Biblical Psychology*, Clark's tr. p. 113 ff.—ED.

of Jehovah, who is a holy fire, consuming all that is unclean. In general, in all the prophets who speak of the sin of Israel, that sin is some form of ungodliness, some course of conduct, whether in worship or in life, having its source in false conceptions of Jehovah. Hosea traces all Israel's evil to this: there is no knowledge of God in the land. The prophetic statements regarding sin are mostly, if not always, particular, having reference to the conditions of society around them, and to Israel the people of God; they rarely rise to the expression of general principles, and do not make abstract statements in regard to sin or its principle. It is not of mankind, but of Israel that they speak, though they say of Israel what other parts of Scripture say of mankind. Israel had a period of innocency, succeeded by its fall, which ended in death: when Israel transgressed through Baal he died.

In the prophetic period, when, of course, already sin in these various forms had arisen and all the various conceptions of it had been formed, and nothing new appeared in regard to it except perhaps a deeper sense of it, and to some extent, as society became more complex, a more alarming spread and self-manifestation of it, all statements that we find regarding it will be altogether particular. There need be looked for no generalising of it or its principle. But this holds good also of the Mosaic and even of the pre-Mosaic period; and indeed in all the Old Testament, except in the single element of Christology, the development is not a development of objective truth so much as of subjective realising of the truth. It matters little, therefore, whether we carry on our inquiry in the region of the prophetic literature or in that of the earlier Scriptures.

On the question of *sin*, just as on other questions, we are not entitled to expect in the Old Testament anything more than popular language—not that of science. It may be made a question, indeed, whether what we call the language of common-sense, especially in regard to moral subjects, has not been largely formed on Scripture; whether

our habitual ways of thinking may not be largely due to its
influence on the human mind for so many ages ; and whether
thus the agreement of Scripture statements with what we
call common-sense and men's ordinary ways of thinking
be not a coincidence but an identity.   It becomes a
problem, indeed, seeing things are so, how far, if philosophy
should succeed in resolving the ordinary ideas of life into
other forms, simpler or higher, Scripture may be capable
of this transformation, or will necessarily undergo it.   No
doubt there is very inconsiderable cause for disquietude.
The philosophers have not yet made much way in this process of resolving our ideas into other forms, each generation
being fully occupied in bringing into sight the failures of
its predecessor.   In any case, when we speak of the infallibility of Scripture, we must remember it is not a
scientific or philosophic infallibility, but the infallibility, if
I may say so again, of common-sense.   And, however it
may be with questions of that kind, what we do find in
Scripture corresponds, particularly in all that concerns
morals and life, to what the unscientific mind thinks
and feels.

(1) Thus, to begin with, Scripture lays down at its
beginning the categories of *good* and *evil*: "God saw
everything which He had made, and behold it was very
good" (Gen. i. 31); "It is not good that the man should
be alone" (Gen. ii. 18).   There is *good* and there is
not good.   Probably in such passages 'good' means little
more than, in the one, *answering to its design,* and in the
other, *conducive to his well-being.*   'Good' in both cases
may be capable of being further resolved.   But here at
least is a general idea embracing particulars under it.
Opposite to good, Scripture places the category of 'evil.'
The two are so irreconcilable that they are named as the
two poles of human thought and experience : "Ye shall
be as God, knowing good and evil" (Gen. ii. 5).   The
existence of Elohim Himself is bounded by these two
walls.   And so radical is the distinction, that the prophet
Isaiah (v. 20) denounces as sunk to the last stage of

perversity those who in his age confounded the two:
"Woe unto them that call evil good, and good evil; that
put darkness for light, and light for darkness; that put
bitter for sweet, and sweet for bitter!"—although even
those did not question the distinction, but only inverted
the things, saying as another said, "Evil, be thou my
good!"

(2) This distinction then existing, we may inquire
whether in the terms employed to express it there be anything that suggests what the *principle* or *essence* of good or
evil is. This is perhaps hardly to be expected. We shall
find abundance of statements to the effect that particular
things are good and particular things evil; but probably
nothing more than popular or figurative expressions for
good and evil in themselves. Naturally, we need not look
for any support for theories regarding evil which have
sometimes been broached, as that evil is defect of being, as
if *omne esse* were *bonum*, and *non-esse* were equivalent to
malum; or that evil is the imperfection inherent in the
finite existence, and eliminated only by the passage of the
finite into the infinite; or that it is, if not identical with
that imperfection which is synonymous with the finite, a
necessary antithesis in thought and life looking to the
development of the creature, an obstacle to be overcome, a
drag to call out the energy of vitality, a resistance to develop
strength of will, an impulse to move it, and thus a factitious
but designed element in the universe. Thus, though called
an evil, and necessarily so thought of (otherwise it would
be inoperative), it becomes in reality a good, or at least
the means to good, and in itself nothing. Such reflections
naturally do not occur in Scripture. But Scripture uses
terms of a different kind, which do add something to our
knowledge.

The Old Testament has a variety of terms for moral
evil which, though they are figurative, tell us something of
how its nature was conceived. There is no language that
in ethical things has a richer vocabulary than the Hebrew
Its terms are all heaped together in certain passages, such

as Ps. xxxii. and li. God spake to Cain, when he was angry because of the rejection of his sacrifice, saying: "If thou doest well, hast thou not the pre-eminence? and if thou doest not well, *sin* (חַטָּאת) croucheth at the door" (Gen. iv. 7). Here *sin* is named for the first time, and personified as a wild beast crouching at the door, and ready to spring upon the man who gave any inlet to it. The word חָטָא, like the corresponding Greek word ἁμαρτάνω, means to *miss*, as the mark by a slinger, the way by a traveller, and even to find *wanting* in enumerating. There is the idea of a goal not reached, a mark not struck. Again, Cain, when in despair he surveys his fate under the curse of his hasty murder, cries out: "My sin (עֲוֹנִי) is greater than can be borne" (iv. 13). The root of *Avōn* is עָוָה, to *pervert* or make *crooked.* Evil is that which is not straight, or, as we say, right. There are several related ideas borrowed from the properties of matter and used for *good*, such as צֶדֶק, *right*, in the sense of linear straightness; יָשָׁר, *uprightness*, as I think, in the sense of superficial *smoothness*; with their antitheses as expressions of evil. And, of course, there are many similar ideas and antitheses; but they are all popular, and such as are the common property of mankind, as *sweet* and *bitter*, *clean* and *unclean*, *light* and *darkness*, etc. The commonest of all words for evil, רַע, perhaps expresses properly the *violence* of breaking, or the *noise* of it.

It may be admitted that something is gained by these terms. Sin is of the nature of failing to reach a mark; it is of the nature of what is crooked compared with what is straight; of the nature of what is uneven contrasted with what is smooth; of the nature of what is unclean compared with what is clean, and so on. The physical ideas are transferred to the moral sphere. There underlies all such transferences, of course, also the idea that that which hits the mark and does not fail is straight and not crooked, is clean and not unclean, is in that outer physical sphere 'good' and its opposite 'bad.' 'Good' in this physical sphere might perhaps be resolv-

able into 'convenient,' 'pleasant,' and suchlike; but it
would not follow that 'good' in the moral sphere, though
it might be resolvable also into other forms, was resolvable
into these same forms 'convenient,' 'pleasant,' and the
like. It is, of course, an old question whether we can observe in these physical expressions the genesis of the ideas
of good and evil, or whether what we see is the expression
in various forms of an antithesis inherent in the mind, and
merely clothing itself in these material forms. But such
questions as these belong to the general theory of morals.
They are hardly raised by anything in the Old Testament.

What Scripture exhibits to us is this : a national consciousness, or at least a consciousness in the highest minds
in the nation, filled with moral conceptions and sentiments
of the strongest and most pronounced description. These
conceptions and feelings are in lively operation. They
exist, and conduct is estimated by the public teachers
according to them. These moral conceptions and sentiments are neither in the process of formation—the national
mind had long advanced beyond such a moral stage; nor
are they yet in process of analysis or decomposition, as
among ourselves at present—the national mind had not
proceeded to any such state of reflection.

Two results follow from the use of the terms referred
to : *first*, the strong, accountable antitheses before remarked; and, *second*, something in the two sets of things
representing good and evil that shows not only that the
things are different, but that they differ with a difference
that is essential and universal, and that there is some effort
made by the mind to conceive good and evil as such.

The question, however, remains, whether in these
modes of speech we have the *genesis* of the ideas of good
and evil, or only the expressions in various forms of an
antithesis inherent in the mind, and merely clothing itself
in these material forms. In the physical sphere *bad* might
be resolved into *unfit* for the purpose desired, but *bad* in
the moral might not be so resolvable. In the physical
sphere the thing is *bad* because it is *crooked*. In the

moral sphere is it not named *crooked* because it is *bad*? Probably there is a circle out of which there is no escaping. But at least there is in such classes of words, as we have said, the evidence of a strong distinction and a strong effort to render it into external expression. And in any case the *origin* or *genesis* of such moral distinctions lies far behind Scripture. The ideas are formed and in full operation long ere any part of it was written.

From the fact that Scripture is always dealing with actual life and presenting rules for conduct or passing judgment upon it, no such thing as a *definition* of the nature of evil is to be expected. What we find is concrete designations of actual evil in various spheres. To this evil there is always something opposite in the particular sphere which is good or right, although this is often not expressed, but assumed as lying in the common mind. Scripture simply exhibits a consciousness in the nation filled with moral conceptions and sentiments, as we have said, which are in operation, but are not themselves ever subjected to analysis.

But the Old Testament is uncommonly rich in its ethical vocabulary. For example, in the sphere of the *Wisdom*, and opposed to it, there is a rich gradation of stages of evil. There is the פֶּתִי, the *simple*, the natural man, undeveloped almost in either direction; still without fixed principles of any kind, but with a natural inclination to evil, which may be easily worked upon so as to seduce him.

Next to that is the כְּסִיל, the man who is sensuous rather than sensual, fleshly in the milder sense—one still capable of good, though more naturally, from his dispositions, drawn to evil.

Then there is the fool who is rather negatively than positively evil, חֲסַר לֵב, ' destitute of mind,' who, from want of understanding rather than a sensuous propensity, becomes the victim of sin. In Job (ix. 12) this man is called a *hollow* man (אִ' נָבוּב). This person is rather defective in intellect, and is thus led to pass unwise and precipitate

14

judgments on providence, and in general on things above him. So he runs into impiety.

Then, further advanced is the fool actual and outright (נָבָל), or the ungodly man—*i.e.* the person who moves in a region altogether outside of the Wisdom, which embraces not only intellectual truth, but religious reverence.

And, last of all, there is the scorner (לֵץ), the speculatively wicked, who makes his ungodliness and folly matter of reflection, and consciously accepts it and adheres to it.

Again, in another region, that of truth, evil is falsehood, כָּזָב, or vanity, שָׁוְא, what has no reality in it ; or it is a *lie* in the concrete, שֶׁקֶר.

In the region of social morals and brotherly kindness evil is generally expressed by the word חָמָס *violence, i.e.* injurious conduct; and a higher stage is שֹׁד.

Again, in the region of theocratic holiness evil is what is *unclean,* טָמֵא, *profane,* חֹל, etc.

There are certain other words which express a somewhat different conception; for example, the word פֶּשַׁע, usually translated *transgress.* This is a mistranslation. The word rather means to *secede from, deficere,* to rebel against, and suggests a conception of sin which is of importance. It describes sin as a personal, voluntary act. It also implies something rebelled against, something which is of the nature of a superior or an authority. And, further, it implies the withdrawal of one's self by an act of self-assertion from under this superior or authority. The particular authority is not stated, for all these terms are general ; but the emphasis is laid upon the self-determination of the person, and his consequent withdrawal from the authority. The word could not be used of the withdrawal of an equal from co-operation with another equal. It is said that Israel ' rebelled against ' the house of David (1 Kings xii. 19). Again Jehovah says : " I have nourished and brought up children, and they have rebelled against Me " (Isa. i. 2); and frequently in this sense.

Now these words suggest two lines on which men thought of what we call *sin.* In the one case it was failure to hit, or to correspond to an objective standard ; in the other it was an attitude taken by a person in reference to another person who was his superior. In the former case 'sin' was the opposite of righteousness. Righteousness (צֶדֶק) is conformity to a standard. The man is righteous in any sphere of conduct or place, when his action or mind corresponds to the acknowledged standard in that sphere. The standards may, of course, be very various, differing in different spheres. In common life the standard [1] may be what is called custom, whether moral, or social, or consuetudinary law, which, as almost the only law in the East, is very strong. Or in a higher region, that of the Covenant, the standard may be the general and understood requirements of this covenant relation. Or in the widest sphere, that of general morals, the standard is the moral law, which all men carry in a more or less perfect form written on their minds. Usually the standard is perfectly well understood, and righteousness is conduct or thought corresponding to it, and sin is failure to conform to it. So in this sense God is called *righteous* when He acts in a way corresponding to the covenant relation. This relation would lead Him to forgive and save His people ; hence He is a *righteous* God and a *Saviour*, the two meaning very much the same thing.

No doubt the breach of the covenant by the people released God, so to speak, from obligations of a covenant kind ; and this caused the prophets to move a step further, going behind the historical covenant, and falling back on the nature of God which prompted Him to form the covenant. And His own nature becomes the standard of His action. What might be called the tone or disposition

---

[1] While the idea of *righteous* or *right* seems to imply a standard, it is doubtful whether, when moral judgments are passed, there is in general any reference in the mind to a standard. The mind passes judgment now from its own standard ; it has attained a condition, a way of thinking and feeling now habitual, from which, without any reference to an external standard, it passes judgment and calls a thing right or wrong. That this condition of mind may have resulted from external teaching may be true ; but this lies further back now when in Scripture we find men passing moral verdicts

of His being is a redemptive disposition towards men; for in creation He contemplated an orderly moral world, purposing the earth to be inhabited, and not subject to the devastations caused by evil in men or due to the cruelties and perversities of idolatry. And He becomes righteous in the highest sense when He acts according to this inherent saving disposition. Righteousness becomes the action corresponding to the nature of the one true God.

This conception of sin as a want of correspondence with an external objective standard has been adopted in the doctrinal books of the Presbyterian Churches of Scotland. There, sin is defined as "any want of conformity unto, or transgression of, the law of God." In this definition the words 'of God' must be very strongly emphasised in order to keep up the sense of relation to a living person; otherwise if sin be thought of as mere breach of an external law, we should fall into mere dead Phariseeism. It may be a question, indeed, whether the words 'the will of God' would not have been more in correspondence with the idea of Christianity than the 'law' of God. It may be certain that we shall never be able to dispense with the idea of *law*, but it is scarcely in the form of law that God commends His will to us in Christ. His will comes to us now not under the one complexion of legality, but coloured with the hues of all the motives that move men to obedience. The very idea of Christianity is the removal of the conception of legality, the mere bare uncoloured, absolute command, and to bring the whole nature of God, with all that is in it fitted to move us, into connection with all in our natures that is likely to be moved. And the operation of the Spirit on the mind is to make obedience or righteousness instinctive, and the spontaneous action of the mind itself. Perhaps it would be impossible rightly to define sin. Practically the will of God is a sufficient standard; that is, if you start with the idea of a standard outside of the mind. Although in point of fact there can never be any disagreement between the will or action of God and that which is right, the Old Testament touches occasionally upon a more general conception, implying that right has a self-existence, and is not a mere creation of the will of God: "Shall not the Judge of all the earth do right?" (Gen. xviii. 25). We should distinguish probably between *wrong* and *sin*, making *sin* the action in its reference to God.

And this is the Old Testament view in general: sin has reference to God the Person, not to His will or His law as formulated externally. And in this view the term פֶּשַׁע is a more accurate definition of it than חֲטָא, although the latter term is also used quite commonly of sinning against a person.

The prophets, being public teachers, occupy themselves with the life of the people. And the standard which they apply is just, as a rule, the covenant relation, *i.e.* the Decalogue. Hence Israel's sin is usually of two kinds: either *forsaking* of Jehovah, God of Israel, or social *wrong-doing* of the members of the covenant people to one another. But what gives its meaning to all they say is their vivid religious conception of Jehovah as a person in immediate relation to the people. Sin is not a want of conformity to the law of Jehovah, so much as a defection from Himself, the living authority, in the closest relation to them, and appealing to them both directly by His prophets and in all the gracious turning-points of their history. The prophets speak directly from Jehovah; they appeal little to external law. Even external law was always living; it was Jehovah speaking. And this consciousness of Jehovah's presence made all sins to be actions directly done against Him. So it is, *e.g.*, in Joseph's exclamation, "How then can I do this great wickedness, and sin against God?" (Gen. xxxix. 9). And the Psalmist, although confessing wrong against his fellow-men, says: "Against Thee, Thee only, have I sinned" (Ps. li. 4).

This idea of sin, as something done directly against a person, naturally led to a deepening of the conception of it. For a person cannot be obeyed apart from some relation to him of the affections And as the party obeying was the people, this proper relation of the affections was difficult to secure. And this difficulty led, no doubt, to that singular habit of personifying the community which we observe in Hosea and the last chapters of Isaiah. The prophets thus created out of the community an ideal individual, from whom they demand the obedience of affection; and they so manipulate this idea as to reach the profoundest conceptions. Yet, perhaps, so long as the prophets began with the community and descended from it to the individual, thinking of the individual only as sharing in the general feelings of the whole, the deepest idea, whether of sin or of righteousness, could not be reached. They had difficulty in reaching a true ethical foundation for want of a true ethical unit to start with.

It was naturally the progress of events in God's providence that opened the way to further conceptions. The actual destruction of the State put an end, for the time at least, to the relation of Jehovah to the community; the community no more existed. Yet Jehovah and His purposes of grace remained. The prophets and people were thus thrown upon the future. That had happened to them which happened to the disciples afterwards, and which our Lord said was good for them: "It is expedient for you that I go away" (John xvi. 7). The life of prophets and people became one of faith absolutely. And hence the clarification of their religious ideas, and the religious purity and spiritual splendour of the ideal constructions of the future kingdom of Jehovah which are due to the period of the Exile. The destruction of the State as a kingdom of God made religion necessarily, so far as it was real, a thing of the individual mind. It had, of course, been this really at all times. Yet the kingdom of the Lord had a visible form before, which now was lost. And, so far as religion lived, it lived only in the individual mind, and as a spiritual thing; for in a foreign land external service of Jehovah was impossible. The Sabbath, as the token of His covenant, could be kept, and was the more tenaciously clung to. The Lord could

be served in mind; and Jeremiah exhorts the people in
Babylon to lead quiet and peaceable lives, and to pray
to the Lord in behalf of the country that sheltered them.
The transition to a spiritual religion was in point of fact
effected.

With all this, however, the inextinguishable hope
remained of a Return and a reconstruction of Jehovah's
kingdom on more enduring foundations. The history of
the past revealed the cause of former failures. It was due
partly just to the nature of the Old Covenant, which was
a covenant with the people in a mass—with them as a
people. Its virtue descended down to the individual from
the whole. But now this splendid fabric was shattered
in pieces, and its only enduring elements, the individuals,
lay scattered about. It was an imposing idea, that of the
Old Covenant, the idea of a religious State, a State all the
functions of which should be arteries and channels for conveying religious truth and expressing service of God. It
is an ideal which has attracted men in all ages, and an
ideal which the Old Testament never gives up—least of all
such prophets as Jeremiah and the Second Isaiah. If
these prophets differ from earlier prophets, it is not in their
ideal, but in the way necessary to reach it. The true
kingdom of God cannot be established by a lump operation
like that of the Exodus. It cannot be called into existence
by a stroke of the magician's wand—even if the wand be
in the hand of God. For it consists in making godly
human minds, and gathering them together till mankind is
gathered; and human minds can be made godly only by
operations that correspond to the nature and laws of the
human mind.

Hence the prophets of this age set themselves to re-
construct on opposite principles from those formerly used.
They begin with the individuals. The broken fragments
of the old house of God were lying all about, as individual
stones. And they gather these up, putting them together
one by one: "I will take you one of a city, and two of
a tribe, and I will bring you to Zion" (Jer. iii. 14). The

need, not of a reformation, but of a fundamental regeneration, is clear to the prophet: "Break up the fallow
ground, and sow not among thorns. Circumcise yourselves to the Lord, and take away the foreskins of your
heart, ye men of Judah and inhabitants of Jerusalem"
(iv. 3, 4). And conformable to this fundamental necessity
is Jeremiah's conception of Jehovah's work, for he is well
aware that appeals to men to regenerate themselves are
vain, he asks : " Can the Ethiopian change his skin, or the
leopard his spots ? " (xiii. 23). Therefore the Lord Himself
will make a new covenant. He " will put His law in
men's inward parts, and write it in their hearts ; and they
shall all know Him, and He will remember their sins no
more " (xxxi. 33). The ethical unit becomes the individual
mind, and sin and righteousness become matters of the
relation of the personal mind to God.

The Exile might appear to us the greatest disaster
that could befall the kingdom of God. Yet it no doubt
helped to clarify the minds of the people in regard to the
religion of Jehovah, enabling them to see that it did not
perish though its external form came to nought. And
though not interfering with the great hope of a community
to arise in the future as the kingdom of the Lord, yet it
permitted and caused the individual to feel his independence,
and to understand that religion was a thing between him
and God immediately. The clear recognition and expression of this Christian truth was greatly helped by the
destruction of the State, and many of the most profound
expressions of personal religion in the Psalter very probably
are not anterior to this period.

It is not necessary, however, to say very much of the
Old Testament doctrine of sin. The anthropology of the
Old Testament is a reflection of its theology : the sense
or thought of sin corresponds to the conception and fear
of Jehovah. And as the thought of the spirituality and
purity of Jehovah rose, so did the sense of what was
required of man to correspond to Him and be in fellowship with Him ; and therefore the sense of sin deepened.

Consequently, the development is not so much intellectual or in ideas, as in a tendency to inwardness, to look less at the mere external actions than at the mind of the actor. But the Old Testament teaching regarding sin does not differ from that of the New Testament. It teaches, first, that all individual men are sinners. Second, the sinfulness of each individual is not an isolated thing, but is an instance of the general fact that mankind is sinful. And, thirdly, the sin of man can be taken away only by the forgiveness of Jehovah: "Who is a God like unto Thee, pardoning iniquity?" (Mic. vii. 18). This forgiveness is of His mercy, and in the latter age a New Covenant will be extended to all His people: their sins He will remember no more. He will be their God, and they shall be His people. As to the first point, testimonies need not be multiplied: "If Thou shouldst mark iniquity, who could stand?" (Ps. cxxx. 3). "Before Thee no flesh living is righteous" (Ps. cxliii. 2). "There is no man that sinneth not" (1 Kings viii. 46).

It might be worth while, however, to look for a moment at the second point, with the view of inquiring how far the Old Testament goes in regard to the sinfulness of mankind, and the connection of the individual with the race. That large numbers of mankind may be taken together and form a unity in many ways, whether for action on their own part or for treatment on the part of God, is manifest. The human race is not a number of atoms having no connection; neither to our eye, at least, does it seem a fluid pressing equally in all directions, and conveying impressions received over its whole mass. It is very probable that it is this, although the influence communicated cannot be traced by us beyond a certain circle. But just as Achan's sin affected, in God's estimate, the whole camp of Israel, the sin of any individual may seem to Him to affect the whole race of mankind.

The view of the Scripture writers is sometimes not so broad. The penitent in Ps. li. exclaims: "Behold, I was shapen in iniquity, and in sin did my mother conceive

me." His evil was so far at least hereditary. The prophet
Isaiah exclaimed : "Woe is me! for I am undone; for I
am a man of unclean lips, and I dwell among a people
of unclean lips" (chap. vi. 5). He shared in the sinfulness
of his people. And not to stop short of the most general,
Job asks in reference to mankind : " Can a clean come out
of an unclean ? There is not one" (xiv. 4). And his
opponent Eliphaz asks : "Shall man be righteous with
God ? shall man be pure with his Maker ?" (chap. iv. 17).
So the Apostle Paul regards all sins among mankind as
but the development, the details, of the original παράπτωμα
of Adam. All sin is one sin of the race. The unity of
the race is a consistent doctrine of the Old Testament.
It was האדם, man, when created as a single individual. It
spread over the earth and was still האדם, man. It was
כל בשר, all flesh, that had corrupted its way before the Flood.
Mankind is, as a whole, corrupt ; and, corresponding to this,
each individual is unclean. Smaller sections of it, as
families, nations, are also sinful, and he that is born in
the one, or belongs to the other, shares the sinfulness.

As we have seen, the Old Testament does not ascribe
any sinfulness to the flesh. It often ascribes weakness
and feebleness to the flesh, i.e. to man as a creature of
flesh, and deprecates God's rigid judgment of man for this
reason : "Man that is born of woman is of few days, and
full of trouble : . . . and dost Thou open Thine eyes upon
such a one, and bringest me into judgment with Thee ?"
(Job xiv. 1–3). But the feebleness is not directly moral.
Though teaching that evil is inherited, it does not appear
to speculate upon a condition of the nature of the individual prior to his own voluntary acts ; though it seems
occasionally to recognise what is technically called habit,
as when Jeremiah says : "The heart is deceitful above all
things, and desperately wicked" (xvii. 9). It has not yet
a general doctrine of human nature distinct from the
personal will, or from the concrete instance of the nature
as it appears in the individual.

Probably the Old Testament does not go the length

of offering any rationale of the fact that each individual is sinful, beyond connecting him with a sinful whole. The doctrine of *imputation* is a moral rationale of the sinful condition of the individual when he comes into existence, and prior to his own acts. And certain things in the Old Testament have been fixed upon as sustaining that doctrine. It is doubtful, however, if the Old Testament offers anything beyond just the historical facts that Adam fell from righteousness, and that we observe his descendants universally sinful, as it is said: "The wickedness of mankind became great upon the earth" (Gen. vi. 5). And God repented that He had made mankind; and He resolved to destroy mankind; and then He determined no more to destroy mankind, though the imagination of the heart of mankind was only evil from its youth. Passages like that in the law: "visiting the iniquity of the fathers upon the children unto the third and fourth generation of them that hate Him" (Ex. xx. 5), and occurrences like the destruction of the whole dependents and family of Korah along with him (Num. xvi.), are usually cited as analogies. They seem, however, to fail just at the point where the analogy is wanted. They afford instances of persons, themselves innocent of a particular sin, suffering from their connection with the person guilty of the sin. But, of course, the whole life of mankind is full of instances of this. The point of the doctrine of imputation, so far as it is a moral or judicial explanation of the sinfulness of all individuals of mankind, lies in the idea that Adam was the legal representative of all the individuals of the race, each of whom, therefore, is held guilty of Adam's sin, and his corrupt nature is due to his own offence of which he was guilty in his representative. This is the moral side. The individual's physical connection with Adam is only the channel through which this moral law takes effect. It is probable, however, that the Old Testament presents merely the physical unity, without yet exhibiting any principle.

The question is of interest as to what was the idea in

the Old Testament when it was said that the iniquities of
the fathers were visited upon the children, or that the
fathers ate sour grapes, and the children's teeth are set on
edge (Jer. xxxi. 29); or in such a case as that of Korah
and his children and dependents.   The Old Testament
idea does not appear to have been the idea of *representation*.   The idea of representation implies that the
descendants are held guilty of the representative's act.
There is no sign of this idea.   The conception was rather
this.   The father or head was alone had in view.   The
children or dependents were embraced in him; they were
his, were part of him.   When the chastisement embraced
them it was only in order completely to comprehend him;
when it pursued his descendants, it was really still pursuing
him in his descendants.   That is, as yet the father or head
alone was thought of, the place or right of the children or
dependents as independent individuals was not adverted to.
In short, the conception was really the same kind of conception as that according to which the covenant of Jehovah
was with the nation as a whole.   That this was the idea
appears from a passage in Job xxi. 17–20.   Disputing
with his friends, who maintained that a man was always
chastised for his sins, and that great sufferings were proofs
of great sins, Job drew attention to the fact that oftentimes the sinner escaped all punishment.   How often is
the candle of the wicked put out?   There is no such
universal law.   To which his friends replied: " God layeth
up his iniquity for his children."   If he escapes himself, his
children suffer.   To which Job replies: " Let his own
eyes see his destruction : for what concern has he in his
house after him ? "   The argument of both parties implies
that the visitation of the father's sins upon the children
was regarded as a punishment of the father.   And the
argument of Job is that as such it fails; the father
escapes, for he has no concern in his house after him, and
no knowledge of it.

The argument of Job does not lead him to find fault
with the supposed providential law on the score of its

injustice; he argues that it is no case of punishing the actual sinner. It is at once perceived that Job's argument implies that to his mind the father and the children are distinct,—the children are independent persons,—and what touches them does not touch the father.

Of course, the proverb referred to above is a way of expressing the idea that the calamities of the end of the State and the Exile were due to the sins of former generations—the fathers, perhaps the generation under Manasseh. In the prophets Jeremiah and Ezekiel, however, the supposed providential law is repudiated on account of its injustice. Jeremiah touches the question lightly, saying merely that the law, the fathers ate sour grapes, and the children's teeth are set on edge, shall no more prevail in the new dispensation: he that eats sour grapes, his own teeth shall be set on edge. But Ezekiel enters into the question fully. He sets it forth in every possible form, especially in chaps. xiv. and xviii., of which the sum is this: 'If a righteous man have an impenitent son, the son will not be saved by his father's righteousness: he shall surely die. And if a sinful father beget an obedient son, the son shall not die for his father's iniquity; he shall as surely live as his father shall die. If a once righteous man turn away from his righteousness . . . his righteousness shall not be remembered; in his sin that he has sinned, he shall die. And again, if a wicked man turn away from his sins and do that which is right, he shall live. . . . *All* souls are mine, saith the Lord; as the soul of the father, so also the soul of the son is mine: the soul that sinneth it shall die. . . . The son shall not bear the iniquity of the father, neither shall the father bear the iniquity of the son. . . Therefore I will judge you, O house of Israel, every man according to his ways.'

The teaching of the prophet is intended, first of all, to comfort his brethren of the Exile. They thought they were under the pressure of an iron law, suffering for the sins of their fathers, enduring a penalty which must be exhausted, whatever their own state of mind and conduct might be. And they stood in despair before this spectre of an irreversible destiny: "Our transgressions and our sins be upon us, and we pine away in them, how then should we live? Say unto them, As I live, saith the Lord, I have no pleasure in the death of him that dieth" (Ezek. xxxiii. 10, 11). But the prophet takes occasion to go very much further, and to teach the freedom and the responsibility immediately to God of the individual—not only his freedom from all consequences of the actions of others, but also his freedom within the limits of his own life. No man, as regards his relation to God, is the victim of a destiny outside of him; and no man is the victim of a destiny created by his own past life. Before God, and in relation to Him, each man is a free moral agent, at liberty to determine; and, as he is at liberty to determine, so the duty of determining lies upon him and cannot be shifted.

This is all the doctrine the prophet is interested in teaching. Modern writers have ridiculed this teaching of Ezekiel, as if he imagined that human life was not a continuous thing, but could be cut up into sections having no moral dependence on one another; and that God treated a man just according to the particular frame in which He found him at the moment, with no regard to his past. But this hardly does the prophet justice. To understand him we must look at his circumstances, the ban under which the people were lying, due to the past, and the former conceptions prevailing among the people. His teaching is part of the new sense of the freedom of the individual, and the worth and place of the single person, which was due to this age. This truth is a general one. We know, indeed, how near external circumstances come towards creating a destiny for many men; and we also know how each is in danger of forging a destiny for himself in the future by his life in the past. Yet in spite of all this the truth which the prophet was interested in teaching remains true—men have a personal relation to God which is not conditioned by the acts of others; and there is a personality in each which can be distinguished in some measure from his own nature; and however much his past may influence his nature, and even his personality, yet the personality can take up a new position towards God, and thus gradually overcome even the evil of its own nature.

This is what the prophet was interested in teaching. It is too true that no man can sin without the sin reacting upon his nature, leaving an imprint upon it, and in some way enfeebling it. And thus as by a law every man bears his own sin. Yet can this be said to be the only sense in which sin might have to be borne? Are there not a multitude of other ways in which we might have to bear sin, besides this reflex influence of sin on the nature? And are we not, when forgiven sin by God, freed from having to bear it in these other ways?

It is true that His forgiveness does not in itself free us from having to bear it in this reflex way. But it would perhaps be a mistake to suppose the laws of mind to have the same kind of rigidity as physical laws. For the moral nature is of such a sort that it can draw in evil itself into the category of remedial influences, and thus our very moral enfeeblement becomes a means of causing us to have more constant recourse to the strength administered by God. St. Paul gloried in his infirmity, because God's strength was made perfect in his weakness (2 Cor. xii. 9). And so even with another inevitable evil consequence of sin, to wit, remorse and its pain—the moral nature is capable of drawing that, too, in among things that are remedial, just as was the case with St. Paul's remorse that he persecuted the Church of God. This sense of remorse magnified to him the mercy of God—" that in me primarily, above all others, He might show His long-suffering " (1 Tim. i. 16). And in other ways. So that even the effects of our past evil may be drawn in among the remedial measures that minister to our general godliness.

Of course, there are two questions: (1) the relation of the individual personality to God—what might be called the spiritual relation; (2) the external history or life of the individual person. Ezekiel is mainly interested in the first. But he may not yet have disentangled the two questions from one another. The point was never clearly understood in Israel. It was felt that the second question must always be resolved in terms of the first—felicity or adversity. So far as the prophet Ezekiel is concerned, he is concerned mainly with the spiritual relation of the individual to God. The outer relation he teaches will correspond to this. His feeling is that he is standing before a new age, when the spiritual relation will realise itself also visibly; the righteous shall 'live,' life being that which we call life in the final state.

From the Old Testament, then, so much can be established, namely:

First, that the human race is in God's estimation a unity—as much so now as it was when it was summed up in Adam, whose acts, of course, were the acts of humanity.

Second, that sin is as much a unity as humanity, and that as the one man developed into millions, the one sin multiplied into millions of sinful acts; but the παράπτωμα of Adam was what all the while abounded. Humanity is one, its sin is one.

Third, that thus when any one sins, it is humanity that sins; it, which is one, propagates its one sin. But, of course, that does not take away from the other truth that the individual sinner is guilty of his individual act. The individual Adam was guilty of his sin.

Fourth, the sin of Adam being the sin of the race, the displeasure of God against the race followed, and the penalty. So when any one in the race sins, it is a manifestation of the sin of the race, and will be chastised upon the race. The chastisement may not extend over all the race, but only perhaps over some part, *i.e.* not over all the individuals. But it will extend, in general, over many more than are personally guilty. It is a chastisement of the race. The persons chastised are not as individuals held guilty of the sinful acts. But the unity which we know as humanity is held guilty of them. The act was an expression of the sin of the world, and it calls down a judgment on the world.

Fifth, of course, the person who committed the sin is as an individual guilty of the sin, and the judgment which falls on him falls on him as an individual sinner. But is there not a twofold treatment of the human race, a treatment of it as a unity, each individual being part of it and acting as part, and therefore for the whole, and the consequences of his acts falling upon the whole; and a treatment of it as individuals, when the individual is dealt with for himself?

The further conclusion to which the passages of the Old Testament lead us are these: *first*, that what is specifically called *original sin* is taught there very distinctly, *i.e.* "that corruption of man's whole nature which is commonly called original sin," and that it is also taught that this sin is inherited; *second*, that no explanation is given in the Old Testament of the rationale of this inherited corruption beyond the assumption that the race is a unity, and each member of the race is sinful because the race is sinful. In other words, in conformity with the Old Testament point of view the individual man is less referred to than the race.

The question, What is the explanation of an individual corrupt before any voluntary act of his own? does not seem raised in the Old Testament. When raised, as it has very much been, various answers have been propounded to it. Some, *e.g.*, Julius Müller in his work on *The Christian Doctrine of Sin*, have had recourse to a pre-existent state to explain it. Müller feels that such a thing needs explanation; punishment implies antecedent guilt. This guilt must have been contracted antecedently to this life, for the punishment is seen in the earliest stages of the present state of existence. It must have been contracted, therefore, he thinks, in a previous condition of existence.

The same difficulty has been felt by all thinkers. And an explanation somewhat similar is the generally accepted one among orthodox theologians. Müller teaches an actual pre-existence. They teach a legal pre-existence of the individual—a pre-existence in the person of one who represented them, and for whose acts they are responsible, and the consequences of whose acts they each bear. I think this way of *explaining* the difficulty does not occur in the Old Testament, for the *difficulty* does not seem to occur there. There is, indeed, very much in the way of dealing with men which this way of explanation fastens upon as favourable to itself. Yet it is doubtful if there be anything really favourable. For every case seems to differ just in the point where it ought to agree. The Old Testament shows innumerable cases of men who suffer for the sins of others, without, however, these sins being imputed to them in any other sense than this, that they do suffer for them. But this theory explains their suffering by the previous imputation of the guilt of the sin. In the Old Testament the imputation of sin and the suffering of its consequences are the same thing—it is nowhere more than a being involved in the consequences of the sin; in this theory imputation of the sin is distinct from the suffering of its consequences, antecedent to it, and the cause of it. In the Old Testament the explanation of the suffering is the unity of man, or the unity of a family, or the unity of a nation, or, at least, some piece of humanity which is an organism; in this theory the explanation is the legal representation by one of all those individuals who suffer on account of him. The two theories proceed on different conceptions of humanity.

I do not know that the Old Testament raises the question which is discussed under the terms *Creationism* and *Traducianism, i.e.* the question whether the soul of each individual be a work directly of the Divine hand or be propagated like the body. But the answer on Old Testament ground would, I think, certainly be in favour of Traducianism,—although the Old Testament way of representing all results as immediate effects of the Divine activity might cause a phraseology distinctly creational

But such a phraseology would apply to the body as well as the soul. It may perhaps be true that God is represented as the Father of spirits oftener than the Creator directly of the body; but that arises from the greater similarity of the spirit to God, and the natural referring of it, therefore, immediately to Him. But unquestionably Scripture represents God as forming the body directly, *e.g.* in Ps. cxxxix., as well as the soul.

And if the general inference from the Old Testament would be in favour of Traducianism there are some special facts that go in the same direction. We notice three, namely:

1. This very doctrine of inherited sin, so distinctly an Old Testament doctrine.

2. The kind of representation employed when the creation of woman is described. She is taken out of man; there was no breathing into her nostrils of the breath of life: in body and soul she is of the man.[1]

3. The way of looking at things which appears in the history of creation in general. It had an absolute end in man. God rested from all His works which He had made in creation. Henceforth creative activity ceased. In the one man was *created* all the race—it is but a development of him.

2. *The Consciousness of Sin.*

We have noticed the terms expressing the idea of *sin* in Israel. Of these the term פֶּשַׁע perhaps was the one

---

[1] It is certainly to be expected that Scripture will not stop short of supplying some rationale of the fact that men are born with a propensity to depravity, which must be regarded as a disability and evil with which each is afflicted, and of which there must be some explanation. It may be the case that the Old Testament does not give any explanation further than insisting upon the unity of the race, and indicating that men receive from their parents the corrupt nature they possess, and that this process of reception mounts up to Adam. The expectation is raised that Scripture subsequent to the Old Testament will analyse this unity of the race, and that the analysis will make it appear not to be a physical unity, but a moral one.

that went most to the root of the conception, that sin was defection from God.

The prophets, being practical teachers, naturally refer to sin as it shows itself in the life of the people. They have no occasion to speculate on its origin, or on its fundamental idea. They regard it as universal. Even Isaiah says of himself, " I am a man of unclean lips." And if we observe a progress in their ideas of it, it is in the direction of a more inward view of it. They direct attention more to the state of mind which the external sinful act implies.[1]

It was less easy for them, dealing with the community, to reach the profoundest thoughts of it. In Amos, the sins mentioned are chiefly those of men against men. But Hosea, through his profound personification of the community as the spouse of Jehovah, is enabled to exhibit the state of the heart of the people, its alienation from the Lord. No prophet has anything higher to say than what he says, either on the side of Jehovah or on that of the people. For, as Jehovah's mind toward the community is that of love, the mind of the community has turned away from Him in alienation of affection and consequent outward sin. Here it is no more external acts on either side that are thought of by the prophet. It is the relation of two minds, mind and mind; love on Jehovah's part, and alienation of affection on the part of the community. These ideas which Hosea struck run more or less through all the prophets.

In Isaiah we look for, and, of course, find, an independent view. His thought of God is not that of Hosea, neither, therefore, is his idea of sin the same. To him Jehovah is the Sovereign, *Kadosh*, the transcendent God, who, however, contradiction as it may seem, is the *Kedosh*

---

[1] It is probable that sins of ignorance were properly such offences as were inevitable, owing to the limitations and frailties of the human mind. The idea is expressed accurately in Ezek. xlv. 20, where the sin-offering is made "for every one that erreth, and for him that is simple"—that is, for inadvertent breaches of law due to the limitations of the human mind in general, or to the natural slowness of individuals. But it was necessary in practice to extend the idea over some offences scarcely coming under it originally.

Yisrael, the holy One of Israel,—who, as the Second Isaiah
expresses it, inhabits eternity and dwells "in the high and
holy place with him also that is of a contrite and humble
spirit" (lvii. 15). Corresponding to his idea of God is
his idea of sin in man. This idea is equally inward with
that of Hosea, but it has another complexion. Sin is
pride. Hence Jehovah has a day against every one that
is proud and lofty—"the lofty looks of man shall be
humbled, and the haughtiness of man shall be bowed down,
and the Lord alone shall be exalted in that day" (ii. 11).
He has nourished and brought up children, and they have
rebelled against Him (chap. i.). It is but another aspect
of this idea when he calls their sin want of faith: "If ye
will not believe, ye shall not be established" (vii. 9). And
but another aspect of it still, when he charges the people
with insensibility to the Divine; people whose hearts were
'fat,' and their ears heavy, and their eyes 'shut' (vi. 10).
Throughout the prophets, sin is estimated in its relation
to Jehovah, and each prophet's conception of it varies with
his conception of Jehovah. Yet though it was difficult
to reach so inward a conception of sin, when the community was the moral subject or unit, it is evident from
these expressions of Isaiah and Hosea how profoundly
inward their ideas were, and how far from true it is to
say that they refer only to external acts, and take no note
of the condition of the mind or affections. "They draw
near unto Me with their lips, but their heart is far from
Me" (Isa. xxix. 13).

God in His providence broke up the outward form of
the community. It ceased to be the kingdom of God.
It was no more a question of its relation as a community
to Jehovah, and of external conduct as a community. The
factors now became different. They were Jehovah and the
individuals. The national existence was interrupted, the
national service in a foreign land was impracticable. There
was nothing now between the single personal heart and the
Lord. It may even seem a strong thing to say, but this event,
the breaking up of the national existence, was the greatest

step, next to the calling of Israel, towards Christianity.
It revolutionised men's conception of religion.   It made
it, as no doubt it had to some extent been always, a thing
exclusively personal. No doubt the idea of the community
remained an idea. It is this idea that plays so splendid a
rôle in the second half of Isaiah, under the name of the
Servant of the Lord—the idea, which was not merely an
idea, but had a nucleus of godly individuals, especially in
Babylon, to which it attached itself; over which, if I can
say so, it hung like a bright canopy, a heavenly mirage
reflected from the kernel of the people on earth.   This
ideal Israel could not die; so far from dying, it possessed,
in Jehovah's calling of it and holding it fast by the right
hand of His righteousness, a vitality which should yet impart life to all the scattered fragments of the people, and
reconstitute them as out of the grave into a new nation.
But ere that time nothing held them together except their
individual faith.

It is at this point that Jeremiah stands, who despairs
of the community as it now is, as all the prophets do,
but who looks forward to a new Church of God made
up of members, gathered together one to one by an
operation of Jehovah with each.   Hence Jeremiah's idea
of sin is not only national, but profoundly personal:
"The heart is deceitful above all things, and desperately
wicked" (xvii. 9); "this people hath a revolting and a
rebellious heart" (v. 23); the house of Israel are "uncircumcised in heart" (ix. 26); "I will give them a heart
to know Me" (xxiv. 7); "Blessed is the man that trusteth
in the Lord . . . I, the Lord, search the heart, I try the
reins" (xvii. 7, 10); "I will write . . . My law upon their
heart" (xxxi. 33).   And the reconstruction which such a
prophet looks forward to, or which is looked forward to in
the second half of Isaiah, is, so far as its moral and religious
character goes, nothing short of, and nothing else than,
Christianity.   These prophets expect it soon.   They couple
it with the restoration from exile; they bring it down upon
a condition of the world externally resembling that in

their own day. We have to distinguish between their religious thoughts themselves and their ideal reconstructions of the external world. These were constructions which, living in that ancient world, they had to make ; for no other materials were at their hand. But the ideas which they expressed through their great fabrics of imagination abide, the inheritance of all the ages. They built on the true foundation gold, silver, precious stones. Time wastes even these costly but earthly fabrics, and we, as we live age after age, have to replace them with materials to serve our use, which shall probably decay too, and future generations will have to body out the eternal ideas in other materials. But the ideas *are* eternal.

Here we see that, in the sphere of religion, sin is idolatry, or service of Jehovah of a kind that profaned His holy name ; that, in the sphere of speech, truth is right-eousness, and sin *falsehood* ; that, in the sphere of civil life, justice is righteousness, and sin is *injustice*, want of con-sideration, also evil speaking, and much else ; and that, in the sphere of the mind of man, sin is *want of sincerity*, either towards God or towards men, *guile* ; *purity*, the opposite to this, being purity of heart, simplicity, openness, genuineness. The Old Testament teaching regarding sin does not differ from the teaching in the New Testament, though probably there is less approach towards generalis-ing and to statement in the form of categories. The Old Testament is so entirely of a practically religious nature, that deductions of a general kind are not quite easy to make.

Perhaps we acquire a better idea of the consciousness of sin in the mind of Old Testament saints from some continuous passages than by any induction based on individual terms. And there is no more remarkable picture of the consciousness of sin in Israel than that shown in Ps. li. The tradition preserved in the heading of the Psalm is that it is by David. Modern writers are inclined to bring it lower down. For our present purpose this question is not of importance. We learn more from such a picture of the feelings of an individual mind in regard to the thoughts of sin in Israel than we could from any investigation into the meaning of the mere terms by which sin is described. My impression of the Psalm is that it contains only a single prayer, namely, that for forgiveness. The cry, "Create in me a clean heart," is not a prayer for what we call renewal. The 'heart' is the conscience; and the prayer is that God would by one act of forgiving grace create, bring into being, for this penitent a clean conscience, on which lay no blot either to his feeling or to God's eye.

The main points are these. The petitioner begins his prayer with what we might call an outburst of feeling: "*Pity me, O God.*" The cry has been long repressed; his feelings have chafed behind his closed lips, demanding an outlet; but he has stubbornly kept silence. At last they break through like confined waters—"*Pity me, O God, according to thy loving-kindness*"; then comes a laying bare of his consciousness to support his cry for pity.

First, he utters such expressions as these, "cleanse me," "wash me," "sprinkle me with hyssop, and I shall be clean." Perhaps the Psalmist has here before his mind what we call the *pollution* of sin, its evilness in itself. It is of the nature of a stain on the nature of man, apart from its consequences, and without bringing in subsidiary ideas of its relation to God and of its liability to punishment. And when he speaks of washing him thoroughly, he perhaps has in his mind the idea of a cloth into which stains have entered and have dyed its very tissues; just as in the words 'cleanse me' he refers to the disease of leprosy, a disease that more than any other almost is constitutional, and, though appearing externally, pervades the whole body. And very beautiful is the contrast which he would present when forgiven and purified: "I shall be whiter than the snow." Still I should not lay much stress on this, because such terms as 'wash,' etc., are all used of forgiveness.

Second, he says: "Behold, I was shapen in iniquity; and in sin did my mother conceive me." This sin is inherited; not he alone, but all about him are sinful. The Psalmist does not plead this as an extenuation of his act, but rather as an aggravation of his condition. It deepens the darkness of his state which he presents before the eye of God, and is an intensification of his plea for 'pity.' In opposition to this condition of his he places what he knows to be the moral desire of God: "Thou desirest truth in the inward parts: in the hidden part make me to know wisdom." He supports his prayer, both by the desperate condition of nature and conduct in which he is himself, and by what he knows to be the gracious desire of God, that no creature of His hand should remain, or be, in such a condition.

Third, he uses these expressions: "Against Thee, Thee only, have I sinned. Hide Thy face from my sin." This is an additional idea—sin is against God. The words *against Thee only* mean *against Thee, even Thee*; as: "I will make mention of Thy righteousness, of Thine only," that is, *even of Thine* (Ps. lxxi. 16). The words express the judgment of the conscience regarding sin; it is against God. No doubt you might confirm this judgment by reflection. All sins are against God, for God is present in all the laws that regulate society; when we offend against men, it is against Him in truth that we are impinging. He is behind all phenomena; He is in every brother man whom we meet. Yet this is scarcely before the Psalmist. The words are the expression of conscience, which, when it opens its eye, always beholds God, often beholds nothing but God. The world is empty, containing but the sinner and God. The Psalmist feels all else disappear, and there is only the full, luminous face of God bearing down upon him.

Fourth, he uses such phrases as: "Cast me not from Thy presence"; "Take not thy holy Spirit from me," and the like. The two expressions mean much the same. God in the world is the Spirit of God. The holy Spirit is the name for all godly aspirations, as well as for the cause of them; it is that quickened human spirit which strives after God, and it is that Divine moving which causes it to strive, and it is that God even after whom there is the strife. Its taking away would leave the soul without any-thing of all this. And the Psalmist by his prayer seems to imply that he had felt himself as if on the brink of this abyss—his sin seemed to him to carry in it the possibility of this consequence, when he should be without God in the world.

These are some of the thoughts of sin in the mind of this penitent, causing him to cry, *Pity me*. Not less pro-found is his concluding petition : " Restore to me the joy of Thy salvation"; "then will I teach transgressors Thy ways"; "Open Thou my lips; and my mouth shall show forth Thy praise." This is still a prayer for forgiveness; but it contains an outlook into the Psalmist's future. The words express the Psalmist's idea of that which should lie at the basis of all life, of any life—the sense of forgiveness. Of course, he does not mean by opening his lips, giving him boldness after his great sin to come before men with ex-hortations, who might reply to him: Physician, heal thy-self. It is not courage to speak, but a theme of which to speak to men that he desires. There is a singular sincerity in his mood. He cannot, in speaking to men, go beyond what he has himself experienced. His words are : " Blot out my transgressions; then will I teach transgressors Thy ways "—Thy way in forgiving. " Open Thou my lips; then shall my mouth show forth Thy praise." "Who is a God like unto Thee, pardoning iniquity ? " By " open my lips " he means " enable me to speak," *i.e.* through imparting to him the sense of forgiveness.

These are some of the thoughts of sin—its pollution; its being inherited; its being in truth, whatever form it may have outwardly, against God; its tendency to encroach upon and swallow up the moral lights of the soul, till all that can be called the Holy Spirit is withdrawn; and the true idea of a life in the world and an activity among men which is founded on forgiveness. And, of course, there is to be observed, what runs through all the Psalm, faith in God's forgiving mercy: " Have pity on me, according to Thy goodness : according to the multitude of Thy tender

mercies, blot out my transgressions." Similar thoughts
are contained in many other passages, such as Ps. xxxii.;
but multiplication of examples would not add anything
to the points just referred to.

VIII. THE DOCTRINE OF REDEMPTION.

1. *The Covenant.*

The only aspect under which Scripture regards the
constitution of Israel, is its religious aspect. The Israelitish State is everywhere regarded as a religious community;
in other words, as that which we call the kingdom of God
or of Jehovah. To the Scripture writers it has no other
aspect of interest. But under this aspect they embrace
all its fortunes and vicissitudes. These have all a religious
meaning. Its deliverance out of Egypt, its settlement in
Canaan, its peaceful abode there, and its ejectment out of
that land, have all a religious significance. They express
some side or some aspect of its relation to Jehovah, God
of Israel. In other words, Israel is the people of God,
and all that happens to it illustrates in some way its
relations to God. This is the fundamental position to be
taken in reading the Scriptures, or in any attempt to
understand them.

Further, though Israel be the people of God, and
though it is as the people of God only that it is spoken of
in Scripture, this, of course, does not make its external form
of no estimation. Its external form is of the highest
consequence, because it is only through this form that its
existence as the people of God is revealed; it is through
this form that its consciousness of what it was manifests
itself; and it is through this form that God's dealings
with it reach its heart and act upon it, quite as much
as God acts upon a man through the vicissitudes of
his bodily life and his social history. This external
form, which it had as a State or people among peoples,

was not a form essential to a Church of God, but
it was the form in which the community of God then
existed. The reasons why God gave it this form to begin
with may, some of them, lie deeper than we can fathom,
but we can see many of them. In a world which was
idolatrous all round, it was well to enlist on the side of
truth, patriotism and popular sympathy, and national self-
consciousness and honour, in order to conserve the truth,
lest it should be dissipated and evaporate from the world,
if merely consigned to the keeping of individuals. And,
no doubt, there were wider designs in contemplation, such
as to give to the world the ideal of a religious State, as
a model for the nations of the world to strive after, and
to be attained when the kingdoms shall be the Lord's.
For the social and civil life of the nations must yet, no doubt,
ultimately be embraced under their religious life, although
the one need never be identified with the other.

But perhaps, in reflecting on this question, this fact
should always be kept in mind, that God's treatment of
men in some measure accommodates itself to the varying
state of the world at the time. At this early time each
nation had its own national god. The national idea and
the religious idea were closely united. Thus Micah, iv. 5,
says: " Every people walketh in the name of his god, and
we will walk in the name of the Lord our God for ever
and ever." Religion, especially among the Shemitic nations,
was national. It was not monotheism, but monolatry, or
particularism ; the nations worshipped each their own
god. So, perhaps, this peculiarity was accepted as the
basis of God's revelation of Himself to Israel. Through
this idea the people were gradually educated in true
thoughts of God. Their history, interpreted by their prophets, taught the people how much greater Jehovah was
than the national God of Israel. To have, and to worship,
one God was, in itself, a great step towards realising that
there was no God but one.

The characteristic, however, of the Old Testament
Church was found first to lie here, that all the truth

revealed to it, and all the life manifested in it, had this concrete and external form—partly national and partly ritual. The truth and the life were embodied. That is, every truth had a hull or shell protecting it—a cosmical form or form of this world. The truth and the life were not strictly spiritual, but manifested always through a body. In other words, the religion was in almost all cases *symbolised*. And this was partly that wherein the inferiority of the Old Dispensation lay. This condition of inferiority endured till Christ came, when there passed over the Old Testament a transformation, and it became new. The spiritual truths broke through the husks that had been needful for their protection till the time of their maturity came, and they stood out in their own power as universal.

Another point of inferiority lay in this, that the truths had been made known piecemeal, and were not understood in their unity. But with Christ, the scattered fragments came together, bone to his bone, and stood upon their feet, organic bodies, articulated and living. It was the same truths of religion which Old Testament writers were revealing, and Old Testament saints believing and living by; it could not be any other, if they were truths of religion; but the truths were scattered and disjointed, and were not apprehended in their organic oneness, and they were also clothed in material forms. This is all that is needful to be held of what is known as Typology.[1] It is not implied that the pious Israelites knew the particular future reference of the things they believed. All Israel knew that they had a future reference in general. But they were present religious truths, clear enough to live by, although many might desire more light. And the symbolism of them aided in bodying out to men's minds the

---

[1] On this see more at length in the author's *Old Testament Prophecy*, pp. 210–241 ; also Dr. Patrick Fairbairn's *Typology of Scripture* ; J. Chr. K. von Hofmann's *Weissagung und Erfüllung* ; Franz Delitzsch's *Die biblisch-prophetische Theologie* ; Diestel's *Geschichte des Alten Testaments in der Christlichen Kirche*, etc.—ED.

meaning of the practices enjoined upon them, and the life demanded from them. And everything in the Old Testament pointed towards the future. The very symbolism was prophetic ; for a symbolism from its nature always embodies ideas in their perfection. Thus the priests' robes, clean and white, taught men's minds that only perfect purity can come before God—the man whose hands are clean and whose heart is pure; but as no man then came up to that ideal, the thought and the hope were awakened of One who should attain to it, or of a time when all should reach it. We should distinguish between symbolism and typology—that is, between a ritual and national embodiment of religious truth so as that it had a concrete, material form, and any merely future reference of the truth or the symbol. The future reference, so far as appears, was nowhere expressly taught contemporaneously with the institution of the symbol. The symbol expressed truth as a present possession of the Church which then was. The bent of the national mind, its sense of imper-fection, its lofty idealism, gradually brought to its con-sciousness that the time for realising lay in the future. The perfection of the idea and the imperfection of the attainment, with the longing that the one should be equal to the other, made the symbolism, whether ritual or national, to be prophetic—that is, converted it into what has been known in the Church as a typology. But in this technical sense typology does not concern us much in our efforts to understand how prophets and righteous men thought and lived in those Old Testament times.

(1) Now we never have in the Old Testament formal statements of an abstract kind. What we have is the expression of a consciousness already long formed. The Old Testament people were in the condition of the people of salvation. This relation had been long formed. And any utterances relating to it are not general statements of what it should be, or even of what it is; but rather expressions of the feeling of realising it—religious, not theological utterances. The fundamental redemptive idea

in Israel, then, the most general conception in what might be termed Israel's consciousness of salvation, was the idea of its being in covenant with Jehovah. This embraced all. Other redemptive ideas were but deductions from this, or arose from an analysis of it. The idea of the covenant is, so to speak, the frame within which the development goes on; this development being in great measure a truer understanding of what ideas lie in the two related elements, Jehovah on the one side and the people on the other, and in the nature of the relation. This idea of a covenant was not a conception struck out by the religious mind and applied only to things of religion; it was a conception transferred from ordinary life into the religious sphere.

The word בְּרִית, connected perhaps with בָּרָא, בָּרָה = to *cut*, means any agreement entered into under solemn ceremonies of sacrifice. Hence, to make a covenant is usually כָּרַת בּ to *cut* a covenant, *i.e.* slay victims in forming the agreement, giving it thus either a religious sanction in general, or specifically imploring on one's self the fate of the slain victims if its conditions were disregarded. Anything agreed upon between two peoples or two men, under such sanction, was a covenant. Two tribes that agree to live at amity, to intermarry or trade together, make a *covenant*. When a king is elected, there is a covenant between him and the people. The marriage relation is a covenant. The brotherly relation of affection between Jonathan and David was a covenant. So one makes a covenant with his eyes not to look sinfully upon a woman (Job xxxi. 1), with the beasts of the field, to live at peace with them (Job v. 23). The victor makes a covenant with the vanquished to give him quarter and spare him. A covenant may be made between equals, as between Abraham and Abimelech (Gen. xxi. 32); or between parties unequal, as between Joshua and the Gibeonites (Josh. ix. 15); or when one invokes the superior power of another, as when Asa bribed Benhadad with all the silver and gold of the Lord's house (1 Kings xv. 19); and in other ways. Generally there accompanied the forming of such agreements, sacrifice, and eating of it in common as is described in Jer. xxxiv. and in other parts of Scripture.

The covenant contemplated certain ends, and it reposed on certain conditions, mutually undertaken. Although it might be altogether for the advantage of one of the parties, as in the case of Joshua and the Gibeonites, both parties came under obligations. There arose a right or *jus* under it, although none existed before, and although the formation of it was of pure grace on one side. The parties contracting entered into understood relations with one another, which both laid themselves under obligation to observe. Jehovah imposed His covenant on Israel. He did this in virtue of His having redeemed Israel out of Egypt. The covenant was just the bringing to the consciousness of the people the meaning of Jehovah's act in redeeming them; and, translated into other words, reads: 'I will be your God, and ye shall be My people.' The covenant bore that Israel should be His. This was the obligation lying on Israel, and the obligation He laid on Himself was, that He should be their God, with all that this implied. Henceforth, Israel was not in a condition towards Jehovah which was absolutely destitute of rights and claims. Jehovah had contracted Himself into a relation. He was God of Israel, under promise to be Israel's defence and light and guide; to be, in short, all that God was. Even when Israel sinned, He was restrained by His covenant from destroying Israel, even from chastising Israel beyond measure. No doubt, when Israel failed to fulfil the conditions of the covenant, it might be said to cease. That would have held of a covenant between equals, or if both had sought mutual advantage from it. But Jehovah had laid it upon Israel. And the same love and sovereignty which chose Israel at first were involved in retaining Israel in covenant; and when the old covenant failed, Jehovah, as true to Himself, promised to make a new covenant with Israel which could not fail of securing its objects.

We touch a very peculiar question, and one of profounder character, here. When the prophets and writers of Israel speak of the *justice* or *righteousness* of Jehovah, and consider that it implies that He will save His people, they move, so to speak, within the covenant. Salvation is due to them as a people of Jehovah. He is righteous in delivering them. But when they themselves have broken the covenant, then they must fall back on the *nature* of Jehovah, on that in Him which led Him to take them to Himself as a people. The fact of His entering into relation with Israel suggests what His nature is; and on that larger basis they build their hopes. But it may perhaps be said that prophets and psalmists do not appeal much to the covenant, and to Jehovah's obligations under it. When they say, " Remember the covenant," it is = " Remember the past, the old relation—that with Abraham," etc.

(2) It is important to remember that the covenant was made with the people as a whole, not with individuals. This is the Old Testament point of view. The people are regarded as a whole, and individuals share the benefit of the covenant as members of the nation. The religious subject or unit in the Old Testament is the people of Israel. This subject came into existence at the Exodus, when Jehovah delivered the tribes from Egypt. Henceforth the people feels itself a unity—a subject, and Jehovah is its God. There subsisted between Jehovah and this people a relation of mutual right in each other. Jehovah as God of Israel bound Himself to protect the nation by His almighty arm in all its necessities arising from its relations without; to instruct it with laws and prophecy, and with the teaching of His wisdom in all its national organisations within; to be to it the Head in every department of its national life. He was its King—King in Jeshurun—King of Jacob. He inspired its teachers. Amos sketches the *two* lines along which Jehovah's grace ran. (1) The *temporal*: " I destroyed the Amorite before you "; " I led you forty years in the wilderness to give you the land of the Amorite " (ii. 9, 10). (2) The *spiritual*— to the prophet the greater: " I raised up your young men

16

to be prophets and Nazirites" (Amos ii. 11). He led its armies; its watchword on the field was: "The sword of Jehovah and of Gideon" (Judg. vii. 18). And the Psalmist laments that He no longer, in the time of its downfall, went forth with its armies (Ps. xliv. 9).

And the people was His, devoting all its energies to His service. Hence there was in Israel no priestly class, as in other nations, privileged in their own right to draw near to Jehovah to the exclusion of others. The priests but represented the nation. The high priest bore the names of the tribes on his breast. In him all drew near. They were a kingdom of priests, and an holy nation (Ex. xix. 6). This possession of each other, so to speak, was not only positive, but also *negative*. It was *negative*; for though the earth and all people were Jehovah's, He was God of no people as He was of Israel. As Amos says: "You only have I known of all the families of the earth" (iii. 2). And though Israel was among the nations, it was not one of the nations. It was debarred from imitating them; from relying on horses and fenced cities for its preservation, as they did (Hos. i. 7, viii. 14, etc.); from following their manners, or practising their rites. This attitude of the prophets towards an army and fenced cities might seem to us mere fanaticism; it was certainly faith in Jehovah as the Saviour of the people of a very lofty kind. The nation was cut off, and separated; and Isaiah recognises that it was near its downfall when he could say that it was filled from the east, and full of silver and gold, and filled with sorcerers like the Philistines (ii. 6; cf. Mic. v. 10–15).

It was also *positive*. For Jehovah poured out in Israel all His fulness. Thus He bestowed on them the land of Canaan (Jer. ii. 7), to perform the oath which He sware unto their fathers to give them a land flowing with milk and honey. And Israel dedicated all to Him; itself and its property. That the manhood of the nation was His, was symbolised by the dedication to Him of all the firstborn. That the increase of the land was

His, was shown in the devotion to Him of the first-fruits. That its life and time were His, appeared from the setting apart of the Sabbath, and the stated times of feast. The seventh week, the seventh year, the seventh seventh or fiftieth year, the year of Jubilee. These are all laws as ancient as the nation. We sometimes hear the opinion expressed that the idea of the Sabbath was only *rest*, cessation from toil, and that thus it was a merely humanitarian institution. But this is to entirely mistake ancient institutions. All institutions were an expression of religion. The Sabbath expressed a *religious* idea—the acknowledgment that *time* was Jehovah's as well as all things. The day was *sanctified*, that is, dedicated to Jehovah. The householder allowed his servants to rest, not, of course, with the modern idea that they might have time to serve God, but with the ancient idea that the rest of his servants and cattle was part of his own rest, part of his own full dedication of the day to God. Hence in the Deuteronomic law the duty of keeping the Sabbath is based on the Lord's redemption of the people from Egypt.

On the position of the individual, Riehm expresses himself thus:—

"The moral and religious significance of the individual personality is not yet fully recognised. God stands in relation to the whole people, but the individual does not [yet] call him Father [though the people do, Isa. lxiv. 7]. Only the people as such is chosen [or elect], and merely as a member of the same has the individual a portion in this choice. Every disturbance of the relation of fellowship between God and Israel is not only felt by him to be painful, but it is also felt as a disturbance of his own personal relations to the Most High. But along with the people [as a whole], the greater and smaller circles within it exercise also an influence upon the relation of the individual to God. So the sin of the fathers is visited upon the children; the punishment inflicted upon the head of the family embraces also all that belong to him [*e.g.* Korah]. It is only later that the meaning of the individual

personality, its personal responsibility, and the determination of its relations to God by its own free moral decision
receive full recognition. For example, the belief that the
children bear the sins of the fathers is limited both in
Jeremiah and Ezekiel, in the clearest way, by insisting on
the essential dependence of punishment upon personal
guilt " (*Alttest. Theol.*, p. 28). This tendency in the Old
Testament to push the individual into the background
helps to explain many things, *e.g.* the little prominence
given to the idea of personal immortality until a comparatively late period. The immortality that the prophets
speak of is that of the State or kingdom. The doctrine of
personal immortality followed the doctrine of personal
responsibility.

We must beware, however, of pressing the national
idea to an extreme, so as to go the length of saying that
Jehovah had no relation to individuals, or that individuals
had no consciousness of personal relation to Him. This is
extravagance. One cannot read the history of Abraham
in the Pentateuch—part of it anterior to the prophets—
without being convinced that this is an exaggeration. This
idea throws the whole Psalter and the Proverbs into the
post-exile period. It is true that in Jeremiah and Ezekiel
the individual rises into a prominence not seen in earlier
prophets; but these retain the idea of the *national* relation
to Jehovah as much as earlier prophets.

That the dedication expressed in the covenant was not
a dedication on the mere ground of nature, but one the
meaning of which was the lifting up of the people out of
the sphere of nature life into the pure region of morals
and religion, was shown by the rite of circumcision, which
symbolised the putting off of the natural life of the flesh;
and by the Paschal sacrifice, which implied the redemption
of the nation with blood. All was Jehovah's to such an
extent that no Israelite could become the owner of another
Israelite; slavery was forbidden, and the year of release
(seventh year) set the bond-servant free. And even the
land could not be permanently alienated. It was not

theirs, but, like themselves, Jehovah's. This idea, that the nation was the Lord's, appears particularly in the prophets, who deal exclusively with the nation. Thus we have such expressions as these in Jeremiah: that Israel is Jehovah's *firstborn* (xxxi. 9); that he is the *first-fruits* of His increase (ii. 3); and the fuller expression of the same idea: " As the girdle cleaveth to the loins of a man, so have I caused to cleave unto Me the whole house of Israel and the whole house of Judah, saith Jehovah; that they might be unto Me for a people, and for a name, and for a praise, and for a glory " (xiii. 11). Hence such figures as are common, to express the covenant connection; for example, the married relation, the figure of a flock, etc. Hence such names as *Lo Ruhamah, unloved; Lo-ammi, not My people.* Hence also such terms as: " Hear the word of the Lord against the whole family which I brought up out of the land of Egypt " (Amos iii. 1). It is a frequent formula of the prophet's, indeed, " I am the Lord thy God from the land of Egypt " (Hos. xiii. 4).

(3) The agreement which the prophets refer to under the name of covenant was that made at Sinai. This was the era of Israel's birth as a nation. Then Jehovah created them, as the word is used in Isa. xl. ff. Then He became their father. As Malachi says: " Have we not all one father? hath not one God created us ? " (ii. 10)— language used of Israel in opposition to the nations. No doubt this was not the only or the first covenant which God had formed with men. For the Old Testament is far from regarding the rational spiritual creature man as a being at any time without rights in his relations to God; and the God of the Hebrews is far from being an arbitrary despot, subject to no law except His own cruel caprice. He limited Himself even in relation to new created man, and made a covenant with him. His very creation of a reasonable and moral creature brought Him into covenant. God, when He came down from His Godhead and con-descended to create, thereby entered into close relations with man and all things made. This was a covenant with

all His works. When He looked upon His creation which He had made, He found it 'good,' and He ceased to create. It was an arena suitable for the display of all that He was; and He reposed in satisfaction. And this repose and satisfaction expresses His relation to the creation. And of this condition of God's mind toward creation, the Sabbath was a symbol. It was the sign of His covenant with creation. It is the earthly correspondent to what is the condition of Jehovah's mind towards creation—this is creation's response to His satisfied and beneficent mind towards it; hence the Old Testament also speaks of the land enjoying her Sabbaths (Lev. xxvi. 34, 43). It is creation's entering into covenant with Jehovah — the expression of this on its side.

Again, when He had asserted Himself as the moral governor of men, He made another covenant with the new race that survived the Flood. This was also, so to speak, a covenant on the basis of nature, though directed to the human family chiefly. Its conditions were abstaining from blood, and the sacredness of human life. The sign was the light in the heavens appearing on the face of the cloud; the symbol of the new light of God's face and of life shining on the dark background of the watery firmament. Again, He made a covenant with Abraham. But here the covenant passes from the region of nature to that of grace; from the wide area of creation and of natural human life, to the moral region and to the redeemed life. The conditions of this covenant were the Promises. The sign of it was circumcision, the symbol of a putting off the natural and entering upon a new spiritual life. Thus these three express a gradual progression: (1) The Sabbath; a covenant with creation. (2) The Noachian covenant; a covenant with man, expressing the sacredness of natural human life—consciousness of man as belonging to Jehovah. (3) The covenant with Abraham; a covenant of grace, of spiritual life. But the covenant of the prophets is the covenant of Sinai, in which Jehovah became God of the nation.

(4) The motive to the formation of this covenant on Jehovah's part was His *love*. It is important to notice that the idea of a covenant is a moral one; the formation of it implies free action on the part of Jehovah, and the motive is a moral one—love. The relation of Jehovah to Israel is not a natural one. In Shemitic heathenism the god was the natural father of the people; Jehovah is the redemptive Creator and Father. In Shemitic heathenism the female worshipper was spouse of the god; but this was because she surrendered herself to prostitution in honour of the god through those who represented him. In such prophets as Hosea the idea of the people being sons of the living God, and of the people being the spouse of Jehovah, has no element of this naturalism in it; the prophet's conceptions, even when he uses phraseology of this kind, which seems to have some resemblance to that employed in Shemitic heathenism, are all spiritual and moral.

It is singular, again, that in the older prophets very little is said of the covenant. The ideas which it expresses are present, but the word is not found. It does not occur in Joel, Amos, or Micah, although Amos expresses the idea of it when he says for God to Israel: "You only have I known of all the families of the earth" (iii. 2; and cf. i. 9). Neither does it appear in Obadiah, Zephaniah, or Habakkuk. But it appears in Hosea more than once, as, "They have transgressed My covenant, and revolted from My law" (viii. 1); and again: "But they, like Adam, have transgressed the covenant" (vi. 7). And in a form very interesting in Zechariah, in a section which is generally recognised to belong to an ancient prophet of that name: "As for Thee also, by the blood of Thy covenant I have sent forth Thy prisoners" (ix. 11). It is in Jeremiah that the term first comes into very prominent use to designate the relation of Jehovah to Israel. There was a reason for this. This prophet lived at a critical juncture in Israel's history. The constitution was breaking up. The old order was changing, giving place to new. And the prophet's attention was sharply directed to it. Its meaning was vividly brought before him; its purposes, its provisions, its defects now becoming apparent, and its failure. And as the circumstances of his time brought his mind to bear upon the nature of that covenant which had proved vain, so he was enabled to rise to the conception of the new covenant which Jehovah should make with His people, the nature and provisions of which would ensure its success. He is the first to prophesy of this, saying, " Behold, the days come, saith Jehovah, that I will make a new covenant with Israel . . . not according to the covenant that I made with their fathers in the day that I took them by the hand to bring them out of the land of Egypt; which My covenant they brake . . . but this shall be the covenant that I will make with the house of Israel; After those days, saith Jehovah, I will put My law in their inward parts, and write it in their hearts; and I will be their God, and they shall be My people " (xxxi. 31–33).

And the writer of the Epistle to the Hebrews, with the singular insight which he has, not into the meaning of texts of Scripture in themselves, but into the meaning which the context gives them, thus speaks: " In that He saith, A new covenant, He hath made the first old. Now that which decayeth and waxeth old is ready to vanish away " (viii. 13); an exact description of the condition of things in Jeremiah's days. What took place in the mind of Jeremiah in regard to the covenant was directly paralleled by what took place in the mind of another prophet in regard to the idea of Israel, the people of God, of whom was salvation. The meaning of Israel, God's purposes with regard to it, its position in the world, its endowments, the determinations of a spiritual kind, impressed upon it as the prophetic people, destined to be the light of the Gentiles, and to bring forth righteousness among them, as the Servant of the Lord, and the like—this conception of Israel on all its sides in God's plan of redemption was raised in the mind of that prophet to whom we owe Isa. xl. ff., by the sense or the fear of Israel's annihilation as a people by the Babylonian power.

2. Why the Covenant with Israel and not another?

The question naturally occurs, Why did the Lord love this people to the exclusion of others; this people, and not some other? This question resolves itself, of course, into the other, Why one, and not all? For if He had chosen any other, the same question would have arisen, Why this and not that? The prophets see the love and grace of God in the choice. They do not speculate on the question, Why they, and not others?—in the earlier time. But later they give at least a practical answer to the question, to wit, that the Lord chose them to be the medium of His choice of others and of His grace to others. So especially in Second Isaiah. The answer is hardly sufficient; but the same objection or difficulty would apply everywhere. There were, no doubt, positive reasons. These must have lain partly in the peculiarities of the Shemitic mind to which Israel belonged; partly, perhaps in the degree of religious advancement among the Shemitic peoples. For, (1) The Shemitic peoples are no doubt distinguished by what is called a genius for religion. "If in antiquity [in general]," says Riehm, "the religious feeling and the consciousness of dependence upon the Deity was particularly lively and powerful, so that the whole national life was governed by it, it was among the Shemitic nations, even in antiquity, that the religious spirit unfolded its highest energy. . . . We perceive how exclusively the religious spirit drew into its service the whole national life, even among the Arabs. It was the same among the Assyrians, the Moabites, and other nations, where kings show the liveliest consciousness of standing in all their undertakings in the service of the national god, for whom it is that they carry on war and make conquests" (*Alttest. Theol.* p. 48).

(2) There is the stage of religious advancement which the Shemitic people had attained in the age of revelation. Even if the religion of the Canaanite and trans-Jordanic nations was not monotheism, it was what might be called

henotheism or monolatry.   Each nation had its own one god, as Chemosh, Milcom, Baal, etc.   It is possible that these are but different names for the same god, expressing the people's idea of the god under slightly different modifications.   But this was a condition very unlike that of Greece or Rome, which, even if they had one highest god, had a multitude also of minor deities whom they worshipped. This henotheism was a stage of religious attainment very advantageous to start from.   Probably the difference between the religion of Israel and that of their neighbours lies chiefly in the ethical character ascribed to Jehovah.

(3) We might also say that the characteristics of the Shemitic mind very well fitted one of this nationality to be the depositary of a revelation.   The Shemitic mind is simple and emotional, without capacity for speculative or metaphysical thought.   Hence the revelation committed to Israel retains its practical simplicity, and remains a religion without ever becoming a theology.   We know the influence of the Greek mind on Christianity, and the effort of this age is rather to get back behind the Greek influence, and teach Christianity as the Shemitic mind presented it and left it.

(4) Be this as it may, this glorious conception of Israel's meaning in God's purpose was the rainbow created by that dark cloud of desolation which the Babylonian captivity threw upon the prophet's horizon.   All these things show how it was Israel's national history that was of significance, and how out of its vicissitudes God's great purposes became revealed.   And it was these vicissitudes that recalled to the prophets the meaning of the covenant, although it had been long expressed before, and made them dwell upon the unchanging basis and motive of it, the *love* of God.   Hence Jeremiah says : " With an eternal love—or a love of old— have I loved thee " (xxxi. 3).   This love manifests itself in *choice*.   It is in the second half of Isaiah and in Jeremiah that this idea appears most frequently.   But it is also in the Pentateuch.   Thus, " Jehovah hath not set His love upon you, and chosen you, because ye are more than all

nations; for ye are the least of all nations: but because Jehovah hath loved you" (Deut. vii. 7). And this choice was irrevocable, for the gifts and calling of God are without repentance, as it is expressed in Isa. xli. 8, 9: "But thou, Israel, My servant, Jacob whom I have chosen, the seed of Abraham my friend. Thou whom I took from the ends of the earth . . . and said unto thee, Thou art My servant; I have chosen thee, and not cast thee away"—words which St. Paul echoes when, standing, like this prophet, before the desolation and disbelief of Israel, he exclaims: "Hath God cast away His people? God forbid" (Rom. xi. 1).

(5) The conditions of the covenant are, of course, the ten words given at Sinai. It is not necessary to dwell on this. But the remarkable thing is,—which all our reading in the prophets reveals,—how entirely the prophets regard the constitution of Israel as a moral constitution, and how little place ritual and ceremony have in their conception of it. In answer to the anxious demand of the people, wherewith they should come before Jehovah: "Will the Lord be pleased with thousands of rams, or with ten thousands of rivers of oil?" the prophet responds: "He hath showed thee, O man, what is good; and what doth the Lord require of thee, but to do justly, and to love mercy, and to walk humbly with thy God?" (Mic. vi. 6–8). And a remarkable passage in Jeremiah seems to exclude the ritual from the basis of the covenant, as it was no doubt only a means to its preservation: "Thus saith Jehovah of hosts; Put your burnt-offerings unto your sacrifices, and eat flesh. For I spake not unto your fathers, nor commanded them in the day that I brought them out of the land of Egypt, concerning burnt-offerings or sacrifices. But this thing commanded I them, saying, Obey My voice, and I will be your God, and ye shall be My people" (vii. 21, 22). Such passages as these do not contain any condemnation of sacrifice in itself; but only a condemnation of the exaggerated weight laid on it by the people. As Hosea says: "I desire goodness, and not sacrifice; the knowledge of God more than burnt-offerings" (vi. 6). The moral side

of the covenant is to the prophets its real meaning; and—what is very peculiar in the earlier prophets—it is this moral side of it which even the priests are charged to teach. It is their failure to teach this that is blamed in their conduct, as in Hosea.

The covenant contained as its conditions the ethical ordinances of the law. But of course an ancient religion could not exist without public worship. This worship was by means of sacrifice and offering. The fundamental principles of the covenant might thus be developed along two lines, ethical and spiritual religion, as by the prophets; and, secondly, ritual of worship — probably among the priests. But the two did not develop co-ordinately and without contact and mutual influence. In particular, the ethical ideas of the prophets reacted largely upon the form of the ritual. It is probable that the ritual was valued in the main for the ideas which it expressed. The particular details, e.g. what animals were to be sacrificed, and how many, and such matters, would be left in the main indefinite.

But the two things to be maintained are: first, that from the beginning the religion of Jehovah contained both an ethical or spiritual side, and a ritual of service or worship. And, secondly, that both, tracing their origin to Moses, gradually expanded in the course of ages, received additions, and underwent changes as circumstances required. The law, i.e. the ritual, grew in contents just as much as the ethical elements of the religion did. The two streams went on increasing side by side, but the Law tended always to take up into itself and embody the loftier elements of the prophetic teaching.

3. The Terms descriptive of the Covenant Relation.

Something must be said, however, of the words which express this covenant relation of Israel and Jehovah. These are the words *holy, holiness, sanctify,* and the like— the root קדשׁ and its derivatives. These words, with their

English equivalents, are: קָדַשׁ, to be holy; Pi., Hiph., to sanctify, hallow, consecrate, dedicate; קֹדֶשׁ, holy thing, holiness, sanctuary, thing hallowed; and equal to 'holy' in connection with a noun; מִקְדָּשׁ, sanctuary, holy place; adjective קָדוֹשׁ, holy; also as noun, *saint*, holy one. Now these words are applied in the Old Testament: (*a*) to things; (*b*) persons; (*c*) and to Jehovah; and it is not an uninteresting inquiry, what is their meaning when so applied?

Now, in pursuing this inquiry, it will be best to disregard opinions stated by others, and follow out merely a brief induction of passages. But perhaps I may state, to begin with, the result to which I think comparison of the passages will lead. These results are: (1) The word 'holy' does not originally express a moral attribute, nor even a moral condition as the blending of many attributes, when applied either to God or men. (2) When applied to Jehovah, it may express any attribute in Him whereby He manifests Himself to be God, or anything about Him which is what we should name *Divine*; and hence the name 'Holy,' or 'Holy One,' became the loftiest expression for Jehovah as God, or it expressed God especially on the side of His majesty. It was the name for God as transcendental. (3) When applied to things or men, it expresses the idea that they belong to Jehovah, are used in His service or dedicated to Him, or are in some special way His property.

(1) With regard to things and men. Of course, *holy* or *holiness* said of things cannot denote a moral attribute. It can only express a relation. And the relation it expresses is, *belonging* to Jehovah, *dedicated* to Godhead. Nothing is *holy* of itself or by nature. And not everything can be made *holy*. Only some things are suitable. But suitability to be made holy and holiness are things quite distinct. For example, only clean beasts could be devoted to Jehovah. A beast so devoted is holy. But all clean beasts were not so devoted. The ideas of 'holy' and 'clean' must not therefore be confounded. Clean-

ness is only a condition of holiness, not that itself. For example, it was forbidden to defile the camp in the wilderness, because this made it unfit for the presence of Jehovah; as it is said, "That they defile not their camps, in the midst whereof I dwell" (Num. v. 3). Everything dedicated to Jehovah, and belonging to Him, was holy. For example, the tabernacle where He dwelt was called מִקְדָּשׁ or קֹדֶשׁ, *a holy place*. Mount Zion, the hill where His presence in the tabernacle was manifested, was *a holy hill*. Jerusalem was the holy city. The sacrifices, as belonging to Him, were *a holy thing*, קֹדֶשׁ. So were the shewbread, the tithes, the oil, the first-fruits, everything, in short, dedicated to Jehovah. In that which was holy there might be gradations. Thus the outer part of the tabernacle was the holy place, but the inner part was ק' קְרָשִׁים, most holy place; it was especially dedicated to God, and none dared enter it. So all flesh offerings were holy; but some were *most* holy things, such as the sin-offering.

The meaning does not seem to be this, that these things being dedicated to God, this fact raised in the mind a certain feeling of reverence or awe for them, and then this secondary quality in them of inspiring awe was called holiness. No doubt things as dedicated to God had this quality. But what the word *holy* describes is the primary relation of belonging to Jehovah. This appears from a passage in which those are described who are to be priests, as indeed it appears quite evidently in the passage where Israel is called *an holy nation*, which is parallel to the other designation, *a kingdom of priests* (Ex. xix. 6). Korah and his company objected to the exclusive priesthood of Aaron, saying: "Ye take too much upon you, seeing all the congregation are holy, every one of them, and Jehovah is among them. And Moses answered, To-morrow will Jehovah show who are His and who are holy" (Num. xvi. 3). Hence the priests are said to be *holy unto Jehovah*, *i.e.* they are His property and possession. The term *holy*, therefore, whether applied to things or men in Israel, or to all Israel signifies that they are the possession of Jehovah; hence the term expresses what is elsewhere expressed by the word סְגֻלָּה, a *peculium*, or *peculiar* people.

But naturally with this idea of belonging to Jehovah other ideas are allied. That which is His is separated out of the region of common things. Thus in Ezek. xlv. 4 a certain part of the land, the portion of the priests, is called קֹדֶשׁ מִן־הָאָרֶץ, a holy thing taken out of the land. Hence *holy* is opposed to *profane*, חֹל. The latter word means that which lies open, is accessible, common, not peculiar. Hence in *holy* there lies the idea of being taken out of the common mass of things, or men, or nations; and with that naturally the notion of being elevated above the common. Again, there quite naturally belongs to it the idea of being inviolable, and those who lay their hands upon it the Divine nature reacts against and destroys. Hence Uzzah, who put out his hand to stay the ark, perished; and likewise those of Beth-shemesh who looked into it. Hence the offerings could not be eaten by any but the priests, God's peculiar servants. So it is said of Israel in his youth, that he was "a holy thing unto the Lord (קֹדֶשׁ ל), . . . all that devoured him incurred guilt, *i.e.* as putting forth their hand against what was Jehovah's" (Jer. ii. 3). Further, it is quite possible that this formal idea of relation to Jehovah might gather unto it, if I might say so, a certain amount of contents. Only clean things could be dedicated to Jehovah. Only men of a character like His own could be His property. And it is possible, therefore, that the word holy may occasionally be used to cover this secondary idea. But this is not its primary use, and in any case is rare.

(2) A more difficult question presents itself when we inquire what is meant when it is said, "Jehovah is holy." First, it is out of the question to say that, as Israel is holy, being dedicated to Jehovah, so Jehovah is *holy*, as belonging to Israel; and that the language, *be ye holy: for I am holy*, means nothing more than "be mine: for I am yours." That sentence means, at all events, *be My people: for I am your God.* Holy, on the side of Israel, meant devoted to

God—not devoted in general. The conception of God was an essential part of the idea. But this suggests at once that *holy*, as applied to Jehovah, is an expression in some way describing Deity; *i.e.* not describing Deity on any particular side of His nature, for which it is a fixed term, but applicable to Him on any side, the manifestation of which impresses men with the sense of His Divinity. For instance, Ezekiel (xxxvi. 20) says of the heathen among whom Israel were dispersed, that they profaned Jehovah's holy name when they said to Israel, "These are the people of Jehovah, and are gone forth out of their land." What is implied in this language of the heathen is a slur upon the power of Jehovah. He was unable to protect His people. Hence, they had gone into exile. This thought on the part of the heathen was profanation of the holy name of Jehovah, *i.e.* it reduced His majesty and might to contempt.

Thus the Divine greatness and power are elements of His 'holiness.' Hence He will 'sanctify' His *great* name, *i.e.* His revealed greatness, by restoring Israel. Again, in a similar way, He *sanctifies Himself* in Gog by giving him over to destruction; *i.e.* He shows Himself by His power to be God (Ezek. xxxviii. 16). And thus the words, "I will sanctify Myself," and "I will glorify Myself," are almost synonymous. Compare Lev. x. 3, where it is said : "I will be sanctified in them that come nigh Me, and before all the people will I be glorified." So it is said in Ps. xcix. 3 : "Let the nations praise Thy great and terrible name, for it is holy." So Moses is chastised because he failed to sanctify Jehovah's name at the waters of Meribah (Num. xx. 12, 13) —*i.e.* failed to impress upon the people His power and Godhead. The cry of the seraphim in Isaiah is, "Holy, holy, holy, the whole earth is full of His glory" (vi. 3), *i.e.* His Divine majesty ; and the word *holy* must here be very much the same as God, *i.e.* God in His majesty. Thus the name comes to express Jehovah on some side of His Godhead, or perhaps on that side which, to men, is specifically Divine, His *majesty*. Hence the name becomes, in Isaiah and the prophets after him, a name of Jehovah as God ; He is the Holy One of Israel, *i.e.* God in Israel, the name implying an effort on the part of men's minds to express Divinity in its highest sense. " *Holy* is the name," says Baudissin, " for the whole Being of Jehovah, God revealed in Israel." Hence it may be used without the article. " To what will ye liken Me, saith קָרוֹשׁ "—the incomparable—the God of majesty. Wisdom is the knowledge of Providence as the ways of God. Hence it is said in Proverbs, " I have not learned Wisdom, so that I should have knowledge of קָרוֹשׁ. The fear of Jehovah is the beginning of wisdom, and knowledge of קּ is understanding."[1]

Two points yet deserve some notice : *first*, the *etymology* ; and, *second*, the *extended usage* of the name to express special attributes. The latter will depend upon the special character under which God is presented with a view to influence men.

Etymology is rarely a safe guide to the real meaning of words. Language, as we have it in any literature, has already drifted away far from the primary sense of its words. Usage is the only safe guide. When usage is ascertained, then we may inquire into derivation and radical signification. Hence the Concordance is always a safer companion than the Lexicon. The word קרשׁ is perhaps related to other words beginning with the same letters, *e.g.* kad., cut, cedo, and the like. If so, its meaning would be to *cut off*, to *separate*, to *elevate* out of the sphere of what is ordinary and set *apart*. If this be its meaning, we can readily perceive how it came to be applied to God. He is the lofty, the heavenly, separated in space from men— dwelling on high. More, He is the majestic, the morally lofty, separated from the human, not only as the finite material creature, but particularly as the sinful, impure creature. The Hebrews hardly distinguish, to begin with, the physical from the moral attributes of God. Majesty and moral purity are hardly separated. In both respects God is separated from man and elevated above him, and

[1] See his *Studien zur semitischen Religionsgeschichte*, ii. p. 79 ff.—ED.

in either way He is holy; and when men's eyes suddenly behold Him, His nature repels the profanity, and men die. If this was the line of thought along which the name 'פ was applied to Jehovah, it perhaps follows that the name was imposed upon men and things in a secondary way as belonging to Him.

Thus (1) we see *Holy* as a designation of Jehovah; having reference to His Godhead, or to anything which was a manifestation of His Godhead.

(2) We have it as used of men and things. These it describes as belonging to Jehovah, dedicated to Him, devoted or set apart to Him. Primarily, therefore, it expressed merely the relation.

(3) But naturally the conception of dedication to Jehovah brought into view Jehovah's character, which reacted on the things or persons devoted to Him. Hence a twofold filling up of the circumference of the word 'holy took place.

(a) As to men devoted to Him, they must share His character, and thus the term 'holy' took on a moral complexion.

(b) As to things, they must be fit to be Jehovah's. Even when 'clean' is used here by the prophets, it denotes moral purity (Isa. vi. 5). Hence the word took on what may be called a ceremonial or æsthetic complexion; differing little from clean, ceremonially pure.

But the name as applied to Jehovah expresses the efforts made by the Hebrew mind to rise to the conception of God as transcendent. It was the name for God absolutely. Hence the highest expression of the national life was: "Be ye holy: for I am holy"; that is at first, *be ye Mine: for I am God*. But what God was is not expressed. And always as the conception of God enlarged and clarified, more was felt to lie in the expression 'פ; and the calling of a people who was His, was felt to be more elevated.

But it will be easily seen how various the shades of significance may be that lie in 'פ. When we use the name *God*, it is not a mere empty name—we have always a feeling in the background of what God is morally, or in power or wisdom. Hence 'p, being used in the same way, may, in certain cases, emphasise special attributes of God, according as circumstances brought these into prominence; in opposition, for example, to the sins of those who were His people, or their disbelief, or their forgetfulness of their covenant relation to Him, or the like.

4. *The Second Side of the Covenant—the People a righteous People.*

The two parties to the covenant are God and Israel, His people. The covenant was made with the people, not with individuals. The people was the unit. The relation of Jehovah to the people made Him King. He was King of Jacob, the Creator of Israel, their King (Isa. xliii. 15). And their relation to Him was that of subjects owing allegiance and obedience. Again, they were a *people*, united by ties to one another, and owing duties to one another. Thus conduct, whether of the nation as a whole or of individuals, was estimated rather under the aspect of civil actions. A people necessarily forms a commonwealth, and its conduct was right when it fulfilled its obligations to its king, and the conduct of the individuals was right when they fulfilled their duties to one another. Yet, on the other hand, this King was Jehovah, God of Israel, and this people was the people of Jehovah. Thus what might seem at first merely civil became religious.

This second conception allowed room for a very great deepening of the idea of the people's relations to one another, and of their relation to their King. It might be made a question, indeed, which of the two conceptions, the civil or the religious, was the prior conception. To answer this question is of little importance. Probably the very asking such a question betrays a modern point of view, and one from which the Hebrew mind never regarded things. The Hebrews regarded all things from the religious point of view. Civil government and the conduct of men to one another alike belonged to the religious sphere, with the more direct acts of Divine service. If we observe a progress in the thinking of the people as represented by their writers, it is not a progress in the direction of dividing men's actions into two spheres, one civil and the other religious, but in the direction of a deeper conception of the nature of actions. All things continued with them to be religious. They were all done to God, but the conception deepened of what the meaning of doing anything to God was.

To begin with, an external obedience to the laws of their king was thought religion; but later it was felt that a true state of the heart towards God must go along with the outward act to make it right. At first, perhaps a citizen considered he had fulfilled his obligations to his fellow-citizen when he gave him his external civil right, when he was just to him; but later it was felt that humanity and mercy and love must be shown by one to another. There is always some danger of generalising too hastily, and finding the steps of progress from one idea to another, or from one stage to another, clearly shown by different writers. We may go so far safely enough. We may say certain authors represent this idea, and certain others another idea. An examination of the writings of one prophet may enable us to say with fairness, this and not another is the prevailing conception in him; and in another prophet who came after him a different and a deeper conception prevails. Yet it may be hardly safe to say that the deeper conception had not yet been reached in the time of the former prophet. Much may depend on his idiosyncrasy. And we require to move with very careful steps in making inductions in regard to the progress of ideas in Israel. In the prophet Amos the prevailing conception is that of righteousness. Jehovah is the righteous ruler of men, who vindicates on all, Israel and the heathen alike, the law of morality. And what the prophet demands from the people is righteousness—that is, just dealing with one another. " Let righteousness run down your streets like water" (Amos v. 24). A succeeding prophet, Hosea, has another, and what is to us a profounder, conception. He abandons the region of law and right, and enters the region of affection. Jehovah is not to him the righteous King, but the loving father of Israel. "When Israel was a child, I loved him, and called My son out of Egypt" (Hos. xi. 1). He is the husband of Israel, who is His spouse. And He complains not of the want of righteousness among the people to one another, but of the want of mercy, חֶסֶד—that is, humanity in the highest sense, goodness, love. Where Amos says: "I will not regard your burnt-offerings; but let justice run down as waters, and righteousness as a never-drying stream" (v. 24), Hosea says: "I desire goodness, and not sacrifice; and the knowledge of God more than burnt-offerings" (vi. 6).

Now, undoubtedly there is a profound advance from the one of these conceptions to the other. The former conception is not abandoned; at least all that it covered is retained, but reduced under a more religious idea. And a succeeding prophet, Micah, combines the ideas together: "What doth the Lord desire of thee, but to do justly, and to love mercy"—חֶסֶד—goodness? (vi. 8). Yet we might go too far in saying that the idea of Hosea was wholly new; for even Samuel had said: "To obey is better than sacrifice, and to hearken than the fat of rams" (1 Sam. xv. 22). And had we fuller records, we might find among earlier prophets much that seems to us now the conceptions of later ones. We cannot be wrong, however, in signalising certain prophets as the great expounders of certain conceptions, though we may find in their idiosyncrasies and their circumstances some explanation of their giving such ideas so great prominence.

We found that what brought perfection to the people of God, so far as that depended on God and the Divine side of the covenant, was the presence of God in His fulness among the people. Sometimes this presence is His presence in the Messianic king, and sometimes it is

His presence, so to speak, in Himself. These two lines cannot, of course, remain separate; and the New Testament unites them in one by making those passages which speak of the Lord's presence in His own Person, also to be Messianic passages. In doing so the New Testament writers stand on history. They have the history of Jesus behind them, and this history has interpreted much of the Old Testament to them. That splendid passage, Isa. xl. 1–11, which speaks of Jehovah coming in strength, *i.e.* in His fulness, and feeding His flock like a shepherd, is interpreted in the Gospels of the Son. It was in the Son, or as the Son, that Jehovah so manifested Himself. By the Old Testament prophet a distinction in the Godhead was not thought of; but subsequent revelation casts light on the preceding. The Lord, the Redeemer and Judge, is God in the Son.

Now the perfection of the covenant relation was reached when Jehovah thus came in His fulness among His people. It is difficult to realise what idea the Old Testament prophets had of this—how they conceived Jehovah present. They are obliged to adopt figures. His glory is seen, and physical images are employed to body out the spiritual ideas. The most brilliant pictures are in the second half of Isaiah. But there are some passages in this book where the prophet seems to show us what in his less exalted, or at all events more realistic, moments he probably really conceived Jehovah's presence to be. In xliv. 23 he says: "The Lord hath redeemed Jacob, and glorified Himself in Israel." In xlix. 3: "Thou art My servant, O Israel, in whom I will glorify Myself." In lx. 1, 3: "Arise, shine . . . for the glory of the Lord is risen upon thee . . . And the Gentiles shall come to thy light." These passages would seem to imply that Jehovah is presented in His presence through Israel itself, not as an independent glory; the glory of Israel is His glory. He and Israel are not two, but glorified Israel reflects His glory. And there is a singular passage (xlv. 14, 15) which perhaps confirms this view: "Thus saith the Lord,

The labour of Egypt, merchandise of Ethiopia and of the Sabeans, men of stature, shall come over unto thee . . . they shall fall down unto thee . . . saying, Surely God is in thee. . . . Verily thou art a God that hidest Thyself, O God of Israel, the Saviour."

It is worth observing here that the Servant of the Lord, whomsoever that remarkable conception represents in the mind of the prophet, does not appear as a distinct personage among Israel redeemed. He either is Israel redeemed, or he is not considered separately from them in their condition of glorified redemption. In chap. liii. Israel redeemed looks back upon the time when he was among them in his humility, and they confess how sadly they misapprehended him. "Who believed what we heard? and to whom did the arm of the Lord manifest itself? . . . We thought him smitten, and afflicted of God; but it was our sins that he bore: by his wounds we have been healed." But after chap. liii. the servant does not appear, except perhaps in chap. lxi. 1, 2, a passage the point of view of which is anterior to the redemption: "The Spirit of the Lord is upon me; because he hath anointed me to proclaim liberty to the captive; . . . to proclaim the acceptable year of the Lord, the day of vengeance of our God." The prophet, after chap. liii., speaks no more of the Servant of the Lord, but of the servants of the Lord—the people are all righteous, and taught of God; while before he spoke of "my righteous servant, whose ear was opened as that of one taught" (l. 4). Perhaps this point is in favour of those who think that the Servant of the Lord is not an individual. If an individual, it is strange that he wholly disappears when Israel is ransomed through his great sufferings. We should expect him to be at the head of the people. But the people have no head but Jehovah Himself. There is a very remarkable passage in chap. lv. 3 f., where the people are addressed: "Incline your ear, and come unto me . . . and I will make an everlasting covenant with you, even the sure mercies of David. Behold, I made him a witness to the peoples, a leader and commander of the peoples. Behold, thou shalt call nations that thou knowest not, and nations that know not thee shall run after thee for the sake of Jehovah thy God, and for the Holy One of Israel; for He hath glorified thee." Here the people, redeemed and glorified, are served heirs to the great promises made to David.

There is one other point here which I need only touch upon. The place of Israel glorified and of God present is, of course, in all the Old Testament writers the earth. God descends; His tabernacle is among men; men are not translated into heaven. The earth is transfigured, but it remains the earth, and abode of men. There is a new heavens and a new earth, but the two are still distinct; and the new earth is the inheritance of the saints. Of course, the conceptions of prophets are very various on this final condition of things. It was not given to them to see clearly here.

Now the word that describes the proper condition of the people on their side of the covenant relation is *righteous*. The difference between 'holy' and 'righteous' must be observed. 'Holy,' קָדוֹשׁ, is a term that expresses the being in covenant. It is equal to belonging to God, *i.e.* being His people; but *righteous* expresses the condition morally of those who are His people. This latter is the word that describes how the people should be at all times, and how it shall be at the end. And Isaiah mournfully exclaims: "How is the city that was faithful become an harlot! she in which righteousness dwelt; but now murderers" (i. 21). And in the later chapters of the book it is said of the restored and perfected Israel: "Thy people shall be all righteous" (lx. 21); "They shall be called trees of righteousness, the planting of our God, that He might be glorified" (lxi. 3); and again: "Ye shall be named the priests of the Lord; men shall call you the ministers of our God" (lxi. 6); and again: "I will greatly rejoice in the Lord . . . He hath covered me with the robe of righteousness, as a bridegroom decketh himself with ornaments" (lxi. 10). It is obvious that the term 'righteousness' is one that admits of considerable variety of use, and may cover wider or narrower meanings. We may refer a little to the usage of the word; and, second, to the general idea conveyed in the expression "the people shall be righteous." We shall inquire what this means when said of the people on their side of the covenant.

(1) As to the usage of the words צָדַק, צַדִּיק, צֶדֶק, and צְדָקָה—verb, adj., and noun.

In general, we may remark that the radical idea of these words is extremely difficult to detect. Most Hebrew words now applied to express ethical conceptions expressed, no doubt, originally physical ideas. In some cases we can reach these original conceptions. For example, the word יָשָׁר, translated *upright*, means 'plain' or 'level,' in a physical sense. Perhaps the radical idea in קָדוֹשׁ is "cut off, separated, removed to a distance." But the radical notion of צדק seems not to have survived. There is probably no passage in the Old Testament where it can be detected. Some, indeed, have thought they found it in Ps. xxiii. 3, מַעְגְּלֵי־צֶדֶק, "paths of righteousness," *i.e.* even or straight paths; but it is probable that there the meaning is the same as in other passages—"right paths" or "righteous paths," *i.e.* such paths as are conformable, appropriate to the requirements of sheep, or paths which are righteous, the figure being deserted. In Arabic the root means "to be true," *i.e.* to correspond to the idea and reality. The lexicographers, with some subtlety, say that a man to speak *ṣidq* must not only say what conforms to the reality, but at the same time what conforms to the idea in his own mind. Thus, if a man said: "Muhammed is the prophet of God," that, to be *ṣidq* or truth, must not only correspond to the fact, which of course it does, but also to his own idea, *i.e.* he must also believe it. Lexicographical subtleties of this kind are rarely very helpful; it is safer, first of all, to look to usage. Then it is possible that etymology may give an idea that binds the usages into one, or give a stem conception out of which all the other conceptions may be seen to have branched off.

If we consider now, first of all, the verb צָדֵק, imperf. יִצְדַּק, which is often translated *shall be justified* in English, as in Gr. δικαιωθήσεται, we find that the proper sense of it is, to be *right*, to be *in the right*, to have right on one's side. The idea is juridical, or, as it is called, forensic—belonging to the forum, or court of law. The Hebrews were fond of this conception, when a question arose between two persons, or when one blamed another, or the like; the parties were very readily conceived as parties to a suit before a judge. And when one defended another in any way, he was said to plead his cause. Thus Jehovah summons the nations and their gods to an imaginary tribunal: "Let them draw near; let us enter into judgment together (Isa. xli. 1). And so when the people are conceived as having a plea which they can bring forward of being true to the covenant obligations, the Lord says: "Let us plead together; declare thou that thou mayest be justified" (xliii. 26). Now the verb צָדֵק was said of the person who in such a real or imaginary plea was found by the real or supposed judge to be in the right, to have right on his side. Examples of this do not need to be multiplied. The one just cited from Isaiah is a good instance: declare לְמַעַן תִּצְדָּק; here there is no question of ethical righteousness, but of simple juridical right—having right on one's side. And, similarly, the passage in xliii. 9: "Let them bring forward their witnesses" (*i.e.* witnesses of their predictions), "that they be justified," found to have right, in this contested matter, on their side.

This is the idea of the simple stem. The causative or Hiphil agrees in meaning; it is to *find in the right*, to find, in one's action as a judge, a person to have right on his side; or, with other modifications, such as to *regard* one as in the right, or to *treat* one as in the right; as, *e.g.*, "I will not justify the wicked" (Ex. xxiii. 7)—treat the רָשָׁע as צַדִּיק. Of course, as a judge finds this by declaring it, the sense may be to declare one to have right on his side; but, properly, it is to find that one is in the right. It does not mean to *make* a man *ethically pure*. There seems no passage in the Old Testament where such a sense is possible, except, perhaps, Dan. viii. 14. To find right, or in the right, is the meaning of the Hiph., or to *justify*; or, with slightly different shades of meaning, to declare to be in the right, or show to have right on one's side. Thus the Servant of the Lord (l. 8) exclaims: "He is near that justifieth me," קָרוֹב מַצְדִּיקִי; "who will enter a plea against me?" (מִי יָרִיב אִתִּי). And in words almost identical, Job—whom God calls "My servant"—says: "I know that I shall be found in the right (אֶצְדָּק); who is he that will enter a plea with me?" (xiii. 18, 19).

Now this is a general mode of conception, applicable in a hundred ways. Any question, or charge, or claim may be brought under this juridical idea. The point on which a man may be arraigned, or suppose himself arraigned, may be a trifle—a point of etiquette, or the question of his life before God. To be in the right, or to have right on his side, may be equally various: it may be in a matter of speech, as speaking truth or no; a matter of custom or consuetudinary law; a matter of common morals; or a matter of his relation to God. The standard may be simply a fact, or any understood norm or rule, whether human or Divine, according to which conduct is measured. When Judah said in regard to Tamar the harlot צָדְקָה מִמֶּנִּי "she is in her rights as against me" (Gen. xxxviii. 26), and when the Psalmist cries: "In Thy sight shall no man living be justified" (יִצְדָּק), *i.e.* be right, or found in the right (Ps. cxliii. 3), they both use the word in the same sense, although the spheres referred to are widely apart. There is always a standard, always a cause; a man's conduct in a particular matter, or his life as a whole, is in question; and there is always a judge, real or imaginary. The standard may be very various, so may be the point or cause; the person is צדק when, before the judge, his act or life is in correspondence with the standard

Of course, in many cases the standard itself may be conceived as the judge, as when a man is condemned by his conscience, or by the popular customs, or by the principles of the covenant. Two passages in Job illustrate the flexibility of the usage in the higher sphere. Eliphaz, arguing against Job's complaints, says: "Shall mortal man be just (יִצְדַּק) with God?" (iv. 17), *i.e.* be found in the right as to his life.[1] To which Job replies: "Of course I know that it is so, How should man be just with God?" (ix. 2). Eliphaz means that, brought to God's bar, no man will be found righteous; Job means, no man can make his righteousness, though he have it, valid against God, or at God's bar, He being unwilling that he should; because His omnipotent power will hinder man from sustaining his cause. "I know that I have to be guilty," he elsewhere exclaims (ix. 15, 20). Thus it may be said in regard to this verb: (1) that it is not much in use in the older language; (2) that it is always used of persons; (3) that it means to be in the right, according to some standard, chiefly in a juridical sense; and (4) that this standard being sometimes the general law of conduct, the moral law, the word shows a tendency to be used of this conformity, or as we use *righteous* in an ethical sense, the juridical idea falling away. This tendency shows itself more and more in the language, *i.e.* the standard becomes more and more the great general principles of morals and religion.

Now the same things can be said in general of the adjective צַדִּיק righteous, in regard to which we need only remark: (1) that it is never used in the feminine; a curious fact, explained, perhaps, by the primary use being juridical, where the interests of men alone came into discussion—and it is only used of persons, with perhaps one exception

---

[1] On the interpretation of Job iv. 17 see the author's *The Book of Job with Notes*, etc. ("Cambridge Bible for Schools and Colleges"), p. 33, where he briefly discusses the competing renderings, and decides on the whole for *Can man be righteous before God?* This, he thinks, is most in harmony with the *time* at which the charge comes in, the scope of the following verses, and the general aphorism in v. 6, 7.—ED.

(Deut. iv. 8); and (2) the ethical notion begins to prevail over the juridical.

The use of the nouns צֶדֶק and צְדָקָה, which hardly differ in their general meaning, is of great interest, especially in Isaiah. The same general idea belongs to this word—that which has the quality of צֶדֶק, which is conformable to a norm or standard. This appears most plainly, first of all, when the word is predicated of things like measures and weights, e.g. אֵיפַת צ׳ a righteous ephah, אַבְנֵי צ׳ righteous weights, מֹאזְנֵי צ׳ a right balance. Our word *right* perhaps comes nearest to the meaning, *i.e.* conformable to the idea of an ephah, weights and balances. So Ps. iv. 5, זִבְחֵי צ׳, right sacrifices, such sacrifices as are agreeable to the idea of sacrifice. Perhaps even מִשְׁפַּט צ׳, right judgment, judgment such as it should be. Here again the norm or standard may vary indefinitely. That has the characteristic of צ׳ in any sphere which corresponds to the admitted norm in that sphere— whatever is *right* according to an understood standard.

The transition from this to conduct or actions is easy. The standard may be propriety, popular custom, what is due socially, or what is required in morals or religion. Naturally, in judging of actions, the last named standards will be those that are chiefly thought of. But as the standard deepens in its idea, righteousness will also acquire more inwardness and condensation. When said of men, the use of the word is readily understood, and hardly needs illustration.

But there can be little doubt that the same general idea appears when צ׳ is predicated of God. The point of difficulty here is naturally to discover the standard by which the action of God is estimated. There appears in the mind of the prophets, when they speak even of God, the generel feeling that there is a moral standard which is not merely God's will. Probably a difference between this standard and God's will rarely occurred to them—the two coincided. But there appears the feeling of the existence of such a standard. Even Abraham says: " Shall not the Judge of all the earth do right ? " (משפט, Gen. xviii. 25).

And in the Book of Job, the most modern of Hebrew books in its ways of thinking, Job openly charges God with injustice; and in one remarkable passage the patriarch proclaims his resolution to adhere to righteousness, though God and man alike should show themselves unjust (xxvii. 5, 6). But usually such a distinction probably was not drawn. God's will and action coincided with righteousness, and God's will was the norm of righteousness on that account practically, without its being the source of it absolutely, or to be identified with it. When God's actions, therefore, were estimated, they were naturally judged by the same standard as was applied when men's were judged. God acted righteously when He acted as a just man would have acted in the circumstances. This makes His righteousness often to be what is called retributive righteousness. And this is a common usage.

But in such passages as those in the second half of Isaiah manifestly this sense will not suit. God's righteousness there is a course of action conformable to a rule; but the rule is not that of the general law of morals. The word belongs to another sphere, namely, the redemptive sphere. The standard is not the moral law in God's mind as sovereign ruler; but some other standard in His mind as God of salvation. When He acts according to this standard, the attribute of 'צ belongs to Him or to His actions. Now this standard, of course, might be a general purpose in His mind in regard to Israel, in which case the standard would be the covenant relation. He acts בצ' when He acts as it becomes God in covenant with Israel. As the covenant was a redemptive one, this comes to much the same thing as to say that He acts as the God of salvation. The interesting point, however, is whether the idea of the prophet has not gone so far as to rise to this as the true conception of God. The purpose of salvation is not a purpose which He has formed, but is the expression of His very Being. It is His characteristic as God. When the prophet says of Cyrus: " I have raised him up in 'צ," that might very well be simply " in the region of a redemptive

purpose " (Isa. xlv. 13). And so when 'צ calls one to
follow it, or when God calls him in 'צ to follow Him, as
He elsewhere speaks of going before him. So when He
says to Israel, " I have chosen thee; I strengthen thee; I
uphold thee with the right hand of My righteousness "
(Isa. xli. 10), this might mean that He acts to Israel on
the lines of His relation to Israel and of His purpose.
And with this agree the many passages where 'צ is
parallel to salvation : " My salvation is near to come, and
My righteousness to be manifested " (lvi. 1).

But there are other passages which seem to go further,
and to show that Jehovah's actions, which are 'צב, were
some of them anterior to His relation to Israel, and
that His forming this relation illustrated His 'צ—in other
words, they rise to the elevation of making the salvation
of Israel, and through Israel that of the world, to be the
thing which is conformable to the Being of Jehovah, and
expresses it. For instance, Jehovah says to Israel : " I have
called thee in righteousness "—the entering into covenant
with Israel was in 'צ (xlii. 6). And in a remarkable
passage, xlv. 18 : " Thus saith the Lord that created the
heavens ; He is God, that formed the earth ; He made it
to be inhabited. I have sworn by Myself that to Me every
knee shall bow ; look unto Me, and be saved, all the ends
of the earth." Here the salvation of the world and the
original creation are brought together, and the first seems
anterior in idea to the second.

5. *Righteousness in the People.*

The Old Testament runs out its idea of the final
state and perfection of the kingdom of God and its
universality, more on the external side, in events and in
the relations of the nationalities of the world to one
another and to the Church. The various prophets differ
according to their circumstances in their idea how the
relations of Israel and the nations were to be adjusted.
In all, however, the heathen are brought into a relation

of submission and subordination to Israel; the Church at last overcomes and absorbs the heathen world.

In the same way the relations of the various classes within Israel are finally adjusted, as at the day of the Lord. All evil is judged and destroyed—the people are all righteous. And with the perfection of the Church comes in also the perfect state of creation. The earth yields her increase; there is abundance of corn even on the tops of the mountains; it shakes like Lebanon—the desert blossoms like the rose, and God's blessing is upon the people (Ps. lxxii. 16 ; Isa. xxxv. 1).

Of course, all Old Testament prophecies are written from the point of view of things as they then were, when Israel alone was the Church, and the nations were outside the covenant. And one of the most interesting and also most difficult tasks of the interpreter of prophecy is to decide how much of the prophetic form may have to be stripped off when applying the prophecies to our own dispensation. In the days of the Apostle Paul a state of things had entered that seemed almost the reverse of the state of things which formed the point of view from which the Old Testament was written. Israel seemed no more the Church, but outside of it. And this state of things raised the question to him in one way as it does to us in general, how the prophecies in regard to Israel were to be fulfilled. He fell back on the covenant; the gifts and calling of God are without repentance. The covenant formed with Israel secured their presence in the Church. The Church was indeed founded in Israel, which was the stock into which Gentiles were only grafted in. The natural branches broken off should be grafted in again, and all Israel should be saved (Rom. xi.). On the spiritual side alone is it that the apostle's reasoning is carried on. This leaves us without any guide so far as restoration to the land is concerned. We are thrown upon general considerations suggested by the ways of God upon the whole.

But how does the Old Testament run out its idea of

the consummation of the kingdom of God on the *inner* side—through such media as redemption from sin, righteousness, and immortality? Only very general statements can be made on this, at least on the two points of *righteousness* and *sin*. And in the Old Testament itself we need not look for more than general statements here. We need not look for such dogmatic passages as are found in the Epistles of St. Paul. The truth will be everywhere expressed in connection with concrete instances. The points of interest will be whether the truth, so far as it is expressed, agrees with the teaching of the New Testament, and how far it is expressed.

(1) *Righteousness.*—If we look at the point of *righteousness* in the Old Testament, we find this quite generally conceived at first. It is looked at always as manifesting itself in concrete cases, and as consisting in conduct. No doubt there are always two presuppositions; these are, first, the idea of God, to whom men are related; and, second, the idea of a moral order, binding on men in their relations to one another. These two ideas always go together. For a moral order of which God is not the Guardian and Upholder does not occur to Old Testament thinkers. No doubt, in the Book of Job—the most modern, perhaps, if again I may use the expression, of Old Testament creations —such an idea as that of a moral order in which God is not the Guardian is found. The sufferer there gives expression to it—momentary expression, however, only. Conscious of his rectitude, and yet receiving no recognition of it from God, but, on the contrary, being plagued every day, he is forced to the conviction that God is an arbitrary and unrighteous tyrant. Rectitude does not find her home and support in God. And Job rises to the highest grandeur to which he attains, when he declares that, though God be unrighteous, he at least will not let go his righteousness, but hold by it all the more firmly : "The righteous shall hold on his way, and he that hath clean hands shall wax stronger and stronger " (xvii. 9).

But ordinarily the ideas of God and the moral order

of life coincide. And to be righteous is to be found in practical harmony in one's conduct with this moral order. Hence on the widest scale Israel is the righteous nation in opposition to the heathen nations. And God's deeds in behalf of Israel are righteous acts; as in the New Testament the great saviours of the people are said, when their deeds in behalf of Israel are referred to, to have ' wrought righteousness.' On a smaller scale, those who live in harmony with the public law and customs of Israel are called ' righteous,' in opposition to those whose life is not governed by such principles—who are wicked (רָשָׁע). Hence an offence is what ought not to be done, or, more exactly, offences are things not done *in Israel*; and the doing of them is to work *folly* in Israel. They contradict the public conscience and law; in many instances an unwritten law, which was regulative of the people's life, and the standard of righteousness.

Righteousness consisted in a right attitude towards the existing constitution, and in conduct in harmony with its traditions. This general idea of righteousness as practical conduct in harmony with the laws of the constitution, explains several things. For one thing, it enables us to understand how saints are found making such strong assertions of their own righteousness, claiming from God the recognition of it, and appealing to His righteousness as that in Him which should make Him interfere on their behalf: " Hear me when I call, God of my righteousness " (Ps. iv. 1); " Judge me, O God, according to my righteousness, and according to mine integrity that is in me" (Ps. vii. 8); " Hear the right, O Lord " (Ps. xvii. 1); " The Lord has rewarded me according to my righteousness, according to the cleanness of my hands hath He recompensed me" (Ps. xviii. 20). And even in Isaiah the Church complains, " my right is passed over by my God ' (xl. 27) It is probably quite true that here we discover a state of mind which we should find no more in our dispensation ; and that where an Old Testament saint appeals to God's righteousness, we should rather make our appeal to His grace. Yet the point of view of these Old Testament saints must be understood. Otherwise we should judge them unfairly, and put them on a lower level than that on which they stand. They stand within a constitution, the principles of which are acknowledged. What they are conscious of is no more than rectitude, an upright and true attitude towards that constitution, in opposition to those against whom they complain. Their claim of righteousness is not a claim of sinlessness. It has little to do with this. The saint who confesses his sins in Ps. xxxii. proclaims his righteousness in Ps. vii., and appeals to God to acknowledge it in Pss. iv. and xvii., and declares that God has rewarded him according to the cleanness of his hands in Ps. xviii. The same Job who boldly declares, at what he knows to be the risk of his life, " I *am* righteous " (xxxiv. 5), and of whom God Himself speaks as " My servant Job, a perfect and upright man, one that feareth God and escheweth evil " (i. 8). elsewhere acknowledges his sins, and speaks of God as making him to possess the sins of his youth (xiii. 26). The righteousness of Old Testament saints is no more than what the New Testament calls a true heart, even when estimated at its highest. It is an upright attitude towards the covenant, and an honest endeavour to walk according to its principles.

And this covenant had for its fundamental principle that for sins of infirmity, sins not done wilfully against the covenant itself, there was forgiveness. It is this which they call the *righteousness* of God. *Righteousness* and *grace* really did not differ within the covenant relation. The righteousness of God in the Old Testament is, no doubt, rather an obscure point, but righteousness within the covenant was, in truth, grace. God's covenant meant that He would be gracious to men's infirmities; and He was righteous when He verified in men's experience the ideas and principles of the covenant which was founded on His grace. So far as what we might call the frame of the conception of Old Testament saints goes, there is nothing amiss in it.

Perhaps it is wanting in innerness, laying more stress on right external conduct than on the right condition of the heart. Still, with the right external conduct there is always combined a reference to the attitude of the mind towards God. The prophets lay real stress on justice and humanity ; and on the social duties—to perform these is to be true to the idea of the covenant. But the great embracing idea in their minds is that of the covenant itself, which God has imposed and upholds; and this causes conduct to have a reference always to God. Hence those epitomes of righteousness which we find often made in the Old Testament, as in Pss. xv., xxiv., while they contain mainly reference to conduct, always include a reference to God. He who shall ascend into the hill of the Lord is the man with clean hands, but also with a pure, *i.e.* upright, heart; who has not lifted up his soul or desire to vanity, *i.e.* to aught that is untrue, any order of life or thought in regard to the conception of Deity not embraced in the constitution of Israel. And Micah defines righteousness to be to do justly, to love mercy, *i.e.* humanity, and to walk humbly with God (vi. 8). In short, righteousness, as it comes before us in the Old Testament, is, as a rule, a practical thing. It is right conduct according to the idea of the constitution of Israel; and this conduct is, of course, regulated by, and reflects a right state of mind towards, the constitution.

Now, when we go a step further, and seek to get at the essence of what such a state of mind is, we come nearer to what we have in our minds when we inquire what righteousness is, *e.g.* when we put the question, How is a man righteous before God ? Practically, righteousness is spoken of as exhibited in conduct and in an attitude of mind. And the Old Testament hardly goes beyond this practical way of speaking. Nevertheless, we may reach what is considered the essence of righteousness. It need not be said that it is not to be sought in sinlessness, for such an idea nowhere appears. If a man calls himself, or is called by others, or is regarded by God as righteous, this is not because he is sinless, but because in some particular matter he has acted rightly according to the principles of piety or humanity embodied in the constitution of Israel, or generally that his life as a whole is in harmony with these principles. But such phraseology as is often met in Scripture—" If Thou shouldst mark iniquities, O Lord, who shall stand?" (Ps. cxxx. 2); "in Thy sight shall no flesh living be righteous" (cxliii. 2)? "for there is no man that sinneth not" (1 Kings viii. 46) —shows that sinlessness did not constitute righteousness before God. And the constitution, providing in its sacrificial system an institution for forgiveness, indicated that the people, though the idea of Israel was that of a righteous people, was not considered as a whole or in its members sinless.

Now the constitution was a covenant of God with the people. The covenant was made by God with Israel; He took the initiative. The idea of such a covenant is that God draws near to men. The idea of such a drawing near is that of favour or grace. This is the most general conception; it is in goodness, in self-communication, in giving to the people of His own fulness, that God draws near to men. Again, on the other side, i.e. on men's side, to correspond to this there must be the attitude of acknowledgment of this, of understanding this attitude of God towards them, and acceptance of it in thankfulness and humility. These are the great conceptions that constitute the framework of the covenant relation. Within this general frame there may be room for much variety, both in God's way of drawing near, i.e. in the operations He performs, in the ways in which He manifests Himself, and in the gifts He communicates, as those of knowledge and life, and also in man's conduct and way of thinking, which will vary according to the knowledge he receives, the life that is awake within him, and the circumstances in which he is placed. But variety of this kind, however great, is within the limits of the great general relation of the two parties to one another. The external frame is, so to speak, very elastic, permitting growth and expansion to any degree within it.

6. *Righteousness, Grace, and Faith.*

Now, that this great general conception was the main thing—the idea of this general relation of God and the people—is shown by the constitution itself. What was required of the people was an attitude of mind and heart corresponding to this relation of God to them—a receptivity and acceptance on their part of God as He drew near to them. Within this general attitude which was required, the life of the individual might be a very chequered one, marked by great imperfections, and even by sins which might be voluntary. Such sins were great evils, which it was the object of the covenant relation more and more to overcome; but they did not involve suspension of the relation itself. Only sins like that of unbelief, as Israel's in the wilderness, or idolatry, which was a denial of the idea of the covenant with Jehovah, involved the suspension of the covenant, and were followed by cutting off from the people. Such sins infringed that general attitude of mind toward God which was demanded as a response to His approach to the people. Now, if we ask what terms express the idea of God's drawing near to men on the one side, and the idea of their reception of this and right bearing of mind towards it, there are no terms that do so but *grace* and *faith*. It is quite true that at one time God's grace might be much fuller than at another. He might unveil His face more fully, impart knowledge in greater abundance, communicate His Spirit in greater power. All this, however, does not alter the general and the essential in His attitude towards the people, or its loving grace. It is equally true that men's feeling of His love might be deeper, their thankfulness profounder, their dependence more absolute, their trust more perfect and implicit, as time advanced. But all this does not touch the essence of the attitude at all times, which was *faith*.

In the general Old Testament way of speaking, a man

may be found righteous in regard to his individual acts, or in regard to his general life. But it is to be observed that this is the case of a man within the covenant, not of one outside of it. And his being within the covenant presupposes and implies his general attitude towards God of faith. Unless by his conduct he shows the reverse, and is cut off, this is assumed. And here lies the essence of his being right with God, his response by faith to His grace, in accepting the covenant and the continued exhibition of this condition of mind in the man's life and conduct. The righteous acts for which he is found righteous are only the exhibition of his attitude towards God and His covenant of grace. The covenant was made with the people as a whole, and its blessings became the possession of individuals as members of the general body. This is the Old Testament conception, and for a long time this conception remains intact.

But, of course, though this be the general conception, in point of fact the individual must exhibit for himself the condition of mind demanded of the whole; and as the people as a whole were endowed with God's Spirit, this was also the possession of the individual as a member of the whole. It is only in the later prophets, like Jeremiah, that the individual rises into the prominence which he receives in the Pauline conception of righteousness, or something like prominence. But what I wish to indicate at present is, that the same general conceptions in regard to grace and righteousness are characteristic of the first covenant as of the new. To be righteous is to be right, *i.e.* to be found taking towards God's covenant, which is a thing having as its principle grace, the right attitude; and this attitude is faith.

Of course, this faith is not conceived as an abstract thing; it is faith in the particular circumstances of the people's condition. It is always practical. It is the faith of James: "I will show thee my faith by my works" (ii. 18). And it naturally always desired to see the response of God to it in deeds of salvation on behalf of the people. Circumstances, however, tended to clarify this faith, and give it a profounder and more strictly spiritual character. The time came when any interference of Jehovah on behalf of the State was hopeless. Its destruction was inevitable. The people's minds were drawn away from the present, and fixed upon the future. Faith was cut away from its connection with any form of national life or external condition, and it became a spiritual relation to God. And by the same process it became less a national thing than a condition of the individual mind. Israel's national ruin cut the people into two classes, and faith found refuge with one—with those that looked for the consolation of Israel. Again, it is quite probable that even in this faith there may have been elements that required sifting and clearing away; but faith rose to be a spiritual trust in the unseen, "the substance of things hoped for, the evidence of things not seen" (Heb. xi. 1).

One thing else may be referred to as indicating that the essence of man's relation to the covenant was faith in Jehovah. That is the fact that idolatry, denial that Jehovah alone was God of Israel, was followed by cutting off from the people. This struck at a point behind the covenant, and threw the sinner outside the sphere where Jehovah was gracious: it was general retribution over against His grace. The same idea rules the institution of sacrifice. Only for sins of ignorance or infirmity were sacrifices available. Sins wilful, or done with a high hand, again struck at the fundamental conception of the relation; they were direct attacks upon the principle of the covenant, and they could not be atoned for.

Now, exactly corresponding to this negative point was the positive point of the *law*. The law was given to the people in covenant. It was a rule of life, not of justification; it was guide to the man who was already right in God's esteem in virtue of his general attitude towards the covenant. The law is not to Israel a law of morals on the bare ground of human duty, apart from God's exhibition of His grace. It is a line marked out along which the life of the people or the person in covenant with God, and already right with God on that ground, is to unfold itself. No assumption of sinlessness is made, nor, indeed, is such a thing demanded. The institutions of atonement provided for the taking away of sins done through infirmity, and the law was a direction to the believer how to bear himself practically within the covenant relation. A man's conduct shows him to be righteous; he is justified by works. But this is not the technical use of the term *justification* now in use. It is another use quite legitimate, not to be opposed to the technical use, but possible alongside of it. Faith precedes this justification; it is a right attitude within the covenant. If we may say so, it is not the man himself that is justified by works, but his faith. This is one way of thinking, and it may have some affinity with the line of thought in the Epistle of James.

But another line of expression and feeling may also be observed. That touches the idea of a *righteousness imputed*. First, we observe it most clearly in the life of individuals. It is connected with the consciousness of sin. Generally, perhaps, some more flagrant sin had awakened the conscience, and given a deeper sense of the sinfulness of nature in the sinner, and led him to seek refuge immediately in God's forgiveness, as in Psalms xxxii. and li. But, no doubt, without the commission of flagrant sins the sense of man's sinfulness became deeper as the national life progressed. The great sorrows to which individuals were subjected in the time of the dissolution of the State caused deeper thought on the causes of their misfortunes, imparted a profounder sense of the alienation of the mind from God, and sharpened the conviction that righteousness could be obtained only in God's forgiving mercy. Secondly, we observe the same line of reflection in the prophets. The nation was, in their view, incurably sinful; it had broken the covenant; righteousness under the first covenant was no more to be hoped for. Only in a new covenant, the very foundation of which was a complete Divine forgiveness, could the people be found righteous.

We see the steps of this thought, as always, most clearly in Jeremiah. He begins with preaching repentance to the people; only by repentance can the calamity of destruction be averted. Suddenly, in the midst of his calls to the people to repent, the question seems to occur to him, Can they repent? Is there any ability in them to do what is demanded of them? Can the Ethiopian change his skin, or the leopard his spots? All hope from the side of the people or of man is over. Only in God can righteousness for them be found. He is " the Lord our righteousness " (xxiii. 6). Hence he finds refuge in the conception of a new covenant in which God bestows righteousness: " I will forgive their iniquity, and remember their sin no more " (xxxi. 34). We perceive in the Old Testament the same general conceptions as in the New, although they are presented more practically and in a less precise form.

7. Suffering and Imputation.

There was a corresponding development of thought on the subject of *suffering*, the *imputation* of sin, and the relation of the individual to the family and the nation.

In the earlier Scriptures these questions did not come into prominence. There the doctrine is taught that God visits the iniquity of the fathers upon their children unto the third and fourth generation. The idea seems to be that the fathers are still punished, their punishment falling on them in their children. The standing of the children as individuals is not thought of, nor the question what relation the calamity has to them. The idea of unity is the uppermost; and the idea that the descendants belong to the original offender, and that he is still suffering God's anger in his children. It was naturally to be expected that in the age of Jeremiah, when the relation of men to God as individuals, and in their own right, so to speak, came to be more prominently treated, this question of the punishment of one's descendants for his sin should come up also. And so we find it in the prophets and writers of that age. The people perhaps felt that they were suffering for the sins of their ancestors. They said: "The fathers have eaten a sour grape, and the children's teeth are set on edge" (Jer. xxxi. 29). In some way they abused this doctrine, either in the way of self-exculpation, or in the way of charging God with unrighteousness. The prophet Jeremiah takes up the proverb. Its use raised the question in his mind. He seems to perceive in the method of God's dealing with men, which this proverb suggests, what is the essence of the old covenant method—the method of dealing with men in the mass, or with Israel as a community; a method which obliterated the rights of the individual, or under which, at least, the individual did not come into the prominence that belonged to him. And he foresees the time when this method shall no more prevail.

But if this method no more prevail, its cessation will be because God and the individual heart will become the two factors in the covenant relation. The external organism will come to an end. All that made Israel distinctive as a community, its external organisation, its old palladiums of redemption and salvation, its orders of teachers, like priests and prophets—all this will come to an end. Men shall no more call to mind the ark of the covenant; they shall no more teach every man his neighbour; the law and ordinances shall no more be external. Hence this proverb comes to an end simultaneously with the coming in of the new order of things called the New Covenant: "Behold, the days come, saith the Lord, . . . that as I have watched over them to pluck up and to break down, so will I watch over them to build and to plant, saith the Lord. In those days they shall say no more, The fathers have eaten a sour grape, and the children's teeth are set on edge. But every man shall die for his own iniquity. Every man that eateth the sour grape, his teeth shall be set on edge. Behold, the days come that I will make a new covenant with the house of Israel . . . I will put My law in their inward parts and write it in their hearts . . . they shall all know Me" (xxxi. 29–34).

That the principle of punishing the children for the sins of the fathers was much speculated on in this age, appears also from the fact that the same proverb is referred to by Ezekiel (xviii. 2), and its further prevalence denied. And in the Book of Job, where all such questions concerning evil are focused, Job repudiates the doctrine, and holds the procedure unjust. He points to the fact that a man is often not punished for his sins in this life. His friends reply that the punishment falls on his children. To which he answers, Let God chastise the man himself; what concern hath he in his house after him when the days of his own life are completed? Job's reply is to the effect that the method of Providence referred to is unjust, and in point of fact fails as a punishment on the man himself, seeing he is all unconscious of the incidence of God's anger on his descendants (xxi. 16–34).

What made the question of such profound interest was this. God's external treatment of men was held to reflect His true relation to them. Chastisements were indications of His anger. A distinction was not yet drawn between God's external providence and God's true mind towards men. In the Book of Job we perceive this distinction in the very course of being arrived at. Yet Job, though he knows the two things, calls them both God, and appeals to the one against the other: "Mine eye poureth out tears to God that He would procure justice for a man with God"[1] (xvi. 20). Thus God's external dealing with men being the reflection of His true relation to them, the injustice of inflicting anger on the children for the sins of the father was manifest so soon as the idea of individual rights occurred to one. Hence Jeremiah has no help but to demand a complete reversal of this pro-

[1] In his commentary on *The Book of Job* ("Cambridge Bible for Schools and Colleges "), Dr. Davidson puts it so—" Job now names his Witness, and states what he hopes for from Him.

"20 My friends scorn me :
    Mine eye poureth out tears unto God,
21 That He would maintain the right of a man with God,
    And of a son of man against his neighbour."—ED.

ceeding; and he seems to require that evil shall not fall on a man's descendants because of a man's sins. We know that this involvement of others in a man's sin continues to be the case, and must be. But we draw the distinction between evils of this kind and God's true relation to the individual. Salvation is to be distinguished from this more external sphere. No doubt the two will influence one another, as a man's condition or circumstances may influence his knowledge of God, or his will to receive the truth. The Apostle Paul has carried back this principle into the history of Israel from the beginning, distinguishing between God's treatment of the nation and His relation to individuals.

The elevation of the individual into religious prominence, and the constituting him, so to speak, the religious unit instead of the people, had wide consequences. No doubt the community was made up of individuals, and the teaching of the prophets, though directed to the nation, must at all times have been taken home by individuals to themselves. And in order fully to realise the life of Israel, we have to take into account the Psalms and the Wisdom books as well as the Prophets. It is in these more subjective writings that the life of the individual and his thoughts find expression. It is extremely difficult to place these writings with any certainty in their true historical place. It is also at all times difficult, no doubt, to detect in history the causes that brought into prominence certain questions. But at all events the dissolution of the State as a religious unit naturally brought into prominence the standing of the individual towards God. The extreme hardships also borne by many pious men at this period forced upon men's thoughts the relation of evil in God's providence to sin and to righteousness. Even the destruction of Israel as a nation, and its subjection to heathen conquerors, might have raised this question.

No doubt, in many minds the deep consciousness of the sin of the nation was sufficient to allay and remove doubt. These heathen conquerors were but instruments of chastisement in Jehovah's hand; the Assyrian was "the rod of His anger" (Isa. x. 5). Yet, on the other hand, Israel was, in comparison with these idolatrous, cruel nations, the righteous people, the servant of God. The truth was in Israel; there was a holy stock in it. Such thoughts would arise, perhaps, only later, when the oppressions of the Exile had been long continued, and there seemed no hope of release from it. Then the problem of evil became oppressive to the mind of godly men. And it was the subject of much reflection, and received, perhaps, various solutions.

One remarkable book in the Old Testament is devoted to the discussion of it, the Book of Job. This book may discuss the *evils* of Israel or those of Judah, but probably its theme is suggested by the *calamities* that befell either the Northern or the Southern State. It may be going too far to say that Job is a type of the people; that is, that the people are spoken of personified under his name. That is scarcely probable, and the supposition is not necessary. It is the sufferings of individuals, godly individuals, that are exhibited. Job is but a specimen, an idealised specimen. But the solution proposed by the author of the book is that these sufferings are not for sin, for Job is perfect and upright, fearing God and eschewing evil (i. 1); they are a trial of righteousness, and if borne in patience and devoutness, lead to a restoration and a higher blessedness. This view makes Job's sufferings only have meaning if they are but examples of the sufferings of many who suffered like himself. Job's sufferings have no relation to any but himself. Job is not in his sufferings a Messianic type. His history is consoling to sufferers, whose sufferings may be severe or mysterious—to religious men; it has not a higher value. The solution of the meaning of sufferings which is given by the prophet Isaiah in the second half of his book, is much more profound. There the Servant of the Lord suffers innocently, too, like Job; but his sufferings are for the sins of the guilty.

There is, again, this case of the descendants of sinners, who suffer the evils of their forefathers' sins. The circumstances of the time brought this question into prominence. The godly exiles were bearing the iniquities of their fathers. And men's thoughts were turned to the old doctrine of retribution enunciated early, that God visits the sins of the fathers upon the children unto the third and fourth generation. The question is of interest, because we see the minds of the wise of that age working their way towards a truth, or at least towards setting forth prominently a truth, which, though always a truth, does not receive much prominence before this time—the truth, namely, set forth by St. Paul, that they are not all Israel who are of Israel (Rom. ix. 6); that within the outer frame of Israel, the nominal people of Jehovah, there is an inner circle to whom, in truth, God is communicating the blessings of the covenant. We perceive this great truth receiving prominence at this epoch in two forms, both leading, however, to the same result, one in the Book of Job, and another in such prophets as Jeremiah. The truth is set foith in the form that God's external treatment of the individual, or the people, is not the index of God's true relation to either. In other words, religion is divorced from any connection with what is external, and is driven into the heart, and made to be a relation of the spirit to the Lord, which no proofs in the shape of external blessings may attend. The calamities of Job were no proof that God's heart was not towards him ; the dispersion of the nation, or at least the breaking up of the external forms of the religious state, did not invalidate religion

This may seem a commonplace to us, but perhaps it was little short of a revolution in the thinking of many in Israel. For the fundamental idea, so to speak, of the Old Covenant was that the people's relation to the Lord was reflected in their external circumstances. The external blessings were the seal to them of God's favour ; calamity was the token to them of His anger. It was the same in the case of the individual. Perhaps for long they could hardly realise God's favour out of connection with the external tokens of it. The fundamental conception of the Wisdom was, that it was well with the righteous and ill with the wicked. This general principle, no doubt true as a general principle, was taken up as without exception. And, in like manner, it needed God's severe dealing with them to bring home to them their sense of sin ; or at least they saw His anger reflected in calamity. The conflict between Job and his friends on the meaning of calamity, and their pertinacious maintenance of the theory that suffering is always due to sin, indicate to us the kind of questioning that was going on in men's minds in this age. And when the author of the book allows Job to drive his opponents from the field on this point, we perceive that it was his purpose to discredit the doctrine, in the shape in which they advanced it, as one that could not be maintained. While, when he brings forward his own doctrine, that calamity may not be for sin, but as a trial of righteousness, we see at least one other solution of the question, one applicable not only to individuals, but to the suffering nation.

But what is more interesting is the conflict in Job's own mind, and his successful effort to realise to himself that, in spite of God's severe chastisement of him, God and he are still in true fellowship. The way in which he expresses this is singular enough, but also intelligible enough. To his mind God was the immediate author of every event. His sufferings came direct from God's hand. And he, unlike the author of the book, still held that sufferings indicated the anger of God, or at least that God was holding him guilty of sins. Yet he rises to the assurance that God knows his innocence; one God holds him guilty, another knows his innocence, and he appeals to the one against the other. This is but his Hebraistic way of affirming that God's heart as He is in Himself is toward him, though His outer providence be against him. But this half solution, as we may call it, which is forced to make two out of the one God, indicates to us the struggles which it cost men at this time to rise, even under the teaching of God's providential dealings, to the idea that religion was a thing altogether of the relation of the spirit to God, and that it might exist with no external tokens of God's favour.

IX. DOCTRINE OF REDEMPTION—SUPRAHUMAN GOOD AND EVIL.

1. *Angels.*

Something has been said of the ideas of evil entertained in Israel and expressed in Scripture, and of the consciousness of sin and guilt among the people of God. But another question presents itself, which is of great interest, and also of some importance. That is the question of the existence of evil outside the sphere of the human mind and human society. Are there traces of a belief in the existence of a superhuman evil to be found in the Old Testament as in the New? And if so, to what extent of development had this belief attained among the covenant people in the prophetic age in particular? This is a large question; and to speak in a judicious manner upon it requires an extensive observation of individual passages scattered largely about in many writings, and a careful weighing of the amount of meaning to be fairly attached to them in the circumstances and connections in which they are found. The question has two sides: one, the existence of evil in regions lying outside human life, and among the creatures of God not belonging to the human race; the other, the influence of beings of this kind upon the destiny of man in general, and upon the self-determination of individual minds among men in particular. Both these questions receive large illumination in the New Testament. All that can be looked for in the Old Testament will be traces of beliefs going in the same direction

as the more fully developed New Testament doctrines
And the most interesting question will be whether such
traces be actually discoverable, and to what distance in
this direction they may be followed.

Now, *first*, the raising of such a question brings us face
to face with another question, namely, the question of the
existence of beings not creatures of God such as men are,
but standing in moral relations to Him as men do, and as
all beings in the universe must do.   For the God of Israel,
who is also the God of the whole universe, is no mere
unmoral force in the universe, nor the unmoral sum of all
the forces in the universe ; He is, above all things, an ethical
Being.   His physical nature is hardly ever alluded to in
the Old Testament.   It does not even go the length, which
the New Testament does, of calling Him Spirit, though it
gives numerous predications regarding Him, and assigns
numerous attributes to Him, which show that the conception of His spiritual essence underlay all current ideas and
modes of expression regarding Him.   There is, I think,
only one passage in the Old Testament which approaches
to saying in words that He is Spirit.   It is the passage
already alluded to in Isaiah : " The Egyptians are men, and
not God ; their horses are flesh, and not spirit " (xxxi. 3).
The Old Testament has no place for speculations upon the
physical essence of God.   It does not say that He is
Spirit ; it says that He has a Spirit, which is the source
of all life and organic existence in the world.   But its
main interest lies in defining God as an ethical Being,
and placing all other beings in the universe in ethical
relations to Him.

And these ethical relations cover the whole forms of
existence and every manifestation of the life of these other
beings.   We are fond, in our scientific analytic manner, of
dividing man into two elements, soul and body ; and so
does Scripture in a general way.   But Scripture never goes
the length that we are apt to go of calling the body a
material organism, and regarding it as subject to the laws
of organisms ; that is, laws different from moral laws, and

applying to the body of man as a thing outside the region
of moral law.   In the Old Testament, man, body and soul,
is a unity; and that unity is a moral unity, standing in
relations to the great moral Being in the universe; and
man, in his body as well as in his soul, *i.e.* man as a whole,
belongs to the region of the moral world.   All that he does
is estimated on moral principles; all that happens to him
illustrates moral principles; and if any part of him, as his
body, falls into another region, where other laws prevail,
e.g. the region of material organism, this is because something has occurred in his history which has disrupted the
unity of his being, and thrown the elements of his nature,
for a time at least, into another region, and subjected it to
the laws that prevail in that sphere, namely, to the laws of
material dissolution and decomposition.   But this is the
effect of evil, and is only temporary.   The scheme of restitution retrieves it.   And the Scripture doctrine is that
when he is restored, man again becomes a unity, and all
the parts of this unity enter together again into the moral
sphere, and the unity takes up the right moral relation to
God and retains it for ever; a doctrine which is expressed
in words not unfamiliar to us: "Their bodies being united
to Christ, do rest in their graves till the resurrection"
(*Shorter Catechism*),—*i.e.* the new man is united to Christ,
both in his soul and in his body, as an indivisible unity.
But this being the conception of the Old Testament, it
being just its characteristic that it passes this moral judgment on all beings, it is to be looked for that if it assumes
the existence of other beings besides man, it will not leave
undetermined the moral sphere to which they belong.   If
there be angels, they will be either good or bad angels.

Now, *first*, that there are beings called *angels*, Scripture
does not prove, but everywhere it assumes.   No person
denies that the people of Israel and the writers of Scripture believed in the existence of beings so named, or that
Scripture makes the belief its own.   The question which
some persons have raised, or have been supposed to raise,
is not whether Scripture makes this belief its own, but

whether, after all, it may not be just an opinion current in those days and among that Eastern people, which, though made its own by Scripture, yet, not being of the essence of religion, may be in our day legitimate subject for discussion, with the view of arriving at scientific conclusions on the subject. With the question in that form we do not deal here. It is part of the general question of Scripture itself.

But the question may appear in another form. It may be put thus: Does not Scripture sometimes so speak of angels as to show that in the minds of the writers their personality was not always very clearly conceived; that though on many occasions this personality seems clearly grasped, on other occasions it is dim, and the angelic being melts away into a mere manifestation of the providence of God in some form, as when it is said: "He makes winds His angels, and a flame of fire His messengers"? (Ps. civ. 4). And the question is put, Is it not this class of passages that we should regard as giving the key to the true Biblical conception of the angels? Are they not mere manifestations of God's providential and redemptive activity, first idealised into living agencies, and then further adorned with personal attributes, those of strength, holiness, and the like, which are characteristic of God's action in providence and in grace? Now, that is a question which is not like the other one lying behind Scripture; it is one raised on the stage of Scripture itself, and no one need be afraid to discuss it.

I shall only say in regard to it, that the view appears to me to invert the Scripture method of conception. The angels are in Scripture the agents and ministers of God in His providence and grace. They are, according to the later generalisation regarding them, "all ministering spirits, sent forth to minister for the sake of them who shall be heirs of salvation" (Heb. i. 14). They carry out God's will, and communicate to His saints strength or light. But as doing so they are personal beings; and the phraseology which uses the name of angels for the mere providence of God and His care of men, is a later phraseology, which reposes upon the more strict and usual conception of what the angels are, and applies it in a looser way. Passages of this sort may be found, perhaps, in Ps. xxxiv. 7 : " The angel of the Lord encampeth round about them that fear Him"; and Ps. xci. 11 : " He shall give His angels charge over Thee, to keep Thee in all Thy ways. They shall bear Thee up in their hands, lest Thou dash Thy foot against a stone." It may be difficult in particular cases to decide between the strict use of the name to indicate personal agents, and its more colourless use for God's providential care. The colourless use, however, is not the primary, but the secondary application, and reposes on what is more strict; it is a figurative mode of speech, which is based, however, on what many times is actual fact.

Now, *second*, Scripture uses certain names for these superhuman beings. And these names are of two kinds : first, those which define their nature, or the class or grade of being to which they belong, in contrast with the race of men ; and, second, those which describe their office, in regard to God or men. Names of the first kind are אֱלֹהִים or בְּנֵי א', אֵלִים or בְּנֵי א'. They are called *Elohim*, or *sons of Elohim; Elim*, or *sons of Elim.* This expression is no doubt wrongly translated in our Version 'sons of God.' The name *Elohim* is used both for God and for angels. The angels are *Elohim* ; and as a family or class they are 'sons of Elohim,' just as prophets are *Nebi'im*, or *sons of Nebi'im.* The idea that they are called 'sons of God' because they stand in close relation to God, or because they share in the purely spiritual nature of God, is not contained in the expression ; neither is the idea present that they are the *adopted sons* of God, having stood the period of probation with success, and now received into His family. This cannot be meant ; for in Job the Satan appears among the 'sons of Elohim,' and is one of them. We found the name *Elohim* to mean 'mights,' 'powers,' and it is with this meaning that the name is given to the angels. In contrast with man, angels belong to the class of Elohim. In Ps. xxix. 1 our Version reads quite rightly if the name is to be interpreted, "Give unto the Lord, O ye mighty, give unto the Lord glory and strength"—literally: "Give unto the Lord, ye sons of Elim." The 'sons of Elim' form the attendants and ministers around Jehovah; and in the end of the Psalm it is said: "In His palace doth every one say, Glorious!" In Ps. lxxxix. 6 the same expression is translated "sons of the mighty": "Who in heaven can be compared with Jehovah, who among the sons of the mighty —*Bene Elim*—can be likened unto the Lord?"

The angels, therefore, in contrast with the human race, belong to the class of Elohim. They are sons of Elohim. The exegetical tradition firmly reposes on this fact. And perhaps in some cases it may apply the name *Elohim* to angels where it properly means *God*, as in Ps. viii. 6 : "Thou hast made him a little lower than Elohim"; in the Septuagint 'angels,' though modern interpreters prefer 'God.' I am not sure whether the exegetical tradition here be not more in accordance with the modes of thinking in the Old Testament.

It might be an interesting question how the same name *Elohim* came to designate God and this class of beings. Perhaps we should be satisfied with the general explanation, that the name, meaning 'powers,' is applied from the standpoint of men to all that is above man, to the region lying above him. Though the same name is given, the two are never confounded in Scripture. But if this answer does not seem satisfactory, our inquiries will throw us back into a prehistorical period, a period where the genesis of the general name Elohim and its general applications must be investigated. From the beginning of Scripture we find God and these Elohim called by the same name; He is surrounded by them; they are His servants, and they minister to His purposes of grace and providence. We can quite well perceive, however, how this broke open a line of thought in another direction. The false gods of heathenism were also *Elohim*; and in this way certain classes of angels and these gods were brought into connection or identification, and the gods of the nations became *demons* or evil angels. There is a curious fluctuation in the exegetical tradition, due, perhaps, to this mode of conception. In Ps. xcvii. 7 it is said: "Confounded be all they that serve graven images, that boast themselves of idols: worship Him, all ye gods"; but the Septuagint renders: "worship Him, all ye angels."

These Elohim, or sons of Elohim, form the council of Jehovah. They surround Him, and minister to Him. He and they are Elohim. And it is from this point of view that some explain the use of the plural in such passages as "Let us make man" (Gen. i. 26); "Let us go down and there confound their language" (Gen. xi. 7). In character these angels are said to *excel in strength*, and to be *mighty* (Ps. ciii. 20); they are styled קְדֹשִׁים (Job v. 1, xv. 15; Ps. lxxxix. 6, 8; Zech. xiv. 5; Dan. viii. 13). And from their ministering office the representation appears in Job that they interpret to men God's afflictive providences with them; and, on the other side, might be supposed to receive men's complaints of this too severe chastisement: "Cry then; is there any that will answer thee? and to which of the 'ק wilt thou turn?" (v. 1). The passage is poetical, and merely touches upon a supposed turn that Job's mind might take. It does not go the length of teaching that it is part of the office of angels to intercede, or even to represent. Although these excel in purity far above men, the profound consciousness of the Creator's holiness in Israel represents Him as finding something to blame in them: "He charges His angels with error" (Job iv. 18). Names are also given to these angels as having certain characteristics, or filling certain offices, as *seraphim, cherubim*.

There is another class of names given to these beings, however, which is of great interest. They are called angels, מַלְאָכִים, *i.e. messengers*, and מְשָׁרְתִים, *i.e. ministers*. These names describe their office, and the place they have in the providence of God. All the Old Testament is filled with illustrations of their operations in this sphere, and examples need not be cited. "The angels represent in a personal manner," says Hermann Schultz, "God's care of His people; they are the medium of His government of His kingdom, and of His interference in the affairs of the world. They reveal the will of God in reference to the present and the future, call men of God to the undertaking of great deeds which God will accomplish by their hand (as Moses, Jerubbaal), deliver the pious out of danger, and execute the judgments of God against the sinful world, or the disobedient in Israel, as in the case of David. When they manifest themselves among men, it is always as armed with some commission from God, which they come to execute." [1]

2. *The Angel of the Lord.*

As God's manifestations of His will and His interferences in the world are predominantly in the way of carrying out His purpose of redemption, the angels usually appear on missions of mercy or in furtherance of the salvation, either of individuals, or of the people as a whole. Prominent among those who labour in this direction stands one angelic figure, who has always attracted largely the attention of interpreters, and regarding whom very diverse judgments have been passed, 'the Angel of the Lord.' It has not been uncommon to find in him a manifestation of the Logos or Son of God, and in his appearance among men a pre-intimation of the incarnation. With regard to the name 'Angel of the Lord,' of course any angel may bear this name. And in many places where such a name is applied, there is no reason to consider that the angelic being to whom it is given is in any way distinguished from others. Thus in 1 Kings xix. 5, it is said that as Elijah lay under a juniper tree an angel touched him; and then further on in the narrative: "And the Angel of the Lord said unto him." The definiteness here arises from the fact of the angel having been already mentioned. So in the history of David it is said that the angel stretched out his hand upon Jerusalem; and then it is added that the angel

[1] *Alt. Theol.*, i. p. 560.

of the Lord was standing by the floor of Araunah the Jebusite (2 Sam. xxiv. 16). Passages of a similar kind are numerous.

But there are many passages of a different kind, where the definiteness of the expression 'the Angel of the Lord' cannot be explained in this way, and where things are said of this angel that are scarcely applicable to ordinary angelic messengers. Thus at the period of the Exodus, the Angel of the Lord led Israel; and it is said regarding him: "Behold, I send an Angel before thee, to keep thee in the way and to bring thee into the place which I have prepared. Beware of him, and obey his voice, provoke him not; for he will not pardon your transgressions: for My name is in him. But if thou shalt indeed obey his voice, and do all that I speak," etc. (Ex. xxiii. 20–23). And in Ex. xxxii. 34 it is said: "Mine Angel shall go before thee"; which in Ex. xxxiii. 14 is varied: "My presence (פָּנַי, My face) shall go, and I will give thee rest"; and in Isa. lxiii. 9 the two are combined: "In all their affliction he was afflicted, and the Angel of His presence (פָּנָיו, i.e. the Angel of His face, the Angel who was His face) saved them; in his love and in his pity he redeemed them." Here regarding this Angel two things are said: that Jehovah's name, i.e. His revealed character, is in him; and that he is Jehovah's face, i.e. the face of Jehovah may be seen in him. They who look upon him look upon Jehovah, and in him all that Jehovah is is present. Hence he saves, and will not pardon transgression, though he has the power. With these passages are to be combined others which describe the emotions of those to whom the Angel appeared, e.g. Jacob said: "I have seen God face to face, and my life is preserved" (Gen. xxxii. 30); and when he recurs to this event in his dying prophecy, he says: "The Angel which redeemed me from all evil, bless the lads" (xlviii. 16).

These passages indicate that in the minds of those to whom this angel appeared, it was an appearance of Jehovah in person. Jehovah's face was seen. His name was revealed. The Angel of the Lord is Jehovah present in

definite time and particular place. What is emphatic is
that Jehovah here is fully present. In particular providences one may trace the presence of Jehovah in influence
and operation. In ordinary angelic appearances one may
discover Jehovah present on some side of His being, in
some attribute of His character; in the Angel of the Lord
He is fully present, as the covenant God of His people, to
redeem them. It is the fulness of the manifestation that
is emphasised in the name. Now, it may be difficult to
say whether the pious in Israel conceived this full manifestation as effected through the medium of an angel like
other partial revelations of God's will and of His power, or
considered it a thing quite distinct. On the one hand,
while freely considering that Jehovah used instruments to
effect His purposes by, they were jealous of ever seeming
to confound Jehovah with His agents. On the other, the
manifestation is called the *Angel* of the Lord, like other
manifestations. Undoubtedly also Jehovah is not conceived
as present in this Angel in such a manner that there is not
still preserved the distinction between him and Jehovah.
The Lord speaks of him as 'My Angel,' and the 'Angel
of My face.' But of course there would be a distinction
between Jehovah manifest for purposes of redemption and
Jehovah in Himself.

This particular point, therefore, is not easily settled.
But one can readily perceive what Messianic elements
lay in the idea of the Angel of the Lord,—who was at
least a full manifestation of Jehovah in His redeeming
power,—and how far the ancient Church was on right
lines when it believed it could trace here the appearance of the Son of God. The question whether we are,
from our more enlightened point of view, to consider this
Angel of the Lord a manifestation of the Son or a manifestation of God, is not of much moment. On the one
hand, further revelation has revealed that God manifested
is God in the Son, and it is not unnatural with the ancient
Church to suppose that these preliminary theophanies of
God in human form were manifestations of the Son, who

at last was manifest in the flesh. To Old Testament saints, of course, this view would not occur. The truth which such theophanies would suggest to them was that God truly manifested Himself among them, at least on great occasions, for their redemption ; in His full personality, in the form of man, He came and was seen by them. He did not yet abide among them ; but both the possibility of this, and the hope of it, and the longing for it, must have been awakened in their minds.

We have thought it not improper to run out one side of angelic manifestation and operation to its culminating point. But we must now return and take up the other. God's providence is not exclusively benevolent or redemptive. Or if you assume that upon the whole it is so, and that a large goodness characterises all that He does, and that His redemptive purpose is strictly His whole purpose, embracing all within it, there are at least particular providences that in themselves, whatever they may be as parts of a great whole, are not benevolent. God often interferes in the world to judge or to destroy. In a way less severe He interferes to punish and chasten. And even in a way less severe still, though full of pain, He interferes to prove and try. Now, on these three lines of providence not distinctively benevolent, the angels also appear as mediating the interference of God in the affairs of men. The angel of death, or destroying angel, smote the Egyptians, and slew their firstborn. The angel of the pestilence stretched his sword over Jerusalem, and chastised Israel for their own sin and the pride of their king. And in connection with the tempting or proving of the saints, the most remarkable instances of angelic activity that Scripture presents to us are to be found.

It is to be observed that, as a rule, the angels who execute God's commissions in providence are mere ministers. Any personal share or sympathy with the operations that they perform is not brought out. They are so far neutral, or morally indifferent. The destroying angel is not called a bad or cruel angel. And the angels that hurry Lot out

of Sodom are not represented as acting out of pity to the
old man. They merely perform with skill and promptitude
the commission entrusted to them. The angels are generally, when enacting the providence of God, mere servants,
whose sympathy with the operations they perform is not
dwelt upon. In other connections the angels are called
'holy ones,' are regarded as greatly more pure than man,
and are described as continually praising Jehovah. But as
His servants among men their moral character generally
retreats. It is necessary to remember this, otherwise we
might draw conclusions that would be too hasty, or at least
too broad, in regard to those angels whom we observe subserving God's purpose in His providences that are afflictive.

3. *Satan.*

In the prologue to the Book of Job, and in the 3rd
chapter of Zechariah, we observe an angel who perhaps
represents in his operation the culmination of angelic service
in the line of providences not strictly benevolent. The
representations in these two passages are highly dramatic
and in some respects ideal, and they must be handled with
circumspection. In Job the scene presented is something
like a cabinet council of heaven. The King, Jehovah, is
on His throne, and His ministers appear to stand before
Him. These ministers are the sons of Elohim. Among
them one presents himself, also one of the sons of Elohim,
who is named the *Satan,* or *adversary.* The presence of
the article with the name shows that it had not yet become
a proper name. *The adversary* describes this angel's
function. The word *Satan* means one who opposes another
in his purpose (Num. xxii. 22, 23), or pretensions and
claims (1 Kings xi. 14, 23, 25 ; Zech. iii. 1); or generally.
'The Satan' is that one of God's ministers whose part it
is to oppose men in their pretensions to a right standing
before God (Zech. iii. 1 and in Job i.); that is, the minister
who represents and executes God's trying, sifting providence. He is one of God's messengers, who appears with

other sons of Elohim, before Jehovah's throne, to report his service, and to receive commissions, parts of God's will, which he is to execute. It is in the exercise of this office that he comes into contact with Job, and gives expression to the sentiments to which we shall immediately refer.

The scene in Zechariah, chap. iii., is not materially different from that in Job. The people had just been restored from exile. Their restoration was the token of God's favour, and of their right standing with Him. His anger was turned away, and He comforted them. Yet the restoration was a miserable restitution of the ancient glory of Israel. Old men who remembered the former Temple wept at the sight of the meanness of the new one; and the people had few of the manly virtues and little of the deep godliness of their fathers in the best times of Israel. And the thought could not but rise in men's hearts of the unworthiness of the present people, and doubts of the truth of their repentance; and whether, in fact, God had returned and been reconciled to them, and was founding anew His kingdom among them. These feelings and doubts are dramatically expressed in the scene where Joshua, the high priest, the representative of the people, is exhibited as standing, clothed in filthy garments, before the Lord, and the Satan standing at his right hand to oppose him. Both in this passage and in Job the Satan comes in between God and men; he opposes men in their pretensions to a right standing before God; in other words, he represents the severe, trying, searching side of God's nature and providence, in opposition to the side of His love and grace and complaisance in men.

So far all is plain. And the representation might go no further, and we should be obliged to concede that, as is frequently the case, the Satan is left a mere minister, and, so far as appears, morally indifferent. But obviously, in Job at least, the representation goes further. Even in Zechariah there seems a reflection on his uncompassionate and inhuman performance of his office: "The Lord rebuke thee, Satan: is not this a brand plucked from the burning?" (iii. 3).

This insistence on human weakness and guilt, and the
general raggedness of human nature and the Church before
God, as seen in the filthy garments of Joshua, was over-
done. There was satisfaction to him in this condition of
men; he desired to hinder the reconciliation of Jehovah and
His people. In the case of Job he has nothing outwardly
to found upon, but he insinuates selfishness in Job as at the
root of his religion. He is no believer in human virtue.
He envies and hates the man who is the subject of God's
love and trust, and misleads God to destroy him.   He
hopes to break the bond of faith that unites Job to God,
by means of the severe and inexplicable calamities which
he brings upon him.   The heart of the Satan is already in
his work.   He begins to carry it on on his own account.

It would not perhaps be fair to draw more from these
passages; subsequent revelation will supply additional
details. We naturally put the question, Is the Satan here
a fallen spirit? Of course, there is no allusion to anything
in his history. All that is touched upon is that one of the
Bene Elohim is called the *Satan*, and that his function is to
oppose and accuse men in their relations to God, to make
it apparent that these relations are not right, or to produce
a displacement of these relations.   This is all that meantime is stated.   But we must recall to remembrance here a
peculiarity in early revelation, and indeed in all revelation,
but one particularly conspicuous in the Old Testament—
its tendency to refer all things back to God.   As Isaiah
says: "I form the light, and create darkness: I make
peace, and create evil: I the Lord do all these things"
(xlv. 7). Hence the evil spirit that troubled Saul, for
example, is called "an evil spirit from the Lord"
(1 Sam. xvi. 14). In the remarkable passage in 1 Kings
xxii. 20–22, where the false prophets persuade Ahab to
go up to Ramoth-gilead, it is said: "And the Lord said,
Who will persuade Ahab, that he may go up and fall at
Ramoth-gilead? . . . And there came forth a spirit, and
stood before the Lord, and said, I will persuade him.   And
the Lord said unto him, Wherewith?   And he said, I will

go forth, and will be a lying spirit in the mouth of all his prophets. Now therefore, said Micaiah, the Lord hath put a lying spirit in the mouth of these thy prophets." And what is emphasised in the passage in Job is not whether the Satan be an evil spirit or no, or a fallen spirit, but this, that he is in the hand of God, and that whatever he performs is only under permission of God and in further-ance of His designs.

This element in our idea of a fallen spirit, namely, that he is filled with hatred of God Himself, and an eager desire to counteract His designs, is nowhere visible in the Old Testament. Perhaps in our popular theology we exaggerate this idea, and give to the kingdom of evil an independence of the Divine will, and assign to it an antagonism to God who is over all, which goes beyond what Scripture warrants. Godet goes the length of saying that Job's trials were inflicted just to show the Satan that his insinuations against Job were false. But this elevates the adversary into a prominence and an importance which is not at all in keeping with Old Testament conceptions of the relation of God to evil, and its subordination to Him. The Satan in Job does not come into such prominence as to be a party at all. He is simply God's minister to try Job, and when his work is done he is no more heard of.

Godet in his interesting essay on Job introduces this idea into the words of Satan—"Does Job serve God for nought?"—which he considers a covert attack on God Himself. "If it be so, God is nothing more than a poten-tate flattered by cowards; He has no friends, no children, nothing but mercenaries and slaves. . . . Satan has then discovered the vulnerable point in God Himself. The in-stinct of hatred has served him well . . . while shooting that fiery dart, which reduces to ashes the piety of Job, it is really at the heart of God that he has aimed," etc.[1]

However the words of Satan may serve to suggest this idea, the idea appears to me one quite foreign to the Old

[1] See *Godet's Biblical Studies on the Old Testament*, edited by the Hon. and Rev. W. H. Lyttleton, p. 199 ff.—ED.

Testament. The Satan is the servant of Jehovah, and the idea is rather that he is zealous for God's honour, than that he is the covert and sneering foe even of Jehovah Himself.

It may also be remarked that, as it is the office of the Satan to try God's saints in the present economy where sin has entered, and as all trial may have the effect of seducing them and tempting them to evil, there is nothing *a priori* against the idea that he may have been employed in God's hand to try those innocent, but whose innocence was not yet confirmed by voluntary determination to maintain it. And thus there is nothing against the idea that the tempta- tion in the form of a Serpent, recorded in Gen. iii., proceeded from the Satan. It is true, Old Testament Scripture does not say directly anywhere that the Satan and the Serpent were identical, or that the one used the other. The first direct statement that Satan was the tempter in the Garden occurs in an Apocryphal book. In the Wisdom of Solomon ii. 23 it is said: "For God created man to be immortal; . . . nevertheless through envy of the Devil came death into the world." There are, however, passages in the Old Testament which form a transition to this, where the Serpent is spoken of as the foe of God and of His people, and the like.

There is one other prophetic passage which has to be noticed. The gods of the heathen nations were, of course, called *Elohim*. So were the angelic beings. It was not unnatural, as we have said, that they should be brought into connection and identified, and that the gods in this way should become *demons, i.e.* evil angelic spirits. And already in the Book of Daniel each nation is represented as having a guardian spirit, who in the heavenly or super- human world is its prince; and in this superhuman world conflicts are waged, which decide the relations of nations to one another on earth. This idea is but a transference into heavenly places of the conflict between the God of Israel and the gods of the nations, which is usually waged on earth.

But the identification of the gods with the angelic Elohim was helped on another line. The heathen nations worshipped the hosts of heaven—the visible powers of which, sun, moon, and stars, were to them but embodiments of spiritual powers behind. In this way it was natural again to bring these gods of the heathen into connection with the *Bene Elohim*, or to identify them with them. The expression 'the hosts of heaven,' though properly meaning the mere visible starry hosts, acquired then the deeper sense of the heavenly powers. Even when Jehovah is called Jehovah of hosts, the idea is that He can lead hosts of angels, as Christ speaks of receiving to aid Him more than twelve legions of angels if He should desire it (Matt. xxvi. 53). And it is certainly in this sense that the passage in Isa. xxiv. 21, 22 is to be interpreted : " It shall come to pass in that day, that the Lord shall punish the host of the high that are on high, and the kings of the earth upon the earth. And they shall be gathered together, as prisoners are gathered in the pit ; and they shall be shut up in prison, and after many days shall they be visited." This judgment is that of the ' day of the Lord.' It falls on kings of the earth upon the earth, and on the host of heaven that are in heaven. Both shall be shut up in the pit, and after many days they shall be visited, *i.e.* released.

But one perceives ideas that afterwards became more clear—of spirits reserved in chains and darkness, of a binding of Satan, and a loosing of him again to deceive the nations. The Old Testament ideas originate in a variety of ways, and only gradually unite to form the general conceptions which we find in the New Testament.

The increasing light of revelation threw the figure of the Satan into deeper shadow, and with the full manifestation of redemption came a clearer knowledge and exhibition of his power and malignity. Our Lord is said to have been "manifested that He might destroy the works of the Devil" (1 John iii. 8). And at that time the antithesis between the redemptive power and the destructive

20

came very strongly out in a hundred points. And the Apocalypse, which may be called the drama of Christ, throws the action into the form of a conflict between Satan himself and those whom he inspires and in whom he is incarnate, such as the Beast on the one hand, and the Saviour with His Saints on the other. But there is no dualism, no power of evil co-ordinate with God: " Greater is He that is in us than he that is in the world" (1 John iv. 4). And this view prevails very strongly in the Old Testament, and it is not amiss for us to recur to it when weary or like to faint in our minds.

X. DOCTRINE OF REDEMPTION—PRIESTHOOD AND ATONEMENT.

1. The Priest.

The four great ideal, or as they are sometimes called typical, figures in the Old Testament, namely, the Prophet, the King, the Priest, and the Servant of the Lord, have each their special significance. They have this both in themselves and in the ideal character in which they point to that which shall be when the perfect and final condition of the theocracy is realised. The last-mentioned, sometimes the *saint* or the ' holy one,' sometimes the *people*, is, as the name indicates, one who serves the Lord, that is, in bringing His truth to the nations. The service rendered by this ' Servant of the Lord ' is a public redemptive service ; and what makes the figure of this personality so remarkable is the suffering which he undergoes in his great vocation of serving Jehovah. At present, however, we look at certain points relating to the *Priest*.

It is remarkable that in the Old Testament the *priest* himself is not to so large an extent a redemptive figure as we should anticipate. And the features which are attributed to him in the New Testament are partly borrowed from the more sublime figure of the Servant of the Lord in

Isaiah. The sacrificial system is left in the Old Testament without explanation as regards redemptive relations, except in a general way. Throughout the Scriptures, till we reach the final chapters of Isaiah, the animal sacrifices receive no explanation, and are not lifted up into any higher region. In the final chapters of Isaiah a step is taken which is of the profoundest significance. Sacrifice is translated out of the animal sphere into that of the human. The Servant makes himself an offering for sin. To us who are familiar with this idea the immense advance made in this conception is apt to be overlooked.

The word *priest* means, perhaps, *minister*, that is, one who serves Jehovah in worship. The covenant is a state of relation between God and men, in which He is their God and they are His people, which means His worshipping people. The term which expresses their translation into the state of fitness to serve Jehovah in all the exercises of worship is 'sanctify.' *Sanctification* or *consecration* is effected through a sacrifice of purification, by which the people is cleansed from sins to serve God. The term expressing this condition of the people in covenant with God as His worshipping people is 'holy.' Now the covenant was made with the people. Hence they were a 'holy nation,' that is, a nation dedicated to Jehovah for His service. The idea of service is an essential element of the idea of sanctity or holiness in the people; because this is the only sense in which moral beings can belong to Jehovah, namely, as His worshippers, doing Him service. Now, to serve Jehovah thus in His worship is to be a priest. Hence Israel is called a 'kingdom of priests.' The nation was priest or minister of the Lord, and every member of it was privileged to draw near to Him in service.

Now, it is very necessary to maintain this point of view; for otherwise some things in the history of Israel will remain unexplained. Israel is a priestly people, and ideally no Israelite has any privileges over another in drawing near and presenting offerings before Jehovah. Throughout the history of Israel we find this privilege largely taken advantage of. Any Israelite felt himself entitled to offer sacrifice before the Lord. Gideon, Manoah the father of Samson, King Saul, David, Solomon, every person, where duty prompted, offered sacrifice to the Lord. It was the privilege of Israelites.

This privilege of individuals, however, did not interfere with a public and national worship, any more than this later superseded it. The covenant was made with the people, which was a unity. And the worship of this unity was carried on in a central sanctuary. Further, it is evident that it had to be carried on by a representative body called priests, for the whole nation could not at all times assemble within the central sanctuary. It had to be carried on by a smaller body for other reasons also, chiefly in order to indicate what the conditions of such service were, and in what state of sanctity those must be who approached to worship Jehovah. The parallel may be drawn between the condition of things in Israel and that in the Christian Church. Worship and mutual edification are the objects had in view by the Christian people, and for these ends they meet in public worship. But it is manifest that the general body must, so to speak, resolve or condense itself into a smaller body of persons who become in a manner its representatives, if these great ends are to be well carried out. It was the same in Israel. The priestly body were the representatives of the people. But the existence of the priestly class as representatives of the people did not supersede or absorb the priestly privileges of the individual, any more than the ministry of the Church supersedes the ministry in prayer and exhortation of the father and the individual.

The selection of a priestly class to minister before the Lord was necessary from the nature of the circumstances in which the people were placed; but, besides being necessary, it was very suitable for the purpose of impressing upon men's minds what the true requirements of serving the Lord were. Those who draw near in service to Him must be like Him in character and mind. This necessity, if it could not be actually realised, could at least be symbolised in so graphic a way as to teach it. The imperfect holiness of the holy nation made the priesthood necessary. As Ewald says: "In the sacred community of Jahveh the original purity which, strictly speaking, ought always to be maintained there, is constantly receiving various stains, noticed or unnoticed, expiated or unatoned for . . . and the whole community, while it felt the necessity for strictest purity, felt also that Jahveh's sanctuary dwelt in the midst of the countless impurities of the people, and was never free from their defilement. Between the sanctity of Jahveh and the perpetually sin-stained condition of the people there is therefore a chasm which seems infinite. All the offerings and gifts which the members of the community bring are only like a partial expiation and payment of a debt which is never entirely wiped out. To wipe out all these stains, to bear the guilt of the nation, and constantly to restore the Divine grace, is the final office of the priest. How hard a one duly to fulfil!" (*Antiq.*, Solly's trans., p. 271).

If a sacerdotal caste is to maintain for Israel the relations with Jehovah which Israel ought as a whole to maintain, this caste must possess in a greater degree than Israel the qualities of sanctity and purity essential to fellowship with Jehovah. In order to secure this, an elaborate system of selection and purification was carried on. First, the basis of the priestly caste was made very wide. The sanctuary and presence of Jehovah was surrounded by a deep mass of specially consecrated persons, the outer circle of which stood far away from it, although nearer it than the ordinary Israelite. There took place within the class of priestly servants a process of exclusion and narrowing, reducing the number and elevating the sanctity, as the approach was made to the presence of the Lord. First a special tribe was set apart, that of Levi, which alone was privileged to perform any act of service connected with the tabernacle. Then, second, within this wider circle was the narrower one of the priests, or sons of

Aaron, who alone could minister directly before God, although they were only admitted to the mediate nearness represented by the holy place. And, finally, gathering up all the virtue and sanctity of the class into himself, there was the high priest, who alone could enter the holiest of all, although even he could enter only once a year.

The other line of sanctification consisted not in diminishing the number of the caste, but in the symbolical acts of purification. Had it been possible to secure really greater godliness in the priest, it would have been demanded. But what could not be secured in reality was expressed in symbol. The priest must be bodily free from all deformity. Then he went through numerous lustrations and purifications by many kinds of sacrifices. Then to exhibit the purity needful for his office he was clothed in linen clean and white.

Notwithstanding these distinctions between the priesthood and the people, the strictly representative character of the priests, particularly of the high priest, is the important point in the institution. In the services of the priesthood Israel was itself serving the Lord. The priesthood was an idealised and purified Israel performing the service before Jehovah. In the priesthood Israel offered its sacrifices to the Lord, and in the priesthood it carried away the blessing, righteousness from the God of salvation.

The meaning of the sacrificial system is of importance here. The great primary fact to start from is that of the state of covenant relation between God and the worshipping people. Though in covenant, the people were not thought of as sinless. They might fall into errors, and they were compassed with infirmities. For these sins of infirmity, or ignorance as they were called, an atonement was provided in the sacrificial system. This is the meaning of the system. It is an institution provided of God for sins committed *within* the covenant. For some sins there was no atonement; sins done with a high hand cut a man off from the covenant people. But for all sins of error, which included not only sins done ignorantly, but sins of infirmity

offering of sacrifice prior to Moses, maintaining perfect silence regarding such sacrifices as that of Noah after the Flood, those of Abraham and the patriarchs, and all preceding the Exodus. But the author's silence can hardly be treated as any evidence of his view of the origin of sacrifice in general, but only of the sacrifices operating in Israel. This work is a history of Israel's sacred institutions—institutions which, at the time when the book was written, had attained their full development, and were in that sense God's final revelation to His people as to how He desired to be served. And (2) the universal prevalence of sacrifice among the heathen nations seems to imply that sacrifice was in some way a natural expression of man's sense of his relation to God. The hypothesis of a primitive revelation, the remains of which lingered among all the peoples of the world, and which expressed itself through sacrifice, is precarious. It certainly cannot be proved; and to explain sacrifice by it must leave the origin of that institution involved in the same precarious and hypothetical condition.

But this leads to the other question, What was the primitive idea underlying sacrifice? The answers have mainly run on two lines, the ethical, and what might be called the physical. It has been supposed that man's sense of evil, of his own inadequate service to God, and of God's holiness, made him feel that reparation was due to God, and that he deserved death. Hence, to express this feeling, he brought living creatures to God as his own substitutes, inflicting on them the penalty of death deserved by himself. Sacrifice was thus from the first piacular and propitiatory. The objection to this idea is, that it seems to assume ideas present in the mind of primitive man as the subject of his own sin, and of death as the deserved penalty of it, which rather belong to an advanced period of ethical reflection. And the same objection applies, though in less degree, to a variety of the above view, which regards sacrifice as the expression of homage and dependence; in other words, a sort of acted prayer

Action rather than words, it is argued, is what is to be expected of primitive life; and this act was sacrifice. So, *e.g.*, F. D. Maurice. See his *Theological Essays* and his *Doctrine of Sacrifice deduced from the Scriptures.*

This view differs not very greatly from another one, that sacrifice or offering was of the nature of a gift to please the deity, and so obtain from him what was desired, whether it was the pacification of his anger and the cessation of calamities, or success in the struggle with enemies, or, in a higher stage of thought, the joy of fellowship with him, and the sense of being pleasing in his sight.

These views all move more or less on ethical lines.

Quite a different view has been advocated by Professors Robertson Smith and Wellhausen.[1] In the view of these scholars the essential idea of sacrifice is to be observed in the sacrificial meal—the communion of the deity and man in a common sacramental food. The god and the tribe were one; or, if the god was estranged, it was only a temporary estrangement. The idea that a common partaking of food united in a bond of friendship or covenant those who so partook, was a usual one. The idea was transferred to the sphere of Divine and human relations. The common sacrificial meal, as it cemented the union of men with men, cemented also the union of the deity and men; or if the union had been partially or temporarily strained, —it could never be more, for the god was one with the tribe,—it restored it. The participants on the human side, by eating food in common, confirmed their union one with another; and by giving the god part of the sacrifice, *e.g.* smearing the blood on stones which he inhabited, and which more lately developed into an altar, they allowed him also to participate, and so cemented his union with them. He was thus one with them, their help and stay in all the vicissitudes of their life. As thought advanced, this action carried moral meaning with it; although originally the idea was more that of a physical union,

[1] See the *Skizzen und Vorarbeiten* of the latter, and *The Religion of the Semites* of the former.—ED.

the common material food binding all who partook of it into one physical body.

A fragment of this primitive theory is supposed still to be seen in the Hebrew sacrificial meal after offering to the God. It is doubtful if this construction of the meaning of the sacrificial meal anywhere appears in the Old Testament; but it is common for a usage to maintain itself long after the original idea which it expressed has ceased to be connected with it.

Those who maintain this theory have considerable difficulty in explaining how this primitive idea gradually ramified into the conceptions connected with sacrifice which we find prevailing from the beginning of the historical period among the Hebrews. If sacrifice was a common sacramental meal between men and the god, how did such a sacrifice as the כָּלִיל or עוֹלָה arise,—the whole burnt-offering, which was wholly given to the deity, and of which men did not partake at all?

The explanation is connected with the advance in social conditions, which suggested new ideas. In the earliest times, it was the tribe that had existence and owned property, it and the god in common. All sacrifices were tribal, cementing the union of the tribe and the god. The individual had no property, no separate being or place. This was the condition in a nomad state. But when the people passed into an agricultural life he had something really his own, his land, his cattle. If he owed them to the god, still they were his in the sense that they did not belong to the tribe or the people. He was, so to speak, in personal relation to the deity. If the old idea of a sacramental meal still prevailed, he could present his offering for himself. But naturally the idea would arise in his mind that he could now present a gift to his god,—it might be out of thankfulness and in return for much that he had received, or it might be to placate the god's anger if he seemed estranged, or it might be for other reason. Sacrifice began to express the idea of a gift to God with the view of pleasing Him.

Whatever the historical evolution of the idea of sacrifice, or whatever its primary idea, it seems certain that this idea of a gift or offering to God is the prevailing idea in the Hebrew religion from the earliest. The sacrifices of Cain and Abel are called a מִנְחָה, *a present.*

If there is dissidence and diversity of opinion between prophets and people, it is not on the general idea that an offering or service is pleasing to the Deity, but on what is the offering that is pleasing,—these material offerings of flesh, or the service of the mind in obedience and righteousness.

3. *Atonement and Forgiveness*

We may notice here a few points, particularly some distinctions, which it is useful to keep in mind, and which are helpful to the understanding of the Old Testament view on these subjects. (1) A distinction is drawn in the Old Testament, as we have seen, between sins of ignorance or inadvertence and sins done with a high hand or of purpose. The former are called chiefly שְׁגָגָה, the latter are said to be done בְּיָד רָמָה. The former class embraced more than mere involuntary or inadvertent sins. The class comprehended all sins done not in a spirit of rebellion against the law or ordinance of Jehovah—sins committed through human imperfection, or human ignorance, or human passion; sins done when the mind was directed to some end connected with human weakness or selfishness, but not formally opposed to the authority of the Lawgiver. The distinction was thus primarily a distinction in regard to the state of mind of the transgressor. In point of fact, however, it was convenient to specify in general the offences that belonged to the class of sins done with a high hand, and upon the whole they were the sins forbidden by the moral law. No doubt, in certain circumstances even these sins if committed involuntarily, were treated as sins of error and the penalty due to them was averted by certain extraordinary arrangements; as for example, when a murder was committed by misadventure, the manslayer was allowed to flee to a city of refuge. Otherwise the consequence of his deed would overtake him in the ordinary penalty attached to such an offence, which was death.

(2) Corresponding to this distinction among offences was another. Only sins of ignorance, as we have said, were capable of being atoned for by sacrifice. The class of offences said to be done with a high hand were capital, and followed by excision from the community. The sins of error or ignorance could be removed by sacrifice and offering. In other words, the Old Testament sacrificial system was a system of atonement only for the so-called sins of inadvertency.

(3) This distinction may be put in other terms—in terms of the covenant. The sins done with a high hand threw those committing them outside the covenant relation. They were an infraction of the fundamental conditions of the covenant union. Such a sin as idolatry, homage to another deity than Jehovah, infringed the first principle of the covenant relation, the basis of which was that Jehovah was God of Israel. The sinner who had committed such an offence had withdrawn himself from the sphere within which Jehovah was gracious; there stood nothing between him and the anger of Jehovah for his sins, and especially for this the greatest possible sin. The sins of ignorance, on the other hand, were sins of human frailty, offences not amounting to an infraction of the very conditions of the covenant; but though disturbing to the relations between a God of holiness and His people, offences that were not immediately destructive of these relations, and permitting the relations to continue, provided they were removed by the means appointed by Jehovah for that purpose, and not voluntarily persevered in or neglected. And the sacrificial or Levitical ritual system was the means appointed for obviating the consequences of these inevitable offences.

The sacrifices were thus offered to a God already in relations of grace with His people. They were not offered

in order to attain His grace, but to retain it—or to prevent
the communion existing between Him and His people being
disturbed or broken by the still inevitable imperfections of
His people, whether as individuals or as a whole. It is
argued by some that such a conception as this of a people
in communion with their God, a communion only liable to
be disturbed now by such mere offences of frailty, points to
a period in the people's history posterior to the prophetic
age, when idolatry and the gross offences assailed by the
prophets no longer existed. It must be admitted at once
that at no period of the people's history prior to the
return from exile did the condition of the people and this
idea embodied in the sacrificial system correspond in fact.
But that would not at once entitle us to infer that the
ideal itself was not of much greater antiquity. At all
events the Old Testament sacrificial system belonged to
the worship of the people of God, conceived as truly His
people, believing in Him and in fellowship with Him.
And it was a means of maintaining this fellowship, of
equating and removing the disturbances which human
frailties occasioned to this communion. Hence the prevailing conception of Jehovah in all the ordinances of the
system is that of holiness—a purity as of light which
human imperfections disturb, and which when disturbed
reacts and becomes a fire that consumes.

It cannot be denied that this idea of the Divine
holiness in the law draws up into it not merely moral
holiness, that is, freedom from and reaction against all
moral evil, but also a considerable æsthetic element. The
Divine holiness re-acts against much that is on man's
side merely an uncleanness, and requires its removal
by washings, before the fellowship can be maintained or
renewed. A deeper study of these points, such as the
uncleanness arising from touching the dead, the woman's
uncleanness from childbirth, and much more, might reveal
to us some moral conception underlying the ordinance.
If the ritual system be late, this supposition would become
even more probable; if it were very early, we might

perhaps more readily acquiesce in the idea that the moral and the physical were not yet strictly distinguished. There were thus in Israel two streams of conception regarding God, running side by side. In the one—as seen in the historical and prophetic literature—Jehovah is a King, a righteous Ruler and Judge, who punishes sin judicially, or forgives it freely of His mercy, requiring only repentance. In the other, Jehovah is a holy person, dwelling in a house among His people, who approach to worship Him; a being, or a nature, sensitive in His holiness to all uncleanness in that which is near Him, and requiring its removal by lustrations and atonement.

On the other hand, the other class of sins referred to threw the offender outside the sphere within which God was continuously gracious. There was no sacrifice for such sins. The offender was left face to face with the anger of God. Here the offender has to reckon not so much with the Divine holiness, as with the Divine righteousness, and wrath against sin. At all events he has no refuge to flee to except God Himself. And these cases are of extreme interest because they polarise, so to speak, the Divine nature itself—the two poles being His wrath against sin and His mercy. And the latter appears the more powerful of the two, and ultimately prevails, although not usually at once, nor without some terrible illustration of God's wrath against evil. It is, of course, with this class of sins that the prophets deal almost exclusively— sins throwing the nation outside the covenant limits. And they express the consciousness of the true nature of these sins and their inevitable consequences. And some may think that just here lies the explanation of their assaults upon the sacrificial system. The people thought that redoubled assiduity in ritual and increase in the splendour of their gifts would atone for their offences, however great. But their idea was a misconception of the very principle of the ritual system, which had respect only to those true to the fundamental conditions of the covenant relations which they had transgressed. Of course, many other false conceptions were mingled together in their minds, due partly to the fact that the sacrifices were of the nature of a gift to Jehovah.

(4) But now this distinction between the two classes of sins being had in mind, and the distinction between sins and persons for whom sacrifice is available and those for whom it is not being remembered, the next point is that of *atonement*, and the means by which it may be effected. The word which has been translated 'atone' is, in Hebrew, כִּפֶּר. Now, in point of fact, this term is used both of sins done within the covenant and sins which threw the offender outside the covenant. The former sins were atoned by the sacrifices, more specifically by the blood of the sacrifices; the latter could not be atoned by this means—at least, in general. Now, it is evident that in order to obtain a general view of the Old Testament teaching on atonement, both classes of sins and their treatment must be kept before us.

The sacrifices atoned for the sins of those who were truly Jehovah's people; they were ordinances of God already in fellowship with men, to whom He was gracious, in fact. They had not respect at all to Jehovah's actual wrath—they had respect only to His holy nature, and the danger that it might react against uncleanness or sin in those who approached Him as His people. Atonement of offences in this relation could hardly furnish us with a general conception of what atonement is. No doubt, the principle may be the same in all cases. But at all events the other class of cases will be more instructive in this at least, that they will show us the Divine mind in a greater variety of conditions. Even any inferences we might draw, however, from atonement of sins that in theory and principle were outside the covenant, may scarcely be held available to form a general and abstract idea of atonement applicable universally; because even when Jehovah was dealing with the sinners who had broken His covenant— they were the sinners of His people, He remembered in them the kindness of their youth (Jer. ii. 2)—they were the seed of Abraham His friend, whom He had chosen and not cast away (Isa. xli. 8). And how far the principles observed even in His treatment of the covenant-breakers of Israel might be applied to the sinners of mankind generally, might need consideration.

There are two classes of passages which have to be considered. They express different shades of conception regarding the Divine Being. The one class bears upon His holiness, the other on His righteousness.

In the class having reference to worship, the Divine nature is considered more as something which instinctively reacts against human unholiness. The worshippers coming into His courts are in His personal presence,—His nature and theirs come into direct union,—and hence the danger to a nature impure. In the other class of cases the sinner is not in Jehovah's presence. Jehovah is rather the ruler, and His action is strictly moral. His will and moral righteousness, rather than His physical nature, come into prominence. It may be best to take this class of passages first.

The word כִּפֶּר, rendered *atone*, means properly to *cover*. Hence its synonym כִּסָּה is not unfrequently employed instead of it, as in Ps. xxxii.: "Blessed is he whose transgression is *covered*." Naturally a covering may be protective, or it may have the effect of making the thing covered inoperative; it may invalidate its natural effect, or annul it. Hence Isaiah says (xxviii. 18): "Your covenant with death shall be disannulled, וְכֻפַּר." Now it is with some such general sense that the word is used of sin; it is covered so that its operation is hindered, its effects are invalidated. In what sense this is done will best appear if one or two points be stated in order.

(*a*) In these cases of extra-ritual atonement the *object* of atonement is the *sin*, or offence, of whatever kind it be, *e.g.* Ps. lxv. 3: "Iniquities prevail against us: as for our transgressions, Thou shalt atone them, תְּכַפְּרֵם," E.V. "purge them away." Ps. lxxviii. 38: "But He, being full of compassion, atoned iniquity," יְכַפֵּר, E.V. "forgave." Isa. vi. 7:

"Thine iniquities shall depart, and thy sin shall be atoned, תְּכֻפָּר." Jer. xviii. 23: "Thou, Lord, knowest all their counsel against me to slay me: atone not Thou their iniquity, אַל־תְּכַפֵּר." Instead of כפר, the verb of similar sense, כָּסָה to *cover*, is sometimes used; Ps. lxxxv. 3: "Thou hast taken away the iniquity of Thy people: Thou hast covered all their sin," כִּסִּיתָ. The immediate effect of the covering is upon the sin. It is of importance to notice that it is never primarily an effect produced upon Jehovah Himself, nor upon His face, nor upon His wrath. The atonement may take place before the Lord, or in His presence (Lev. vi. 7), but the Lord Himself is never the object. His face or eyes are not covered so that He does not see the sin or offence or unholiness of the sinner; the sin is covered and withdrawn from His sight. Similar ideas are expressed by the phrase, "I am He that blotteth out thy transgression like a cloud" (Isa. xliv. 22); and by such figures as casting the people's sins into the depth of the sea (Mic. vii. 19), casting them behind His back (Isa. xxxviii. 17). It might seem that the difference is not great between covering a sin so that God's eyes do not see it, and inducing Him to turn away His eyes from it; and the Psalmist (Ps. li. 9) actually prays: "Hide Thy face from my sin." Still there must be something in the usage, and it no doubt suggests these general ideas: (1) that the sin itself must in some way be done away, and made invalid; (2) that without this no gifts can operate on the Divine anger—He is not induced by influences from without, but moved from within Himself.

(*b*) A second point in this class of offences is that the subject who atones is usually God Himself—He covers the sin. Ps. lxv. 3: "As for our transgressions, Thou dost atone (or, cover) them." In general this is the representation, though occasionally another subject intervenes, as Moses the mediator of the covenant, and others who represent the people. The meaning of atoning sin, then, may, in general, be said to be this, it is covering it so that the eyes of Jehovah do not behold it, and His anger

21

against it is quenched; and none but Himself can effect this.

(c) The means whereby sin is covered in these extra-ritual cases are various. The fact that He Himself is represented as the subject who performs the covering or atonement, shows how profoundly the feeling had taken possession of the people's mind that in whatever way sin was to be invalidated, and its effects neutralised, ultimately its removal must be due to God; that He was not moved by something or anything outside of Him, but that the movement came from within Himself, whatever the immediate means were of which He made use. Hence in the widest sense, His own sense of Himself, considerations taken from His whole being, and His relations to men, may intervene between men's sin and His anger; Ps. lxxix. 9: "Help us, O God of our salvation, for the glory of Thy name . . . cover our sins, for Thy name's sake." "Who is a God like unto Thee, pardoning iniquity?" (Mic. vii. 18); or less widely, some one prevailing attribute, such as His compassion; Ps. lxxviii. 38: "But He, being full of compassion, covered their iniquity." As has been said, the effect of sin was, so to speak, to polarise the Divine nature, and to draw out powerfully the consuming anger; yet the prevailing tone of His nature might come between and cover the iniquity, so that His anger was turned away. There is, perhaps, no passage that illustrates the general idea that atoning or covering of sin must proceed from the Lord Himself, whatever means He employs, better than the passage in Isa. vi. The ideas of the passage have undoubtedly a certain resemblance to the Pentateuchal passages, though the means of atonement are very general. The prophet's uncleanness was removed by a messenger sent from the presence of the Lord; and, second, by a coal taken from His altar, where He is Himself most present. And the coal had in it a Divine power; both the agent and the means came directly from the Lord.

I am afraid these remarks leave the question somewhat indefinite; but probably it is left somewhat indefinite in the Old Testament, the definite points being only these: that it is the sin that is covered; that 'covering' it means withdrawing its power to provoke the anger of God; that usually it is God Himself who covers it; that the motives are drawn from His own nature, and the initiative is His; and that the means, where mentioned at all, are appointed by Him, though the motives and the means are usually identical.

There are two or three historical passages of considerable interest; for example, the instance of the golden calf made by Aaron (Ex. xxxii.), and the instance of the whoredom of the people in the plains of Moab in connection with Baal Peor (Num. xxv.). In these instances there are several things: (1) a breach of the covenant; (2) an outbreak of Divine wrath in the form of a plague; and (3) the intervention of a human agent: in the one case Moses, who interceded with Jehovah; and in the other Phinehas, who executed vengeance upon the chief transgressors. In both cases the covering of the sin of the people followed. Now the two points of interest are: (1) that the Divine anger to a certain extent took effect in the plague and slaughter. It was manifested and illustrated so far as in some degree to satisfy it. And (2) a human agent intervened to effect the covering of the sin. On what ground was the action of Moses or Phinehas a covering of the people's sin? It was, perhaps, on the principle of solidarity. The anger of Jehovah was kindled against the whole people, and threatened to consume them utterly. But these men were of the people. Moses was a mediator and representative of the people, and not in any way involved in their sin; and he was a prince and leader, and showed his zeal for the Lord. In point of fact, though many had broken the covenant, it had not been broken by the people as a whole. And God had respect to His covenant, and covered the offence of the sinners. It is this principle of solidarity, perhaps, that explains the intercession of the prophets. Amos twice interceded and was heard. But both Jeremiah and Ezekiel are warned that their intercessions will not be listened to.

But the other point is of chief interest in regard to the prophet Isaiah. Of course, to punish for sin and to cover sin are ideas opposed to one another. If the people bear their sin in Divine chastisement, there is no covering of it. But it is to be noted that the penalty of breach of the covenant is not mere chastisement, but destruction. Now the question suggests itself, whether chastisement to a less degree than destruction might not be held a covering of sin in God's mercy. Strictly, it was not a covering, but might it not be considered so? In this case there would be a union of means acting as 'covering': first, the satisfaction so far of the punitive wrath, and, second, the mercy of God intervening to regard it as enough—as it is said in Isa. xl. 2: "She has received of the Lord's hand double for all her sins."

4. *Atonement by Priest and High Priest.*

Anticipating in some measure what has to be noticed further on, we may say here that the points in connection with atonement in the sacrifices that entered into worship are not numerous, although they are of importance. They are two.

(1) The subject who atones in this case is no more God Himself, but the priest, or, when the atonement is made for the whole people, the high priest. This is not, perhaps, a great change, as the priest is appointed of God. But the procedure of atoning is now something ordinary, and not left to the mercy of God. In particular instances He has appointed standing ordinances and persons for accomplishing it. It is still an ordinance, proceeding in all its parts from Him; but it is now a standing ordinance.

(2) The object of atonement is still the sins of the offender, whether individual or people. In this case, however, the language differs considerably from that previously used. It is more commonly not the sins of the offenders, but the *persons* or *souls* or *lives* of the offenders that are covered. The change is due to the circumstances. The

persons in question now are not strictly sinners afar from God. They are His worshippers entering into His courts; and the danger is of His nature reacting against them and consuming them, as in Isa. vi. Of course the danger in the other class of cases was to the person of the sinner ultimately; but in these cases the sinner was not a worshipper in Jehovah's presence, and it was rather God's judicial sentence that he had to fear. If anything were needed to show that the danger feared is, so to speak, from the nature of God and His presence, it is the fact that not only the persons drawing near to Him needed to be atoned or covered by blood, but the same necessity existed for the tabernacle, or house itself, and all its furniture. These contracted uncleanness, perhaps, from the presence in them of sinful men, and they had to be covered by sacrificial blood. This is a very profound idea of the Divine holiness; and when we extend it from the mere idea of worship to His universal presence, it becomes very suggestive.

(3) The means of atonement in this case are always the blood of the sacrifice. Sometimes the efficacy appears to be ascribed to the whole sacrificial arrangement, but never unless the arrangement contained a bleeding sacrifice. The chief atoning sacrifices are the sin-offering, the guilt-offering, and the whole burnt-offering.

The passage in Lev. xvii. 11 gives the fullest account of the principle of atonement. " The life of the flesh is in the blood: and I have given it to you upon the altar to make an atonement for your souls: for the blood atoneth in virtue of the life." This law prohibits the eating of blood, and states the reason. The life is in the blood, and the blood is given to make atonement; and this atonement the blood effects in virtue of the life which it contains. Atonement is here represented as made not for sins, but for souls or persons. The blood makes this atonement, covers the persons: it does so because it contains the life. But no explanation is given of the principle how the blood with the life in it covers the persons, *i.e.* atones. The passage is silent on the principle; but the ordinance is an ordinance of God: "I have given it to you upon the altar."

Thus the Old Testament doctrine of atonement runs on two lines, which perhaps, in the Old Testament, do not meet or coincide.

The Christian doctrine, as expressed by St. Paul, has united the two, taking from the first that which creates the necessity of atonement, the moral righteousness of God; and from the second the means of atonement, the blood of sacrifice, and making the one answer the other. The apostle, of course, lays down universal principles applicable to all men, Jews and Gentiles. He regards all sins as inferring the wrath of God. All sins, in his view, belong to the category of sins done with a high hand; at least all men are guilty of such sins. Knowing that such things are worthy of death, they not only do them, but have pleasure in those that do them. All men are guilty of sinning wittingly. Thus the relation of God to all men is to St. Paul the same as His relation was to sinners in Israel with a high hand. He is Ruler and Judge; His righteousness and the sin come into connection. Of course, the apostle refers forgiveness to the same source as the Old Testament, the mercy or grace of God.

Then, as has been said, he unites the means used in the second class of offences with this primary class, making the sacrifice the means of atonement. The Old Testament has not gone so far as this. It recognises the moral righteousness of Jehovah, which manifests itself in wrath against sin. But for such sin there is not sacrificial atonement; the sinner's refuge is only in God Himself, in the prevailing direction of the Divine mind, which is towards mercy and compassion. And, secondly, it recognises infirmities and impurities adhering to men even when truly in fellowship with God as His people. And these infirmities of His worshipping people disturb the Divine holiness, which is in danger of manifesting itself destructively in opposition to these imperfections of men, and the infirmities must be atoned or covered. And the means of this covering is the

blood of sacrifice in virtue of the life which it carries.   It
is not easy to remove from this second conception the
elements of a relative kind which it contains, and the shade
of physical conception of the Divine nature peculiar to it,
so as to reach a pure general idea universally applicable.

5. *The term 'Atone.'*

The references in the Old Testament are scattered
through it, and have regard to particular cases.   There is
no single passage that states a formal or full doctrine upon
the subject.   It is probable that a full doctrine of *Atonement* can hardly be obtained from the Old Testament even
by combining the passages.   But traces of general ideas
may be discoverable, which lead in the direction of the
more complete New Testament doctrine.

(1) The word 'atone' כִּפֶּר is not now used in the Kal.
In Gen. vi. 14 : "Thou shalt pitch it with pitch," the word
is a denominative from the noun כֹּפֶר, 'pitch.'   The word
is now used only in Piel and its derivatives.   Further, the
word is no more used in Scripture in its literal and
physical sense, but always in a transferred metaphorical
sense.   The original meaning of the word, however, was
certainly to *cover*, and so put out of sight, or do away
with.

In the cognate languages it is used in the sense of to
deny, i.e. conceal a fact.

That the word means to 'cover' originally appears
from the synonyms, *e.g.* כָּסָה, to *cover*, put out of sight, and
so out of activity or influence, to annul or invalidate,
parall. to מָחָה, *blot out.*   See Jer. xviii. 23 : אַל־תְּכַפֵּר עַל עֲוֹנָם
וְהַטָּאתָם מִלְּפָנֶיךָ אַל־תֶּמְחִי.   Neh. iii. 37 (iv. 5) quotes this thus :
אַל־תְּכַס עַל עֲוֹנָם וְחַטָּאתָם מִלְּפָנֶיךָ אַל־תִּמָּחֶה.   So Ps. lxxxv. 3 :
"Thou hast taken away the guilt of Thy people, Thou hast
covered (כִּסִּיתָ) all their sin " ; Ps. xxxii. 1 : " Blessed is the
man whose sin is covered."   In this extra-ritual use of
כפר that which is atoned or covered is sin or guilt; and
from the passage in Jeremiah it appears that it is covered

from Jehovah's sight—מִלְּפָנֶיךְ.¹ With this idea may be compared Ps. xc. 8 : " Thou hast set our iniquities before Thee, our secret sins in the light of Thy countenance." Similar figures, as we have said, are to *remove* or *take away* sin, Isa. vi. 7 ; Ps. xxxii. 1 ; to *blot it out*, Jer. xviii. 23 ; Isa. xliii. 25, xliv. 22 ; to *cast into the depth of the sea*, Mic. vii. 19 ; *to cast behind the back*, Isa. xxxviii. 17 ; cf. Ps. cix. 14 : " Let the iniquity of his fathers be remembered with the Lord ; and let not the sin of his mother be blotted out." And so in the New Covenant, Jehovah remembers sins no more. All these figures express the idea that the sin is covered so as to have all effects from it removed ; it is put out of sight, invalidated, undone. In particular, Jehovah no more sees it, and it exerts no influence upon Him. Hence the Psalmist prays : " Hide Thy face from my sins," Ps. li. 9. This sense of undoing or annulling or invalidating appears in several passages, *e.g.* Isa. xxviii. 18, already referred to : " Your covenant with death shall be disannulled " (תְּכֻפַּר) ; and Isa. xlvii. 11 speaks of a calamity which "thou shalt not be able to neutralise." And there is the interesting passage in Prov. xvi. 6 : " By goodness and truth guilt or sin is atoned (יְכֻפַּר) for," which means done away with, the results of it obviated ; it does not mean that *reparation* is made by goodness and truth. In all these passages the use of the word is metaphorical ; the sense of literal covering no more obtains (cf. Gen. xxxii. 20 ; Prov. xvi. 14). It may, no doubt, be made a question, seeing the word כִּפֶּר is used in parallelism both with the word כִּסָּה *cover*, and also with מָחָה *blot out*, which of these

¹ If כִּפֶּר mean to *cover*, and כֹּפֶר be a *covering*, the question, as we have said, may be raised, and has indeed been raised, whether it be the sin that is covered or God. Are God's eyes covered so that He does not see the offence, or is the offence covered so that it is not seen by Him ? The phrases used may suggest both sides, *e.g.* the second in the language, "Hide Thy face from my sin !" and the opposite, to "set our sins in the light of His countenance." The effect is the same, whether God does not see the offence, or it be not seen by Him, being invisible to Him. The questions remain : (*a*) What produces this effect ? (*b*) How does this produce the effect ?

two ideas is the primary one in כִּפֶּר. Some even think that כִּפֶּר is a denominative from כֹּפֶר, *a ransom.* But כֹּפֶר, *ransom*, is so named because it covers. כֹּפֶר is properly ransom money from a death penalty: "Save him from going down to the pit; I have found a ransom" (Job xxxiii. 24), *i.e.* the ransom money covers the offence.

(2) In these extra-ritual passages the subject or agent who atones (כפר) is, as we have said, usually God Himself. He covers the sin; and in this usage 'cover' or atone is almost equivalent to 'forgive,' although the figure is present to the mind of the writer. See the passages already cited—Jer. xviii. 23: "Cover not their sin"; Ps. lxv. 3: "Iniquities prevail against us: as for our transgressions, Thou wilt atone them—cover them" (תְכַפְּרֵם); Ps. lxxviii. 38: "But he, being full of compassion, atoned — covered — their iniquity." To these add Ps. lxxix. 9: "Help us, O God of our salvation! atone, cover our sins for Thy name's sake"; Ezek. xvi. 63: "Thou shalt open thy mouth no more because of thy shame, when I have forgiven—atoned or covered to thee—all that thou hast done." It is to be observed that in these passages Jehovah does not first atone or cover the sin, and then follow this by forgiveness; the atoning or covering is merely a figure for forgiveness. It might be that כפר in the sense of *forgive* was a secondary usage, derived from the primary sense of to *cover* or *atone*, either by a life ransom or by a sacrifice; and that the sense "forgive" was properly to *declare atoned for.* It is a question of the genesis of the sense *forgive.* If this were its genesis, *forgive* would express properly the result of the covering or atoning the sin; and as this result always followed, the word *cover* or *atone* would come to have the sense forgive when the subject is God. However the usage arose, the sense *forgive* is the usual one. Considering that כִּפֶּר is used in the ritual and non-ritual sense, it is probable that even in the *ritual* 'cover' has not a literal, but a metaphorical sense; and that it is not said in regard of the blood being literally laid on the object covered; for in most cases it is not; it is

brought before God, and even in the ritual it might be He (or His eyes) that is covered.

(3) There is the question of the *means* that lead to Jehovah's atoning or covering of sin, or the *motives* that induce Him. This point opens out rather a wide inquiry. It may be said, however, negatively, that sacrifice or offering is never the means. None of the prophets, not even Ezekiel, refers to sacrifice as the means of atonement for the sins of the people; God forgives of His grace and mercy alone. It is possible that in Isa. liii. the sacrificial idea may be present. There is, indeed, one passage (1 Sam. iii. 14) where reference seems to be made to a possible use of sacrifice wider than that which it ordinarily has: " I have sworn that the iniquity of Eli's house shall not be atoned, covered, with sacrifice nor offering for ever." There is another passage also of interest (1 Sam. xxvi. 19), where David says to Saul, when remonstrating with him for his persecution of him: " If it be the Lord that hath stirred thee up against me, let Him smell an offering." The ideas here are : David regards Saul's persecution of him as an aberration of mind, possibly caused by God. If caused by God, it must be in punishment of some inadvertent or unremembered sin of which Saul had been guilty. Therefore for this sin let him offer a sacrifice, that Jehovah may remove the punishment—the aberration of mind under which the king suffers. This is, however, just the proper use of sacrifice, namely, for sins of inadvertency.

There are several cases which at first sight look like instances of sacrifice which are not so. One is the case in Deut. xxi. 8. This was the case where a murdered body was found, without its being possible to trace the murderer. The elders of the city nearest to which the body was found were to take an unblemished heifer, never subjected to the yoke, bring her to a valley with running water, and there slay her by breaking her neck. The elders were to wash their hands over the heifer, and protest their innocence, " Our hands have not shed this blood . . .

And they shall answer and say, Atone, O Lord, for Thy
people Israel . . . suffer not innocent blood to remain
in the midst of Thy people. And the blood shall be
atoned (or, covered) to them." This is no sacrifice, but
a symbolical judicial action. That the animal was not
a sacrifice, is certain from the fact that her neck was
broken; a thing absolutely forbidden in sacrifice, where
the blood must always be separated from the flesh. By
the murder, guilt was brought on the land, which of
right could be removed only by the death of the murderer.
In this case he could not be found, and a symbolical
execution was performed; which, illustrating the principles
of justice, was held sufficient. A similar though more
painful and tragic instance occurs in 2 Sam. xxi. A
famine of three years afflicted the land in David's days, and
on inquiring the cause of the Lord, David was answered:
" It is for Saul and his bloody house, because he put to
death the Gibeonites." The narrator then explains to us
that the Gibeonites were not Israelites, but of the remnant
of the Amorites; but the children of Israel had sworn to
them to spare them (Josh. ix.), and Saul sought to slay
them in his zeal for Israel. Receiving this answer, David
turned to the Gibeonites, asking: " By what means shall I
make atonement (בַּמָּה אֲכַפֵּר), that ye may bless the heritage
of the Lord?" They answered: " The man that devised
evil against us . . . let seven men of his sons be delivered
unto us, and we will hang them up unto the Lord." Now
this is not a sacrifice, but again of the nature of a judicial
transaction. Guilt lay on the land because of Saul's sin;
this guilt was punished by God with famine: the guilty
person could no longer be made amenable himself, and he
was made amenable in his descendants. The case is
entirely analogous to that in Deuteronomy. They both
illustrate the principles of justice and of God's government.

The case of the Gibeonites is entirely similar to the
case of the manslayer, Num. xxxv. 32, 33: " Ye shall
take no ransom for the life of a manslayer who is guilty
of death. . . . So ye shall not pollute the land wherein ye

are: for blood polluteth the land: and no expiation can be made for the land for the blood (לְאָרֶץ לֹא יְכֻפַּר לַדָּם) shed therein, but by the blood of him that shed it." These words are from the Pentateuch, and the idea is expressed in terms of *holiness* and *pollution*.

As it is Jehovah who covers or atones sin, naturally the motive is usually found in Himself. And here a preliminary point requires to be remembered. The effect of sin upon Jehovah, whatever the sin was,—whether idolatry, wrong-doing, or disobedience,—was to arouse His anger or wrath. The Divine wrath, of course, is not an attribute like His righteousness. Wrath in God is what it is in men, —an affection, a pathos,—and is transient. The Divine nature is capable of wrath, although God is slow to anger. Then the natural result of wrath is punishment of the wrong-doer. But as wrath is but an affection, and not the fundamental character of the Divine mind, which rather is long-suffering and compassion, this prevailing disposition may so restrain the anger that no chastisement follows, but there is forgiveness; Ps. lxxviii. 38, 39: "They (the people) were not faithful in His covenant. But He, being full of compassion, forgave their iniquity, and destroyed them not: yea, many a time turned He His anger away, and stirred not up all His wrath. For He remembered that they were flesh." Very often God is represented as restraining His anger "for His name's sake." The phrase is peculiar to the later books, and embraces a variety of ideas. In Isa. xl. and in Ezekiel this is the idea expressed by the phrase: "Jehovah is God alone, but He has become God of Israel." The nations know Him only as Jehovah, the God of Israel. Therefore He can reveal Himself to the nations only in connection with Israel, for they know Him only as God of Israel. His purpose is to reveal Himself to all flesh. But this purpose can be effected only through Israel. Hence His name, His honour as God alone, is involved in Israel's history, whose God He is. He has begun a redemptive work in the world with Israel, a work which is to embrace

the nations, and He cannot undo this work however Israel
may sin. This consideration restrains His anger against
Israel. So it is in the poem, Deut. xxxii. 26, 27 : " I
would make the remembrance of them (Israel) cease from
among men, were it not that I feared the provocation of
the enemy, lest their adversaries should misdeem, lest they
should say, Our hand is exalted."

In Ezek. xx. the whole course of Israel's history is
explained on this principle. That which has prolonged
the existence of Israel as a people, and given them a
history, is Jehovah's regard for His own name. He is
conscious of being God alone, and He has become God
of Israel ; in this light alone the nations know Him,
only thus does knowledge of Him reach the nations.
Therefore His name would be compromised in Israel's
destruction ; His work of redemption and revelation of
Himself to the nations begun upon the earth would be
obliterated and made of none effect. His preservation and
final redemption of His people Israel is that which reveals
His name, His sole Godhead, to the nations. Hence, even
when the trials of the Exile had failed to turn the hard
hearts of the people, Jehovah exclaims : " For My name's
sake do I defer Mine anger . . . that I cut thee not off.
I have refined thee, but not as silver " (*i.e.* not with the
result with which one refines silver). " For Mine own
sake, for Mine own sake do I do it : for how should My
name be profaned, and My glory will I not give to
another " (Isa. xlviii. 9–11). Naturally the expression,
His 'name's sake,' expresses many other things besides
this, such as the fact that Israel is His people whom
He hath redeemed, and His affection for their forefathers.
Thus in Deut. ix. 26–29, Moses prays : " O Lord God,
destroy not Thy people and Thine inheritance, which Thou
hast redeemed. . . . Remember Thy servants Abraham,
Isaac, and Jacob ; look unto the stubbornness of this people
. . lest Egypt say, Because the Lord was not able to
bring them into the land which He promised them, and
because He hated them, therefore He slew them in the

wilderness. Yet they are Thy people and Thine in-heritance." We have the same circle of ideas in Ex xxxii. 10–14 and Num. xiv. 15–20. In the latter passage, Moses prays: "If Thou shalt kill this people as one man, the nations which have heard the fame of Thee will speak, saying, Because Jehovah was not able to bring them into the land which He swore to give them, therefore He slew them in the wilderness. And now . . . let the power of my Lord be great, according as Thou hast spoken, The Lord is slow to anger, and plenteous in mercy . . . Pardon, I pray Thee, the iniquity of this people according to the greatness of Thy mercy. And the Lord said, I pardon according to thy word."

(4) There is another aspect of the case which is illustrated in the history of the people in the wilderness, and in all the prophets. In the history of the Exodus the anger of God against the people's rebellion expressed itself in plagues; and in the prophets, in the people's subjugation by the nations and ejection from their land, with all the terrible sufferings connected with the Exile. Yet a full end was not made of the people. The eyes of the Lord are upon the sinful kingdom to destroy it, saving that He will not altogether destroy the house of Jacob (Amos ix. 8). The point here is that the righteous anger of Jehovah displayed and enforced itself. It received, so far, a certain illustration. Jehovah did not stir up all His wrath, nor make a full end of the nation, which would have been the natural penalty of their disobedience; but His righteous anger was displayed, and His rule vindicated so far. In His returning mercy He might even feel that He had chastised too harshly. "Speak comfortably to Jerusalem and say unto her, She hath received double for all her sins" (Isa. xl. 2).

(5) And one other point may be referred to. A few cases occur where human intercession is had respect to, and God averts His anger and forgives. We have the instance of Abraham in Gen. xviii. 23–33. There is the case in Amos (vii. 4–6). Preparations for destroying

Israel were shown him, and he prayed: "O Lord, forgive,
I beseech Thee: how shall Jacob stand? for he is small."
And the Lord said: "It shall not be." Jeremiah, again,
frequently intercedes for Israel, though both to him and
to Ezekiel the intimation is given that the time for intercession is past: "Though Moses and Samuel stood before
Me, My mind could not be toward this people: cast them
out of My sight" (Jer. xv. 1). In the wilderness, when
the people made the golden calf, Moses interceded with
effect: "The Lord said: . . . it is a stiff-necked people.
Now therefore let Me alone, that My wrath may wax hot
against them, that I may consume them: and I will make
of thee a great nation" (Ex. xxxii. 9, 10). Moses prayed,
making the representations already quoted in the passage
in Num. xiv. And the Lord repented of the evil which
He thought to do to Israel. In a subsequent part of the
chapter there is recorded a slaughter of three thousand
men which the Levites made among the people. And
Moses said on the morrow to the people: "Ye have sinned
a great sin: and now I will go up unto the Lord; per-
adventure I may, make an atonement (אוּלַי אֲכַפְּרָה), for your
sin." Moses prayed: "Oh, this people have sinned a great
sin. Yet now, if Thou wilt forgive their sin—; and if
not, blot me out of Thy book which Thou hast written."
Moses acknowledges the sin, and will not outlive the destruction of the people. It is not certain what is meant
when he says: "Perhaps I may atone (or, cover) for your
sin"; whether it is that he himself will be able to remove
it from God's sight, or that he will be able so to intercede
that God may cover it. The latter is probably the meaning, for Moses prays Jehovah to take away the people's sin.
So that his intercession does not *atone* in the technical
sense. Moses identifies himself with the people, devotedly
refusing life to himself if the people are to perish; then
he profoundly feels and acknowledges the people's sin,
which from the relation he assumes to them may be considered their confession.

There is an important passage in Num. xxv. 10-13.

The case is that of the sin of Israel with the Midianitish women. Phinehas, seeing an Israelite bring in a Midianitish woman for purposes of fornication, smote them both through with a dart. And the Lord said: "Phinehas hath turned My wrath away from the children of Israel, in that he was jealous with My jealousy among them, so that I consumed them not in My jealousy. Therefore I give unto him my covenant of peace, because he was jealous for his God, and made atonement for the children of Israel" (וַיְכַפֵּר). This fornication appears to have been part of the religious worship of the Baal of Peor. Here it is the zeal of Phinehas that atones, his zeal expressing itself in the act of vengeance upon the sinners. It does so because this zeal is the zeal of Jehovah. Phinehas enters into Jehovah's mind, acts in His mind, and thereby magnifies and sanctifies Him. This atones.

In one instance, Num. xvi. 46 (Heb. xvii. 11), when the plague had broken out among the people because of the rebellion of Korah, incense atones: "Moses said unto Aaron: Take a censer, and put fire therein from off the altar, and put on incense, and go quickly into the congregation, and make atonement for them . . And he put on incense, and made atonement for the people. And he stood between the living and the dead, and the plague was stayed." This is the only case where incense alone has atoning power. The passage, however, ought rather to be classed among the ritual passages.

The result of this examination of passages in regard to *forgiveness* and *atonement*, though not very large, is of interest. The chief points are these:

1. God alone forgives sin and covers it. To cover or atone for it, when said of God, is a mere figure for forgiveness, and means obliterating it, as the other word 'blot out' implies.

2. Though sin excites the anger of God, anger is with Him but a passing emotion, as the Psalmist (Ps. xxx. 5) says: "His anger is but for a moment; His favour for a lifetime." The prevailing tone of His nature is mercy, and

on penitence and confession He is ready to forgive, apart from all sacrifice or what is called atonement : " I said, I will confess my trangressions unto the Lord ; and Thou forgavest the iniquity of my sin " (Ps. xxxii. 5).

3. Motives to forgiveness, which He finds in Himself, are many, *e.g.* His compassion, His memory of His former servants the patriarchs—"for My servant David's sake," respect to His covenant, and for His own name's sake ; which last embraces a multitude of considerations, particularly His universal redemptive purpose, which has been begun in Israel and can be accomplished only through Israel, whose God He is known to be, though he be God alone.

4. The wrath called forth by the sin of individuals or of His people often expresses itself in plagues on the people ; and in all the prophets, in their humiliation under the nations and exile from their land. Thus His righteous anger receives a certain satisfaction—it is displayed ; as Isa. v. 16 expresses it, He is magnified in judgment and sanctified in righteousness. His nature is revealed. His righteousness is declared or shown (Rom. iii. 25). Yet a full end is not made. He does not stir up His wrath, but restrains it.

5. In another way satisfaction is rendered to Him, and His anger is appeased—namely, when men enter into His just resentment, and, feeling it, act in the mind of God ; as when the Levites intervened to chastise the people for their idolatry in worshipping the calf, or when Phinehas was jealous with the jealousy of the Lord, and did judgment upon the Israelitish prince and his Midianitish paramour. More simply, God's anger is turned away, and sin covered (atoned), by the intercession of His nearest servants, as Abraham, Moses, Samuel. There is a solidarity between these men and the people. Their confession of the people's sin is the people's confession. And yet they are different ; they are near to God. He has respect unto them. Their intercession usually sets before God those great motives in Himself from which He acts—His compassion, His covenant,

22

His redemptive purpose already begun, His name's sake, *i.e.* His sole Godhead, and yet His being known alone in Israel. With the intercession there is always confession of Israel's sin.

These are the main points in early literature. What elements of the Christian doctrine they show is easily seen.

Taking all these points together, three main principles appear:

1. God's nature is gracious; from His nature He will take away the sin of the world.

2. There may be in His operation in doing this, first, a display of His righteous anger against sin; and, second, also on the part of sinful men or their representative, an entering into this righteous indignation.

And, 3. On the part of those forgiven there must be repentance, and trust in God's mercy.

6. *Ritual use of the Term.*

From *Atonement*, as it appears in the extra-ritual books of the Old Testament, we pass now to the ritual atonement. The law or ritual legislation is very extensive, and not altogether homogeneous, and does not formally give any account of atonement. It regulates the offerings, but it introduces us to the ritual system as already in operation, without giving any account how it began, or what are the principles embodied in it. Its two fundamental positions are that all sacrifices must be offered at one place; and that only the priests, the sons of Aaron, can offer or make atonement. There is one writer, however, who stands half-way between the extra-ritual or prophetic Scriptures and the ritual law, the prophet Ezekiel; and we gain a clearer view of the nature and purposes of the ritual law from him than we acquire from the law itself. The last nine chapters of his book furnish a key that opens the ritual law more easily than anything which we find in the law itself.

The Book of Ezekiel, although probably not much read, is perhaps, apart from occasional difficulties, the easiest understood of all the prophetic books. The book was probably written late in life, and the writer has so disposed it as to make its mere order accurately express his general conceptions.

(1) In chaps. i.–iii. there is the great vision of God borne by the cherubim, and the initiation by the God who thus manifests Himself, of the prophet into his office of a watchman among his people. The vision in chap. i. is a vision of God as the prophet conceived Him. Then God, thus present symbolically, makes the prophet conscious of his inspiration and of the fact that Jehovah is with him in all he speaks, by presenting to him the roll of a book, containing all Jehovah's words, which he eats, and which he feels sweet to his taste. The sweetness was not due to this, that though the book, being full of lamentation and woe, contained bitter things at first, at the end it was filled with promises which were sweet. The sweetness was rather due to this, that the things written were from God, whose bitter word is sweet; as we have it in Jer. xv. 16 : " Thy words were found, and I did eat them; and Thy word was unto me the joy and rejoicing of mine heart : for I am called by Thy name, Jehovah God of hosts." The prophet's idea of what we call his inspiration is perhaps more precise and stringent than that of Isaiah. In the inaugural vision of Isaiah, " there flew one of the seraphim having a live coal in his hand, . . . and he laid it on my mouth, and said, Lo, this hath touched thy lips, and thine iniquity is taken away " (vi. 6, 7). And immediately on this an impulse seized the prophet to enter on Jehovah's service. " Here am I, send me." All that Isaiah felt needful to make him a prophet was the forgiveness of his sin. There was in him a strength and power of character which needed only the removal of the moral hindrance to set them free. But both Jeremiah and Ezekiel were weaker men. Ezekiel, as is usual with him, makes Jeremiah his model, who says, " The Lord said unto me, Whatsoever I

command thee, that shalt thou speak. . . . Then the Lord put forth His hand, and touched my mouth, saying, Behold, I have put My words in thy mouth" (i. 7-9). Both the later prophets represent themselves as speaking not merely the word, but the ' words' of Jehovah.

Now, from this point onwards Ezekiel's book has a clear order.

(2) Chaps. iv.-xxiv. contain prophecies announcing the destruction of Jerusalem, and symbolical actions prefiguring it. These actions, or at least many of them, were not actually performed. They passed as symbolical representations before the prophet's mind, for he thought in figures, and he narrated them to the people. With great wealth and variety of representation the prophet exhibits in these chapters the certainty and manner of the destruction of the city, and the ruin of the kingdom of Judah; and the necessity of it from the persistent sin of the people, and the nature of Jehovah, who must display His holiness in judgment. There is much in these chapters that is very powerful as well as beautiful—some things which show that if Ezekiel had lived in our day he would have risen to the highest rank in moral imaginative writing. His xvith chapter is an allegory of Jerusalem under the figure of a foundling child who became a faithless wife. Though marked by a breadth with which modern taste is unfamiliar, the allegory is powerful; and when the details are forgotten, and only the general conception remains in the mind, the prophet's creation is felt to be artistically beautiful as well as true. Jerusalem and Jehovah are represented. An outcast infant exposed on the open field, and weltering in its blood, was seen by the pitying eye of a passer-by. Rescued and nourished, she grew up to the fairest womanhood, and became the wife of her benefactor, who lavished on her all that could delight and elevate. But the ways into which he led her were too lofty to be understood, and the atmosphere around her too pure for her to breathe; the old inborn nature (her father was an Amorite and her mother a Hittite) was still there beneath all the refinements

for which it had no taste, and at last the native taint in her blood asserted itself in shameless depravity and insatiable lewdness.

(3) Chaps. xxv.–xlviii. As in the first half of his book Ezekiel's thoughts are occupied with the coming destruction of Jerusalem and Judah, so in the last half he is occupied with the restoration and final felicity of Israel. There are three steps in his delineation—(a) judgments on the historical nations around Israel, in order to prepare for the restoration of Israel (chaps. xxv.–xxxii.); (b) the process of Israel's restoration itself (chaps. xxxiii.–xxxix.); and (c) finally, a picture of Israel's restored and perfect condition (chaps. xl.–xlviii. 5).

We may look at each of these. First, chaps. xxv.–xxxii. *The judgments on the nations.* — Israel occupies a place of universal significance in the history of the world; for it is the people of Jehovah, who is God alone. He who is God alone, we are again taught, has become God of Israel, and it is through Israel that He is known to the nations, and through Israel and her history that He will fully reveal Himself to the peoples of the world. The perfect manifestation of Himself will be seen in Israel's restoration, when His glory shall be revealed, and all flesh shall see it together. But this restoration of Israel cannot be without great judgments on the nations who have hitherto harassed her or seduced her. These judgments will awaken the nations to the knowledge of who the God of Israel is: they shall give them to know that He is Jehovah, God alone; and they will ensure that in the future His people shall not be troubled or led astray. Chastisement overtakes the nations for two sins, first, because of their demeanour towards Israel, the people of the Lord; for they had taken part in Jerusalem's destruction, as Edom, or had rejoiced over it, as Ammon and Moab; or they had been a snare to Israel, inspiring false trust and seducing her from the true God, as Egypt. And, secondly, judgment falls on them because of their ungodly pride and self-deification, as in the case of Tyre and Egypt, and their failure to acknowledge

Him as God who is God alone. And the issue of His judgments in all cases is, that the nations know that He is Jehovah, God alone; and thus in the future all the peoples around Israel will no more injure her. When restored, she shall dwell in perfect peace.

Second, chaps. xxxiii.–xxxix. *The process of the restoration of Israel itself.*—It is in these chapters that the main part of the prophet's contributions to Old Testament theology lies, such as his teaching on the place of the individual soul before God (chap. xxxiii.). In general, he reviews all that was evil or calamitous in the past, and intimates how it shall be reversed and remedied. For example, the shepherds of the people, the royal house, had destroyed alike themselves and the flock. But the Lord Himself will take in hand the gathering of His scattered sheep together, and the feeding of them henceforth; He will appoint His servant David over them to lead them (chap. xxxiv.).—Here belongs the splendid vision of the valley of dry bones. The nation is dead, and its bones bleached; but there shall be a resurrection of the dead people, and a restoration of them to their own land. Two kingdoms shall no more exist there; but the Lord's people shall be one, and His servant David shall be prince over them for ever (chap. xxxvii.). There is one passage in these chapters, where the redemptive principles illustrated in these future blessings and in all Israel's history are stated, which is very remarkable. That is chap. xxxvi. 17–38 : "Son of man, when the house of Israel dwelt in their own land, they defiled it by their doings . . . wherefore I poured out My fury upon them . . . and scattered them among the nations. And when they came among the nations they profaned My holy name, in that men said of them, These are the people of Jehovah, and they are gone forth out of His land. Therefore say unto the house of Israel, I do not this for your sake, O house of Israel, but for Mine holy name, which ye have profaned. . . . And I will sanctify My great name, and the nations shall know that I am Jehovah. . . . For I will take you from the nations, and will bring you into your own land. And I will sprinkle clean water upon you, and ye shall be clean. A new heart also will I give you, and a new spirit will I put within you. . . . And I will put My spirit within you . . . and ye shall keep My judgments, and do them. Then shall ye remember your evil ways, and ye shall loathe yourselves because of your iniquities." Probably no passage in the Old Testament offers so complete a parallel to New Testament doctrine, particularly to that of St. Paul. Commentators complain that nobody reads Ezekiel now. It is not certain that St. Paul read him, for he nowhere quotes him. But the redemptive conceptions of the two writers are the same, and appear in the same order: 1. Forgiveness—" I will sprinkle clean water upon you"; 2. Regeneration—" A new heart and spirit"; 3. The Spirit of God as the ruling power in the new life—" I will put My Spirit within you"; 4. The issue of this new principle of life, the keeping of the requirements of God's law—" That the righteousness of the law might be fulfilled in us, who walk not after the flesh, but after the Spirit (Rom. viii. 4)"; 5. The effect of living 'under grace' in softening the human heart and leading to obedience—" Ye shall remember your evil ways and loathe yourselves"—" Shall we sin because not under law but under grace?" (Rom. vi.–vii.). And, finally, the organic connection of Israel's history with Jehovah's revelation of Himself to the nations (Rom. xi.).

Third, the last section of the prophet's book (chaps. xl., xlviii.). This contains his vision of the new temple, with all its measurements, including those of the outer and inner courts (chaps. xl.–xlii.). Then there is a vision of the return of Jehovah, who had left Jerusalem, and His glorious entry into the new house prepared for Him, by the east gate, by which He had gone out; which gate therefore shall remain for ever shut (chap. xliii.). There follow certain regulations as to who shall serve Him in sacrifice and offering, namely, the priests the sons of Zadok; and who shall be subordinate ministers to guard the portals of the house, slaughter the victims and the like, namely, the Levites, the former priests at the high places, now degraded to inferior functions for their idolatry Then follow regulations for two half-yearly atonements for the people and the house. And finally comes a description of how the restored tribes shall be settled in the land.

Now, in order to understand this vision, all the preceding parts of the prophet's book must be kept in mind. This passage contains no teaching. All that the prophet wished to impress upon his people regarding Jehovah and the principles of His rule, His holiness and wrath against evil, has been exhausted (chap. iv.–xxiv.). All that he desired to say about the revelation of Jehovah's glory to the nations, that they may know that He is Jehovah, and may no more exalt themselves against Him in self-deification, and no more disturb or seduce His people, has been said (chaps. xxv.–xxxii.). And the great operations of Jehovah's grace in regenerating His people and in restoring them have been fully described (chaps. xxxiii.–xxxix.). All this forms the background of the present section. The last words of chaps. i.–xxxix. are: "And I will hide My face from them no more: for I have poured out My spirit upon the house of Israel, saith the Lord God." The people have been washed with pure water, a new spirit has been given them. The Spirit of Jehovah rules their life, and they know that Jehovah is their God.

Therefore this section gives a picture of the people in their final condition of redemption and felicity. It does not describe how salvation is to be attained, for the salvation is realised and enjoyed; it describes the people, and their condition and life now that redemption has come. This accounts for the strange mixture of elements in the picture, for the fact that there is " so much of earth, so much of heaven," in it. To us who have clearer light, the natural and supernatural seem strangely commingled. But this confusion is common to all the prophetic pictures of the final condition of Israel, e.g., Isa. lx., and must not be allowed to lead us astray. We should go far astray if, on the one hand, fastening our attention on the natural elements in the picture, such as that men still exist in natural bodies, that they live by the fruits of the earth, that death is not abolished, and that the prince has descendants and the like, we should conclude that the supernatural elements in the picture, such as Jehovah's abode in glory in the new House, and the issue of the stream from the temple, spreading fertility around it and sweetening the waters of the Dead Sea, were mere figures or symbols meaning nothing but a higher spiritual condition after the Restoration, and that the Restoration foreseen by Ezekiel was nothing more than that natural one which took place under Zerubbabel. Ezekiel's Restoration is one that is complete and final, embracing all the scattered tribes; it is a resurrection of the nation, and it is the entrance of Israel upon its final perfection. On the other hand, we should go equally far astray if, fastening our attention only on the supernatural parts of the picture, such as Jehovah's presence and the river of life issuing from the temple, we should conclude that the whole is nothing but a gigantic allegory, that the temple with its measurements, the courts with their chambers and kitchens for cooking the sacrificial meals, the priests and their ministrations,—that all this in the prophet's view is nothing but a lofty symbolism representing a perfection to be eventually reached in the Church of Christ. To put such a meaning on the temple and its measurements, the courts and chambers and kitchens, is really to bid defiance to language. The whole is real and literal. And it is of interest to us because it reveals more simply and clearly than anything else the meaning of the Levitical system and ritual.

1. The salvation and blessedness of the people consists in the presence of Jehovah in His temple among them. His people, though all righteous, are not free from the infirmities and inadvertencies incidental to human nature. But as, on the one hand, the presence of Jehovah sanctifies the temple in which He dwells, the land which is His, the people whose God He is; so, on the other hand,

any defilement in the people, the land, or the temple disturbs His holy being, and must be sedulously guarded against or removed. Hence the elaborate care taken to prevent all profaning of Jehovah, and to keep far from Him all that is common or unclean. First, the sacred oblation, the domain of the priests and Levites, is placed in the centre of the tribes. In the midst of the oblation is the portion of the priests, and in the middle of the priests' portion stands the temple. This is a great complex of buildings, first surrounded with a free space, then by a great wall, then by an outer court, then by an inner court; then the house has also gradations—first a porch, then an outer house, and, finally, the Most Holy place, in which Jehovah is present. All these circumvallations are for the purpose of protecting the absolute holiness of His Being; they are not symbols, but realities. His people, however, though forgiven and sanctified, are not removed from the possibility of erring, and all error on their part is reflected on the holy nature of their God; and the uncleanness must be put away by the blood of the sacrifices, sin-offering and burnt-offering, which He has appointed to atone. Here we have the key to the strange fact that it is only for unwitting faults that the sacrifices are provided. These are the only faults of which the redeemed and restored people will be guilty. Yet even these inadvertencies are uncleannesses which disturb the perfect holiness of God in the midst of them, and must be atoned or invalidated, that Jehovah may continue present among them.

The idea in Ezekiel and that in the law are identical. Only in Ezekiel the situation is real; in the law it is somewhat ideal. In the prophet the restored people are holy, led by the Spirit of God; and the sins they commit are only inadvertencies, for which the ritual sin-offerings are provided as atonement. In the law this ideal condition is assumed, so to speak, imposed upon the people, and set before them as something to be striven after. The people are regarded as holy; the same inadvertent sins only are supposed to be committed, and the same atonements are provided for them, and the same care is manifested to preserve the holiness of Jehovah from all invasion or disturbance. On this subject the following points suggest themselves :—

The law knows nothing of ceremonies. Both the law and Ezekiel embrace all that Jehovah is under the conception of holiness. The extra-ritual Scriptures speak mainly of Jehovah's righteousness. He is a Ruler, a King, and Judge. When He deals with the sin of men, it is judicially. The law and Ezekiel do not name Jehovah's righteousness. They speak of His holiness. But 'holiness' in these books embraces all that Jehovah is. His attributes of righteousness and power, His majesty and the like, are all embraced under His holiness. These are two distinct modes of conception in regard to God.

But this is worth notice. Besides those attributes of Jehovah called moral which are embraced under holiness, certain other things are also brought under that idea— certain other things in Jehovah. Holiness has a certain respect to the nature of Jehovah, to what might be called His æsthetic nature—to feelings and sensibilities in regard to that which in our view is not moral.

To men's minds, besides the things that are considered wrong, there are many things, objects or conditions or actions that are disagreeable, which are either repulsive, or from which they shrink, or which cause a revulsion in the feeling. There are many natural actions in regard to which civilized men have a feeling which prevents them doing them in public. There are diseases, and even conditions of the body, from which the feeling shrinks; and there are objects, such as some of the lower creatures, and especially, perhaps, the body in death, which cause a recoil of feeling. These things affect our nature, not at all our moral judgment.

Now, the peculiarity of the law is that it has attributed this class of feelings to the Divine nature. The objects or conditions or actions referred to affect the Divine nature as they do human nature—they are obnoxious to it, they disturb and offend the Divine holiness. Therefore, when any of these things occur in His people, or are done by them, they act upon the holy nature of Him who is their God, and with whom as His people they are in fellowship, and who dwells among them. As it is said, Lev. xx. 24, 26 : " I am the Lord your God, which have separated you from the peoples. Ye shall therefore separate between the clean beast and the unclean. . . . Ye shall not make yourselves abominable by beast or fowl . . . which I have separated from you as unclean. But ye shall be holy unto Me: for I the Lord am holy." An extreme instance of the Divine sensitiveness or holiness is the regulation regarding the priests' clothing when ministering in the inner court. They were prohibited from wearing anything woollen, on the ground that it caused sweat (Ezek. xliv. 18).

It is manifest that the conception that Jehovah was locally present among the people, in a house or tabernacle in the midst of them, would facilitate this tendency to draw in under His holiness those æsthetic feelings which refined men share. It was His presence that sanctified or made holy that which was locally near Him ; for example, the tabernacle or temple, making it a holy place, making Zion also a holy hill, Israel a holy nation, and Canaan a holy land. And so, on the other hand, when anything unclean came into His house or land, it defiled it, and when it came near Himself it profaned Him—it touched on His nature, which reacted against it.

Entirely parallel to the conception of the Divine holiness, embracing in it what we call the æsthetic, was the conception of all sin as uncleanness. All sins, moral as we name them, and others which we call ceremonial, are named uncleanness in the law and in Ezekiel. For example, those several enormities enumerated in Lev. xviii. In regard to them it is said, Lev. xviii. 26–28 : " Ye shall keep My statutes, and shall not do any of these abomina-tions : that the land vomit you not out also, when ye defile it." And so the idolatries are uncleannesses. And so with other things similar : " Turn not unto them that have familiar spirits, nor unto wizards: seek them not out, to be defiled by them: I am Jehovah your God" (Lev. xix. 31). And, of course, all those other conditions or actions to which reference has been made are called uncleannesses. But our modern distinction of ceremonial and moral is not one known to the law. Equally unknown to it is the idea that the Levitical purifications and ritual offerings were symbolical—operations performed merely to suggest the ideas of *moral* purity in God and the necessity for it for men. On the contrary, the Levitical defilements were real; they were offences to the absolute purity of the Divine nature. And the Levitical purifications were equally real—the washings removed the uncleanness if of a lesser kind, and the blood of the sacrifice atoned for it if it was of a more serious nature. It is just those defilements, such as that arising from touching the dead, that are called *sins*, and the offering to atone for them is called the *sin-offering*. An instructive instance is that of the Nazirite, Num. vi. 2–12: "When either man or woman shall make a special vow, the vow of a Nazirite, to separate himself unto the Lord . . . all the days of his separation he is holy unto the Lord . . . he shall not come near to a dead body. And if any man die very suddenly beside him . . . he shall bring two turtle-doves to the priest, and the priest shall offer one for a sin-offering . . . and make atonement for him, for that he sinned by reason of the dead."

Now, with regard to this *ritual atonement*, it is distinguished in several ways from the *atonement* previously referred to.

1. In the first place, there are stated and regular means appointed for it. It is not left to the compassion of God, or the intercession of men, or Jehovah's consideration for His name's sake. The stated means are the sacrifice, and specially the blood of the sacrifice.

2. The person who atones in this case, as has been already stated, is no more God Himself, but the priest; or, when the atonement is made for the whole people, the

high priest. The priest, of course, is appointed of God. But the procedure in the atonement is now something ordinary; both the means to it and the persons accomplishing it are fixed ordinances.

3. A certain difference of phraseology also appears. In the extra-ritual atonements, that which was atoned or covered was the sin. In the ritual atonements, that which is atoned or covered is the persons or souls of the offenders; or it may be, for even things are atoned for in the ritual, the altar or the sanctuary in which Jehovah is present. The difference of construction is perhaps not of great importance, being due to the different conception entertained of sin in the ritual law. In the extra-ritual Scriptures sin is conceived as an offence which the sinner is guilty of. The offence is seen by the eye of the righteous God, the Judge and Ruler. It incurs His anger, and draws forth penalty. But the sin is not considered as adhering to the sinner; hence, when it is atoned it is covered and done away. But in the ritual atonements sin is regarded as an uncleanness, and this necessarily adheres either to a person or a thing. Hence, when atonement is made, the person is covered, or, as the case may be, the thing—the altar or the dwelling-place which contracts defilement from the presence of the people.

Here two questions arise—first, what is the idea of atonement in the ritual? and, secondly, what is the principle? As to the idea, it seems still, as in the extra-ritual, that of covering, putting out of sight, or doing away with the uncleanness. The use of the word atone (כִּפֶּר) is still figurative. There are other terms, however, which have less of figure in them. These are:

$$\left.\begin{array}{l} \text{חִטֵּא to un-sin} \\ \text{טַהֵר to cleanse} \\ \text{קִדֵּשׁ to sanctify} \end{array}\right\} = \text{כִּפֵּר atone.}$$

The *fact* is, that the sacrifice or blood removes the sin, or cleanses, or sanctifies; the *figure* is, that it covers the sin or uncleanness, and so removes it from the sight of God,

or obviates all effects of it. There is an element of the
ideal still in the operation. When the altar or sanctuary
is atoned for, the blood is literally applied to them, so that
the uncleanness adhering to them is literally covered. But
when persons are atoned for, the blood is not usually
applied to them, it is merely brought before the sight of
God, being applied to His altar. Sometimes, however, as
in the consecration of the high priest, it is applied to the
person; and when applied to the sanctuary, there is the
idea that the uncleanness of the people cleaves to the
sanctuary. Hence, on the day of atonement, the sacrifices for the people are regarded as cleansing the sanctuary
as well as the people; the things are identical.

Ritschl has argued that the ritual atonement moves
entirely in the region of nature, in the sphere of that which
man and God are, so to speak, physically; that man needs
to be covered by the blood of sacrifice when approaching
God, because of what he is as a finite creature in the presence of the natural majesty of God. But the terminology
appears to be against this, which speaks of specific acts of
uncleanness, and calls them *sins*. Riehm, in his valuable
book on *Old Testament Theology*, and in his *Essay on Atonement*, argues against this transference of the operation of
atonement into the mere physical or natural region; but
agrees with Ritschl to this extent, that the *necessity* for
atonement, for the covering of the sinner's uncleanness by
blood, lies in the danger to the sinner from the holiness
of God, which would react against the sinner's uncleanness if he approached uncovered by blood, and destroy the
sinner.[1] That is, the covering of the sinner is regarded as
a *protection* of him against the reaction of the Divine holiness, which would destroy him. But this idea, that the
necessity for covering by blood lies in the danger to the
sinner from the reaction of the Divine holiness against him

---

[1] See the discussion in Ritschl's *Die christliche Lehre von der Rechtfertigung
und der Versöhnung*, vol. ii. ; Hofmann's *Schriftbeweis*, ii. 191 ff. ; Weiss's
Biblical Theology of the New Testament, Clark's tr., i. 419 ff., and ii. 220 ff. ;
etc.—ED.

in his uncleanness, appears to have no support in the language of the ritual. It is nowhere intimated that there is any danger to the sinner because of his uncleanness. If he neglects the appointed means of purification, he is threatened with *being cut off*; but this is because of his disobedience to the ordinance of God, not because of his uncleanness. The idea appears to be rather that the uncleanness or sin of the individual or people is incompatible with their being the people of God. It disturbs the holiness of God, who is their God, and abides among them. It makes His fellowship with them impossible; if not removed, it would make His abode among them as their God no more possible, and lead, as it did of old, to His withdrawal. The explanation lies in the words, " Be ye holy : for I am holy " (Lev. xx. 7).[1]

7. *The Principle of Atonement.*

Finally, as to the principle of atonement by the sacrifice or the blood of sacrifice, this, I fear, must remain obscure The law appears nowhere to give any rationale or explanation of the ordinance that blood atones or covers the sin or defilement. The passage in Lev. xvii. 11 comes nearest an explanation, though without supplying it. " The life of the flesh is in the blood, and I have given it to you upon the altar to make an atonement for your souls ; for the blood atones in virtue of the life." The law here is not occupied immediately with the question of atonement; it is a law against eating of blood. Eating of blood is prohibited, because the life is in the blood, and the blood has been

---

[1] In the Epistle to the Hebrews, where the same idea prevails, there seems no allusion to any obstacle to the sinner's drawing near to God on the part of God, the obstacle lies exclusively in the conscience of sin on the sinner's part ; and it is when his conscience is purified from dead works that he can serve the living God. Pre-Christian sin is ignorance. And another New Testament writer seems to touch on the same idea—" the times of this ignorance God winked at, but now commandeth all men everywhere to repent " (Acts xvii. 30).

And even our Lord Himself says : " If I had not come and spoken unto them, they had not had sin " (John xv. 22).

given to make atonement; and this atonement the blood
effects in virtue of its being the life. We must be on our
guard again against fancying that we have symbolism here.
There is no symbolism, but reality. The blood is not a
symbol of the life, it is the life, or contains it. The offering
of the blood to God is the actual offering of the life. The
slaying of the victim and the offering of the blood are not
two separate acts. They are one act, which consists in
offering the life or victim to God. The death is not to be
regarded as a mere means of getting the blood; the death
and the offering are the giving to God of the life of the
victim. But while stating the fact that the life thus
given atones, the ritual law offers no explanation. The
traditional explanation has been that the death of the
victim was a *poena vicaria* for the sin of the offerer. And
it is probable that this idea did become attached to sacrifice.
It is questionable, however, when other things are considered,
if it be found in the law. When we consider such things
as these: first, the fact that whatever older or more primary
ideas of sacrifice may have been, in the Old Testament at
least sacrifice is of the nature of a gift to God; secondly,
that the kind of offences for which sacrifices made atonement were sins of inadvertency, in regard to which there
does not seem evidence that they awakened the wrath of
God, although, notwithstanding that they were done un-
wittingly, they disturbed His holiness and endangered His
fellowship with His people and His abode among them; and,
thirdly, that these sacrifices were offered in the main for a
people in His covenant fellowship, for those already His
worshipping people, and that the prophet Ezekiel regards
these atoning offerings as necessary, and as continuing even
in the final condition of the people, after their forgiveness
and final restoration, and when they are all led by God's
Spirit,—when these and other things are considered, it
does not appear probable that the death of the victim was
regarded by the law as a penalty, death being the highest
possible penalty.

On the other hand, though the sacrifices were of the

23

nature of a gift, in this case the use of the blood in virtue of the life for atonement is an express appointment of God. And it is said that the blood in virtue of the life atones for the souls or lives of men. It is possible that the compilers of the ritual law satisfied themselves with just enunciating this fact, refraining from stating any principle, or assuming that the principle was known. The ritual law is the culmination of a multitude of ritual practices and probably ritual conceptions, and the compilers have satisfied themselves with legalising the practices without condescendence on the principles. The view of Riehm, that the blood atones simply because it is God's appointment or ordinance; and that if the question be put why He appointed blood, there was no reason for His appointment beyond this, that there is a certain congruity in life being appointed for life,—the *nephesh* of the creature for the *nephesh* of men,—is not altogether satisfactory. It may be assumed that the grounds for the Divine appointment are deeper than this; but so far as the Old Testament is concerned they are not distinctly revealed. At all times the blood was sacrosanct. Life belonged to God, and must in all cases be given back to Him, and not used by men as flesh might be. It is probable that deeper and mystical ideas gathered around the blood, and that men, if they did not see more in the offering of the life for atonement of sin than a mere ordinance of God, felt there was more in it; that there lay grounds under the ordinance which they might not see. Meantime the law has contented itself with stating the fact that the offering of a life to God atones. Subsequent revelation may go further.

But thus in the Old Testament there are two lines on which atonement moves: that of the righteousness of God in the extra-ritual Scriptures; and that of the holiness of God in the ritual law. In the former, He deals with sin as the righteous Ruler and Judge of men. In the latter, He deals with it as a holy person with whom men have fellowship, who draw near to Him, and among whom He graciously abides. But there is one other Old Testament passage which may give additional light (Isa. liii.).

Although the form in which the sacrifice is put in the law be that it is the giving of the life of a creature to God, naturally the other side of such a transaction. when the case of the creature is concerned, is that it is the death of the creature. In earlier times. perhaps, the former side of the idea was more prominent — the idea of a gift to placate God; in later times the other side, that the death of the creature was of the nature of penalty, by the exaction of which the righteousness of Jehovah was satisfied. This idea seems certainly expressed in Isa. liii.; at least these two points appear to be stated there, that the sins of the people, *i.e.* the penalties for them, were laid on the Servant and borne by him; and, secondly, that thus the people were relieved from the penalty, and their sins being borne, were forgiven.

New Testament scholars seem as much perplexed in seeking to discover the principle of atonement in the New Testament as we are in the Old. There is one passage in the Epistle to the Hebrews (x. 1–10) which has been interpreted by New Testament scholars, such as Bishop Westcott, and indeed most, in a way which is very doubtful. The passage runs thus : " For it is not possible that the blood of bulls and of goats should take away sins. Wherefore when He (*i.e.* Jesus) cometh into the world He saith, Sacrifice and offering Thou wouldest not, but a body hast Thou prepared Me. In burnt-offerings and sacrifices for sin Thou hadst no pleasure. Then said I, Lo, I am come . . . to do Thy will, O God. Above when He said, Sacrifice and offering . . . Thou wouldest not . . . (which are offered by the law), then said He, Lo, I am come to do Thy will, O God. He taketh away the first that He may establish the second." Now the general interpretation of this passage is that it substitutes for the mere material sacrifices of the Old Testament an ethical service, obedience to the will of God. But this, I think,—though it may be the meaning of the Psalm quoted (Ps. xl.), as it is the

doctrine of the prophets,—is obviously not the meaning of
the author of the Epistle to the Hebrews. The author's
argument is that Christ having done what was declared in
Scripture to be God's final will in regard to sacrifice, His
sacrifice is final. "By one offering He hath perfected for
ever them that are sanctified." It is not the general will
of God that he refers to, but His particular specific will
that Christ should offer His body. What are contrasted
are not two disparate things, namely, the material sacrifices
offered according to the law and the moral sacrifice of
obedience; but two things of the same kind or class,
namely, Old Testament sacrifices, the blood of bulls and
goats, and the offering of the body of Christ once for all—
the blood of Christ. For it is said, "Sacrifice and offering,
i.e. the legal offerings, thou wouldest not, but a body hast
Thou prepared Me." He willed not sacrifices, and He
willed the offering of the body of Christ; "by, or in,
which *will* we have been sanctified through the offering of
the body of Christ once for all." The Epistle to the
Hebrews merely throws the New Testament sacrifice into
the mould of the Old Testament, but furnishes no principle:
"If the blood of bulls and the ashes of an heifer sanctify to
the purifying of the flesh, how much more shall the blood of
Christ purify your conscience from dead works to serve the
living God?" It is not a new principle, but a more con-
clusive application of the old principle. The death of Christ
takes away sin because it is the death of *Christ*.[1]

XI. THE DOCTRINE OF THE LAST THINGS—
THE MESSIANIC IDEA

1. *Distinctive Contributions to the Doctrine.*

In the times of the early prophets it is the nation
as a whole that occupies the view of the prophet, its

[1] On this see more at length in the author's *The Epistle to the Hebrews
with Introduction and Notes*, pp. 189-194.—ED.

relation to Jehovah, its approaching fall; yet the in-
destructibleness of Jehovah's kingdom, its rise again in
the future, to be universal and all-enduring. Under this
general conception of the future, the eschatology of the
kingdom of the Lord, fall those prophecies which are
called Messianic. And the Messianic Hope is the transition to the Doctrine of the Last Things.

When we pass from this early region and this
general subject, the people or kingdom of the Lord, we
have to consider the individual, his condition and destiny.
This raises many questions regarding, *e.g.*, human nature
in the elements composing it—body, soul and spirit; sin
and its atonement; as well as death and immortality—the
eschatology of the individual. The most of these questions
came into prominence a century or two later down the
history than the period of the early prophets. In all the
earlier prophets the religious unit, so to speak, is the
people, as we see, *e.g.*, in Hosea. The individuals occupy
a secondary place, and share the fate, disastrous or happy,
of the people. It is but exceeding slowly that in the
thoughts of the Old Testament the individual man acquires
prominence and comes to the rights and the responsibilities
assigned to him in Christianity. It can readily be seen,
however, how God's providence in the history of Israel
gradually led to this result. So long as the State, North
and South, endured, the unit, the people, was apt to be
alone thought of. But when the State fell, first the
North and then the South, this unit no more existed.
Yet the individuals existed, and their God existed; and
the individual rose into the consciousness that all those
things which had been spoken of the people, its duties and
relations to Jehovah its God, had a reality as regarded
himself, and meantime had no other reality. Even
before the actual dissolution of the State, the many
calamities that befell the people in common could not
but awaken the individual's consciousness, and lead
him to a clearer conception of his true relations and
worth. The interpretation put by the prophets upon

the people's disastrous history led men to reflect and to discriminate.

While the interpretation that calamity was due to the sins of the people, might be just when the people as a unity was considered, yet many were conscious that they did not share in the sins and idolatries denounced by the prophets. Still the disasters of defeat and exile fell on them even with a more crushing weight than on the sinners of the people. It was the *élite* of the nation, the best-informed, and purest, and most godly, that were deported from their country. They could not but say, as one of them does: "Verily I have cleansed my heart in vain, and washed my hands in innocency. For all the day long have I been plagued."—"Lo, these are the ungodly who prosper in the world" (Ps. lxxiii. 12–14). Hence arose the proverb, "The fathers ate sour grapes, and the children's teeth are set on edge"; or, as it is expressed in Lam. v. 7: "Our fathers sinned, and we bear their iniquities." It is in the two prophets Jeremiah and Ezekiel, who both lived partly before and partly after the Exile, that the individual man fully comes to his true place before God. Indeed, in the xviiith and xxxiiird chapters of Ezekiel we may say that we see the birth of the individual mind taking place before our eyes: "All souls are mine, saith the Lord: as the soul of the father, so also the soul of the son" (xviii. 4). The prophet disentangles the individual from the people as a mass, and even from his nearest ancestors; he shall not be involved in the consequences of their sins: "The soul that sinneth, it shall die." But the prophet goes much further than this, and asserts for the individual a moral freedom, in virtue of which he can break with his own past and deliver himself from its consequences. He is not under the *ban* of the past. There is an *ego*, an *I* in man, possessed of moral freedom, which can rise above even that which may be called nature in him, and not only break with it, but take the rule of it, and shake off its moral shackles, and, in the favour of God, redeem himself from its consequences. Perhaps there are hardly any more important passages in the Old Testament than these two chapters of Ezekiel. The religious unit, so to speak, that subject between which and God religion is the bond and in which religious experiences take place, is the individual mind.

The period between the earlier prophets and those of later time, when problems of the individual life fill the minds of Scripture writers, such as the author of Job, for instance, and the authors of many of the Psalms,—this long period is of the greatest importance. There belong to it some, we may almost say most, of the profoundest parts of the Old Testament; those parts, indeed, many of which have come nearest Christianity. Examples are the Book of Deuteronomy, with the revolution which its discovery and promulgation occasioned; the prophecies of Jeremiah, in a moral and personal aspect—perhaps because he analyses himself and dissects his own mind and experience to us— the most Christian of the prophets; the Book of Ezekiel, on whom modern writers pass a very slighting, but probably not very profound judgment; who, at any rate, is not without his part in leading on the people of God towards great New Testament truths; the exquisite little collection of elegies, called the Lamentations, written shortly after the fall of the city, and reflecting the condition of the people's mind after this event. These poems exhibit to us the mind of religious men stunned by the magnitude of the blow, especially by the reflection that it was Jehovah their God who had inflicted it. Then they show us the profound sense of sin awakened in men's minds by these reflections; and no doubt it was just the people's history as a whole, under the interpretation of it by the prophets, that more than anything else deepened the sense of sin in the nation's heart. And, finally, they show us the inextinguishable faith in Jehovah, the Saviour of His people, a light which the darkness, however deep, could not swallow up. We may refer specially to the 3rd chapter of the Lamentations, perhaps the most singular piece of reflective meditation and weighing of considerations for and against the hope of God's mercy, which the Old Testament contains.

And, finally, there is the prophet of the second half of Isaiah,—who touches problems of sin and forgiveness more profoundly than any of his predecessors.

Many difficult questions are raised by Deuteronomy which we cannot discuss here. Perhaps a careful reader of it will feel inclined to come to the conclusion that it is the reflection of the teaching of the three earliest prophets of Israel, Amos, Hosea, and Isaiah, particularly of the last two ; for if a distinction can be drawn between the two things, it is more distinctively religious than moral. It will certainly be best understood when read after Hosea and Isaiah. This, at any rate, is its historical position, so far as it influenced and modified religious life among the people. Its teaching might be somewhat generally summed up in four points : 1. Jehovah, Israel's God, is one Jehovah, who cannot be represented in any form. The right disposition men show towards Him is love, and love is His disposition towards His people : "Hear, O Israel : Jehovah our God is one Jehovah : and thou shalt love Jehovah thy God with all thine heart" (vi. 4). "And Jehovah chose them because He loved them" (iv. 37). 2. The humanity which is everywhere inculcated in the book. It is not necessary to dwell on this. How often the widow, and the orphan, and the stranger are commended to the consideration of the people, because they were themselves once strangers in Egypt ! How the gleanings of field and vineyard, the sheaf forgotten in the field, and the seventh year's crop are to be left them that they may be well and rejoice before the Lord ! This spirit of benevolence and goodwill extends even to the nations, as, e.g., to Egypt. One can hardly fail to see the teaching of Hosea reflected in both these points. 3. The holiness of Jehovah is greatly emphasised, and the necessity that His people should be holy. And here the doctrines of Isaiah are probably reflected. But an effort is made to bring the prophet's ideal hopes as to the future into the present. In the picture which he draws of the final condition of Jerusalem, every one that is left shall be called 'holy.' Deuteronomy seeks to realise this great ideal in the present life of the people. Under this general idea fall all the prescriptions regarding cleanness, and purifications, and the like. It is this conception that gives unity to these laws, and enables us to understand them. And to this head belong all those denunciations of the impurities of the Canaanites, and the overwhelming moral earnestness of the warnings against having part in them, and the terrible threatenings against practising the religious rites or customs of these peoples.   4. And, finally, as the corollary of this law of holiness and the unity of Jehovah their God, and as the necessary means of realising this holiness, there is the law of the one altar where sacrifice to Jehovah is to be offered, that at Jerusalem. This is by no means, as is often represented, the chief burden of Deuteronomy. It is the least part of it, and only a consequence of other doctrines.

As the book is all spoken by Moses, the way in which the law is represented is this. It is not a law that is to come into effect on their entry into Canaan; it is to be observed from the time that Jehovah shall have given them rest from all their enemies round about; that is, from the times of David, or, more particularly, Solomon; for only when the temple was built did that place become known which Jehovah had chosen to place His name there. The main idea of the book is the holiness of Jehovah and the necessary holiness of His people To 'sanctify' Jehovah is to recognise Him to be the God that He is; God alone, spiritual, and above all ethical. To 'sanctify' Him in thought is to recognise this; in act, it is to live as the people of such a God should do—to be like Him. The opposite of to 'sanctify' is to 'profane'; and the people profane His name when, being His people, they engage in the impure worship of the Canaanites, or serve Jehovah in a false way, as under visible forms; and when, being His people, they practise the moral impurities of the nations about them. It is probable that 'holy' in Isaiah is mainly a moral idea, but in Deuteronomy and the law it is extended over a multitude of outward conditions; and ideas such as clean and unclean, perfect and imperfect physically, are drawn very largely into it. This great ideal of 'holiness' was set before the people; and they were taught by a multitude of prescriptions to seek to realise it.

Jeremiah had already been five years a prophet when Deuteronomy was made public law in 621. He does not appear to have had any hand in the promulgation of the law; nor in Josiah's reformation, which abolished all the rural high places of sacrifice, and confined the ritual worship of Jehovah to the temple at Jerusalem. It is probable that he saw this reform with satisfaction, but probably cherished few illusions in regard to it. It was good in its way, but it was not the good which he and men like him desired to see and required. The prophets were men never satisfied. When a reform was effected they accepted it, but always went further. Jeremiah soon had reason to see the effects of Josiah's reformation to be anything but good in all respects. The temple of the Lord, where worship was alone carried on, became to men's minds a kind of fetish: "the temple of the Lord, the temple of the Lord, are these" (Jer. vii. 4). The people thought it indestructible. And they thought their service of Jehovah at one place, as He had commanded, condoned all other offences and sins. "Will ye steal, murder, and commit adultery, and walk after other gods; and come and stand before Me in this house, and say, We are delivered?" (vii. 9). "Is this house that is called by My name a cave of robbers," where, after committing their depredations, they find refuge and think themselves safe?

It is indeed an interesting position that is occupied here by Jeremiah. That prophet's relation to the people and to Jehovah made him continually tossed between the two, and neither listened to him. He interceded for the people before God, but was rejected. "Though Moses and Samuel stood before Me, My heart could not be toward this people" (xv. 1). He carried Jehovah's word to the people, and he was persecuted because of it.

God seemed to ask much from him and to give him nothing. Yet He gave him Himself. And He gave him His word. On this the prophet fed. " Thy words were found, and I did eat them; they were unto me a joy, and the rejoicing of mine heart: for I am called by Thy name, O Jehovah God of hosts" (xv. 16). To know God, to be His servant, to have His ear to pour out his sorrows and perplexities and hard experience into, was enough. Success he had none—only defeat on every side; yet he was himself victorious amidst defeat. His teaching is little else than an expression, a transcription of his own pious life, of his intimate fellowship with God. It is personal religion become conscious of itself. Though not in the same formal way as Ezekiel, Jeremiah took great steps towards giving prominence to the individual mind.

Several things combined to secure this result. First, there was the isolation of the prophet. He felt himself, especially in opposition to the false prophets, the only true man in the State. This isolation, combined with his singular tendency to introspection and self-analysis, enables us to see his mind better than we see that of any other prophet. It was perhaps his isolation that compelled him to practise introspection; it required him to analyse his own mind, and to bring clearly before himself his relation to Jehovah, and perceive wherein the essence of that relation lay. And all this being the case of an individual, it established the position of the individual once for all. Secondly, another thing led to the same result, namely, his conception of Jehovah. Jehovah is to him a purely ethical being, and consequently His relation to the subject in fellowship with Him is a purely inward one. It must, therefore, be a relation to the individual mind. And, conversely, the service rendered to Him must be a service of the mind.

From this position follow the main things which appear in his prophecies, *e.g.*, 1. His condemnation of the whole past religious history of the nation; it has been no service of Jehovah (chaps. ii., iii., vi.).   2. The futility of external service and material symbols, such as sacrifice, ark, and the like: the time is coming when these shall no more be called to mind (vii. 21–28, vii. 9–11, iii. 16–18). 3. Hence his dissatisfaction with or indifference to the reforms of Josiah,—reforms on which the people prided themselves.   It is not reform but regeneration that is required: "Break up the fallow ground, and sow not among thorns; circumcise your hearts" (iv. 3; *cf.* references to the heart, iv. 4, 14, v. 23, xi. 20, xvii. 9, xxxi. 33).   4. Hence the stringent demand for morality in the individual, the subject of Jehovah's fellowship (v. 1, vii. 26–28, ix. 1–6, xviii.).   5. Hence prophecy has lost what was extraordinary and intermittent in it,—it becomes little else than an exalted piety.   Jeremiah has reached the condition spoken of by the Servant of the Lord: "He wakeneth my ear, he wakeneth morning by morning" (Isa. l. 4). Prophecy is a continuous standing in the counsel of God. It is that which he himself predicts of all: "They shall all know Me" (xxxvi. 19).   His conception of prophecy is that of a relation of mind to mind, conscious and reasonable, and his scorn is for the 'dreams' and 'visions' of the false prophets (xxiii. 21–32), and their mechanical supernaturalism.   The verification of prophecy lies in the consciousness of the true prophet, and in the moral nature of his prophecy; it is only prophecies of 'peace' to sinners and a sinful nation that require justification by the event (xxviii. 7–9).   6. Hence the calmness with which Jeremiah contemplates the ruin of the State as a State, buys a field on the eve of the city's fall (chap. xxxii.), and counsels submission to the king of Babylon (xxi. 9, xxix. 1–7, xxxviii. 17).   Though the State falls, the individuals of the people remain, and Jehovah remains, and religion and life to him remain; and 7. To the same effect is his view of the nature of the New Covenant.   The Lord writes it on the heart of the individual, and graves it on his inward part; and each man knows the Lord (xxxi. 33).

5. *The Consummation of the Kingdom.*

The great thoughts of salvation which the prophets give forth gather around certain conspicuous figures in the people of Israel. One of these figures is the theocratic or Davidic king. The idea of the king occupies a large place especially in prophets like Isaiah and Micah. In the various lights in which it is set, and the glorious colours with which it is invested, it becomes the most fruitful Messianic conception in prophecy. In the second part of Isaiah we have another figure, less conspicuous and imposing in grandeur, but, if possible, more singular in the attributes with which it is invested, and suggesting thoughts equally profound, although in an altogether different region—the figure of the *Suffering Servant of the Lord.* We can trace the character of the theocratic kingdom, and see what efforts the prophets make to set forth the glories of the theocratic king, rising in their conceptions of him till at last they reach the unsurpassable height of naming him: " God with us—Mighty God," and teaching that in him God shall be wholly present with His people. The point to which that delineation of the theocratic kingdom and king carries us, is perhaps the most favourable place for gathering together some of the things which the prophets say about the issue and final condition of the kingdom. This issue of the theocracy into its final condition takes place at a time and under circumstances which make up what the prophets call ' The day of the Lord.' These two great figures, the King and the Servant, suggest almost all the conceptions in the Old Testament which we are accustomed to call Messianic or Christological. It is probable that Old Testament writers themselves did not yet identify these two figures, or come to the conclusion that the attributes of both would yet be combined in one person. History, however, shows that this was to be the case. The Messianic conceptions and hopes in Israel are mainly connected with the last days, the period of Israel's perfection and final peace and blessing. This restoration of Israel and its perfection are realised througù this event, ' The day of the Lord.'

Now, to begin with, all Israel's spiritual blessings came from God, and even all Israel's blessings of whatever kind. He taught Israel's arms to fight, and made him tread on his high places. Salvation belonged unto God. And in whatever form or degree salvation was attained, it was through Him. All the strength of the nation arose from being strengthened with might by His Spirit, when all the channels of their life were filled and flushed with the Spirit poured into them. God Himself was Israel's highest blessing. He was the portion of her cup. His nearness brought salvation near. His presence in its fulness was the end of all development in Israel and Israel's glorification : " Arise, shine; for thy light is come, and the glory of the Lord is risen upon thee " (Isa. lx. 1). This was the meaning of the covenant relation.

With regard to the covenant, the two great factors in it are, of course, God and the people. Under the former head is discussed what is properly called theology, under the latter what is named anthropology. The Messianic teaching might be taken as a part of the first, and the doctrine of immortality as a part of the second. These two in some respects correspond. They form respectively the eschatology of the two departments ; or rather the Messianic doctrine belongs to the eschatology of the nation or people ; immortality, to the eschatology of the individual. Even the Messianic doctrine is not strictly a distinct thing in the Old Testament ; it is an element of the eschatology or final condition. There does not, I think, run through the Old Testament a distinct hope, to be called the Messianic hope. What is interpreted as *Messianic* in the New Testament, is rather everything in the Old Testament that is ideal of its own kind, whatever that kind may be,—an idealism only to be realised in the last times, whether, for example, it be the king, or the people, or the priest, or the individual saint.

Being thus some form of the final and perfect condi-

tion of the kingdom or people of Jehovah upon the earth,
being a picture of this, or of this in some of its aspects,
or of some great outstanding personage who is influential
in the introduction of this perfect state, or in maintaining
and perpetuating it,—that which we may call the *Messianic*,
—using the word in that general sense, as nearly equivalent
to *eschatological* in reference to the kingdom,—may assume
very different forms, and bring into ideal prominence
different persons or agents in the work of perfecting the
kingdom, or in its condition when perfected. We can
perceive that Jehovah's own operation and His own presence will be the essential Messianic element. Then we
have the state and conduct of the people as a whole; and
then, again, the theocratic king idealised as he shall be
in the latter day, when the kingdom of God is perfect;
or, because he was representative of Jehovah and the
destinies of the kingdom were in his hand, the individual
saint in his sufferings and deliverance.

The *Messianic*, as it is called, will thus differ very
greatly in different ages. The prominent agent in the
particular age will be idealised. At all times, of course,
Jehovah's work and presence may be dwelt upon. Also
at almost any time the condition of the people may be
idealised. During the monarchy the prominent personage
will be the Davidic king, and so on.

Dividing the history into periods, the prominent figures
seem these:

1. Jehovah, in His work and presence, at all times.
And this is of special importance, because it lays the
foundation both for the work and the person of the Messiah.
Whoever he is, it is Jehovah in him that is Saviour.

2. In the pre-monarchical period it is chiefly the people,
or mankind, as in the protevangelium, the promises to
Abraham and the patriarchs: "In thee and in thy seed";
and in the poems of Balaam.

3. During the monarchy it is the Davidic king,—
the Messianic king as *representative* of Jehovah,—though
also, of course, many times, of His people. This is parti-

cularly the case during the Assyrian conflicts, because
the destiny of the State was greatly in the hands of the
kings, and because the Davidic monarchy was threatened
with extinction in Isaiah's days and in Micah's. The
Davidic king is *intra-Israel*; the Servant of the Lord is
much wider, *intra-national*. The widening ideas of the
time could not but create a larger subject, giving him a
larger scope.

4. After the destruction of the monarchy, the Messianic
or eschatological hopes again centre in the people, as in
the second half of Isaiah ; the personal Messiah, as Davidic
king, drops out of sight; the *Divine* in this case is the
revelation of God incarnated in Israel.

5. At the Restoration, as was to be expected, the
priest becomes more prominent, or the union of the
priestly and the kingly becomes so, because the greater
sense of sin brings the idea of *atonement* into prominence.
So in the prophets of the Restoration, Zechariah, Haggai,
and Malachi.

It is remarkable that the *prophet* plays little part in
the eschatological view. Except in the passage in Deuteronomy, he has no place, though the prophetic function of the
people is the main conception of the second half of Isaiah.

But in the view of the prophets themselves, their
own function would be superseded in the perfect State.
Jehovah would write His law on men's hearts, and one
should no more teach his neighbour. The Spirit of God
takes the place of the prophet—He is poured out on all
flesh, and they all prophesy ; all the Lord's people are
prophets. With regard to Daniel, my impression is that,
in that book, it is the people, the saints of the Most High,
who shall receive the kingdom, and that the " son of man "
in that prophecy is a symbol of the people, and not of
an individual. This point, however, is somewhat obscure.
When the idea of the covenant relation was realised in
God's full presence in Israel, then Israel had reached the
end of her desires and attained perfection. The idea of
salvation in the Old Testament is *fellowship* with God.

That this union of God with Israel should yet be realised, all the prophets firmly believe. No doubt ere that time come there shall be great sorrows, and Israel shall seem abandoned of God. All the prophets predict the dissolution of Israel; but they look across the dark stream of death, and behold a new life on the other side. They usually put the two, destruction and restoration, side by side in abrupt opposition to one another. One prophet, like Micah, may first describe, as in his first three chapters, the dissolution of Israel: "Zion shall be ploughed like a field, and Jerusalem shall become heaps"; and then in the following chapters paint the restoration of the pristine kingdom, and the revival of the House of David: "It shall come to pass in the latter day that the mountain of the house of the Lord . . . shall be exalted above the hills, and all nations shall flow to it." Another prophet, like Isaiah, may begin with this prediction, and run out the development of calamity from his own present till this time of perfection is reached. Usually the prophets do not bridge over the chasm between Israel's dissolution and her restoration. They move usually in the higher region of Divine procedure. And as God chastises Israel by dispersing her in His anger, so He gathers her together again in His returning mercy. But, in the earlier prophets, the internal processes within Israel which explain, or at all events accompany, this different dealing, are usually only hinted at.

In later prophets, on the other hand, or at all events in prophets whose point of view is that of a later time, as in the second part of Isaiah, we have laid bare to us the wonderful internal process going on within Israel, the atonement of her sin and her repentance, which mediate the Restoration. We have it also in Zechariah: "I will pour out on Israel the spirit of grace and of supplications, and they shall look on Him whom they have pierced, and mourn" (xii. 10). The prophets may not express, they may not even represent, to themselves the means of Israel's restoration, except that God shall accomplish it; but they

24

all believe in it. And in the prophecies, certainly in
those of Isaiah, we have the idea of continuity, and the
holy seed indestructible blossoms out into a new people.
When they accompany to the grave, with bitter lamentations, the bier on which is laid the virgin daughter of
Israel, they sorrow not as those that have no hope. She
shall rise again : "Thus saith the Lord God, Behold, O
My people, I will open your graves, and cause you to
come up out of your graves, and bring you into the land
of Israel" (Ezek. xxxvii. 12).

Now the author of all this to Israel being God, the
fulness of Israel's life and the perfection of her attainment is
often described as the *coming of God*. What precise conception the prophets formed of this *coming* of God may not be
easy to determine. But it was not merely a coming in
wonders, or in the word of His prophets, or in a spiritual
influence and a change in His people's minds. It was something objective and personal : " Behold, the Lord cometh in
might, with His arm ruling for Him. The glory of the
Lord shall be revealed, and all flesh shall see it together."
When He came He came in His fulness. The age behind
was wound up and a new age commenced. The processes
that had been long going on ran out, and new lines of
movement began. This coming was not only the perfection of Israel, it was also the restitution of all things,
the renovation of the world. And it was a thing which
not Israel alone, but the inanimate world, had longed for
and rejoiced in : " The Lord is King ; let the earth rejoice ;
let the multitude of isles be glad thereat" (Ps. xcvii. 1).
During the past, the former age, God had often seemed
apathetic. He slept ; He let the reins of government
slip from His hands. He winked at men's wickedness.
Now He awoke. He grasped the reins of power ; He
took to Him His power and reigned. The kingdom was
the Lord's.

Now this is the fundamental thing,—Jehovah in person was present with His people. But this coming of
Jehovah is not always represented as being accomplished

in the same way. Sometimes the direct appearance of Jehovah in person is asserted, and the question how His appearance shall be realised is answered. Sometimes the coming is accomplished in the line of the Messianic hope—Jehovah comes down among His people in the Messiah, His presence is manifested and realised in him. The Messiah is " Immanuel—*God with us,*" he is *El Gibbor,* 'mighty God.' God is fully present, for purposes of redemption, in the Messianic king. This is the loftiest Messianic conception. It places the Messiah in the line of the perfect realisation of the hopes of Israel. Her highest hope was the perfect manifestation of God and His abode among the people; and when this hope is conceived as finding verification through the line of the Messiah, the Messiah becomes in himself the personal appearance of God.

The Messianic hope in the early prophets ran chiefly in the line of the theocratic kingship, and this hope blossomed into extraordinary splendour on two great occasions. The first was the glorious reign of David and the early monarchs of his house. This gave rise to hopes, and suggested conceptions, and disengaged, if I may say so, ideals which constituted the loftiest Messianic revelations. These are contained in the Messianic Psalms, such as Pss. ii., lxxii., cx., and others. Such passages seem to repose on the promise made to David by Nathan, that his house should never cease to bear rule in the kingdom of Jehovah. This promise is often alluded to in Scripture. It is formally stated in 2 Sam. vii. 12 ff.; alluded to in Pss. lxxxix., cxxxii., and in David's last words, 2 Sam. xxiii. ff., 1 Kings xi. 13, 36; while Ps. ii. and others are based on it. It is also present to the mind of all the prophets, even the oldest, as Amos and Hosea. The other occasion was when danger threatened the Davidic house, or when the certain dissolution of the kingdom was before the prophet's mind. Here two chief periods may be mentioned as giving rise to conceptions called Messianic : (1) the age of Hezekiah; (2) the age of the Exile. Perhaps we should give a third later age—an age of the study of the old predictions. Then the inextinguishable faith of the prophets in God's promises reacted against the appearances and dangers of the present, and they recalled to mind the 'sure mercies of David,' and the 'covenant ordered in all things'; and Isaiah gave the prophecies of the *Virgin's Son* and the *Mighty God*; while Micah saw rising on the ruins of Jerusalem a new Zion, and the former kingdom restored to it. This was the inspired protest of faith in the face of danger, or in view of the dissolution of the kingdom, now perceived to be inevitable. This continued, and is repeated, *e.g.*, in Jeremiah.

But when the kingdom had been long destroyed, and the Davidic house long in abasement, these ideas became less prominent. Circumstances turned the thoughts of the prophets in other directions, and made them move on other lines. God's providential treatment of Israel raised new conceptions of the future. The struggling nationality in Babylon attracted interest especially. Its faith amidst its exile, its constancy amidst its persecutions, its permanence and enduring individuality amidst defections, and the wearing hardships and enticements from the heathenism about it,—these drew the attention of the prophets. The idea of the people of God, the other side of the great covenant relation, rather than that of the theocratic king, was what filled their minds. And there floated before them glorious idealisations of that people, of its endowments by God, of its destinies, of what it should accomplish in the world, and what it should be when God returned to it and restored it to its own land. Then comes to light the meaning of Israel's sufferings, and the holy figure of the Suffering Servant rises before the prophet's view.

In this way a new and most fruitful Messianic conception is struck—profounder, if possible, than any previous. But it is a conception wholly different from the former one, though it comes in to supplement it. The former Messianic conception made prominent the Divine side. Its highest expression was *God with us*. In the Messiah, Jehovah came to His people. But, as was said, the prophet left unreconciled the antithesis between a sinful Israel and an Israel among whom God was to be present for ever in peace and fatherly protection and care. God could abide in this way only among a purified people. And now the chasm is filled up. Israel is purified by the sufferings of the Servant of the Lord: "*By His stripes we have been healed*" (Isa. liii. 5), and Jehovah dwells for ever among them. But this Servant rises out of the people. He is Israel itself. He realises in himself all that Israel should be, and therefore atones for Israelites who have not such characteristics. But he is a figure suggested by the sufferings of godly Israel, the holy kernel of the people in exile. He is the Messiah, but not the King Messiah. It is doubtful if the prophets identified in their own minds the Servant of Jehovah and the King Messiah. Later revelation showed them to be one. But, in the Old Testament, Messianic truth runs in many streams, far apart, all pursuing their own way, and regarding which one far up the stream would be unable to say that they would yet meet in the same sea.

Again, in Zech. iii. the Branch is the Messiah. And the conception of atonement struck in Isaiah reappears, though it is doubtful if it is in quite the same sense. There is another very difficult passage in Zechariah where the same conception of suffering seems to appear: "They shall look unto Him whom they have pierced" (xii. 10).

And, finally, the Book of Daniel is, as a whole, Messianic, though whether in the more general and wide sense of eschatological, or in the narrower sense of personally Messianic, will depend on our interpretation of the phrase, 'a son of man,' *i.e.* it is not quite clear whether this son of man be a real person, the Messianic king, or a personification of the people of the saints of the Most High; represented as human in opposition to the beasts which represented the heathen kingdoms. Without doubt the former interpretation became very prevalent before the time of our Lord, and the Book of Daniel is a very important element in the formation of the Messianic hope of his time.

As has been remarked, however, the prophets, regarding Jehovah's presence as Israel's salvation, dwelt much on His coming. It is not necessary to multiply references. The first eleven verses of Isa. xl., of which the climax is, " Say to the cities of Judah: Behold your God"—" the Lord cometh in strength," are an example; and among the Psalms the cii[nd], " Thou shalt arise, and have mercy upon Zion. . . . So the heathen shall fear the name of the Lord, and all the kings of the earth Thy glory; when the Lord shall build up Zion, He shall appear in His glory " (ver. 13 ff.). Now the authors of these passages, and others like them, had not in their mind the Messiah. They spoke of the appearance of Jehovah Himself, without connecting it with the Messianic hope. But Jehovah's appearance in glory could not in reality take place on two lines, and subsequent revelation fitted these passages into the line of Jehovah's manifestations in the Messiah. These manifestations of Jehovah were either for salvation or for judgment. But for these ends Jehovah appeared in the Messiah. All judgment is committed into his hand. Hence, in the New Testament, these passages are all referred to the manifestation of God in the Messiah.

3. *The Day of the Lord.*

But to be more specific. This manifestation of Jehovah is conceived as occurring at a set time, and with certain characteristics accompanying it; and in this aspect it is called *the day of the Lord.* It is possible that in Hebrew as in Arabic the *day* means the day of battle; the day of Badr is the battle of Badr, and this may be the primary sense of the phrase in Hebrew. And, in fact, in Isa. ii., where it is used, it may refer to the Lord's battle day—through His instruments the Assyrians. But naturally the phrase soon acquired a wider sense in Hebrew. It is not, however, to be regarded primarily as an *assize*, a day of judgment; judgment always took place in an external manner, in the form of chastisement at God's hands through His instruments—often in war. It is a day that is a special time; and it is the day of the Lord, belongs to Him, is His time for working, for manifesting Himself, for displaying His character, for performing His work—His strange work upon the earth. Hence Isaiah says: "For the Lord of hosts hath a day upon every one that is proud and lofty . . . and he shall be brought low" (ii. 12); "And the Lord alone shall be exalted in that day" (ver. 17).

Now, as to this day, these things may be observed:

(1) As it was a day of the manifestation of Jehovah, God of Israel, in His fulness, and therefore in a way to realise His purposes, which, with Israel and even with the world, were those of grace, it is fundamentally a day of joy to Israel and also to the world. "Let the children of Zion be joyful in their King" (Ps. cxlix. 2). "The Lord is king; let the earth rejoice; let the multitude of the isles be glad thereof" (Ps. xcvii. 1). "Say among the heathen that the Lord is king. . . . Let the heavens rejoice, and let the earth be glad; let the sea roar (*i.e.* for gladness), and the fulness thereof. Let the fields be joyful, and all that is therein. . . . Before the Lord: for He cometh, for He cometh to rule the earth: He shall rule the world with righteousness, and the peoples with His truth" (Ps. xcvi. 10–13). That Jehovah should reign, and that He should come to the earth as King, must, in spite of all the terrors that might attend His coming, bring to the world a pervading gladness. For the falsehood and injustice that had cursed the earth so long would disappear, and the longing of men, who were ever, in words or sighs, crying, 'Show us the Father, and it sufficeth us,' should be satisfied. But it would be a day of satisfaction, above all, to Israel, when He should plead her cause; for the day of vengeance was in His heart, and the year of His redeemed was come. Naturally an accompaniment of the manifestation of Jehovah was the disappearance of the idols. "Ashamed, turned back . . . are all they that frame graven images; Israel is saved with an eternal salvation" (Isa. xlv. 17). "On that day men shall cast their idols of silver and their idols of gold to the moles and to the bats" (ii. 20).

But in the view of the prophets the gigantic oppressions which the empires of Assyria and Babylon meant
to Israel, were but projections of their idolatry, with
its cruelties and inhumanity, and licentiousness and pride.
The later prophet, Daniel, condenses this idea into a graphic
enough and expressive figure, when he represents the
heathen monarchies under the image of various savage
beasts, while the kingdom of God is represented under the
image of a man.   These kingdoms were embodiments of
the qualities of the brute ; in the kingdom of Israel man
rose to his place, and the true attributes of humanity found
full play and embodiment.   Hence the grand tone of all
descriptions of the day of the Lord is a certain joy, which
is willing to face the terrors of His coming for that which
shall follow upon it.   Behind the tempest the sky breaks
clear.   The terror, and the joy that is in spite of it, are
finely displayed in the hymn of Habakkuk (chap. iii.).

(2) To those in Israel who looked for Jehovah's coming,
apart from the natural terrors of it, it was unmixed satisfaction.   And it would have been so to all Israel had fidelity
to her relation to Jehovah been universal.   But this was
far from being the state of Israel.   The condition of Israel
was mixed.   Hence the ' day of the Lord,' while as a whole
a day of salvation, had another side, which made it a day
of judgment.   To Israel as the people of God it was a day
of salvation, and consequently it was a day of vengeance
and judgment upon the people's foes, i.e. all the heathen
round about.   Thus Obadiah (vers. 15–17) says : " For the
day of the Lord is near upon all the heathen : as thou hast
done (to Israel), it shall be done unto thee : thy reward
shall return upon thine own head, . . . but upon Mount
Zion shall be deliverance, and there shall be holiness."
But there were many in Israel who belonged to Israel
only in race.   They were " filled from the East, and were
soothsayers like the Philistines " (Isa. ii. 6).   They shared
the idolatries and practised the sins of the nations; and,
as Jeremiah charges it upon them, their sin was double :
" Hath a nation changed their gods, which are no gods ?

but My people have changed their glory for that which doth not profit. . My people have committed two great evils: they have forsaken the fountain of living waters, and hewn out unto themselves cisterns, broken cisterns, that can hold no water" (ii. 11–13). Therefore the day of the Lord came upon Israel also as a day of terrors and destruction. And the true prophets find it necessary to warn the people against a superficial national conception of the day of the Lord, as if it was a mere interference of Jehovah in behalf of Israel as a people, and not a manifestation on strict moral lines, and a revelation of the righteous judgment of God. So early even as Amos this perversion of the idea had crept in: "Woe unto you that desire the day of the Lord! Wherefore will ye have the day of the Lord? It is darkness, and not light. As if a man did flee from a lion, and a bear met him. Shall not the day of the Lord be darkness? even very dark, and no brightness in it?" (v. 18).

Hence the 'day of the Lord' acquires a double-sided character. It is a day of salvation and judgment, or a day of salvation through judgment,—a day of judgment on the heathen world and the Church's foes, but also upon the apostate, impure Church itself,—and a day of salvation behind this. Sometimes one side is prominent and sometimes another. Sometimes it is represented as a process of sifting, or a process of refining. Thus Zephaniah, whose book is just a detailed delineation of the day of the Lord, says: "The day of the Lord is at hand; the Lord hath prepared a sacrifice, and He hath bid His guests" [Israel is the society, and the nations who execute His wrath are the guests]. . . . "And it shall come to pass at that time, that I will search Jerusalem with candles, and punish the men that are settled on their lees" (i. 7–12). And another prophet says: "I will turn My hand upon thee, and purge away thy dross" (Isa. i. 25); and yet another: "Who may abide the day of His coming . . . for He is like a refiner's fire . . . and He shall sit as a refiner and purifier of silver" (Mal. iii. 2, 3). Sometimes both sides

of the Divine manifestation are brought forward, as in Joel:
"I will pour out My Spirit upon all flesh; . . . and I will
show wonders in the heavens and in the earth, blood, and
fire, and pillars of smoke. The sun shall be turned into
darkness, and the moon into blood, before the great and
terrible day of the Lord come. . . . And it shall come to
pass, that whosoever shall call on the name of the Lord
shall be delivered" (chap. ii. 28–32).

It is in connection with this side of the day, which
is judgment, that all the terrible pictures of it are drawn
with which we are familiar. That day, says Amos, is
"darkness, and not light" (v. 18). According to Joel, it is
a "day of darkness and of gloominess, a day of clouds and
of thick darkness" (ii. 2) . . . "the sun and moon shall
be dark, and the stars shall withdraw their shining" (ii. 10).
Isaiah describes it as a day of terrors: "Men shall go into
the holes of the rocks and into the caves of the earth for
fear of the Lord . . . they shall say to the mountains,
Cover us; and to the hills, Fall on us" (ii. 19). "Behold,
the Lord maketh the earth empty, and maketh it waste,
and turneth it upside down, and emptieth out the inhabitants thereof . . . the earth shall reel to and fro like a
drunkard, it shall shake like a booth . . . and it shall fall,
and not rise again" (Isa. xxiv. 1–20). "Behold, the day
of the Lord cometh, cruel both with wrath and fierce anger,
to lay the earth desolate . . . therefore I will shake the
heavens, and remove the earth out of her place, in the
wrath of the Lord of hosts" (Isa. xiii. 9, 13). For this
wrath shall be universal and indiscriminate: "I will
utterly consume all things from off the earth, saith the
Lord. I will consume man and beast; I will consume the
fowls of the heaven, and the fishes of the sea   . and I
will cut off man from off the earth, saith the Lord. Hold
thy peace at the presence of the Lord God: for the day
of the Lord is at hand" (Zeph. i. 2–7).

(3) From this character of the day as a manifestation
of God we may understand how it is that the prophets
connect it with many different things. It is a manifesta-

tion of God—of God as what He is truly, and in the
whole round of His being. Hence it displays His whole
character, and sees His whole purpose effected. Hence it
has universal bearings. But all manifestations of Jehovah
are on moral lines. God wholly revealed is only in perfection that which He is partially seen to be every day.
His perfect work is but the completion of the work which
He can be seen at any time engaged in performing. The
final state of things was but the issue of operations going
on always. The prophets are in the dark as to the time
of that day, but they are in no ignorance of the principles
of it. And the feeling that these principles, retarded by
many obstacles in their operation now, counteracted by
the opposing wills of men, and by their insensibility to
Jehovah's work among them, may at any moment overcome the obstacles and throw off the hindrances that
impeded them, and run out into perfect realisation, was
ever present with them. Thus, when they observed a
quickening of the currents of providence in any direction,
whether of judgment or salvation, the presentiment filled
their minds that it was the beginning of the day of the
Lord. Hence Joel attaches that day to the plague of
locusts and drought ; this extraordinary judgment seemed
to him the first warnings of the universal judgment.
Another prophet (Isa. xiii.) connects the day with the
violent upheavals among the nations that accompanied
the overthrow of the Babylonian monarchy by the Medes :
" The oracle of Babylon . . . the noise of a multitude . . .
a tumultuous noise of the kingdoms of nations gathered
together . . . they come from a far country, even the
Lord, and the weapons of His indignation, to destroy the
whole earth. Howl ye, for the day of the Lord is at
hand " (xiii. 1–6). And yet again, in the second chapter,
the prophet connects it with the wickedness and pride of
Israel, and with the feeling that God's vengeance must fall
upon it : " The land is full of idols . . . the lofty looks of
man shall be humbled . . . for the Lord hath a day upon
every one that is proud and lofty " (ii. 11–12). And other

prophets connect it with other great movements in the world, in which Jehovah's presence was conspicuously seen.

These prophets moved much amidst presentiments. It was mainly moral necessities that they spoke of. They had a finer sensibility than others to detect the currents of things. Their hearts were full of certain issues, and they were constantly looking for them, although the exact time of their coming was hid from them. And as one in the darkness thinks he hears the approach of an evil which he dreads, these prophets, when the sound of Jehovah's goings was more distinctly heard than usual, deemed that what they heard was the warning of His coming to shake terribly the earth. This was not a mere subjective feeling. For His final appearance was closely connected with these manifestations in great providences, as the outermost ring in the pool is but the widening of the innermost. For there moves a current under all things, bearing them on its bosom towards results affecting all. Often its motion is imperceptible. But sometimes it receives a mysterious quickening, and men become conscious whither things are moving. Every wave that runs up and breaks upon the shore is the precursor of the full tide; and every act of judgment or of salvation is a premonition of the day of the Lord. To say that this frame of things shall never reach a goal, is to put God out of it as effectually as to say that it never began. But it shall not end in a manner which cannot be guessed at. It shall end on the lines on which it is at present moving. And the ear that is wakened by Jehovah, and sharpened by His touch, may detect in the sounds of any signal providence the final issue of things, as surely as one can hear the full tempest in the first drops that fall sharp and measured upon the leaves in the sultry stillness of the air.

A distinction, of course, must be drawn between the faith of the prophets and their presentiments. Their expectation of the day of the Lord was a belief, an assur-

ance, as much as our own; but the feeling they had about
its nearness on any occasion was more a presentiment.
It is somewhat difficult for us to realise this peculiar
feeling which the prophets had of the nearness of the day
of the Lord. Yet, perhaps, it is not really so difficult.
The prophets wrote and spoke usually amidst very stirring
scenes. Great events were passing around them. It is
only, speaking generally, amidst convulsions that rend
society deeply that they came forward. In these great
events about them they felt the presence of Jehovah. He
was nearer than before. The noise of falling empires, the
desolations of the kingdom of God, the revolutions in men's
thoughts, revealed to their ear His footsteps; they heard
in them the sound of His goings. God was so near that
His full presence, which He had promised, appeared imminent. Speedily His glory would be revealed, and all
flesh would see it together, as the mouth of the Lord
had said. Thus their belief in the nearness of the Lord's
coming was more a feeling than a thought, more a presentiment of their heart—a religious presentiment—than a
mere intellectual calculation of time. Still the feeling was
of such a kind that we cannot imagine them thinking His
coming could be long deferred.

(4) Another thing follows from the last two particulars.
Though the 'day of the Lord,' as the expression implies,
was at first conceived as a definite and brief period of
time, being an era of judgment and salvation, it many
times broadened out to be an extended period. From
being a day it became an epoch. This arose from the fact
that under the terms *day of the Lord, that day*, or *that time*,
was included not only the crisis itself, but that condition
of things which followed upon the crisis. Frequently, also,
there was included under it the condition of things that
preceded the crisis. Now this condition of things that
issued in the day of the Lord was frequently one of some
duration, being sometimes a calamitous period in Israel's
history, and sometimes a period of great commotion among
the nations. The *day* is usually considered a period when

it is brought into connection with the Messianic age or
identified with it. The Messianic age, as we observe it,
for example, in Isa. ii., the prophecy of the mountain of
the Lord, or in Isa. xi., the prophecy of the shoot out
of the stem of Jesse, is a period entirely homogeneous.
There are no occurrences within it. It is the perfect
condition of Israel, and there are no events or breaks
within it. It has characteristics, but no internal development. It is a period of light, and peace, and the knowledge
of the glory of the Lord which covers the earth. But it
has no movement. "It shall come to pass in that day,"
says Zechariah, "that the light shall not be clear and dark,
but it shall be day only . . . not day and night . . . but
it shall come to pass that at evening it shall be light"
(xiv. 6). Subsequent revelation has broken up the coming
of the Messiah into a coming and a coming again, and
intercalated between the two an age full of developments
and vast changes. But the prophets embrace all in one
period, over which there hangs a Divine light. The
characteristics they assign to the Messianic age are those
characteristics in the main which we assign to the age
which the Second Coming shall introduce. These characteristics are the result of the first coming and the natural
expansion of its principles, and to the prophets the principles and their realisation all seem condensed into one
point. But in this way, as was said, the day of the
Lord widens out into a period, homogeneous, no doubt,
but extensive.

(5) Again, the condition in which the day of the Lord
leaves the external world is variously represented. For,
as the prophets were not interested in giving mere predictions of external events or conditions, but in setting
before the Church the moral developments and issues of
the kingdom, it sometimes happens that they bring down
these issues in their completed form upon an external
condition of the world which is just that existing in their
own day. There is a perfection and realisation of moral
principles ; but the condition of the world, in its kingdoms

and the like, remains unchanged. Thus to Micah the
Assyrian still exists in the Messianic age.

But, ordinarily, this is not the case. The heathen
monarchies entirely disappear. The heathen nations are
utterly destroyed, as in Joel; or they are absorbed into
Israel, as in most of the prophets. "In that day shall
Israel be the third with Egypt and with Assyria: when
the Lord of hosts shall say, Blessed be Egypt My people,
and Assyria the work of My hands, and Israel Mine
inheritance" (Isa. xix. 24, 25). "Egypt shall be a desolation, and Edom a desolate wilderness . . . but Judah
shall dwell for ever" (Joel iii. 19, 20). "The house of
Jacob shall be a fire . . and the house of Esau for
stubble; and they shall devour them . . . they of the
south shall possess the mount of Esau; and they of the
plain the Philistines . . . and Benjamin shall possess
Gilead" (Obad. 18, 19). In many of the prophets this
conquest of the world by Israel is through the religion of
Israel. Many nations shall say, "Come, and let us go up
to . . . the house of the God of Jacob; . . . He will teach
us of His ways, and we will walk in His steps" (Isa. ii. 3).
The issue is the same in all, but it is realised in many different forms.

And, finally, in many of the prophets what is declared
is not only a great change upon the condition of the earth,
but an absolute transformation. An order of things wholly
new is introduced upon the world. It is not quite certain
what that prophet quoted both by Isaiah and Micah means
when he says "that the mountain of the house of the Lord
shall be exalted above the hills" (Isa. ii. 2; Mic. iv. 1);
whether he speaks of real physical changes on the face of
the world, or uses only a figure to express religious prominence. But it is certain that the prophet Zechariah
contemplates physical changes when he says: "The land
shall be turned into a plain from Geba to Rimmon south
of Jerusalem: and it shall be lifted up," i.e. elevated, "and
inhabited in her place, from Benjamin's gate unto the
place of the first gate"; and so on (Zech. xiv. 10). But

the transformation of the earth assumes larger proportions in many of the prophets, and becomes a complete transformation of all things. There is not so much a transformation as a transfiguration: "Behold, I create new heavens and a new earth, saith the Lord" (Isa. lxv. 17; cf. iv. 2, xi. 6–16, etc.).

As the prophets are mainly interested in the moral destiny of Israel, there are two characteristics which are always announced as present in that great day:

a. Israel is truly the people of God. The people shall be all righteous. Jehovah dwells in Zion. He is Israel's glory, and she needs no more the light of the sun and moon. He makes a new covenant with Israel, and writes His law upon her heart. Sorrow and sighing flee away. The Lord rejoices over Israel as the bridegroom over the bride. Jerusalem shall be holy; the uncircumcised and the unclean shall pass through her no more.

b. Israel in that day shall be fully restored. Ephraim shall not envy Judah, nor Judah envy Ephraim. Jehovah will lift up a signal to the nations, and they will bring Israel's children from afar, and plant them in their own land. The former kingdom shall return, and all the nations on which Jehovah's name is named shall be again subject to Israel, in a new manner. But we shall have occasion to speak of this again when considering the Restoration of Israel in itself.

4. *The Day of the Lord in Deutero-Isaiah.*

So much importance belongs to the Second Isaiah in this connection, however, that it is necessary to look more particularly to the conceptions of *Redemption* and the *Day of the Lord* which appear in that great section of prophecy. Something has been said of the *day of the Lord* as the idea is represented in most of the prophets. The prophet whom we shall now specially consider does not, I think, use this expression, but the idea is present to him when he says: "The Lord God cometh in might, His arm ruling for Him.

Behold, His reward is with Him, and His recompense before Him (xl. 10). "The glory of the Lord shall be revealed, and all flesh shall see it together" (xl. 5). And the issue of Jehovah's coming shall be that He will "feed His flock for ever, like a shepherd." And in another passage (xlii. 13–17): "The Lord shall go forth as a mighty man; He shall stir up ardour as a man of war. . . . I have too long holden my peace, now will I cry out like a travailing woman. I will make waste mountains and hills . . . and I will lead the blind by a way that they know not . . . they shall be turned back and ashamed that trust in graven images." See also the splendid passage in lix. 16, etc.

We have seen, then, that it was Jehovah who was the Saviour of His people, and that this salvation consisted in His coming to them in His fulness; for then was fulfilled the idea of the covenant, that He should be their God and they His people. It is remarked by Franz Delitzsch that it is always Jehovah in the Old Testament, and not the Messiah, that is the Saviour of the people. The remark is true; and it is a truth profoundly important when we consider it in connection with Messianic statements in the Old Testament. We find that, though Jehovah alone is Saviour of His people, and though the salvation is often represented as realised in His coming in person in the day of the Lord, this is not always the case. Sometimes He comes not, so to speak, in person or independently, but in a presence manifested in the Messianic King; and in such cases there is no additional presence of Himself in person. This elevates His presence in the Messiah, and the Messiah in whom He is present, to a very lofty significance. It may be doubtful, as we have already observed, if the Old Testament went so far as to identify the Messiah with Jehovah, or to represent the Messiah as Divine. It went the length of saying, however, that Jehovah would be present in His fulness in the Messiah, so that the Messiah might fitly be named 'God with us,' and 'Mighty God.' It is thus just the very idea that Jehovah alone is the Saviour of His people that

25

makes this representation, viz., that He saves them in His presence in the Messiah, so remarkable, and elevates the Messianic conception to so high a level. It was not a difficult step to take, to infer that the Messiah was Himself God, and that because He was God He was Saviour; and then to apply even those passages which speak of Jehovah's coming in person to His coming in the Messiah.

We have seen also that each of the prophets represents the day of the Lord as arising out of the condition of the people of God and of the world in his own day, and therefore as near. Isaiah, for instance, in his first discourse (chaps. ii.–iv.) represents the day of the Lord as a moral necessity, to humble the pride and to chastise the sin of men of his day. Again, in chap. xiii. it is represented as following the convulsions of the nations which were to issue in the downfall of Babylon. The chapters we are now considering represent it in the same way as following on the conflict of Cyrus with the idolatrous kingdom. Probably it is not too much to say that all students of prophecy now acknowledge that this peculiar mode of representation characterises the prophets. It was not so, however, with scholars of older date, such as Hengstenberg. That redoubtable Berlin theologian expressed the opinion that the prophets and psalmists would have made themselves ridiculous by cherishing such a notion. In reply to this, Kurtz, in an excellent paper on the "Theology of the Psalms," remarked: "It is once for all the case that not only the subjective hopes of the pious in Israel at all times conceive the time of the Messianic fulfilment as near, but the objective prophecies of the prophets of the Old Covenant so represent it"; and he adds, "and so it is in the New Testament; for the apostles represent the advent of the Lord as near, even immediately near."

Perhaps these two remarks require still to be made on the term *Day of the Lord*. One is, that of course there is no such thing as *a* day of the Lord, it is always *the* one day of which the prophets speak. It is a great religious conception, in the minds of the prophets, of unknown

antiquity; for even Amos refers to the conception as
having already been corrupted. The day of the Lord is
the day when the Lord Himself comes, manifesting Himself
in His fulness. It is never *identified* with plagues or convulsions; these are but the tokens of its nearness, or, at
most, accompaniments of it. "The sun shall be turned
into darkness, and the moon into blood," says Joel, "before
the great and terrible day of the Lord come" (ii. 31).
The second remark is this,—although to the prophets,
amidst the great events taking place around them, in which
they saw the presence of Jehovah, the day seemed near; yet
this was not a judgment of the mind so much as a surmise
of the heart; it was not an intellectual calculation, it was
rather that they threw their faith and their hope of the
coming of Jehovah in His redemptive fulness into the events,
and His coming seemed imminent. I make such suggestions
in explanation of this peculiarity on the part of the prophets. I am doubtful if they will quite satisfy others, for
they do not quite satisfy myself. But however we explain
the peculiarity, its existence cannot be doubted, and it is
of great importance in interpretation.

Another thing which appears with regard to the *day
of the Lord* is, that, being perfect redemption, a condition
of full religious fellowship with the Jehovah, it was this
religious side that was present to the prophets chiefly; and,
having a presentiment of its nearness, they often bring the
perfect kingdom into a condition of the world such as they
saw in their own time. Of course it need not be said
that such an idea as that which we call 'heaven,' an abode
of the saints in a transcendent sphere different from the
earth, is not yet an idea of the Old Testament revelation.
The perfect condition of the Church was not to be realised
by translating it into heaven, to be with God there, but
by Jehovah coming down to be with men here, when the
tabernacle of God was with men. Ordinarily, however,
the prophets conceive the earth as renewed so as to be a
fit abode for God's perfect people; and sometimes a new
heaven and a new earth are prophesied of.

One other point may be referred to. The day of the Lord, or His coming in His fulness as Redeemer, was to bring perfect redemption to His people. But the question arises, what did the prophets understand by *redemption*, and who were His *people*? We must always remember the condition of the world in the prophets' days, because redemption was conceived as coming to the Church and world that then existed. Now the people of God in the prophets' days was Israel, and no other. And redemption in that day, while the essence of it was the same as redemption to us, namely, the forgiveness of sins, and the perfect fellowship of God consequent on this, was not yet conceived as consisting exclusively in these spiritual blessings; because the Church of God was a people, and a local dwelling and land was necessary to it. And, further, the minds of men in those days were not able to realise to themselves that they possessed the favour of God, and had His fellowship and were His people, unless they had also external prosperity. It was not the external blessings themselves that they coveted; but these external blessings, possession of Canaan and the like, were a kind of sacramental sign to them. They were seals of God's forgiveness and His favour. Hence in this prophet the *righteousness* of the people is put in parallelism with their *salvation*. This righteousness was imputed to them or bestowed on them by Jehovah, but they were able to realise it only when it was manifested externally in their restoration and outward well-being.

Now, keeping these few points before our minds, we are able to place ourselves in the circumstances of the prophet, and to understand his construction or conception of *Redemption*, and how it was to be effected.

Throwing ourselves into the world of the prophet, we perceive easily the phenomena and forces which made up that world. These were Jehovah, God alone, and the false gods; the people of God, in bondage to that mighty world-empire of Babylon, which was but an incarnation of its own idolatry; the irresistible career of Cyrus, raised up and directed by Jehovah, and the prostration of the idol-worshipping nations before him. The prophet did not look on these things as other men did. His eye saw in them what he brought with him to the observation of them. He animated them with his own religious faiths and hopes. The external conflict became to him a conflict of principles, and out of the conflict the eternal truth rose victorious; the kingdom of the Lord was ushered in,—the kingdom of Him besides whom there was no God, no Saviour.

To many an eye the world might have seemed only confusion, and it did fill many of the prophet's contemporaries with despair. They shared in the alarm of the other nations at the advance of Cyrus, fearing he might but forge heavier chains for them than those that now bound them. But they were comforted against this fear: "But thou, Israel, my servant, fear not: for I am with thee; I hold thee by the right hand of My righteousness" (xli. 8–10). They were faint-hearted: "Why, when I am come, is there no man?" (l. 2). They were captious, and criticised the ways of Jehovah in delivering them: "Woe to him that striveth with his Maker!" (xlv. 9). But though to many minds in Israel all things might appear in confusion, they could not appear so to a prophet of the Lord. It was a great Divine drama that was being played, complicated and extended, and only a prophet could foresee how it would develop itself. He could foresee, because to his mind the principal, or rather the only actor was Jehovah Himself; and he knew beforehand what He was and what His purposes were: "Look unto Me, and be ye saved, all the ends of the earth: for I am God, and there is none else" (xlv. 22). The thought of Jehovah, like the morning light breaking into the darkness, turns to the prophet's view the confusion into order. Under his eye there starts and proceeds, step by step, the evolution which ushers in the kingdom. This evolution has two sides, an outer and an inner; but the power moving and operating in both is Jehovah.

The outward evolution is the career and work of

Cyrus. This Cyrus, who was spreading consternation among the heathen, treading down kings, and exciting terror even in the breasts of the captives, was the 'anointed' of Jehovah, whom He had raised up, and who was come, obedient to His bidding; and His raising him up was not a mere display of power, but a great operation within the sphere of redemption: "I have raised him up in righteousness: he shall build my city, and let go my captives" (xlv. 13). Other prophets had spoken of heathen conquerors as Jehovah's instruments. The Assyrian was the 'rod of His anger' (x. 5) to chastise His people in early times; and later, in Jeremiah, the Lord speaks of "My servant Nebuchadnezzar" (xliii. 10).

But in two particulars this prophet goes beyond others: first, in the great scope of the task which he assigns to Cyrus, which is to crush the heathen world-power, and thereby abolish idolatry; and to set the Lord's captives free and build His temple, that the law might go forth from Zion and the word of the Lord from Jerusalem; and, second, in the intimacy with Jehovah Himself into which he brings the Persian hero. Cyrus is no mere instrument, as the Assyrian was, to be flung away or broken in pieces like a rod when God's purpose was served with it. Cyrus is the anointed of the Lord, whose right hand Jehovah holds (xlv. 1), whom He even 'loveth' (xlviii. 14), whom He called by name when he did not know Him, and who shall even call on His name (xli. 25); and whom He has raised up with the widest purpose, even that men may know from the rising of the sun and from the west that there is "none beside Me" (xlv. 6). These passages suggest one of the most interesting questions that these prophecies raise, the question, what thoughts the prophet had of the religion of Cyrus, and whether he entertained the hope that the king might be won over to the religion of Jehovah. No thought was too lofty or too wide for the prophet in the passion of enthusiasm which the vision of a restored nation and a regenerated world raised within him. And, obviously, if such a thought occurred to him, it would facilitate to his mind the solution of the problem that attracted his thoughts, namely, how the nations could be gained over to the true faith and become the kingdoms of the Lord.

In this way what might be called the external frame of the prophet's conception of the universal kingdom of the Lord was set up,—the idolatrous empire was laid low, the idols demonstrated to be vanity (xli. 29), those that served graven images were turned back and put to shame (xlii. 17); and, on the other side, the ransomed of the Lord were restored to Zion with everlasting joy upon their heads (li. 11), and Israel saved with an everlasting salvation (xlv. 17). Such language, however, is proof enough how ill suited such a phrase as 'external frame' is to express the prophet's conception. The work of Cyrus was, in truth, the work of Jehovah. Its whole meaning to the prophet lay in its being a religious work,—a great stride taken by the kingdom of the Lord towards its full victory over all that was evil and false. Nothing could demonstrate how entirely all the prophet's interests are religious so much as his eagerness to bring Cyrus, the great agent in Jehovah's work, himself into true and personal relations with the Redeemer of Israel, and God over all.

But there is also a process of internal evolution needful to realise the perfect kingdom of the Lord. The prophet's idea is complete; he has comprehended the problem in all its details. The work of Cyrus in the world only overthrows the idol-serving empire, and eternally discredits the idols and the idolaters. The nations are not thereby enlightened in the knowledge of the true God, and right. It is the mission of the Servant of the Lord to bring forth right to the nations, and the countries shall wait on his instruction. Not to raise the question of the Servant here, whether he be Israel or another, when the prophet says in xlii. 6 and xlix. 6 that the Servant shall be "the light of the Gentiles," and in chap. lx. says of Zion glorified, "Arise, shine . . . the Gentiles shall come to thy light," it appears manifest at least that his idea is that the Servant shall reach the Gentiles only through Israel restored. Any missionary enterprises of individuals, however exalted, could scarcely occur to the prophet. Like all prophets of the Old Testament, he operates with nations and peoples. And if the nations are to receive light through Israel, it will be through Israel again a people before the world's eyes; just as the Lord goes forth from Zion, and the word of the Lord from Jerusalem. And this clearly enough shows what the prophet means by the *Restoration*. It is no return of a few or many exiles from Babylon; it is the reconstruction of the people in its former integrity.

Delitzsch (with whom Cheyne agrees) maintains that the covenant which the Servant makes or is, is made with the true spiritual Israel. Of course, it is a truism that the covenant cannot be made with those who will have none of it,—"There is no peace, saith my God, to the wicked" (xlviii. 22). But the language which the prophet uses when he speaks of the Servant as a "covenant of the people," whose mission is to set up the tribes of Jacob and restore the preserved of Israel, and when the Lord says: "I will say to the north, Give up: bring My sons from afar; even every one that is called by My name" (*i.e.* belongs to the people of Jehovah) (xliii. 6), sufficiently indicates the extent of the prophet's hopes. And, speaking expressly of the new covenant, the Lord says: "Ho, every one that thirsteth, come ye to the waters. Incline your ear, and I will make an everlasting covenant with you . . . let the wicked forsake his way, and the unrighteous man his thoughts: and let him return unto the Lord, and He will be gracious" (lv. 1–7). This language shows the extent of the covenant, and that the prophet's hopes were the same as those of the Apostle Paul: "And so all Israel shall be saved" (Rom. xi. 26). But this restoration of the people could not take place apart from the true conditions of it: "Let the wicked forsake his way, and . . . let him return unto the Lord, and He will be gracious." To the prophet's mind, Israel's exile and afflictions were due to its sin, and its restoration must be preceded by its repentance and forgiveness. This forgiveness it mediated through the sufferings of the Servant of the Lord. But it is he also who kindles within Israel the glow of a new faith in Jehovah, which secures their spiritual unity, and thus leads to their restoration. But here again, if we would observe the prophet's thoughts, we shall find that he attributes all to Jehovah. He called the Servant in righteousness, and took hold of his hand, and will keep him, and make him a covenant of the people, a light of the Gentiles (xlii. 6): "Behold my servant, whom 1 keep hold of; I will put My spirit upon him" (xlii. 1). "For the Lord God will help me; therefore have I set my face like a flint, I know that I shall not be ashamed. He is near that justifieth me; who will contend with me?" (l. 7, 8).

Deferring reference to the Servant's atoning sufferings for the present, I may notice three passages which describe the Servant's operation and methods. The first is in chapter xlix., which shows that the Servant also operates in the direction of restoring Israel; it is not, however, in an external way, like Cyrus, but by awakening a new faith and a new spirit in the scattered exiles. For this is even more necessary than the external interposition in their behalf of Cyrus. Jehovah thus speaks to the Servant: "I will preserve thee, and make thee a covenant of the people, to raise up the land, and make them inherit the desolate heritages; to say to them that are bound, Go forth; to them that are in darkness, Show yourselves. They shall feed by the ways; they shall not hunger nor thirst, neither shall the sun smite them. I will make all my mountains a way. Lo, these shall come from far: and these from the north and from the west; and these from the land of Sinᵢn' (xlix. 8–12). Two things, surely, are made evident by such a passage: first, that the Servant is a contemporary of the Exile and that the land is desolate, seeing he helps to its repopulation; and, second, that the imperative condition of the people s restoration is their repentance and new faith, which the Servant produces in their minds: "I will make thee a covenant of the people, in order to raise up the land; to make them inherit the desolate heritages."

The second passage, showing the general method of the Servant's operation, is the one previously quoted in chap. l.: " The Lord Jehovah hath given me the tongue of disciples, that I may know how to comfort with words him that is weary: He wakeneth mine ear morning by morning to hear as the disciples. He opened mine ear, and I was not rebellious. I gave my back to the smiters: I hid not my face from shame and spitting. For I knew that I shall not be ashamed. . . . He is near that justifieth me" (l. 4–8). Here the Servant sets forth these three things: (a) his consciousness of having the true word of the Lord, and his acceptance of the mission entrusted to him as having it; (b) the inevitable sufferings in the work of the Lord,—he who is Servant of the Lord will suffer; and (c) his invincible faith, founded on Jehovah's help; and the assurance that through Jehovah he shall yet succeed. To this passage should perhaps be added the beautiful one in chap. lxi. 1 : " The Spirit of the Lord is upon me. He hath anointed me to preach glad tidings to the meek,' etc.

The third passage I shall cite is in chapter xlii. 1 ff., describing the Servant's bearing and method with the Gentiles: " Behold My Servant. I will put My spirit upon him: he shall bring forth judgment to the Gentiles. He shall not strive, nor cry. The bruised reed he shall not break: he will bring forth judgment to the Gentiles; and the isles shall wait on his instruction." The only instrument which the Servant employs is the word of the Lord. This word is powerful, because it is not a mere dead letter; the Lord Himself is in it: " For as the rain cometh down, and the snow from heaven, and returneth not thither, but causeth the earth to bring forth seed to the sower, and bread to the eater ; so shall My word be: it shall not return to me void, but shall accomplish that which I please. For ye shall go out with joy, and be led forth with peace" (lv. 10, 11; comp. li. 16). The Servant does not so much wield the word of God, he is rather an impersonation of it: "He made my mouth a sharp sword . . . He made me a polished shaft, and said unto me, Thou art My Servant" (xlix. 2). The Servant is the word of the Lord incarnate in the seed of Abraham.

But thus the prophet's construction is complete. Jehovah, God of Israel, is God alone. Being so, the nations are related to Him no less than Israel. As the one true God, He must reveal Himself to all men, and destroy their confidence in that which is no God, no Saviour: "My glory will I not give to another" (xlii. 8). To Him every knee shall bow. Yet though God over all, He stands in a special relation to Israel. This relation is now about to be manifested through His Servant. He will turn the hearts of His people to Himself, and, gathering them from all lands, will appear in His glory among them. And through them, thus restored, His relation to all mankind will also be manifested: His Servant will bring forth right to the Gentiles, the nations will walk in Zion's light, and kings come to the brightness of her rising.

Much more might be said of this prophet's conception of the people Israel or Jacob.

5. *Redemptive Righteousness in Deutero-Isaiah.*

But, passing that by, it will be enough to refer to his peculiar use of the word *righteousness* as a redemptive term. There are three terms: (1) the verb צָדֵק; (2) the adjective צַדִּיק; and (3) the two nouns צֶדֶק and צְדָקָה. The word 'righteous' is used in two ways: first, in a juridical or forensic sense; and, second, in an ethical sense. The verb is almost exclusively used in the forensic sense, to *be in the right*, with the idea of a court or judge in the background; or to be *found in the right*,—as our Version goes, to be *justified*. Naturally, to be *found* in the right is very near to be *pronounced* in the right. Hence Hiph. to *find* in the right, *pronounce* in the right, or *justify*. Of course, there may be a multitude of situations, some important and others less so, in which one may be found in the right or justified; but the word has the same sense everywhere, and generally it is used in the sense of being right before God. The adjective is chiefly used in the ethical sense. It is the two nouns, however, which are used somewhat peculiarly in these prophecies.

The word 'righteousness' is used both of Jehovah and of the people.

First, in relation to Jehovah. The word is used in reference to all His redemptive operations. These are done 'in righteousness,' בצדק; they are צדקה, 'righteousness.' For instance, "Who raised up him from the east, whom 'צ calleth to follow it?" (xli. 2). "I have called him (Cyrus) in righteousness: he shall rebuild My city, and let go My captives" (xlv. 13). And of the people: "But thou Israel, My servant, fear not . . . I keep hold of thee with the right hand of My righteousness . . . all they that are incensed against thee shall be confounded" (xli. 10, 11). And again of the Servant: "I called thee in righteousness, and took hold of thy hand, and will keep thee, and make thee a light of the Gentiles" (xlii. 6). And frequently Jehovah's righteousness is put in parallelism with His salvation: "My righteousness is near; My salvation is gone forth" (li. 5). "My righteousness shall be for ever, and My salvation to all generations" (li. 8). And, again, the people are represented as asking of Jehovah 'ordinances of righteousness,' i.e. deeds of salvation on their behalf (lviii. 2); and Jehovah's *righteousness* sustains him, and His arm brings salvation unto him (lix. 16).

Now, of course, we must not identify righteousness with salvation. Salvation is something objective; it is a condition in which the Lord puts the people, including restoration and, what precedes that, forgiveness of sins. When righteousness is put in parallelism with salvation, that word also has a certain objective sense, meaning deeds or operations which are illustrations or embodiments of Jehovah's righteousness, or a condition of the people brought about by Jenovah operating in righteousness. In othei words, salvation is, so to speak, the clothing, the manifestation of Jehovah's righteousness. So we have it in the remarkable passage, xlv. 21, "a righteous God, and a Saviour," where the two expressions are identical in sense; or the point may be that His being Saviour is the necessary consequence of His being righteous. Thus salvation is a result, a manifestation of His righteousness. How then is this ?

Now, we might find the explanation of this way of regarding salvation as righteousness manifested in the relation of Jehovah to Israel. He is Israel's God, His covenant is with Israel. They are His people; it is therefore *right* that He should interpose in their behalf. He is righteous in saving them; and of course He is also righteous in inflicting vengeance on their oppressors. No doubt this conception will cover a number of the passages. And a similar idea is, that Israel's salvation is due to Jehovah's *faithfulness, i.e.* not merely to His word or promise, but to His whole relation to Israel as their God.

There are passages, however, which this idea of righteousness merely in regard to His covenant with Israel will hardly explain. They are these: xlii. 6, where He says to the Servant, "I called thee in righteousness, and took hold of thy hand"; and xlii. 21, "the Lord was pleased for His righteousness' sake to give a law great and broad." Both these passages refer to the very beginning of Jehovah's relation with Israel, and imply that even the initiation of the covenant illustrated His righteousness. And, once more, li. 5, "My righteousness is near; My salvation is gone forth, and Mine arm shall rule the people; the isles shall wait on Me, and on Mine arm shall they trust." Here, not the salvation of Israel only, but that of all mankind, illustrates or embodies the righteousness of Jehovah. And this wider expression makes it questionable whether we were right in explaining even those passages which spoke of Israel's salvation as righteousness, merely of what was *right* or righteous in Jehovah in view of His relation to His people.

Various attempts have been made to explain this usage. In an excellent paper on the root צדק, Kautzsch [1] defines 'righteousness' to be conformity to a norm; and in his exceedingly good treatise on the theology of these chapters, Krüger [2] defines the norm in this case to be Jehovah's will, which is a redemptive will, upon the whole. Hence He is righteous when He acts along the line of this redemptive will, or in conformity to it; or, in other words, according to His redemptive purpose.

But does it not seem that these definitions are rather abstract? And when it is said that righteousness is conformity to a norm, is not that either false, or to say nothing more than that righteousness is righteousness? A man would not be righteous who habitually lied, though he would speak according to the norm of falsehood. Is there not in the norm itself the idea of *righteousness*? Does not the existence of a norm imply a prior judgment as to what is right, and the norm is the expression of this judgment? Conformity to a norm is not righteousness unless the norm be right, or embody righteousness. Correspondence is only the evidence of righteousness, not righteousness itself. A particular act or general conduct is righteous, because it is an instance of that general of which the norm is an embodiment. Therefore, to say that Jehovah's redemptive acts are righteous because they are in correspondence with His general will, which is a redemptive will, is hardly true; they are righteous only because that redemptive will to which they correspond is righteous. And thus we come back to the question, why are 'a righteous God' and 'a Saviour' identical expressions? [3]

---

[1] *Die Derivate des Stammes* צדק *im Altt. Sprachgebrauch.*

[2] *Essai sur la Théologie d'Ésaïe 40–66*, par F. Hermann Krüger. Paris: Fischbacher.

[3] From what appears elsewhere, we gather that Dr. Davidson's answer to this question was that, while in other books the term 'righteous' and its cognates convey legal ideas, in Second Isaiah at least they express the constancy of God's purpose regarding Israel, His trustworthiness in all His dealings with His people, even in His chastisements.—ED.

6. General Considerations on the Eschatology of the Old Testament.

On this whole subject of the Eschatology of the Old Testament the following remarks may also be made with regard to its rise, its development, and its contents:

(1) It is, of course, now a commonplace to say that Amos taught that Jehovah is absolute righteousness, the impersonation of the moral idea; that moral evil alone is sin; and that the only service Jehovah desires is a righteous life—although Amos also teaches that Jehovah is good and compassionate (ii. 9, vii. 1); that Hosea represents Jehovah as unchanging love, which no ingratitude of His people can weary or alienate; and that to Isaiah, Jehovah is the transcendent Sovereign and universal Lord,—whose glory fills the whole earth,—the קדוש of Israel. Both Hosea and Isaiah insist much on the inwardness of religion. It is a state of the mind, a prevailing consciousness of Jehovah. The want of this consciousness, insensibility to the Lord the King, is sin; and it is the source of all sin, of the levity of human life, and the self-exaltation both of men and nations. Further, the prophetic *ideas* form but half of the teaching of the prophets; the greater half lies in their own life and personal relation to God.

(2) Taken as a whole, the prophetic teaching amounts to the full ethicising of the conception of Jehovah. And the *moral* is of no nationality; it transcends nationality, and is human. The righteous God is God universal, over all. The principles of the human economy have at last clearly reflected themselves in the consciousness of the prophets, and human history is seen to be a moral process. It has, at all events, a moral aim, and will have a moral result. The universalism of the prophetic idea of God, and its influence on the prophetic notion of history, is most clearly seen in Isaiah. The movement of the prophetic thought towards the universalistic idea of God may have been aided by the entrance of the universal empires of Assyria and Babylon on the stage of history. This gave them a

new conception—that of the world; and it created a new correlation—Jehovah and the world.

(3) What is called Eschatology,—the doctrine of τὰ ἔσχατα,—the last things, the final condition of the world, could not have arisen earlier than this. The idea of a final condition of the world could not arise apart from a general conception of the meaning of human life and history; and what suggested the meaning of human history to the prophets was their conception of the moral being and the universal rule of Jehovah. An eschatology; a condition of final result; a condition of mankind and the world at the end of Jehovah's operations, arose very naturally.

(4) The Old Testament, however, is what might be called Theocentric. Jehovah operates; He accomplishes all; and He finds the motives of His operations in Himself. Hence the final condition of the world is not in the Old Testament the issue of a long ethical development in human society, ending in a perfect moral world or kingdom of righteousness upon the earth. The final condition is rather due to an interposition, or a series of interpositions, of Jehovah. These interpositions, of course, are all on moral lines; in the interests of righteousness they are to make an end of sin and bring in everlasting righteousness, and the issue is a kingdom of righteousness. But the issue is due to a sudden act, or a sudden appearance, of God, and is not the fruit of a growth in the hearts of mankind.

(5) It is not enough, however, simply to say that an eschatology, the conception of a final condition of mankind, could hardly have arisen before a general conception of the nature of the human economy, or at least of those things that are needful to man's perfection and felicity, had become general. There is the question, *had* such a conception come to the prophets? Now the answer to that question is, that the meaning of human history, or the understanding of its tendency, of its movement towards an eschatological goal, was not revealed to Israel by study the life of mankind, but by reflection on the nature

of God as revealed. God was the real Maker of history. To the prophets there are no such things as mere events or occurrences; all events are animated, so to speak, with a Divine energy. God is the author of the events, and His mind, His will, or His purpose is in them. Hence, when so broad a view as that of human life or history as a whole is taken, it is, so to speak, secondary. It is the reflection of the view taken of God, of His being, and therefore as an inference from His being, of His purpose, and of what the issue will be when He realises His purpose, or, as we might say, when He realises Himself in the history of mankind. So soon as the ethical being of Jehovah was conceived, and His oneness as God, there could not but immediately follow the idea also that human history, which was not so much under His providence as His direct operation, would eventuate in a kingdom of righteousness which would embrace all mankind.

No doubt the way in which this is conceived is that this kingdom of righteousness is first realised in Israel, and that through Israel it extends to all mankind; for the nations " come to Israel's light, and kings to the brightness of its rising," this light being the glory of Jehovah dwelling in Israel. But the unity of God creates the unity of mankind.

(6) So we have an eschatology of two kinds : that of the *kingdom*, and that of the *individual*. The former is what is taught concerning the perfection of the nation or people of Israel, or on a universal scale of the nations or mankind; and the latter, so far as the individual is considered in himself as distinct from the people, would constitute the doctrine of immortality. But one of the things that surprise us more and more in the Old Testament is the place given to the individual. How little the individual bulks in it, how greatly the individual loses himself in the community,—thinks of himself always as part of it, has hopes for himself only so far as he has hopes for his people. Pure or true individualism, *i.e.* the individual's consciousness of himself in relation to God, and

26

as having a destiny of his own to work out or to inherit out of all relation to the destiny of the community, and independent of all other men—this kind of individuality appears in the Old Testament only in a few great instances.

XII. DOCTRINE OF THE LAST THINGS— IMMORTALITY.

1. *Differences in Modes of Thought.*

In much of the teaching of the Old Testament, as we have seen, it is the destinies of the People of God as a people that are specially in view. But there is the question also of the *Individual,* and what the Old Testament has to say of him. This comes into view in connection with the Old Testament conceptions of *sin, death, life,* and *immortality.* Very much of what is taken up into the Christian doctrine of *Immortality* appears in the Old Testament in connection with what is said of the *People* or the *Kingdom* of God, especially in the prophetic teaching. But there is much more than that in the New Testament doctrine; and in the Old Testament itself there is an Eschatology of the Individual as well as an Eschatology of the Kingdom or People.

In entering now on the teaching of the Old Testament on the subject of a *Future Life,* we have to notice certain matters of general interest, and certain broad considerations which have an important bearing on the view we take of the Old Testament position. These must be borne in mind if we are to understand aright the Old Testament conception of a future life.

We may notice, in the first place, the point which has just been referred to, namely, the relation of the Eschatology of the Individual to that of the Kingdom or the People. A large portion of the contribution which the Old Testament makes to Christian Eschatology is derived from the Eschatology of the Nation. To this belong such points as these: (1) the manifestation or advent of God; (2) the universal judgment connected with the Day of the Lord; (3) behind this judgment, the incoming of the perfect kingdom of God, when all Israel shall be saved, and the nations shall be partakers of their salvation; (4) the *finality* and *eternity* of this condition, that which constitutes the blessedness of the saved people being the presence of God in the midst of them; (5) the form which this view of the presence of God Himself (which corresponds to the Christian view of heaven) takes in such Messianic prophecies as Isa. ix. 11, etc., where Jehovah is represented as present in His fulness in the Messianic King.

Now, most that is said in these connections is said of the people as a people. The people is immortal, and its life eternal; and this life is conceived as lived in this world, although this world is also said to be destined to be transfigured, so that there shall be a new heaven and a new earth (Isa. lxv. 17). But the question must arise, Are the individuals of the people immortal, or is there only an immortality of the people as a people ? Is the life of the individuals, however prolonged and blessed, yet finally closed by death ? In most passages the prophets have in view the destiny of the people as a unity, the ultimate fate of individuals not being present to their mind. In some passages, however, the destiny of the individual is referred to, and perhaps a progress may be observed.

It is important to observe, therefore, how the Old Testament ways of thinking on man's future differ in certain respects from ours. The chief difference, perhaps, lies in this, that when the Old Testament speaks of immortality, eternal felicity, or what is equivalent to heaven, it usually speaks of the immortality and eternal felicity of the nation. This immortality and felicity shall be entered upon at the manifestation of Jehovah at the day of the Lord and His judgment. We, on the other hand, think of the individual and immortality, and apply the latter term to the individual's destiny after death. But in the Old Testament the immortality of the people does not raise the question of *death*. There is a change,—a being made perfect, an entrance upon a new age,—but only a change.

The Old Testament position appears precisely like that which, if New Testament scholars be right, was the early Christian position—when the hope of the Second Coming continued vivid. This Coming would change the world and the Church, but the Church would pass living into perfect blessedness. And of course individuals would share in the change—"We shall not all sleep, but we shall all be changed" (1 Cor. xv. 51). Now, this was very like the state of feeling in the Old Testament. The individual would share in the transition of the community. The day of the Lord would break, and the living would enter into fulness of life without tasting death.

Thus the greater part of what is said of immortality in the Old Testament being said of the people, death is not a thing referred to in such connections.

But even when the individual is spoken of, or is the speaker, his hopes may be connected with the destinies of the people. He may share in these,—entering into enduring blessedness, without seeing death,—he being part of the people. In passages, also, in which this is implied, death is not contemplated. There is an immortality, a continuance of being, which does not pass through death or arise behind it. Now that the Second Coming has ceased to be a vivid part of Christian faith, and death is looked on as the inevitable fate of us all, the state of the question becomes somewhat changed, and immortality is looked at exclusively as something involving death.

The passages, however, in the Old Testament where death is contemplated are not numerous, because the hope of the nation was so vivid, and this hope was shared in by the living individuals.

True individualistic hope, therefore, is expressed only in those passages of the Old Testament where death is contemplated,—where it seems near or certain. Then the individual person is cut off from sharing in the hope and destiny of the nation, and he is thrown upon his own individual relation to God to sustain him.

Again, it has always been felt to be strange that the teaching in the Old Testament regarding immortality should be so obscure, or at least so indirect and inexplicit. This seems not only strange in itself when the case of some other nations, such as the Egyptians, is considered, in whose minds questions of death and immortality occupied so prominent and engrossing a place; it becomes doubly strange when we take into account the very clear and elevated teaching given in the Old Testament regarding other truths of religion, and the true conditions of living unto God. The faith in a future life is so important a part of our religion, that we are surprised to find it appearing with so little explicitness in the religious thoughts of the Old Testament saints. This has, indeed, appeared to some writers—Warburton, for example [1]—so surprising, that they have concluded that the revelation of the doctrine was of purpose kept back, with the view of serving some other ends. This idea, however, belonged to the time when views of the nature and methods of revelation prevailed which were rather artificial. In the present day we are more inclined to conclude that the methods pursued by revelation were simple, and, if we can say so, natural; that is, that its great object was to enable men in each age practically to live unto God, and that at all times it gave them light sufficient for this; but that on other subjects it left them very much with the ideas which they had.

In other words, it took men as it found them, setting before them at all times, and in each successive age, what was needful that they might walk before God in holiness and righteousness, and, as it taught them this, penetrating and transforming other modes of thinking on many non essential matters which they cherished. If, therefore, we find explicit teaching on this question of immortality postponed, we may infer that it was not unnatural that it

[1] In his *Divine Legation of Moses.*

should be so; that there was something in the ways of thinking on the part of the people which, for a time at least, supplied the place of it, or at all events made it not a necessity to a true life with God and a walk before Him in righteousness. And we may perhaps also infer that at a later time events occurred in God's providential ruling of the history of the people, which modified their former modes of thinking to such an extent that more explicit statements on this question were requisite, and so when requisite they were supplied.

Again, our life now is very strongly individual, and so is our religion. Some make it a charge against Christianity at least as practised and lived, that it is too individualistic, that it is so even to selfishness. However this be, it cannot be doubted that a different way of feeling prevailed in Israel. The individual was always apt to lose himself in some collective, such as the family, the tribe, or the people. He was part of a greater whole, and felt himself to have meaning only as belonging to it. This is perhaps an Oriental way of thinking; and if so, revelation in some respects accommodated itself to it. It did not wage war against it, but left the positive truth which it gave to act upon it, and gradually disintegrate and dissolve it. The covenant was made not with individuals, but with the people. The prophets address their oracles to the State, to the leaders and rulers in the kingdom of God. It is the destinies of this kingdom that they pursue out to the perfection of it. The individual has his part in the blessings of the kingdom, but he has it as a member of the people.

This conception of solidarity and the repression of individualism are considerations always to be kept in view in judging the Old Testament. They explain many things, and give a different colour to some things which are apt to offend us. The sweeping away, for example, of the whole family and dependents of a man along with himself because of his sin or offence, was a practice due to this idea of solidarity. The children and dependents were not regarded as having an independent existence or a standing

of their own. They were part of the father, of the head of
the family, and he was not held fully punished unless all
that were his shared his fate. Such a practice would
appear now to us an immorality, because of our strong
sense of the independence of each individual; but from the
point of view of solidarity then prevalent it had not this
aspect. And in the same way the tendency of the
individual in early times to sink himself in the collective
unity, the tribe or the people, helps to explain what seems
to us the defective aspiration of the individual after
immortality or life. What Jehovah had founded on the
earth was a kingdom of God. This was eternal. In the
days of the King Messiah this kingdom would be universal,
and the people would be perfect. And the individual had
his immortality in that of the theocracy. His great interest
was in it. His hopes found realisation there. His labours
were perpetuated in it, even if he ceased to live. He saw
the good of Israel, and he continued to live in the fuller
life of his people. But this immortality of his hopes and
purposes was not all. In his children he continued to
live. He was there in them; for he regarded them as
himself, furthering God's work and enjoying His favour.
So, too, his remembrance was not cut off—" the righteous
shall be held in everlasting remembrance" (Ps. cxii. 6),
This kind of feeling is illustrated in Isa. lvi., 3, where the
prophet, encouraging strangers and eunuchs to attach themselves to the new community of the Restoration, addresses
the latter: " Let not the eunuch say, Behold, I am a dry
tree." The feeling of these persons was that, having no
children, they would have no permanent place in the community, no endless share in the kingdom of God. To them
the Lord replies: " I will give them in Mine house and
within My walls a place, and memorial, an everlasting
name that shall not be cut off" (lvi. 5). The passage is
a pathetic one; for all that the prophet is as yet able
to promise the individual, however high the worth of the
individual is now considered to be, is an immortality in the
memory of God and of men. A true personal immortality

is not yet promised; not he, but his memory, shall be immortal.

Yet it must be acknowledged that here lay an imperfection which could not but be felt. This kind of immortality in the perpetual existence of the kingdom of God, and in the perfection of the people in which the spirit of the individual lived, must have been felt by the man to be too shadowy to satisfy his heart. The individual spirit struggles against the idea of being poured out into the general stream of the spirit of mankind or even of the people of God, and claims a place for itself. And this claim will be the more resolutely pressed the more the individual becomes aware of his own worth and of the meaning of the personal life. Now, in the providential history of Israel, the time came when the State or people in which the individual was apt to lose himself came to an end. At the Exile the people ceased to exist, being scattered into every land. But though the people and State had disappeared, Jehovah their God remained, and religion remained, and there remained the individuals of the nation; and thus all that significance and those responsibilities and hopes, which belonged to the people before, were now felt by the individual to belong to him. We might think the downfall of the kingdom of Judah a great calamity, yet in a religious sense it was the greatest step towards Christianity taken since the Exodus. It made religion independent of any locality; it showed that the people of God could exist though no longer in the form of a State or nation. It changed the religious centre, so to speak, making it no more the conscience of the people, but the conscience of the individual. Hence in a prophet of the Exile we find such words as these: "All souls are Mine, saith the Lord; as the soul of the father, so also the soul of the son is Mine" (Ezek. xviii. 4). To each individual spirit the Lord stands in the same relation. Naturally, when this stage has been reached the craving for individual immortality would immediately arise. And speedily the idea would be extended; even the dead of past generations would be drawn in under the general conception. They, too, would be made to share in the blessings of the perfect kingdom, and thus faith in the resurrection also would arise, as in Dan. xii.

There is another way of thinking, common now, which makes us wonder how the doctrine of a future state could for long be so obscurely stated in the Old Testament. We wonder how morality and religion could exist without the support of those eternal sanctions supplied to the mind in the faith of a future retribution. Now the difference between our way of thinking and that prevalent for long at least in Israel, does not lie in any difference as to belief in retribution. It lies here. We may relegate this retribution to a future world; Israel believed that it prevailed fully now and was seen in this world. The universal faith of the people is compressed in Prov. xi. 31 : " Behold, the righteous shall be recompensed on the earth ; much more the ungodly and the sinner." Or as it is in the 1st Psalm. To our minds now the anomalies of providence bulk much more largely than they did to early Israel at least. We may detect general principles in providence, we may see the direction the movement pursues ; it may in a general way plainly make for righteousness, but there are many hindrances, and the current is often hemmed, and to appearance even turned aside. But in the early literature of Israel such a feeling hardly appears. Even in the Book of Proverbs, a book occupied almost exclusively with the doctrine of providence, with God's rule of man's life, there seems to be hardly one complaint regarding any anomaly of providence, any hardship or infelicity to the righteous or any prosperity or felicity to the wicked. In later books, such as Ecclesiastes and Job and some Psalms, complaints are abundant. But in the earlier literature the faith in an inflexible retribution in this life prevails. This, indeed, may be said to be just the essence of the prophetic teaching— balanced or tempered, of course, by God's enduring mercy and His purpose of grace, which nothing could frustrate, and towards which even His righteousness in retribution worked.

It may be made a question how this very stringent doctrine of retribution in this life arose. It is probably due, as
almost all other doctrines are, to the very powerful theism
of Scripture and of the people. God was all in all. Events
were all His work, and all immediately His work. All the
changes on the earth and in life were but the effects of an
unseen power operating within all things. And this God
was righteous, and His rule, therefore, in each particular
event a display of His righteousness. As there was one
God, there was one world. His rule prevailed alike everywhere. The universe was a moral constitution. The
physical had no meaning in itself; it was but the medium
for the manifestation of the moral. Thus that sphere
where retribution finds full realisation, and which we have
learned to transfer to some transcendental state, early
Israel found to exist in this present world. Sin was
punished and righteousness rewarded. There was no
anomaly here. The anomaly was the existence of evil, and
that it was permitted to continue, and not finally purged
away. Yet this condition was but temporary, and would
terminate soon; it might terminate at any moment. The
day of the Lord might break on the generation then living.
The glory of the Lord would be revealed, and all flesh
would see it together. He would come, His arm ruling
for Him, His reward with Him, and His recompense
before Him. He would perform His short work on the
earth.

Of course, here again, in this idea of a retributive rule
of God on earth, there was an imperfection, and the feeling
of it led to further developments. In the early and happy
condition of the kingdom and society the well-being of the
righteous might seem realised, and under good government
the wicked might be cut off. The law of retribution had
effect. Yet later, when the State began to stagger under
the blows dealt it from abroad, and when morals within
became dissolute, the faith in a perfect retributive rule of
providence in this world would receive rude shocks. The
fall of the State, indeed, was its most perfect illustration

when the State was considered as a moral person,—as the prophets from Hosea downward consider it. But in the disastrous time that followed it was just the righteous individuals that suffered the most grievous hardships, and that often just because of their righteousness—"For Thy sake are we killed all day long" (Ps. xliv. 22). And then this ideal of a perfect retributive providence in this world began to break up. Men felt it giving way under their feet. And profoundly interesting is it to observe the perplexities, we might say the agitation and alarm, which the discovery occasioned. The unrighteousness prevailing on the earth was immediately transferred to God as the author of it; for He was the author of all events. The very sun of righteousness in the heavens seemed to suffer eclipse. The reason of pious minds almost tottered under the suggestion that God Himself was unrighteous, as the author of Job makes him say: "It is God that makes my heart soft, and the Almighty that troubleth me" (Job xxiii. 16); "The earth is given into the hands of the wicked: He covereth the face of the judges thereof; if not He, who then is it?" (Job ix. 24). By and by a higher teaching calmed these feelings by suggesting considerations, such as that these afflictions of the righteous might serve beneficent ends, even in regard to the righteous themselves. And further, it calmed them by opening a glimpse, if no more, of the truth, that though pious minds might end their life on earth amidst darkness, a light might still arise after death. This appears the position assumed in Job xix. 25: "I know that my Redeemer liveth . . . and after this my body is destroyed, I shall see God: whom I shall see for myself, and mine eyes shall behold, and not another." Apparently also in Pss. xlix., lxxiii., and possibly xxxvii. But of these we shall speak again.

There is yet another point of view from which, to us now, the want of clearness in the Old Testament doctrine of a future life appears somewhat strange. We are surprised that the Old Testament saint seemed satisfied with the conditions, necessarily imperfect, of a religious life with

God upon the earth; that he did not feel the need of a closer fellowship with God than is possible amidst the imperfections of earth; and that dissatisfaction with earth did not lead him to demand, and to believe in, a more perfect condition of existence and a nearer vision of God Now, in this there may be some imperfection in the manner of thought and feeling of the Old Testament saints. Here at least we touch upon a point in which we have been taught to diverge from them, and which in some respects is just the point of difference between the Old Testament and the New. In order to judge these Hebrew saints fairly, however, we must look closely at their way of thinking; and if we do so, perhaps we shall be prepared to admit that we may have diverged from them, not indeed in fundamental faith, but practically further than was necessary. We have come to feel strongly the imperfections of the most perfect life upon the earth, and to believe that only in a world that is another can full fellowship with God be found. However true this be, it is possible that the very axiomatic nature of the truth leads occasionally to the undue depreciation of this life, and to an unnecessary disparaging of the possibilities it offers in the way of living unto God. So far as the Old Testament saints were concerned, if we examine the utterances very numerously scattered over the Scriptures, we do find evidence of a very vivid consciousness of the presence of God with them, and of the possession of His fellowship: "Whom have I in heaven? and on earth there is none I desire beside Thee" (Ps. lxxiii. 25). "When I awake I am still with Thee" (Ps. cxxxix. 18). "I have set the Lord before me; He is at my right hand" (Ps. xvi. 8). "Nevertheless I am continually with Thee" (Ps. lxxiii. 23). This consciousness of God's nearness and fellowship seems to exceed that which men ordinarily have now. We might speculate to what it was due.

In some respects it might be due to the extremely emotional and the highly intuitive nature of the people's mind, which realised God more powerfully than our minds do. There was, no doubt, something supernatural in the visions of God which such prophets as Isaiah and Ezekiel saw, but there must also have been a peculiar mental characteristic which lent itself readily to such revelations. Perhaps another thing which helped the people to realise the presence of God so vividly with them was just this, that He did in fact dwell in a house among them where He had placed His name. When the worshipper came to this house, he felt he was near unto God; there he appeared before Him. We are familiar with the vividness with which God's presence was realised, and with the longing of saints to be near the place of His abode: "One thing have I desired . . . that I may dwell in the house of the Lord all the days of my life, to behold the beauty of the Lord" (Ps. xxvii. 4). But to whatever this vivid realising of God's presence was due, it certainly existed in the minds of His people, and the religious meaning of it is not affected. That which constitutes the essence of the future world to men now, the presence of God, the Israelite profoundly enjoyed on earth.

But no doubt a significant point of difference between the modes of thought among Old Testament saints and those now current emerges here. The difference lies in the different views of what constitutes life. To the Israelite, 'life' meant what we ordinarily call 'life in the body.' Life was the existence of man in all his parts. When Adam was created, God formed him of the dust, and breathed into his nostrils the breath of life; and he became a living person (Gen. ii. 7). He lived; and in the fellowship of God his life was perfect. And so the pious Israelite always continued to think. To him, separation of the spirit from the body was what he called death. He was far removed from the philosophical view that the body was a prison-house, released from which the spirit could spread its wings and soar into purer and loftier regions. Neither yet had he attained to the Christian view, that there is a perfection of the spirit even apart from the body His view of life was the synthetic one; it was the existence of man in all his parts, living in the light of God's face. He stood before that analysis, so to speak, which experience teaches us takes place in death; and his view corresponded to that new synthesis which the New Testament teaches, when the dissolved elements of human nature shall be reunited in the resurrection life. And his nomenclature corresponded with that of the Apostle Paul; he called the existence of man in the *body* 'life,' as the apostle names existence in the *resurrection body* 'life.'

But of course, *life* being understood in this sense, a physical sphere was necessary for it. Hence, as the earth was the abode of man, it was to be his abode for ever. A transcendental sphere of existence, such as we conceive heaven, could not occur to the Israelite. He was far from being insensible to the imperfections that accompanied life. Though he enjoyed God's presence, it was not yet God's presence in its fulness. In a sense, therefore, the Israelite believed in a future life, and longed for it. But it was not a life in a transcendental sphere; it was a future life upon the earth. In the perfection of the people of God they would not be translated to be with God in heaven, but God would come down and reveal Himself in His fulness among men; the tabernacle of God would be with men, and He would be their God, and they His people. Then God would make a new covenant with men, forgiving their sin, and writing His law upon their hearts. And the kingdom would be the Lord's. And simultaneously with this manifestation of Jehovah among men, the earth would be transfigured, and all hindrances to a perfect life with God removed: "Behold I create a new heavens and a new earth, and the former shall not be remembered" (Isa. lxv. 17), This manifestation of Jehovah in His fulness was felt as if it were imminent; the salvation was ready to be revealed. And here, perhaps, just as much as anywhere, lies the explanation of the want of the kind of faith which we now have. The eternal abode of man was the earth; perfection lay in the perfect presence of Jehovah; but His perfect presence was always near in hope,—living men might behold it.

2. *Fellowship with God the Fundamental Idea.*

These considerations may tend somewhat to remove our surprise at the absence of explicit teaching about immortality in the Old Testament. The pious Israelite had in truth, or felt he had in essence, all those things that constitute heaven. No doubt he had them in idea rather than in the fulness of reality. He had that sense of perfect retribution which to us seems to belong to the future, although the time came when painful doubts arose, and suggested that something was wanting. He had that presence of God which is that which gives its meaning to heaven. It was this that made up the joy of life to him—"Thou art the portion of my cup . . . the lines have fallen to me in pleasant places" (Ps. xvi. 5–7). So that the acute remark made by the authors of the work called the *Unseen Universe* is true, who say: "Not from want of religion, but from excess of religion, was this void [specific thoughts about future immortality] left in the Jewish mind. The future life was overlooked, overshadowed by the consciousness of the presence of God Himself" (p. 9). Yet this presence of God was not in such fulness as to satisfy, and in this sense the pious Israelite looked for a future life, when God would be present in His glory. But this perfection was one the scene of which still remained the earth; there was no translation of man into a transcendental sphere of spiritual existence.

It is to this point of the enjoyment of God's fellowship and life in His favour upon the earth that the chief developments of the Old Testament doctrine of immortality attach themselves. The event of death interrupted this fellowship, and turned the joy of life with God into darkness. For, to the Israelite, death was truly death; and the dead were cut off from fellowship with the living, whether man or God. It may seem surprising that the references to death are so few in the Old Testament. Yet, if we count them up, the passages are pretty numerous. Naturally, these passages are generally of the nature of reminiscences

of feelings that were present when the prospect of death
was near.   Hence they are all personal, and not of the
nature of abstract teaching; though they often rise to the
expression of principles, particularly the principle that
fellowship with God constitutes an indissoluble bond, which
death cannot sever.   The kind of immortality demanded,
or inferred or prayed for, is always a religious immortality, the continuance of that life with God already
lived on earth.   The mere existence of the spirit after
death is never the point, for this was never doubted; it is
the existence in the fellowship of God and in the light of
His face that is supplicated for or assumed.   Hence every
contribution made to the question is of a practical religious
kind.   It is a demand of the religious mind, what seems to it
of the nature of a necessity; or it is a flight of ecstasy of
the religious experience; or it is what seems involved in the
very relations of God and the mind of man.

To the Old Testament saints, immortality seemed the
corollary of religion, for immortality was the continuance of
fellowship with God.   If religion was true, *i.e.* if God was,
then that experience which religion was would continue,
and men would live.   The teaching of the Old Testament
is summed up by our Lord: " God is not the God of the
dead, but of the living " (Matt. xxii. 32).   The prophets
and saints of the Old Testament kingdom of God were not
speculative men.   They did not reason that the soul was
immortal from its nature; this was not the kind of immortality in which they were interested, though for all that
appears the idea that the immaterial part of man should
become extinct or be annihilated, never occurred to them.
They did not lay stress, in an objective, reflective way, on
man's instinctive hopes of immortality, though perhaps they
may be observed giving these instinctive desires expression.
They could not, with the patient eye of inductive observation, gather up what we call analogies to the passage of
beings from a lower to a higher life, such as we conceive
our own death to be, as the entrance of a fuller life.   They
did not reason : they felt, and they knew.   They set the

Lord before them; and because He was at their right hand they were not moved, and every element of their being rejoiced. They had life with God, and they felt that immortality was involved in their communion with Him. He was their God; and He was not the God of the dead, but of the living. This communion was the object of their hopes and the ground of their faith. Their faith in immortality was but a form of their faith in God. It was entirely subjective and religious,—the corollary not of reason, but of experience drawn from their actual life with God. And even if it had remained but a record of subjective conditions, of postulates of faith, of demands not of reason, but of religious life, without any objective verification, it would have been a distinct contribution to the belief of men in immortality, a contribution in a region and from a side altogether different from those in which other nations made their contributions—the contribution not of man's reflection, but of his religious nature.

But the Old Testament age did not pass away without these subjective aspirations receiving an external seal. In Christ these subjective hopes and demands of faith and man's heart became real outward facts. In His life they passed into history.

3. *Preliminary Questions as to Man's Nature.*

Any question concerning death and immortality and resurrection must be preceded by other questions relating to the nature of man. For if death be in some sense a dissolution, and that which is simple is incapable of separation, the nature of man must be compound; and its elements will demand consideration, the dissolution of which is death, the continued separation of which is the state of the dead, and the reunion of which is resurrection. But there is no question more difficult in Biblical Theology than the question of the nature of man. Not only is there no certain answer given to it in the Old Testament, but the New Testament seems to leave it equally unsettled

27

That man possesses a soul and a body is clearly taught. That is the simplest and most general form in which the teaching appears. That death may be defined as the separation of these; that their localities during death remain distinct; and that in resurrection they are united,—these are all general statements, true indeed, but concealing within them a number of minor undetermined problems. With regard to the body, except in the matter of its resurrection, there is not much complication. But on the side of the soul there is such a variety of terminology employed, and such apparently irreconcilable predications are made concerning it, that certain results seem hardly to be expected from any investigation. The first and most prominent fact is that Scripture constantly uses two words for this side of human nature, *soul* and *spirit*, which it does not employ indiscriminately by any means. It seems to regard the latter as the primary, the union of which with body gives rise to *soul*. But whether this *soul* that so arises be itself something distinct from the *spirit* which, uniting with the body, gave rise to it, or whether it be not that *spirit* itself conceived in this state of union and in all the relations incidental to it, so that the naked essence unrelated would be called *spirit*, and the same essence in vital union with the body would be named *soul*, is a question to which answers very diverse have been returned. Moreover, as to this *spirit* itself, its relation to God's nature is very obscurely set forth in Scripture; for it seems sometimes called His. He gives it, and men live; He takes it away, and men die. It returns to God who gave it. He is " the God of the spirits of all flesh " (Num. xvi. 22, xxvii. 16). And sometimes it is called man's. Thus we are at a loss to say whether this spirit which God gives man, and which, coming from God, may be called God's (as the apostle also exhorts us to glorify Him in our bodies, which are God's, Gal. vi. 20), and which, given to man and belonging to him, may be called man's,—be really a permanent part of man at all, or merely God Himself abiding in every creature, sustaining life, and when He withdraws, causing that from which He withdraws to fall into death. There are thus two very obscure sides to the question concerning man's nature : one is the relation of man's *spirit* to man's *soul* ; and the other is the relation of man's *spirit* to God's *Spirit*. Are *soul* and *spirit* in man essentially or substantially, or only relationally distinct ? Are man's spirit and God's Spirit numerically distinct, or is the same spirit called man's because possessed by man, and God's because given by God? And being given by God, is it man's inalienable possession or only a temporary gift ? These are questions on which one cannot profess to be able to declare any very definite results. But they deserve consideration, partly because they are of great interest in themselves, and partly on account of their bearing on the larger question of immortality. For this latter strikes its roots very deep down into the Old Testament views of the primary and essential relations of man with God.

With regard to the essential or substantial distinction of soul and spirit in man, there are certain statements in the New Testament, to which we may return here,[1] as they might seem and have indeed been considered by many, undeniably to establish it. There is the passage in 1 Thess. v. 23: "And the very God of peace sanctify you wholly ; and I pray God your whole spirit and soul and body be preserved blameless unto the coming of our Lord Jesus Christ." Here, to use the words of Ellicott, the prayer " is threefold : *first*, that they may be sanctified by God, the God of peace ; for sanctification is the condition of outward and inward peace, wholly ὁλοτελεῖς in their collective powers and constituents ; *next*, that each constituent may be preserved to our Lord's coming ; and, *lastly*, that each so preserved may be entire and complete in itself, not mutilated or desintegrated by sin ;—that the body may retain its yet uneffaced image of God, and its unimpaired aptitude to be a living sacrifice to its maker ; the appetitive soul its purer hopes and nobler aspirations ; the spirit, its ever blessed associate, the Holy and Eternal Spirit of God " (*Destiny of the Creature*, p. 107).

[1] See pp. 184–187.—ED.

This New Testament passage certainly names three constituent elements of human nature, names them all co-ordinately, and speaks of each as needing sanctification, and capable of preservation. Are we to consider the distinction between soul and spirit as real, or only, so to speak, functional; as a distinction of organs or substances, or only of the different relations or conditions of a single element ?

In Heb. iv. 12, too, there occurs, as we have seen, a similar passage: " For the word of God is quick, and powerful, and sharper than any two-edged sword, piercing even to the dividing asunder of soul and spirit, and of the joints and marrow, and is a discerner of the thoughts and intents of the heart." The word of God has four qualities assigned to it: (1) it is living, ζῶν ; (2) it is active, ἐνεργής ; (3) sharp; (4) reaching even to the dividing, i.e. even as far as to divide, ἄχρι μερισμοῦ, of soul and spirit. The word μερισμός is rather the noun of action, dividing, than the place, division ; the words do not mean entering in so deep as to reach the place of division of soul and spirit, the limit of boundary between them, where the two meet, where the line of division runs between them ; but entering so deep as to divide the soul and spirit, as to effect a division of them. Yet it is left ambiguous whether the sharp Word of God, which enters so deeply that it divides, effects this division between the soul and spirit, and between the joints and marrow, or within the soul and spirit ; that is to say, whether it separates between the two, or cuts asunder each into its parts, lays it open, or, as we should say, dissects both soul and spirit, both joints and marrow.

So far as our question goes, a decision on this point is not important. The passage recognises two things : one called soul, which is not merely the animal life, and another called spirit. These are so substantial and independent, that either they may be separated by a distinction and a line of division drawn between them,—a sharp distinction, it is true, but one which the Word of God, sharper than

any two-edged sword, is qualified to effect,—or each of
them may be severally divided and cut open into its own
elements. As was said, the view which considers the
division not to be made between the two elements, soul and
spirit, but within each of them, seems the true one; for
one does not divide joints from marrow, but rather divides
joints themselves, and goes so deep as to cut open even
the marrow. But in any case the question is: Does
Scripture, while speaking of two such distinct and even
antagonistic things, mean really two things, or only two
aspects and relations, two sides of the one individual thing,
which, considered in itself, in its nature, is called *spirit*,
and as such is pure and Divine; and considered as related
to the flesh, is called *soul*, and in this relation may be
degraded and covered with the sensuous? I suspect there
is no passage which can be adduced at all so clear as those
two, and to some these have seemed decisive, but to others
quite the reverse.

These passages raise only one of the two questions over
which obscurity in this matter hangs. The other question,
namely, that of the relation of man's *spirit* and God's *Spirit*,
is raised as soon as we turn to the Old Testament. In the
account given of the creation of man (Gen. ii. 7), something
is said both about the origin and about the elements of his
nature: "God formed man of the dust of the earth, and
breathed into his nostrils the breath of life; and he became
a living soul." There are three things or stages in the
process. *First*, God formed man of עָפָר, dust, the most
immaterial of the material elements of earth. If you
contrast man's formation with that of the beasts, you find
that it is the result of a specific decree on God's part, and of
a particular independent act of formation. The earth and
waters at the command of God *brought forth* the other
creatures. But man's formation is the issue of deliberation
and distinct workmanship on God's part. *Second*, his body
being formed, God breathed into his nostrils the breath
of life, נִשְׁמַת חַיִּים, *i.e.* the breath which is the origin and
font of life, rather than the breath which is the index of

life. This is the point around which the controversy
turns. The word *breath* is not used, I think,—there is one
disputed passage,—of the life-breath of other creatures
besides man. The act was real and symbolic. God
breathed. What He breathed was נְשָׁמָה; this became in
man חיים 'נ, *breath of life*. *Third*, this done to man, man
became a living soul, נֶפֶשׁ חַיָּה. The difference of construction of these words is to be observed : *soul*, 'נ, has always an
adjective qualifying it,—man is a *living soul*, the soul lives,
is the bearer of life, within it all life's functions go on, and
all life's phenomena are realised ; and so Paul says : " the
first man, Adam, was made a ψυχὴ ζῶσα " (1 Cor. xv. 45).
The word *breath*, 'נ, however, or elsewhere *spirit*, 'ר, has no
adjective to qualify it, but a noun in construction with it.
You do not speak of a *living spirit*, but of a *spirit of life*,
—one which confers or bestows life, one from which life
issues forth ; it is *the spirit that giveth life*, τὸ πνεῦμά ἐστι
τὸ ζωοποιοῦν (John vi. 63). The soul lives ; but it has
not life in itself, the spirit gives it life.

If we recur for a moment to the second step in the
process, without discussing the word *became*, it is evident
that although the act was symbolical, and might seem to
be limited in meaning to the mere calling into operation
the inspiring and expiring processes of man's respiration,
and the putting within him that which is the sign of life,
namely, his breath ; yet the expression *breath of life* can
hardly mean merely breath, which is the *sign* of life here.
The action is not to be taken as merely symbolical of
putting breath in man. For that which God breathed
into man could not be mere atmospheric air, and besides
there is the same double use of words in Hebrew that
appears in all languages, the word for breath and spirit
being the same. And further, in point of fact, this נֶפֶשׁ
here said to be breathed into man is, as breathed, elsewhere
said to be the cause of understanding in him : " the
breath (or inspiration) of the Almighty giveth understanding," נ' שַׁדַּי תְּבִינֵם (Job xxxii. 8). The narrative is simple,
and might seem merely to allude to the putting of breath

into man, which is the sign of life; but in conformity
with the usage of 'ﬡ elsewhere, we must hold that it is
also the spirit or breath of God which is the source of
life in man.

But now, on the other hand, what was this which God
breathed into man? Was it His own Spirit? On the one
hand, we might strictly adhere to the figure, and say: No
man breathes his own spirit—that principle, namely, whereby his own personal existence is continued, and whereby he
breathes; but only that whereby his existence manifests
itself, viz. breath. And thus what God breathed into man
stood related to Himself, as a man's breath is related to
him; it was not His own Spirit, but something else, His
breath. But, on the other hand, the spiration of a spirit
is spirit; the spiration of God gives subsistence to His
Holy Spirit. And thus many Psychologists, such as Oehler
Hofmann, and others, hold that there was a real communication of God's own Spirit, which, thus communicated,
became, or gave origin to, 'ﬡ, or *soul.* Thus Oehler says ·
" 'ﬡ nil aliud nisi inclusam in corpore, spiritus divini, ut ita
dicam, particulam." He thinks it needful to defend such
a theory from the charge of Pantheism and Emanationism,
and he considers it sufficient for that purpose to assert that
God communicated His spirit *willingly.* But if every
creature's spirit be God's Spirit, so far as spirit is concerned, Pantheism is the result, though there may not
attach to such a pantheistic theory certain characteristics
which usually attach to pantheistic theories, such as un-
consciousness in that which is *Pantheos.* On the other
hand, this passage in Genesis does not teach that this 'ﬡ
which was put into man was created. It came out of God.
He breathed it into man. To our feeble thinking—I
ought, perhaps, to apologise for saying feeble, for to some
the rigorous and sharp distinction of creation and emanation, and the denial of any other kind of origin whatever,
may seem strength,—to our thinking there may be no
middle thing between bare external creation and coarse
materialistic emanation, and consequent partition of the

Divine; but our thinking may not be entitled to be considered the measure of possibility on a subject so profound. One has a repugnance to believe in the creation of spirit as he does in the creation of matter. And there is a difficulty attaching to the conception of it quite distinct from the difficulty attaching to the conception of creation as such. That any Being, even God, should be able to produce substances and natures the same as His own, by mere outward creation and not by some internal process of generation, is so altogether unlike what we see or can conceive as harmonious in the nature of things, that we almost claim to be allowed to repose in some middle effort of the Divine nature, which shall not be altogether generation nor altogether creation. Scripture calls God "the Father of our spirits." No doubt it does elsewhere say that He formeth, יֹצֵר, the spirit of man, within him, Zech. xii. 1.

But thus you will see how the question is encumbered, and that in matters concerning the state of the dead we may find expressions both hard to understand in themselves and not easily reconcilable with one another. Probably all that can be determined meantime with certainty, though it leaves the questions which were raised very vaguely answered, is this: Whether the *soul*, נ׳, in man be distinct substantially from the *spirit* or no, the soul is the seat of life and of personality in man, and having received subsistence, no more loses it. At death it parts from the body; if the person who died be restored to life, the soul returns to the body. It has existence apart from the body in *Sheol*, and the personality is still attached to it in that region. The Old Testament, I think, does not call that which is in Sheol *soul*, nor yet *spirit*; it does not condescend upon the quality of any of the individuals there; it calls them all רְפָאִים, that is, either *soft, tenues, shadowy*, or *long-stretched*. Again, as to *spirit*, whether that be man's permanently, or God's actually and man's only in temporary possession, it is said to return to God who gave it (Eccles. xii. 7). Its presence is the source of life in

tion.[1] The Old Testament represents Sheol as the opposite of this *upper sphere* of light and life. It is " deep Sheol," שׁ׳ תַּחְתִּיָּה, Ps. lxxxvi. 13 : " Thou hast delivered my soul from the lowest hell." It is deep down in the earth, Ps. lxiii. 9 : " Those that seek my soul, to destroy it, shall go down into the lower parts of the earth." Corresponding to this it is the region of darkness, as Job, mournfully looking to it, says : " A land of darkness, as darkness itself ; and of the shadow of death, without any order, and where the light is as darkness " (x. 22, 23). Of course, there is no formal topography to be sought for in Sheol. It is in great measure the creation of the imagination, deep down under the earth, even under the waters, and dark, and all within it chaos. The shades tremble " underneath the waters, and their inhabitants," Job xxvi. 5. Hence it is often decked out with the horrors of the grave. The prophet Isaiah, xiv. 9, represents the king of Babylon as going into Sheol : " Sheol from beneath is moved for thee to meet thee at thy coming. Thy pomp is brought down to Sheol, and the noise of thy viols : the worm is spread under thee, and the worms cover thee." And so in Ezek. xxxii. 21–23 : " The strong among the mighty shall speak to him out of Sheol . . . Asshur is there and all her company : his graves are about him : all of them slain, fallen by the sword : whose graves are set in the sides of the pit."

That is a representation, according to which Sheol is a vast underground mausoleum, with cells all around like graves. But it may be asserted with some reason that nowhere is Sheol confounded with the grave, or the word used for the place of the dead body. Sheol is the place of the departed personalities—the Old Testament neither calls them ' souls ' nor ' spirits.' It is the place appointed for all living, the great rendezvous of dead persons ; for a strict distinction is not drawn between the body and its place, and the soul and its place. The generations of one's forefathers are all there, and he who dies is gathered

[1] The supposed discovery of Sheol in Assyrian Sualu (as affirmed by Friedrich Delitzsch, Jeremias, etc.) is denied by Schrader, Jensen, etc.

unto his fathers. The tribal divisions of one's race are there, and the dead man is gathered unto his people. Separated from them here, he is united with them there. And if his own descendants had died before him, they are there, and he goes down, as Jacob to his son, mourning. None can hope to escape passing down among that vast assemblage of thin and shadowy personalities: "What man is he that liveth, and shall not see death? that shall deliver his soul from the hand of Sheol?" (Ps. lxxxix. 48).

But it may be of use to put under distinct heads a few things about Sheol.

(1) The state of those in Sheol. As death consists in the withdrawal by God of the spirit of life, and as this spirit is the source, in general, of energy and vital force, the personality is of necessity left feeble and flaccid. All that belongs to life ceases except existence. Hence Sheol is called אֲבַדּוֹן, *perishing*, it is called חֶרֶל, *cessation* (Isa. xxxviii. 11). The personalities crowding there are power-less, and drowsy, and still and silent, like those in sleep. Hence they are called רְפָאִים (Job xxvi. 5; Isa. xiv. 9). The state is called דּוּמָה, silence: "Unless the Lord had been my help, my soul had almost dwelt in silence" (xciv. 17). It is the land of forgetfulness (Ps. lxxxviii. 12); "the living know that they must die: but the dead know not any thing. Also their love, and their hatred, and their envy, is now perished" (Eccles. ix. 5). Yet though they are feeble, as those in Sheol confess to the Babylonian king, "Art thou become weak as one of us?"—חֻלֵּיתָ (Isa. xiv. 10), *thinned*, as one worn by sickness,—they know them-selves and their state, as this representation shows, and also others. They even seem to keep a kind of shadowy life of their own, a dreamy pomp and ceremonial, sitting with invisible forms upon imperceptible thrones from which they are stirred, with a flicker of interest and emotion, to greet any distinguished new arrival. It is the shadow of earth and its activities; wavering shades of the present life. The things said are not presented to us as matters of faith, they are the creations largely of the writers' imagination.

One can see that there is no knowledge on the part of the
writers concerning this underworld. They shudder at the
thought of it, and their imagination paints it dark and
distant. The grave suggests a deep cavernous receptacle
to them. The sleep of death causes them to deem it a
land of stillness and silence. The flaccid corpse makes
them think of the person as feeble, with no energy or
power of resistance. All is taken from the circumstances
of death, and can have no reality or truth to us as an
article of belief. Only this is certain, that there was a
belief in the continued existence of the person. Death
puts an end to the existence of no person.

(2) There seems to be no distinction of good and evil in
Sheol. As all must go into Sheol, so all are represented
as being there. Sheol is no place of punishment itself, nor
one of reward. Neither does it seem divided into such
compartments. The state there is neither blessedness nor
misery. It is bare existence. " There the wicked cease from
troubling, *i.e.* from the disquietude which their own evil
causes them, and the weary are at rest." " The small and
great are there alike, and the servant is free from his
master " (Job iii. 17, 19). To-morrow, said Samuel to the
king whom God had rejected, " to-morrow shalt thou and
thy sons be with me. Then Saul fell straightway all along
upon the earth, and was sore afraid, because of the words of
Samuel " (1 Sam. xxviii. 19). " The dead know not anything," says the Preacher, " neither have they any more a
reward " (Eccles. ix. 5).

There are, perhaps, a pair of passages from which critics
have surmised that there was in the Old Testament
a belief in a deeper Sheol than the ordinary, a ἅδης
σκοτιώτερος, a darker Hades. In Isa. xiv., a passage
so rich in contributions to our knowledge of Hebrew
thought concerning the things of the dead, the Babylonian
is said to be thrust down to יַרְכְּתֵי בוֹר, " the sides of the
pit "; he who had said presumptuously, " I will set my
throne on the sides of the north, in the mount of God "
(יַרְכְּתֵי צָפוֹן). But the expression is evidently used in anti-

thesis to "the sides of the north," and cannot be held to signify a deeper Hades than that where the ordinary dead are assembled. And the same must be said of the only other passages where traces of such an opinion have been found by some scholars, as, *e.g.*, Ezek. xxxii. 23, already quoted, and Isa. xxiv. 21 : "The Lord will punish the high ones that are on high, and the kings of the earth upon the earth. And they shall be gathered together, as prisoners are gathered in the pit, and shall be shut up in the prison, and after many days shall they be visited." Neither can the fervent prayer of Balaam, "May I die the death of the righteous, and may my last end be like his" (Num. xxiii. 10), have any reference to that which he feared after death, or to any faith which he had in a distinction in the positions of the righteous and the wicked in Sheol. Rather his prayer is that he may live such a life as he sees before Israel, rich in God's blessings, and therefore peaceful and long; so that he should die old and full of days, and be carried to the grave like a shock of corn coming in in his season.

It is doubtful, therefore, if in the Old Testament any traces of a distinction in Sheol between the good and evil be found. The distinction that begins to appear is that indicated in Ps. xlix., that while the wicked are congregated in Sheol, the righteous overleap and escape it. Towards the close of the Hebrew commonwealth, another idea began to rise—that of a gloomy vale of horrid sufferings through the torturings of fire. This was Gehenna—first the valley of Hinnom, where the cruel rites of Moloch were performed, and children passed through the fire to the horrid king. Then this idea seemed to be transferred to the state of the dead, and the wicked were conceived to be subjected to such torments of fire. Already, ere New Testament times, this advance upon the old doctrine of Sheol had been made, and in the parable the rich man is represented as tormented in flames (Luke xvi. 23–28). And probably some traces of the idea may be found in the Old Testament, as in the end of Isaiah, "for their worm

shall not die, neither shall their fire be quenched"
(lxvi. 24).

(3) But this last passage leads to some other questions,
e.g., as regards the connection of the personality in Sheol
with the body of which it had been deprived, with the
outer world, and with God.

As to connection with the outer world, that is completely broken off. The dead can neither return, nor does he
know anything of the things of earth; even the fate, happy
or miserable, of those he is most bound up with, is a
mystery to him. "His sons come to honour, and he
knoweth it not; and they are brought low, and he perceiveth
it not of them" (Job xiv. 21). "As the cloud is consumed
and vanisheth away: so he that goeth down to the grave
shall come up no more" (vii. 9). Yet with the strong
belief in the existence of the persons in Sheol, there was
naturally a popular superstition that they could be reached,
and that they could be interested in human affairs, of the
issues of which they must have deeper knowledge than
mortal men. This belief among the Hebrews gave rise to
the necromancy so sternly proscribed in the law, and
ridiculed by Isaiah: "Should not a people seek unto their
God? should they seek for the living to the dead?" (viii.
19); and the belief is not extinct among ourselves. That
it was not a mere superstition, but an unlawful traffic, was
shown by the case of Samuel; for there is no reason to
suppose this a delusion of Saul's, or a trick of the woman.
At all events the incident bears testimony to the prevalent
belief in the existence of those who had died in this life.
Yet how far the practice in general was carried on by mere
working on the superstitions of the people, one cannot say.
There is no other case in the Old Testament but that of
Samuel of any dead person appearing and returning to
Sheol. The relation between the dead in Sheol and God
is not close: "Shall the dead praise Thee?" (Ps. lxxxviii.
10). Of this more hereafter.

The question whether any connection still exists between
the body and the dead in Sheol is interesting, but there

are hardly materials to answer it. No such connection exists between the body and the soul as to interfere with the passage into Sheol, whatever befall the body. The body needs not to be embalmed, as in Egypt, nor burned, nor even buried. It may be thrown out as a dishonoured branch, and yet the descent into Sheol be unimpeded. The want of burial was in itself dishonouring, and it is regarded as having a reflection on the condition of the dead person in Sheol in the estimation of others there. But, on the other hand, there are passages which seem to speak of a sympathetic *rapport* still existing between the body and the person in Sheol. These passages are hardly capable of being pressed further than to the inference that the body, though thrown off, was still part of the man, and was not mere common unrelated dust. Some passages speak of sensibility still remaining in the body ; *e.g.*, Isa. lxvi. 24 : " Their worm dieth not," where the body is represented as feeling the tooth of the corrupting worm. But others go further, and seem to regard the soul as also sensitive, and sharing in the pain of the body : " His flesh upon him shall have pain, and his soul within him shall mourn " (Job xiv. 22). But, as I have said, these statements hardly go further than to show that the body, though cast off, is still considered in some connection with the person.

The main point is that the relation between the deceased person and God is cut off. This is what gave death its significance to the religious mind, and caused such a revulsion against it, culminating in such protests as that in Ps. xvi. Fellowship with God ceases : " In death there is no remembrance of Thee : in Sheol who shall give Thee thanks ? " (Ps. vi. 5). " For Sheol cannot praise Thee," says Hezekiah ; " they that go down to the pit cannot hope for Thy truth " (Isa. xxxviii. 18). And the plaintive singer in Ps. xxxix. pleads for an extension of his earthly life on this ground : " Hold not Thy peace at my tears : for I am a stranger with Thee, and a sojourner,"—the meaning of these words being the opposite of what, with our Christian knowledge, we put into them. The Old Testament saint was a sojourner with God: this life in the body upon the earth was a brief but happy visit paid to Jehovah; but death summoned the visitor away, and it came to an end.

5. *Conception of Death.*

The point of view from which Scripture looks at everything is the moral and religious. This is the point of view from which it regards the universe as a whole. It is a moral constitution. With all its complexity it has a moral unity, all its parts subserving moral ends and illustrating moral truths. Hence, when Scripture describes the origin of things and their gradual rise into order, though it may seem to be physical phenomena that it is describing, its design has not respect to these physical phenomena in themselves, but primarily to this, that they occurred through the free act of a Supreme Moral Agent; and that they contemplated as their final result the preparation of a suitable sphere of activity for another free moral agent. This moral purpose of Scripture in everything which it says makes it of less consequence for it to describe events precisely as they occurred. It may use liberties. It may so group phenomena and so colour events that the moral meaning of them may shine out to our eyes more clearly than if it had adhered in its description to prosaic literality. It is quite conceivable that some parts of ancient history are so written in Scripture. Its design never being to record facts merely for facts' sake, but for the sake of the moral teaching which they contain, it is a supposition not to be at once rejected, that in order to exhibit to our dull eyesight the ideas of history, it may idealise the history. This principle, however, if admitted, must be carefully guarded; and no doubt the difficulty would be to guard it when once admitted. It must be guarded for the reason that Redemption is historical. Our salvation consists of historical facts: " If Christ be not risen, your faith is vain; ye are yet in your sins" (1 Cor. xv. 17) A redemption consisting wholly of ideas would, of course, be only an ideal redemption, and leave us precisely where we were. But the historicity of salvation as a whole being conserved, nothing stands in the way of our admitting that some of the historical occurrences whereby it was illustrated or realised may have been set by subsequent narrators in an intenser light than that in which they first appeared.

If the point of view from which Scripture regards the universe as a whole be moral, much more will it regard man in this light. Man has, no doubt, according to Scripture, just as God has, a nature and a 'self.' But his essence and meaning lie so exclusively in his 'self,' in his personality, that only when the just equilibrium between his nature and his 'self' has been disturbed, do the former and its elements come into prominence. His centre of gravity as well as centre of unity lies in his moral constitution. That remaining as it was by creation, he will remain as he was in creation a living man, a unity embracing all his parts; for this is what Scripture means by *life*. The author of the well written but not very exhaustively thought out treatise on *The Christian Doctrine of Sin*, says: "Death as a simple physical fact is unaffected by moral conditions." But such a statement requires limitation in several ways. We observe moral conditions to be of great influence in reference to disease, in keeping off infection, for instance, and in neutralising the effects of poison. We read in the Gospel history of some who had faith to be healed, and on the other hand of the infliction of mania through the operation of evil intelligences on the mind; and what is true of disease is, of course, true also of death, for the two are identical. The forty days' fast of our Lord in the wilderness shows sufficiently the enormous power exercised over the body by the mind in a high state of spiritual tension. Who does not perceive that such a statement as that death is unaffected by moral conditions, is a mere begging of the question?

It is true that ultimately all, moral and immoral, die; just as it is true that death is inherent in all organisms with which we are familiar. But that implies merely that death affects all the limited varieties of moral conditions now appearing in the race since sin has intervened, and that death is inherent in human organisms such as we now know them. But that fact can support no inference as to how death or disease would behave in the presence of a perfect moral condition, and what would occur to the organism of such a human being; for the difference between the highest morality that exists and a perfect one, is a difference not of degree, but of kind. Experience affords us no data here on which to go; or if we refer to the case of Christ, who was sinless, we read nothing regarding Him which implies that He ever suffered any ailment, or that the seeds of natural death were sown in His body. We can form no judgment from direct observation. We could at most infer from what we see of men at present. But such an inference would certainly be to beg the question against Scripture, which expressly recognises the two conditions of a perfect and an imperfect moral state, and teaches that the organism of human nature is not a thing under the government of physical laws only, but is lifted up by the spiritual nature of man into another plane, and subject in its destiny to the operation of moral laws.

Coupled with this view, that death is inherent in all organisms, and that, consequently, the death threatened to Adam could not mean mere physical death, is the view of the writer quoted, that death as there threatened was merely the *moral* consequence of transgression, namely, what we call spiritual death, together with the terrors that gather about dying to a sinner. This irruption into our theological nomenclature of the term *death* to describe the spiritual condition of a sinner, has been a great misfortune, not only because it affords a foundation for the kind of views propounded by this author, but because it diverts our minds from the Scripture way of regarding death and life. In the Old Testament and in St. Paul, *death* always includes what we popularly call *dying*; and in the Old

Testament *dying* includes *remaining dead, i.e.* all the destiny
of the dead ; and so *life* includes the life of the body,—
in Paul the resurrection life, which, as man is a unity, alone
is life.   Even the expression, ' dead in sins ' (Eph. ii. 3, 5),
does not mean spiritually insensible in the practice of sin,
but subject to death as a penalty in the element or region of
sins.   There are, no doubt, certain expressions, particularly
in this Epistle to the Ephesians, that may seem to go
against this view, such, *e.g.*, as this : " You hath he quickened,
who were dead in trespasses " (ii. 1) ; " raised us up together,
and made us sit together in the heavenly places " (ii. 6).
But this difficulty disappears as soon as the apostle's true
manner of looking at Christianity is understood.   He
always, in the theoretical portions of his Epistles, looks at
it as a whole.   He uses terms of it which embrace and
describe its perfect results ; not the beginning, but the
end of its development.   What it will yet achieve is to
him already achieved.

His statements are not empirical and bounded by the
actual experience of Christians, but ideal, and reaching out
to the future consummation of things.   Nay, he even in his
ideal descriptions employs the terms suitable for the future
and perfect to describe the small beginnings of the present.
Hence to him believers are as much sanctified as they are
justified ; they are saints, complete in Christ.   It is only in
the practical parts of his epistles, when he descends to deal
with the actual condition of the Churches and his converts,
among whom, alas ! this ideal of Christianity is far enough
from yet obtaining, that he analyses the effects of redemption
into those that already are and those that shall be.   Then
sanctification is seen to be incomplete.   Then the perfect
Church splits asunder, and what we name the Church
Visible is the subject of treatment, at least in its members.
But neither the imperfect saint nor the Church Visible
belongs to the region of the ideal of Christianity, and
consequently they find no place in the early and theoretical
parts of the Epistles.   And so, speaking to the Ephesians,
he uses terms descriptive of salvation as perfectly realised,

to indicate what believers are really in possession of. His language is in a sense proleptic. Believers do not yet sit with Christ in the heavenly places; but faith and grace, when they shall have their perfect work, will issue in their resurrection; and this issue is involved in those beginnings of power which God has already put forth among them. Consequently the apostle does not employ the terms 'quickened' and 'raised' to describe a mere spiritual change which has already been produced. He uses them literally, although by anticipation, to remind the Ephesians of what is contained in God's gift to them, and what shall yet accrue to them, namely, the redemption of the body.

I quite admit that, after all, the two views may coalesce, and that it may be the vitalising of the soul with spiritual life which really quickens the body; for the new body is not in Scripture regarded as alien matter, but is the old body vitalised and become spiritual. And the new life instilled into the soul by God's Spirit may become so intense, that, like a flame, it stretches itself out and communicates its fire to the body, still its own and not yet altogether extinct. We know so little of what life is, and how it operates to gather a body about it. But just as we see the somewhat languid life of our present existence gradually add element to element and accumulate in the slow course of twenty years a mature full body to itself, so the intenser life that we shall yet inherit may on the resurrection day draw a body around itself in an instant, accomplishing in the twinkling of an eye what is the work of many years at present. But what I am anxious to emphasise is, that Scripture makes very little in this region of physical cause and effect. Man is under a moral constitution. Death is the *penalty* of sin, not that spiritual feebleness which may be but another name for sin itself. And life is the *reward* of righteousness, not righteousness itself. The wages of sin is death; but grace reigned *through* righteousness *unto* eternal life (Rom. v. 21; vi. 23)

6. *Life and its Issues.*

But we must leave this New Testament region, which is always so fascinating, and return to the Old Testament and its statements on the subject of *Sheol*, the receptacle of the departed. There, in that underworld, good and evil, according to the Old Testament, appear alike immured; and the condition in which they subsist is not *life*, but bare existence, dreary and infelicitous. Does the Old Testament give any light as to the permanence of this condition? Sheol does not appear to be a place of reward or punishment. Is there any escape from it for the righteous, or is there any intensification of its evils awaiting the unjust? There is no question that is stirring men's minds with a greater intensity at present than this one of the destiny of the wicked. Does the Old Testament go any way to solve it?

Besides the view which may be said to be the ordinary and hereditary one in the Churches, there may be said to be at present three others current, besides minor ones which I do not mention, regarding the destiny of those dying impenitent. First, there is the Universalistic view, according to which all shall be restored. Second, there is the view, stopping short of this, which demands a place of repentance and a sphere of development beyond the grave, and which, assuming infinite gradations of salvation, finds a place for at least most of the race. And, third, there is the view, which calls itself that of Conditional Immortality, according to which those finally evil shall ultimately be annihilated. Has the Old Testament anything to say to the question as stated in these views?

Now, of course, such questions will not be decided on Old Testament ground, but in the light of the clearer revelation of the New. But so far as the Old goes, it does not, I think, favour any of these views. From all that we have seen, you will perceive that the Hebrew view of things is a view essentially concerned with things on this side. Salvation is to it a present good. The moral constitution of the world exhibits itself already here. In this life righteousness delivers from death. This vivid manner of conceiving the moral order of the present constitution of things, accounts for the fact that attention is confined to what falls on this side almost exclusively. Whatever principles are involved in the relations of God and men, these exhibit themselves completely in the present life. It is well with the righteous,—the lines fall to him in pleasant places —God is the portion of his soul. As to the wicked, he says to God: I desire not the knowledge of Thy ways. His feet are set in slippery places. He is brought down in a moment amidst terrors. The principles prevailing in life come out always to perfect manifestation in death. The manner of dying is certain to express the true relations of the righteous and the wicked. And the manner of dying fixes the condition of the dead; and this condition abides. All is yet general; only great principles of moral government appear. But, so far as the Old Testament is concerned, no change seems indicated in the state of the unjust, either in the way of release or in the way of an intensification of the evils of Sheol. They die estranged from God, they remain estranged; the estrangement does not appear aggravated into positive misery. In Ecclesiastes, indeed, it is said that God will bring every work into judgment; but it cannot be said with certainty that this judgment differs from that passed on every one at death, and illustrated in his manner of dying. Neither in the Apocryphal writings that arose on the soil of Palestine proper is there any advance upon the Old Testament doctrine, at least till quite close to the Christian era. In the Greek Apocrypha the case is different.

Scripture is chiefly concerned with the destinies of the righteous. And on this side there is great advance on the dreary doctrine of Sheol, which is the popular basis of the doctrine of the dead. And to that I will devote a few remarks.

The passages adduced already touching the place and state of the dead are perhaps more poetical than dogmatic, and little can be concluded from them beyond the continued existence of the persons that once lived upon the earth, their consciousness of themselves and of others, their complete exclusion from the world of life, and their silent, feeble form of subsistence. But there are also passages which show the other side of the picture. Perhaps as those formerly adduced could not be held to contain statements which we should be justified in treating as part of a religious conviction, but were rather expressions of an imagination very vivid and greatly stirred, exercising itself upon what was unknown, and clothing it in robes woven out of the things seen in connection with death; so we might not be justified in attributing dogmatic significance to the statements regarding life and immortality. They may be but jets of religious feeling, spasmodic upleapings of the flame of love of existence or love of God, which flickers most wildly and convulsively just when it is about altogether to expire. What value to attribute to them is a thing that perhaps cannot be decided without bringing them into relation to the doctrine regarding future things now fully revealed in the New Testament, But that these beliefs appear in the Old as bursts of religious feeling, as demands of the living soul for continuance in life, as longings of the soul in fellowship with God for closer and eternal fellowship with Him, as expressions of an instinctive shrinking from death, so far from impairing their validity or depriving them of meaning, only adds to it, by showing how deeply seated the desire of immortality is in the nature of man as given by God; how it rises higher the higher the nature is purified by God's fellowship; and how probable, therefore, in itself it is that immortality shall be its goal and reward.

Man, so far as we can gather from the narrative in Genesis, was made neither mortal nor immortal. He was not made so that he *must* die, for the narrative represents him surrounded by the means of living for ever; nor was he so made that he *could not* die, for the event has too clearly shown the reverse. He was made capable of not dying. with the design that by a free determination of his activity rewarded by God's favour, he should become not capable of dying. He sinned, and when he sinned he died. But death is thus a foreign thing, an evil befallen man, the child of sin. Where sin is, death is. But surely the other thought could not but be immediately suggested, —seeing if sin had not been, death would not have been,— that when sin should be overcome, death would be vanquished also. To overcome sin is to live. This is everywhere the doctrine of the Bible. Yet in the earliest portions of Scripture the truth is not put quite in this manner. It is not freedom from sin that *gives*, or that *is*, life, so much as fellowship with God. Sin is regarded as an enfeebling of the soul, a drugging of the soul by a deadly narcotic, an impairing of its vital energy. That which pours life into the enfeebled, paralysed spirit is God's Spirit, and so is God. In Him, with Him, is life. Thus the early Scriptures overleap a step. They do not so much speak of *righteousness being life*, as of *God*, who is the cause of righteousness, *giving* life.

This is perhaps the state of the belief in the earliest times. This seems the idea at the root of the Mosaic economy. There is no allusion there to a future life. Yet there are life and death set before the Israelite. Are we to suppose it was only earthly life, worldly goods, the quiet heritage of Canaan, freedom from peril and sword ? Life lay in God's favour, in His presence and fellowship. The religious life of Mosaism was as real as our own, and as true. What the patriarchs are represented as looking forward to was not the rest of Canaan, but abiding with God,—a settled nearness to Him and fellowship with Him. They sought 'a country'—which the New Testament writer, from his point of view, interprets as a heavenly one (Heb. xi. 16). They looked for the "city that hath the foundations, whose builder and maker is God" (Heb. xi. 10). What thoughts they may have had, one can hardly imagine. Yet what they sought, and what they felt called to, in all their wanderings, was some stable place of abode,—some country, some city of God, where He dwelt, and where they should dwell with Him; where their life should run on for ever parallel to God's. He was the element of satisfaction that they sought, and that constituted their life.

And so it was with the pious Israelite when settled in Canaan. He thought nothing good, nothing to be desired, which was severed from the fellowship of God. The external goods which he enjoyed, he considered but the pledge of this. But there is little, if any, sign of that analytic tendency, which we cannot resist, to distinguish between this world and another. To the Israelite both worlds were united in one. He enjoyed both. He drew a distinction between this world without God and this world with God. The wicked had the former and he the latter. God was his portion, and the lines had fallen to him in pleasant places. The future he seldom strove to unveil. Still, if he did, we can imagine what feelings the thought would arouse: it would either be a pitiful entreaty that God would not interrupt that blessed fellowship by death: "I said, O my God, take me not away in the midst of my days" (Ps. cii. 24):

> "Return O Jehovah, deliver my soul:
> O save me for Thy mercy's sake.
> For in death there is no remembrance of Thee:
> In Sheol who shall give Thee thanks?" (Ps. vi. 4, 5).

or it would be a violent resistance and putting down of the thought of death. It could not, it must not be, that this blessed fellowship should ever be broken: "I have set the Lord always before me: because He is at my right hand, I shall not be moved" (Ps. xvi. 8).

So far, what we have seen was the certain faith in God and life in Him. This was conviction and thought. Rising out of that was, perhaps, more the emotional feeling of immortality—the dread of dying, the passionate longing for life—the refusal to conceive or to admit that this life with God lived on earth could come to an end. Yet perhaps there was no intellectual presentation to the mind itself of the way in which it could be continued. Still certain things narrated in the Pentateuch might suggest to the saints of those and after times even a way. That wonderful glory recorded to have been vouchsafed to Enoch, of whom it was said that he "walked with God," showed that the reward of the closest fellowship with God might be rapture into God's presence without tasting of death— "for God took him" (Gen. v. 24). And this word *took* laid deep hold of men's minds in this connection. For the sorely troubled Asaph, when he came to clearness and peace, at last comforted himself that God would *take* him also:

> "Thou shalt guide me with Thy counsel,
> And afterward *take* me to glory" (Ps. lxxiii. 24).

This glory of Enoch's was what few could hope for as it had fallen to him; yet the way in which Asaph conceives it, was the way those contemporary with Enoch and subsequent to him could hardly help conceiving it. What had befallen him who walked with God marvellously, in this marvellous way, would befall them who walked with Him in an ordinary way, in a manner equally real if less marvellous. And, in addition to this, there was the general faith in God's power, and that He was able to bring again the dead. Thus Abraham, being strong in faith, staggered not at the promise of God through unbelief, but offered up his son when commanded, though the promise was made to him, accounting that God was able to raise him up even from the dead (Heb. xi. 19). Such miracles, too, as are narrated of Elijah would also familiarise men's minds with the possibility of the dead again living.

Thus we should anticipate that the minds of Old Testament saints would run in two lines in this matter of the hope of immortality,—one line emotional and another reflective, though the emotional may also have under it reflection of various kinds, chiefly on the evils or the inequalities of life. The emotional utterances will chiefly rise from the feeling of fellowship with God, which is life, and take the form of protests against the thought of its being broken in upon; and these reaches of feeling into eternity will be brief and rarely sustained, and seldom

reasoned. Indeed, they will generally ground themselves
with a certain absoluteness simply on the sense of fellowship, and refuse to take all other facts, even death,
into consideration. The reflective utterances, again, will
naturally accept of facts, such as the universality of death,
and seek to dispose of them. Thus, what the emotional
utterances bring forward will rather be *immortality, i.e.* never
dying. What the reflective utterances bring forward will
be *resurrection.* And, as was to be anticipated, the expressions of emotion will appear in lyrics, in plaintive
elegies,—the productions of deeply exercised religious men.
The expressions of reflection will rather come from prophets,
men who have a clear outlook into the things of the future,
and who are set to indicate with authority to the Church
the final developments of her history.

We cannot fully pursue these two lines. It must
suffice to project them, and to linger for a little at one
point in each. The passages where the Old Testament
saint appears striving to maintain his fellowship with the
living God in spite of all vicissitudes, are chiefly Pss. xvi.,
xvii., xlix., lxxiii., and the Book of Job. The state of the
believer's mind in Ps. xvi. does not materially differ from
that disclosed in the great passages of Job. But there is
another psalm which forms the fitting background to this
one, at which we may look for a moment, Ps. xc., headed,
' A Prayer of Moses the man of God.' Whether the Psalm
be so old or no, it is very old, and little that is plausible
can be said against its traditional age. It might be called
an elegy on the brevity of human life. But such general
subjects never were treated alone by a Hebrew poet. If
he deplored an evil, he was always struggling for a remedy.
The remedy of this he finds in the eternal God. The
Psalm might be headed : ' The eternal God a refuge for man,
shortlived by reason of his sin.' First, the poet posits the
relation of God to men : " Thou hast been a dwelling-place
for us in all generations." This relation of God to men is
the theme of the Psalm, which consists, then, of a further
statement how God is this, and how men need it, and,

finally, of a prayer that God would cause the relation to be fully realised in the case of those now praying. The words "in all generations" suggest the eternal sameness of God, over-against the brevity of man's life. "From ever-lasting to everlasting, Thou art God. Thou turnest man to destruction," *i.e.* Thou seest men, generation after genera-tion, perish, Thyself still eternal and living: for a thousand years in Thy sight are but as yesterday. Men are like the grass, which, springing in the morning, withereth ere night. But this short-livedness of men in opposition to the eternal, unmoved duration of Jehovah, is not without a cause. It is not merely that He lives and they die each from his appropriate nature. They die because they are consumed in His anger. He hath set their sins in the light of His face, turned His full face with awful light upon them.

This is the condition of men, sinful and perishing because they are so. The Psalm expresses general and universal relations. God eternal, men of transient exist-ence, and that because God's wrath carries them away in their sins. Yet, also, there is another general relation to be added: "Thou art our dwelling-place, our refuge, in all generations." He who carries sinful men away with a flood, the overflow of His wrath, is their refuge. In God is the hiding-place from the anger of God. In Him, the Eternal, man that is of few days finds his refuge. And so the Psalmist concludes with the prayer: "Return, O Lord; how long? and pity Thy servants. Satisfy us in the morning with Thy goodness; that we may be glad, and rejoice all our days." This may be the cry of a generation worn out with wanderings, and sick with disappointed hopes, and sated with plagues, dropping down one after another like an enchanted caravan in the wilderness; but it is fit to be the cry and the confession and the prayer of a worn and heavy-laden human race, to God, under whose anger it perishes.

What is spoken generally in Ps. xc. is expressed par-ticularly in the words of a single person in Ps. xvi

Who the person is we cannot certainly say. But David's favourite word heads the Psalm, חָסִיתִי בָךְ, "I have fled for refuge to Thee," as in vii. and xi.; and the tradition puts his name in the heading. What the dangers were which threatened him, must remain unknown; but we know that it was a mortal danger. His life was at stake; and he presses close to Jehovah, the living God, to protect him from the death that sought to assail him.

First when he begins to speak, he has already taken refuge in Jehovah; pursued by dangers, he has sought safety in Him: and being in Him he prays that He would not deliver him up to his pursuers: "Keep me, O God: for I have fled to Thee." Speedily in that refuge his terror seems to pass away, and he speaks calmly, and even with assurance, of eternal safety. Partly he addresses God and partly he soliloquises. It is the believing consciousness thinking aloud. And the thoughts that would fill a mind at such a time would be something like these: first, there would be joy in Jehovah; which might very naturally suggest the unhappy lot of those who sought their joy in aught else. And, as the mind passed from antithesis to antithesis, this thought would drive it back again with increased intensity to the feeling of its own blessedness. And then, when from its refuge it looked abroad on its foes, that had just pursued it to its dwelling-place, this blessedness would throw its colour over them all, and a bold defiance of them would be felt.

This seems just the line of thought in the Psalm. First, the mind's joy in Jehovah: "I said to Jehovah, Thou art my Lord, my joy; delight is in none but Thee." The use of the word *Lord* seems to indicate the complete devotion of the speaker to Jehovah. Then comes the natural passage of the mind to other minds, unlike itself, finding their joy in something else, אַחֵר; "their sorrows are many who seek for themselves aught else": "I will not pour out their drink-offerings of blood, and I will not take their names on my lips." If the Psalm be Davidic, these expressions must be taken figuratively. It is not probable that in his day there was any party actually practising idolatrous rites in the kingdom. But there were, no doubt, many irreligious men, chiefly among the supporters of Saul's dynasty; and many who secretly, and some who openly, repudiated Jehovah, the God of David. In words of strong aversion, the Psalmist speaks of their religious services as drink-offerings of blood.

But, with a natural swing, the mind reverts to its own blessedness: "*Jehovah* is my portion," ver. 5,—'Jehovah' being put emphatically at the head of the clause. And every possible figure is heaped together to express the idea that Jehovah is the possession of the speaker, and to convey what the joy of this possession is to him. "Jehovah is the portion of my inheritance and my cup: Thou art my constant lot. The lines have fallen to me in pleasant things." And, unable to restrain himself, he breaks forth into the exclamation, "I will bless the Lord."

But, finally, from being occupied with the contemplation of his position, and his joy there, he now looks out upon his foes; and he feels confident that where he is they cannot come. In that hiding-place to which he has fled he is secure, all secure, his whole man—not secure merely, but triumphantly confident: "My heart is glad, and my glory rejoices; my flesh also resteth securely." For that Sheol, which opened her mouth wide to swallow him, God will beat back; and that pit, which yawned for him, he shall not see: "Thou wilt not leave my soul over to Sheol, nor give Thine holy one to see the pit." What he shall experience will be life,—"Thou wilt make me know the way of life,"—the way to life. Not death, but life, shall be his portion.

Now, if we consider the lie of the Psalm, first the flight of the suppliant to God to protect him from some mortal danger, then his soliloquising with himself over his blessedness in God, and then his outlook from his place of refuge, from which he dares to face and to defy his pursuers, we can hardly escape the conclusion that what, in his lofty moment of inspiration, he expresses, is the assurance of immortality. He shall not die, but live. God, to whom he has fled, will not leave him to Sheol; it shall not be permitted to have its desire upon him, to swallow him up; neither will He allow him to see, *i.e.* to have experience of the pit. He to whom he has fled will save him from those dark enemies that would devour him. Also He will save him wholly. He the living man, in the fellowship and protection of the living God, shall live. He does not contemplate dying and being restored again to life. Rather these gigantic personalities, Sheol, Shachath, that open their mouth for him, shall have no power over him. He shall be made to know the way to life. And it was life such as then he lived, only fuller; not spiritual life, nor bodily life, but personal life, embracing all. These distinctions, which we insist so much upon, vanish in the excitation of such a moment. And it is ridiculous to imagine that the hopes of one who speaks thus went no further than delivery from some particular mortal danger that threatened him at the time. Some such danger may have started the train of thoughts and feelings which here run out to so sublime a height, but the expressions here are absolute. He who trusteth in God shall live; Sheol and Shachath shall have no power over him.

We need not stop to discuss how far such feelings are true, and how even death is not death to the righteous. For such is not strictly the meaning of the Psalm. We shall only say that, although to all appearance the Psalm expresses the idea of not dying, yet it may be applied to any who, having died, cannot be held of death. The Psalm teaches that those who have perfect fellowship with God shall not die. It does not go into the grounds of this, as other parts of Scripture do, which show God to be life and giving life; and that the creature in such fellowship with Him partakes of His immortal strength, and dieth not. It only expresses the relation, and the consequences that flow from it. But anyone in such perfect fellowship cannot die. If death fall upon him, it must be out of the course of things, the result of a special economy, in which that which is the natural order is suspended. But when this suspension is removed, things will flow in their accustomed order. He who died under a special economy will live under the natural law. And hence the words of this Psalm may be very fitly applied to such an One as in Acts ii. 31.

A superficial criticism used to find in our Lord's proof of the resurrection, taken from the words of God to Moses in 'the Bush,' "*I am the God of Abraham*," an artificiality. His commentary is, God is not the God of the dead, but of the living; and His conclusion, therefore, Abraham shall again live. If I might say so, our Lord's argument is an Old Testament commonplace. It is the argument, so far as it can be so called, of all Old Testament saints. It is the argument of this Psalm and of all the Psalms. What they postulate from fellowship with God is *life*,—escape from Sheol, not experiencing Shachath; and if, in fact, they have fallen into the power of these, neither their faith nor their words can be satisfied without release from them. And, again, what their words and their faith require is not an immortality of the soul; such a thing would have sounded strange to them. They knew of persons only, not souls; and their faith demanded the life of the whole person. But, in strictness, the argument for the resurrection here is not direct but constructive. It is an argument for immortality, for not dying, — an argument that ignores facts like death; and only when this fact of death comes in its way does it become modified into an argument for resurrection. The apostle expresses this view when he says: "The body, indeed, is dead because of sin; but the Spirit is life because of righteousness" (Rom. viii. 10).

The hope of Job differed altogether from the hope of this Psalmist; because Job, when he spoke, was in estrangement from God. And in this life he could not hope for reconciliation; for his malady, which betokened God's anger, he saw, would be mortal. Yet what his faith, in spite of appearances, made certain to him was, that he would see God in reconciliation and in peace. It is a reuniting that his faith demands. Whether it is of his whole being or no is left by the words rather obscure, though the general drift of the Old Testament would point to the former. But this Psalmist has not words enough to express his present blessedness in union with God, and what he protests against is any interruption of it. His faith demands that his whole spirit and soul and body be preserved entire in fellowship with God for ever. The other Psalms which have been named add little if anything to the details of Ps. xvi.

The other point from which immortality was viewed was *reflection*; and as this, unlike emotion and faith, which ignored facts, took facts into consideration, it produced the doctrine of a *resurrection*. It was the prophets who raised and prosecuted this thought specially; and, as was proper to their office, it was in connection with Israel as a people that they chiefly proclaimed the resurrection. Israel in fellowship with God would have lived for ever; but, like Adam, Israel sinned and died: "When Ephraim offended in Baal, he died," says Hosea (xiii. 1). And all the prophets downwards are familiar with the idea of Israel's dissolution from which nothing can now save him. But with the sentence of dissolution came also the promise of restitution. Isaiah embodies this hope, in the very image used by Job as unsuitable to man, the image of the tree sprouting again (lxv. 22), and in plain words: "The remnant shall return." But his contemporary Hosea, who employs the figure of death, employs also that of resurrection: "Let us return unto the Lord. After two days He will revive us: and the third day He will raise us up, and we shall live in His sight" (vi. 2). And the power of death over them shall be altogether destroyed: "I will ransom them from the power of the grave; I will redeem them from death: O death, I will be thy plagues; O grave, I will be thy destruction" (xiii. 14).

These things are certainly said of the people, for the plural refers to the tribes rather than to individuals. But

29

the idea of resurrection is very broadly presented, and we wonder whether it is for the first time that it arises, or whether it be not rather an idea, already more or less familiar, applied to a new subject. On the one hand, such miracles as those narrated of Elijah must have powerfully affected men's minds, even although those raised by him ultimately succumbed to death. Such events would at least furnish the imagery used here, and make it both intelligible and very well fitted to inspire hope. On the other, it is certainly first in connection with the tribes and people that the idea of resurrection is plainly expressed, and the individual Israelites share it because Israel shares it. But the idea once struck by the prophet Hosea is familiar to every succeeding prophet; and whether Hosea used the term *raise* figuratively or no, succeeding prophets use it literally. In some cases, as in the great prophecy of Ezekiel of the valley of dry bones, we may be in doubt whether the prophet refers to the actual raising of individuals dead, or to the restoration of dismembered tribes, and a renewal of the national life. But even if it is to the latter, his imagery reposes on the familiar thought of individuals rising. The valley seemed full of bones, very dry; but bone came to his bone, and flesh came up upon them, and by the breath of God they lived, and stood upon their feet.

If, in the case of Hosea, the idea of the national resurrection was first, and was transferred to the resurrection of the individual, in Ezekiel the order of thought is certainly the reverse; the national resurrection reposes on the fully won idea of that of the individual. Again, in the singular prophecy in Isa. xxvi. this is quite as true: "Thy dead men shall live; awake and sing, ye that dwell in the dust." And in Daniel it is no more said of the people, but of individuals directly, though, from the contested age of Daniel, we cannot be certain how early the passage is: "There shall be a time of trouble, such as never was since there was a nation even to that same time: and at that time thy people shall be delivered, every one that shall be found written in the book. And many of them that sleep in the dust of the earth shall awake, some to everlasting life, and some to shame and everlasting contempt. And they that be wise shall shine as the brightness of the firmament; and they that turn many to righteousness as the stars for ever and ever" (Dan. xii. 1, 2). While in other passages only a resurrection of Israel is spoken of, and where individuals are referred to we have only a resurrection of the just; here there seems taught a resurrection both of the just and of the unjust.

Now, of course, these utterances are of the nature, much of them, of subjective hopes. They are based upon the relation to God—a relation of fellowship and love. This relation, the soul demands, shall not be interrupted. It protests against death. It overleaps Sheol in the vigour of its faith. This is the position of the Old Testament saint. Has his hope been verified? In Christ it has been verified, in Him as an Old Testament saint, as One who was truly a Holy One. And in Him those united to Him by faith shall have the verification of it also in themselves.

The history of the creation presents man living and in true relations with God. This is the ideal condition of man, and the idea of its permanence is implied in the relation. The conception of man is entirely a moral one. This relation to God is the central point. This remaining, all other things are permanent. Such ideas as that the soul is immortal from its nature, or, on the other hand, that the body is necessarily subject to decay from its nature, do not occur. The Old Testament strictly knows nothing of such elements of the being of man; the living man as a whole person is the subject of its contemplation, and he lives in the continuance of his true relations to God. This is the point of view of the history of creation. It is also the point of view of the *Wisdom* literature in its earliest stage, the stage of what might be called principles, where only the ideal conceptions of man and the world, and their relations to God, appear. Such conceptions are expressed in proverbial form in these terms: " In the way of righteous-

ness is life, and the pathway thereof is immortality"; "The
hoary head is a crown of glory; it is found in the way of
righteousness" (Prov. xii. 28, xvi. 31).   The E.V. misreads
the latter passage, and obscures its teaching by translating
"*if* it be found in the way of righteousness."   The meaning
is as in the other passage: "The fear of the Lord pro-
longeth days; but the years of the wicked shall be shortened'
(Prov. x. 27).   Such passages do not refer to cases only;
they state a *principle*.   To the Hebrew mind this life in
the body was the normal life.   He had no doctrine of a
transcendent place of happiness different from earth, where
the principles of God's government, impeded in their flow
here by many obstacles, should roll on smooth and straight.
He saw these principles realised here.   The blessedness
of the just, arising from the fellowship of God, was enjoyed
here.   And in the contemplation of this, the *fact* of death
was ignored.   At least this is the point of view in the early
Wisdom literature,—in the deep flow of the principles that
regulate the relation of God and man, death is submerged.

The theory that the doctrine of immortality was kept
hid from Israel in order that the attention of the people
might be fastened on the conditions of a moral life here,
fails to take into account this point of view from which
we must always start.   A normal life here *was* immortality.   The doctrine of immortality was already given
to the people in this conception: life was the existence
of the whole man in the body, this life was had in
fellowship with God, and this fellowship was indissoluble;
for in the conception they had of the world their
condition in it, truly represented the relations of God to
men.   Of course, all this was in some respects *ideal*, and
facts were opposed to it.   But the doctrine of immortality
was given in the idea and in the consciousness of the living
saint; and the task of after revelation was to move out of
the course the obstacles that stood in the way of the idea
being realised.   To us, on the contrary, the obstacles bulk
so largely that we begin with them, and we are scarcely
able to conceive a condition of the mind that could give

death a secondary place, or sweep it away in the rush of great principles regarding God and the universe, or sink it in the intense ecstasy of conscious life with God.

7. *Problems of Righteousness and their Solution.*

In many passages of the Old Testament the idea of immortality is connected with the problems of the Wisdom. The hope, the necessity, of immortality appears as the solution of problems which, it was felt, received no just solution in this life. As the Wisdom aimed at detecting and exhibiting the operation of fixed principles in the world and life, it became practically a doctrine of providence in a wide sense. And in a world where moral anomalies were so abundant, a doctrine of providence took oftentimes the shape of a theodicy or justification of the ways of God to man; and as this justification was seen to be imperfectly comprehended in this life, the necessity was felt of projecting the final issue into a region beyond death.

In no nation were the principles and conditions of well-being and misfortune so clearly distinguished as among the Hebrews. The lawgiver set out by laying before the people blessing and cursing. Though the kingdom of God was administered as to its principles in no way different from God's government of other nations, there was this great difference, that there was always present the inspired consciousness of the prophets and teachers of the people, in which was immediately reflected the meaning of God's providence with them. And it is possible that, though the principles of God's government of Israel were the same as those by which He governs other nations, there was a more immediate connection in their case between sin and misfortune, than there is among other peoples. There is in all cases the same connection; but it may be made a question whether, in addition to having the connection clearly set before the people by the prophets, the connection was not more strict and immediate in God's rule of His people.

In addition to this general law, the individual was also taught the same lesson. When he sinned, there was immediately, in the ceremonial disability that ensued, a punishment of his offence. Thus that fundamental connection between sin and suffering being extremely prominent, it took possession of men's minds with a very firm hold. And, no doubt, this was intended. The law was a ministration of death; its purpose was to educate the people in the knowledge of sin and retribution. In the theology of Paul, the law stands not on the side of the remedy, but on the side of the disease. It came in to aggravate the malady— that the offence might abound. It had other uses, and this view of it is not meant to be exhaustive. But as an intermediate institution, coming in between the promise and actual redemption, this was one of its effects and purposes. It augmented the disease in the consciousness of the mind struggling with its demands, and perhaps also, as Paul argues, it increased the disease in fact by provoking the sinful mind to oppose it. It revealed both sin and its consequences: "By the law is the knowledge of sin"; "when the commandment came, sin revived, and I died" (Rom. iii. 20, vii. 9). The covenant of Sinai and its administration brought out very conspicuously the principles of all moral government.

It was natural in this way for a member of the Hebrew State to apply the principle of retribution very stringently and universally. All evil he knew to be for sin, any evil he concluded to be for some sin. Where there was evil, there must have been sin to bring it forth. Evil was not an accident, nor was it a necessary outcome of the nature of things; it arose from the sinful conduct of men: "Affliction cometh not forth of the dust, neither doth trouble spring out of the ground; but man is born unto trouble,—*i.e.* born so that he acts in such a manner as to bring trouble upon himself,—as the sparks fly upward" (Job v. 6, 7).

This stringent application of the law was more natural in a state of society like that existing in the East than it

would be with us.   There, society is simple, and its elements
more detached from one another.   The tribes live apart,
and draw their subsistence from the soil in the most direct
way.   One class does not depend upon another ; indeed, there
are no classes, no such complex and intricate interweaving
of relations as in modern society.   Hence the incidence of
a calamity was generally direct ; it did not pass through
several sections, or ramify on all sides, affecting most
severely those who were innocent of the evil.   The movements of life were simultaneous, and a calamity was seen
to fall generally where it was deserved.   In this way, not
in Israel only, but throughout the East, the principle of
retributive righteousness was held very firmly : with the
man who doeth well it is well ; with the sinner it is ill.
This was right under the rule of a just God ; for this rule
was particular, and embraced every occurrence.

But even in such an approach towards organised society
as was made on the settlement of the people in Canaan, this
simple faith must have received rude shocks.   In the happy
times of the early monarchy, indeed, when the kingdom of
God was everywhere prosperous, and heathen States on
all sides bowed before it, and when justice was administered
with equal hand, and society still preserved its ancient
moral authority, the principle was receiving continual verification.   But in later times, when great heathen monarchies
rose in the East and trampled the kingdom of God under
their heel, the principle could not but come into danger of
question.   At first, indeed, the principle itself afforded an
explanation of these calamities—they were the just judgment of God upon the sin of the people.   And, so far as
the nation was concerned, the explanation might satisfy the
pious mind.

But the case of individuals was different.   In the
fate that overtook the different classes of the people the
failure of the principle was most signally manifested.
It was the most godly of the nation that suffered the
severest calamities.   The disloyal, ethnicising party, agreeing with their conquerors, or at least submitting to their

idolatries, escaped suffering; while the true theocratic-hearted men, whether those left at home or those carried into exile, were the victims of extreme hardships and indignity, both at the hands of their enemies and from their false brethren. And even in regard to the nation, though the sense of the national sinfulness might compose the mind and humble it more deeply before God, there could not but rise occasionally in the heart thoughts of a disturbing kind. Though the people had deeply sinned, and though their sin was aggravated by the fact that they had sinned against the knowledge of the truth, yet by comparison the people of God, though sinful, stood above those idolatrous powers into whose hand their God had delivered them. Already this thought appears in the prophet Habakkuk, when he compares Israel and the Chaldeans, which latter acknowledge no right but force, and no God but their own right hand. And, further, as time wore on under the sorrows of the Exile, and a new generation arose who had not been guilty of the sins that caused the national dispersion, and yet continued to suffer the penalty of them, there arose not only a sense of paralysis and helplessness, as if they lay under a cruel ban which no conduct of their own could break, but also questionings as to the rectitude of God.

Now, these questionings were met in three ways. First, in the prophet Ezekiel, himself an exile, the old conception of the national unity is subjected to analysis. The unity is resolved and decomposed into individuals, and the relation of the individual to Jehovah is declared to be direct and immediate; the son does not suffer for the sins of the father, nor the individual for the sins of the nation, —the soul that sinneth shall die. This was an emancipation of the individual from the ban of national sin, and a profound advance towards a spiritual religion. Of course, the prophet's conception is true only in the region of spiritual relation to God; externally, the individual may be involved in national calamity, but his own conduct is that which determines God's spiritual relation to him. It may not be quite certain that the teaching of the prophet is presented with all the limitations necessary to it. But great truths are everywhere presented broadly, and the limitations come in their own time.

A second line was that of hope in the future, as we observe it in the second half of Isaiah. The very calamities of the Exile and the apparent dissolution of the nation led to a profounder meditation upon what the people of God was,—what designs Jehovah had in calling it to be His servant,—and a deeper conception of what Jehovah Himself was, and of the scope of His purposes. Thus it became plain what it was to know the true God, and what must yet, in spite of all appearances, be the issue of the fact that there was a true God, and that the true knowledge of Him had been given to Israel, His servant. When we look at the circumstances of the time, at that which was powerful in the world, and at the state of Israel scattered in every land, the faith of this prophet in the destiny of his people becomes one of the most surprising things in the Old Testament. But this was only part of the conception. A judgment was formed of the meaning of the chastisement of the people, and hope found satisfaction in the idea that these chastisements exhausted the nation's sin and atoned for it. The precise form of the prophet's conception, as we saw, is matter of difficulty; but his general idea, that the sorrows and evils of the Exile, falling on some element in the people, removed their guilt, is plain.

But a third line is also followed. In the second half of Isaiah the sorrows of the people are due to their sins. Their sorrows are the expiation of their sins, and the national unity is still firmly retained. But in another book the distinction is drawn between the godly and the sinful among the people, and the question is raised, What is God's purpose in the chastisements which He inflicts upon the godly ? This question is put and answered in the Book of Job. Though Job be an individual, it is scarcely possible to avoid regarding him as a type of the godly portion of the nation; the character as drawn in the book is broader and larger than that of an individual. The answer given to the question is, that the afflictions of the righteous are a trial of their righteousness, and when borne with steadfastness they issue in a higher religious condition and a closer fellowship with God, through a more perfect knowledge of Him. "I had heard of Thee with the hearing of the ear: but now mine eye seeth Thee" (xlii. 5).

These were thoughts which consideration of the sin of the nation and its sufferings suggested. Of equal, if not greater, interest were thoughts suggested to the mind by the sufferings and history of the individual. The general principle, that it was well with the righteous and ill with the sinner, was seen to be broken in upon on two sides. The wicked were many times observed to be prosperous, and, on the other hand, the righteous were plagued every day. Now, relief was sought from this anomaly of God's providence in various ways. First, the pious mind sought to comfort itself and other minds in similar distress, with the consideration that the triumphing of the wicked was brief; it was but a momentary interruption to the general flow of God's providence, which would speedily be removed. This is the consideration in some of the Psalms. Or, at any rate, whether brief or prolonged, it would come to an end. The true relation of the wicked to God would be manifested sometime in this world; they would be destroyed, with terrible tokens of His displeasure. This is taught in other Psalms. In the Book of Job this solution no longer satisfies, it is a solution not found universally valid. The wicked not only pass their life in prosperity, but go down to the grave in peace: "They spend their days in wealth, and in a moment (*i.e.* in peace) go down to the grave. He is borne away to the grave, and men keep watch over his tomb. The clods of the valley are sweet unto him, and all men draw after him, as there were innumerable before him" (chap. xxi. 32). When this point is reached there is evidently only the alternative, to leave the question unsolved, or to project the solution beyond death. Secondly another consideration which afforded comfort to the righteous mind was a deeper analysis which he was able to make of that which was to be called true life and true prosperity and blessedness. In all the passages where the question is raised of the outward prosperity of the wicked, the righteous comforts himself with the thought that he has the blessedness of God's favour,—except in the Book of Job. Even in the xxxviith Psalm the pious mind exhorts others: "Delight thyself in God, and He will give thee the desire of thy heart." Yet in this Psalm this delight in God is not regarded as sufficient or altogether satisfying to the mind; there is the demand also that the anomaly of the prosperity of the wicked should be removed, and that the righteous should be externally prosperous. In Ps. lxxiii. the pious mind dwells more upon its own blessedness in possessing the favour of God: "Nevertheless, I am continually with thee"; but the problem of providence is still found a trouble, which occasions great disquietude to the mind. And a solution of it is anxiously sought. In two remarkable Psalms, however, the xlixth and xviith, the problem seems to have been entirely overcome. In the first of these two passages the author comes forward with a philosophy of the question, and in the other he calmly surveys the prosperity of the wicked almost as if it were a thing of course. This life belongs to the wicked, but there is another which belongs to the righteous. In both these passages the solution seems thrown into the region beyond death. And this is also the solution in the xixth chapter of Job, although the conclusion is there reached in a somewhat different way. One is almost compelled to think that both Ps. xlix. and Ps. xvii. are later than the Book of Job.

8. *Ideas of an After-Life in Psalms xvii., xxxvii., xlix., lxxiii.*

A brief reference may be made to each of these typical passages. The simplest resolution of the problem is that seen in Ps. xxxvii. There the condition of the perplexed mind is not very aggravated, and the relief administered is simple. The difficulty of the prosperous wicked and the afflicted righteous man was felt, but the difficulty was simply a practical one. The fact that many wicked were rich and prosperous, and that righteous men were in distress, led to envy and irritation on the part of the just. And relief is administered in the form of an advice often repeated, with a reference to the great principle of moral government: " Fret not thyself because of evil-doers . . . cease from anger, and be not wrathful . . . fret not thyself in any wise to do evil." And the consideration urged is that the prosperity of the wicked is *brief*; it is an inter-ruption to the general scope of things, but it is speedily overcome by them, and the current flows on in its accustomed channels: " Fret not thyself because of evil-doers : for they shall soon be cut down like the grass . . the wicked plotteth against the just; but the Lord laugheth at him, because He seeth that his day is coming," And, on the other hand: " Trust in the Lord and do good, and thou shalt inherit the earth." The Psalmist satisfies himself and others by affirming the general principle, and by saying that the exception to it is of short duration.

This is a practical solution, sufficient when the evil has gone no further than to occasion discontent. The difficulty that there is exception at all, does not bulk largely in presence of the acknowledged brevity of its duration. The other side of the question, the felicity of the righteous in God, is touched upon, though but slightly ; it is touched upon in the course of an exhortation to keep the faith even amidst present confusions, because out of these the true moral order will speedily arise: " Delight thyself in God, and He shall give thee the desires of thine heart." This is one way of reading the Psalm. It may be questioned, however, whether it is sufficient. It makes the Psalmist's doctrine somewhat abstract, and hardly does justice to the manifest eschatological references in it, as that the meek shall inherit the earth. The ' meek ' is technical language for the godly ; and inherit the earth refers to the final condition, when the kingdom of God has come. The Psalm, therefore, appears to be a real eschatological national Psalm; comforting the righteous with the hope of the nearness of the day of the Lord, and the triumph of the right.

In Ps. lxxiii. an advance is made both in the problem and in the solution. The problem is felt to be more serious. The Psalmist's mind is in a more disquieted condition. The question is no more a mere practical one, but has become a real religious and speculative difficulty, what the writer calls an *amal*, so great that his faith in God was in danger of being overthrown: "As for me, my feet were almost gone. Behold, these are the ungodly, who prosper in the world. . . . Verily I have cleansed my heart in vain." Only after much anxiety had the Psalmist been enabled to return again to peace. In the sanctuary of God a light was shed upon the fate of the wicked which enabled him to walk without stumbling. And just as the problem is more seriously grasped than in Ps. xxxvii., so the solution is also profounder. This solution consists in a contrast between the condition of the wicked and that of the righteous, with the necessary consequences of this condition. The whole is thrown into the form of an analysis of their respective relations to Jehovah. The prosperity of the wicked is a thing merely apparent; it has no substantiality, because of the necessary attitude of Jehovah to sin. The prosperity of the wicked is as "a dream when one awaketh"; so, when "Jehovah awaketh, He will despise their image." The relation of God to them must display itself; and when it displays itself they will perish amidst terrible manifestations of His anger. The righteous, on the other hand, is ever with God: "I am continually with Thee: Thou wilt (or, dost) direct me with thy counsel. . . . It is good for me to draw near unto God . . . all they that go far from Thee shall perish." The essential thing is the relation of men to God. This contains in it the fate of men. And this fate will yet reveal itself.

The Psalmist considers that this fate, so far as the wicked is concerned, will reveal itself in their visible

destruction.   It is, indeed, possible that both in this Psalm
and in Ps. xxxvii. the prophetic conception of the day of
the Lord may be present to the Psalmist's mind, and the
destruction of the wicked be that which will overtake them
on that day.   This is one of the main points, indeed, to
which, in studying these Psalms (xvii., xxxvii., xlix., and
lxxiii.), attention has to be directed   Is the Psalmist
contemplating his own death ? or is he contemplating that
change which will supervene at the coming of God, on the
day of the Lord and the judgment, when the sinners of the
people perish, but the godly pass into the peace of God ?
However this be, the Psalmist sees in the relation of
men to God the certain issue of their history.   The
question is of interest, however, whether he does not
pursue the destiny of the righteous beyond death.   It is
possible that he might have satisfied himself with stating
the general principle, with leading back the destiny of the
righteous and the wicked alike to that which is really essential, their relation to Jehovah ; and assuring himself that the
destiny of all will be determined by this.   And some scholars
understand the words " thou wilt take me to glory " in this
sense ; meaning that God would take the saint to His care
and protection.   But (1) the passages adduced by Ewald
and Riehm to support this sense are hardly in point.   And
(2) the same phrase occurs in Ps. xlix., where it can hardly
refer to protection and providential care in this life.   It is
therefore more natural, I think, to regard the phrase as
having a reference to that which is beyond death; at
any rate, it must have a reference to the eternal relation of
the saint to God.   And the words, " my flesh and heart
faint and fail," not unnaturally refer to death.   The hope
of the believing mind lies in its relation to Jehovah :
" Whom have I in heaven but thee ? and on earth I desire
nought beside Thee."   And his assurance that it shall be
ill with the wicked, is based equally upon their relation
to God.

Ps. xlix. is even more remarkable.   Its reference to the
condition after death, in regard both to the wicked and to

the righteous, can scarcely be mistaken. First, the Psalmist begins with a promise to all men, high and low, rich and poor, that he will clear up a mystery. Whatever his theme and the lesson he is going to teach may be, it is no more a truth which he is wringing out of circumstances; it is no more a thing reached only by a struggle, and attained only as a necessity of faith. It is an objective doctrine, an assured principle. Again, though he speaks in the first person, what he says applies to all men. His proposition is, 'Why should I fear in the evil day?' He has no reason to fear; and this feeling of security arises from his contemplation of mankind. He sees that all men die; this is the universal fate: wise men die, the brutish and foolish perish together. So far as this is concerned, the lot of men is the same, and common to all. Thirdly, the question to which he presents a solution is that of the prosperity and riches of the wicked; and also, on the other hand, the misery of the good, the calamities of the evil day. The riches of the wicked cannot deliver them from death. None can redeem his brother, or give unto God a ransom for him so that he should live and not see the pit. He shall see it; for all men die. And none can carry his riches to the grave with him. Thus the riches and prosperity of the wicked do not avail the wicked; he as well as poorer men comes to the grave at last. Still, if this were all that could be said, there would be an advantage in riches—in this life, at least. If all die, and if this were the end, the wicked, if rich, would be better than the righteous, if poor.

But it is just at the point when death intervenes that the difference appears. Man, being in honour, without understanding is like the beasts that perish. Like sheep, the ungodly are laid in Sheol, and Death shepherds them: their end is to be for the consumption of Sheol. It is probable that there may be a transference to Sheol of that which takes place in the grave. There is no likelihood that the passage teaches that the deceased persons in Sheol are consumed, so as to cease absolutely to subsist. But the point, on the one hand, is that at death the wicked, however prosperous in life, really become the prey of death—they may be compared to the lower creatures; while, on the other hand, the righteous live: "God shall redeem me from the hand of Sheol: for He will take me." Sheol, the place of the dead, is escaped; the hand of God takes the righteous soul across its gulf to Himself.

Now, these points in this passage are remarkable: first, what the author teaches is put forward as an objective principle, no more a mere demand of faith, but a dogma of religious belief; second, it is a doctrine which assumes and is based upon the acknowledged fact that death is universal, wise and foolish alike falling a prey to it; third, the doctrine itself touches the point of the prosperity of the wicked in this life, and the evils that befall the righteous; and, fourth, the solution is thrown entirely into the region beyond death. The destiny of men is looked at as a whole, both in this life and as extending beyond death. And this destiny depends on their relation to God. The wicked's prosperity in this life cannot save him from death; and death to him remains death. The evil are gathered like a flock into Sheol; death is their shepherd. The Old Testament teaches no aggravations in death. Death is itself the highest aggravation,—*i.e.* death and continuance in the state of death, according to the popular notions of what this was,—Death *shepherds* them. But God redeems the righteous from the hand of Sheol; for He takes him.

The phrase 'he will take me' looks like a reminiscence of the language used of Enoch,—"He was not; for God took him" (Gen. v. 24). The date and the authorship of the xlixth Psalm is doubtful. It might be supposed that this remarkable conception would scarcely be early. The passage belongs to the writings of the Wisdom, as the introduction shows. And it is quite conceivable that in certain circles of the people a more advanced faith might have prevailed than was to be found among the bulk of the nation. At all events, the plain sense of a passage ought not to be made dependent on questions of date or authorship.

It is possible that Ps. xvii. may have the same meaning. It draws the same kind of distinction between two classes of men: those whom it calls men of the world, whose portion is in this life, whom God loads with earthly joys and blessings; and another class, whose portion God is Himself. This character of the two classes furnishes the key to their destiny. The Psalmist, though he appears to regard the prosperity of the wicked in life as a thing natural and of course, their portion being in this life, anticipates their destruction eventually at the hand of God. But for himself, he will "see God's face in righteousness." The language in which the Psalmist expresses his hope is remarkable, though of somewhat uncertain meaning: "I shall behold Thy face in righteousness: when I awake, I shall be satisfied with Thine image." The phrase 'in righteousness' might mean 'through righteousness,' more probably 'in the element of righteousness.' The expression 'thine image,' תְּמוּנָתֶךָ, is remarkable. The word is used to express what we call the species or genus of a thing: "Thou shalt not make unto thee any generic likeness of anything in the heavens" (Ex. xx. 4). When such a thing is seen, the beholder must be face to face with it—in its very presence, and looking on it. The language is thus in favour of an immediate vision of God; as in Deuteronony it is denied that any 'ת of God was seen in His manifestations of Himself on earth (Ex. iv. 12). In the xixth chapter of Job, too, the assurance of Job, that he shall see God, is one having reference to a state after death.

If this sense be adopted, then the expression 'when I awake' would have a quite natural sense, though a very large one. It is very improbable that the word should mean merely 'when I awake out of sleep in the morning,' or 'every morning'; as if the meaning were that each morning, as soon as consciousness returned, his joy in God would return; and he would realise God's image, and be satisfied with it. Neither is the sense very natural, 'when I awake out of this night of darkness and calamity now lying on me, in the morning of prosperity' (Riehm). On the other hand, if the word refer to the history

30

of man after death, the passage seems to go further than even Ps. xlix., and to refer to the awakening out of death, when God has brought in His perfect kingdom, which departed saints would live again to share. This doctrine is certainly found in Daniel; and from the date of that book onward it is the faith, at least, of the Pharisees. It is quite probable that it may have been cherished in Israel long before the age of Daniel, if that book be of the late date to which it is now usually assigned. It is certainly also found in Isa. xxvi. 19—a passage the age of which is very obscure—" Thy dead shall live, my dead ones shall arise. Awake and cry for joy, ye dwellers in the dust: for a dew of light is thy dew, and the earth shall bring forth the dead." The heading of the present Psalm ascribes it to David. Such headings are not very good evidence; though, being in the first book, this Psalm is probably not a very late one. But again our duty is to accept the natural sense of words, leaving questions of date and authorship to take care of themselves.

9. *The Idea of an After-Life in Job.*

In endeavouring to ascertain what hopes of immortality were entertained by Old Testament saints, how these hopes arose, and on what they were grounded, special attention must be given to the Book of Job. Something might be said even for the propriety of beginning with it. For the opinion that once prevailed, that the book was of Arabic origin, or, at least, not of native Israelitish extraction, is now altogether obsolete. The work has every mark of a genuine Jewish authorship. And though the belief that once also held the field regarding the extreme antiquity of the book cannot now be maintained in face of modern criticism, yet even if we admit the actual authorship to be pretty late, the scene and the circumstances are those of very early times. Job himself is represented as living in the patriarchal age; and it is the author's aim to exhibit events and opinions as they existed then. It is, no doubt, quite possible that the beliefs and the condition of society in his own days may sometimes form the background of his picture, or even give some of its colour to the light which he throws over it. But probably such a thing, if it be the case, will very little interfere with the truth of the representation of the ideas; for we find substantially the same views expressed on this subject in such Psalms as the xvith and xviith, and in the very late prophet Malachi. It is difficult to know how far to distinguish between the author of Job and his hero. For, on the one hand, as we must take very much of the speeches and opinions put into the mouths of Job and his friends to be due altogether to the author, and certainly to be sympathised with by him, while yet, on the other, he shows very great power in giving objectivity to his personages and maintaining very distinctly their individualities, it will always remain somewhat doubtful how far he shared in the views which he makes his characters express.

In order to realise fully the meaning of the passages bearing on this subject in Job, it will be of use to refer to the general contents and the problem of the book.

(1) As it now lies before us, the book consists of five parts. First, the prologue, in prose, chaps. i.–ii. This describes in rapid and dramatic steps the history of Job, his piety and the prosperity and greatness corresponding to it; then how his life is drawn in under the operation of the trying, sifting providence of God, through the suspicions suggested by the Satan, the minister of God's providence in this aspect of it, that his godliness is but selfish (" *Does Job serve God for nought ?* "), and only the natural return for the unexampled prosperity bestowed on him. If stripped of his prosperity, he will renounce God to His face. These suspicions bring down two severe calamities on Job, one depriving him of all external blessings, children and possessions alike; and the other throwing the man himself under a loathsome and painful malady. In spite of these afflictions, Job retains his integrity, and imputes no wrong to God. Then the advent of Job's three friends

is described, Eliphaz the Temanite, Bildad the Shuhite, and Zophar the Naamathite, who, having heard of Job's calamities, came to condole with him.

Second, the body of the book, in poetry, chaps. iii.–xxxi., containing a series of speeches in which the problems of Job's afflictions and the relation of external evil to the righteousness of God and the conduct of men are brilliantly discussed. This part is divided into three cycles, each containing six speeches, one by Job and one by each of the friends (chaps. iii.–xiv., chaps. xv.–xxi., and chaps. xxii.–xxxi.), although in the last cycle the third speaker, Zophar, fails to answer. Job, having driven his opponents from the field, carries his reply through a series of discourses, in which he dwells in pathetic words upon his early prosperity, contrasting with it his present misery and humiliation. He ends with a solemn repudiation of all the offences that had been insinuated or might be suggested against him, and with a challenge to the Almighty to appear and put His hand to the charge which He had against him, and for which He afflicted him.

Third, a youthful bystander named Elihu, the representative of a younger generation, who had been a silent listener to the debate, now intervenes, and expresses his dissatisfaction with the manner in which both Job and his friends had conducted the case, and offers what is scarcely to be called a new solution of the question, but some arguments which the friends had overlooked, and which ought to have put Job to silence (chaps. xxxii.–xxxvii.).

Fourth, in answer to Job's repeated demands that God would appear and solve the riddle of his life, the Lord answers Job out of the whirlwind. The Divine Speaker does not condescend to refer to Job's individual problem, but in a series of ironical interrogations asks him, as he thinks himself capable of fathoming all things, to expound the mysteries of the origin and subsistence of the world, the phenomena of the atmosphere, the instincts of the creatures that inhabit the desert; and, as he judges God's conduct of the world amiss, he is invited to seize the reins himself and gird him

with the Divine thunder and quell the rebellious forces of
evil in the universe, chaps. xxxviii.–xlii. 6. Job is humbled
and abashed, and lays his hand upon his mouth, and
repents his hasty words in dust and ashes. No solution
of his problem is vouchsafed ; but God Himself effects that
which neither the man's own thoughts of God nor the
representations of his friends could accomplish ; the Divine
Speaker but repeats in another form what the friends had
said and what Job had said in a sublimer way, but now
it is God who speaks. Job had heard of Him with the
hearing of the ear without effect; now his eye sees Him,
and he abhors himself, and repents in dust and ashes.
This is the profoundest religious depth reached in the book.

Then, fifth, comes the epilogue, also in prose, chap. xlii.
7–17, which describes Job's restoration to a prosperity
double that of his former estate, his family felicity, and
long life.

(2) If, now, we pass from this outline of the contents
of the book to inquire what is the idea of the book or
the design of it, we must not expect to find this in
any particular part of the poem, but partly in the sentiments uttered especially by Job, partly in the history
of mind through which he is made to pass, and partly in
the author's own contributions, the prologue and epilogue.
Job is unquestionably the hero of the work ; and in the
ideas which he expresses, and the history through which
he passes, taken together, we may assume that we find the
author speaking and teaching. The discussion of the question of the meaning of suffering, between Job and his friends,
occupies by far the largest part of the book ; and in the
direction which the author causes this discussion to take,
we may see revealed the main didactic purpose of the
book. When the three friends, the representatives of
former theories of providence and of previous views in
regard to the meaning of evil and the calamities which
befall men, are reduced to silence, and driven off the field
by Job, we may be certain that it was the author's purpose
to discredit the ideas which they represent. Job himself

offers no positive contribution to the doctrine of evil; his position is negative, and merely antagonistic to that of the friends. But this negative position, victoriously maintained by him, has the effect of clearing the ground; and the author himself supplies in the prologue the positive truth, where he communicates the real explanation of his hero's calamities, and teaches that they were a trial of his righteousness. It was, therefore, the author's purpose in his work to widen men's views of the providence of God, and set before them a new view of suffering. This may be considered the first great object of the book.

This purpose, however, was in all probability no mere theoretical one, but subordinate to some wider practical design. No Hebrew writer is merely a poet or a thinker. He is always a teacher. He has men before him in their relations to God. And it is not usually men in their individual relations, but as members of the family of Israel, the people of God. Consequently, it is scarcely to be doubted that the book has a national scope. The author considered his new truth regarding the meaning of affliction as of national interest, and to be the truth needful for the heart of his people in their circumstances. But the teaching of the book is only half its contents. It contains a history, and this history furnishes the profoundest lesson to be learned. It exhibits deep and inexplicable affliction, a great moral conflict, and a victory. The author meant the history which he exhibits and his new truth to inspire new conduct and new faith, and to lead to a new issue in the national fortunes. In Job's sufferings, undeserved and inexplicable to him, yet capable of an explanation most consistent with the goodness and faithfulness of God, and casting honour upon His steadfast servants; in his despair, bordering on unbelief, at last overcome; and in the happy issue of his afflictions,—in all this Israel should see itself, and from the sight take courage and forecast its own history. Job, however, is scarcely to be considered Israel, the righteous servant under a feigned name; he is no mere parable, though such a view is as early as the Talmud.

Without doubt, there is a connection between the second half of Isaiah and the Book of Job. The linguistic affinities are manifest. And in both the problem is the same, the sufferings of the righteous servant of the Lord. But 'My servant Job' is scarcely the same as 'My righteous servant' in Isaiah, although in Job there may be national allusion. The solution of the problem differs in the two. In Job, sufferings are a trial of faith which, successfully borne, will issue in restoration. In Isaiah they are vicarious, borne by one element in the nation in behalf of the whole, and issuing in the national redemption. Two such solutions can scarcely be entirely contemporaneous. That of Isaiah is the profounder truth, and may be later. But Job is hardly to be identified with the 'servant of the Lord.' It is the elements of reality that lie in the tradition of Job that make him of significance to Israel. It is these elements of reality common to him with Israel in affliction, common even to him with humanity as a whole, confined within the straitened limits set by its own ignorance, wounded to death by the mysterious sorrows of life, tormented by the uncertainty whether its cry finds an entrance into God's ear, alarmed by the irreconcilable discrepancies which it seems to discover between its necessary thoughts of Him and its experience of Him in His providence, and faint with longing that it might come unto His place and behold Him, not girt with majesty, but in human form, as one looketh upon his fellow,—it is these elements of truth that made the history of Job instructive to Israel in the times of affliction when it was set before them, and to men in all ages.

(3) Two threads, therefore, requiring to be followed, run through the book. One, the discussion of the problem of evil between Job and his friends; the other, the varying attitude of Job's mind towards heaven,—the first being subordinate to the second, and helping to determine it. Both Job and his friends advance to the discussion of his sufferings and of the problem of evil, ignorant of the true cause of his calamities, as that is laid before us in the

prologue,—Job strong in his sense of innocence, and the friends armed with their theory of the righteousness of God, who giveth to every man according to his works.

The principle with which the three friends came to the consideration of Job's calamities was the principle that calamity is the result of evil-doing, as on the other hand prosperity is the reward of righteousness. Suffering is not an accident or a spontaneous growth of the soil: man is born unto trouble as the sparks fly upward; there is in human life a tendency to do evil, which draws down on men the chastisement of Heaven. The form in which the principle is enunciated by Eliphaz, from whom the other speakers take their cue, is this: where there is suffering there has been sin in the sufferer; not necessarily deadly sin, though where the suffering is great the sin must have been heinous. Not suffering, however, in itself, but the effect of it on the sufferer, is what affords a key to his fundamental character. Suffering is not always punitive; it is far oftener disciplinary, designed to wean the man, who is good though still a sinner, from his sin. If he sees in his suffering the monition of God, and turns from his evil, his future shall be rich in peace and happiness,—so happy is the man whom God corrects, and who despises not the chastening of the Almighty. His latter estate shall be more prosperous than his first. If he murmurs or resists, he can only continue under the multiplying chastisement which his impenitence will provoke. For "irritation killeth the foolish man, and indignation slayeth the silly one" (v. 2).

Now this general idea is the fundamental principle of moral government, the expression of the natural conscience, —a principle common more or less to all peoples, though perhaps more prominent in the Shemitic mind because all ideas are more prominent and simple there,—not suggested to Israel first by the law, but found and adopted by the law, although it may be sharpened by it. It is the fundamental idea of prophecy no less than of the law; and, if possible, of the wisdom or philosophy of the Hebrews more

than of either.   The friends did not err in laying down
this general principle, they erred in supposing it a principle
that would cover the wide providence of God.

Job agreed with his friends that afflictions came directly
from the hand of God, and also that God afflicted those
whom He held guilty of sins.   But his conscience denied
the imputation of guilt, whether insinuated by his friends
or implied in God's chastisement of him.   Hence he was
driven to conclude that God was unjust; that He sought
occasions against him, and perverted his right.   The position
of Job appeared to them nothing else but impiety, as it came
very near being; while theirs was to him mere falsehood,
and the special pleading of sycophants in behalf of God,
because He was the stronger.   Within these two iron walls
debate moves with much brilliancy, if not strictly of
argument, at least of illustration.   The progress of the
argument is not important to us meantime, the other
thing, namely, the progress of Job's mind in his relation
to heaven, being the thing in which for our present purpose
we are interested.   There is one remark only which may
be made.   To a reader of the poem now it appears strange
that both parties were so entangled in the meshes of their
preconceptions regarding God as to be unable to break
through to broader views.   The friends, while maintaining
their position that injustice on the part of God is inconceivable, might have given its due weight to the persistent
testimony of Job's conscience as that behind which it is
impossible to go.   They might have found refuge in the
reflection that there might be something inexplicable in
the ways of God, and that affliction might have some other
meaning than to punish the sinner, or even to wean him
from his sin.   And Job, while maintaining his innocence
from actual and overt sins, might have bowed beneath the
rod of God, and confessed that there was such sinfulness in
every human life as to account for the severest chastisement from heaven, or, at least, have stopped short of
charging God foolishly.   Such a position would certainly
be taken up by an afflicted saint now; and such an explana-

tion of his suffering would suggest itself to the sufferer, even though it might be in truth a false explanation.

But perhaps all this was designed on the part of the author. The rôle which he had reserved for himself was to teach the truth on the question in dispute, and he accomplishes this by allowing his performers to push their false principles to their proper extreme. The friends of Job were religious Orientals, men to whom God was a Being in immediate contact with the world and life, effecting all things with no intervention of second causes; men to whom the idea of second causes was unknown, on whom science had not yet begun to dawn, nor the conception of a Divine scheme pursuing a distant end by complicated means, in which the individual's interest may suffer for the larger good. The broad sympathies of the author and his sense of the truth lying in the theory of the friends, are seen in the scope which he allows them, in the richness of the thought and the splendid luxuriance of the imagery—drawn from revelation, from the immemorial consent of mankind, the testimony of the living conscience, and the observation of life—with which he makes them clothe their views. He felt it needful to make a departure from a position too narrow to confine the providence of God within; but he was not unmindful of the elements of truth in the theory which he was departing from, and, while showing its insufficiency, he sets it forth in its most brilliant form.

Then in regard to the position maintained by Job, that God was unjust—the extravagance of his assertions was occasioned mainly by the extreme position of his friends, which left no room for his conscious innocence along with the rectitude of God. Again, the poet's purpose, as the prologue shows, was to teach that afflictions may fall on a man out of all connection with any offence of his own, and merely as a trial of his righteousness. Hence he allows Job, as by a true instinct with respect to the nature of his sufferings, to repudiate all connection between them and sin in himself. And, further, the severe conflict into which the suspicions of the Satan brought Job could not be exhibited without pushing him to the verge of ungodliness. But in all this the poet is true to the conditions of his time. Under the Old Covenant the sense of sin was less deep than it is now. In the East, too, and especially in the desert, men speak boldly of God. Such a creation as Job would be an anomaly in Christian drama. But nothing would be more false than to judge the poet's creation from our later point of view, according to a more developed sense of sin and a deeper reverence for God than belonged to antiquity. It is in complete contradiction to the idea of the book to assume, as Hengstenberg, for example, does, that Job's spiritual pride was just the cause of his afflictions, and the root of bitterness in him which must be killed down ere he could become a true saint. The fundamental idea, on the contrary, is that Job before his afflictions was a true saint. This is testified by God Himself, and is the radical idea of the author in the prologue, and the fundamental conception of the drama. Job's complaints, indeed, proved that he was not perfect or sinless. But this was never supposed. Yet it was not his sin that caused his afflictions. They were the trial of his faith, which, maintaining itself in spite of them, and becoming stronger through them, was rewarded with a higher felicity.

Now it is this inner movement of the drama that is of interest to us here—not the outward controversy between Job and his friends regarding evil, but the successive attitudes taken by Job's mind towards God. This is of extreme interest in the general, and it is of more interest in the question with which we are immediately concerned.

(4) It is scarcely necessary to call attention again to the *character* which the book has in common with all other parts of the Old Testament—its *religious* character, the word being used in the strict sense. The poem is not philosophic or moral. Job in all his utterances starts from himself, from his own case and experience, and not from any aspect which men or the world without him presented. He at times includes others, even all mankind,

in his misery and trial; he had seen or heard of their straits and sorrows too, and he draws the colours with which he paints his own misery sometimes from the common sorrows of the race. But his position is properly personal first; what draws his attention to the world and the relations of God to it is his own case. A jar had occurred there, a displacement of his own relations to God. Formerly, he had been at peace with God; suddenly, through a single step of reasoning, his sufferings, he beholds God in anger with him. How far his belief that God was angry with him, as he concluded He was from the construction he put upon his sufferings, alienated his mind from God, is not easy always to perceive. That his sufferings would perfectly alienate his mind was the prediction of the Satan, and his hope in plaguing him. He was disappointed. But the very problem of the book is this ultimate condition which Job's heart will settle into; and what the chief part of it is occupied in showing is the ever-varying, wavering attitude of the sufferer's spirit, sometimes standing firm and sometimes swaying as if it would altogether fall, until at last it settles into a composure that nothing can shake.

Hence the greater part of Job's speeches are monologue, or speech to One absent and resolutely refusing to hear. The friends are present, but their presence is subordinate. Their shallow theories occasionally irritate and provoke a sarcasm: *Ye are the people, and wisdom will die with you*; their perverse attempts at consolation sometimes increase the solitude and wretchedness of the sufferer, and he pathetically beseeches them to be silent: *Miserable comforters are all of you; would that ye were silent, and it should be your wisdom.* But they are too insignificant to detain him, he has to do with Another; and their words form but starting-points from which the spirit begins its appeals to Him. Like one sick who has been drawn into half-consciousness by the entrance of some visitor, and utters some words of apparent recognition, but straightway relapses and soliloquises with himself, or speaks to someone absent who is thought near, Job is for a moment drawn into controversy as each new comforter delivers himself of his solution of the mystery of the universe; but speedily he turns from them, or, though before him, they make no impression on his eye, which is fascinated by the awful form of Another, or strained so as to pierce the deepest heavens that it might come to His place. And thus to Him he pours out his heart, pleading his former relation of love to Him: *Oh, that I were as in months past!*; seeking to startle Him with the certain consequences of his treatment: *Thou wilt seek me, but I shall be gone*; calling passionately that He would come and solve the mystery of his troubles, and sinking into hopelessness when He refuses to appear or to hear him; provoked apparently by this obstinate silence, and flinging indignant words against Him who uses His omnipotent power to crush a moth; looking all around and proclaiming all on earth to be impenetrable darkness; and yet again, in the midst of all this darkness and confusion, groping his way back to Him, like a child who has fled in tears and anger from the hand of a chastening father, sure that He is his Redeemer and will yet show that He is this, and will return to him and yearn over the work of His own hands. It is needful to understand the exact mental condition out of which the thoughts of immortality spring, in order to estimate properly the thoughts themselves. And nothing is further from the truth than to regard the hopes of immortality expressed in Job as the results of philosophical reasoning. They are the broken cries, after the light of God's face, of one to whom around God the clouds and darkness seem to have immovably settled.

Before the friends' arrival, we find only one allusion from Job to the other world: "Naked came I out of my mother's womb, and naked shall I return thither" (i. 21)— an allusion that indicates nothing but the forced composure with which he looked forward to it. But when the friends arrived, their amazement and dumb sympathy, combined with his protracted anguish and those regrets which he many times utters so pathetically over a too brief life,— all this made him break out in the bitter lamentations of

chap. iii., where we have from him a full picture of the
state of the dead. It is curious that his pictures vary
with the point of view from which they are seen. Chap.
iii. is a paroxysm of human sorrow, which the sight of
sympathising men brought upon him. And from the side
of the wretchedness of human life, at least such as his, the
state of the dead seems the profoundest blessedness :

" Why died I not from the womb ?
  Coming out of the womb, why gave I not up the ghost ?
  Why did the knees hold me up ?
  And the breasts that I should suck ?
  For now should I have lain down and been quiet ;
  I should have slept : then would there have been rest to me
  With kings and counsellors of the earth,
  Who built desolate places for themselves ;
  Or with princes who had gold,
  Who filled their houses with silver :
  Or as a hidden untimely birth, I should not be ;
  As infants that never saw light.
  There the wicked cease from troubling ;
  And there the weary are at rest.
  The prisoners rest together ;
  They hear not the taskmaster's voice.
  The small and great are there alike ;
  And the servant is free from his master " (iii. 11-19).

That which makes misery and sorrow overpowering is
not the pure evil, but that element of tenderness which the
memory of former things mixes with it. Had he not been
cruelly cared for, he would have died ; and the stillness and
majesty of death ravish his sight and carry him away.
His words become calm, and he forgets his anguish,
thinking himself one of the happy dead. That rest which
he would have enjoyed is unbroken and profound like
deep sleep ; royal and in state ; princely and with the
rich of the earth ; broken by no sharp pains, but unconscious and still as the unmoved faces of infants born before
their time ; common to all, the evil and the good, the
wicked ceasing their unquiet life of evil, and the weary
being at rest. The two ideas most prominent in this picture
of the condition of the dead are the splendour and pomp

of death, where all the great who played famous parts in life congregate, and even the meaner men are admitted to their fellowship; and the freedom and the painlessness of it, for it is the common refuge of all who are wretched here. These two things are in contrast with the squalor and degradation of Job's present condition, and with the unbearable anguish of his disease. All that can fairly be inferred from such a passage is the belief in the existence of a place of the dead, where good and evil alike are assembled; but the colours in which it is painted are borrowed largely from the grave, and the condition of the body in death.

With reference to the problem of the book, it may be asked: Does Job's mind show any progress in this chapter towards disowning God to His face? And it may be replied that it does. For where he alludes to God, the nature of his allusion seems to show the beginnings at least of alienation; he will not name Him, but speaks indirectly, as of one distant, *Why gives He light to him that is in misery?* And though it is chiefly an outburst of pure human grief that we have in chap. iii., and while it might be admitted to be excessive and therefore sinful, without being a sin of the kind called disowning God to His face,—as it can hardly be contended that the similar complaint of Jeremiah, who uses almost the same words, formed a sin of that kind; yet it is not improbable that the whole complaints are tinged with that same religious feeling which appears in the only allusion to God in the chapter.

The next allusion to the place or state of the dead adds nothing to that already given, except that the brevity of this life is lamented and contrasted with the unalterable condition of death:

" My days have been swifter than a weaver's shuttle,
And are spent without hope. . . .
The cloud consumes and is gone,
So he that goeth down to Sheol shall come up no more.
He shall not return again to his house,
And his place shall know him no more" (vii. 6).

The sleep of death is unbroken and eternal. No doubt human feeling and regret might utter such words even still, having in view the present manner of earthly life to which none shall ever return. And it may be difficult to infer with certainty from such language anything about Job's belief. Yet the language here and in chap. xiv. :

> "Till the heavens be no more, they shall not awake,
> Nor be roused out of their sleep,"

hardly permits us to suppose that the hope of a resurrection was an element of his ordinary faith.

Again, in the chapters from which these passages are taken, the progress of his mind in alienation from God is decided. He has no hesitation in declaring the treatment meted out to him to be injurious and unjust, and demands of the friends whether he be not able to say whether he be justly afflicted or no :

> "Is there falsehood in my tongue?
> Cannot my taste discern what is perverse?"

And then he passes on to a description of the sad condition both of all men and of himself in particular, rising into a sarcastic remonstrance with Heaven over its treatment of him, as if he was and must be coerced :

> "Am I a sea, or a monster of the sea,
> That Thou settest a watch over me?"

In his indignant bitterness he travesties the viiith Psalm to express the Deity's incessant occupation with him :

> "What is man, that Thou shouldst magnify him,
> And set Thy thoughts upon him?
> That Thou shouldst visit him every morning,
> And try him every moment?
> How long wilt Thou not look away from me?"

He even ventures, with incredible boldness, to ask the Almighty, supposing he had sinned, how such a thing could affect Him, and to reproach Him with His too watchful scrutiny of wretched men :

> " If I have sinned, what do I unto Thee,
> Thou observer of men ?
> And why wilt Thou not pardon my transgression,
> And take away mine iniquity ? "

Here we have the beginning of a singular distinction
which the mind of Job begins to draw in the Divine Being.
There is an external God and there is a hidden God ; the
one but an arbitrary Omnipotence, the other the Father of
Mercies. To the endless harpings of the three, who were
' the people,' that God was just, Job ironically replies : Of
course He is, *I know that it is so* ; because no one can
vindicate his right against omnipotence :

> " How can a man be just with God ?
> If he should desire to contend with Him,
> He could not answer Him one of a thousand.
> Wise in heart, and strong in power :
> Who can oppose Him and prosper ? . . .
> Though I were righteous, my mouth would condemn me :
> Though innocent, it would pervert my cause.
> I am innocent ! "

But though he is innocent, this arbitrary Might has determined to hold him guilty :

> " I know Thou wilt not hold me innocent.
> I have to be guilty ; why then should I weary myself in vain ?
> Though I wash myself with snow,
> And cleanse my hands with lye ;
> Thou wilt plunge me into the ditch,
> And mine own clothes shall abhor me."

That God holds him guilty is the interpretation put by Job
upon his afflictions :

> " I will speak in the bitterness of my soul.
> I will say unto God, Do not hold me guilty ;
> Show me wherefore Thou contendest with me."

And we might almost imagine that the Satan's prediction
had come true, and that Job had renounced God to His
face, when he proclaims the government of the world
to be indiscriminately cruel :

> " He destroys the righteous and the wicked.
> When the scourge slays suddenly,
> He mocks at the distress of the innocent " ;

31

or when, in a passage in which he reaches the climax of
extravagance, he asserts in the face of God that all the
skill and care and seeming affection which He lavished on
his creation and early years, were but in order that He
might the more ingeniously torture him as now He does:

> " Didst not Thou make me flow as milk,
>   And thicken me like the curd ?
> Clothe me with skin and flesh,
>   With bones and sinews interweave me.
> Life and favour Thou didst grant me,
>   And Thy providence preserved my spirit.
> Yet these things Thou didst hide in Thy heart ;
>   I know that this was in Thy mind :
> If I sinned, Thou wouldst observe me,
>   And wouldst not absolve me of my sin.
> Were I wicked, woe unto me ;
>   Were I righteous, I must not lift up my head.
> Filled with shame, and the sight of my misery,
>   Should I lift it up, Thou wouldst hunt me like a lion,
>   And show Thy wonderful power upon me " (x. 10–16).

Yet even here, where he reaches perhaps the highest point
of alienation to which he comes, there is no direct renuncia-
tion of God.   For even amidst these loud and bitter cries
there are heard undertones of supplication to the Unseen
God, the ancient God of his former days, the real God who
is behind this menacing angry form that now pursues him:—
" Thou wilt seek me, but I shall be no more "; " Thy hands
have fashioned me and made me, and yet Thou dost destroy
me "; " Oh that a clean might come out of an unclean ";
" and dost Thou open Thine eyes upon such a one, and
bringest me into judgment with Thee ? " (vii. 21, x. 8,
xiv. 3, 4).

The thoughts that had taken complete possession of
Job's mind were that his afflictions were direct inflictions
on him by God in anger, and that the afflictions were of
such a kind that they must very speedily prove final.
God's anger would pursue him, he saw well, even to the
grave.   We must consider him a man in middle life, older,
perhaps, than some of the younger of his comforters, yet
much younger than the eldest of them.   And thus he saw

himself cut off in the midst of his days. And over the grave absolute darkness hung before him. It was:

> " A land of darkness and of death shade ;
> A land of gloom, like the thick darkness ;
> Of death shade, and disorder,
> Where the light is as thick darkness " (x. 21, 22).

Many times all these thoughts gather together and press upon him, and he falls into a paroxysm of sorrow. Yet it is out of these very paroxysms that new and bolder thoughts spring, and that new hopes are engendered, which, if they are transient, yet by their momentary glory still the wild motion of the heart and soften the feelings towards Heaven.

One of the most remarkable of these is in chap. xiv. There he breaks into a sorrowful wail over the wretchedness of man, and his inherent weakness,—man born of woman is of few days and full of trouble,—and the rigid treatment of him by God—" Oh that a clean might come out of an unclean ; and dost Thou open Thine eyes upon such a one?"; and over the complete extinction of his life in death, as complete as that of the waters which the sun sucks out of the pool, more to be lamented in this than are the trees which, if cut down, will sprout again. The very extremity of the misery of man, so awfully realised in himself, forces into his mind the thought that there might be another life; that when God's anger was passed, which now consumed him, He might remember His creature and awake him to life and blessedness : " Oh that Thou wouldst hide me in Sheol; that Thou wouldst appoint me a set time and remember me " (xiv. 13). Yet the thought is but a momentary flash of light, serving only to show the darkness, and in a moment is swallowed up by the gloom about him,—" if a man die, shall he live again ? " Still the phantom, for he will not believe it to be quite a phantom, is too glorious to lose sight of, and he will, in spite of reason and experience, pursue it,—" All the days of my appointed time would I wait till my change came, Thou wouldst call, and I would answer ; Thou wouldst yearn after the work of Thy hands." Such would be the meeting of the creature and his reconciled Creator, whose anger had turned away.

The thought that dawns upon Job here is certainly that of a new life in the body; for it is to this alone that the rising objection applies: If a man die, shall he live again ? And however momentary the thought be, yet it is once started. And it is certainly probable that the author of the passage was himself not unfamiliar with such thoughts. Else he could hardly have let his hero give expression to them. But what is always to be observed is the ground on which the hope of resurrection or any hope is founded; it is the complete reconciliation and reunion of the creature with God. Here there is estrangement; in Sheol the separation is wider. As the xlixth Psalm expresses it, in this brief life upon the earth the living man is a sojourner, a guest with the living God; but his visit ends, and he departs at death. But what both the creature and the Creator yearn for is complete fellowship—that their joy may be full; and this fellowship must be of the whole person—body and spirit.

Between this passage and the even more remarkable one in chap. xix. there is a step which cannot be omitted. In chap. xiv. the hope of meeting God can hardly sustain itself at all. It is little but a rainbow that melts again into the dark cloud. The hope consists of two elements, the overpassing of God's anger, and the reunion of the creature with Him in blessedness, which depends on that. But this overpassing of His anger, how shall it be hoped for ? Job's solution of this comes from that double representation of God which has been alluded to. The outer God is pursuing him, but the Unseen heart of God sympathises with him. The outer God holds him guilty, but the consciousness of God knows his innocence. He appeals from God to God. He asks God to procure the recognition of his innocence with God. The outer God—which is God in that aspect of Him that is the cause of Job's sorrows—will pursue him to death, and his blood will lie upon the earth. But he can appeal to the earth not to cover it, as

innocent blood, till it be avenged; and that there is an
Avenger in heaven, he knows:

> " My face is inflamed with weeping,
> And a shadow of death is on my eyes;
> Although no violence is in my hands,
> And my prayer is pure.
> Oh earth, cover not thou my blood,
> And let my cry have no resting-place.
> Even now, behold, my witness is in heaven,
> And He who can attest me is on high.
> My mockers are my friends,
> My eye droppeth unto God;
> That He would do justice to a man with God,
> And between a man and his fellows !
>
> .   .   .   .
>
> Give a pledge, I pray Thee,
> Be thou my surety with Thyself " (xvi. 16, xvii. 3).

He weepingly implores God to do him justice with God; to
procure that God would acknowledge his innocence. He
prays God to give him a pledge that He will use means
with God that his righteousness be confessed.

This is one of the most singular passages in the book.
Job is not able to present to himself otherwise these two
things, namely, the thought that his afflictions are proof of
God's anger, and show that God holds him guilty; and his
own consciousness of his innocence, and assurance that
God is also aware of it. This was the only way in which
an Oriental mind could express such an idea. We take
refuge in a scheme of providence, a great general plan, the
particular developments of which do not express the mind
of God towards individuals. But to the Oriental, God
was present in each event; and each event befalling the
individual expressed God's feeling towards him.

The other expression of confidence in chap. xix. is
reached in the same way. It follows that hardest of
passages in which Bildad, with concealed insinuations,
pictured the awful fate of the sinner. Under his terrible
picture he wrote, *These are the habitations of the wicked*, and
held it up before Job. It was meant for him. The terrible
distemper, " the first-born of death," which consumes the

sinner's limbs, was too plain an allusion to his leprosy to
be mistaken by him.   The brimstone that burns up the
sinner's habitation is also the fire of God that fell on Job's
cattle.   The tree, withered at the roots and cut down,
reminds Job too easily of his own wasted state, and the sad
calamities that had lopped off his children from him.   He
is the sinner.   To every sentence of his oration Bildad adds
' Thou art the man.'

Against this application Job's whole soul protests and
maintains his innocence.   But while maintaining it he
realises with new distinctness his dreary isolation, God
and men having alike turned against him; which he
describes in most pathetic words.   Yet so profound and
unalterable is his conviction of his innocence, that as with
a desperate leap out of the depth of his misery he rises to
the assurance that his innocence shall yet be revealed, that
God will publicly declare it, and that he himself shall hear
the declaration and see the Redeemer that makes it.   The
joyful anticipation of this overcomes him, and he faints
with longing—" My reins are consumed within me."

It is the lowest ebb of sorrow that precedes the flow
of this full tide of faith.   God not only afflicted him with
trouble, but removed from him all human sympathy.   There
is something more breaking to the heart in the turning
away of men from us, than in the acutest pain.   It crushes
us quite.   We steel ourselves against it for a time, and rise
in bitterness to it and resentment.   But it breaks us at
last, and we soften and are utterly crushed.   And this
seems the way, whether men frown on us with justice or
no.   So there comes on Job, when he sets before himself
his complete casting off by men, by his friends and his
household, and even by the little children who mocked his
attempts to rise from the ground, a complete breakdown,
and he bursts into that most touching of all his cries :
" *Pity me, O my friends !   Why do ye persecute me like God ?* "
But his appeal is vain.   Those Pharisaic muscles will not
move.   The rigidity of that religious decorum no human feeling shall break.   Secure as they are in their principles and

their piety, their countenance shows but austere reprobation of their wicked friend. They will be more austere because he is their friend, and because they feel it a sacrifice to be austere. And, looking into their hard eyes and set faces, Job reads only their unalterable verdict against him. So he turns away from them, and the desire suddenly seizes him to make his appeal to posterity, to record in writing his protestation of his innocence, to grave it in the rock that it might last for ever, and that all generations to the end of time might read, when they listened to his story, the solemn denial of his guilt. "Oh that my words were written, that they were graved upon a book! That they were inscribed with an iron pen and lead in the rock for ever!" The words are not the words about his Redeemer which follow, but his protestation of his innocence.

But if that were possible, how small a thing it would after all be! He needs more, and shall have more. His invincible confidence in his innocence makes him feel that behind all the darkness there looks a face that shines upon him. There is a living God who knows his innocence, who shall yet declare it to him, to men, publicly, visibly,—whom his eyes shall see. That life behind lived in God's fellowship cannot go for nothing,—these endearments are not for ever broken off. "I know that my Redeemer is living: whom I shall see, and mine eyes shall behold Him; and my reins faint within me."

The passage is of much difficulty. The main points are these :—ver. 25, "But I know that my Redeemer liveth, and in after time, as an afterman, will stand upon the earth." Job dies under his afflictions, unacknowledged and held guilty; but there is one that liveth, who stands in such a relation to him that he calls him his Redeemer. Whether גֹּאֵל mean next of kin, *i.e.* one on whom as next of kin it devolves to take up his cause and right it, or more generally one who will right him and deliver him from the wrongs which he suffers, matters very little. The thing is that there is such a Deliverer, and that He lives, though Job dies; and that when Job is dead this Redeemer will stand

upon the earth. The word אַחֲרוֹן may mean an *afterman*,
either as one after me, taking my rights, or simply as one
coming after me. In the one case it repeats the idea of
גֹּאֵל, in the other the idea of *liveth*. And the word עָפָר, *dust*,
seems used for the *earth*, not without reference to it as the
place where the sufferer himself lies in death. The ideas
contained in the verse are simply these—that he has an
avenger, a sustainer of his rights; that this Redeemer
liveth, dieth not; and that He will manifest Himself upon
the dust, whither He returns to uphold the cause of the
afflicted innocent, and declare his innocence.

> "And after my skin which is destroyed—this here,
> Even without my flesh shall I see God:
> Whom *I* shall see,
> And my own eyes behold, and not another's;
> And my reins faint within me."

Two things were needed for his vindication—one, that his
innocence should be publicly proclaimed among men. This
is expressed in ver. 25. But how small a thing that would
be! His sorrow lay chiefly here, that God was estranged
from him. His heart and flesh cry out for the living God.
The other half of his assurance concerns himself—he shall
see this Redeemer, who shall appear on his behalf.

The expression נִקְּפוּ־זֹאת is a relative clause, and זֹאת
seems used δεικτικῶς—pointing to his body: "After this
my skin, which they consumed"; and וּמִבְּשָׂרִי is the apodosis
—"then without my flesh." What Job looks for is an
appearance of God, a vision of Him for himself, an interposition of Him on his behalf. He faints with longing for
that joyful sight. Now the question, of course, is much
agitated among interpreters—When does Job anticipate
this appearance of God to be made on his behalf? Various
views are contended for, which all depend on the different
renderings of וּמִבְּשָׂרִי in verse 26. Some render, '*And
from my flesh* shall I see'; that is, I in my flesh—
looking from it—shall see God. This translation leads to
two views: (1) That Job shall see God even though he
be reduced to a mass of flesh—his skin gone through his

disease; or (2) that, endowed with new flesh, he shall see God—in a new resurrection body. Now the first of these views seems out of the question: a distinction between his skin and his flesh is inconceivable. Elsewhere he says, " my bone cleaveth to my skin and to my flesh " (xix. 20). His skin and his flesh cannot be put in antithesis, but must mean the same thing. This seems also to go against the second view, and it is improbable that Job would have called his new body, had he imagined such a thing, *my flesh*, or that he would have called his present body his *skin* merely, without adding his *flesh* also. Others render, ' *and away from my flesh* shall I see God'—*i.e. and without my flesh*. This, again, is taken differently—(1) by some in a comparative sense, without my flesh—a mere skeleton, but of course still alive in this life; and (2) by others absolutely —stripped of my flesh, disembodied, no more in this life. In the one case Job is assured he shall see God in this life, however great the ravages be which disease has made on him; in the other, he shall see God only after this life is ended. Now, I think that between these two views the truth lies, and that no other sense is possible. On this alternative the following remarks may be made:

(1) It is above all things to be noticed what to Job's own mind is the main point. It is that he shall see God. The connection of the whole is: But I know that my Redeemer liveth, and . . . I shall *see God*. The question, whether *here* or *elsewhere*, is not the main point. His afflictions were to Job the seal and token of God's anger, —in being afflicted Job felt God's face withdrawn from him. God was imputing sins to him. And so were his friends, arguing on his calamities. What Job is assured of is, that God knows his innocence—is still in friendship with him. And this invincible assurance is the basis of the other invincible assurance, that this relation of God to him will yet be manifested. It will be manifested to his own joy—his eyes shall see God, and to the conviction also of men. Nothing speculative mixes in the question. It is purely a personal faith. The future or the present is

indifferent so far as the true point of Job's position is concerned.

(2) A second point is this. I think it must be conceded that Job does not anticipate restitution to health and prosperity in this life. Neither in this chapter nor anywhere does he express such an opinion, but always, and consistently, an opposite one. He calls such a view, when expressed by his friends, *mockery* (xvii. 2). In one of the most remarkable passages of the book, chap. xvi. 18, he says: "O earth, cover not my blood,"—alluding to the idea that the blood of one unjustly slain, like himself, will not cover, but lies on the face of the earth, appealing for vindication. Here he anticipates that he shall have to die an unjust death. Immediately after these words he adds: "Even now, He who shall witness for me is in heaven, and He who shall testify to me is on high." Now this might seem a revocation of his view that he shall die a martyr's death; but it cannot be so from what follows. A few verses further on he says of his friends: "They change the night into day—*i.e.* their promises are, that the night of affliction will soon give place to a day of restitution. To which he answers: "If I have said to corruption, Thou art my father; to the worm, Thou art my mother; where then is my hope? It shall go down to the bars of Sheol" (chap. xvii. 12). To the same effect is his desire in xix 23, that his protestations of his innocence should be graven in the rock as a testimony to all generations when he is no more.

And that the new idea of a restitution to prosperity does not appear in chap. xix. seems proved by what follows. In chap. xxiii. 14 he says that God will "perform, or complete, the thing appointed for him"—*i.e.* will bring him to death through his malady. And, again, in his last words, chap. xxx. 23, he says: "For I know that Thou wilt bring me to death." To the former passage, xxiii. 14, he adds—"and many such things are with him." Dying an unjust death, as Job now does, is a common occurrence in God's providence. And this idea appears in all the chapters that follow the xixth. Job misses the Divine rectitude in the history of men,—men die in affliction though they be righteous, and the wicked die in peace though they be sinners, chaps. xxiii.–xxv. Hence, in chap. xxiv. 1, Job asks why men do not see God's judgment days—His days of assize, when He shows His rectitude in governing the world. The point of the speeches after chap. xix. is that this rectitude of God fails to manifest itself during the whole life of some men. Such an argument could hardly have been carried on if Job had, in chap. xix., risen to the assurance that God would visit him with prosperity and health in this life.

(3) This *seeing* of God, therefore, which Job anticipates, if it take place in this life, will not be accompanied by restoration to health and prosperity. But could such a thought have occurred to Job? Job's disease was to him the very seal of God's estrangement from him—his calamities *were* God's hiding His face from him, and proofs of His anger. Hence, in chap. xiv., he contemplates being hidden in Sheol till God's wrath was past, and *then* being recalled to a new life. And it seems impossible that Job could have conceived God reconciled to him *while* He continued to afflict him with his malady.

These arguments seem to point to the conclusion that Job does not anticipate this appearance of God on his behalf in this life—that is, prior to his death through his disease. There are many individual points that go in the same direction. The word *Goel* naturally suggests a reference to the vindicator of the deceased. Admitting that it would not necessarily do this if it stood alone, it remains that no account of the word חי, *liveth*, can be suggested which does not imply an antithesis between Job dead and his living Goel.

It is a great mistake to regard any of Job's utterances in any of his speeches as extravagances, or to suppose that he is allowed by the author even to contradict himself, or to rise to an idea in one verse out of all connection with its surrounding context, or which he dismisses as not further

to be pursued. On the contrary, he usually flings out
ideas first, generally or vaguely, which he resumes and
pursues till he has given them full expression. This makes
it probable that the conception of a new life thrown out
in chap. xiv. is not a mere isolated idea, like a flash of
light swallowed up for ever in the darkness. It is rather
the commencement of a progress which finds its climax in
chap. xix. This progress has three stages, first, that of
presentiment in chap. xiv. :—" If a man die, shall he live
again ? Thou wouldst call, and I would answer Thee ! "
Second, that of *prayer* in chaps. xvi.–xvii. :—" My witness
is in heaven, and He who shall testify for me is on high.
Mine eye droppeth tears unto God that He would maintain
the right of a man with God, and between a man and his
fellow." These are words which follow the other words :
" O earth, cover not my blood." And, third, that of *assurance*, in chap. xix. : " I know that my Redeemer liveth—
whom I shall see."

(4) If, as seems necessary, we assume that Job expected
this appearance of God on his behalf not previous to his
death, we must not attempt to fill up the outlines which
he has drawn. We must take care not to complete the
sketch out of events that have transpired long after his
day, or out of beliefs reposing on these events that are
now current among ourselves. The English Version has
done so at the expense of the original. The main point
of Job's assurance is, that God will appear to vindicate him,
and that he himself shall see Him in peace and reconciliation. It is for this that he faints with longing. This is
the point that absorbs his attention. And, probably, this
so absorbed his imagination that the surroundings of the
event were hardly thought of. These surroundings hardly
form a positive part of his assurance at all. We must
lay no stress on them as parts of his conception or vision.
We should be wrong to say that Job contemplates a purely
spiritual vision of God. And we should be wrong to say
that he contemplates being invested with a new body when
he sees God. He was a living man when he projected

before his own mind this glorious vision; and probably he fancies himself to see it, when it is realised, as a living man. This seems likely, because he threatens his friends with God's anger when He appears. But he had not in his mind at the time any thought of the necessary pre-liminaries — such as being invested with a new body. He sees the coming appearance of God, and he sees himself present with it, and he fancies himself a living man.

It is a fundamental thought, then, in Job's mind, that God's anger will pursue him to the grave. Restoration in this life is an illusion, a false issue, which the friends hold up before him. But he knows better. The certainty which he expresses is a certainty which concerns him after death—without his flesh he shall see God. *He* shall see Him; and *his* eyes, not another's, behold Him. Other eyes may see Him too,—but *his* shall. Job's sorrow was that God was unseen, that He eluded his search—" Oh that I knew where I might find Him." But this hiding of Himself shall not always continue; and the thought of seeing Him overcomes him, so that he cries out: " My reins faint within me."

Now it is necessary to consider what Job was,—in his *righteousness*; this is the very basis of all,—a just man, fearing God and eschewing evil. A man in union with God —living by faith on God. The writer puts him outside of the Israelitish community; he is not one of the cove-nant people. He has not much about him to fall back upon, no public life embodying God's relations to men, no great society of believers on whose experience to lean and draw support from, nothing but his own history—his *consciousness*. For, whatever supports one may have in what is without, in ordinances and a church life and a visible organisation, as proofs to him that there is a God—a God of grace, and that He has revealed Himself to men, and is dwelling among them in very truth,—all these things but help to form his consciousness—are but outer food to be turned into personal nourishment, and must be so used; and one's own history and experience may be in extreme circumstances enough, just as it is in all cases necessary.

Further, looking merely at the things here said, they are very singular, they are all concrete things, and not general; but if turned into generals, we hardly yet know more. First, there is One who upholds the cause of men, who shall yet stand upon the earth and declare of everyone according to his deeds. There is a Redeemer, a righter of men from the wrongs and sorrows of the world and the malice of Satan. This shall be public, before the eyes of all. What this man reaches through his troubles, and affirms of his own case, must be true of all. Second, there shall be to the righteous a complete reunion with God. Estrangements, whether explicable or no, shall be reconciled, and the eye of the just shall see God.

The question must be put,—Does Job contemplate the vindication of himself before men and his own vision of God as contemporaneous ? There seems no certain answer to be returned to this question. In the Old Testament it is ideas and things that appear, not times and seasons. It is fragments, not wholes. Here, two things are certainly affirmed with irrefragable certainty : A public confession by God of the just before the world, and a union of the just with Himself in blessed vision. That the things are contemporaneous may not be here taught. Nor can we conclude with certainty in what condition the sufferer thought himself to be when seeing his Redeemer. On the one hand, the Vindicator shall rise upon the dust—and even without his flesh Job shall see Him. This implies that not in this life or with this body he shall behold Him. But, on the other hand, the *goel* and *afterman* stands upon the earth, and there might be a return here to the bold anticipation of the xivth chapter. If there is not, then it is left to us to put the two anticipations together and make a whole out of them.

Once more, if we conceive Job's case in its true breadth—who, at bottom, was his accuser, the Satan ; who ultimately it is that, as Judge and Vindicator, shall stand upon the earth, He to whom all judgment is committed, being the Son of Man; what eyes it is that are needful to see Him who came in the flesh, even eyes of flesh, when to those who look for Him, He shall come the second time, for salvation—we shall have the elements for a construction greater than that yet reared in the Old Testament. In treating the Old Testament scientifically, we show the materials of the fabric not yet reared; in treating it practically, we may even exhibit the fabric fully reared.

The vision of his meeting God in peace so absorbed Job's mind, that the preliminaries which would occur to a mind in a calmer condition, and which immediately occur to us, were not present to his thoughts. Yet I do not know but that to Job's mind all the religious essentials were present which we associate with the future life. And though the ancient and traditional interpretation of the passage was in many respects exegetically false, and imposed on Job's mind our more particular conceptions, it seems to me that it seized the true elements of Job's situation in a manner truer to the reality than can be said of some modern expositions.

The situation of Job differed from that of the Psalmists whose words we have in Pss. xvi., xlix., and lxxiii. These men were, when they spoke, in fellowship with God. What they demand is the continuance of it. But Job had lost it. This saint has a double difficulty to overcome. His invincible faith in God's relation to him at heart, in spite of a darkness which will last all this life, enables him to overcome it, and to rise to the assurance that this estrangement of God shall be removed, and that he shall see Him in peace. This is a very profound faith.

10. *The Hope of an After-Life in relation to the ideas of Life and Death.*

The Old Testament view of Immortality is a very large one. It embraces a variety of elements which require careful study, and which may seem at first obscure. It may be best understood if we look at these three points in particular:—first, the Old Testament view of *death*; second, the Old Testament view of *life*; and, third, the *reconciliation* of the two—or the way in which life overcomes death. It might seem to be more natural to speak first of *life*, but it may conduce to clearness if the question of *death* be put first.

On such questions as *life*, *death*, the *body* and the *soul*, there are several witnesses who offer us their testimony There is science; there is speculation, ancient and modern; and there is Scripture. We naturally compare their testimonies. This is inevitable. And on comparing them, or any two of them, say science and Scripture, it may turn out that they do not agree. But there is an important preliminary question regarding the witnesses—Are they witnesses of the same kind? The question is not whether the one is more or less credible than the other, but whether they really be witnesses that speak to the same things; whether, though they all speak about the world and man and the body and soul, they do not speak of these looking at them from quite different points of view. If the latter is the case, these witnesses, though giving different testimonies regarding these subjects, may not be in conflict.

What students of the Old Testament have rather to complain of is, that its testimony on all matters which are also matters of science is virtually suppressed, through the assumption that it is a witness of the same kind with the scientific witnesses, and that its testimony moves in the same plane. Hence the trepidation lest there should be contradiction, and the rash haste to effect a harmony The maxim that the Bible and nature having the same Author cannot contradict one another, in itself a right maxim, may become mischievous if we set out with unjust notions of the two, or assume that the Bible and science deliver testimony within the same sphere. The result is to lead to a comparison of science as the interpreter of nature with Scripture, to attempts at harmony, to explanations sometimes forced; in the course of which it happens either that scientific results are denied, or said to be so immature that nothing can be founded on them, or else such a haze is thrown around Scripture that practically all meaning is denied to it. The latter is usually the case; for in this conflict theology generally suffers a defeat, and the result is scarcely less disastrous to Scripture than the open ascription of error to it. For while its authority may be formally upheld, it is made to be so obscure that on a large class of subjects it cannot be taken into any practical account.

Now, unquestionably science and Scripture look at all the things on which they speak in common from different points of view. Science busies itself, whether it speak of the world or of man, with a physical constitution under physical law. This is an idea unknown to the Old Testament. In its view the world is a moral constitution, all the phenomena of which illustrate moral law and subserve moral ends. Now it is of great importance to keep this general distinction before our minds. It would be of great utility to go through Scripture under the guidance of this general principle which pervades it, collecting all that it says about the world or man, before bringing its testimony into any comparison with what science says. We might find that though the testimonies were very different, yet Scripture in making moral affirmations regarding the universe did not contradict science in making physical affirmations. And we should always be justified in saying of any apparently physical affirmations which Scripture makes, that to make such affirmations is not its direct object. Such physical statements are only the vehicle or indirect means of making moral statements.

(1) As to *death*. The Old Testament means by that what we ourselves mean when we use the word. It is the phenomenon which we observe, and which we call *dying*. But in the Old Testament this, so to speak, contains two things, death itself or dying, and the state of the dead. Now, on the one hand, all parts of the Old Testament indicate the prevalence of the view that at death the person who dies is not annihilated. The person who is dead has not ceased

32

to exist, though he has ceased to live. But, on the other hand, death is not merely the separation of body and soul, the body falling into decay and the soul continuing to live. The Old Testament does not direct its attention to the body or the soul so much as to the person, and the person who dies remains dead. Death paralyses the life of the person. The person who has died continues dead. He descends into the place where all dead persons are congregated, called in the Old Testament *Sheol*, and in the New Testament *Hades*. The dead person is there not nonexistent, but dead, and all the consequences which we observe to follow death here pursue him there,—he is cut off from all fellowship with the living, whether the living be man or God.

Of course, the Hebrew view of death is not materialistic. Just as in the history of creation God formed man out of the dust of the ground, and breathed into his nostrils the breath of life, just as the body is represented as complete while not yet inhabited by the soul, which was drawn from elsewhere and entered the body; so the soul leaves the body in death, but does not become extinct. Yet the Old Testament does not call that which descends into Sheol, the place of the dead, either *soul* or *spirit*. It is the deceased person. And this person, though dead, was to such an extent still existent, that he was supposed capable of being evoked by the necromancer, as in the case of Samuel. The person still subsisted, though dead.

Again, the Hebrew view is far from being akin to the philosophic theory, which held the body to be the spirit's prison-house, from which when set at liberty the spirit rejoiced in a fuller life, and could expand its faculties to a greater exercise of power than was possible to it when cramped in the narrow material cell. Such a view of the body is far from being Scriptural. But, on the other hand, we must equally dismiss from our minds ideas which Christianity has made familiar to us,—ideas of a culmination of the spirit at death into moral perfection, and the drifting away of all clouds which obscure the face of God to it here on earth. This view is the end, the result, of the development and the struggles of faith which we observe in the Old Testament. But it must not be assumed at the beginning of them.

Dismissing, then, all these ideas from our mind, we have to adhere to the representations in the Old Testament. And the point that requires to be kept firm hold of is, that the person who dies remains dead, not merely in the sense that he does not live on earth, but in every sense; life is paralysed in whatever element of our being it may be supposed to reside. The state of the dead is a continuance, a prolongation of death. A few passages may be cited to illustrate what was thought of the state of those dead.

(a) There are certain strong expressions used at times in the Old Testament regarding death, from which it might be inferred, indeed, that it was believed that the existence of the person came to an end absolutely, e.g. (Ps. cxlvi. 4): "His breath goeth forth, he returneth to his earth; in that very day his thoughts perish" (Ps. cxlvi. 4); "O spare me, that I may recover strength, before I go hence, and be no more" (Ps. xxxix. 14); "Why dost thou not pardon my transgression? for now shall I sleep in the dust; and thou shalt seek me earnestly, but I shall not be" (Job vii. 21). "For a tree hath hope, if it be cut down, that it will sprout again; but man dieth, and wasteth away: man giveth up the ghost, and where is he? Man lieth down, and riseth not; till the heavens be no more, they shall not awake, nor be raised out of their sleep" (Job xiv. 7). But these are merely the strong expressions of despondency and regret over a life soon ended here, and that never returns to be lived on earth again. The very name and conception of Sheol, the place of the dead, is sufficient answer to the first impression that they produce. The word Sheol, as has been said, is of uncertain meaning; but it probably is connected with the root that signifies to *gape* or *yawn*, and may mean a chasm or abyss, and thus differ little in meaning from our own word *Hell*, connected with the word to be *hollow*. A word often used in parallelism with it is *pit* and in the New Testament *abyss*. This place, where dead persons are assembled, is represented as the opposite of this upper world of light and life; it is spoken of as deep down in the earth: "Those that seek my soul, to destroy it, shall go down into the lower parts of the earth" (Ps. lxiii. 9); or it is under the earth, "the shades tremble underneath the waters" (Job xxvi. 5). Corresponding to this it is a land of darkness, as Job says: "A land of darkness, as darkness itself; without any order, and where the light is as darkness" (x. 22).

Of course there is no formal topography to be sought for Sheol. It is in great measure the creation of the imagination, deep down under the earth, or under the waters of the seas. It is the abode of departed persons, the place appointed for all living. The generations of one's forefathers are there, and he who dies is 'gathered unto his fathers.' The tribal divisions of one's nation are there, and the dead is gathered unto his people. Separated from them here, he is united to them there; and if even his own descendants had died before him, they are there, and he goes down, as Jacob to his son, to Sheol mourning. None can hope to escape entering among these dead personalities: "What man is he that liveth, and shall not see death; that shall deliver his soul from the hand of Sheol?" (Ps. lxxxix. 48).

(*b*) We have seen that, as death consists in the withdrawal by God of His spirit of life, and as this spirit is the source of energy and vital force, the personality in death is left feeble. All that belongs to life ceases except bare subsistence. Hence Sheol is called *Abaddon*, 'perishing'; it is called *cessation*. The persons there are still and silent as in sleep. They are called *shades*. The condition is called 'silence': "unless the Lord had been my help, my soul had dwelt in silence" (Ps. xciv. 17). It is the land of forgetfulness: "the living know that they must die: but the dead know not anything. Also their love, and their hatred, and their envy, is now perished" (Eccles. ix. 5); "Art thou become weak as one of us?" is the salutation with which the mighty king of Babylon is greeted by the shades. Yet this passage in Isa. xiv. represents the dead as having a kind of consciousness of themselves and others, a memory of the past, and as enjoying a kind of subsistence, which, though not life, is a dim reflection and shadow of life upon the earth. The social distinctions that prevail on earth are continued in Sheol. Shadowy kings sit upon imperceptible thrones, from which they are stirred with a flicker of interest and emotion to greet any distinguished new arrival. Respectable circumcised persons refuse to mingle with the uncircumcised.

But all this, it can be readily seen, is partly poetry and partly effort of the imagination. It is not doctrine. It is the product of the imagination operating on the circumstances connected with death. The grave suggests a deep cavernous receptacle as the place of the dead. The sleep of death causes them to deem it a land of stillness and silence. The flaccid, powerless corpse makes them think of the person as feeble, without energy or power. Only this amount of certainty seems deducible, that the dead persons still in some way subsisted. Death puts an end to the existence of no person.

(c) My impression is, as has been stated, that so far as the Old Testament writings are concerned, there appears nowhere any distinction between good and evil in this place of the dead. Sheol is no place of punishment itself nor of reward. Neither is it divided into any distinct, retributive compartments. The state there is not blessedness nor misery. It is subsistence simply. There is a distinction drawn in the Old Testament between the righteous and the wicked. But it is not a distinction in regard to their condition in Sheol. It is a distinction anterior to Sheol,—a distinction according to which the righteous do not fall into Sheol at all, as will appear immediately.

(d) There is one more point in regard to the dead that is of importance. Connection with the world of life is completely broken. The dead man cannot return to earth, nor does he know anything of the things of earth; even the fate, happy or miserable, of those he was most bound up with, is unknown to him: "His sons come to honour, and he knoweth it not; they are brought low, and he perceiveth it not of them" (Job xiv. 21). Yet, with the strong belief in the existence of the personalities in Sheol, there was not unnaturally a popular superstition that they could be reached, and that they could give counsel to the living. The belief probably was not that the dead must have more knowledge than the living, from the mere fact of their having passed into another state. It was not thought that there must be wisdom with great Death. More likely the dead to whom recourse was had were persons who were eminent when living, such as prophets or great ancestors, and who might still be supposed capable of giving counsel or light to the living in their perplexity. This appears to be the meaning of Saul's desire to consult Samuel. The prophet Isaiah, however, ridicules the idea: "Should not a people seek unto their God? should they seek for the living unto the dead?" (viii. 19). But the main point is that the relation between the deceased person and God was held to be altogether severed. This was what gave death its significance to the religious mind, and caused such a revulsion against it, culminating in such protests as that in Ps. xvi.

Now these points regarding death and the state of the dead perhaps are hardly to be called Scripture teaching; they are rather the conceptions lying in the popular mind which Scripture presupposes, and which are made the foundation on which what may more fairly be called Scripture teaching is reared. But all kinds of men are represented in Scripture as giving expression to these sentiments, the pious as well as others. They are elements of the national mind. They form, in fact, the convictions against which the faith of the pious struggles; and in this struggle really lies the contribution made to the doctrine of immortality in the Old Testament. How general these convictions are may be seen from Pss. vi., xxx., and Hezekiah's prayer, Isa. xxxviii. In the first it is said, " Return, O Lord, deliver my soul : for in death there is no remembrance of Thee ; in Sheol who shall give Thee thanks ? " In the second, " I cried unto the Lord, What profit is there in my blood, when I go down to the pit ? Shall the dust praise Thee ? shall it declare Thy truth ? " And in the last, " For Sheol cannot praise Thee, death cannot celebrate Thee : they that go down to the pit cannot hope for Thy truth." And the plaintive singer in Ps. xxxix. pleads, as Job often does, for an extension of his earthly life on this ground : " Hold not Thy peace at my tears : for I am a stranger with Thee, and a sojourner," the meaning being, as has been noticed, nearly the opposite of what the Christian mind would read into the words. To the Old Testament saint this life on earth was a brief but happy visit paid to the Lord ; but death summoned the visitor away, and it came to an end. This is always the significant element in the popular view of death, that it severed the relation between the person and God.

2. As to *Life.*—As by death, so by life the Old Testament means what we mean by it. It starts from the idea not of the soul, but of the person. ' Life ' is what we so call ; it is the existence of the complete personality, in its unity, body and soul. Man was made a living person, such as any one of us is, and the maintenance of this condition is *life*. But in the Old Testament there is always an additional element. What might be called the centre of gravity of life is not physical, but moral or religious. Man was created a living person, in a particular relation to God ; and this relation to God would have maintained him in the condition of a living person. The bond of unity in the elements of man's nature is his moral relation to God. So that *life*, as the Old Testament uses the term, is what we name *life*, with the addition of the fellowship of God. This was the condition of the original man—he was a living person. This is *life*, and the continuance of it is *immortality*. The

idea of immortality which the Old Testament teaches, or is engaged with, is not a doctrine of the subsistence merely of the immaterial part of man's being. It is a doctrine, first, of the subsistence of the whole of man's being, body and soul; and, secondly, not of the subsistence of this merely, but its subsistence in the fellowship of God. The mere subsistence of the dead person was never questioned. Scripture has no need to affirm it, but presupposes it. What it is occupied with is a religious immortality, an immortality which shall preserve and prolong that life with God actually enjoyed by the living saints here upon the earth.

The early chapters of Genesis illustrate what is meant by *life* and *immortality*. They tell us that Adam was made a living person,—a person such as we are, and living as any of us lives. This man lives in fellowship with God. The passage, from its way of speaking, appears to assume that life is to continue; for a warning is given that it will cease in certain events. Apart from these events it is destined to flow on. The question is not raised as to *how long* it will flow on; but no cessation is contemplated, except in the case of a particular occurrence. The man who lives is not a body nor a soul, but a complete person. No question is raised whether the soul be immortal from its nature, nor whether the body be from its nature liable to dissolution. The passage says nothing of the body or the soul, it speaks of the person, who lives as we understand life to be. This is life in the primary condition of man, in the fellowship of God, and this life has an indefinite flow onward, provided a certain occurrence do not intervene. When we pass across the record of many generations, and come to the story of the Patriarchal and Mosaic ages, we perceive the same conceptions prevailing There is no allusion in the literature of the periods to a future life of reward; yet life and death are set before Israel. What is this life that is spoken of? It is life as we behold it in the case of any living man, but always with an additional element. It lay in God's favour. External goods were good, when God's presence and favour were in them. They were seals to the pious Israelite of God's good pleasure with him. In the joyousness of existence and in the clea: light of God's favour the Old Testament saint in his full bodily existence upon the earth, in the language of Scripture, had *life*.

It has always been surprising to readers of the Old Testament that there is so little reference in it—in many parts of it no reference at all—to what we call a *future life*. And there is, no doubt, some difficulty in conceiving the modes of thinking that prevailed in Israel. In point of fact, our modes of thinking and theirs form two extremes. We have been taught by many things to feel that a true or perfect religious life with God cannot be lived upon the earth; that only in another sphere can true fellowship with Him be maintained. It is possible that what is true in this idea may have been pursued to an extreme, to the undue depreciation of this life, and the undue limitation of its possibilities in the way of living unto God. The Hebrew stood at the other pole. This life seemed to him the normal condition of man. Life with God was possible here—was indeed life. It was this that gave life its joy—"The Lord is the portion of mine inheritance and my cup" (Ps. xvi. 5). It was this possession of Jehovah that made life to the pious mind of old. The Hebrew saint did not think of the future, because he had in the present all that could ever be received. Hence it was only on occasions when the presence of God was like to be withdrawn or lost, as when death threatened, that the question of a future life rose before the mind. So that when we feel surprise at the small reference to future immortality in the Old Testament, we must take care that we do not pass a mistaken judgment on the Old Testament saints, and suppose that the reason why they thought and spoke so little of the future was that they were entirely occupied and satisfied with the material joys of this earthly life.

The true state of the case is very much the opposite

of this. The Hebrew saint called that "life" which made the existence of the complete person in all his parts, body and soul. Anything else was not life, but death. And he had this life upon the earth, and God's presence with him filled it with joy; he had life in its perfect meaning. Therefore our surprise, if legitimate, must be directed to these two points, namely: How the Old Testament saint could fancy a life on earth, with all its imperfections, to be a satisfying life with God; and, secondly, How he was so little given to reflection, that the thought of death, so inevitable to us, did not oftener intrude and disturb his joy, and force him to contemplate the future. Now, we must not forget in what age of the world we live, and in what age the Old Testament saints lived. There lies behind us all the speculation of mankind upon death; the history of Christ and all the light cast by Christianity. The Old Testament saint stood before all these things; he was only sowing seeds here and there, of which we now reap the harvest. But, in reference to the first question, it may perhaps be admitted that a deeper sense of the evils which pervade this world, the impediments which the evil of mankind lays in the way of the principles of the Divine government—in a word, a deeper sense of the sinfulness of mankind and of the holiness of God, might have suggested the necessity of another sphere where evil should be eliminated and the fellowship of men with God be complete.

And in point of fact we perceive this thought in a certain form in Job, who, baffled before the complexities of God's providence, is compelled to look to the future, and enabled to assure himself that beyond this life he will see God's justice vindicated. But in earlier times there was a strong feeling of the unity of God and His universal efficiency in the rule of all things; and this carried with it also the feeling of the unity of the world, which was the sphere of His rule, and no distinction was drawn between this world and another. There was one world, as there was one God ruling everywhere. His efficiency and will pervaded the universe; no change of place could make any alteration. Hence the idea, now familiar to us, of heaven as an abode of the righteous, had not yet been reached. That which makes the essence of our idea of heaven, the presence of God, they had as much as we. But this presence was enjoyed on earth.

In the perfect state of God's people, when the covenant should be fully realised, when Jehovah should be truly their God and they His people, the saints would not be translated into heaven to be with God, but He would come down to earth and abide among them. The tabernacle of God would be with men. That state of blessedness which we transfer to heaven, they thought would be realised on earth. They were not insensible to the evils that were on the earth, nor did they suppose that God would dwell with men upon the earth, the earth remaining as it is. On the contrary, the coming of the Lord would destroy evil, and the earth would be transformed: "Behold, I create new heavens and a new earth" (Isa. lxv. 17). Yet it remained the earth; and in the new and transfigured world the principles of God's present rule were but carried to perfection. Hence essentially, though not perfectly, the pious Israelite had, in God's presence with him, what we name heaven, although upon earth; and though he might long and look for the day of the Lord, when God would appear in His glory and transform all things, this change did not create another world, but brought in the religious perfection of the present one. In other words, what we call, and what is to us, *heaven,* the Israelite called *earth,* when the Lord had come to dwell in His fulness among men; there was no translation into another sphere. There were not two worlds, but one.

And this coming of the Lord was regarded as imminent. The pious mind saw the Lord in everything, especially in any great calamity or convulsion among the nations; He was present there, and His full presence was ready to be revealed. And this feeling of the nearness of the Lord's coming helps greatly to explain the paucity of

the references to the death of the individual. I suspect
we might find the same paucity in the apostolic writings,
and for the same reason. The mind of the Church in
Israel corresponded greatly to the mind of the early Christian Church. The great object of expectation was the
coming of the Lord. The salvation was ready to be
revealed. The living generation might see it. Living
men could take up the words of the apostle—"We that
are alive and remain at His coming" (Thess. iv. 15).
Hence the death of the individual had not the significance
which it has come to have among us. Our point of view
is changed. We may look for the coming of the Lord;
but, however certain in itself, its time is uncertain, while
our own death, besides being certain, cannot be very far
off. And, consequently, the death of the individual has
now come to usurp the place which, both in Israel and in
the early Christian Church, was held by the coming of
the Lord.

(3) *The conflict of the view of life with the fact of death.*
—Life, as has been said, was that which we name so, the
existence of the person in all his parts, body and soul, in
the fellowship of God. Death was a severance of the
person from God's fellowship. Hence arose a conflict; and
in the triumph of faith over the fact of death, lies largely
the Old Testament contribution to the doctrine of immortality.

(a) Now, first, I suspect it must be admitted that sometimes, especially in the earlier periods, the Old Testament
saint acquiesced in death; he accepted it even under the feeling that it was severance from God. One of the strangest
things in the Old Testament is the little place which the
individual feels he has, and his tendency to lose himself in
larger wholes, such as the family or the nation. When
in earlier times the individual approached death, he felt
that he had received the blessing of life from God, and had
enjoyed it in His communion. His sojourn with God had
come to an end; he was old and full of days, and he
acquiesced. However strange his acquiescence may seem to

us, he consoled himself with the thought that he did not
all die, the memory of the righteous was blessed.   He
lived, too, in his children and in his people; he saw the
good of Israel; his spirit lived, and the work of his hands
was established.   The great subject was the people, the
nation.   Jehovah had made His covenant with the nation;
the individual shared its blessings only in the second
degree, through the prosperity of the people.   And he was
content to lose himself in the larger whole; to have poured
his little stream of life and service into the tide of national
life, and in some degree swelled it.   This was particularly
the case in earlier times.   But when the nation came to
an end with the Captivity, and national religion and life
no more existed, the individual rose to his proper place and
rights; he felt his own worth and his own responsibility.
Though the nation had fallen, God remained and religion
remained; but it remained only in the heart of the individual.   The religious unit, formerly the people, now
became the individual person.   With the fall of the
nation, religion took a greater stride towards Christianity
than it had done since the Exodus.   Hence the problems
of the individual life rose into prominence, particularly the
problem of death.

The efforts of faith, as we have interpreted them, seem
made on two lines: (a) First an appeal is taken, in a way
not quite easy for us to understand, against the fact of death,
a demand for not dying,—a protest against the fellowship
of the living man here with God being interrupted.   It is
probable that the examples of this may be to be referred
to particular circumstances, when death might be actually
threatening; and this fact helps us somewhat to understand
them.   But the language used, the demand made for continuance of life, the lofty assurance expressed by faith, that
from the relation of the person to God life cannot be interrupted, rise to the expression of principles, and are by no
means merely an assurance that God would save the person
from death on this particular occasion.   They express what
the religious mind demands; what it feels to be involved

in its relations to Jehovah, absolutely and apart from all circumstances. (*b*) Secondly, we observe the faith of the Old Testament saints operating in a less ecstatic way, which to us is more comprehensible. The first was a protest against death, and a rising up to the enunciation of the principles involved in the relation of the living believer to God. This second is rather a protest that dying is not death ; it is an analysis of the popular conception of death, and a denial of its truth. According to the popular conception, dying and the state after death were one : the dead person descended into Sheol, and was severed from God. Faith now reclaims against this view. The death of the saint is not this : he does not descend into Sheol, he overleaps the place of the dead.

(*c*) Further, it is evident that in analysing the idea of death, and concluding that in the case of the righteous it did not imply descent into the place of dead persons, there was also an analysis of the human being into elements. Death made this analysis inevitable. The body fell into decay, and faith was only able to assure itself that the *person* was taken by God. There is no means of knowing what view was entertained of the condition of the person. It may be doubtful if, with the strong view had of life, as the full existence of the person in the unity of all his parts, body and soul, they would regard the condition, even of those whom they described as taken by God, as properly to be called life. Faith needed to supplement itself. This it did by the doctrine of the *resurrection of the body*. It was chiefly the prophets who brought up this side ; and the idea of resurrection is presented first as the raising up of the dead nation, as in Ezekiel's vision of the dry bones of Israel. There is, however, one very beautiful passage where the idea occurs in connection with the individual (Job xiv.). As has been said, Job regarded his malady as proof of God's estrangement from him. Further, he regarded his malady as mortal ; God's estrangement would endure to the end of his life. With these feelings in his mind the thought suddenly presented itself, that this life

on earth might not be the only one—life might be renewed ,
out of Sheol and the grave he might be called by God's returning favour to a second life. " O that Thou wouldest hide
me in Sheol till Thy wrath be past; that Thou wouldest
appoint a set time, and remember me ! " But while pursuing the thought he becomes conscious of what is involved
in it—If a man die, shall he live again ? But, without
answering the objection, he pursues his original dream of a
second life : " All the days of my appointed time would
I wait till my change came. Thou wouldst call, and I
would answer Thee ; Thou wouldst yearn after the work
of Thine hands."

11. *The Moral Meaning of Death.*

We have drawn attention to a number of passages in
the Old Testament with the view of exhibiting the way in
which the Hebrew mind regarded death and the state of
the dead. These passages are to a large extent popular,
some of them poetical, and therefore not fitted to bear the
weight of dogmatic inferences being built upon them. But
they are sufficiently plain to enable us to reach the popular
way of thinking regarding death. It may be of use now to
indicate the views given of the moral meaning of death and
its opposite. Much depends here on the method on which
we approach the investigation of Scripture on such questions. In a work entitled *The Christian Doctrine of Sin*,
by the late Principal Tulloch of St. Andrews, the following
statements are made, among others, on this question of
immortality: " But what of physical death ? it may be
asked—Is not this also immediately connected with sin
as its consequence ? Is it not so specially in St. Paul's
Epistles ? What then are we to make of this ? To the
modern mind, death is a purely natural fact. It comes in
course of time as the natural issue of all organism, which
by its very life spends itself, and hastens towards dissolution as an inevitable end. We cannot conceive any
individual life perpetuated under the existing laws of the

external world. . . . The physical fact of death therefc cannot be traced to sin as its sole cause. Nor can Pau₁ be said to do this. Even when he speaks of death as the dissolution of the body, it is not only this dissolution that he means, but death with all its adjuncts of pain and sadness and spiritual apprehension" (p. 163). "Death as a simple physical fact is unaffected by moral conditions. Its character may be greatly altered, and no doubt has been greatly altered, by the fact of sin; but its incidence is natural, and lies in the constitution of things. . . . Physical dissolution did not directly follow the act of sin, and is not connected with it as immediate cause and effect" (pp. 76–77). "The dissolution of the physical system is nowhere in St. Paul nor in Scripture represented as solely the result of sin. The death of Adam, the death of sin, in St. Paul is always something more than mere physical death. It may include the death of the body—it does this plainly and prominently in the passage before us [Rom. v. 12], but it always includes more; . . . It is beyond doubt that death itself in the mere sense of decay is inherent in all organism; that the conditions of life, in short, are death; and that infant organic structures consequently should die when weak or imperfect or ready to vanish away, is no more remarkable than that any other organism should perish" (p. 188).

These passages are specimens of many others in the volume. It may strike one that the consistency of some statements in the extracts with others is not apparent at once. For example, it is said that the "dissolution of the physical system," i.e. natural death, "is nowhere in St. Paul represented as solely the result of sin"; and yet immediately after it is admitted that in Rom. v. 12, where Paul says, "As by one man sin entered into the world, and death by sin," the death of the body is "plainly and prominently" included. It is added that more is always included; but it is hard to see how the inclusion of more excludes this. And in another passage the writer says: "If the apostle's view of the consequences of sin included death as an external fact, the special meaning of the fact for him . . . was spiritual" (p. 164). What is meant by saying that the meaning of death as an external fact was *spiritual* may be left an open question; but it is difficult to reconcile the admission that Paul's view of the consequences of sin included death as an external fact, with the assertion that the dissolution of the physical system is "nowhere in St. Paul . . . represented as solely the result of sin." The author's use of the words 'sole' and 'solely' is peculiar. For he says plainly "death as a simple physical fact is unaffected by moral conditions," and again, "it is beyond doubt that death itself in the mere sense of decay is inherent in all organism"; and then he says "the physical fact of death, therefore, cannot be traced to sin as the sole cause." But however we may criticise words, the general drift of the author is unmistakable, which is, that natural or physical death in man is not due to sin, but is the result of his constitution, being inherent in organism; and that when it is said "the wages of sin is death," what is meant by death is a certain condition of man's spirit, not any fact in his history. I cite these passages not for the purpose of controverting as unscriptural the views presented in them, though I consider them to be unscriptural, but to draw attention to the viciousness of the method of investigation adopted, namely, that of mixing up the views of Scripture and the results of science, and attempting to identify them before any thorough investigation of what the view of Scripture is, and particularly before ascertaining what its point of view is.

The Old Testament certainly has a view on this subject which is neither that of modern science nor that of ancient speculation. I do not say that its view is in contradiction to either of these views, but it differs from them. And in order to ascertain the real truth on any question, it is well to allow each witness to give his testimony separately, and from his own point of view, without making premature attempts at reconciling one evidence with another.

Now the general scope of Scripture on such broad

33

questions as death, sin, God, and the like, can be ascertained. One thing, indeed, that characterises Scripture in distinction from modern literature—looking at it as a national literature—is that its deliverances on any subject are consistent throughout. There is no such violent antithesis of opinion on these questions as occurs in modern literature. From beginning to end of the Bible the view taken of *death*, for example, and *sin*, is self-consistent. But the full view is nowhere presented at once; and hence, in order to pass a just judgment as to Scripture teaching on such a subject, we have to familiarise ourselves with the whole of Scripture.

The acquiring of this familiarity is not an easy thing. It takes, I might say, the labour and experience of a lifetime. For Scripture is a literary work written in the language of life, and not in that of the schools, whether of Philosophy or Theology or Science; and whatever ways of thinking and speaking men have, will appear in it. All forms of human composition that the genial, subtle, various, calculating, enraptured human mind may employ to express itself, may be looked for in it. The ways of reaching its sense are a thousand. One must lay bare all his sensibilities, and bring himself *en rapport* with it on every side, and weigh general statements, and make the necessary deduction from a hyperbole, and calculate the moral value of a metaphor, and estimate and generalise upon sentiments that are never themselves general, but always the outcome of an intense life in very particular conditions, and even take up with his dumb heart "the groanings that cannot be uttered." But these two positions are to be firmly maintained, *first*, that Scripture has a meaning and a view of its own on most moral and religious questions; and not more than one view really, although, of course, different writers may present the view with all the variety natural to different minds and diverse circumstances; and that this view is not to be inferred from any single text, but from the whole general tenor of thought of the Scripture writers; and, *second*, that the meaning of Scripture is capable of being ascertained from Scripture alone, and ought not to be controlled by anything without—that, for example, our interpretation of prophecy ought not to be made dependent on historical events now occurring or that have occurred, and that our interpretation of Scripture statements regarding creation or the constitution of man ought not to be submitted to the judgment of geologists or writers on physiology.

Having regard, then, to the point of view of Scripture, the possibility of finding its meaning, and the duty of seeking it, from itself alone, we may look again at the question in hand. Now, the cause of life in man is viewed as in God. God lives, and is the source of life. He sends forth His Spirit, and man lives. He withdraws His Spirit, and man dies. The life or death of man depends on the will of God, and is due to an influence exerted by God. Here, no doubt, we enter a region of some difficulty. The 'Spirit of God' seems sometimes to be identical with, or to be the cause of, the mere physical energy which we call life, while at other times it is identical with moral power and spiritual vitality ; and Scripture writers sometimes so speak as if they regarded these two things as ultimately the same, and held a decline in moral vigour to be equivalent to a decline in vital energy. But however this be, there is no doubt that the prevailing view taken of God in Scripture is not physical, but ethical. He is spoken of as personal, and having a character. It is true that He is living, has life in Himself, and communicates life by communicating Himself ; but it is taught, above all, that this communication of Himself is the free act of a Person, and is the consequence of His goodness and love, which is His character.

But the same is the case with man. He has been created in the image of God ; he is a free person, and has a moral character. And his relations to that which is without him are the expressions of his freedom and character. God and man are alike in this. The difference is that God communicates and man receives. Whether what passes between them be a physical influence or a moral influence, the conditions of it are on both sides moral Man is not considered in Scripture as a duality, but as a unity, though a unity composed of elements; and the principle of this unity, the centre of it, is his moral relation to God. This binds all his parts into one, and retains his constitution entire as he came from God. The narrative beginning with chap. ii. of Genesis places man thus created before us in true relations to God, and living; it describes how God called to man's consciousness these relations, concentrating them into a particular point; and how He set before him death as the penalty of any change in these true relations: "Thou shalt not eat: in the day thou eatest thereof, thou shalt die." He ate, and died. This was the penalty attached to eating the tree. In the day man ate, he died. He became mortal, in the sense that he must die. Death laid his hand on him, and called him his own from that moment. From that moment he was dead in sin; dead as the consequence of sin. He could be called dead in the language of Paul, who says to men who still lived: "The body, indeed, is dead because of sin."

It really scarcely requires to be argued that 'death' in Scripture, as well as 'life,' and indeed all other terms of a similar kind, is used as part of the language of 'common sense.' The term *death* is not a synonym for sin or sinfulness any more than life is a synonym for righteousness; at least not in the Old Testament, nor, I think, in the writings of St. Paul. Everywhere in the Old Testament and in St. Paul 'death' is regarded as a thing distinct from 'sin,' of which it is the consequence, and it always embraces what we know as physical death. And everywhere 'life' is distinguished from 'righteousness,' and always embraces life in the body, and in the New Testament the resurrection life. The expression 'dead in sin,' which we use to signify what we call spiritual deadness, is not Scriptural language for that idea. Indeed, it is the very converse of the language of Scripture.

That state in which the natural man is when sin reigns, before ever the moral ideal has risen before the mind and disturbed the placidity and naïve instinctiveness of the sinful actions, is not called *death* by the apostle, but *life*: "I was alive without the law once" (Rom. vii. 9). It is the second stage that is called *death*, when the commandment has been introduced into the mind, and has decomposed its unity, and made its elements fly to different sides and take part one half of it with the law and the other half with sin, "When the commandment came, sin revived, and I died." Then he was dead in sin; doomed to die in the element of sin. Both in the Old Testament and in the New man is regarded as a unity; and when it is said in the Old, "In the day thou eatest thereof thou shalt surely die" (Gen. ii. 17), and in the New, "The wages of sin is death" (Rom. vi. 23), death is used in its ordinary full sense; just as when it is said, "In the path of righteousness is life" (Prov. xii. 28), and "Grace shall reign through righteousness unto eternal life" (Rom. v. 21), life means in the one case this compound life which men live in the present body, and in the other the new life which men shall live in the new body. Of course, 'death' is a large word; it includes not only dying, but remaining dead. It embraces all that has been said above of the condition of the dead. The views then exhibited expressed the general mind of the people; but this might be subject to further enlightenment, *e.g.* a distinction might be made between the condition of the righteous and that of the wicked, etc.

Still the question comes, What ideas were entertained of the effects of this natural death? What was the fate or condition of the soul? First of all, the Old Testament view was not materialistic. Just as the story of creation represents the body as complete, while not yet inhabited by the soul, which was drawn from elsewhere and entered the body; so the soul leaves the body in death, but does not become extinct. When the dead man is raised, the spirit or soul comes again to the body. The necromancer can evoke the dead. Death is the extinction of no person. But, again, the Hebrew view is far from being akin to that ancient philosophic theory which held the body to be the spirit's prison-house, which when set at liberty rejoiced in a fuller life, and could expand its members to a greater exercise of power than was possible to them when cramped in their narrow material cell.

The terms as they are used popularly embrace all that we usually associate with life and death, the joy on the one hand, and the fears, regrets, darkness, and the like, on the other. For death being the consequence of sin, what lends terror to it, in addition to the shrinking of a living being from it, is the consciousness of this. And in addition to this it may happen that seeing death is now, so to speak, normal (through the effect of sin, sin being universal); any-thing extraordinary about it, any aggravation of it, *e.g.* its suddenness, or prematureness, or disastrousness, may be specially regarded as the judgment and punishment of sin, and not the mere death itself, seeing it is a common fate. But this does not hinder that death itself is always included; and that, though the awful death is specially the judgment on the wicked, even the death of the righteous is an awful evil. Neither does this hinder that death may sometimes, as in Job's case, be looked at as a relief. That is only relative. Death is essentially an evil. It is always an effect of sin, an intensification of the effects of sin, namely, separation from God. It is the greatest possible separation.

In the xvth chapter of 1 Corinthians, Paul writes: "As by man came death, by man came also the resurrection" (ver. 21). Could it be argued here that not the fact of death, but only the moral consequences of it, came by sin? No man in his senses would so argue. Or could it be argued that spiritual torpidity came by man, and spiritual resurrection by Christ? This was the very error that the chapter was written to confute. Or could it be argued that the expression 'by man' meant that death was a necessary consequence of his constitution, he being an organism? Now, certainly the apostle says that the first man was 'earthy' and not 'spiritual,' and that 'flesh and blood' cannot inherit the kingdom of God. He certainly believed that the condition in which Adam was created was not one in which he could enter into the kingdom of God. And it might be supposed that he considered man mortal by nature, and that he must pass through death in order to attain a spiritual body. But this would not be an inference in the line of his reasoning. For he says even of men as now constituted: "We shall not all sleep; but we shall all be changed" (ver. 51). This shows that he distinguished between dying and that change of the earthy into the spiritual which must take place in order to enter the kingdom of God or perfect Messianic kingdom, and that man's being χοϊκός, or earthy, did not in his view imply the necessity of death. Of course, the capacity of death is implied. Immortality was not inherent in the nature of the original man as a quality of it. Scripture says nothing of such a thing; but in the moral condition of man as a righteous, religious being, immortality was inherent.

When, therefore, it is said that the penalty of sinning was death, we must start from death as we know it. The dead are insensible to all that is. Fellowship with the living ceases. Fellowship with all ceases, even with God. The soul exists; but it has no conscious relations.

The cause of this is separation from God. The Hebrew people took a certain view of evil, including physical evil. They always regarded evil as evidence of the anger of God. This is the fundamental idea in Job on both sides. Even to Job himself his calamities were proofs of God's anger, though the anger was undeserved. Perhaps the book was written partly to break in upon this view and modify it. But the view everywhere prevailed. The suppliant prayed that God would not visit upon him the sins of his youth. Evil was the consequence of God's anger. Hence, of course, death, the greatest evil, was the extreme consequence. The people saw in evil the signature of God's feeling towards them. He had left them when He chastised, left them

altogether when He chastised unto death. It may be doubtful, on the other hand, if they realised the absence of God
except in these evils. Despondency or spiritual depression
outside of trouble perhaps did not assail them. That state
of feeling which we name the sense of desertion by God
did not produce itself in them except through calamities.
These calamities were to them the proof, and gave rise
to the sense, of being forsaken. Hence also Christ felt
forsaken in the midst of His sufferings, and never before.
He was a true Old Testament saint. But in His sufferings He realised this abandonment by God as truly as the
Old Testament saint did. In death He was abandoned;
in it He realised His abandonment. Thus on both sides
there was no feeling of God's anger except through
suffering and death; on the other side, there never was
suffering and death without the feeling of God's anger.
Death expressed this.

To die was to become separate from God; to be dead
was to continue in this state of separation. This is the
meaning of death in the Old Testament. Hence the
terrors that gathered around dying. Throughout the Old
Testament the ideas that usually come to expression on
the subject of death are dark indeed. They are so dark
as to suggest at once the question whether so gloomy a
view could have prevailed exclusively. To this we may
reply that such a view could prevail only where God's
grace had not begun to manifest itself. Death was separation from God, but the very idea of a covenant is union
with God, and union with God is 'life.'

This, then, is death, which is the wages of sin. The
picture given of it can perhaps scarcely be called Scripture
teaching, it is rather the preliminary to Scripture teaching;
it is the dark ground upon which Faith is enabled to paint
her brighter views, but the ground itself is not wholly
matter of revelation. It is the expression rather of the
moral consciousness of a people on whom the sense of
human sin and of God's holiness had taken a profound
hold, and who were ignorant of any final and thorough

means of their reconciliation. These pictures of death and the state of the dead, though drawn by saints, are usually drawn by saints in sickness. The complainer in Ps. vi. is sick unto death. So was Hezekiah; so was Job. Now it is not only that in such circumstances the imagination mixes even still darker colours. There was a special oppression upon the mind. Sickness and all other evils, especially of the same direct character, were the tokens of God's anger; and His anger was for sin. This was the source of Job's extreme perplexity. The Psalmist pleaded that God would not chasten him in His hot displeasure, for such chastisement would be unto death; and another Psalmist humbly deprecated being visited with the sins of his youth. Sickness brought profoundly home the sense of sin, and this sense shed a lurid light, which made the darkness of Sheol even darker. Perhaps the Old Testament saints did not realise the anger or the absence of God, except in these evils. Despondency or spiritual depression did not perhaps assail them out of trouble. That state of feeling which we name the sense of desertion did not produce itself in them except through calamities. But the sense of sin and of God's estrangement was always reflected from evil. And, on the other hand, the sense of God's favour was realised in prosperity and health. Thus the man *lived* in the light of God, and his candle shone upon his head.

To the saint thus living and blessed in the present an outlook into the future did not occur. In his calm or ecstatic felicity there was no room for the exercise of that restless analytic that is ever distinguishing between this world and another. To him there was but one world, one system of things. Or, if there were two, it was this world with God, and this world without Him. The wicked had the latter; he, the former. In that unity with God, which might be called essential, there was no room for distinction or change.

The cause of the fluctuation in the mind of the Old Testament saint was his inability to dispose of the question of sin. No mode, satisfying to the reason, of disposing of sin was known by him. It was not possible that the blood of bulls and of goats could take away sin. His ceremonies could not make him perfect as pertaining to the conscience. There was a remembrance made of sin every year. And as the sense of God's favour or the feeling of sin prevailed, the mind fluctuated between the light of heaven and the darkness of Hades. But to us all this is altered. We too have the advantage of having seen the subjective hopes of the Old Testament saints realised in a case, and fellow-ship with God maintain itself even through death.

12. *Further on the Reconciliation between the Idea of Death and the Idea of Life.*

We found it necessary to dismiss from our minds many ideas connected with death which are familiar to us who have the light of a fuller revelation. Denuding ourselves of these, we have also to remember that such ideas are not ideas that lie at the beginning of the Old Testament development, are not even ideas that in their fulness are to be found anywhere along the course of the Old Testament history and thought, although they may be seen springing up and receiving expression in some measure there. They are ideas that are, so to speak, wholes made up of many fragments that lie scattered up and down the Old Testament; and that which has given them unity as well as force, changing them from their character of anticipations and demands of faith or religious reason into stable convictions, has been the life of Christ, in whom all these ideas—mere postulates or ecstasies of faith before—have been converted into historical facts. We have to dismiss also from our minds many modes of thinking not even drawn from Christianity directly, but inherited rather from the traditions of European thought, which have passed into our Christian thinking, and been, so to speak, adopted by it. Questions of the nature of the soul in itself, or of the nature of the body, are foreign

to Scripture. Now by death we found to be meant for
the whole person an insensibility to all that is life, and
a seclusion from it, whether the living be God or man.
A full representation of all that is said in Scripture on
this point would occupy much space; but the essential
thing in it is what has been stated. Questions might be
raised whether the separation from life and God which
was involved in death was always held due to sin, or
only afterwards became connected with the idea of sin.
To answer such questions, we should probably have to
travel into regions of thought among the Shemitic peoples
that lie beyond the confines of history. Probably as soon
as we enter upon Old Testament times, that which causes
separation from God will be found to be sin, and death
will be found to be regarded as due to sin. There are
passages in the Old Testament in which death seems
regarded as a natural event. Such passages, however,
are not distinctively religious, and do not bring the event
strictly into connection with its original cause, but merely
refer to it as a thing now natural to men. But this does
not show that it is natural in any other sense than that
it has become naturalised; and we ourselves employ the
same methods of thought and speech.

The Old Testament idea of *life*, too, was seen to be
just that of our natural life in our present personal condition. And the person is composed of body and soul.
No doubt this is not equally so. The personality belongs
to the soul rather than to the body. The deceased in
Sheol do not lose personality in the sense that the individual soul evaporates or melts away into a general
spiritual element. Such an idea is wholly foreign to
the Old Testament. Individualism or personality is one
of its strongest ideas, and the identity is never lost.
And of course, of the elements of which the living
person is composed, the soul is by far the nobler and the
more energetic, so that the personality is considered to
adhere to it when it separates. But this does not hinder
that to a true and full person the body is essential. Now

this being life, that is, our existence in full personal condition, that which gave it was God. It was an efflux from Him; His Spirit communicated it. This is sometimes spoken of as if it were a physical relation between men and God. And of course, in some sense it is so. There is no point perhaps more obscure in the Old Testament than its method of speaking of the Spirit of God as the spirit of life. But without entering into that, both God and man are chiefly conceived as ethical. Their relations are moral. Even when God communicates to man a physical influence, this communication is made under ethical conditions on both sides. Thus life is had in the fellowship, the moral and emotional fellowship, of men with God. This life is enjoyed here. It is the fact and experience of its enjoyment here that is the basis and ground for the hope and the faith of it at any future time.

Now, one can readily perceive how, based on this experience of the possession of life, the expression of the faith in its continuance would arise, as in point of fact we see it to have done, in two ways. One way might be the calm and contemplative expression of the principle. I am not sure but we have raised, and perhaps rightly, in our Christian thinking, as it has come to be current among us now, certain ideas into a prominence over other ideas, which they did not at all possess in Old Testament times. One of these ideas is the idea of sin. In the Old Testament, sin is far from being ignored; but it takes its place rather within than above the general idea of God's relation to men. This idea embraces it, rather than is composed of it. In the viiith Psalm, for instance, which describes the place which God has assigned to man in the world, sin is not specially alluded to. This is not because the Psalm describes man's condition before sin entered; which it does not do. Nor because the Psalm describes his condition after sin has been eliminated; for neither does it do this, though the description of the Psalm being ideal, when it is realised, may correspond to this. But the Psalm does not specially mention sin nor yet redemption, because it includes them both.   It seizes upon that which in a world where both exist it sees to be the prevailing tendencies, what amidst all the elements which surround him in his relation to God man's ideal position is.   And this is what makes it a prophetic Psalm, pointing to the world to come, when this ideal shall find verification.

Now this is the character of very much of the Old Testament, particularly of the early Old Testament writings. They are written in the midst of a world where sin and redemption both exist, and they seize man's relation to God not on one side or the other, but on the whole.   And naturally the larger idea prevails over the smaller, the whole view absorbs that which is partial.   This is the point of view of the early Wisdom as seen in the Proverbs. In the condition of the country that then prevailed, when the land had rest and the social virtues were still un-corrupted, the true principles of God's relation to men were seen realising themselves without interruption or hindrance, and the religious philosopher finds his highest enjoyment in meditating on these principles and giving them expression.   These relations are conceived as essen-tial and unchangeable, and the fellowship between God and the persons of men is, so to speak, absolute.   From what he sees the wise man rises to the conception of a relation that cannot be interrupted.   And when he says that 'the pathway of righteousness is immortality,' his words express not the temporary phenomenon, but the eternal truth.   And death has no place, but is swept away before the irresistible wave of unchangeable principles.

Again, expression is given to the same idea in very different circumstances, and consequently in a very different way; not now in philosophic calmness expressing what it sees, but in moral perturbation protesting against what it fears or demanding what it fails to see.   Such expression is given by the mind of a person feeling himself in danger of death, from which he recoils and against which he protests.   The danger brings before him the thought of his relation to Jehovah, his blessedness in Him, which he cannot think of being interrupted.

But now we come to the reconciliation of a faith of this kind with the fact of death on the one hand and with the idea of death just described. Such a faith, indeed, as that just described, which would have none of death, and resolutely bade it be gone, could not be always sustained in the face of the inexorable fact. The expression of it, whether in the Wisdom books or in the Lyrics, would perhaps only be found during the healthy vigour of a man or the nation. A decaying nationality or a dissolving nature could not sustain it. It is a faith of this sort to which the Preacher, the author of Ecclesiastes, seeks to recall himself or the people in the declining stages of the commonwealth, with but little success, owing to the overpowering depression which adverse circumstances laid upon his own heart and that of the nation: "Fear God, and keep His commandments" (xii. 13); and, "There is nothing better for a man than that he should eat and drink, for this is his portion from God" (ii. 24). A joyous life with God upon the earth was his theme. But the times were too late for these far-off and faint echoes of a stronger time to be listened to, and the outlook was too gloomy. And even long before this time it could not fail that the question of *Sheol* should often rise and demand some solution satisfying to the reflecting mind. And we have seen how the pious Hebrew was enabled to analyse what we call death, and rise to the faith that it involved no separation from God, according to the old idea of it.

And there is the other half of the solution. The Old Testament saint, in the vivid consciousness of the life which was his in his fellowship with God, made the demand that this life should not be interrupted by death, could not think of it as thus interrupted. This was a demand for the immortality of the whole man, of the saint in the unity of his being. The protestation, too, which was made by him when he had to face the fact of death, that dying was not death in the popular sense, and did not involve separation from God, was a demand for an immortality in the religious sense—of the soul. But this latter had to be supplemented by the idea of the participation of the body in the same, which we find chiefly in the prophetical writings. The one was the natural complement to the other, and thus the great primary demand for the continuance of the whole person in life was revealed. This idea of a resurrection is pursued in more than one form by the prophets. It is a national rather than a personal hope at first and for a time. First, the covenant which God made with Israel was a national covenant. What He founded was a kingdom of God. This was eternal. In the King Messiah this kingdom would be universal and perfect. The individual saint had his immortality in the theocracy. His great interests were centred in it. His hopes found realisation there. His labours were perpetuated in it, and his spirit lived in it, even if he died. He saw the good of Israel. But this immortality of his hopes and purposes was not all. In his children he lived, he was there in them furthering God's work, enjoying God's favour. So, too, he was remembered for ever—" the memory of the just shall be in eternal remembrance " (Ps. cxii. 6). This is the kind of immortality that is taught in the Book of Wisdom, the finest of all the apocryphal writings.

Yet this kind of immortality in the perpetual existence of the work and kingdom of God, into which he had flung his energies and in which his spirit lived, must have been felt by the individual to be too shadowy to satisfy his heart. The individual man struggles against the idea of being a mere drop in the general stream of humanity, and claims a place for himself. The doctrine that, though the leaves fall off, the tree remains undying, does not satisfy the individual demand for life. This demand for a place for the individual life was expressed in the doctrine of the restitution of Israel.

It was natural, as has been said, that the prophets, whose minds were always directed rather to the whole community than to individuals, should bring up this side

of the idea of life. Israel in fellowship with Jehovah
would have lived for ever as a people; but, like Adam,
Israel transgressed the covenant and died: "When
Ephraim offended in Baal, he died," says Hosea (xiii. 1).
And all the prophets downwards are familiar with
Israel's dissolution. But with the sentence of dissolution came also the promise of restitution. Hosea,
who employs the figure of death for the dissolution, uses
the figure of resurrection for the restoration: "Let us return unto the Lord: after two days He will revive us;
and the third day He will raise us up, and we shall live in
His sight" (vi. 2). The power of death over them was to
be destroyed: "I will redeem them from the power of the
grave: I will redeem them from death: O death, I will be
thy plagues: O grave, I will be thy destruction" (xiii. 14).
These things may be said here of the people; but the
language seems to imply that the idea of a resurrection of
individuals was familiar. The great prophecy of Ezekiel
also concerning the valley of dry bones probably refers to a
resurrection of the members of the nation scattered and
wasted in every land, and their reconstitution into a living,
united body; for the people say: "Our bones are dried,
we are cut off for our parts." But, as in Hosea, the idea of
a resurrection of individuals lies under the imagery. And
in other prophets the idea deepens, and that which these
prophets say of the people, which seemed to them in its
disjointed, wasted state to be like dried bones scattered
over the valleys, is said with immediate reference to individuals on whom death has passed. The restitution of
Israel embraces also all Israel of the past. This view appears in Isa. xxvi., but most fully in Daniel: "At that
time thy people shall be delivered, every one that is found
written in the book. And many of them that sleep in the
dust of the earth shall awake, some to everlasting life, and
some to shame and everlasting contempt. And they that
be wise shall shine as the brightness of the firmament; and
they that turn many to righteousness as the stars for ever
nd ever" (Dan. xii. 1).

But before we close, it may be in place to refer to other aspects of the case which are of great interest. One of these is the relation of the Old Testament ideas to the question of the destiny of the wicked. On this subject several views are current.

There is the universalistic view, according to which all shall be restored. Then there is the view, stopping short of this, which demands a place of repentance and sphere of development beyond the grave, and which, assuming many gradations of salvation, finds a place for at least most of the race. And there is the view which calls itself that of conditional immortality, according to which those finally and persistently evil shall be annihilated. These views are in addition to the one which has been generally accepted. Now, of course, such questions will not be decided on Old Testament ground, but in the light of the clearer revelation of the New Testament. I do not wish, therefore, to speak with great decision on such a question; but my impression is, that the whole scope of the Old Testament is in favour of the ordinary opinion. In all those Psalms which have been alluded to, faith in the future sustains itself by planting its foot on the present. The view of the Old Testament saint is chiefly confined to the present,—the future is to him, so far as he himself is concerned, and so far as the wicked are concerned, but the prolongation of the present. Salvation was to him a present good. The moral constitution of the world exhibits itself on all its sides here. This is the very postulate of the thought of the Hebrew mind, and the fundamental idea of the Old Testament theocracy. Whatever principles are involved in the relations of God and man, exhibit themselves in life here. So much is this the case, that any deviation from this position which occurs, as in the prosperity of the ungodly or the adversity of the just, occasions extreme disquietude. And it is obviated by the reflection that it must be brief, that at least in death the true relations of God and men will exhibit themselves; and what is after death is but the

34

prolongation of what precedes it. No doubt, in the Book
of Job this principle is assailed by Job on both its sides,—
necessarily on the side of the just,—for he was a just
man, and on this side he would never see good; but he
carries the same principle out on the other side, giving
examples of men ungodly and yet dying in peace, and
honoured by imitation at least after death. Yet as Job
expresses his assurance of seeing God's face after death,
this might seem to carry also the opposite, that the wicked
would have no such vision.

But Scripture, both in the Old Testament and the
New, is chiefly interested in pursuing the destiny of the
just. This is in the very nature of the case. For
the representations which are given in the Old Testament of death and Sheol are not strictly Scripture
teaching. They are the expressions of popular feeling,
though all classes of men, pious and evil alike, are represented as giving utterance to them. The revelation, or
the Scripture teaching itself, consists rather in the efforts
of faith to rise above them. The consequence of this is,
that the Old Testament doctrine of the future life is
one-sided. The doctrine is developed only so far as it
concerns the righteous; it is left entirely undeveloped as
concerns the wicked. In Ps. xlix. the wicked are brought
like sheep into Sheol, and Death, personified as a keeper,
shepherds them; but no further exposition of their destiny
appears. In Isa. xxiv. 21 it is said that the Lord will
"punish the host of the high ones on high, and the kings
of the earth upon the earth. And they shall be gathered
together, as prisoners are gathered in the pit, and shall be
shut up in the prison, and after many days they shall be
visited." But the meaning of this visitation is very obscure.

Such passages require to be carefully looked at. They
probably contain germs which were afterwards more fully
developed. But that is the most that can be said of them.
Between the close of the Old Testament Canon, indeed, and
the Christian era, the doctrine as it concerns the destiny of
the evil seems to have received expansions. These expan-

sions appear in the parable of the Rich Man and Lazarus, and in the New Testament expression, the "Gehenna of fire." This Gehenna was properly originally *Ge Hinnom*, the valley of Hinnom, used as a burial-place, or a place where impurities were burned. The last words of Isaiah have been brought into connection with this: "They shall go forth, and look upon the carcases of the men that have transgressed against Me: for their worm shall not die, neither shall their fire be quenched; and they shall be an abhorring unto all flesh" (lxvi. 24). This is a remarkable passage. The circumstances are those of the final felicity of the Church,—here, those that are represented as looking on the carcases of the wicked; there, the carcases of the wicked, which are represented as exposed to unceasing corruption and consumption by fire. This, however, is something that is represented as transpiring not in Sheol, but on the face of the earth: the godly go and look upon the evil; and it is their carcases. The destruction of the transgressors is complete, and men shudder at and abhor their remains. But any question of a further kind is not answered. The representations in the Old Testament are generally of this fragmentary kind, and it requires skill and fairness when one seeks to combine them, or draw general inferences which fit into more advanced revelation from them. So far as the Old Testament is concerned, a veil is drawn over the destiny of the wicked in death; they descend into Sheol; death is their shepherd; they die in the old sense of death, and nothing further seems added in regard to them. I think there is no indication of any aggravation of misery or positive torment being their lot in the Old Testament; neither is there any indication that their personality in Sheol ceases, or that they are annihilated.

In reading the Old Testament, we must remember that it is a book of beginnings. Thoughts of God never thought before are showing themselves; presentiments in regard to man and his destiny, hopes or dreams in regard to life, are seen rising up from the deepest heart of the pious, like air-bells to the surface. The life and immortality brought to light in the gospel are being reached from many sides, in fragments, and many times only by the arm of faith reached out and striving to grasp them as brilliant rainbow forms. In the Old Testament, truth has not yet attained its unity. But everywhere in it the ground of hope or assurance is the spiritual fellowship already enjoyed with God. Our Lord's argument, " God is not the God of the dead, but of the living," is the expression of the whole spirit of the Old Testament on this great subject. The temple of truth is not yet reared, perhaps the idea of it hardly conceived in its full proportion. Yet everywhere workmen are employed preparing for it, and all around there lie the exquisite products of their labour; and here we may see one laying a foundation, and there one carving a chapiter, and there another wreathing a pillar or polishing a corner-stone, working singly most of them, able only to take in the idea of the one piece on which he is engaged, till the master-builder comes in whose mind the full idea of the temple bodies itself forth, and at whose command each single piece of workmanship arises and stands in its fit place.

NOTES OF LITERATURE.

———◆———

I. BIBLICAL THEOLOGY AND THE THEOLOGY OF THE OLD TESTAMENT GENERALLY.

AMMON, C. F., *Biblische Theologie*, Erlangen, 1792, 2 Aufl. 1801-2, 3 vols.

BAUER, G. L., *Theologie des Alten Testaments*, Leipzig, 1796 and 1800-2, 4 vols.

ZACHARIAE, G. T., *Bib. Theologie*, 4 Theile, 1772-75.

BAUER, G. L., *Biblische Moral des Alten Testaments*, Leipzig, 1803-5, 2 vols.

KAISER, G. PH. CH., *Die biblische Theologie, oder Judaismus und Christianismus*, Erlangen, 1813-21, 2 vols.

DE WETTE, W. M. L., *Biblische Dogmatik Alten und Neuen Testaments, oder kritische Darstellung der Religionslehre des Hebraismus, des Judenthums und des Urchristentums*, Berlin, 1813; 3 Aufl. 1831.

BAUMGARTEN-CRUSIUS, L. F. D., *Grundzüge der biblischen Theologie*, Jena, 1828.

CÖLLN, D. VON, *Biblische Theologie*; hrsg. von D. Schulz, Leipzig, 1836, 2 vols.

VATKE, W., *Die Religion des Alten Testaments in der Geschichtlichen Entwickelung ihrer Prinzipien dargestellt*, Berlin, 1835.

BAUER, B., *Die Religion des Alten Testaments*, Berlin, 1838 ff., 2 vols.

KNAPP, J. G., *Biblische Glaubenslehre*, Halle, 1840.

BECK, J. T., *Die christliche Lehrwissenschaft nach den biblischen Urkunden*, 1 Theil, Stuttgart, 1841; 2 Aufl. 1875.

STEUDEL, J. CH. F., *Vorlesungen über die Theologie des Alten Testaments*; hrsg. von Oehler, Berlin, 1840.

OEHLER, G. F., *Prolegomena zur Theologie des Alten Testaments*, Stuttgart, 1845.

HÄVERNICK, H. A. C., *Vorlesungen über die Theologie des Alten Testaments*; hrsg. von Hahn mit Vorwort von Dorner, Erlangen, 1848; also 2 Auflage mit Anmerkeng von Hermann Schultz, Frankfort a. M. 1863.

LUTZ, J. L. S., *Biblische Dogmatik*; hrsg. von Ruetschi, mit Vorwort von Schneckenburger, Pforzheim, 1847, 2 Ausg. 1861.

NOACK, L., *Die biblische Theologie. Einleitung ins A. u. NT*. Halle, 1853.

SCHULTZ, HERMANN, *Alttestamentliche Theologie, Die Offenbarungsreligion auf ihrer vorchristl. Entwickelungsstufe*, Frankfort a. M. 1860, 2 vols. ; 2 Aufl. 1878, 1 vol. ; 5th ed., Göttingen, 1896 ; English translation (from 4th ed.) by J. A. Paterson, 2 vols., Edinburgh, 1892 (T. & T. Clark).

HOFMANN, J. CH. K. VON, *Der Schriftbeweis*, Nördlingen, 1852–55, 2 Theile ; 2 Aufl. 1857–60.

EWALD, H., *Die Lehre der Bibel von Gott, oder Theologie des alten und neuen Bundes*, 4 parts, Leipzig, 1871–76 ; also an English translation of the first volume by T. Goadby under the title of *Revelation, its Nature and Record*, Edinburgh, 1884 (T. & T. Clark).

OEHLER, G. F., *Theologie des alten Testaments*, 2 vols., Tübingen, 1873, 1874 ; 3 Ausg. hrsg. von Th. Oehler, Stuttgart, 1891 ; also English translations by Ellen D. Smith and Sophia Taylor, 2 vols., Edinburgh, 1874, T. & T. Clark, and George E. Day, 2nd ed., New York, 1884.

BENNETT, W. H., *The Theology of the Old Testament*, London, 1896.

DILLMANN, A., *Handbuch der alttestamentlichen Theologie*. Aus dem Nachlass des Verfassers hrsg. von R. Kittel, Leipzig, 1895.

DUFF, A., *Old Testament Theology ; or, The History of the Hebrew Religion from the year 800 B.C.*, London, 1901.

DUFF, A., *Theology and Ethics of the Hebrews*, London, 1892.

GRAU, D. R. F., *Gottes Volk und sein Gesetz. Bruchstücke einer biblischen Theologie Alten Testaments*, Gütersloh, 1894.

LOTZ, W., *Geschichte und Offenbarung im Alten Testament*, 2 Ausg., Leipzig, 1892.

SCHLOTTMANN, K., *Kompendium der biblischen Theologie des Alten und Neuen Test.* ; hrsg. von E. Kühn, 2 Ausg., Leipzig, 1895.

DRIVER, S. R., *Sermons on Subjects connected with the Old Testament*, London, 1892.

HITZIG, F., *Vorlesungen über biblische Theologie und messianische Weissagungen des Alten Testaments* ; hrsg. von Kneucker, Karlsruhe, 1880.

PIEPENBRING, CH., *Theologie de l'Ancien Testament*, Paris, 1886, English translation by G. H. Mitchell, New York, 1893.

KAYSER, AUGUST, *Die Theologie des Alten Testaments in ihrer geschichtlichen Entwickelung dargestellt* ; hrsg. von K. Marti, 1894.

RIEHM, ED., *Alttestamentliche Theologie* ; hrsg. von K. Pahncke, Halle, 1889.

SMEND, S. R., *Lehrbuch der alttestamentlichen Religionsgeschichte*, Freiburg u. Leipzig, 1893.

FOSTER, R. V., *Old Testament Studies ; an Outline of Old Testament Theology*, Chicago, 1890.

GABLER, J. P., *De justo discrimine theologiæ biblicæ et dogmaticæ*, 1787.

DAVIDSON, A. B., paper on "Biblical Theology" in his *Biblical and Literary Essays*, London, 1902.

KÄHLER, M., article on "Biblische Theologie" in Herzog's *Real-Encyclopädie*, 2nd ed.

II. THE HISTORY AND THE RELIGION OF ISRAEL.

BAUDISSIN, W. W., *Studien zur semitischen Religionsgeschichte*, Leipzig, 1876–79.

WELLHAUSEN, J., *Prolegomena zur Geschichte Israel*, Berlin, 1883.

DIESTEL, L., *Geschichte des Alten Testamentes in der christlichen Kirche*, Jena, 1869.

HENGSTENBERG, E. W., *Geschichte des Reiches Gottes unter dem Alten Bunde*; also English translation in Clark's "Foreign Theological Library," Edinburgh.

KUENEN, A., *Religion of Israel*, Haarlem, 1869; Eng. tr. 3 vols. 1875.

MONTEFIORE, C. G., *Religion of the Ancient Hebrews*, Hibbert Lecture, 1893.

CHANTEPIE DE LA SAUSSAYE, *Lehrb. der Religionsgeschichte*, 2nd ed.: *Religion of Israel*, by Valeton, 1897.

OESTERLEY, W. O. E., "The Development of Monotheism in Israel," *Expositor*, vi. 6, p. 93.

III. GOD AND THE DIVINE NAMES (additional to literature referred to on p. 52).

On "Jehovah," etc.

DILLMANN'S Note, Commentary on *Genesis*, p. 74 (T. & T. Clark).

SKIPWITH, G. H., "The Tetragrammaton" in *Jewish Quarterly Review* x. p. 662.

GRAY, G. B., article on "Names" in *Encyc. Bibl.* iii. 3320 ff.

BLAU, *Das altjüdische Zauberwesen* (1898).

STADE, in *Gesch. d. Volkes Israel*, vi. 1, 130 ff.

PINCHES, "Ya and Jawa in Assyro-Babylonian Inscriptions" in *Proceedings of Soc. of Bibl. Archæology*, i. pp. 1–13.

KÖNIG, "The Origin of the Name יהוה," *Expository Times*, x.

HOMMEL, *Ancient Hebrew Tradition*, 115.

WELLHAUSEN, J., *Skizzen*, iii. 169.

LAGARDE, P., *Mitteilungen*, p. 96 ff. (1884).

DAVIDSON, A. B., article on "God" in *Dict. of Bible*, ii. p. 199 (Clark).

KUENEN, *Religion of Israel*, Eng. tr. 1874.

KÖNIG, *Hauptprobleme der altisr. Religionsgeschichte*, 1884.

SELLIN, *Beiträge zur semit. Religionsgeschichte*, 1896–97.

HUNNIUS, C., *Natur u. Char. Jahves nach d. vordeut. Quellen d. Bücher Genesis-Könige*, Strassburg, Heitz.

König, E., "War 'Jahve' eine Kana'anäische Gottheit?", in *Neue Kirchl. Ztsch.* 13.

Weber, H., "Die alttest. Schätzung d. Gottesnamens," in *Deutsch-Amer. Ztschr. f. Theol. u. Kirche*, 3.

Johns, C. H. W., "The Name Jehovah in the Abrahamic Age,' *Expositor*, vi. 8, p. 282.

On " Elohim," etc.

Fleischer, *Kleine Schriften*, i. 154 ff.

Delitzsch, Franz, Note, Commentary on *Genesis*, p. 48 (1887) (Clark)

Nöldeke, article in *Zeitsch. d. Morg. Gesell.* xi. 174.

Dillmann, Note, Commentary on *Genesis*, i. 1 (Clark).

Nestle, article in *Theol. Stud. aus Würt.* p. 243 ff. (1882).

Baethgen, *Beiträge*, 271 and 297 ff.

Gray, G. B., article on "Names," *Encycl. Bibl.* iii. 3323.

On " Lord of Hosts."

Gray, G. B., article in *Encycl. Bibl.* iii. 3328.

Löhr, *Untersuchungen zum B. Amos*, 37 ff. (1901).

Kautzsch, articles in *Ztsch. f. altt. Wiss.* vi. 17 ff., and in *Real-Encycl. f. Protest. Theologie*, xvii. 423 ff.

Smend, *Altt. Religionsgeschichte*, 2nd ed. p. 202.

Wellhausen, J., *Israel. u. jüd. Geschichte*, 3rd ed. p. 25.

IV. Typology, Prophecy, and the Prophets.

Fairbairn, Patrick, *Prophecy viewed in respect of its distinctive Nature, its special Function, and proper Interpretation*, Edinburgh, 1856.

Lee, Samuel, *An Inquiry into the Nature, Progress, and End of Prophecy*, in three Books, Cambridge, 1849.

Davison, John, *Discourses on Prophecy*, 6th ed., Oxford, 1856.

Hofmann, J. Ch. K. von, *Weissagung und Erfüllung*, Nördlingen, 1841–44.

Fairbairn, Patrick, *The Typology of Scripture, viewed in Connection with the whole Series of the Divine Dispensations*, Edinburgh, 2 vols. 6th ed., 1876.

Kirkpatrick, A. F., *The Doctrine of the Prophets*, Cambridge, 1892.

Bredenkampf, C. J., *Gesetz und Propheten. Ein Beitrag zur alttestamentlichen Kritik*, Erlangen, 1881.

Orelli, C. von, *Die alttestamentliche Weissagung von der Vollendung des Reiches Gottes*; Eng. tr.

Delitzsch, Franz, *Die biblisch-prophetische Theologie, ihre Fortbildung durch Chr. A. Crusius und ihre neueste Entwickelung*, 1845.

König, F. E., *Der Offenbarungsbegriff des Alten Testaments*, 2 vols. Leipzig. 1882.

SMITH, W. R., *The Prophets of Israel and their Place in History to the Close of the Eighth Century*, Edinburgh, 1882 ; new edition, with Notes, by T. K. Cheyne, 1895.

MAYBAUM, S., *Die Entwickelung des israelitischen Prophetentums*, Berlin, 1883.

DUHM, BERNH., *Die Theologie der Propheten als Grundlage für die innere Entwickelungsgeschichte der israelitischen Religion*, Bonn, 1875.

KUENEN, A., *De Profeten en de profetie in Israel*, Leiden, 1875 ; also, *The Prophets and Prophecy in Israel, a Historical and Critical Inquiry*. Translation from the Dutch by A. Milroy, London, 1897.

THOLUCK, A., *Die Propheten und ihre Weissagungen*, 2nd ed. 1887.

SCHWARTZKOPFF, P., *Die Prophetische Offenbarung*, 1826.

KÖNIG, F. E., *Das Berufsbewusstsein der Altt. Propheten*, 1900.

EWALD, H., *Die Propheten des Alten Bundes*, Göttingen, 1867–68 ; English tr., *Commentary on the Prophets of the Old Test.*, London, 1875–81.

KITTEL, R., *Prophetie und Weissagung*, 1899.

MICHELET, S., *Israels Propheten als Träger der Offenbarung*, 1898.

DARMESTETER, J., *Les Prophètes d. Israel*, 1892.

CORNILL, C. H., *Der Israelitische Prophetismus*, 1896.

CORNILL, C. H., *The Prophets of Israel* ; tr. by S. F. Corkran, Chicago

DAVIDSON, A. B., *Old Testament Prophecy*, 1903 (T. & T. Clark).

DAVIDSON, A. B., " Prophecy and Prophets" in *Dict. of Bible*.

SMITH, W. R., and T. K. CHEYNE, article on " Prophetic Literature" in *Encycl. Bib.* iii. 3853 ff.

V. ON MESSIANIC PROPHECY AND PARTICULAR PROPHETS.

RIEHM, ED., *Die Messianische Weissagung*, Gotha, 1875 ; also English tr., *Messianic Prophecy* (T. & T. Clark), 2nd edition, 1900.

BRIGGS, C. A., *Messianic Prophecy*, 1886 (T. & T. Clark).

STANTON, V. H., *The Jewish and Christian Messiah*, 1886 (T. & T. Clark).

WOODS, F. H., *The Hope of Israel*, 1896 (T. & T. Clark).

VOLZ, P., *Die vorexilische Jahwe-prophetie u. der Messias*, 1897.

HÜHN, *Die Messianischen Weissagungen*, 1899.

DELITZSCH, FRANZ, *Messianische Weissagungen in gescht. Folge*, 1890.

DILLMANN, A., *Die Propheten des alten Bundes nach ihrer politischen Wirksamkeit*, 1868.

BÖHL, E., *Christologie des Alten Testamentes, oder Auslegung der wichtigsten Messianischen Weissagungen*, Wien, 1882.

CHARLES, R. H., "The Messiah of O. T. Prophecy and Apoc. and the Christ of the N. T." in *Expositor*, 6th Series, 5.

DUHM, B., "Das Buch Jesaia übersetzt u. erklärt," Nowack's *Hand-Kommentar z. AT*.

GIESEBRECHT, F., *Der Knecht Jahves d. Deuterojesaia*, Beyer, Königsberg.

DAVIDSON, A. B., articles on "The Theology of Isaiah," *Expository Times*, vols. v. and vi.

DAVIDSON, A. B., article on "Jeremiah" in *Dict. of Bible.*

ERBT, W., *Jeremia und seine Zeit.* 1902, Göttingen, Vandenhoeck und Ruprecht.

HACKSPILL, M., "La vocation de Jérémie," *Bull. de Litt. Ecclesiastique*, 1902.

PLÜDDEMANN, R., "Jeremias u. s. Zeit.," *Deutsch-Amerikanische Zeitschrift f. Theol. u. Kirche*, 1902.

MARTI, *Der Prophet Jeremia von Anatot*, 1889.

DAVIDSON, A. B., "The Prophet Amos," *Bib. and Lit. Essays*, London, 1902.

PROCKSCH, O., *Geschichtsbetrachtung und Geschichtsüberlieferung, b. d. vorexilischen Propheten*, 1902, Leipzig, Hinrichs.

MEYER, F. B., *Sacharja d. Prophet d. Hoffnung*, Hagen, Rippel.

DAVIDSON, A. B., "The Prophet Hosea," *Bibl. and Lit. Essays*, London, 1902.

BOEHMER, "Grundgedunken der Predigt Hosea" in *Ztschr f. wiss. Theol.* 1902.

SMITH, W. R., and CHEYNE, T. K., "Obadiah" in *Encycl. Biblica.*

BUDDE, "Nahum" in *Encycl. Biblica.*

SELBIE, J. A., "Zephaniah" in *Dict. of Bible.*

NOWACK, "Zechariah" in *Dict. of Bible.*

On the Poetical Books.

MÜLLER, EUGEN, *Der echte Hiob*, 1902, Rehtmeyer, Hannover.

DELITZSCH, FRIED., "Das Buch Hiob," *Neu übersetzt u. kurz erklärt*, 1902, Leipzig, Hinrichs.

KRIEGER, H., "D. Leiden d. Gerechten" in *D. B. Hiob im Lichte d. NT*, Wehlau, Fock.

KIRKPATRICK, A. F., "The Book of Psalms" (*Cambridge Bible*).

VI. COVENANT.

DAVIDSON, A. B., article in *Dict. of Bible.*

GUTHE, H., *De foederis notione Jeremiana*, Leipzig, 1877.

KRAETZSCHMAR, *Die Bundesvorstellung im Alt Test.*, Marburg, 1896.

DILLMANN, A., *Handb. d. altt. Theol.* pp. 107 ff., 419 ff.

SMEND, *Lehb. d. Altt. Religionsgeschichte*, pp. 24 ff. and 294 ff.

SCHULTZ, H., *O. T. Theology*, Clark's tr. ii. p. 166.

RIEHM, E., *Altt. Theol.*, p. 68 ff.

VALETON, *Ztschr. f. altt. Wiss.* xii. xiii.

VII. ATONEMENT; DAY OF ATONEMENT, ETC.

STADE, *Geschichte d. Volkes Israel*, vi. 2.

SCHULTZ, H., *O. Test. Theology*, i. p. 307 ff., ii. p. 402 ff.

DELITZSCH, FR., article in Riehm's *Handwörterbuch d. bibl. Alterthums.*

RITSCHL, ALB., *Die christl. Lehre von d. Rechtfertigung u. d. Versöhnung,* vol. ii.

WEISS, B., *Biblical Theol. of N. T.*, vol. i. p. 419 ff., and vol. ii. p. 202 ff.

THOMASIUS, G., *Christi Person und Werk.*

SMITH, W. R., on כפר, *Old Test. in Jew. Church,* p. 43 ff., and 2nd ed. p. 381 ff.

DRIVER, S. R., article on "Propitiation" in *Dict. of Bible.*

RIEHM, E., *Der Begriff der Sühne im AT,* 1877.

NOWACK, *Archäologie,* iii. 220.

DAVIDSON, A. B., article on "Atone" in *Expositor,* Aug. 1899.

DILLMANN, A., *Commentary on Leviticus,* chap. iv. 20.

CURTISS, S. I., "The Semitic Sacrifice of Reconciliation" in *Expositor,* 4th Series, 6.

PATERSON, W., article on "Sacrifice" in *Dict. of Bible.*

VIII. DOCTRINE OF MAN.

RIEDEL, W., "Die Gottesebenbildlichkeit d. Menschen," *Altt. Untersuchungen,* Leipzig, 1902.

CURTISS, S. I., "The Physical Relation of Man to God among Semites" in *American Journal of Theology,* vi.

ROOS, M. F., *Fundamenta Psychologiæ ex S.S. collectæ,* 1762.

OLSHAUSEN, H., *Opuscula Theologica,* 1834.

BECK, J. T., *Umriss der bibl. Seelenlehre,* 1843, 1871 ; Eng. tr. (Clark).

DELITZSCH, FRANZ, *System der bibl. Psychologie,* 1861 ; Eng. tr. (T. & T. Clark) 1867.

WENDT, H. H., *Die Begriffe Fleisch und Geist im bibl. Sprachgebrauch.*

HEARD, J. B., *The Tripartite Nature of Man,* 1882.

ELLICOTT, C. J., *The Destiny of the Creature,* 1883.

WHITE, E., *Life in Christ,* 1878.

DICKSON, W. P., *St. Paul's use of the terms Flesh and Spirit,* 1883.

IX. ESCHATOLOGY.

KEICHER, "Die Eschatologie des Hiob" in *Der Katholik,* 82.

BEER, G., *D. biblische Hades,* Tübingen, Mohr.

UMBACH, S. L., "Lehre d. Unsterblichkeit im AT" in *Deutsch-Americanische Ztschr. f. Theol. u. Kirche,* 3.

WÜNSCHE, "Die Poesie des Todes im alttest. Schrifttum," Haupt's *Deutsch-evang. Blatter.*

SCHWALLY, FR., *Leben nach dem Tode.*

DAVIDSON, A. B., article on "Eschatology of O. T." in *Dict. of Bible.*

BOETTCHER, *De Inferis,* 1846.

OEHLER, G. F., *Vet. Test. Sententia de rebus post mortem futuris,* 1846.

SCHULTZ, H., *Voraussetzungen der christl. Lehre v. d. Unsterblichkeit,* 1868.

DAVIDSON, A. B., "Modern Religion and O. T. Immortality," *Expositor*, May 1895 ; and *Biblical and Theol. Essays*, London, 1902.

SALMOND, S. D. F., *Christian Doctrine of Immortality*, 5th ed. 1903 (T. & T. Clark).

SCHREINER, J., *Elysium u. Hades*, Braunschweig, Sattler.

SCHMIDT, F., *Die Unsterblichkeits- u. Auferstehungsglaube in d. Bibel*, Brixen, Buchh. d. Kath.-pol. Pressvereins.

NOWACK, W., *D. Zukunftshoffnungen Israels in d. Assyr. Zeit.*, Festschrift f. Holtzmann, Tübingen, Mohr.

COCORDA, O., "L'immortalita dell' anima nell *Archico* Testamento" in *Riv. Crist.* 1902.

CHARLES, R. H., "The Rise and Development in Israel of the Belief in a Future Life," *Expositor*, vi. 7, p. 49.

X. MISCELLANEOUS.

Priesthood.

BAUDISSIN, W. W., *Die Geschichte des altt. Priesterthums untersucht*, Leipzig, 1889.

BENZINGER, I., *Hebräische Archäologie*, 1894, vol. ii. pp. 405-28.

NOWACK, W., *Lehrbuch der heb. Archäologie*, 1894, vol. ii. pp. 87-138.

SCHÜRER, E., *Geschichte des jüdischen Volkes im Zeitalter Jesu Christi*, 3rd ed. 1898, ii. pp. 214-99 ; Eng. tr., *History of the Jewish People in the Time of Jesus Christ*, 1885-90.

Angels.

DAVIDSON, A. B., article in *Dict. of Bible*.

HACKSPILL, "L'angelologie juive à l'époque neo-testamentaire" in *Rev. bibl. internationale*, 11.

Faith, etc.

LUTZ, W., *Bib. Dogmatik*, p. 312.

SCHULTZ, H., "Gerechtigkeit aus dem Glauben im AT and NT" in *Jahrb. f. deutsche Theologie*, 1862, p. 510.

WARFIELD, B. B., article on "Faith" in *Dict. of Bible*.

DAVIDSON, A. B., "The Wisdom of the Hebrews," *Bibl. and Lit. Essays*, London, 1902.

SKINNER, J., article on "Righteousness" in *Dict. of Bible*.

BOEHMER, JUL., *D. alttest. Unterbau d. Reiches Gottes*, Leipzig, Hinrichs.

INDEX OF SCRIPTURE PASSAGES.

35

INDEX OF MATTERS